An Introduction to Work and Organizational Psychology

To Tansy, Kim, and Rees

An Introduction to Work and Organizational Psychology

A European Perspective

Second Edition

Edited by Nik Chmiel

Blackwell Publishing

© 2008 by Blackwell Publishing Ltd

BLACKWELL PUBLISHING
350 Main Street, Malden, MA 02148-5020, USA
9600 Garsington Road, Oxford OX4 2DQ, UK
550 Swanston Street, Carlton, Victoria 3053, Australia

First published 2008 by Blackwell Publishing Ltd

1   2008

Library of Congress Cataloging-in-Publication Data

An introduction to work and organizational psychology : a European perspective / edited by
Nik Chmiel. – 2nd ed.
p.   cm.
Includes bibliographical references and index.
ISBN 978-1-4051-3276-3 (pbk. : alk. paper)   1. Psychology, Industrial–
Europe.   2. Organizational behavior–Europe.   I. Chmiel, Nik.   II. Title: Work and
organizational psychology : a European perspective.
HF5548.8.I576 2009
158.7–dc22
2008002784

A catalogue record for this title is available from the British Library.

Set in 10.5 on 13 pt Galliard
by SNP Best-set Typesetter Ltd., Hong Kong
Printed and bound in the United Kingdom
by TJ International Ltd., Padstow, Cornwall

The publisher's policy is to use permanent paper from mills that operate a sustainable forestry
policy, and which has been manufactured from pulp processed using acid-free and elementary
chlorine-free practices. Furthermore, the publisher ensures that the text paper and cover
board used have met acceptable environmental accreditation standards.

For further information on
Blackwell Publishing, visit our website at
www.blackwellpublishing.com

Contents

List of Contributors

Neil Anderson, Professor and Head, HRM and OB Group, Amsterdam Business School, University of Amsterdam, the Netherlands

J. H. Erik Andriessen, Faculty of Technology, Policy and Management, Delft University of Technology, the Netherlands

Dave Bartram, Research Director, SHL Group Ltd., Thames Ditton, UK

Felix C. Brodbeck, Chair of Industrial and Organizational Psychology, Department of Psychology, Ludwig Maximilians University, Munich, Germany

Nik Chmiel, Director of Occupational Psychology, Past President of the European Association of Work and Organizational Psychology, Queen's University Belfast, UK

Nicole Cunningham-Snell, Shell Services International, London, UK

Marco Depolo, Faculty of Psychology, University of Bologna, Italy

Clive Fletcher, Professor Emeritus, Department of Psychology, Goldsmiths University of London; Honorary Professor, Warwick Business School, University of Warwick; Managing Director, Personnel Assessment Ltd., London, UK

Franco Fraccaroli, Faculty of Cognitive Sciences, University of Trento, Italy

Michael Frese, University of Giessen and London Business School, Past President of International Association of Applied Psychology, Giessen, Germany

Guido Hertel, Work, Industrial & Organizational Psychology, University of Würzburg, Germany

G. Robert J. Hockey, Department of Psychology, Sheffield University, UK

Gerard P. Hodgkinson, Professor of Organizational Behaviour & Strategic Management and Director of the Centre for Organizational Strategy, Learning & Change, Leeds University Business School, UK

Henry Honkanen, OD Consultant, Organizational Psychologist, Arena Nova Ltd, Helsinki, Finland

Jan de Jonge, Department of Technology Management, Subdepartment of Human Performance Management, Eindhoven University of Technology, the Netherlands

Binna Kandola, Pearn Kandola, 76 Banbury Road, Oxford, UK

Asli Kücükaslan, Department of Management, Faculty of Economics and Administrative Sciences, Marmara University, Istanbul, Turkey

Pascale Le Blanc, Department of Social and Organizational Psychology, Utrecht University, the Netherlands

Chris Lewis, Aver Psychology, St. Ives, Cambridgeshire, UK

Vicente Martínez-Tur, Department of Social Psychology, University of Valencia, Spain. Member of the Spanish CONSOLIDER Project on Work and Organizational Psychology

Kerri McDonnell, Occupational Psychologist, Police Service of Northern Ireland, Belfast, UK

Micaela McGinley, Occupational Psychologist, Police Service of Northern Ireland, Belfast, UK

Cornelia Niessen, Work and Organizational Psychology Unit, Department of Psychology, University of Konstanz, Germany

Jan Noyes, Department of Experimental Psychology, University of Bristol, UK

Sandra Ohly, Work and Organizational Psychology, Johann Wolfgang Goethe University, Frankfurt, Germany

José M. Peiró, Department of Social Psychology, University of Valencia and IVIE, Spain. Member of the Spanish CONSOLIDER Project on Work and Organizational Psychology

Ivan Robertson, Managing Director, Robertson Cooper Ltd, Manchester, and Leeds University Business School, Leeds, UK

Susannah Robertson, Consultant, Robertson Cooper Ltd, Manchester, UK

Bruno Ruettinger, Institute of Psychology, Darmstadt University of Technology, Germany

Jesus F. Salgado, Departamento de Psicologia Social, University of Santiago de Compostela, Spain

Juergen Sauer, Department of Psychology, University of Fribourg, Switzerland

Wilmar Schaufeli, Department of Social and Organizational Psychology, Utrecht University, the Netherlands

Sonja Schinkel, Department of Organizational Psychology, University of Amsterdam, the Netherlands

Ute Schmidt-Brasse, PSYCON Psychologische Unternehmensberatung, Integrative Organisations-, Team- und Personalentwicklung; Interkulturelle Beratung, Wildeshausen, Germany

Noel Sheehy, School of Psychology, Liverpool John Moores University, Liverpool, UK

Handan Kepir Sinangil, Organizational Behavior Division & Graduate Program Chair, Faculty of Economics and Administrative Sciences, Marmara University, Istanbul, Turkey

Sabine Sonnentag, Work and Organizational Psychology Unit, Department of Psychology, University of Konstanz, Germany

Andrew J. Tattersall, School of Psychology, Liverpool John Moores University, Liverpool, UK

Matti Vartiainen, Laboratory of Work Psychology and Leadership, Department of Industrial Engineering and Management, Helsinki University of Technology, Finland

Michael A. West, Professor of Organizational Psychology and Head of Research, Aston Business School, Aston University, Birmingham, UK

Marion Wittchen, Work, Industrial & Organizational Psychology, University of Würzburg, Germany

"Observation and experience can and must drastically restrict the range of admissible scientific belief, else there would be no science. But they cannot alone determine a particular body of such belief. An apparently arbitrary element, compounded of personal and historical accident, is always a formative ingredient of the beliefs espoused by a given scientific community at a given time."

(Kuhn, 1962)

Introduction

Nik Chmiel

The industrial revolution started in Great Britain in the eighteenth century. Before it the social unit was still the village, and most families owned some means to make a living: land, or the right of common pasture, or simple wooden machines. In 1769 Arkwright patented the spinning machine, which could do the work of 12 women, and was driven by water power. The power loom was invented by Cartwright in 1785, and perfected some 30 years later. Weavers became factory employees (Halliday, 1995). The change to an economy dominated by factory production and urbanization necessitated constant effort in pursuit of production, and the development of large manufacturing towns such as Manchester (Messinger, 1985). Britain led the way to industrialization, and for most of the nineteenth century reaped the economic benefits of being first, consolidating an empire in the process. By the turn of the twentieth century, however, both the USA and Germany began to overhaul the UK.

Landy (1997) suggests that "Industrial and Organizational Psychology was peculiarly American in its inception" (p. 467), and its early history concentrated on individual differences. A key book, *Psychology and Industrial Efficiency*, was published in an English edition in 1913 by Munsterberg, one of the pioneers in American I-O Psychology (although originally from Germany). By the 1930s in the USA there were several universities and colleges offering training in I-O Psychology, and during 1937–8 the American Association for Applied Psychology (AAAP) came into being, which included an Industrial and Business Psychology Section. The American Psychological Association (APA), formed in 1892, merged with the AAAP after the Second World War, creating a division of Business and Industrial Psychology (Division 14). Katzell and Austin (1992) note the emergence of a separate discipline of Applied experimental and Engineering Psychology (Division 21 of the APA) embracing biology, engineering, systems analysis, and computer science, as well as psychology.

In Britain studies were begun in 1915, under the auspices of the Health of Munitions Workers Committee, investigating industrial fatigue and factors affecting the personal health and efficiency of workers in munitions factories. The Industrial Fatigue Research Board, later renamed the Industrial Health Research Board (IHRB), was set up in 1918 to continue the work. Subsequently responsibility for the IHRB was assumed by the Medical Research Council. In 1921 the National Institute of Industrial Psychology (NIIP) was established to "promote and encourage the practical application of the sciences of psychology and physiology to commerce and industry by any means that may be found practicable." When Morris Viteles, an American I-O psychologist, visited Europe he noted that industrial psychology in both England and Germany was expanding at a rapid rate and was more extensive in its scope than in the USA (Shimmin & Wallace, 1994).

Contemporary Work and Organizational Psychology in North America and Europe, as well as elsewhere, emphasizes a scientific basis for understanding people at work. Medawar characterized scientific enquiry "as a logically articulated structure of justifiable beliefs about nature. It begins as a story about a Possible World – a story which we invent and criticize and modify as we go along, so that it ends by being, as nearly as we can make it, a story about real life" (1969, p. 59). Nonetheless "real life" can be explained from many differing perspectives. Karl Popper (1991) argued that science itself was a social institution, and therefore knowledge produced by its practice was necessarily influenced by politics, social considerations, economics, and the particular interests and experiences of the scientists involved. This book is based on a European perspective in that the authors live and work in Europe and have been asked to consider the European context in their writing. Nonetheless observations and explanations of the nature of work can be drawn from any appropriate source when a story about real working life requires justification.

The second edition of *An introduction to work and organizational psychology*, like the first, can be read in many different ways. Reading and understanding one chapter does not depend on reading any of the other chapters. All the chapters in the book have been written taking account of developments in the field since the first edition. Thus there are differences in content in established areas, and new areas have been introduced. First, there is much more emphasis on the organization of work, reflecting developments in the field. *Inter alia*, the section on technology reflects its importance in chapters on virtual team-working and telework, the section on organizations at work includes chapters on mergers and acquisitions and strategic management, and the chapter on job analysis reflects the contemporary importance placed on competency approaches. Second, the new edition gives added recognition to the applied and practical nature of work and organizational psychology by including a separate section on theory and application. The aim of the theory and application section is to demonstrate both the types of approach and thinking that can be extended from considering the scientific knowledge that underpins work and organizational psychology to problems in the workplace, and the kinds of practical problem-solving for organizations that ensues. Two chapters consider the changing nature of work and the creation of inclusive organizations, and three case studies present practical solutions to problems relating to people at work, technology, and organizational change. There is also a chapter that explores the issues and steps involved in providing competent consultancy to organizations.

PART I

PEOPLE AT WORK

Work Profiling and Job Analysis

Dave Bartram

Overview

This chapter looks at what job analysis is and at why and how it is carried out. Job analysis is the cornerstone of a range of other work and organizational psychology applications, including training, selection, job design, and performance management. The chapter describes and reviews all the main methods of job analysis. It also considers how job analysis is changing as the world of work changes. It highlights the emergence in the past few years of competency-based approaches and considers how these relate to more traditional methods.

What Job Analysis Is

Job analysis has been defined as the "collection and analysis of any type of job related information by any method for any purpose" (Ash, 1988). The breadth of this definition indicates the difficulty of covering everything about job analysis in a single chapter. People do job analysis for all sorts of different reasons, they use all sorts of different methods, and they apply the results to all sorts of different business processes.

It may help to consider what we get out of a job analysis. Traditionally there are two main types of output from a job analysis: job descriptions and person specifications.

- A **job description** tells us about the nature of the work. It defines a job in terms of the tasks it involves, its functions, the methods and procedures employed and standards of performance that need to be attained if the job is to be carried out effectively. Job descriptions can be work-oriented or worker-oriented.
  - a) **Work-oriented job descriptions** focus on the tasks that need to be accomplished. For example: "Stock levels maintained at specified levels

with appropriate goods." This approach is also referred to as task-oriented.

b) **Worker-oriented job descriptions** focus on the attributes of the worker necessary to accomplish those tasks. For example: "Monitor stock levels on shelves and recognize when stock falls below minimum levels. Know which goods are needed to maintain stock levels above minima." This approach is also referred to as person-oriented.

- **A person specification**, on the other hand tells us about the nature of the people who do the work. It describes the knowledge, skills, ability, and other characteristics (**KSAO**s) a person would need to perform the job effectively. The "other characteristics" typically include a wide range of attributes, such as personality, interests, motivation, training, and experiences and qualifications. Clearly, there is a more direct link between a worker-oriented job description and a person specification than there is with a work-oriented one.

The key to good job analysis lies in identifying what is *important* about a job. An exhaustive list of every action carried out by somebody over the course of a week would be of little value in identifying what the qualities are that someone needs to do the job effectively. The analysis needs to focus on what are the things that make it difficult to do, what are the things that are likely to result in some people being better able to do the job than others or that result in people needing training before they can do the job?

Why Job Analysis is Done

The main reason for carrying out a job analysis is to understand what behaviors are required to do a job effectively. Generally, these behaviors would be carried out by people, but job analysis is just as important (probably more important) when designing jobs for robots to carry out, such as in automated assembly or manufacture plants. For the purposes of this chapter, however, we will stick to jobs done by people. What we want from a job analysis is a model of how human behavior relates to the job in question. In this sense, the person specification is a model or set of hypotheses about the KSAOs people need in relation to the job that is described in the job description.

Imagine that you have just started a new business. You have a factory and offices, you have a product to manufacture and distribute, but you have no employees. You will need to identify what roles and functions you need people for (administration, manufacture, maintenance, warehousing, delivery, storekeeping, supervision, management, etc.), how many people you will need to perform each of the functions, what sort of mix of functions and tasks each person will be required to carry out. You will need to have some system for classifying and grouping your jobs and giving them meaningful titles (warehouse manager, warehouse foreman, warehouse operative, etc.). You'll need to ensure that jobs have been designed to meet relevant health and safety legislation. You will need to find people who fit those requirements and will be effective workers, you need to provide cost-effective training for them, and offer them fair and attractive rates of pay and conditions. Finally you'll need to put in place some system for measuring how well the people are doing so that you can manage their performance and ensure the business is a success.

Job analysis provides the means by which we can do all of the above. We need well-defined "people-models" of jobs for a number of reasons. To optimize the fit between people and their jobs, there are three things you can do: hire people who fit the job (**selection and recruitment**); change the job to fit the people (**job design**); change the people to fit the job (**training and development**). In practice, it is usually a case of doing some mixture of all three.

- Job analysis provides us with the information necessary to produce a person specification that can be used as the basis for deciding what qualities we need to assess in a selection procedure. This is one of the most widely used applications of job analysis.
- By identifying the skills and knowledge necessary to perform a job effectively, and by comparing that specification with an audit of the current workforce's capabilities and skills, job analysis also provides us with the specification for training programs.
- Where people are experiencing difficulty carrying out a job, a job analysis can often identify the causes of these difficulties and be used to suggest ways in which the job might be redesigned to make it easier to perform. Such redesign might relate to improving the ease of use of essential equipment, changing procedures or practices or changing the way in which the various tasks are distributed between jobs and between people.

Job analysis also provides the source of measures for assessing whether people in the job are performing well or not. In this respect, job analysis is the key to the design of **performance management systems** and to the validation of training, job redesign, and job selection procedures. For example, suppose that analysis of a job shows that good written communication skills are an essential attribute. This can then be used to justify the assessment of written communication skill as a selection requirement. It also provides us with an aspect of performance that we should assess in the job to see if people are performing effectively: i.e. how well do job incumbents meet the need to communicate effectively in writing?

Job analysis can also be used to set appropriate rates of pay for jobs (known as **job evaluation** or job compensation models). Job evaluation methods tend to fall into one of two types: job component models and benchmark models.

- By analyzing different job in terms of a standard set of job or task components and by collecting data on the rates paid for different jobs, it is possible to generate equations that predict what the pay rate should be for any new job (so long as the new job is made up of some mix of these standard components).
- Benchmarking is rather different. Information is collected on rates of pay for a number of different jobs and these rates are then used as "benchmarks" against which someone can compare specific jobs. Rather than generating predicted rates from components, the process is to find a benchmark job that seems to best fit the description for the job one is evaluating.

Starting up a new business is one scenario where job analysis is crucial. However, it is also important whenever business changes – and the requirements placed on people change. A major source of change in business comes through mergers and acquisitions and through downsizing. When the organization changes one needs a good basis on which to choose who stays and who goes and to know what the investment in retraining will need to be.

Finally, without a good job description and without a person specification that is clearly related to that job description, we will be unable to justify our selection procedures, we will not be able to make a business case for investment in training, nor will we be able to defend the criteria we use in performance management or the setting of pay rates and bonuses. In the extreme, when an organization is taken to court by an aggrieved worker or by a union over claims of bias or unfairness, its best defense is a good job analysis and a clear audit trail relating that analysis through a person specification to actual workplace performance assessment practices and procedures.

In short, job analysis is needed for

- Recruitment and selection
- Training and development
- Performance management
- Merger and acquisitions and downsizing
- Job design and redesign
- Health and safety requirements
- Classification of job and labeling of jobs
- Human resource planning and effective use of available resources
- Job evaluation and compensation
- Legal defensibility

Job analysis and job classification

Job analysis also provides the basic data that has enabled us to create **job classification systems**. There is an International Standard Classification of Occupations

(ISCO: http://www.ilo.org/public/english/bureau/stat/class/isco.htm), developed by the International Labor Organization in Geneva. However, each country tends to have its own system as well. What is more, these change over time as the nature of work changes. Nevertheless, as you might expect, the various classification systems have a lot in common. Job classification systems define job families (clusters of jobs which are similar in tasks or KSAO requirements).

Probably the most influential job classification system was the Dictionary of Occupational Titles (DOT), developed in the USA by the US Employment Service (USES), using job analysts from all over the country (US Department of Labor, 1965). To properly match jobs and workers, the USES used a standard occupational "language." The first edition of the DOT was published in 1939 and contained around 17,500 job definitions. Blocks of jobs were assigned 5- or 6-digit codes which placed them in one of 550 occupational groups and indicated whether the jobs were skilled, semi-skilled, or unskilled. The last edition of the DOT was published in 1977 and contained over 2,100 new occupational definitions, and several thousand other definitions were substantially modified or combined with related definitions.

The DOT approach, while thorough, was difficult to use, and a new approach was needed. The O*NET (Occupational Information Network: Dye & Silver, 1999) was developed as a more practical job information tool, and it encompassed changes to the DOT that reflected the latest research in job analysis. O*NET contains data describing over 900 occupational groups. What is more, O*NET was designed as an online system (http://online.onetcenter.org). O*NET descriptors for each job include: job titles and alternative names used for the job, knowledge, skills, abilities, tasks, generalized work activities, work context, experience levels required, job interests, and work values/needs. Each O*NET occupational title and code is based on the US Standard Occupational Classification (SOC) system. This means that O*NET information links directly to US labor market information, such as wage and employment statistics. While these latter links are of less use outside the US, the main core of the system is a very valuable general resource.

O*NET is important because as well as being a job classification system:

- It also contains a wealth of job-analysis data.
- It is updated on a regular basis.
- It provides a "crosswalk" capability so that DOT job codes (and other classification system codes) can be used to reference O*NET job descriptions.
- It has drawn from the best work in psychology to define its taxonomy.
- It is freely available for use by anyone, with its ongoing development being funded by the US government.

There is nothing comparable in the rest of the world in terms of amount of detail and quality of information, and although some of the job titles do not translate easily into other cultures, most of the content of the database is usable in any country.

Job Analysis Methods

There is a bewildering array of different job-analysis methods and tools. In this chapter we will review the range that is available, but will not be able to look into these in any depth. The section near the end of this chapter called "The Research Close Up," however, will give a better impression of what a job analysis actually involves.

The methods job analysts use depend on what type of work-related information they are trying to collect. This in turn is a function of why they are doing the job analysis, what sort of aspects of the job they need to focus on, and how much detail they need to go into.

Types of information

McCormick (1976) distinguished a number of different types of information:

1. Work activities – what you have to do.
2. Work performance – how well you have to do it.
3. Job context – the business, social and physical settings in which you have to do it.
4. The machines, tools and equipment you need to do the job.
5. Job-related outcomes, such as material produced or services delivered.
6. Personnel requirements, such as KSAOs.

The first five of these fall into the work-oriented types of analysis, whereas the sixth is purely worker-oriented. However, worker-oriented descriptions can cover all these aspects from the viewpoint of what the person has to do, the standard they need to attain, and so on.

Sanchez and Levine (2001) reflect the changes since the 1970s with a wider range of types of information:

1. Organizational philosophy and structure – how the job fits into the organization and its mission
2. Licensing and other mandated requirements, which may limit the range of people who can do the job and affect the job content.
3. Responsibilities – types and levels of responsibility and accountability.
4. Professional standards – such as the application of national psychological association ethical codes of conduct to psychologists.

5. Job context – the environment physical and social, work patterns (e.g. shiftwork).
6. Products and services – what the worker produces or the service they deliver in the job.
7. Machines, tools, work aids, and equipment – what skills the person needs and the range of tools etc they need to be able to work with.
8. Work performance indicators – including performance standards.
9. Personal job demands – physical, social, and psychological demands the job makes on people.
10. Elemental motions – breaking down complex maneuvers into the detailed elements that make them up
11. Worker activities – a worker-oriented view of what they have to do in the job (e.g. planning, decision-making, etc.).
12. Work activities – looking at the job in terms of the observable behaviors.
13. Worker trait requirements (the person specification). What are the knowledge skills abilities and other characteristics (KSAOs) required by the worker?
14. Future changes – how will the job change in the future?
15. Critical incidents (see below).

The US O*NET (Dye & Silver, 1999) provides a good example of a system that covers all the types of information relevant to jobs. It has a structure that categorizes information into six main areas (see figure 1.1).

Methods and sources of job information

Information for a job analysis can be obtained from a variety of sources in various ways. The main source of information for job analysis is job incumbents. However, supervisors and professional job analysts are also valuable sources of data (for example, the O*NET system is a repository of data collected by many job analysts over many years). Where jobs are being designed, then it is not possible to ask job incumbents about the job – as there will not be any. Job incumbents are also likely to focus on the job as it is now and not on how it may need to be developed to meet the organization's changing needs. People are not the only source of information about jobs; observation methods can also be used. For some jobs there are detailed records of what the job incumbents do (for example, the computerized records kept of call center operators). Electronic Performance Monitoring (EMP) is not new: pilots have been flying with black boxes that record their actions and communications for some time now. Computerization of the workplace has seen this type of real-time monitoring become more common in other areas too.

Sanchez (2000) has noted a number of points of caution regarding the use of job incumbents as sources of information for job analysis.

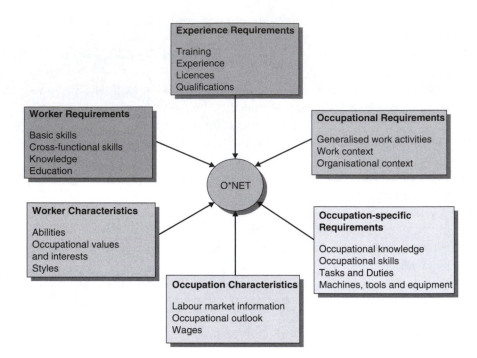

Figure 1.1: The O*Net content model (based on Mumford & Peterson, 1999)

- It takes a lot of time away from their work.
- They may not always be motivated to give an objective and unbiased account of what they do.
- They will be unfamiliar with the job-analysis tools and methods.
- There is no empirical evidence to suggest that they provide more valid job descriptions than nonincumbents.

In practice it is advisable not to rely on a single source of information. After all, there is no "correct" job analysis. All sources of information and methods of collecting data give slightly different perspectives on the job.

The tools used by job analysts tend to fall into two types: those where the job analysts are obtaining direct evidence about the nature of the job and those which rely on the opinions or judgment of other people. In the first category we have:

- Documentation relating to the job (such as job manuals, instruction manuals, maintenance records).
- Observation of job incumbents at work, either directly or through remote CCTV monitoring and multimedia data analysis.
- Diaries kept by job incumbents.

In the second category there are a large number of tools and methods that can broadly be classified as either:

- Questionnaires completed by job incumbents or other Subject Matter Experts (SMEs).
- Various forms of structured interview with job incumbents or other SMEs.

Job-analysis interviews with job incumbents or other SMEs can be structured in various different ways. An increasingly common method is the *future-oriented interview*. This is used to understand what KSAOs a job is likely to require in the future. Many of the questionnaires and other techniques described below are used in a job-incumbent interview where the job analyst uses the questionnaire or tool as an interview guide or device to structure the interview.

Direct data collection methods

One of the first things a job analyst does is to examine prior job descriptions relating to the job in question, if these exist. Training manuals and other training materials will be examined as these indicate what the necessary knowledge and skills are. In some cases there may be well-developed occupational standards, either produced by the organization or adopted from national occupational standards frameworks (like the NVQ system in the UK: http://www.dfes.gov.uk/nvq/).

Other valuable sources of initial data are job databases, like the O*NET, where similar job can be examined and preliminary descriptions produced for checking and verification with job incumbents and local SMEs. Operational staff, the organizations' HR department, and line managers can also provide factual information about the job, its role in the organization, pay rates, and so on.

Having obtained this preliminary information, one of the oldest forms of job analysis is to then observe people at work. Psychologists have watched people at work, sometimes asking questions about what they are doing or why, sometimes even trying to do the job themselves to get a better understanding of it. The main limitation of watching what people do is that for many jobs this provides very little information about the job and even less about the qualities required to do it. For example, watching a screen writer at work producing a script will not identify the personal creative skills that are needed for the job.

Time-and-motion (T&M) studies evolved from industrial engineering as methods to try to make production more efficient. In practice T&M is a collection of techniques that remain useful tools for the job analysis for certain job types, especially where optimizing the work environment and the working processes and procedures is the aim of the job analysis. T&M techniques can be used to analyze how long it takes people to perform various tasks and subtasks and the movements required, and then used in job or equipment redesign or for analyzing training needs.

Hierarchical Task Analysis (HTA) was developed in the 1960s in the UK by Annett and Duncan (1967) and their colleagues (see Shepherd, 2001). It is used mainly in the analysis of complex tasks for work design and training design purposes. However, it can also be useful in identifying job incumbent attributes necessary for selection. As its name implies, it involves identifying goals and subgoals and then breaking them down into details of the tasks and task sequences required to achieve them. HTA requires the use of considerable expertise to do well and is generally a method used by expert job analysts rather than HR personnel.

Computer-based and video-based observation. Nowadays, it is rare to see a job analyst with a clipboard and a stopwatch. For a lot of jobs, performance is recorded on CCTV and examined later using a range of content analysis methods. For some jobs, computer-recoding (EMP) is a built-in part of many tasks (for example, call logging for call-center operators, vehicle movement tracking for ambulance drivers, computerized task logging systems for office workers, computer-based consultancy diary and scheduling systems, and so on).

Job diaries. Job incumbents can also be asked to keep a diary of what they are doing over a typical week. This can provide a lot of useful information for the job analyst, but it is dependent on the worker taking the time to fill in the diary accurately and on this activity not interfering with their work itself. Diary methods are probably best used as a method of getting people to make a note of any critical incidents that occur over a longer period of time, rather than trying to document everything they do. Such records can prove a useful source of information for the Critical Incidents Technique (discussed below). Modern technology provides the opportunity to use diaries in a more creative way. Job incumbents can be provided with hand-held computers that are programmed to ring an alarm at certain times. When the alarm goes off, the PDA can be programmed to provide some questions to be answered, scales to rate, or a set of options to choose from for the person to give some indication of what they are doing, how difficult it is, and so on.

Cognitive task analysis (CTA: Vincente, 1999). All the above observational methods rely on the nature of a job being revealed in what people can be seen to do. However, successful performance in many jobs is more a function of thinking than doing. CTA is a way of getting job incumbents to "think aloud" as they work. It has a long history of use in cognitive psychology – for example, in trying to understand how experts achieve high levels of performance. It is not without its problems, though. The act of thinking aloud is difficult to do and can interfere with the thinking itself. It is very time consuming to do and to analyze, and for most routine job analysis it may add little of practical value. Its main use may be in helping design training and identifying areas where job redesign might be of benefit, especially where costly errors or accidents occur (safety-critical jobs) or where there are persistent performance problems to diagnose.

Task-oriented data collection methods

Task Inventory Analysis (TIA). The most basic approach to job analysis starts with the identification of tasks in order to produce a questionnaire or checklist for a specific job. This approach is job specific, and results in a new questionnaire for every job. Consequently, comparisons between jobs are not possible with this approach. The task inventories are typically generated through interviewing SMS or SME discussion panels and will contain statements about what the worker does in the job, how it is done, and why. The resulting TIA is then used to get information from job incumbents on one or more of the following scales: time spent relative to other tasks, importance, difficulty, and criticality to the job.

Critical Incidents Technique (CIT) was developed originally by Flanagan (1954) in studies for the US Army Air Force. It focuses on identifying the particular aspects of the job that are critical for success, or failure (see box 1.1). To do properly it is a very time-consuming and demanding process. CIT is a very good method of getting a lot of detailed behavioral data about a specific job or role. By its nature, it is difficult to use what is found to make comparisons between jobs, although one can use some standard frameworks to classify the events when carrying out the content analysis.

Functional Job Analysis (FJA) (Fine, 1988) arose from the development of the DOT. It is a technique that aims to generate task statements and identify for each task what the person does, why and how it is done, and what is accomplished by the work. For each task, the analyst also defines the orientation and level of involvement the person has in working with People, Data, and Things (known as the worker functions). Training time is defined by the level of reasoning, mathematics, and language required. The methodology is a mixture of a work-focused approach (task statements), that does not allow for cross-job comparisons, and a worker-oriented approach that does.

Worker-oriented data collection methods

Repertory grid analysis (RGA) (e.g. Dick & Jankowicz, 2001; Honey, 1979) is widely used in job analysis in the UK, but rarely in the USA. It is a method used

> ## Box 1.1:   Five main stages of Critical Incidents Technique
>
> 1. Determine the general aim of the activity or job
>
> 2. Provide a definition of a critical incident: e.g. an incident, the successful or unsuccessful handling of which has had a significant impact upon the performance of the individual or on other people.
>
> 3. Develop a plan and specification for the collection of factual incidents, including deciding who should provide these and how the data will be obtained from them. Generally, this involves developing a standard set of questions the person needs to answer, such as "What were the circumstances leading up to the event?" "What did the person do?" "What was the outcome of the action?" etc.
>
> 4. Collection of the data. This can result in hundreds or even thousands of incident descriptions being obtained. Data can be collected through face-to-face interviews or, for practical reasons, on computer through forms on an organization's intranet.
>
> 5. Analysis of the descriptions. This is carried out using content analysis techniques to identify common themes and dimensions. It will generally be computer-based these days, using qualitative data-analysis software.
>
> 6. Interpretation and reporting. The result of the analysis need to be reported and related to the purpose of the analysis.

to elicit constructs that help define the qualities needed for success in the job. Typically, SMEs are asked to think of between 8 and 12 people, some of whom are successful and some unsuccessful at the job. They may also be asked to include a hypothetical "ideal" job incumbent. They are then presented with subsets of three people drawn from this sample and asked to identify a job-relevant construct that differentiates one of them from the other two. They rate all the people on this construct, and the process is repeated with a new subsample of three people. The final set of construct ratings can then be analyzed to identify what attributes differentiate successful from unsuccessful job incumbents, or ideal employees from others. The same approach can be used where people are asking to think of some work activities rather than people and these are then used to elicit constructs. RGA requires a lot of data if it is to produce reliable results. Typically one needs to spend an hour or so with about 30 people in order to elicit sufficient constructs for an analysis.

The *Job Elements Method (JEM)*, developed by Primoff and Eyde (1988) is designed to identify the behaviors that are significant to job success (see box 1.2). It is mainly focused on identifying worker characteristics important for selection and analyzing training needs. The job elements refer to behaviors and the sources of evidence that can be used to indicate their occurrence. The examples of evidence are described as sub-elements. For example, "reliability" is the behavior of

---

Box 1.2:   Outline of the Job Elements Method procedure

A panel of SMEs is used to identify elements and sub-elements relevant for the job in terms of KSAOs and then evaluate the elements using four scales:

1.   To what extent will a "barely acceptable worker" have the KSAO?

2.   How important is the KSAO for a "superior worker"?

3.   How much trouble is their likely to be if this KSAO is ignored?

4.   How easy will it be to find people who can meet the requirements for this KSAO?

Ratings on the four scales are combined for each element into:

•   An "item index," which indicates the value of the element in a selection context,

•   A "total index," which indicates the usefulness of the element in differentiating between applicants for the job,

•   A "training index," which relates to the importance of including the element in job training.

---

acting in a dependable way (a job element) and it can be evidenced by seeing if someone turns up to work on time, can be trusted to do what they are told, and so on. This approach is very similar to the behavioral competencies approach described later.

Ability Requirements Scale (ARS) developed by Fleishman and his coworkers. Fleishman defined abilities as "relatively enduring attributes of the individual that influence a broad range of task performance "(Fleishman & Mumford, 1988, p. 918). The scales in the ARS are based on extensive research by Fleishman and his colleagues into the structure of human ability. The ARS covers 37 abilities which have either a broadly cognitive (e.g. oral expression) or physical character (fine motor control). The abilities do not include personality, values, interests, or motivation.

Position Analysis Questionnaire (PAQ) (McCormick, 1976; McCormick et al., 1972, 1979). The PAQ is one of the most widely used job-analysis question-naires. It has 195 items. The first 187 are job-element items rated on a five-point scale. They are divided into six sections: information input, mental processes, information output, and relationships with other persons, job context, and other job characteristics. Ratings typically focus on the importance of the item for the job, or its complexity or frequency. The items describe behaviors involved in work activities that are not job specific. As a result the PAQ can be used to make comparisons between jobs. The ratings are used to define 45 dimension scores: 13 from the overall analysis and the rest from analysis of each of the 6 sections. Scale profiles on the dimensions can be linked to person specifications and assessment requirements. The links to person specification are carried out through relationships between the PAQ dimensions and 76 personal attributes. Specification of personal attribute requirements can then be generated from the job element job profile.

The PAQ is best suited to lower-level and mid-level jobs. It is quite difficult to use as a means of describing higher-level management or professional positions. However, McCormick and colleagues later developed a questionnaire to cover this area of the world of work as well: the Professional and Managerial Position Questionnaire (PMPQ) (Mitchell & McCormick, 1979).

Threshold Trait Analysis (TTA) focuses on identifying the personal characteristics that are important for performing a job effectively (Lopez, 1988). It uses a work-oriented approach and covers 33 personal qualities categorized into five groups: mental, physical, learned, motivational, and social. The first three of these are called ability or "can do" factors, and the last two are called attitude or "will do" factors. The "will do" aspects are an addition to what is found in many other early job-analysis systems, though it is a key part of more recent competency-based approaches (see below). "Will do" aspects related to jobs can be found in the O*Net in the Work Values section. The TTA is used by SMEs (a minimum of five per job is recommended) rating the relevance, level and practicality of each of the 33 traits for acceptable job performance. As the traits are general, it is possible to make cross-job comparisons with this method.

The *Personality-Related Position Requirements Form (PPRF)* was developed by Raymark and colleagues (Raymark, Schmit, & Guion, 1997) to generate hypotheses about the importance of various personality attributes for job performance. Twelve scales linked to the Big 5 personality factors are scored in terms of how important they are for effective performance in the job. The scales include, for example, general leadership, interest in negotiation, and achievement striving as subdimensions of extraversion. This approach really has more in common with competency profiling approaches, which are described later, than traditional work- or worker-oriented job analyses.

Work Profiling System (WPS: SHL, 1998) is an example of a computerized job-analysis system that streamlines the process of data collection and interpretation. WPS was developed in the UK but is mainly used in South Africa and the US, where the legal systems require organizations to be able to show a clear audit trail from job requirements to selection assessment methods. WPS has a similar approach to the PAQ, but covers all job types (from blue-collar up to senior management) – see box 1.3 for details – and is also linked into competency modeling methods.

Box 1.3: Outline of the Work Profiling System (WPS)

WPS integrates three databases using algorithms to weight and integrate information between them.

1. Information is initially collected using a behavior-oriented approach (via structured job-analysis questionnaires) and a behavioral profile is created. The behavioral statements in the WPS questionnaires refer to worker-oriented tasks and activities that extend across all jobs in the economy. The questionnaires focus on the actual work done in the job and the work context. SMEs rate the importance and time spent on a range of different tasks. There are three questionnaires, one each for:
   a) Managerial and professional jobs, with 7 sections, 31 task categories, and 344 task statements.
   b) Service and administrative jobs, with 9 sections, 28 task categories, and 298 task statements.
   c) Manual and technical jobs, with 8 sections, 30 task categories, and 325 task statements.

2. A Human Attribute Model (HAM) of the KSAOs necessary to perform various tasks: see figure 1.2. This model is also linked to a general competency framework (described below), from which competency-profile reports can be produced.

3. An inventory of assessment methods (such as personality inventory scales, ability tests, assessment center exercises, etc.) that measure the human attributes defined in the HAM.

Once the job-analysis data has been provided, WPS can generate a range of different reports, including :

- a job description,
- a person specification,
- a performance review form,
- an individual development planner,
- an interview guide for use in selection or development interviewing,
- a specification of recommended assessment tools.

WPS can also generate person specifications in the form of competency profiles (see below: lists of competencies in terms of their relative importance for the job). The tasks in WPS have been mapped to the Universal Competency Framework's 112 competency components (see p. 22). This enables job analysts to generate a competency requirements profile for the job they have analyzed. What is more, by using the UCF's competency modeling tools, the profile can be produced in a form that matches an organization's own competency model.

These competency profiles provide the computer files that can be used together with assessment data from personality, motivation, and ability tests to create "person–job match" reports. These reports provide an indication of how well a person "fits" the competency requirements for a job, and can be used diagnostically to see where the areas of "mis-fit" are and how significant they might be.

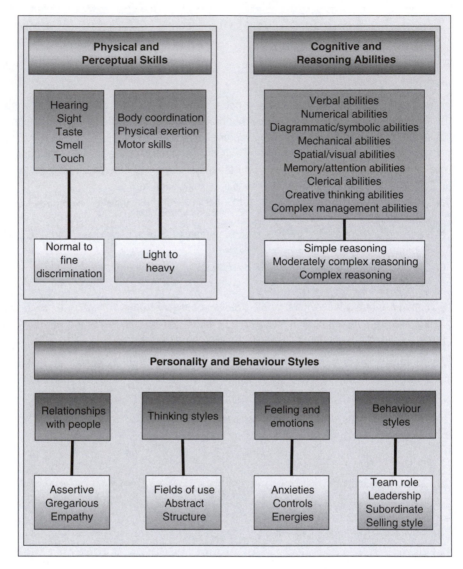

Figure 1.2:   The WPS Human Attribute Model (based on SHL, 2001)

Issues relating to job-analysis methods

All of the questionnaire and interview methods have one or two major potential sources of "error" or bias. Some (TIA, CIT, FJA, JEM, RGA) rely on SMEs to identify which tasks, constructs, or job elements are relevant for the job or to generate these descriptions. All the methods rely on SMEs to give ratings on various scales relating to the relevance of items to the job in question. Thus all these methods are largely dependent on the validity of the opinions of the particular sample of SMEs that have been chosen, and on the ability of those SMEs to make reliable judgments on the questions they are asked.

The direct observation methods get round the problems of SME subjectivity to some degree, but they are limited in other respects. They may provide only a partial picture of what the job involves. As such it is dangerous to rely on them without corroboration from other sources of information.

No single method or source can be said to be the best. They each have advantages and disadvantages. They vary in terms of time required, cost, and resources needed. Nowadays it is fairly simple to get a large number of job incumbents to complete an online job-analysis questionnaire. It takes a lot more time and resources to get the same quantity of data through structured interviews. However, the information obtained from a few interviews may greatly enrich and help to validate the larger quantity of data obtained from the questionnaires.

In terms of formal assessment properties, some job-analysis methods are available as off the shelf tools, with manuals and technical information about their reliability and validity. For example, structured job-analysis questionnaires like WPS or PAQ are backed up by user manuals and technical information that make them comparable to psychometric tests. Use of these helps to ensure that the analysis covers the full range of the tasks that a job incumbent will have to deal with. Other methods are less formally defined and are not standardized. They can provide richer data, but through their lack of standardization can often introduce biases. For example, you would not want to base a person specification on just a visionary interview, as this is likely to give an incomplete picture of the job requirements. However, a future-oriented interview does have value in highlighting qualities that may be needed to as the job changes and evolves in the future.

A typical job analysis may involve use of a questionnaire-based method, like WPS or PAQ, elicitation of some critical incidents, a repertory grid analysis session, and some future-oriented interviews with key SMEs. The job analyst's task is to pull all this information together and produce a balanced overall description of the job and the worker characteristics associated with it. The analysis of reliability and validity of job-analysis data is complex, especially as a wide range of types of data may be involved. Brannick and Levine (2002) provide commentaries on the reliability and validity of a number of methods, and also discuss how to assess reliability and construct validity for job-analysis data in general (pp. 282–90). Usually the main way of assessing reliability is to look at the level of agreement between the various people who are providing job information. The more closely they agree with each other, the more reliable the overall summary of the data will be.

From Job Analysis to Work Profiling

Job-analysis methods have evolved over time using both work-oriented and worker-oriented methods. However, they have different strengths and weaknesses. Worker-oriented approaches tend to produce more general descriptions of human behavior and tend to be less tied to the specifics of the job in question. As such they are more directly suited to the identification of requirements for selection and recruitment, to the design of training programs, and to performance management. Work-oriented approaches on the other hand are more appropriate for work design.

Another difference is that there is considerable evidence to suggest that work-oriented job analysis is less prone to biases and distortions than the worker-oriented approach (Morgerson & Campion, 1997). Worker-oriented approaches rely more on job incumbents and other SMEs providing information about the attributes they need to do the job to an analyst. These reports are more likely to be biased than direct observation by an analyst of the tasks that are being carried out or direct interrogation of job incumbents. A typical bias in reporting from a job incumbent would be to make the job sound more difficult or complex than it is in order to justify higher payment. It is better for the job analysts to decide how difficult or complex the task is having collected information from job incumbents about what they do and why.

However, despite worker-oriented methods being more subject to biases and distortion, they are increasingly being used in preference to work-oriented methods. This is the result of the changing nature of work. People's roles in the workplace are becoming more variable. Many people no longer have a well-defined "job"; rather they are given a set of roles and responsibilities. The exact nature of the tasks is often not fixed. How the person performs is becoming more important than what they perform. There are still many routine jobs that can be specified as a set of tasks that have to be performed according to well-defined procedures. However, we tend to find such routine jobs are being increasingly automated (e.g. the robotization of car production), while people are being expected to deal with the less routine aspects of work.

These changes in the nature of work have resulted in people talking about "work analysis" (Sanchez & Levine, 1999) or "work profiling" rather than job analysis. The new term is intended to capture the idea that people work rather than have fixed "jobs," and the nature of the qualities they need for that work can be defined as a profile of KSAOs. We still end up with a person specification, but the route to it is changing.

Work profiling and competency modeling

As a response to the growing instability of jobs and the inadequacies of the more work-oriented approaches to job analysis, a range of new approaches has developed over the past couple of decades. These include: future-oriented job modeling (Landis, Fogli, & Goldberg, 1998), strategic job analysis (Schneider & Konz,

1989), and strategic job modeling (SJM: Schippmann, 1999). These can all be considered to be extensions of the more traditional worker-orientated job-analysis approaches.

Schneider and Konz (1989) talk about processes through which one can identify the skills required for jobs in the future. Schippmann states that SJM focuses on the "strategic and future-oriented needs of today's organizations." He divides the description of a work position into job description variables and situation variables. The former consist of work activity and competency variables and the latter of work context and strategic context variables. These can be described as the people side and the work side of an equation, where the work side defines requirements and the people side defines the available capabilities. Schippmann see the interface between these two as being via competencies (the fit between those that are required and those that are available). He defines competencies as "measurable, occupationally relevant, and behaviorally based characteristics or capabilities of people" (p. 20). These are broken down into two main categories: "Can do" competencies (relating to knowledge and skills) and "Will-do" competencies (relating to personality and attitudinal factors). These are also referred to as technical competencies and behavioral competencies.

On the "People" side of the equation, competencies sit at the top of a pyramid, with education, training, and experience feeding into them, and with abilities, traits, interests, values, and motivations at the base. On the work side, the specification of competencies required in a position are at the top of a pyramid that has work activities and work context at is middle level and organizational vision, competitive strategy and strategic business initiatives at its base.

There is not space here to go into the further details of Schippmann's model, but it provides a good example of how work profiling integrates an understanding of the nature of the work involved, the personal characteristics required, and the role of the work within the broader organizational context. It is also important for emphasizing the need to express job requirements and person capabilities in the same language (i.e. competencies) if we are to assess the degree of fit between the two.

The ability to set jobs in their organizational context is one of the main reasons for the growing emphasis on competencies, which provide a common language for talking about diverse jobs. Traditional job analysis looks at each job on its own and does not provide the means of linking job descriptions into business strategy. Competency modeling is different. It can start from asking the very broad question of "What is this organization trying to achieve?" The answer to this question should be a set of objectives or outcomes and criteria for recognizing when they have been achieved. One can then ask the question, "How are these going to be achieved? What are the competencies necessary for the organization to be able to achieve these outcomes?" Competency modeling at the strategic level can be used to answer these sorts of questions. Such modeling procedures provide a common language for then talking about what is required from individual positions throughout the organization if the outcomes from people's work in those positions are to contribute to the organization's goals. In this respect, properly used, competency modeling becomes a very powerful performance management tool.

Unfortunately, the word "competency" has had a very checkered career. It was rapidly adopted within the HR community as a term to describe almost anything about people that related to how successful they were in their job. Nearly everyone had their own definition of competency. Some were over-inclusive, like Boyatzis (1982), who said a competency was any underlying characteristic of an individual that was related to effective or superior performance. Others confused the term with standards of performance (or competence).

The plethora of definitions has meant that the construct has been ill-defined and, as a result, has not attracted much attention from the academic community. That is changing, and there is now a growing number of studies that explore the construct of competency and its role in work profiling. A turning point was the report in Personnel Psychology of the Job Analysis and Competency Modeling Task Force (JACMTF: Schippmann et al., 2000). What this report has done it to help provide a "respectable" position for competency modeling within the work profiling toolkit. They also noted the move towards more operational definitions of competencies that will provide the basis for greater rigor in their identification and measurement.

Bartram (2002) defined competencies as "sets of behaviors that are instrumental in the delivery of desired results." This definition underlies the development of a "Universal Competency Framework" (UCF: SHL, 2004) that attempts to capture all aspects of behavior in the workplace as competency components. The UCF model defines 112 component competencies, each consisting of a set of behavioral anchor definitions, which provide the building blocks for creating organization-specific competency models (Kurz & Bartram, 2002). Recent research has also identified eight broad factors that these components fall under and has shown how measures of personality, motivation and ability relate to these performance factors (Bartram, 2005). Box 1.4 contains a description of each of the Great 8 competencies, together with their related underlying psychological attributes.

Further work on this model has demonstrated how rules can be generated that derive competency requirements from job descriptions. Bartram and Brown (2005) describe how they used the O*NET as a source of job descriptions and defined algorithms that linked O*NET job attributes to competency profiles for different jobs (see the "Research Close-up" below). This study showed that it is possible to produce competency profiles from job descriptions in a rigorous way and with a level of reliability greater than the competency profiles produced by a job incumbent.

Box 1.4:   Titles and definitions of the Great Eight Competencies

More detailed definitions of each of the Great Eight are provided by the competency component level of the SHL Universal Competency Framework™ (see Bartram, 2005, Appendix A). The final column shows the hypothesized relationships between the Big Five, General Mental Ability, and Motivation for the Great Eight. Where more than one predictor is shown, the second is expected to be of less importance than the first.

Competency domain title	Competency domain definition	Big 5, motivation, and ability relationships
Leading & Deciding	Takes control and exercises leadership. Initiates action, gives direction, and takes responsibility.	Need for power and control, Extraversion
Supporting & Cooperating	Supports others and shows respect and positive regard for them in social situations. Puts people first, working effectively with individuals and teams, clients and staff. Behaves consistently with clear personal values that complement those of the organization.	Agreeableness
Interacting & Presenting	Communicates and networks effectively. Successfully persuades and influences others. Relates to others in a confident and relaxed manner.	Extraversion, General mental ability
Analyzing & Interpreting	Shows evidence of clear analytical thinking. Gets to the heart of complex problems and issues. Applies own expertise effectively. Quickly takes on new technology. Communicates well in writing	General mental ability, Openness to experience
Creating & Conceptualizing	Works well in situations requiring openness to new ideas and experiences. Seeks out learning opportunities. Handles situations and problems with innovation and creativity. Thinks broadly and strategically. Supports and drives organizational change.	Openness to experience, General mental ability

Continued

Organizing & Executing	Plans ahead and works in a systematic and organized way. Follows directions and procedures. Focuses on customer satisfaction and delivers a quality service or product to the agreed standards.	Conscientiousness General mental ability
Adapting & Coping	Adapts and responds well to change. Manages pressure effectively and copes well with setbacks.	Emotional stability
Enterprising & Performing	Focuses on results and achieving personal work objectives. Works best when work is related closely to results and the impact of personal efforts is obvious. Shows an understanding of business, commerce and finance. Seeks opportunities for self-development and career advancement.	Need for achievement, Negative agreeableness

Note: The titles and definitions in this table are taken from the SHL Universal Competency Framework™ Profiler Cards (copyright © 2004 by SHL Group plc, reproduced with permission of the copyright holder). These titles and definitions may be freely used for research purposes subject to due acknowledgment of the copyright holder.

No one is advocating that job analysis should be replaced by competency modeling; rather, the latter provides some additional value through its focus on the worker, on personal values and personality, on the notion of core competencies that are common across jobs, and on the notion of a person's "fit" to an organization as well as to a job within that organization.

Job analysis remains necessary as a means of identifying competencies (Sparrow & Bognano, 1993). Sanchez and Levine (2001) have commented that the distinction between the two is, in any case, rather blurred – especially when one compares worker-oriented job-analysis methods with some of the more rigorous competency modeling approaches. The key advantage of competency modeling approaches from the business side is the way in which this links business goals and strategies to individual people working in an organization. The key challenge is to apply more scientific rigor to competency modeling methods. This requires us to be very clear about the definition of competencies. The more they can be anchored in observable behaviors the easier it is to measure them with reliability.

We also need to be clear about why certain competencies are important for a job, if the approach is to have any validity. There are two main complementary approaches to this. One is to be able to demonstrate the "audit trail" from desired outcomes or goals, through to the behaviors that are required to achieve these results. The second is to provide empirically validated links between job tasks and job requirements and the personal characteristics that enable people to meet those requirements.

In general, it is recommended that multiple methods and multiple sources are used to analyze jobs whenever time and resources allow. Furthermore, the sort of data, the quantity of data, and the level of specificity of it should be related to why the analysis is being done (job design, training, evaluation, etc). Factors such as the commercial risks involved, health and safety concerns, the number of people or positions affected, and the nature of the interventions will determine the methods to be included in a multimethod approach.

The Future

As the nature of work changes and moves away from being highly task-based to be more role and function based, so the nature of job analysis has to change. We have seen this in the way that the job-analysis methods popular during the last century are giving way to competency profiling and methods that pay more attention to the qualities people need to cope with the demands work places on them. Job analysis is being replaced by work profiling.

Job-analysis methods are not foolproof. A single job incumbent's ratings tend to have quite low reliability, but in practice they are often used as the basis for all sorts of important business decisions. We know that reliability and validity are enhanced through the aggregation of information that has become possible with the advent of facilities like O*NET and computerized job-analysis and data collection tools like WPS. It is almost certainly going to be more valid to use a person specification generated from a well-defined job selected from a database like O*NET, than it is to rely on a single job incumbent to profile their job.

While there are an infinite number of different jobs in the world of work, and everybody's job is unique in some respects, the differences between them in terms of person requirements can be captured by a relatively small number of variables. Differences are therefore predictable in such a way that it will not be necessary to carry out an expensive in-depth job analysis for every job as though it were something new. Job-analysis databases will develop to provide the tools for assessing how well a particular job fits the profiles of jobs in the database, and hence how "transportable" the database content is to that new job.

Summary

Job analysis is a critical step in many different applications of psychology to work. We need to understand the nature of the job requirements and the demands they will make on people in order to better design the workplace, select people for jobs, or train them. A large number of different approaches to job analysis have been reviewed. In practice, none are sufficient on their own. Good job analysis involves a multimethod approach which ensures good coverage of all the important aspects of the role and does not result in job descriptions being biased by common methods factors.

We have seen that as the world of work is changing and as the nature of the demands made on people at work evolves, so job analysis has changed. The emphasis has shifted away from a detailing of tasks, to an understanding of roles and responsibilities. This has been accompanied by the development of competency-based approaches to specifying person requirements.

Job analysis is costly and time-consuming. As a result it is often skimped on by organizations. This is to be regretted because it is such an important underpinning to performance management and to ensuring that organizations and workers share a clear understanding of what they are doing and why.

Discussion Points

Why do we need both work-oriented and worker-oriented approaches to job analysis?

Why has competency modeling become so popular?

Key Studies

Schippmann, J. S., Ash, R. A., Battista, M., Carr, L., Eyde, L. D., Hesketh, B., et al. (2000). The practice of competency modeling. *Personnel Psychology*, *53*, 703–39.

McCormick, E. J. (1976). Job and task analysis. In M.D. Dunnette (Ed.), *Handbook of industrial and organizational psychology* (pp. 651–97). Chicago: Rand McNally.

Further Reading

www.job-analysis.net. An HR website with a lot of useful information about job-analysis methods and uses.

http://online.onetcenter.org/. The O*NET website. Click on "related links" to take you to a whole lot of other material on job analysis, including job-analysis questionnaires: http://www.onetcenter.org/questionnaires.htmlone.

Brannick, M. T., & Levine, E. L. (2002). *Job analysis: Methods, research and applications for human resource management in the new millennium*. Thousand Oaks, CA: Sage Publications. An up-to-date and accessible overview of job analysis.

Gael, S. (Ed.). (1988). *The job analysis handbook for business, industry and govern-* *ment* (Vols. 1 and 2). New York: Wiley. A comprehensive collection of chapters covering all the major methods of job analysis.

Research Close-Up

Abstracted from: Bartram, D., & Brown, A. (2005, Jan.). Generating competency profiles from job descriptions. *Proceedings of the British Psychological Society's Occu-* *pational Psychology Conference*, Chesford Grange, pp. 63–7. Leicester, UK: BPS.

Introduction

This study explored the question: Is it possible to generate valid competency profiles directly from the information contained in an O*NET job description? Job incumbent ratings of the importance of the 20 UCF competencies (SHL, 2004) were used as a criterion measure and then predicted using equations based on combinations of data from the O*NET 5.1 database (http://online.onetcenter. org/). O*NET provides a common language for defining and describing occupations (Peterson et al., 2001). The O*NET Content Model reflects the character of occupations (via job-oriented descriptors) and people (via worker-oriented descriptors). The O*NET Standard Occupational Classification (SOC) divides more than 900 jobs into 23 categories.

Method and procedure

The criterion data set was created by merging data from a number of job-analysis projects, consisting of 444 raters (job incumbents), representing 125 SOC codes covering 18 of the 23 O*NET SOC job families. To generate importance ratings on the 20 Competency Dimensions we have to create a comprehensive and stable map between the O*NET Content Model and the 20 Competency Dimension Model. Using such a map enables us to automatically produce competency importance profiles on demand for all O*NET SOC codes in a systematic and auditable fashion. The mapping was carried out using O*NET Abilities and Values from the *Worker Characteristics* domain, Skills from the *Worker Requirements* domain, and Generalized Work Activities (GWAs) and Work Context from the *Occupational Requirements* domain. To create the mappings we asked the following question: "Which abilities (or skills, values, GWAs, contexts) are likely to influence behaviors associated with Competency X (where X is one of the 20 competencies in the UCF model)?" The final mappings included between 4 and 7 O*NET descriptors as predictors for each of the 20 competencies. After selecting O*NET descriptors best related to each of the 20 Competency Dimensions, unit weighted equations were defined to produce each of the 20 Competency Dimension scores. The resulting scores were defined as O*NET prediction scores.

Results

Profile Similarities (correlations) between the O*NET prediction scores and the job

Continued

incumbent criterion ratings were distributed with a mean of 0.61 and Standard Deviation 0.19. With corrections for unreliability in the criterion measures (the average reliability of the ratings was only 0.50) the average profile similarity is 0.86.

Discussion

This research has shown that it is possible to generate valid competency profiles from a standard job description using an automated process. The correlation of 0.86 represents the level of agreement between the absolute values of ratings generated using the O*NET-UCF prediction equations and a perfectly reliable job incumbent rater. In practice profiles generated by job incumbent are not very reliable. Automated generation from a job database is intrinsically more reliable.

The accuracy with which we could predict criterion ratings was surprisingly high, and provides encouragement to ongoing research that is attempting to apply this approach to a wider range of competency models and other job description systems.

Work Motivation

Guido Hertel and Marion Wittchen

2

Overview

In this chapter, content- and process-related theories of work motivation are described and discussed. Content-related theories focus on reasons *why* individuals are motivated, including personal (e.g., need for achievement, need to belong) and situational factors (e.g., task-related features such as meaningfulness, feedback, autonomy). Process-related theories explain *how* motivation evolves and is transformed into goal-directed action, including decisions between different action options (expectancy theories), the development of action intentions (goal-setting theory), the (self-)monitoring of action (self-regulation theory), and the evaluation of action results (job satisfaction, justice theory). In addition, individual motivation in work teams and the development of work motivation over the life-span are discussed as more recent research fields. After reading this chapter, you should be able to understand the main tenets of the described theories, to evaluate their basic virtues and weaknesses, and to apply them to practical issues.

Introduction

Motivation is a broad and frequently used term referring to psychological processes that initiate and determine direction, intensity, and persistence of voluntary and goal-directed actions (Mitchell, 1987). *Work motivation* refers to internal and external forces that initiate work-related action and determine its form, direction, intensity, and duration (Pinder, 1998). While abilities and training determine whether employees *can* perform the job they are assigned to, motivation determines whether employees *will* do it as best as they can. Crucial questions regarding work motivation are "Why do some individuals show high motivation in their job, while others do not?", and "How is high motivation transformed into effective work behavior?" Potential answers to the first question have to include both personal and task-related factors (cf. figure 2.1), an idea that goes

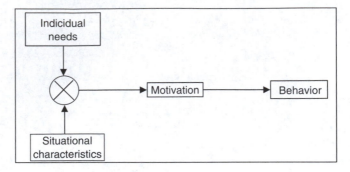

Figure 2.1: Basic motivation model (Rheinberg, 2004)

back to Lewin (1938). *Content-related* theories offer personal needs and interests together with features of the working task as explanations for different motivation levels. In contrast, *process-related* theories focus on the development of work motivation and the transformation into concrete action. First, we will describe and discuss content-related theories of motivation.

Content-Related Theories of Work Motivation

Content-related theories of work motivation explain work-related actions as either determined by certain characteristics of employees, the task, or the job context, or by the interaction of these factors. When they address work behavior that is activated and maintained by person or task characteristics only, they refer to intrinsically motivated behavior that needs no external rewards such as monetary incentives.

The debate is still continued whether external rewards such as payment might undermine intrinsic motivation (Deci, Koestner, & Ryan, 1999; Cameron, Banko, & Pierce, 2001). Meta-analyses have revealed that expected monetary rewards decrease intrinsic motivation mainly during interesting tasks, whereas pay for performance can even *increase* intrinsic motivation during less interesting tasks (Cameron et al., 2001). Moreover, most studies that have demonstrated detrimental effects of tangible rewards were conducted in the laboratory with rather short-time and meaningless tasks, and with school children as participants. The few studies that have examined these effects in organizational settings with grown-up employees and meaningful tasks indicate that pay for performance rather increases than decreases intrinsic motivation (Rynes, Gerhart, & Parks, 2005), signaling competence, autonomy, or the achievement of performance goals. Thus, external rewards are not necessarily in conflict with intrinsic motivation in organizational settings.

In the following section of this chapter, theories on individual needs as antecedents for intrinsic motivation will be discussed.

Individual needs

The concept of individual needs serves to explain individual differences in the striving for specific outcomes or situations. Needs are biological concepts and are assumed to have a genetic base. They guide human behavior usually unconsciously, and can differ in their strength between individuals. Various need approaches have been developed that are relevant for work motivation.

Among the approaches that focus on specific needs, McClelland (1961) suggested that employees differ in their need for achievement, affiliation, and power. *Need for achievement* refers to individuals' tendency to seek and accomplish challenging tasks. Persons with high need for achievement are particularly motivated in challenging jobs where they can show their competence in comparison to performance standards. Moreover, need for achievement has been found to be related to self-reported *personal initiative* at work (Frese, Fay, Hilburger, Leng, & Tag, 1997), i.e. voluntary proactive behavior that is characterized by consistence with organizational goals, persistence, and action orientation. *Need for affiliation* refers to individuals' evaluation of social interaction with others (colleagues, supervisors). Thus, employees with high need for affiliation are particularly motivated by jobs that include interdependent work with others such as teamwork. A related concept is *need to belong* (Baumeister & Leary, 1995), which refers to the individual tendency to build and maintain interpersonal relationships. A strong need to belong motivates people to invest high levels of time and energy into social relationships, and to suffer more than others when they are deprived from enduring and meaningful relationships. Finally, the *need for power* or dominance refers to the interest in influencing others. Thus, persons with a high need of power might be particularly motivated in supervisory and management positions.

An initial measure of the needs for achievement, affiliation, and power was the "Thematic Apperception Test" developed by Murray (1938). In this projective test, ambiguous pictures (see figure 2.2) are presented, and the participants are asked to invent stories based on this picture. It is assumed that these stories reflect participant's motivational disposition. While this procedure is quite time consuming and must be administered by a trained psychologist, a number of more economic and objective paper/pencil tests have been developed more recently (Cassidy & Lynn, 1989; Schmalt, 1999; Stahl, 1983).

Perhaps the most prominent multiple classification of human needs is Maslow's (1943) hierarchical model that postulates five need types as determinants of human behavior. These five types are arranged in ascending order. The first four types are considered as deficiency needs that generate tension and drive to act when they are not satisfied. The first type contains *physiological needs*, such as need for air, water, food, and warmth. The second level contains *safety needs* including lack of danger, threat, and deprivation. The third level contains *social needs* including the need for belonging and social contact. The forth level

Figure 2.2: TAT sample picture

contains *self-esteem needs* including the desire for recognition, appreciation, and respect by others. The final and highest level need type, need for *self-actualization*, is categorized as growth needs. In contrast to deficiency needs, growth needs can not be fully satisfied. Self-actualization is defined as one's full human potential. Maslow's hierarchy has been among the first approaches that stressed self-actualization as important motivator in working contexts, thus supporting human factors at work. However, the preconditions and the measurement of self-actualization are still not well understood. Moreover, the central assumption of Maslow's model that the different need types are activated in hierarchical order is discussed quite controversially. According to Maslow, higher needs such as self-esteem or social needs should determine behavior only when lower needs are satisfied. Convincing empirical evidence for this "satisfaction-progression hypothesis" is lacking.

Due to its heuristic plausibility, Maslow's model is still quite popular, in particular among managers and consultants. However, most empirical tests of the model have failed (Wahba & Bridwell, 1987). Particularly, the number and distinction of the five need categories could not be empirically validated, neither their assumed hierarchical organization. However, this is not to dismiss Maslow's need hierarchy entirely. It should be kept in mind that Maslow developed the model based on logical and clinical insights, not as a testable theory in the usual sense. For instance, he did neither outline ways to test the model empirically, nor did he specify the concrete time span for the described processes (hours, days, years). Thus, the main merit of the model is its normative and philosophical statement about general values of work and organizational psychology as a whole, directing the attention to personal growth and self-actualization as an important need of employees and organizational possibilities to meet them (Muchinsky, 2003).

Table 2.1: Reiss profile of basic motives (adapted from Haverkamp & Reiss, 2003)

Need	Description
Power	Desire to influence others including leadership and dominance
Curiosity	Desire to achieve knowledge
Independence	Desire for freedom and autonomy
Status	Desire for social standing, wealth, and attention
Social contact	Desire for peer relationships
Vengeance	Desire to get even including the desire to compete and win
Honor	Desire to obey a traditional moral code
Idealism	Desire for integrity and loyalty
Physical exercise	Desire to physical exercise
Romance	Desire for beauty and sexuality
Family	Desire to raise own children
Order	Desire for regularity and tidiness
Eating	Desire for food
Acceptance	Desire for approval and self-esteem
Tranquility	Desire for relaxation and security

More recent multiple need classifications have been developed based on inductive empirical procedures. Reiss (2000), for instance, identified 15 basic desires as reasons for initiating and maintaining behavior, including the desire for power (i.e., the tendency to strive for success and leadership), the desire for independence (i.e., the tendency to strive for freedom and autonomy), and the desire for social contact (cf. table 2.1). Supporting the basic model assumptions, Havercamp and Reiss (2003) found correlations between such self-reported motives and actual behavior. For instance, compared to the average sample, athletes were found to score higher on the desires for status and for physical exercise, people volunteering in humanitarian organizations scored higher on the desire for idealism, and students of a training program for military officers scored higher on the desire for power.

In a similar way, Holland's typology of vocational interests as personality aspects (Holland, 1997) was developed in order to explain vocational choice, job satisfaction, and job performance. Holland suggested that employees choose jobs that are compatible with their basic interests, and that they are most motivated and satisfied in work environments that match their personalities. Holland describes vocational interest along six major dimensions (cf. table 2.2). According to the model, the closer the match between vocational personality type and job characteristics, the greater the individual's work motivation and job satisfaction should be.

Characteristics of the work environment

In addition to the personal dispositions of employees, work motivation is also affected by environmental factors such as task characteristics. These factors are addressed by the following theories.

Table 2.2: Vocational types according to Holland (1997)

Personality type	Preferred activities	Matching occupations
Realistic	Mechanical activities, working with tools and machines	Carpenter, technician
Investigative	Working with abstract ideas and theories	Scientist
Artistic	Creating things	Musician, writer, painter
Social	Helping, teaching	Social worker, school teacher
Enterprising	Managing, selling, persuading	Sales representative, entrepreneur
Conventional	Organizing and evaluating data	Bank assistant, secretary

Herzberg's two-factor theory   Herzberg (1966) and his colleagues were interested how the features of a job and job-related activities influence work motivation. Based on a new methodological procedure, Herzberg and his colleagues identified two groups of situational factors that might either influence work motivation or prevent dissatisfaction (cf. see Research Close-Up 1, near the end of the chapter). Similar as with Maslow's model, the basic idea is that a high salary and safe and healthy working conditions are not sufficient to initiate high and sustainable work motivation. Instead, employees also need a meaningful and interesting task, responsibility, and recognition by others.

A major problem of Herzberg's theory is that the two-factor structure could not be replicated with other methodological procedures (King, 1970), suggesting that the results in the original study might be affected by methodological shortcomings. Indeed, part of Herzberg's results might be explained by attribution theory (e.g., Weiner, 1986) which would predict that negative events (dissatisfying work situations) are generally attributed to external factors while positive events (success) are internally attributed to own capabilities and persistence. Despite the criticism it received, the two-factor theory has been appreciated for its main ideas. Herzberg was among the first to stress the importance of a distinction between intrinsic and extrinsic variables (Ambrose & Kulik, 1999), that in turn provided useful implications for the design of motivating jobs (Steers, Mowday, & Shapiro, 2004). Moreover, together with Maslow, Herzberg was one of the pioneers emphasizing the necessity to create motivating work environments, promoting human factors at work. For instance, job enrichment as a strategy to increase the motivation potential of a job traces back to Herzberg's theory. In contrast to job enlargement that merely increases the number and variety of tasks an individual performs (e.g., installation of left and right doors to a car instead of only one door in the production line of a car factory), job enrichment refers to a vertical expansion of jobs, including planning, execution, and output evaluation. Thus, job enrichment contributes to a higher task identity that has been stressed as an important motivator and health factor also by the German action theory (e.g., Frese & Zapf, 1994; Hacker, 1998).

Job Characteristics Model   Extending the ideas of Maslow and Herzberg, the Job Characteristics Model (JCM) by Hackman and Oldham (1976) is a theory-driven approach specifically developed for designing motivating work conditions. Today, the JCM is one of the most influential theories in work and organizational psychology. According to the model, the potential (intrinsic) motivation a task elicits depends on three psychological experiences of the worker: meaningfulness of the task, responsibility for work outcomes, and quantitative as well as qualitative feedback about the actual wok results. As Hackman and Lawler (1971) put it, the model postulates that internal rewards are obtained when individuals *learn* (knowledge of results) that they *personally* (experienced responsibility) have performed well on a task they *care about* (experienced meaningfulness). According to the JCM, these psychological states are determined by the following five core task dimensions (Hackman, 1987):

- *Skill variety* measures the amount of different activities in the task that require different skills and talents.
- *Task identity* indicates the degree to which the task is a whole and identifiable piece of work, including activities from planning over execution to seeing a visible outcome.
- *Task significance* measures the degree to which the job has a substantial impact on the lives or work of other people, either in the organization or in the external environment.
- *Autonomy* indicates the degree to which a task provides freedom, independence, and discretion in scheduling the work and in determining the procedures to be used.
- *Feedback* refers to the degree to which direct and clear information about the effectiveness of the work is provided by the task.

Autonomy and feedback are considered as necessary preconditions for the experience of responsibility and knowledge of the actual work results, respectively (cf. figure 2.3). In contrast, skill variety, task identity, and task significance are linked to the experience of meaningfulness in a way that allows mutual compensation. These different relations are expressed by different mathematical functions determining the motivation potential score (MPS) of a task:

$$\text{MPS} = \frac{(\text{Skill variety} + \text{Task identity} + \text{Task significance})}{3} \times \text{Autonomy} \times \text{Feedback}$$

As can be seen, lack of autonomy or feedback would reduce the MPS score to zero, while lack of single aspects that contribute to the meaningfulness of the task can be compensated by the other two. Imagine, for instance, an employee tightening nuts on aircraft brake assemblies: although skill variety and task identity might be rather low, his job is nevertheless perceived as quite meaningful due to the significance of this activity for others (pilots, passengers, etc.).

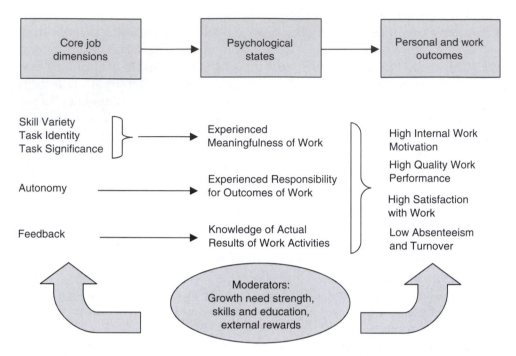

Figure 2.3: Hackman & Oldham's Job Characteristics Model (adapted from Hackman, 1987)

The motivation potential of a task is expected to determine several outcome variables. High motivation potential is expected to lead to high intrinsic motivation, high quality of performance, high job satisfaction, and low rates of absenteeism and turnover. The model components and their interrelations are illustrated in figure 2.3. As can be seen, the JCM also includes person factors such as individual need for self-actualization ("growth need strength") and organizational support as moderators (Oldham, 1996). Thus, not all employees react positively on strategies to increase motivation by enhancing skill variety, task identity, or autonomy. Employees who value family or hobbies much higher than their career (i.e., low job-related growth need) are not very likely to experience higher intrinsic motivation when their job has more responsibilities.

The JCM was tested empirically in numerous studies that often applied the Job Diagnostic Survey as a measure of the five core dimensions. Overall, the evidence is mixed (Morgeson & Campion, 2003). Hackman and Oldham (1976) themselves provided moderately supporting evidence for their model, showing that jobs high on the JCM core dimensions were correlated with high motivation. Particularly, the combination of skill variety, task identity, and task significance predicted the perceived meaningfulness of a task. Moreover, individual growth need strength showed the expected moderating effect. Outcomes of persons high in growth need strength were more likely to be positively affected by the experience of the critical psychological states (cf. figure 2.3). However, no clear evidence could be found for the connection between autonomy and experienced responsibility, and feedback and knowledge of the results, respectively. The assumed multiplicative interplay of autonomy and feedback could not be clearly demonstrated, either. Instead, additive versions of the JCM lead to better results (Evans & Ondrack, 1991). Moreover, the general importance of the critical states as mediating processes could only be demonstrated inconsistently, partly due to measurement problems of these subjective states (Ambrose & Kulik, 1999; Parker & Wall, 2001). On the other hand, the impact of job characteristics on employees is always a subjective process, which might also explain why the core JCM dimensions are better predictors of job satisfaction (correlation about 0.40, cf. Fried & Ferris, 1987) than for objective performance.

Even though the JCM has been explored in numerous studies, there are many questions awaiting further research. Among them are long-term effects of the JCM characteristics on individual needs and skills (Oldham, 1996). For instance, task design might affect the growth need strength of employees in the long run. Imagine how frustrating it can be to work for years on a job with nearly no autonomy, significance, and feedback. Moreover, the causal relation between job characteristics and outcome variables might be bidirectional. For instance, while high autonomy and feedback during work can increase the motivation of workers, for instance in a car factory, high initial motivation of the workers can also lead to higher requests for autonomy and feedback (James & Tetrick, 1986). A final issue for future research is the explanation how the JCM dimensions and the resulting motivation transform into overt behavior. Suggestions are provided by process-oriented models of motivation that are discussed later in this chapter.

Although the JCM has not been confirmed in all details, the basic assumption that job characteristics are linked to important outcome variables has received substantial overall support (Parker & Wall, 2001). Therefore, the JCM provides helpful guidance how working conditions can be designed in order to facilitate high intrinsic work motivation.

Interaction between person and task characteristics

So far, we have discussed person and context factors separately. The following content theory refers to the interaction of task characteristics and personal dispositions of employees.

Flow theory   The concept of "flow" has received increasing attention in recent years (Csikszentmihalyi, Abuhamdeh, & Nakamura, 2005). In his theory, Csikszentmihalyi defines "flow" as the subjective experience of optimal motivational state that occurs when persons are completely engaged in what they are doing (Csikszentmihalyi, 1982). When in flow, persons feel completely absorbed by the activity so that awareness of time and environment can be lost because persons focus on information that is directly relevant to the activity. Flow activities are accompanied by positive affect, intense concentration, and feelings of effortlessness (Csikszentmihalyi et al., 2005). Thus, being in flow combines optimal motivation and concentration with positive affect and lack of fatigue – something that might be quite interesting for daily work processes.

How do workers get into flow? Csikszentmihalyi and his colleagues (2005) assume three basic antecedents of flow:

1. The activity one engages in contains a *clear set of goals and rules* that add purpose and direction to the behavior. They also channel attention so that there is no ambiguity regarding the measures to be taken in order to achieve the goal.
2. *Perceived task demands and individual skills match each other* so that the activity provides opportunities to experience one's own competence.
3. The task provides *clear and immediate performance feedback* that informs the individual how well s/he is doing.

Thus, the initiation of optimal (work) motivation according to this theory is determined by the interaction of task characteristics, particularly the level of task demands, and personal skills. The flow concept has triggered a number of research endeavors lately, applying the concept to very different activities such as computer work, writing, learning, sport, or even graffiti spraying (Rheinberg, 2004). A brief questionnaire measure of flow (in German and English) with initial norm data has been developed by Rheinberg, Vollmeyer, and Engeser (2003). New research directions include whether being in flow is a meta-skill that can be trained (Csikszentmihalyi et al., 2005). However, the concept has also been criticized for its theoretical vagueness. For instance, in the study by Csikszentmihalyi and LeFevre (1989), perceived task challenge was taken as an indicator of flow, although it should be rather a precursor of flow. Moreover, concrete implications of flow theory for task design are difficult to derive because matching task challenges with workers' skills is highly dependent on the subjective experience of employees.

Box 2.1:   Field note: Some principles of motivational work design

In contrast to the mechanistic work design that tries to optimize workflow (e.g., Taylor, 1911), the motivational approach to work design considers job characteristics that might correspond to the needs and interests of employees. According to Hackman (1987), five principles should be considered in job (re)design. *Natural work units* should be formed in order to increase task identity and experienced responsibility for work results, while still maintaining an efficient work structure. Similarly, the principle of *combining tasks* refers to putting fractionalized tasks back together so that employees can see the results of their work and that required variety of skills is increased. *Relationships with customers* should be established to provide employees with contact to the ultimate user of their product or service, which can provide performance feedback, increase skill variety by interpersonal skills, and enhance autonomy by management of customer relationships. In *vertical loading*, the intent is to partially close the gap between executive and controlling aspects of work, thus increasing employees' autonomy. When a job is vertically loaded, employees receive responsibilities that formerly were reserved to management, e.g., autonomy in deciding on work methods as well as flexibilities regarding scheduling and crisis management. Finally, Hackman recommends *opening feedback channels* in order to enable immediate task-related feedback, e.g. by placing quality control functions in the hand of employees, or by computerized online feedback.

Despite the remaining questions and the sometimes mixed empirical support for content-related models, research on the *why* question of work motivation has accumulated important starting points for the understanding and improvement of motivation in work contexts. Interventions derived from these theories have been widely recognized. Moreover, the models have contributed to the normative orientation of work and organizational psychology, emphasizing that employees might need more than just money and a safe job. The second part of this chapter explores *how* work motivation transforms into concrete actions and goal striving over time. Answers to this question are provided by process theories on work motivation.

Process-Related Theories of Work Motivation

Process-related theories explain how people develop work-related motives, values, and interests and transform them into plans and actions. To provide a heuristic structure for the theories available, we refer to a general model of motivated action developed by Heckhausen and Gollwitzer (1987). This model distinguishes four main phases of motivated action (cf. figure 2.4). In the beginning, a person has to choose between different action options. After a concrete action is chosen, the second phase includes the development of action goals including planning and intention building. The third phase includes the execution and regulation of actions towards goal attainment. Finally, during the fourth phase of this prototypical process model, the action results are evaluated. As an example imagine a university professor who decides whether she wants to work on a book chapter, prepare the next lecture, or go to the gym, etc. After deciding to work on the book chapter (first action phase), she then commits herself to the goal of finishing at least five pages in the next two hours (second action phase).

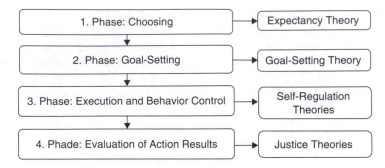

Figure 2.4: Action phases of the general model of motivated action developed by Heckhausen & Gollwitzer (1987) and associated process theories

During the following writing process, she has to monitor herself constantly in order not to get disturbed by phone calls, emails, the smell of fresh coffee, etc. (third action phase). Finally, after the two hours of work she evaluates the result in comparision to her goals, and perhaps by asking others for their opinion.

This general model of motivated action is helpful to structure the various process-related theories of work motivation because most of the latter theories focus only on specific problems and do not cover the whole action process. Moreover, the Heckhausen/Gollwitzer model also provides a general schema to analyze and solve concrete problems related to motivational issues in organizations (cf. table 2.5).

Choosing between action options: Expectancy models

Expectancy models perceive humans as rational beings that try to maximize their outcomes and/or minimize their costs. Thus, a person is generally expected to engage in those actions where she expects to gain most. At least two general components are part of this individual decision-making process: The subjective probability that an action will lead to certain consequences (*expectancy*), and the subjective evaluation of these consequences (*valence*). In performance situations, the expectancy component mainly reflects individuals' belief that she can achieve a certain performance level by means of her own effort (self-efficacy). The multiplicative conjunction of expectancy and valence reflects that small but safe incentives can be more attractive than high incentives that are difficult to achieve: A bird in the hand can be worth two in the bush.

While expectancy models originated in the 1930s, it was Vroom (1964) who applied these concepts to issues of work and organizational psychology and work motivation. He also extended the expectancy model, stressing that performance in work contexts is often not motivated by the task itself (intrinsic motivation) but by certain expected outcomes connected to task performance. For instance, a sales person in a fast-food chain might not be motivated because she enjoys selling burgers, but because she anticipates earning money and receiving recognition from her supervisor. In addition to valence and expectancy, Vroom (1964) included in his VIE theory the concept of *instrumentality* of performance for the achievement of valued outcomes. Thus, expectancy models basically include three different components, their definitions varying slightly with different versions of the theory. The following definitions are combinations of those suggested and intend to clarify the basic principles:

*   Expectancy (E) describes the perceived probability that individual effort put into an action (e.g., working fast) will lead to certain action results (e.g., 20 percent more burgers sold). Since expectancies are thought as probabilities, they range between 0 (no correlation between effort and action results) and 1 (perfect correlation between effort and action results).
*   Instrumentality (I) describes the perceived probability that action results (e.g., 20 percent more burgers sold) are connected with specific consequences (e.g., money, recognition from the supervisor). Instrumentalities are either conceptualized as probabilities, thus also ranging between 0 and 1, or thought as correlations, ranging between +1 (increasing the likelihood of outcomes) to −1 (decreasing the likelihood of outcomes). The latter provides the opportunity that action results can sometimes decrease the attainment of valued consequences, for instance, when high performance is sanctioned negatively by colleagues.
*   Valence (V) describes the extent to which a person likes or dislikes the expected consequences of an action result. Vroom (1964) assumed that valence can take a wide range of both positive values (likes such as money, recognition, etc.) and negative values (dislikes such as stress, extra hours, etc.). A valence of zero indicates that a person is indifferent to the consequence of an action result.

In order to predict the choice of (or effort level during) a specific action, the motivational force of an action is defined as the product of the three basic components according to the general formula:

$$\text{Force} = E \, (I \times V)$$

That is, the valences of all expected consequences (money, recognition, etc.) of an action result (e.g., 20 percent more burgers sold) are multiplied by the perceived instrumentalities of the action result for these consequences. The sum of these products is then multiplied by the expectancy that the chosen action level (e.g., working hard) will actually lead to the action result (e.g., 20 percent more burgers sold). The choice of a certain action by an individual is predicted by comparing the resulting forces of the different action options (see figure 2.5).

Many of the major propositions of the expectancy theory are supported by empirical research, particularly for the *direction* of effort. For instance, in an early

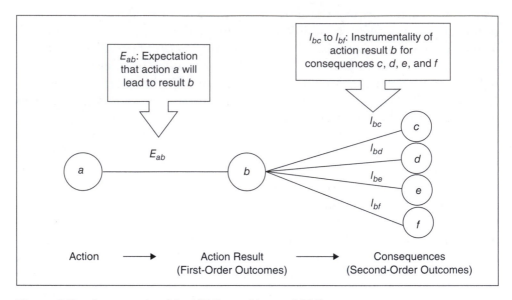

Figure 2.5:   Components of the VIE theory (Vroom, 1964)

Table 2.3:   Correlations of VIE components with behavioral variables according to meta-analytical results (van Eerde & Thierry, 1996)

Criteria	Average correlation with valence	Average correlation with instrumentality	Average correlation with expectancy	Average correlation with VIE product
Performance	+0.18	+0.17	+0.17	+0.19
Choice	+0.27	+0.27	+0.38	+0.25
Reported effort	+0.34	+0.24	+0.26	+0.29
Reported intention	+0.39	+0.29	+0.40	+0.42
Reported preference	—	+0.71	—	+0.74

study of students selecting an employer (Vroom, 1966), organizations that offered positions that were perceived as instrumental for achieving valued outcomes also received high attractiveness ratings. Moreover, 76 percent of the participants chose the organization with the highest subjective instrumentality score. Expectancy models can also predict the *amount* of effort persons choose to exert in a task, although these effects are usually smaller. A recent meta-analysis (van Eerde & Thierry, 1996) confirmed the impact of valence, instrumentality, and expectancy for different behavioral outcomes (cf. table 2.3). However, the authors could not confirm that a multiplicative combination of these factors explained more variance of the behavioral outcomes than using the components alone in a simple main effect model. Vroom himself states in the preface of a new edition of his classic 1964 book (Vroom, 1995) that the main impact of the VIE theory might be more the heuristic value of the three components than their multiplicative conjunction.

Today, expectancy theory has become a standard in research on work motivation and has been used as a framework for a wide variety of studies. Moreover, the conceptualization of the three components provides a helpful heuristic for applied diagnosis and intervention planning in work contexts. For instance, when considering why an employee's motivation decreased lately, it might be fruitful to explore the three VIE components separately as distinct approaches for interventions. Related questions might be if the salary is still high enough (valence), if recent performance of this employee has received sufficient feedback (instrumentality), or if the employee has to accomplish more than she can handle (expectancy).

The theory's limitations mainly arise from its focus on rational and deliberate processes. Very often, persons cannot or do not consider all available information in order to make a rational choice. Instead, persons follow simplifying heuristics or habits. Moreover, strong emotions can bias a person's decision. Another limitation is that intrinsic motivation is not considered in expectancy theory because actions are not assumed to have values by their own. Also, individual differences are neglected. Finally, expectancy theory is less suited to explain the maintenance of action over time, particularly in light of alternative actions and obstacles. The latter is better explained by the following theories.

Focusing on action goals: Goal-setting theory

After persons' choice between action directions and level of initial effort, the second phase of motivated action includes the planning of the action and the activation of sufficient energy and will strength. The latter is also called "volitional process" in order to contrast this phase from the more cognitive deliberations of the first action phase (Heckhausen & Gollwitzer, 1987). One prominent way to activate will strength is the setting of action goals.

The idea of assigning employees a specific amount of work to accomplish, such as a performance standard or a deadline, has already been introduced by Taylor (1911) in his "scientific management" approach. However, a more systematic exploration of why, when, and how goals increase individual motivation and performance has been provided by *goal-setting theory* (Locke & Latham, 1990). The basic principles of the theory have received substantial empirical support and can be summarized as follows:

1. *Goal difficulty*: Challenging goals, which are perceived as just about attainable, lead to higher performance than goals with low or medium difficulty.
2. *Goal specificity*: Challenging goals lead to higher performance when they are specific compared to nonspecific "do your best" goals.

Moreover, goal-setting theory also identifies four underlying psychological processes (*mediators*) explaining how specific and challenging goals are assumed to

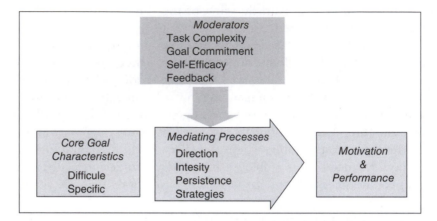

Figure 2.6:   Mediators and moderators of the goal-setting process

affect performance. First, clear and specific goals help individuals to focus their attention on goal relevant information. Second, clear and specific goals have an energizing function leading to increased effort. In contrast, easy goals can lead to suboptimal performance because employees limit their efforts to goal level. Third, clear and specific goals increase the persistence of individuals and help to stay focused. Finally, clear and specific goals improve use and development of strategies relevant for task accomplishment (cf. figure 2.6).

In addition, there are also a number of context factors that affect the goal-setting process. So-called *moderators* not only determine whether the goal-setting process works or not, but also provide important information about necessary preconditions so that goal-setting works best. One of these moderators is the *complexity of the task*. Goal-setting works particularly well in easy tasks where high effort influences performance quite straight and directly (Wood, Mento, & Locke, 1987), presumably because the required work strategies are known. In contrast, in a flight simulator study with Air Force trainees, Kanfer and Ackerman (1989) found that in initial stages of the training process, difficult goals had even nega-tive effects. Moreover, conflicts between quantitative and qualitative task demands are more likely in complex tasks, sometimes leading to increased performance quantity at the expense of quality.

Another moderator of goal-setting effects is *goal commitment*. Goal commit-ment refers to the congruence of assigned and personal goals, and describes the degree to which employees accept their goal, feel obliged to, and persist when obstacles occur. Empirical research has shown that sufficiently high goal commit-ment is a necessary condition for positive effects of goal-setting to occur (Locke & Latham, 1990). There are two general ways to increase goal commitment by employees. One is to enable participation and voice, thus changing goal-setting into goal *agreement* (Hinsz, Kalnbach, & Lorentz, 1997). The second way is to assign challenging and specific goals by supervisors who are trusted by employees and who explain goals thoroughly (Latham, Erez, & Locke, 1988). In both cases, the important difference is that employees perceive the goal-setting process as fair and appropriate instead of arbitrary and exploiting.

A third moderator is the degree to which individuals believe that they are *capable* to accomplish the goals they are assigned to. This moderator is related to the concept of *self efficacy* developed by Bandura (1997), and covers similar aspects as the expectancy component in the VIE theory. In the goal striving process, persons with higher self efficacy choose and accept higher goals, are more committed to them, make better use of their strategies, and use feedback better than people with low self efficacy. Self-efficacy can be increased by adequate role models (supervisors) and sufficient training and personnel development.

A final moderator of goal-setting processes is *feedback* about the progress towards goal attainment. Basically, goal-setting effects are assumed to be strong and positive only when sufficient feedback is available. Please note that this conceptualization is somewhat different from the JCM where feedback is assumed to be rather one of the main factors that cause motivation. Empirical research rather confirmed the conceptualization of goal-setting theory because feedback only had positive effects when provided together with high and specific goals, whereas no effects occurred when such goals where absent (Bandura & Cervone, 1983). In other words, performance information per se does not increase motivation but has to be connected to specific goals that provide meaning to the feedback (i.e., "how close am I to goal attainment?"). Apart from informative value, performance feedback can also trigger emotions (pride, embarrassment, etc.) that provide reward and reinforcement in itself.

As an ensemble, goal-setting theory has been shown to be a powerful and elegant approach to increase motivation and productivity in organizations (Locke & Latham, 2002). Several more complex management techniques build on this theory, such as "Management by Objectives" (Rodgers & Hunter, 1991) or group goal-setting techniques (e.g., Pritchard, Jones, Roth, Stuebing, & Ekeberg, 1988). Moreover, goal-setting processes are also important for self-management strategies that are reviewed in the next section. Among the current challenges of goal-setting theory are the integration of personal differences (e.g., need for achievement, conscientiousness) and of potential changes of goal striving over time. From a more practical perspective, the main challenge is perhaps the development of clear and nonconflicting goals together with sufficient and reliable feedback routines within complex work processes of modern organizations (Hertel, Konradt, & Orlikowski, 2004).

Execution and behavior control: Self-regulation theories

Whereas goal-setting theory often implies external sources of goals (e.g., the supervisor), theories of self-regulation refer to cases when persons set goals themselves. In work contexts, this happens for instance when persons commit themselves to work-related goals, or when they want to change their behavior (e.g., to give more feedback to colleagues). According to Karoly (1993), self-regulation covers all processes that enable individuals to control their goal-directed activities (including thought, affect, behavior, and attention) over time and across changing situational contexts. According to Bandura (1991), self-regulation requires three basic steps: self-monitoring, self-evaluation, and self-reaction. *Self-monitoring* is necessary to collect information about the goal pursuit and depends on accuracy, consistency, and frequency. Moreover, self-monitoring can already have a motivating function in itself when individuals enjoy improving their capabilities. Self-observation provides the basis for *self-evaluation*, which includes comparison of individual performance with personal standards that can either result from comparison with relevant others, from observational learning, or from direct training (Bandura, 1986). Finally, self-reaction includes reward or punishment of one's own behavior based on self-evaluation. Apart from concrete rewards (e.g., a coffee break after completing a difficult problem), self-reactions also include positive or negative emotions such as pride or embarrassment after success or failure, respectively. Persons who reward their goal attainments have been shown to accomplish more than persons who perform the same tasks without self-reactions, even when self-monitoring and goal-setting is given (Bandura, 1986).

Self-regulation is closely related to self-efficacy mechanisms, both as an antecedent and as a consequence (Bandura & Locke, 2003; Vancouver, Thompson, Tischner, & Putka, 2002). On the one hand, self-efficacy beliefs affect choice of aspiration level, perception of own performance, intensity and duration of effort, and evaluation of performance results. On the other hand, consequences of self-regulation, particularly self-monitoring, contribute to self-efficacy beliefs. Together, self-regulation theories combine and extend components and ideas from other successful motivation models, such as goal-setting and expectancy theory, and receive increasing empirical support (Bandura & Locke, 2003; Karoly, 1993). Applied interventions based on self-regulation theories include trainings of goal-setting and self-regulation (e.g., Latham & Frayne, 1990) and coaching interventions.

Evaluation of action results: Justice theories and job satisfaction

In the final phase of motivated action, people evaluate the results and consequences of their actions. In work contexts, these evaluations determine workers' *job satisfaction*, i.e., cognitive, affective, and behavioral reactions. Although the definition of job satisfaction still is a controversial issue, one of the main determining factors is whether expected results and consequences have been attained (Wanous, Poland, Premack, & Davis, 1992). Thus, job satisfaction and work motivation are closely interrelated: The likelihood that a person will achieve satisfying results is determined by the aspiration level and goals a person chooses and commits to during a job sequence. In turn, motivation of this employee in later job sequences is determined by the degree of satisfaction. Of course, job satisfaction is also influenced by numerous other factors, among them person factors such as affective dispositions and personality traits, context factors such as working conditions, stress, supervisor behavior, team climate, etc., as well as the interaction of both (see Hulin & Judge, 2003, for a recent review). However, one of the most central factors that determine the extent of job satisfaction is whether outcomes are perceived as *just*.

In evaluating justice, employees can either focus on the amount of rewards they receive compared to others (*distributional justice*), or on the procedure according to which different rewards are allocated (*procedural justice*). Perceptions of *distributional justice* are explained by *equity theory* (Adams, 1965). Basically, equity theory assumes that individuals reflect their personal gains in light of their investments. For instance, a self-employed computer programmer is likely to ask herself whether the money she receives for a job is fair given the amount of time she has spent on it. Moreover, the theory assumes that persons compare these ratios with perceptions of others' gain/investment ratios. Perceived *underpayment* inequity occurs when persons perceive their gains to be lower than the gains of others who spent the same investments. This inequity results in dissatisfaction and compensatory behavior, such as lowered performance, absenteeism, turnover, and even theft (Ambrose & Kulik, 1999).

The *procedural justice* of work-related actions or decisions (e.g., feedback, promotion), however, depends on whether the acting persons perceive that they have voices and opportunities to express their personal interests and feelings, and whether procedures are consistently applied, free of bias, based on accurate information, and conform with ethical and moral standards (e.g., Leventhal, 1980). It is also important that employees feel treated with dignity and respect, and that the decisions are clearly communicated and explained (Colquitt, 2001). Although distributional and procedural justice are considered as independent, procedural justice can compensate negative effects of distributional inequity (see research close up 2). More recent aspects of perceived justice in organizations are addressed by research on *psychological contracts* which are defined as the subjective beliefs about mutual obligations of employer and employee (Rousseau, 1995). In a study by Robinson and Morrison (2000), the perceived breach of these contracts was particularly connected with intense negative feelings when employees perceived this contract breach to be a purposeful act by the employer, compared to accidental breaches (see also Frese in this book).

What are the consequences of job satisfaction – or, why should employers bother about the satisfaction of their employees? First, there is ample evidence that job satisfaction is positively correlated with important organizational outcomes such as job performance, absenteeism, and turnover. For instance, the mean true correlation between overall job satisfaction and job performance is estimated to be 0.30 (Judge, Thoresen, Bono, & Patton, 2001). Moreover, job satisfaction seems to be even more closely related to voluntary behavior that is not prescribed by job contracts but nonetheless crucial for organizational effectiveness. *Organizational citizenship behavior* (Organ & Ryan, 1995) or *contextual behavior* (Motowidlo & van Scotter, 1994) includes helping others at work, loyalty toward the company, and commitment toward organizational goals. The mean true correlation between overall job satisfaction and organizational citizenship behavior is estimated to be 0.44 for nonmanagerial employees (Organ & Ryan, 1995). Finally, employees' commitment to and identification with an organization are closely related to job satisfaction (e.g., Mathieu & Zajac, 1990). Social identity approaches to organizational behavior (e.g., Haslam, 2004) propose that identification with an organization, i.e., self-categorization as a member of the organization and feelings of belongingness, leads to increased motivation and activities in line with the norms and goals of the organization. These positive effects of identification might be mediated by affective and normative commitment to the organization (Meyer, Becker, & van Dick, 2006). Thus, although more research on the causal mechanisms is desirable, there are several good reasons to support high job satisfaction even from a strictly economic perspective.

Recent Research Directions

In addition to further developments of the motivational theories discussed, current research on work motivation intends to develop more inclusive "mega-theories" that synthesize different content and process-related approaches, and provide more concrete guidance for practitioners (Locke & Latham, 2004). Below, we describe two emerging research fields where integration of different motivational models is needed: Changes in work motivation as a function of age, and work motivation as a function of social processes within work teams.

Development of work motivation over the lifespan

As a consequence of decreasing birth rates and growing life expectancy, many western countries face an ageing workforce, leading to an increasing need to reintegrate older employees in work processes (cf. Fraccaroli & Depolo in this book). Apart from changes in physical and cognitive capabilities over time, this also requires a good understanding of motivational changes as a function of age, particularly because minor age-related decreases in capability might be compensated by high work motivation.

Content-related changes of work motivation as a function of age refer to different priorities of work-related values, interests, and needs. For instance, it is likely that the value of a challenging workplace and multiple feedback decreases with age, whereas safety and security of the workplace together with a positive working climate might become more important over the years (Warr, 1997). In contrast, salary might be particularly important when employees start a family and raise children, but less important in the beginning and the end of people's career. Such initial assumptions are based on plausibility and theoretical considerations and have yet to be tested empirically. What has been shown repeatedly is that job satisfaction increases with age (e.g., Clarke, Oswald, & Warr, 1996). This pattern seems to be mainly due to higher economic resources of older employees rather than to lower standards or expectations of older generations, or earlier retirements of unsatisfied employees (Schulte, 2005).

Process-related changes can be derived by integrating ageing as a moderator in existing models. For instance, in the terms of expectancy theory, Warr (2001) suggested five sources for age-related changes: Adaptation to incentives ("hedonic treadmill"), development of habits over time, social comparison with younger colleagues, effects of age-related stereotypes, and changes in job-related self-efficacy. In a similar way, Kanfer and Ackerman (2004) derive a number of hypotheses about ageing effects regarding valence, instrumentality, and expectancy components. However, most of the described hypotheses have yet to be tested empirically because research on age-related changes of work motivation is just evolving. Nevertheless, the potential of older employees to be motivated and highly performing members of organizations is much higher as some popular stereotypes suggest. Making use of this potential requires organizations to provide appropriate training and working environments.

Motivation in work groups

The theoretical models discussed so far refer to individual work, simply because this is the least complex case. However, work processes today increasingly are organized in teams (cf. West in this book) so that an important question is how individuals' work motivation might be affected when they work together with others in a team. Research exploring this question has already started about 100 years ago, when Triplett (1897) observed that children worked faster on a simple winding task when coupled with a partner. However, in the following years, research on motivation in groups mostly focused on *motivation losses* in groups, i.e., decreases of motivation during group work compared to individual work. Examples of such motivation losses are described in table 2.4. For instance, *social loafing* occurs when individual contributions are not identifiable so that individual efforts have no positive or negative consequences for the team member (e.g., Karau & Williams, 1993). During *free riding*, team members reduce their efforts because they perceive their contribution as dispensable (Kerr, 1983), for instance, because more competent members already solve the task. *Sucker effects* occur when team members reduce their efforts in order to prevent being exploited by other team members who seem to do nothing (Kerr, 1983).

Given these potential motivation losses in groups, is it still rational to let people work in teams? Well, most empirical studies that demonstrate motivation losses in groups were conducted in the laboratory with groups consisting of strangers (usually students) who worked only a short time together on rather artificial tasks (e.g., brainstorming on uses for a knife) that had no important consequences. When teams have a common history and future, including opportunities to retaliate low contributions of members, and work on meaningful tasks that have important consequences, motivation losses are less likely or do not occur at all (Erez & Somech, 1996). Thus, experimental research settings might overestimate negative effects of group work on motivation.

Moreover, more recent research has accumulated evidence that group work might also have positive effects on motivation, leading to *motivation gains* in groups compared to individual work. For instance, team members who highly value the team outcome sometimes compensate expected poor performance of their partners (*social compensation*; e.g., Williams & Karau, 1991). Moreover, team members who realize that their contribution is indispensable for the group outcome often exert additional effort in order not to let their partner down (*social indispensability*; e.g., Hertel, Deter, & Konradt, 2003; Weber & Hertel, 2007). Together, although potential negative effects of teamwork on individual motivation have to be considered, there are a number of good reasons for teamwork from a motivational perspective (Guzzo, Jette, & Katzell, 1985). Whether these potential positive effects can be achieved usually depends on how teams are implemented and managed (cf. table 2.4; see also West in this book).

Beyond research on single effects of motivation losses and gains, integrative theoretical framework for understanding motivation in groups has been developed. The Collective Effort Model (CEM; Karau, Markus & Williams, 2000) builds and extends the classic VIE approach to groups. While valence and expectancy components are conceptualized similar to individual work, the authors extend the instrumentality component suggesting that the contingency of individual effort and individual outcomes are more complex in groups. According to the CEM, instrumentality of individual contributions in groups depends on three perceived contingencies: (1) the contingency between individual performance and group performance, (2) the contingency between group performance and group outcome, and (3) the contingency between group outcome and individual outcome. Thus, probabilities that team members perceive their action results as instrumental are smaller in groups because outcomes are also determined by other group members. Another adaptation of expectancy models to groups is the VIST model (e.g., Hertel et al., 2004) that additionally integrates trust, defined as the expectancy that the other team members will cooperate, as a fourth component that might be particularly relevant for distributed teamwork. Finally, goal-setting theory has been also successfully applied and extended to team work (Pritchard et al., 1988). The best goal-setting results seem to be achieved when both team-related and individual goals are provided and both are not in conflict with each other (Crown & Rosse, 1995).

Table 2.4: Effects of groups on individual motivation

	Effect	Process	Interventions to prevent motivation losses/foster motivation gains
Motivation losses in groups	Social inhibition	Effort reduction due to audience effects	Training (reduction of evaluation anxiety)
	Social loafing	Effort reduction due to lack of expected sanctions	Identifiability of individual contribution
	Free riding	Effort reduction due to perceived dispensability	Training (increase of task-related self efficacy)
	Sucker effect	Effort reduction as reaction to perceived exploitation by other group members	Distributive justice; identifiability of individual contribution
	Soldiering	Collective effort reduction as a reaction to perceived unfairness by the management	Procedural justice
Motivation gains in groups	Social facilitation	Effort increase due to audience or co-actors	Simple or well learned tasks, training (reduction of evaluation anxiety)
	Social comparison, social competition	Effort increase in order to match other's performance level	Low task interdependence, moderate discrepant capabilities between adversaries
	Social indispensability	Effort increase due to perceived indispensability of personal contributions for the group outcome	High task interdependence, partner-related performance feedback, moderate discrepant capabilities between group members
	Social compensation	Effort increase in order to compensate inferior performance by other group members	High value of group outcome, high self-efficacy
	Social laboring	Effort increase in order to improve group status	High group identification, threatening outgroup

Table 2.5:   Typical practitioner questions and related motivation models

Question	Model
Does this job candidate have the potential to be a motivated co-worker?	Need Theories
Which job might be best suited for this person?	Interest Theories
What can be done to redesign the task/job to be most motivating?	Job Characteristics Model
How can I trigger optimal motivation in this task?	Flow Theory
Which arguments do I need in an advertisement to recruit employees for this job?	Expectancy Theories
How should managers explain their employees what they are expected to do?	Goal-setting Theory
How can I support an employee to change her work behavior?	Self-Regulation Theory
How can I myself change my work behavior?	
How should salaries be constructed so that they are perceived as fair by all employees?	Equity Theory
How should promotion decisions made in a fair way?	Procedural Justice Theories
How should teams be managed to prevent motivation losses and enable motivation gains?	Collective Effort Model
	VIST Theory
	Group Goal-setting

Summary

This chapter provides an overview of the relevant theories on work motivation available today. Due to space constraints, some approaches had to be neglected, among them attribution theory, learning theory, social identity theory, and theories of intrinsic and extrinsic motivation. Moreover, theories on job satisfaction have only been summarized. More information on those approaches can be found in our further reading list, and we like to encourage you to make use of it. However, the theories that are reviewed in this chapter provide good ground for a basic understanding of work motivation as well as related diagnosis and intervention planning in the field. As a final overview of the models discussed, table 2.5 provides concrete suggestions about which of the models might be relevant to answer some of the typical applied questions in this area. You can use this table as a test of your understanding by covering the right column and trying to answer the questions for yourself.

Discussion Points

How might individual differences (e.g., need for achievement) moderate effects of expectancy and goal-setting theory? Think of a potential study to test your ideas.

Which components of the Job Characteristics Model are related or similar to components of the VIE theory?

What are the suggestions of the different theories discussed in this chapter for an optimal level of task difficulty?

How does self efficacy affect work motivation, and what measures could be taken by managers in order to increase employees' self efficacy?

How might personality factors and environmental characteristics affect age-related changes of work motivation, and why? Use the main assumptions of the theories discussed in order to develop hypotheses.

Key Studies

In the classic study by Vroom (1966), the basic model assumptions of expectancy theory are explained and tested:

Vroom, V. H. (1966). Organizational choice: A study of pre- and post-decision processes. *Organizational Behavior and Human Performance*, *1*, 212–25.

A classic field study demonstrating goal-setting effects is provided by:

Latham, G. P., & Yukl, G. (1975). Assigned versus participative goal-setting with educated and uneducated woods workers. *Journal of Applied Psychology*, *60*, 299–302.

Further Reading

A highly recommendable introduction to basic motivation theory and research is provided by:

Heckhausen, H. (1997). *Motivation and action*. New York: Springer.

A good review of recent work motivation research:

Mitchell, T. R., & Daniels, D. (2003). Motivation. In W. C. Borman, D. R. Ilgen, & R. J. Klimoski (Eds.), *Handbook of Psychology Vol. 12, Industrial and Organizational Psychology* (pp. 225–54). New York: Wiley.

Interesting suggestions for future research on work motivation:

Locke, E. A., & Latham, G. P. (2004). What should we do about motivation theory? Six

recommendations for the twenty-first century. *Academy of Management Review*, *29*, 388–403.

Good reviews of research on specific process theories:

Van Eerde, W., & Thierry, H. (1996). Vroom's expectancy models and work-related criteria: A meta-analysis. *Journal of Applied Psychology*, *81*, 575–86.

Locke, E. A., & Latham, G. P. (2002). Building a practically useful theory of goal-setting and task motivation. *American Psychologist*, *57*, 705–17.

Bandura, A. (1991). Social Cognitive Theory of Self-Regulation. *Organizational Behaviour and Human Decision Processes*, *50*, 248–87.

Research Close-Up 1

In the so-called *Pittsburgh Study*, Herzberg, Mausner, and Snyderman (1959) asked employees to sample positive and negative work experiences and identify the factors they considered responsible for these events. This method is called *critical incident technique*. Interestingly, two independent groups of situational factors emerged that either caused positive or negative events (cf. figure 2.7). Participants explained positive work experiences predominantly with personal achievement, interesting tasks, responsibility, and recognition/promotion. Herzberg and his colleagues considered these factors as work-related and intrinsic, and termed them "motivators" (or content factors). In contrast, participants explained dissatisfying work experiences predominantly with external factors (context factors), such as company policy and administration, poor relationship with supervisors, peers, or subordinates, and low salary. These external factors were related to dissatisfying experiences only, and unrelated to satisfying events. Herzberg and colleagues concluded from these data that context factors such as salary and working climate, can be utilized to prevent dissatisfaction, but not to increase satisfaction and motivation. Instead, content factors, such as responsibility recognition and a meaningful task, were emphasized as means to increase work motivation.

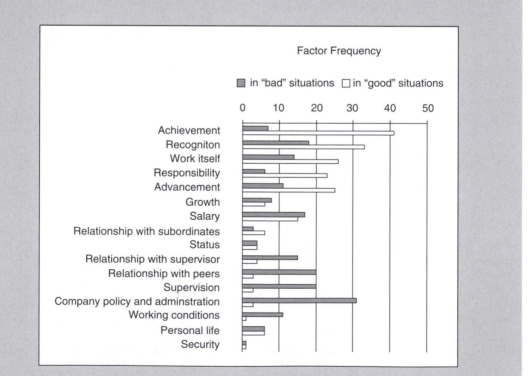

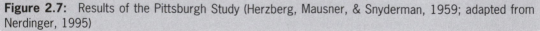

Figure 2.7: Results of the Pittsburgh Study (Herzberg, Mausner, & Snyderman, 1959; adapted from Nerdinger, 1995)

Research Close-Up 2

A field study by Greenberg (1990) provides an interesting example for the interplay of distributive and procedural justice. In two of three factories, the management had to reduce workers' salaries by 15 percent for a period of 10 weeks due to economic reasons (loss of two large manufacturing contracts). Employees were expected to perceive distributional inequity because their working hours were not reduced during this time. In factory A, the necessity for the salary cuts was thoroughly explained to the employees in a 90 minute meeting, and the company president showed respect and considerable remorse about the pay cuts (high procedural justice). In factory B, the salary cuts were announced in a 15 minute meeting without any attempt to explain or justify them, and without expressing remorse (low procedural justice). Factory C, where salaries were not reduced, served as a control condition. Interestingly, employee theft rates significantly increased in factory B after the salary cut relative to other periods in this factory, and also compared to factory A where the salary cut had been thoroughly explained. In factory A, employee theft rate increased only slightly during the salary cut period (cf. figure 2.8). Furthermore, in factory B, significantly more employees resigned during that period than in the other factories.

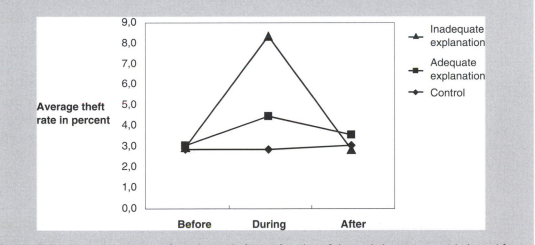

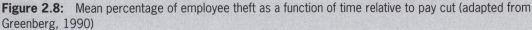

Figure 2.8: Mean percentage of employee theft as a function of time relative to pay cut (adapted from Greenberg, 1990)

Learning and Training at Work

3

Sabine Sonnentag, Cornelia Niessen, and Sandra Ohly

Overview

Learning for and at work is a key topic in work and organizational psychology. Work-related learning occurs both in formal (e.g., training courses) and informal settings (e.g., on the job) and may refer both to learning for a current job and to development for a potential future job. Because of the changing nature of work, including the widespread use of sophisticated technology, change in customer demands, and work within the globalized economy, learning increasingly becomes a life-long necessity for most individuals.

For many decades, research on work-related learning was dominated by concepts and empirical studies on formal training arrangements. In more recent years, research pays increased attention to more informal work-related learning activities. Research has shown that both individual characteristics and situational factors are important predictors of individuals' participation in formal and informal learning activities and of success in their learning endeavors.

The structure of this chapter is as follows. First, we introduce the learning concept. Then we describe the relevance of learning for today's organizations. Next, we focus on learning in formal settings and present training design principles and training methods, and give a brief overview over important steps in the training process. Subsequently, we describe approaches to informal work-related learning. In the next two sections, we provide an overview of the most important individual characteristics and situational factors related to learning. The chapter closes with a brief summary.

---

1 Learning Concept

Learning is a core concept in psychology. In work and organizational contexts, learning processes refer to relatively permanent changes in knowledge, skills or attitudes of individuals or teams (Kraiger, 2003). For example, employees may have to learn how to use a new computer program, how to interact more effectively with customers or clients, or how to supervise a product development team. Learning in the work and organizational context comprises both training and developmental approaches. Training aims at learning processes that result in knowledge, skills or attitudes to be used in the current or near-future job. Development refers to learning processes relevant for personal and professional growth beyond the current job (Noe, Wilk, Mullen, & Wanek, 1997). Learning and development occur in formal and also informal settings (Chao, 1997). Formal learning activities are characterized by structured activities initiated and sustained by the organization. Typical examples are seminars and courses, formal mentoring programs, or planned job rotation as part of formal development programs. Informal learning activities are less structured and typically initiated by the employee themselves. Typical examples here comprise self-managed learning, informal exchange of information with co-workers and persons outside the organization, and on-the-job learning (Sonnentag, Niessen, & Ohly, 2004).

2 Relevance of Learning

Learning is particularly important in today's working life for a number of reasons: First, during the past two decades we are witnessing a tremendous change in the "nature of work" (Howard, 1995). This change refers to the widespread use of sophisticated computer-based technologies, changed management practices including team work arrangements, and increased customer demands (Holman, Wall, Clegg, Sparrow, & Howard, 2003) and implies that employees need more skills and knowledge to meet these changing demands. Particularly, in highly industrialized countries with few natural resources an economy's competitive advantage has to be based on highly developed human skills and specialized knowledge (Martin & Moldoveanu, 2003).

Second, the change in work demands is not a single event. Rather, job requirements are changing continuously, making continuous learning a necessity (London & Mone, 1999). Particularly in fields with very fast technological innovations such as computer science and specific areas of engineering, employees face problems associated with obsolescence (Fossum, Arvey, Paradise, & Robbins, 1986), that is the experience that existing knowledge is no longer useful and needed. In these fields, updating one's knowledge and skills becomes a core job requirement (Pazy, 2004).

Third, also employment relationships and the "psychological contract" (Rousseau, 1995) are changing. This development implies that employees can not any longer expect life-time employment with a single employer or in the job they have been trained for initially. Therefore, in order to succeed on the labor market, life-long learning is a necessity for many employees.

Fourth, many European societies face dramatic demographic changes, particularly an aging workforce. Although all workers are increasingly called on to learn continuously, older workers often have difficulties to meet this demand. However, particularly for older unemployed individuals, continuous learning is important to ensure their employability because it is increasingly difficult for them to keep hold on or change jobs.

Learning is empirically related to favorable work-related outcomes. This positive relationship is well-documented for training interventions. A meta-analysis expressed this relationship as the effect size of Cohen's d (difference between the means in a training and a nontraining group, divided by the standard deviation). This meta-analysis found an effect size of $d = 0.62$ on behavioral outcomes (e.g., supervisory ratings of on-the-job performance) and an effect of also $d = 0.62$ on results (e.g., productivity, company profits) indicating that behavioral outcomes and results were about two third of a standard deviation larger in persons that participated in a training compared to persons that did not (Arthur, Bennett, Edens, & Bell, 2003). However, it has to be noted that for results as outcome variable (i.e., utility of the training program for the organization) some find training interventions resulted in a negative outcome. This implies that a closer examination of the factors that make training successful with respect to results is needed. Other studies addressed the benefits of trainings for organization-level outcomes such as productivity or customer satisfaction. Here, there is some evidence that training is also linked to such organization-level outcomes (Tharenou & Burke, 2002).

With respect to more informal learning approaches there also seems to be a positive relationship between engagement in learning and job performance (for a brief summary cf. Sonnentag, Niessen, & Ohly, 2004). However, definitive conclusions are premature because the number of available studies is relatively small and most research is based on cross-sectional designs. Because effect sizes reported in studies largely vary, it seems that not all formal and informal learning activities result in positive outcomes. Therefore, it is particularly important to examine in more detail which aspects of learning are mostly beneficial for work-related outcomes.

3   Learning in Formal Settings

Learning in formal settings most often takes place in trainings and in development programs. During the past decades, training research has made significant progress (Salas & Cannon-Bowers, 2001). This progress is routed in both theoretical advancements and in a better research methodology. In this section we describe basic training principles and two illustrative training methods. In addition, we refer to important tasks to be accomplished during the training process, particularly before and after the actual training sessions.

3.1 Training design principles and training methods

Research on training has a long tradition and has regarded training as an instructional process that builds on basic learning principles (Kraiger, 2003). Noe and Colquitt (2002) summarized the most important characteristics a training program must meet in order to be effective: First, trainees should understand the objectives, purpose and intended outcomes of the training. Second, the training content should be meaningful and should be relevant for the job. Third, trainees should be provided with useful training aids such as diagrams or models. Forth, trainees should have the opportunity to practice in a relatively safe environment. Fifth, the training should provide feedback for the trainees. Sixth, trainees should have the opportunity to observe and interact with other trainees. Seventh, the training program should be well-coordinated and arranged.

When it comes to more specific training methods, a broad variety of different approaches are available ranging from more traditional methods such as lectures to more modern approaches such as computer-based trainings (Sadler-Smith, Down, & Lean, 2000; Welsh, Wanberg, Brown, & Simmering, 2003). Because a comprehensive overview over training methods of beyond the scope of this chapter, we will focus on one traditional method (Behavior Modeling Training; e.g., Latham & Saari, 1979) and a more recent European approach (Error Management Training; Frese, Brodbeck, Heinbokel, Mooser, Schleiffenbaum, & Thiemann, 1991). For more information on other training methods, readers may refer to Kraiger (2003).

Behavior Modeling Training (BMT) is based on social learning theory (Bandura, 1977) and has been used for training a broad range of different skills. A core assumption of BMT is that learning requires attentional, retentional, reproduction, and motivational processes. Typically, a BMT program first presents a description of the behavior (i.e., skills) to be learned, then if provides a list of learning points and a model of the required behavior (e.g., demonstrated on a videotape). Subsequently, trainees get the opportunity to practice the behavior and receive feedback on this displayed behavior.

A recent meta-analysis (Taylor, Russ-Eft, & Chan, 2005) based on 117 studies found large effects of BMT on declarative knowledge (e.g, written tests with multiple-choice questions; $d = 1.05$) and on procedural knowledge (i.e., skills; $d = 1.09$). Effects of BMT on attitudes and job behavior were smaller ($d = 0.29$ and $d = 0.25$, respectively). Effects of BMT on declarative knowledge slightly decreased as time after training elapsed, procedural knowledge and also job behavior remained stable or even increased over time. This finding implies that trainees' procedural knowledge and job behavior improves also after the training intervention has ended. However, declarative knowledge tends to "get lost" after training.

Procedural knowledge benefited from the use of learning points formulated as rule code. Rule codes formulate learning points as rules to be followed in one's behavior (e.g. "Verbalize clearly at the beginning of a meeting the points you want to discuss") as opposed to descriptions or summaries of the model's behavior that has been presented during the training (e.g., "presented the meeting agenda").

Using models that showed both positive and negative versions of the behavior to be learned resulted in poorer declarative knowledge and attitude change than the use of only positive models. However, job behavior was positively affected by mixed models. Job behavior after BMT was further improved when trainees were instructed to set goals and when trainees' managers were also trained. In addition, a positive relationship between training hours and procedural knowledge was found. This implies that longer training interventions resulted in a better learning of procedural knowledge than shorter trainings.

Error Management Training (EMT) is a training method that capitalizes on the positive functions of errors by giving trainees ample opportunities to make errors during training (Frese et al., 1991). Most often, EMT has been used for training computer-related skills. EMT encourages trainees to actively explore the computer program to be learning. Exploration is also stimulated by providing trainees only with minimal information. During the training, trainees are exposed to situations in which they very likely will make errors. EMT informs trainees about the positive sides of errors by stressing the learning opportunities associated with them. Thus, the core idea of EMT is that trainees make many errors during training and that they experience errors as a inherent part of the learning process, rather than as a stressful experience that has to be avoided. The positive effects of EMT become most evident when the (former) trainee is confronted with a difficult task or a new problem in his or her real work situation (Ivancic & Hesketh, 2000). The Research Close-Up 1 (below) illustrates a typical EMT study (Keith & Frese, 2005b).

Recently, Keith and Frese (in press) conducted a meta-analysis on the effects of EMT. The overall effect size of EMT based on 23 studies was moderate ($d = 0.44$). EMT had a stronger effect on test performance (i.e. performance after the training; $d = 0.58$) than on training performance (i.e., performance during the training; $d = -0.15$). Test tasks that were more complex and difficult than the training tasks were associated with larger effect sizes ($d = 0.80$) than test tasks that were very similar to the training tasks ($d = 0.17$). In addition, effect sizes were larger in trainings with feedbacks with high clarity – as opposed to low clarity feedback. Overall, this meta-analysis shows that EMT is a promising approach for preparing trainees for difficult and complex tasks in the work situation.

3.2   Training process

In order to design an effective training program, it is not only important to choose appropriate training design principles and methods. Also before and after the actual training sessions important tasks have to be accomplished. Here, we describe the most important pre- and post-training tasks: training needs analysis, training evaluation, and fostering training transfer. Readers who are interested in a more detailed description of a practitioner's perspective on the training process will find an overview in a chapter by Winkler (2002).

Training needs analysis   One important step in the development of a good training is the conduction of a training needs analysis (Tannenbaum & Yukl, 1992). Such a training needs analysis should comprise an organizational analysis, a task analysis, and a person analysis. The organizational analysis identifies organizational goals, resources, climate, and environment in order to assess the context and the ultimate objective of the training program. Task (or job) analysis describes the tasks to be performed. It identifies knowledge, skills, abilities, and orientations an employee should possess in order to perform the task well. Thus, task analysis determines the training content. Person analysis focuses on individuals (or groups of individuals) and identifies the persons who should participate in the training. In addition, it describes the prerequisites (knowledge, skills, motivation) with which these persons enter the training process. More recently, Hesketh (1997) has argued that it is not sufficient to conduct a training needs analysis, but that also a transfer of training needs analysis should be performed. Such a transfer of training needs analysis should assess the metacognitive skills (e.g., how to assess one's own skills, how to cope with unexpected situations) needed for training transfer as well as the environmental features that enable training transfer.

Unfortunately, training research has not yet paid much attention to training needs analysis or transfer of training needs analysis (Salas & Cannon-Bowers, 2001). Similarly, also practitioners are often reluctant to conduct a thorough training needs analysis what might make the training less effective (Kraiger, 2003). However, it is important to put effort into a well-conducted training and transfer of training needs analysis because this will help to design the most appropriate training and to identify potential problems early on.

Training evaluation   Training evaluation is an important part of the training process. Training evaluation provides information about whether trainees have achieved the training goals and shows if the training should be improved. In addition, it justifies the costs of the training (Sackett & Mullen, 1993).

Kirkpatrick (1976) proposed a taxonomy for evaluation training programs comprising four criteria: reaction criteria (i.e., training impression and enjoyment of the training, trainee satisfaction), learning criteria (i.e., learning progress as assessed in tests immediately after the training), behavioral criteria (i.e., on-the-job performance), and results criteria (i.e., organizational outcomes such as cost reduction or customer satisfaction).

This taxonomy is widely used in training evaluations with a particular focus on reaction criteria. A meta-analysis however showed that the four evaluation criteria are only weakly correlated (Alliger, Tannenbaum, Bennett, Traver, & Shotland, 1997). The low correlations indicate that for example trainings that are enjoyed a lot by the trainees (reaction criterion) do not necessarily result in improved on-the-job performance (behavioral criterion). As a consequence of their meta-analysis, Alliger et al. suggested that trainees' judgment of the utility of a training is a more useful indicator within training evaluation than pure affective reactions (cf. also Warr & Bunce, 1995).

Training transfer   To ensure that organizational and individual investments in training pay off, it is crucial that employees apply what they have learned to theirs jobs, that is that transfer of training takes place. Baldwin and Ford (1988) suggested that lack of training transfer can not only be attributed to poorly designed or conducted trainings, but also to individual and organizational factors exerting their influences before, during, and after the training. Among others, these factors include trainee motivation, supervisor support, and climate in the work environment.

Training transfer will benefit from the use of specific training principles such as the use of identical elements, focus on general principles, stimulus variability, and variety in conditions of practice (Baldwin & Ford, 1988). In addition, adaptive expertise and goal-setting may help training transfer (Hesketh, 1997). During the post-training phase, workplace characteristics play a core role in fostering versus inhibiting the application of newly learned knowledge and skills. For example, in a qualitative study conducted in a UK social services department, it was found that supervisory social support and opportunity to use what has been learned during training were important factors necessary for transfer of training (Clarke, 2002). In a later section of this chapter when we describe individual and situational factors that are relevant for learning we will summarize a meta-analysis that examined these factors also in their relationship to training transfer (Colquitt, LePine, & Noe, 2000).

4   Informal Learning

Informal learning happens outside formally-arranged training or development activities. Mostly, it takes place at the workplace and is often initiated by the employee him- or herself. Informal learning can aim at improving one's functioning in the present or a near future job, for example in the context of organizational socialization (Chao, 1997) or when adapting to a new job or new job demands (Pulakos, Arad, Donavan, & Plamondon, 2000). Informal learning can also refer to the acquisition of knowledge, skills and behaviors assumed to be helpful for future jobs. Such informal developmental activities are closely related to the concept of "career-related continuous learning" (CRCL; London & Smither, 1999) – although CRCL may also include more formal learning activities (e.g., following a training course).

Informal learning is important for individuals because not all learning needs can be satisfied with more formal learning programs. For example, very specific skills (or a combination of skills) may not be taught in a training course, or no training course may be offered at the time when the learning should take place.

Several approaches are relevant for informal learning at work: experiential learning, situated learning, and deliberate practice. Also research on specific learning strategies is important for work-related informal learning. Experiential learning theory conceptualizes experiential learning as "the process whereby knowledge is created through the transformation of experience," that is through "the combination of grasping and transforming experience" (Kolb, 1984, p. 41). It is assumed that individuals differ in their learning styles when learning from experience. In addition, research has shown that also jobs differ largely in the degree they offer opportunities for learning. Particularly, challenging job situations including job transitions, specific task characteristics, and obstacles enable learning from experience (McCauley, Lombardo, & Usher, 1989; McCauley, Ruderman, Ohlott, & Morrow, 1994). An empirical study has shown that interpersonal and task-related skills may also benefit from learning opportunities outside the job such as parenthood or voluntary work (Ruderman, Ohlott, Panzer, & King, 2002). It is important to note that gaining experience does not necessarily result in good performance. For example, a study in the domain of trade credit management showed that lecturers and students in management (but with no experience in the specific domain) outperformed experienced professional credit managers in a credit judgment task (Summers, Williamson, & Read, 2004). Professional credit managers were only slightly better than laypeople. This result illustrates that experience per se is not associated with better performance. Therefore, more research is needed to identify the individual characteristics, the situational factors, and the interaction between individual and situational variables that are associated with learning from experience.

The situated learning approach regards learning as a social process of constructing meaning and understanding (Lave & Wenger, 1991). In this view, learning can only be understood with respect to the social and physical context within which it occurs. So-called "communities of practice" that "share a concern, a set of problems, or a passion about a topic, and who deepen their knowledge and expertise in this area by interacting on an ongoing basis" (Wenger, McDermott, & Snyder, 2002, p. 4) are assumed to offer such as a learning context. Research on communities of practice is largely based on ethnographic and other qualitative approaches. For example, Hodgkinson and Hodgkinson (2004) described communities of practice among teachers in British schools.

Deliberate practice is a concept developed in the context of expertise research (Ericsson, Krampe, & Tesch-Römer, 1993) and refers to effortful activities pursued with the goal of improving one's current performance level. Typically, deliberate practice occurs in the domains of music and sport. Research has shown that deliberate practice can also be observed in the job context. For example, Dunn and Shriner (1999) found that teachers feel that they can learn from specific planning and evaluation activities such as preparing materials needed for instructional activities or from mentally planning instructional strategies and activities. Another study examined deliberate practice in German insurance agents (Sonnentag & Kleine, 2000). Analyses showed that about two third of the studied insurance agents used at least one deliberate practice activity in a typical work week (e.g., running mental simulations of difficult sales scenarios, asking for feedback, preparing for difficult situations). Insurance agents who were highly involved in deliberate practice showed higher performance than agents spending less time on deliberate practice.

Research on learning strategies covers a broad range of different learning contexts, both in formal and more informal settings. This field of research has it origins in studies on classroom learning but is also highly relevant for learning at work. Warr and Allen (1998) proposed a work-related taxonomy of cognitive, behavioral, and self-regulatory learning strategies. Cognitive learning strategies refer to the rehearsal, organization, and elaboration of material. Behavioral learning strategies comprise interpersonal help seeking, seeking help from written material, and the practical application of newly learned skills. Self-regulatory strategies comprise emotion control, motivation control, and monitoring of comprehension processes (cf. also Warr & Downing, 2000).

Holman, Epitropaki, and Fernie (2001) examined learning strategies among call centre employees in a UK bank and identified three cognitive and three behavioral strategies. The cognitive strategies comprised extrinsic work reflection (i.e., reflection about how one's work relates to that of others and to the company as a whole), intrinsic work reflection (i.e., reflect reflection about one's job and thinking about how new information relates to it), and (low) reproduction. The behavioral strategies comprised (interpersonal help seeking, help seeking from written material, practical application). In future research it would be particularly interesting to include self-regulatory learning strategies in the study of informal learning on the job because these learning strategies might be particularly helpful in the job context.

There is some evidence that specific approaches to informal learning and the use of learning strategies are related to positive outcomes such as increased satisfaction and reduced role ambiguity (Aiman-Smith & Green, 2002; Lankau & Scandura, 2002). However, relationships with knowledge gain tend to be weak (Warr & Downing, 2000). Interestingly, particularly persons with low learning anxiety tend to benefit from the use of learning strategies whereas this is not the case for persons high on anxiety. It might be that highly anxious learners need more specific strategies and support in order to learn.

Taken together, research on informal learning provides promising approaches to work-related learning. However, compared to research on training, knowledge on the most successful ways of informal learning is still limited. Here, more research is needed that systematically evaluates the effects of the various approaches to informal learning and their suitability for different groups of learners.

5 Individual Characteristics

Not all individuals participate to a similar degree in learning activities. Individuals differ also with respect to learning success. In this section we will describe motivational factors (goal orientation, motivation to learn), cognitive abilities, and age as important factors that might influence an individual's learning activities and learning success.

5.1 Motivational factors

An important motivational factor that is related to learning is an individual's goal orientation. Goal orientation is a mental framework for how individuals interpret achievement situations (Brett & VandeWalle, 1999). There are basically two forms of goal orientation, learning goal orientation and performance goal orientation (Dweck & Leggett, 1988). Highly learning oriented individuals focus on improving their skills and on mastering the task whereas highly performance oriented individuals are more focused on achieving a positive evaluation. As a consequence for learning in informal and formal settings, one can expect highly learning oriented individuals to invest more effort into learning activities, to focus their attention on the task to learn and to process information received differently (Sonnentag et al., 2004; Yeo & Neal, 2004). All these behaviors contribute to successful learning (in informal and formal settings). In addition, highly learning oriented individuals can be expected to seek out challenging tasks and to show an adaptive response pattern when difficulties arise. For example, they tend to see errors as informative feedback and to increase their effort. This adaptive response pattern might be especially useful in informal learning settings, when there is less structure than in formal trainings.

Highly performance oriented individuals are expected to show a different behavior pattern in learning settings: they focus more on maintaining a positive self-image and on their performance. Because performance tends to be low when learning a new task, this behavior pattern is detrimental. Furthermore, highly performance oriented individuals tend to choose easier tasks, see errors as a threat to their self-esteem, and exert minimal effort (Sonnentag et al., 2004; Yeo & Neal, 2004).

It is important to note that learning orientation and performance orientation are not opposite poles. One person can be high on both dimensions, and the description above is thus a simplification, as little is known so far about the behavior of those individuals with specific combinations of learning goal and performance orientation. Still, it becomes clear that promoting a learning goal orientation is beneficial to foster learning. This could be done by stating that the goal is to *learn*, not to demonstrate what a person already is capable of, and that no one needs to be afraid of making errors or showing low performance. In addition, a supervisor can stress the same objectives and reward employees' attempts to try out new ways of working. In this way, it becomes clear that learning is valued, and employees will be more likely to adopt a learning goal orientation.

In addition to goal orientation, the motivation to learn is an important factor to identify individuals who are likely to participate in informal learning activities and who benefit from formal learning activities such as trainings. Motivation to learn is "the desire on the part of the trainee to learn the training material" (Colquitt, LePine, & Noe, 2000, p. 681), and has been shown to be related to important learning outcomes. Given these positive results, it is valuable to know which persons generally are motivated in trainings: those who are high on conscientiousness, have an internal locus of control, are achievement-motivated, take their job seriously and feel committed to the organization (Colquitt et al., 2000). In line with the VIE Theory of Motivation, Tharenou (2001) has argued that the desire of individuals to learn can further be specified as the expectancy that putting effort into something will result in a valuable outcome. For example, to be motivated, it is necessary that (1) a training participant is confident that he or she can be successful in learning the material, (2) that learning the material leads to some outcome outside the training (e. g. promotion, interesting work tasks), and (3) that this outcome is of value for the training participant (he or she desires a promotion or more interesting work tasks). This perspective on learning motivation is advantageous because it gives hints about how to promote employees' learning motivation: For example, before employees start with a training course the supervisor or trainer can promote their self-confidence by stressing that they can master the training content, and can announce that valuable outcomes are provided.

The confidence that one can be successful in learning and training is also called learning self-efficacy (Mathieu & Martineau, 1997). Building the confidence that one can master the training material can be seen as an aim of formal trainings: The more a person believes he or she can successfully apply what was learned, the more likely he or she will show training transfer. Indeed, self-efficacy was positively related to the use of new technical equipment in a study on British car mechanics, trained how to use the new equipment in a two-day training course (Warr, Allan, & Birdi, 1999). Self-efficacy can be increased through adequate introduction into the training (basic skills need to be trained first, if not present), by ensuring positive learning experiences early in training (by giving easy trainings tasks), and by assisting training participants in the use of adequate strategies to learn. A training method specifically designed to build self-efficacy is behavior modeling (Gist, Schwoerer, & Rosen, 1989).

5.2   Cognitive abilities

One of the frequently examined individual characteristics in the training literature is cognitive ability. Cognitive ability refers to the capacity to reason, to plan, and to solve problems. Individual differences in this information processing capacity (working memory and processing speed) correlate with differences in learning, especially at initial stages of the learning process, when new information from the environment and recalled knowledge has to be coordinated and processed (Kanfer & Ackerman, 1989; Salas & Cannon-Bowers, 2001).

A strong predictor for training success is general cognitive ability (g), the single factor underlying different cognitive abilities tests (Ree & Carretta, 1998; Schmidt & Hunter, 1998). In a meta-analysis by Schmidt and Hunter (1998) the estimated predictive validity of g was 0.56 for training success. Colquitt et al. (2000) found strong relationships between g and declarative knowledge ($r_c = 0.69$), skill acquisition ($r_c = 0.38$) and transfer ($r_c = 0.43$). r_c is the an estimate of the meta-analytic correlation corrected for unreliability in both variables. For example, Lievens, Harris, Van Keer, and Bisqueret (2003) showed that g positively affected language acquisition of European managers after a cross-cultural training program in Japan. General cognitive ability (g) also affects self-efficacy after training positively.

Some researchers have proposed that there is "not much more than g" (e.g. Ree & Carretta, 1991, p. 321). That means that g assumed to be a strong predictor of training success across a variety of jobs and that specific cognitive abilities do not add incremental validity above and beyond g on training success. However, Colquitt et al. (2000) have shown that motivation to learn has an incremental validity for learning on cognitive abilities: there was "much more than g" (p. 696). Together, the motivation to learn and ability explained 63% of the variance in declarative knowledge, 20% of the variance in skill acquisition, 9% of the variance in post-training self-efficacy, and 20% of the variance in affective reactions to trainings and utility judgments. Moreover, locus of control, conscientiousness, anxiety, age and climate added incremental validity to motivation to learn and cognitive ability (24% for declarative knowledge, 9% for skill acquisition, 77% for post-training self-efficacy, 27% for reactions).

Research also showed that participants benefit from training tailored according to their cognitive ability (Gully, Payne, Koles, & Whiteman, 2002). In a study of Gully et al. (2002), persons with higher levels of cognitive ability seemed to benefit more from error-encouraging training than did individuals with lower ability: Diagnosing and learning from errors led to better declarative knowledge, task performance, and higher self-efficacy in high ability individuals, but not in lower-ability individuals.

Several questions remain open. It is not fully clear through which mechanisms cognitive ability affects learning. Furthermore, persons with lower ability may show the same level of performance as persons with higher abilities when there is enough time for training. In sum, more studies are needed that examine if and how these differences matter in complex real life settings.

5.3 Age

In many industrialized countries, the workforce is aging. In Europe, the proportion of employees between 20 to 29 years of age will decrease by 20 percent and the proportion of people of the 50 to 64 years age group will increase by more than 25 percent during 1995 and 2015 (Commission of the European Communities, 1999; cf. for a detailed review of the research on age, Kanfer & Ackerman, 2004; Warr, 2001). Although all workers are increasingly called on to be engaged in learning at work, there is evidence that older employees participate less in training and developmental activities (Warr & Fay, 2001; Warr & Birdi, 1998). They take longer to complete job-related training with similar performance than younger employees (e.g. Czaja & Sharit, 1998; Salthouse, Hambrick, Kristen, & Dell, 1996; for a meta-analytic review see Kubeck, Delp, Haslett, & McDaniel, 1996). However, the meta-analysis of Colquitt et al. (2000) revealed only a weak negative relationship between age and declarative knowledge acquired in trainings ($r_c = -0.19$) indicating that older individuals' learning performance declines only to a small degree.

One explanation for older employees' difficulties to learn refers to the perceived or factual decline in cognitive abilities (fluid intelligence) with increasing age (Maurer, Weiss, & Barbeite, 2003; Verhaeghen & Salthouse, 1997). This finding does not rule out that within an open learning environment with self-paced tasks and special training or instructional compensation for age-related disadvantages older employees' output will parallel the performance of the younger individuals after a while (Paas, Camp, & R., 2001; Van Gerven, Paas, Van Merrienboer, & Schmidt, 2002). Moreover, research showed that previous knowledge supports learning even of older persons (Beier & Ackerman, 2005; Charness, Kelley, Bosman, & Mottram, 2001). Previous knowledge helps to integrate new information. For example, Gott, Hall, Pokorny, Dibble, and Glaser (1993) investigated the role of existing knowledge structures in a new problem-solving task. Qualitative analysis of thinking-aloud protocols of six technicians indicated that good problem solvers used their knowledge base to interpret new information. Their abstract knowledge structure allowed for a deep understanding of the problem.

Compared to the research activities on cognitive aging, less research has examined noncognitive factors such as motives and social influences (Kanfer & Ackerman, 2004; Warr, 2001). Older employees reported a lower motivation for learning (Warr & Birdi, 1998), but meta-analytic results indicated only a weak effect of age on motivation to learn ($r_c = -.18$; Colquitt et al., 2000). Further analysis showed that older trainees described the need for development as less pronounced than did others (Maurer et al., 2003; Warr, Allan, & Birdi, 1999), more specifically they perceived the training less as an advantage for their career than did younger workers (Guerrero & Sire, 2001).

Motivation and cognition are strongly interrelated. Kanfer and Ackerman (2004) suggested that the motivation for training will decline because reduced cognitive ability slows down learning. Learning becomes more difficult and effortful which might in turn influence learning self-efficacy negatively. Moreover, the time frame for the development of knowledge and skills decreases when people get closer to retirement.

There is also evidence that age discrimination affects learning and development of older workers negatively. Stereotypical beliefs of managers significantly influenced attitudes toward training, promotion and retention of older workers (Chiu, Chan, Snape, & Redman, 2001; Maurer & Rafuse, 2001; Shore, Cleveland, & Goldberg, 2003). Research also showed that not only the chronological age, but also that the relative age to other team members or managers affects learning and development activities (Cleveland, Shore, & Murphy, 1997; Maurer et al., 2003; Shore et al., 2003). A large-scale study of Maurer et al. (2003) revealed that perceived relative age (e.g., being relatively old in a young group) was negatively related to supervisor and co-worker support.

The key problem remains how to encourage older employees to initiate learning activities. There are several proposals for tailored training that take adverse effects into account and that might support learning activities of older employees (Maurer, 2001; Warr, 2001). For example, because older employees show less educational initiative, they have to be encouraged to participate in learning activities by providing rewards (e.g., awards or skill based pay). Training has to be delivered with no time restriction. If necessary, basic skills should be enhanced prior to training. For example, older employees should have to learn basic computer skills before the training course for a complex computer program starts. Moreover, it is necessary to provide appropriate learning strategies and instructions. Additionally, organizational norms, especially negative stereotypes have to be changed, and a positive learning climate for all employees has to be created (for detailed information see Maurer, 2001 and Warr, 2001).

6 Situational Factors

Learning is affected by the organization in which it takes place. For example, the organizational reward system (pay for performance, promotion, skill-based pay) signals the importance of learning and may stimulate or hinder learning activities, either directly (e.g. pay for knowledge acquisition) or indirectly (e.g. pay for promotion attained through skill development; Baldwin & Magjuka, 1997).

Most research examined the impact of social factors as predictors of learning. Support from supervisors and co-workers have a significant influence on the involvement in work-related learning (Maurer et al., 2003) as well as nonwork-related developmental activities (Maurer, Mitchell, & Barbeite, 2002). There is evidence that employees' motivation to learn and self-efficacy before training is affected by supervisor support (for meta-analytic findings see Colquitt et al., 2000). Guerrero and Sire (2001) showed that in addition to perceived supervisor support also the information about the training (i.e., its usefulness, objectives and quality) were positively related to pretraining self-efficacy and training motivation. Supervisor support was also positively related to training outcomes. Meta-analytic findings of Colquitt et al. (2000) showed that supervisor support is positively related to the acquisition of declarative knowledge ($r_c = 0.25$). More specifically, other research has showed that learners seek more feedback when supervisors signal supportive behavior (Williams, Miller, Steelman, & Levy, 1999), which, in turn, might influence learning positively.

However, not only pretraining motivation and self-efficacy as well as training outcomes are positively affected by management support, but also the transfer of what was learned during training to the working place (Bennett, Lehman, & Forst, 1999; Facteau, Dobbins, Riussell, Ladd, & Kudisch, 1995; Tracey, 1995). There is strong positive relationships between supervisor support and transfer ($r_c = 0.43$). For example, in a longitudinal study with technicians, support for transfer expressed by supervisors and peers led to an increased use of new equipment after training (Warr, 1999). Moreover, other researchers showed that transfer was also related to the transfer climate. Transfer climate refers to employees' perception how the work environment helps to use at the workplace what was learned during training. Meta-analytic results revealed a positive relationship between (positive) climate and transfer ($r_c = 0.37$), and job performance ($r_c = 0.26$; Colquitt et al., 2000). Support and perceived organizational climate have also a positive impact on participation in developmental activities (Allen, 1999; Birdi, Allan, & Warr, 1997). Particularly, perceived supervisor support seems to lead to higher self-management for career development (Allen et al, 1999) when employees receive feedback and feel empowered by their supervisors (London, Larsen, & Thisted, 1999).

Often, learning takes place in a collaborative setting with peers and others where various interaction processes can support or constraint learning activities. For example, according to Baldwin and Magjuka (1997) training initiative depends also on group composition that influences trainees' motivation. Trainees can benefit from collaborative training settings in which they can observe each others' actions and where they can help each other (Shebilske, Jordan, Goettl, & Day, 1999). Thus, groups provide opportunities for learning by observation. Moreover, groups can facilitate learning through cooperative norms that include the willingness to support each other (Baldwin & Magjuka, 1997). There is considerable evidence that peer support has a strong relationship with transfer of training ($r_c = 0.84$; Colquitt et al., 2000). In sum, social support from supervisors and peers as well as transfer climate are strong predictors for learning-relevant outcomes.

The organization affects employees' learning also through its technology, which refers to factors such as technical tools and equipment, job design, and work flow design (Porras & Robertson, 1992). There is remarkably little research that examines the impact of these factors on learning. One exception is the study by Aiman-Smith and Green (2002) that investigated how people learn to operate technical systems. Interestingly, it turned out that users needed less time to become competent in operating the new system when the system had a high novelty for the user than when it had a lower novelty. One explanation is that the novelty of the system demands less relearning.

When it comes to job design variables as predictors of learning, Parker and Sprigg (1999) found that high job control and low job demands were important predictors for three learning-related outcomes, namely perceived mastery (i.e., employees' belief that they can control or act on job demands that occur), role-breadth self-efficacy (i.e., employees' confidence that they can carry out a wide range of integrative, proactive, interpersonal activities that go beyond traditional purely technical tasks), and production ownership (i.e., breadth and proactivity of employees' role orientation). Particularly, high job control was positively related to learning-related outcomes. In addition, results of two cross-sectional and one longitudinal analysis of Holman and Wall (2002) indicated that higher job control increases the perception that the job provides the opportunity for skill use and development (skill utilization) as one learning related outcome (see Research Close-Up 2). A longitudinal study with a large sample of Dutch teachers showed that high job control and low job demands predicted learning motivation (Taris, Kompier, de Lange, Schaufeli, & Schreurs, 2003). Parker and Sprigg as well as Holman and Wall measured learning-related variables, but did not assess learning activities directly. However, these promising studies suggest that it is mainly job control that is related to learning.

So far research has been focused on the influence of situational characteristics on learning and development. It might also be interesting to examine the influence the other way around: How do employees who are engaged in learning and development activities affect their work environment? Learning and development change people and this might also have an impact on roles, responsibilities, pay, and social relationships to team members or supervisors.

Summary

Learning refers to relatively stables changes in knowledge, skills or attitudes. In the work context, learning can take place in formal and in more informal settings. Learning at work is particularly important at present times when the nature of work is continuously changing. Generally, research has shown that learning in trainings is related to positive work-related outcomes.

Behavior Modeling Training and Error Management Training are two successful training methods. To make trainings more effective, it is needed to conduct a training needs analysis, to invest in training evaluation, and to pay attention to factors that enhance training transfer. Promising approaches to informal learning at work include experiential learning, situated learning, deliberate practice and the use of cognitive, behavioral, and self-regulatory learning strategies.

Motivational factors play a crucial role in learning participation and learning success. Particularly learning goal orientation and motivation to learn are important. In addition, cognitive ability is a strong predictor of favorable learning outcomes. Older individuals

Continued

have particular difficulties in learning. These difficulties can be attributed to cognitive and motivational processes as well as to age discrimination. With respect to situational factors, supervisor support and climate are important predictors of learning and transfer. Collaborative learning environments can enhance learning outcomes. A high level of job control is positively related to work-related learning.

Discussion Points

When you think about a job you are involved in or know well: What kinds of informal learning activities might be useful for this kind of job?

Thinking about a job you have or have had: What forms of trainings have been provided for you? Do you recognize the principles described in this chapter in your own experience? If the training proved to be unsatisfactory: What would have been more helpful in your opinion?

Imagine that you want to convince the management of an organization that this organization should support informal learning at work both by job design and specific supportive arrangements. How do you argue? Which counter-arguments do you anticipate?

Further Reading

This book describes principles and guidelines to implement and maintain a state-of-the-art training program:

Kraiger, K. (2001). *Creating, implementing and managing effective training & development: State-of-the-art lessons for practice.* San Fransisco: Jossey-Bass.

This chapter provides more details about research on learning at work:

Sonnentag, S., Niessen, C., & Ohly, S. (2004). Learning at work: Training and development. In

C. L. Cooper & I. T. Robertson (Eds.), *International review of industrial and organizational psychology* (Vol. 19, pp. 249–89). Chichester: Wiley.

www.tcm.com/trdev/ lists all kinds of resources for those interested in training and learning: For example job listings, references, discussion groups.

www.bologna-berlin2003.de/pdf/MemorandumEng.pdf is a memorandum issued 2000 by a task force of the European community. It contains examples and reflections of how "life-long learning" can look like in practice.

Research Close-Up 1

Keith, N. & Frese, M. (2005). Performance effects of error management training. *Journal of Applied Psychology, 90,* 677–91.

Introduction

Error Management Training (EMT) has proven to be an effective training method.

Letting training participants explore while having minimal information about the training content, and stressing the positive nature of errors that naturally occur, lead to better performance after training. Nina Keith and Michael Frese wanted to know how exactly this training approach works. They assumed that there are two underlying processes that make error management training effective: emotion control and metacognitive strategies. Emotion control refers to the efforts individuals undertake to minimize their negative emotions (e.g. performance anxiety), for example, to consider calmly how to continue with a task when difficulties arise. The second process, metacognition, is an individual's effort to control his or her thoughts. For example it involves planning how to do the task, and monitoring the process of task accomplishment. Because participants in EMT practice emotion control and metacognition during training, they are expected to also apply both processes when working on a difficult task after training.

Method

Fifty-five students without any previous knowledge were trained how to use a specific software. There were three training conditions: two EMT conditions that only differed slightly in instructions, and a condition where participants were encouraged not to make any errors (i.e. error avoidance condition). First, all participants read a manual describing the basic functions of the software. After that, all participants had to work on tasks using the software. In the error avoidant condition, participants followed a detailed step-by-step instruction to prevent them from making errors, whereas in the error management conditions, participants received instructions emphasizing the positive nature of errors.

To capture metacognition, all participants were instructed to verbalize all their thoughts during training. Their statements were later classified as metacognition or other cognitions. Emotion control was rated by training participants right after training. Then, a performance test followed. Two experts judged the performance.

Results

Analysis revealed that during training participants in the error management conditions made more errors than participants in the error avoidant group, but had a more positive attitude towards errors. Emotion control and metacognition were also higher in the error management conditions, and this was significantly related to the quality of performance in the difficult test.

Discussion

The study supports the positive function of errors for learning in training. Furthermore, it identified two processes that make error management training effective: emotion control and metacognition. This information is useful for adapting error management training to other training contents. If an instructor wants to use an error management approach, he or she needs to make sure that emotion control and metacognition are indeed trained to make this approach effective. This study suggests not only to focus on the training material (what is learned) but also on the kind of information processing that is most promising for learning.

Research Close-Up 2

Holman, D. J. & Wall, T. (2002). Work characteristics, learning-related outcomes, and strain: A test of competing direct effects, mediated, and moderated models. *Journal of Occupational Health Psychology*, 7, 283–301.

Introduction

There is some evidence that learning is affected by work design. The job demand control model (Karasek & Theorell, 1990) suggests that jobs characterized by high demands and high control (i.e., active jobs) are related to a high degree of learning, whereas jobs characterized by low demands and low control (i.e., passive jobs) offer little opportunities for learning. Moreover, these two aspects of work, demands and control, are also well-known predictors for strain (e.g., anxiety and depression). One aim of the study of Holman and Wall (2002) was to examine these work design variables in relation to both strain and learning. They studied skill utilization and self-efficacy as learning-related outcomes. Here, skill utilization refers to the perceived opportunity to use and develop skills.

The second purpose of the study was to test competing models of the relationships between learning-related outcomes, strain, and work design variables. More specifically, Holman and Wall investigated whether (a) work design has independent effects on learning and strain (e.g., control is positively related to learning), (b) mediated effects (e.g., control affects learning, what in turn reduces strain), or (c) moderated effects (e.g., greater control reduces strain only if there is greater self-efficacy).

Method

The participants of the study were customer service agents in three call centers of a UK bank. At Time 1, 571 employees filled out a questionnaire. After one year, 347 employees completed a second questionnaire. Holman and Wall devided the sample into three independent subsamples: (1) respondents that completed questionnaires at Time 1 only ($n = 427$), (2) at Time 2 only ($n = 203$), and (3) at both Times ($n = 144$). Therefore, they conducted two cross-sectional and one longitudinal analysis. The study allowed for comparing the results of the cross-sectional and longitudinal analyses.

Results

The data analysis included two main steps. First, Holman and Wall used structural equation modeling to test the competing models of the relationships between work design, learning and strain on the two cross-sectional subsamples. Second, using longitudinal hierarchical regression analyses they examined the relationships in the longitudinal sample.

The results of the three analyses indicated that the mediated models provided the best fit to the data. The two cross-sectional studies showed that skill utilization fully mediates the effect of control on depression. This result was replicated in the longitudinal analysis. A high degree of control supports employees to use and develop skills. This, in turn helps them to cope with job demands and thus to reduce depression. The second result that was consistent over the three analyses was that depression only partially mediated the effect of control on skill utilization. The data revealed that a low degree of control reduced the opportunity for using and developing skills, and that low control also affect skill utilization through its effect on depression. The study showed no significant relationships between self-efficacy, strain, and work design variables.

Discussion

The study revealed some consistent results over three different samples whereby cross-sectional results could be replicated in a longitudinal study design. The key notion was that there are reciprocal effects between strain and learning-related outcomes: greater control increases skill utilization, which in turn reduces depression. One main limitation is that the results are based on self-report data. Moreover, Holman and Wall measured learning-related variables, but did not assess learning activities directly. However, the study suggests that job control is highly relevant for learning.

Performance Appraisal: Assessing and Developing Performance and Potential

4

Clive Fletcher

Overview

This chapter begins by outlining the purposes of performance appraisal – which include assessing ongoing work performance, giving feedback, trying to increase work motivation and to enhance quality and quantity of output and developing potential. It goes on to examine the various approaches taken to assessing the individual's effectiveness at work, including the use of rating scales, competencies and achievement against objectives. The shift in emphasis of research from assessment issues to studying the social and motivational context of appraisal is outlined, and issues such as reactions to feedback and the personal and political agenda of the participants are discussed. Moving from present performance to potential, methods such as multisource feedback systems are outlined and evaluated. Finally, the impact of organizational change on performance appraisal systems and the emergence of broader performance management strategies are considered.

What is Performance Appraisal?

Just for a few moments, put yourself in the position of a senior manager in a major company. You have five managers reporting directly to you, and another twenty managerial and professional staff reporting to them. How are you going to assess the performance of the people working for you? What criteria will you use to judge whether anyone is not performing well enough, or to decide whether any of them are ready to take on greater responsibilities and perhaps achieve a promotion? How will you seek to drive up performance in your division, and how will you try to motivate and develop your staff to bring this about? These are the questions that managers face every day; they are central to the manager's role. The answers to them are often expressed, in a formal way, through the performance appraisal system that the organization puts in place. Not surprisingly, organizations vary in the kind of answers they come up with, and so the approach taken to appraisal varies widely too. In this chapter, we will look at performance appraisal in its many guises and evaluate it from the viewpoint of theory and research in occupational psychology. First, however, it is necessary to understand in more detail what performance appraisal systems look like, how they work and what they are trying to do.

Essentially, performance appraisal is a generic term used to describe a range of processes whereby a manager and a subordinate meet on a periodic basis to review the work of the latter and to seek to raise performance levels. Box 4.1 presents a fairly traditional example of how the whole process can work, but, as we will see below, more progressive organizations at the present time often go some way beyond this in what they do under the banner of performance appraisal.

Box 4.1:   Steps in the annual appraisal process in a telecommunications company

1. The period for doing appraisals is April to May, so at the end of March the personnel department sends out the appraisal forms and guidance documents (for both those doing the appraisal and those being appraised) to all managers who have staff to appraise.

2. The appraisers then pass on to their appraisees a preparation form, which invites them to make a self-assessment against various competency headings, and also against the objectives they set last year. Meanwhile, the appraiser from his or her own point of view is making those same assessments for each person to be appraised.

3. The appraisal interview takes place, and can last anything between one and two hours. The appraiser will invite the appraisee to comment on his or her performance over the past year, to identify any problems that have arisen and to review progress against objectives set. Discrepancies between the two of them in how they see the appraisee's performance may arise, and will be discussed. Finally, objectives for the year ahead are agreed, as is any development activity needed to help the appraisee.

4. An appraisal report form is now completed – it may have been partly written by the appraiser before the interview, but now it becomes the formal record and is signed by both parties. It includes a set of ratings of the individual on the key competencies associated with the role, a statement of the objectives for next year, an overall performance rating and a list of action points relating to the appraisee's development needs. They each keep a copy of it, and another copy is sent to the personnel department.

5. Various kinds of follow-up activity will take place. The personnel office scans all the appraisal forms for development recommendations that may require their input (to advise on relevant training courses, or to assist in possible job changes). At three-monthly intervals, the progress against objectives set is monitored and discussed by the appraiser and appraisee.

One of the key issues in understanding appraisal – and for research perspectives on it – is establishing the aims of the exercise; what are we trying to achieve? Perhaps one of the most frequently cited purposes is to enable some kind of assessment to be made of the appraisee. But assessment, while constituting a core element of appraisal, is of little value if done simply for its own sake. What it provides is a basis for several central purposes of appraisal, in particular:

1. *Improving performance.* One of the basic psychological principles of learning is that to improve performance, individuals need to have some knowledge of the results they are already achieving. Forming an assessment and conveying it should meet this requirement and help to enhance performance.
2. *Making reward decisions.* If the organization is to seek to distribute rewards in a fair and equitable manner – be they pay, promotion or whatever – then some method of comparing people is necessary. If an assessment of performance is made annually, it can be used to direct rewards to those most deserving of them.
3. *Motivating staff.* There are three ways in which appraisal seeks to motivate employees. Even since the earliest appraisal schemes, it has been an article of faith that giving feedback, quite apart from assisting in task performance, is something that motivates people. And there is some justification for this, as employees in all types of organization frequently express the view that they want to know where they stand, i.e. they desire feedback. The assessment made in appraisal provides the basis for the feedback, and thus contributes to motivation. Second, assessment also increases motivation through its role in facilitating the fair distribution of rewards. Third, setting targets that improve on previous performance is also a motivating device.
4. *Developing subordinates.* People need training, on and off the job, to help them develop, and it is part of the appraisal's role to facilitate this. Identifying what short- and medium-term development needs the individual has, and planning how to meet them, is a key aim for appraisal.
5. *Identifying potential.* By identifying good and poor performers, the appraisal enables the organization to focus succession planning and resources on the individuals who are most likely to respond positively and effectively to it.
6. *Formal recording of unsatisfactory performance.* In its most negative garb, appraisal can be part of the process whereby unsatisfactory performance is documented and used in evidence in disciplinary or dismissal proceedings.

These are some of the purposes that, in theory at least, can be served by an appraisal scheme that includes an element of assessment. On the face of it, they seem very reasonable and entirely justifiable. But together they form a formidable agenda – can we really assess, motivate, reward and develop people all in one annual process that still often consists of a single interview and a report form? To answer this question, we can turn to the psychological research relating to appraisal. Much of the research that has been done splits into two broad themes:

how to assess performance effectively, and the social and motivational context of appraisal.

The Assessment of Work Performance

The rating of performance dimensions

If one is to assess ongoing work performance, the decision has to be made as to how this is to be done: what is to be assessed, and the method used. In the early years of appraisal systems (and they have been around since before the First World War), the tendency was to assess the individual on personality attributes. This became very unpopular with appraisers, who disliked making such fundamental judgments about their staff. From the 1960s onwards, this approach diminished, though Holdsworth (1991) notes that as late as the 1970s one British retailing organization was asking its managers to appraise staff on "moral courage"! In its place, organizations settled on rating job-related abilities, such as "management of staff," "performance under pressure," "decision-making." This kind of approach can still be found, though now what is rated is normally a set of competencies. There are various ways of defining competencies, but in general they can be thought of as observable skills or abilities to complete a managerial task success-fully or as behavioral dimensions that affect job performance (Woodruffe, 2000; Sparrow, 1996). The competency labels may not look very different from the job-related abilities mentioned above, but they will usually have been defined in much more detail, with good and poor performance described in behavioral terms; an example of some of the competencies used to describe performance in a customer-facing role in a high street bank is given in box 4.2.

Box 4.2:   Example of some of the competencies used by a financial institution to describe effective and ineffective performance in a sales role

The two competencies described below were arrived at by rep grid analysis of the constructs elicited from managers of staff in the role concerned. Each manager was asked to think of examples of six or seven good and poor performers among subordinates in this job. The names of these subordinates were then each written on a separate card, and the manager was presented with three of the cards, two of which had the names of high performers, and the other a low performer. The manager's task was to describe in behavioral terms one way in which two of the three differed from the third. With repetition of this for different triads of cards/names, a series of constructs emerges that define the behavioral differences between good and poor performers. In all, eleven competencies were identified as being of primary importance in this job role.

Continued

Competency: Problem analysis and judgment

Effective: Analyses the customer's requirement in a logical fashion. Correctly identifies the combination of products to meet the need. Thinks things through and looks beyond the immediate situation. Displays a capacity for innovation in problem-solving. Makes decisions on a balanced appraisal of the facts.

Ineffective: Focuses narrowly on the immediate problem without looking at the broader perspective. Offers solutions before analyzing the problem sufficiently. Is rigid and unimaginative in matching available products to meet the needs of the customer. Sees things in overly simple, black and white terms. Promises more than can be delivered.

Competency: Planning and organizing

Effective: Organizes the day so that post is dealt with without delay. Plans ahead, looking beyond the immediate situation. Ensures there is cover for absences. Diarizes key dates and events for follow-up. Prioritizes time and effort to maximize opportunities for customer contacts. Does homework on customers and has information that may be required readily accessible. Delegates routine work where possible. Adopts a structured approach to tasks.

Ineffective: Disorganized and unsystematic in tackling the work. Fails to anticipate problems and does not plan ahead. Misses important dates and events that should have been followed up. Double books self. Gives routine and minor tasks equal priority with more important elements of the job. Not punctual.

Identifying which job-related attributes or competencies are of chief importance in performing a role or range of roles should result from a systematic process of job or competency analysis. The methods used (questionnaires, critical incidents etc.) are discussed in chapter 1, and so will not be discussed further here. Turning to *how* these attributes are measured rather than *what* is measured, several different forms of rating scale can be employed. For example, the scale intervals may be simply numerically or alphabetically defined (1–5, a–e), or they may be verbally described (outstanding, very good, good, and so on). Most appraisal forms contain at least one rating – usually of overall performance – and quite often they present a whole series of them relating to different aspects of performance. Rating scales are the vehicle for the quantitative assessment of the individual. Because of this emphasis on the use of ratings in appraisal, much psychological research effort has been expended on trying to find what rating method is the most effective in producing well distributed ratings that differentiate between employees of differing levels of performance in an accurate and reliable way (Fletcher, 2001). In other words, what kind of rating method gives us measures of performance that are – to use the frame of reference we associate with psychological testing – psychometrically sound? Conventional rating scale use has long been recognized as bedeviled with problems (Landy & Farr, 1980); most frequent of these are central tendency (everyone is rated in the middle), halo effect (assessment of one quality of the individual affects the judgment of all his or her other attributes, so all ratings are highly correlated) and positive skew (everyone is rated high – all swans, no geese).

One response to these problems is the development of behaviorally anchored rating scales, or BARS (Smith and Kendall, 1963). These are carefully and systematically derived scales for assessing performance, and seek to put the person making the assessment into a more objective, observational role, rather than a judgmental one. The process for developing BARS is described in box 6.3.

However, the time and cost it takes to develop BARS discourages many organizations from using them widely; quite apart from anything else, BARS by their nature are rather specific to a single role or group of related roles, and cannot readily be generalized to other jobs. Moreover, the research on how effective they are is not altogether reassuring in demonstrating that they show a significant improvement in psychometric characteristics (for example, consistently producing a more even distribution of performance ratings) over more conventional methods (e.g. Jacobs, Kafry, & Zedeck, 1980).

Box 4.3:   Constructing BARS

Although there are a number of variations, the development of BARS usually goes through five stages:

* Examples of behaviors reflecting effective and ineffective job performance are obtained from experts who are knowledgeable about the job to be rated.

* These examples are grouped into a series of separate performance dimensions by the experts.

* Another expert group repeats the second stage, allocating the examples to dimensions.

* This provides an independent check on the relevance of the behavioral examples to each dimension. Any that are allocated differently by the two groups are probably too ambiguous and should be discarded. As a result of this, the dimensions should be quite independent of each other.

* Taking each dimension separately, the examples relating to it are rated on a numerical scale by the experts in terms of the degree of effectiveness they represent. Where an example does not get rated similarly by different expert judges, it will be deleted; a high level of agreement on how an example is rated on that dimension is required.

* The resulting dimensions are expressed as scales, the points of which are anchored by the behavioral descriptions arrived at through the preceding development stages. The number of dimensions can vary according to the job; anything from 6 to 9 would be quite typical.

An example of a BAR in relation to a teamwork competency is given below in figure 4.1.

Continued

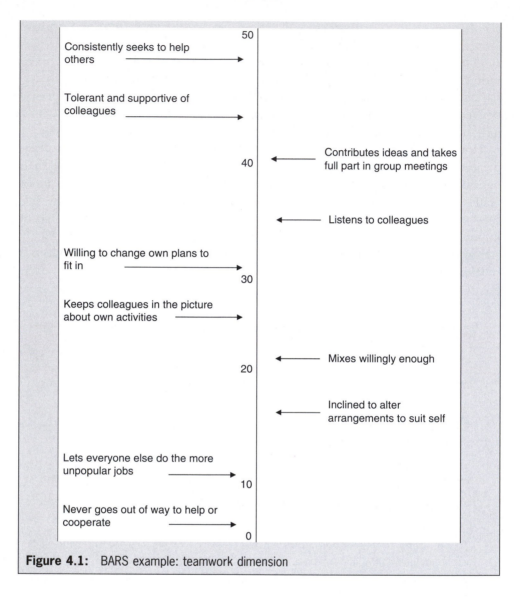

Figure 4.1: BARS example: teamwork dimension

BARS represent a pragmatic, methodological solution to the problems with ratings. Another approach is to try to deepen our understanding of the cognitive processes involved in making performance ratings. This is best exemplified in the program of work carried out by DeNisi (1996). He examines the information acquired by the rater, the cognitive representation of this, how the information is stored and retrieved, and how it is integrated with other factors to come to an assessment decision. This work has produced helpful cognitive models of the rating process, and these have informed some of the various attempts to train people to carry out appraisal ratings. In effect, this is the other major strategy –

instead of focusing on the format of the rating scales, one tries to improve the use made of them by the raters themselves.

There are various ways of doing this:

- *Rater error training*: teaching raters about the typical errors so they are sensitized to them and, in theory, less likely to make them.
- *Performance dimension training*: training raters in the use of the performance dimensions they are rating people on, and ensuring they can differentiate between them, i.e. they are able correctly to allocate a piece of behavioral "evidence" to the dimension it should be rated under.
- *Frame of reference training*: seeks to give raters a clear picture of the standards they are rating people against; for example, by giving behavioral examples that would typify performance at each point on the rating scale.
- *Behavioral observation training*: focuses on the initial data collection by giving the raters training in correct observation and recording of behavior, which should enhance the quality of the ratings they eventually make.

Not surprisingly, the different approaches tend to have different effects and consequences. However, the relatively few studies on the impact of these and similar training methods (e.g. Woehr & Huffcutt, 1994: Lievens, 2001) reflect somewhat mixed results; some improvement in rating quality is observed, though it is neither great in scope nor very consistent. The limited progress made by cognitively oriented research on appraisal has led to a move towards a perspective that emphasizes appraisal as a social process, which is addressed in more detail below.

Finally, one other approach to improving the fairness of appraisal should be mentioned, namely the use of more raters. One aspect of this is involving the person appraised more directly in the rating process. Many appraisal schemes, like that described in box 4.1, invite the appraisee to make a self-assessment and then use this as a background to the discussion of the appraiser's ratings. Self appraisal seems to work best when individuals are asked to make assessments of their strengths and weaknesses relative to their own overall performance, rather than to compare themselves directly with others on each attribute (Fletcher, 2004); in other words, when they are asked to say what they are good at and not so good at, without necessarily implying that the latter means they are less effective than their peers in this respect.

Results-oriented appraisal

This approach has become increasingly popular over the past 25 years or so, and originally stems from the concept management by objectives (MBO, or MbyO), which is a rather wider application of the same principles across the whole organization (Drucker, 1955). Results-oriented appraisal focuses on setting objectives (or goals) and reviewing performance against those objectives. The objectives should relate to key aspects of the job, and provide *quantifiable* performance improvement targets for the individual to achieve *within a specified time period*. Manager and subordinate meet annually or more frequently to review progress against last year's objectives and to agree new ones for the year ahead.

The advantages of this approach are held to be that it is:

- more objective, because it rests on quantified measures;
- strongly job-related;
- less likely to engender conflict (because of its greater objectivity, appraiser and appraisee can see what has or has not been achieved).

The disadvantages are:

- it is not as easy to make direct comparisons between people on the basis of achievement against objectives, because the objectives set will vary somewhat from person to person
- it is far from straightforward to express performance in some jobs, or parts of them, in terms of objectives (for example, would it be a good idea simply to set an objective for a surgeon to carry out 25 percent more operations in a year?)

The most striking thing here is that the research literature strongly supports objective setting. The evidence (e.g. Locke & Latham, 1990) shows that goal setting is effective in raising performance levels – it is claimed that more than 90 percent of all studies on goal setting show positive effects. Some caution should be expressed here, though, as goal setting theory has been criticized for numerous limitations (Donovan, 2001). For example, many of the studies have been done in laboratory rather than field settings. The former obviously offer a degree of experimental control that the latter do not, but possibly at the cost of ecological validity; the nature of the task, the attitude of those participating, the rewards offered and many other factors may be very different from what one would find in real-world work situations. Another caveat is that studies on objective setting have been more concerned with quantity of output rather than quality – and quality is often as important, if not more so, than quantity (think back to the issue of objective setting for surgeons mentioned above). In terms of research on the *process* of objective setting, some of the main conclusions (Locke & Latham, 1990) are:

1. Difficult objectives lead to greater achievement than easy ones.
2. Specific objectives, rather than general exhortations to do well, lead to better achievement.
3. Feedback on performance and achievement is essential.
4. The individual's own level of commitment is also a factor.

So, many appraisal systems today have a strong element of objective setting in them. But, perhaps in recognition of some of the limitations of this approach, they frequently also include some rating scales of competencies or performance dimensions on their appraisal forms.

The Social and Motivational Context of Appraisal

The early research emphasis on ways of assessing performance and on the technical problems of rating scales perhaps resulted in less attention being paid to the social and motivational context of appraisal. In time, though, the latter has become the more dominant perspective. This is not surprising, since no matter how good the technical quality of the appraisal methods used, if those who are to be involved in the process – the appraiser and the appraisee – are not committed to the aims of the exercise, then little is likely to be achieved. Recent survey evidence suggests that 80 percent of British organizations express dissatisfaction with their appraisal schemes (Fletcher, 2004), and whilst there are no comparable figures for other European countries, much the same proportion emerges from web-based surveys in the US, so perhaps they would also be similar. The reason for the dissatisfaction in the UK seems to rest chiefly on the perception that they fail to meet the aims organizations set for them. For example, in one survey a key objective of the appraisal systems operated by the organizations contacted was "motivation," but not one of the managers assessed their system as being very good in achieving this objective.

What are the problems that give rise to this rather dismal picture? A fundamental one is conflicting aims. The typical appraisal system faces the managers carrying out the appraisals with a potential role conflict: on the one hand, they are communicating an assessment to the appraisees, which may not be in line with how the appraisees see their own performance, while in the same session they are expected to play more of a counseling role, helping staff to improve performance and dealing with problems. It has been suggested that these two roles do not sit well together, because if appraisees become defensive about the assessment made of them, they are less likely to be willing to engage in a constructive search for ways of improving performance. The basic conflict here, then, is between the *assessment* function of appraisal and the *motivational* function of appraisal. This in turn is linked to four other aspects of the situation: the quality of the assessment, the way it is conveyed, the implications for rewards and the personal agenda of the participants.

Quality of assessment

As we have seen, there are difficulties in obtaining accurate and objective measures of ongoing job performance. Staff being appraised may feel that their boss has only a limited view of their performance, or is biased in some way, or is not taking account of other factors beyond their personal control that have impacted on what they have achieved. One particular bias that has been shown to operate in appraisal is attributional bias (Mitchell & Wood, 1980). Social psychological research has demonstrated the pervasive effects of "fundamental attributional error," which refers to the tendency to interpret the causes of other people's behavior in terms of their internal dispositions, and to take less account of situational influences than one does in explaining one's own behavior. Clearly, in the context of performance appraisal, this could lead to serious distortions in judgments of the extent to which an individual's performance has been influenced by external factors.

Communicating the assessment

Appraisers are frequently reluctant to convey any critical comments to the appraisee, as they are apprehensive about the defensive reactions they may encounter. When they do make some critical comments, the results are sometimes the exact opposite of what they seek to achieve. Kay, Meyer and French (1965), in their seminal work on the General Electric Company of America found that criticism led to lower motivation and little or no behavior change in those appraised. Another study, by Pearce and Porter (1986), reported a long-term stable drop in organizational commitment as a consequence of staff just being rated as "satisfactory" – as opposed to more favorably than that – when an appraisal scheme was introduced. In fact, Kluger and DeNisi (1996) concluded from their review of the literature that more than one-third of feedback interventions (many of which occur in nonappraisal settings) *decreased* performance. While it is possible to convey feedback on performance limitations in a way that does not cause counterproductive reactions, the levels of skill and the conditions necessary to achieve this are not found all that often. For appraisal feedback to be effective, it has to:

- be specific and clear in content;
- be given soon after the event it relates to;
- be balanced in recognizing strengths as well as weaknesses in performance;
- come from a credible source
- be communicated in a sensitive manner (which may need training to achieve).

Links with rewards

An observation that has been made repeatedly is that direct links between assessments made in appraisal with rewards, such as pay rises and – to a lesser extent – promotion, cause great difficulty (Campbell, Campbell, & Chia, 1998). The reason for this, as has already been noted, is the lack of faith in the accuracy and fairness of the assessments made. If an individual is told that she will not be getting as big a pay rise (or none at all) as she hoped because her performance level does not justify it, and she does not feel the assessment of her performance is right anyway, in most cases her reaction is predictably negative.

Personal and political agenda of the participants

Bernardin and Villanova (1986) found that a majority of appraisers and appraisees felt that inaccuracy in performance ratings was more because of deliberate distortion than inadvertent cognitive errors on the part of the raters. The attitude of managers towards carrying out PA seems to be ambivalent at best. It is frequently observed that they avoid carrying out appraisals. In one UK survey (Industrial Society, 1997) less than two-thirds of organizations reported a better than 67 percent appraisal completion rate – and this is one of the more favorable findings! Why does this rather bleak situation arise? Various writers (e.g. Cleveland & Murphy, 1992) have offered analyses of PA from the point of view of the appraiser. In particular, Longenecker and his colleagues have specifically focused on the politics of appraisal in a number of studies and articles (Longenecker, Gioia, & Sims, 1987; Longenecker & Gioia, 1988; Longenecker, Liverpool, & Wilson, 1988; Longenecker, 1989; Gioia & Longenecker, 1994). Amongst other things, this research identified the following reasons why managers gave unduly favorable ratings of subordinates:

1. a belief that accurate ratings would have a damaging effect on subordinate motivation and performance
2. a desire to improve the subordinate's chances of getting a pay rise
3. a wish to avoid others outside the department seeing evidence of internal problems and conflicts
4. preventing a permanent written record of poor performance coming into being which might have longer-term implications for the subordinate
5. a need to protect subordinates whose performance had suffered from the effects of personal problems
6. wanting to reward subordinates who had put in a lot of effort even if the end result was not so good
7. avoiding confrontation and potential conflict with "difficult" subordinates
8. aiming to promote out of the department subordinates who were disliked or problem performers.

Though less frequently reported, some reasons for deliberately manipulating performance assessments in a downward direction were also uncovered:

9. scaring people into performing better
10. punishing difficult or noncompliant subordinates
11. encouraging unwanted subordinates to leave
12. minimizing the merit pay award(s)
13. complying with organizational restrictions on the number of higher ratings given.

The general observation from this research is that managers frequently allow their appraisal of staff to be influenced by nonperformance issues. Gioia and Longenecker (1994) found that the higher an individual rose in an organization, the more political the appraisal process becomes. (See the Research Close-Up at the end of this chapter.)

From the appraisee's side, personal motives may include wanting to maintain self-esteem, seeking to refute criticism, protecting and enhancing reward and promotion prospects, seeking training opportunities and career development moves (Fletcher, 2002). Although there is ample evidence that subordinates want feedback on performance, this does not mean that they are going to accept it blindly. In some cases, they want to know what their boss thinks of them so that they can give their own side of the story and correct what they may feel are unwarranted criticisms of their performance. The concept of procedural justice is relevant here, as it deals with perceptions of the fairness of the procedures used for distributing rewards within an organization. Having the opportunity to participate and contribute actively to the appraisal – having a "voice" in it – and being able to challenge assessments are found to be important factors in determining perceptions of procedural justice (McDowell & Fletcher, 2004).

The fact is that while organizations have needs that they expect the appraisal system to meet, the people doing the appraisal – and those they are appraising – usually have more personal agendas to follow; these often cause the appraisal process to become less effective in terms of what the organization wanted from it. There is, though, another aspect of appraisal that we have hardly mentioned until now, but that has profound implications for whether appraisal is seen as a motivating force; this is its role in *developing* the appraisee.

Appraising Potential

It is one thing to know how people are performing now, but what about making sure they get the kind of experience and training they are going to need for future roles? And which of them should be promoted to higher levels when the opportunity arises? Appraisal is typically supposed to contribute to answering these questions, but assessing potential to perform at a higher level is not straightforward. One obvious basis to work from is present performance, as reflected in appraisal and other data. But the reason for having an assessment of potential is precisely because present performance is by no means a completely reliable indicator of future performance, hence the so-called "Peter principle": people rise to the level of their incompetence, i.e. you keep getting promoted until you reach the position where you cannot do the job well, so you do not get promoted any more. The other problem is that when managers are asked to assess the longer-term potential of their staff, the assessment task they are being faced with is especially difficult. They are being asked to comment on the ability of an individual to do a job at a level that may be above their own, and which they have no direct experience of.

Because of these problems, organizations have increasingly turned to other methods of assessing potential. One of the simplest is to have career review panels made up of senior managers, who periodically review the career progress of more junior managers and decide what promotion or development steps should be taken in each case. However, they now often use evidence from either psychometric tests or Assessment Centers (and their close relative, Development Centers) to help them make these judgments. As there are dealt with elsewhere in this book, they will not be further discussed here. Instead, we will concentrate our attention on a method that has become widely adopted in recent years, which started out in most organizations as a development activity and that is increasingly being drawn into the formal appraisal process. This is multisource, multirater feedback (MSMR), also known as "360-degree feedback."

360-Degree Feedback and Appraisal

The term 360-degree feedback generally means an individual being rated by subordinates, peers, superiors and – sometimes – clients, as well as doing a self-assessment. These assessments are collected and integrated by either a human resource manager or an external consultant, then fed back to the "target" manager in the form of a profile of his or her competencies as seen from these differing perspectives: see figure 4.2 for an example of a page from a feedback report of this kind. An action plan is then drawn up to tackle any development needs that have been identified.

In recent years, this kind of process has been widely adopted in the UK, perhaps in part because the changes in UK organizations described below have created a new culture and transformed ideas about management, with the result that 360-degree feedback is an idea whose time has come. An example of such a system is given in box 4.4. The actual proportion of companies applying it is hard to gauge, but one report (Kandola & Galpin, 2000) indicated that in a 1999 survey of 350 organizations, 40 percent had experience of such feedback system, while in a later survey of 60 HR departments over 75 percent were using them, confirming its growing popularity. Its popularity in other European countries varies, as is the way it is applied (e.g., see Brutus, Derayeh, Fletcher, Bailey, Velazquez, Shi, Simon, & Labath, 2006).

What do 360-degree feedback systems actually *achieve*? Certainly, many managers receiving this kind of feedback feel it is potent, and they seem to have a broadly positive attitude to it (Fletcher & Baldry, 1999), but does that mean they respond constructively and modify their behavior and style? There is a

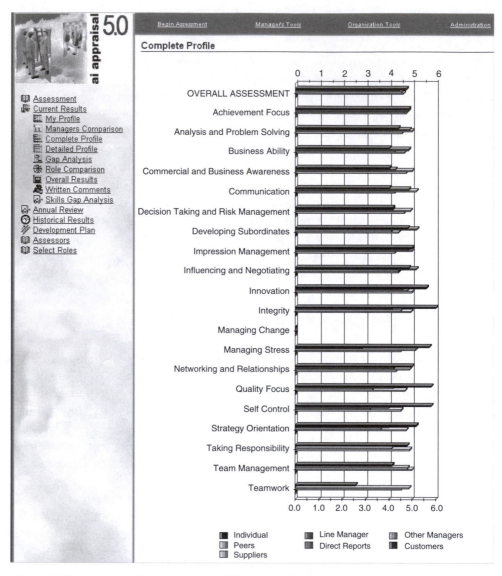

Figure 4.2: Example of a page from a 360-degree feedback report

growing body of research on this. In terms of outcomes, most studies show that focal managers' (that is, the manager who is being assessed) ratings tend to improve over successive feedback episodes, though there is quite a lot of variability in how much change is observed (Smither, London, & Reilly, 2005). Bailey & Fletcher (2002) found that, over time, feedback led to a perception of increased competence and lowered development needs. Much depends on the nature of the scheme, how it is introduced and the culture of the organization.

> ## Box 4.4: An example of 360-degree feedback for development
>
> This was an application of 360 as part of a career review workshop run for middle managers in a public sector organization that deals with financial strategy and regulation. A key element of the workshop was the combined input of psychometric test data and 360-degree feedback, and helping participants to use this to inform their thinking about future career development. The 360 questionnaire covered 7 competencies and was given to participants to distribute 3–4 weeks before the workshop; when completed by the feedback-givers, the questionnaires were returned directly to external consultants who compiled a report for each manager. On the first day of the workshop, a consultant led the participants through a session on psychometric tests (how they should be interpreted), before distributing confidential details of their scores on the personality and cognitive tests they had taken pre-workshop. After they had looked at these and had a chance to raise general questions, the session moved on to look at 360-degree feedback, and how that should be interpreted. The participants were then given their feedback reports and dispersed to read through them individually. The final session of the day was given to talking through general issues and questions arising from the feedback, and how it might relate to the psychometric data. Prior to the second stage of the workshop process, which was a week later, each participant – having had some time to consider the test data and the feedback – had an individual session with a consultant to discuss the implications and possible development steps.
>
> Particular strengths of the approach taken to using 360 in this example were the way it was integrated with psychometric data to give a broader picture, and the extent to which support and assistance was provided to participants in helping them understand the information and its implications, and in formulating development plans accordingly.

This section has looked at the role of performance appraisal in the assessment and development of potential, and has described how this aspect of appraisal has now been at least augmented – and in some organizations completely replaced – by a variety of techniques that fall outside the traditional annual appraisal session. But this reflects part of the wider picture of changes in appraisal practice, and it is this that the chapter concludes with.

Organizational Change and Contemporary Trends in Performance Appraisal

In recent years, performance appraisal systems have begun to take on a very different appearance in some organizations. This is partly owing to the frustration felt with the failure of traditional appraisal methods to deliver what was asked of them, but it also stems from pervasive changes in the nature of organizations themselves. They have taken out whole management levels, downsized, become more international in their operations and so on. They have also had to operate in an increasingly competitive climate and with greater legal regulation. Those changes in themselves necessitate a different way of operating, and this is signified by the adoption of new systems like total quality management, and an increasing interest in relating individual performance to rewards. All this suggests the need for a new approach to appraisal. For example, if you have fewer management levels, it usually means that individual managers have more subordinates working to them, those subordinates may be geographically spread and the manager may see any one of them fairly infrequently – all of which makes fair and accurate appraisal more difficult. This has fuelled the interest in multisource, multilevel appraisal.

An increasing recognition that conventional approaches to appraisal do not motivate people, and the need to make the most of the reduced number of employees, has brought about a greater emphasis on development rather than assessment in appraisal. There is a steady decline of the monolithic appraisal system, which typically involved a universally applied process with an heavy emphasis on the appraisal forms and on using the process primarily for assessment purposes. In its place appraisal seems to be breaking down into three elements:

- A performance planning session that involves reviewing achievement of objectives over the period in question and setting objectives for the period ahead. If performance-related pay comes into the picture, this is often what it is related to.
- A development review, probably based on competencies or skill dimensions, that looks at the training and development needs of the individual. This takes place at a different time of the year from the performance planning session. Where they operate, 360-degree feedback systems may feed into this element of appraisal.
- As has been mentioned, the assessment of potential is now often supplemented by the use of more objective assessment methods, such as psychometric tests or assessment centers.

These elements are now more often properly integrated into the human resource policies of the organization as whole, and referred to as Performance Management Systems. These represent a strategy that seeks to create a shared vision of the purpose, aims and values of the organization, and to help each individual employee to understand and recognize his or her part in contributing to them; the overall aim is to enhance individual and organizational performance. Typically, elements of such a strategy will include developing the mission statement and business plan, objective setting and other methods of performance measurement, developing competencies of employees, performance-related pay (sometimes) and various approaches to improving internal communications.

Embedding appraisal in a wider approach of this kind turns it into a more effective mechanism, and one that can make a big difference to attitudes. Fletcher and Williams (1996) found that better performance management practices were related to job satisfaction and organizational commitment in both public and private sector organizations. And Mayer and Davis (1999) found that implementing a more acceptable appraisal system increased trust in top management. Looking beyond attitudes to the bottom line, it has been demonstrated (e.g. by Patterson, West, Lawthom, & Nickell, 1998) that good HR practices, and especially effective implementation of appraisal, show a close association with organizational performance indicators. Perhaps the most striking example of this is the study by West and Johnson (2002) which looked at the relationship of HR practices and procedures to various performance indicators across 61 hospitals in the UK Health Service. Amongst the findings, the strongest correlation to emerge was between the quality of appraisals and patient mortality rates, with the former accounting for 25 percent of the variance in the latter – even after many other factors such as doctor/patient ratios and size of hospital were controlled for. The researchers concluded that a significant number of lives could be saved by better HR systems, and in particular better appraisal.

So, for all its difficulties, appraisal *can* be successful, but only if it is used in the context of an integrated framework of performance management. If the trend towards applying it like this continues, it may establish itself as a more important contributor to organizational functioning and individual well-being than it has done in the past.

Performance appraisal systems vary greatly, but they are found in one form or another in most large organizations. They usually try to achieve many – probably too many – different ends. Much of the emphasis has been on finding ways of assessing people accurately and fairly, but this has proved problematic in the context of today's complex organizations. The perception that appraisal systems have often failed to deliver the increased motivation and improved performance expected of them has led to changes in the orientation of both research and practice in this field, with more attention being paid to employee development. The assessment of potential is now increasingly determined by assessment centers, psychometric tests, and the use of multisource feedback. Organizations have gone through a huge amount of change in recent years, and this has made more traditional approaches to appraisal less relevant. Instead of a single appraisal mechanism, organizations increasingly use a series of linked processes as part of an integrated performance management strategy.

Summary

Performance appraisal systems vary greatly, but they are found in one form or another in most large organizations. They usually try to achieve many – probably too many – different ends. Much of the emphasis has been on finding ways of assessing people accurately and fairly, but this has proved problematic in the

Continued

context of today's complex organizations. The perception that appraisal systems have often failed to deliver the increased motivation and improved performance expected of them has led to changes in the orientation of both research and practice in this field, with more attention being paid to employee development. The assessment of potential is now increasingly determined by assessment centers, psychometric tests and the use of multisource feedback. Organizations have gone through a huge amount of change in recent years, and this has made more traditional approaches to appraisal less relevant. Instead of a single appraisal mechanism, organizations increasingly use a series of linked processes as part of an integrated performance management strategy.

Discussion Points

What are the aims of performance appraisal, and to what extent are they achievable?

How is performance appraisal supposed to motivate people to improve performance?

Do managers accurately and objectively assess the work performance of those under them?

What are the advantages of using multisource, multirater feedback?

How have organizational changes affected performance appraisal practices?

Key Studies

Pearce, J. L., & Porter, L. W. (1986). Employee responses to formal appraisal feedback. *Journal of Applied Psychology, 71,* 211–18. An example of a study that reflects how appraisal does not always produce the results desired!

Smither, J. W., London, M., & Reilly, R. R. (2005). Does performance improve following multisource feedback? A theoretical model, meta-analysis and review of empirical findings. *Personnel Psychology, 58,* 33–66. A very thorough review of the effects of 360-degree feedback and some of the influences determining them.

Further Reading

Fletcher, C. (2008). *Appraisal, feedback and development.* London: Routledge. A general book, covering most aspects of appraisal, and one that has become a standard for Human Resource practitioners.

Fletcher, C., & Perry, E. (2001). Performance appraisal and feedback: A consideration of national culture and a review of contemporary trends. In N. Anderson, D. Ones, H. Sinangil, & C. Viswesvaran (Eds.), *International handbook of industrial, work and organizational psychology.* London: Sage. A chapter looking both at cultural variables impacting performance appraisal and also at how developments in IT are likely to influence performance appraisal practice in the future.

Patterson, M., West, M., Lawthom, R., & Nickell, S. (1998). *Issues in people management.* IPD Report No. 22. London: Chartered Institute for Personnel an Development. A research report illustrating how good HR practices, especially appraisal, can have a profound effect on the business and its effectiveness.

Williams, R. (2002). *Managing employee performance: Design and implementation in organizations.* London: Thomson Learning (Psychology@Work Series). This book looks more widely at performance management as a whole and describes the various approaches and methods used.

Research Close-Up

Harris, M. M., Smith, D. E., & Champagne, D. (1995). A field study of performance appraisal purpose: Research versus Administrative based ratings. *Personnel Psychology, 48*, 151–60.

Introduction

Cleveland and Murphy (1992) suggest that an appraisal system that is used for one purpose may not (under similar circumstances) yield the same outcome when it is used for a different purpose. Given what we know about the motivations of those doing the appraisal, and particularly their reluctance to be very critical of their staff (see this chapter), this seems likely to be true. Harris et al set out to test, in a field setting, the following hypotheses:

1. that ratings of performance that were collected for the traditional purposes of appraisal would be more lenient (i.e. more favorable) than ratings collected for research purposes, because the latter would not have any real impact on the staff rated

2. that ratings collected for research purposes, because they offered a more "honest" and less lenient assessment would show greater validity against an external criterion measure of performance

Method

Participants

The people rated were 223 first line supervisors working in the manufacturing division of a major US company. The group broke down along these lines – 85 percent were male, 15 percent were from ethnic minorities, and the average age was 33 years. Those rating their performance were managers in the company.

Design and procedure

One group of supervisors was asked to make ratings of their staff purely as part of the validation process for a company assessment center, and that the ratings would not be used to make decisions on the staff concerned and would remain confidential. The ratings they made were then compared with the appraisal ratings recorded for the same staff by these managers during the last appraisal round, approximately 3–4 months earlier. In addition, the assessments made of the staff when they attended the assessment center were compared with their managers' ratings of them – their assessment center performance, as it represented a consistent task situation for all of those attending and was marked by experienced assessors, was

Continued

taken as the measure of the validity of the managers' ratings.

Results

The proportion of staff rated as "needing improvement" was just 1.3 percent in the case of the appraisal ratings, but 7 percent on the research ratings, chi-square analysis showing this to be a significant difference at the 0.05 level. The mean ratings given for the two groups were also significantly different, with the appraisal group getting the more lenient ratings. Turning to the second hypothesis, the ratings made for research were indeed more highly correlated with how the staff performed in the assessment center (a significant correlation of 0.17) when compared to the appraisal ratings (0.11, NS). However, the difference between the two correlations was not significant, so offers only partial support for the hypothesis.

Discussion

This study shows in a real company setting that appraisal ratings are often influenced by factors other than the actual performance of the appraisee; some (but not all) managers gave differing assessments according to the impact they thought the ratings would have, and were reluctant to file an appraisal on staff that might have adverse consequences for them in terms of pay or promotion prospects.

Careers and Aging at Work

Franco Fraccaroli and Marco Depolo

Overview

The chapter examines aging in work organizations and the individual and organizational management of the late career. The first part seeks to show, by citing a series of demographic and macroeconomic data, that these issues are of increasing urgency for the western industrialized societies, and for individuals in the late stages of their careers.

The second part of the chapter describes the results of research in the social sciences (work and organizational psychology, management studies, industrial gerontology) on elderly workers and their strategies to handle the final phase of the work career satisfactorily (for the individual and the organization).

The third section addresses the problem of the late career from the point of view of the individual psychological experience. It examines studies on how aged workers live through this stage of the life cycle, how they prepare for the transition to retirement, and how this specific phase can be studied in terms of the redefinition of personal identity and restructuring of the life-system.

Before these issues are examined, an introduction provides a conceptual frame of reference for the study of careers and marks out the area of analysis.

Introduction

Definitions

A career can be defined as a series of transitions from one role to another within an organization or a social system (Barley, 1989), or as an evolving sequence of a person's work experiences over time (Arthur, Hall, & Lawrence, 1989, p. 8). Nicholson and West (1989, p. 181) use the term "work histories" to denote the sequence of work experiences; they therefore eschew the term "career" on the ground that it is too heavily connoted in everyday language. Arnold (1997b) furnishes a more complete and systematic definition of the career as a sequence of

occupational positions, roles or activities, decisions about that sequence, preparation for future roles, and the meaning attributed by a person to his/her past
experiences.

The theoretical relevance of these definitions to the subject of this chapter is
obvious, and they have at least three aspects with major implications for analysis
of the later career and the experience of aging in organizations.

The first aspect, which dates back to studies by the Chicago school of sociology
(Barley, 1989), concerns the *subjective nature* of a career. The latter is not just an
ascending sequence of objective positions, as hypothesized by classical occupational sociology. According to Hughes (1971, p. 137), the career "is the moving
perspective in which the person sees his life as a whole and interprets the meaning
of his various attributes, actions, and the things which happen to him."

Secondly, the concept of "career" can be applied to *different life domains.* As
Goffman stressed in his celebrated study (1961), although the career is usually
associated with a person's occupational life-course, there are other socially regulated life experiences where individuals can attribute meaning to a sequence of
events and actions which concern them. From this perspective one can talk of
the career of both a worker and a person approaching retirement.

A third distinctive aspect of the notion of career is its close connection with
the way in which people *experience time.* According to Arthur et al. (1989), the
career is how work experiences emerge or evolve over time. Careers can explain
something of the link between time and work (Bailyn, 2004). Through time,
individuals develop a perspective in which their career gives meaning to their
entire lifespan. "Career gives the individual a sense of social time, and we think
to ourselves in terms of a career path which includes the states of past, present
and future" (Hassard, 1999, p. 337). Also more recent studies on the concept
of "career" (Bergmann Lichtenstein & Mendenhall, 2002; Savickas, 2002; Young
& Collin, 2004) stress the dynamic and evolving nature of processes of professional development, assuming them to change constantly over time. A career is
a path of individual development in which the subject gives meaning to the events
and choices in his/her work experience; but it is at the same time a social path
which connects personal experience to external factors – for example, the social
positions occupied by the person in the course of his/her lifetime, historical
events, and facts concerning the organization to which s/he belongs.

A final interesting approach to the career is taken by Heinz (2003), who con-
ceives work trajectories as negotiated careers. Trajectories are ballistic curves like
those of rockets when launched: they are highly predictable, whereas actual work
careers are much more like less ordered pathways negotiated within a frame of
transitions and sequences with no latent meaning of continuity.

Time and Career

The close connection among time, work and career enables the issue of aging
in organizations and the later career to be treated not only as a contingent

problem of people, work organizations, or society as a whole, but also in light of four different theoretical components (Fraccaroli & Sarchielli, 2002).

Individual development in a lifespan perspective. Aging is connected with a person's ontogenetic development, with his/her age-related physical, physiological, cognitive and psychological changes. The difference between young people and the elderly can be explained in terms of different stages of the life-course, This is not to deny the existence of interindividual differences within age groups – people differ in their pace of aging; they handle the passing of the years in distinct ways; and they have diverse initial endowments – and these various factors explain why experiences of aging in workplaces vary so considerably.

Period and historical events. In the course of their lifetimes, individuals encounter various processes connected with historical, economic and cultural events. Labor-market conditions, the nature of the economic cycle, the evolution of jobs and professions, and the structure of production organizations may significantly and varyingly influence organizational behaviors and work careers. Consider, for example, how during the 1990s labor-market dynamics in the Western countries (work flexibility, downsizing, contingent work forces, etc.) altered the structure of careers (Arnold, 1997a; Sullivan, 1999). Length of service and loyalty to the firm, once of key importance in construction of a career, have grown increasingly marginal, giving way to promotion criteria based on skills, an ability to innovate, and individual enterprise. Transition from one role to another role with greater responsibility and prestige is increasingly regulated by the acquisition of new skills (through training) and is not functional on age. Careers have become less linear and more irregular. Career advancement is less automatically seniority-based but requires more initiative and personal investment.

All this heightens the role of the individual in construction of his/her career; see in this regard the notion of the "protean career" developed by Hall (2004), who describes a career orientation where the person's core values drive career decisions, and where the main success criteria are subjective. Finally. consider the organizational space in which they evolve. The notion of the "boundaryless career," put forward by Arthur and Rousseau (1996) and Arthur, Inkson, and Pringle (1999), denotes a sequence of job opportunities that extends beyond the boundaries of a single firm in a more dynamic, unstable and open productive system. Careers are increasingly less determined by an individual organization. They may involve role transitions, job changes, transfers from one organization to another offering greater potential for development. Single individuals assume greater responsibility and autonomy in managing their professional paths, and in accumulating an array of sought-after skills which can be transferred from one organization to another.

Cohort. There are also processes specific to a particular cohort of individuals and springing from events and historical facts that a group of people sharing a life-experience encounter during a particular phase of their development paths. These generational processes may decisively influence the evolution of behaviors and attitudes, giving rise to cohort-specific experiences. Consider, for example, workers whose initial training did not cover information technologies and who,

---

Box 5.1:   What is meant by "late career" and "aged worker"?

It is difficult to establish a precise threshold at which the late career begins or when a worker can be classified as an aged worker. Theories which hypothesize the existence of career pattern stages take age as the parameter with which to identify the passage from one stage to the next. But chronological age is too simplistic a benchmark for the complex processes that regulate the final part of a person's work career. Moreover, an age-based categorization entails the assumption that all individuals of the same age have identical work experiences invariant across work situations. The variability among the organizational behaviors of older workers is often greater than the variability between older workers and other age groups (Farr & Ringseis, 2002, p. 41). Given that aging is a multidimensional process, Sterns and Miklos (1995) identify various approaches to definition of the "older worker" and the "late career":

- *the chronological and legal approach*: this defines the older worker and the late career on the basis of chronological age and a legal definition of age. For example, the European Community has undertaken initiatives in favor of older workers which define them as being over 45 years old;

- *functional approach*: this is a performance-based definition of aging. Individuals are classified as "older" by an objective measure of performance, health, physical capacity, and cognitive ability. This approach recognizes that people of the same chronological age display marked differences in their functioning;

- *psychosocial approach*: this definition is based on the social perception of aging in workplaces and society. An individual is classified as an older worker according to the social perception of what is an "older worker". The definition is also based on individuals' self-perceptions of themselves and of their careers as congruent with the social career timetable;

---

as they have grown older, have had to cope with the massive introduction of computers into their workplaces. Or, on a smaller scale, consider the cohorts of workers who joined an organization at the same time and at the same age, and who have since then shared its fortune.

As we shall see, many of the above considerations concerning the elderly worker can be interpreted as problems specific to a cohort of persons, rather than to general processes of aging. In other words the cohort of workers who will be elderly in twenty years' time may encounter problems and difficulties in many respects different from those experienced by elderly workers today.

Age norms. A further component is the relationship between age and social role. As a person ages, s/he occupies new positions and performs different roles which may be normative (i.e. pertaining to the majority of people of a certain age) or nonnormative (events not specific to a particular age group). Aging can

- *organizational approach*: this defines the "older worker" in terms of aging in organizational roles: it therefore relates to seniority and tenure. Important for this definition are the age norms shared by the members of the organization;

- *lifespan approach*: this approach takes account of the marked variability in the aging process among individuals and the possibility that behavioral change may occur at any point in the life cycle. These factors give rise to the great specificity of individual careers in adulthood, with the consequent difficulty of constructing age-based typologies.

There are, moreover, numerous contextual factors that intervene when the late career or older workers are being defined. An important role is played by the type of job. An extreme example is provided by Jaques (1970) in his well-known article on the crisis of creative work in middle age. Jaques identifies a phase of very precocious decline – at the age of around 35 to 40 – when numerous artists enter creative crisis. As regards less exclusive activities, workers in numerous occupations risk being considered "too old" at the age of 40 because the physical capacities, the attentive resources, the flexibility, and the innovativeness required by particular jobs tend to decline precociously. Conversely, in other occupational areas, like politics or the senior civil service, at the age of 50 individuals still have significant career development possibilities ahead of them. The labels of "late career" and "aged worker" also depend on the legal retirement age in the various productive sectors and in various countries. For example, where organizations have voluntary or mandatory early retirement schemes, the lower the person's retirement age, the sooner the label "older" is applied (Boerlijst, Munnichs, & van der Heijden, 1998, p. 183).

The thresholds for defining the "late career" and the "aged worker" are therefore necessarily vague and indefinite. By convention, we may adopt the range 50–70 years following Greller and Simpson's review (1999). Likewise, we may define an "aged worker" as a person aged over 50 beginning or passing through the final stage of his/her career and who is preparing for retirement.

be regarded as an unpredictable combination of orderly phases and socially structured sequences, on the one hand, and crises, breakdowns, and accidents on the other. The social roles performed by people as they grow older may significantly affect their behaviors, attitudes, expectations and motivations. In other words, an individual is influenced not only by chronological age, historical events, and membership of a particular cohort, but also by the system of expectations – individual and collective – connected with the roles that s/he assumes with the advancement of age. In this regard, studies in organizational demography (Lawrence, 1988) have shown highly consistent perceptions within organizations of where a person should be along a career trajectory at specific ages.

These processes are also manifest in the late career and in the transition to retirement. The "right time" to retire is socially constructed. Likewise, there is a system of implicit and shared norms which make certain processes typical of the late career (career plateauing, motivational decline, restructuring of goals) more or less acceptable to the individual and the community. One can conceive of a socially constructed career timetable for the life-course which determines how a career path should "normally" proceed in relation to a person's age. The term "asynchronism" is used when a person's experience diverges from this socially-defined career calendar.

Labor Market and Older Workers

The final years of the last century saw the advent of radical changes in demographic trends worldwide: principally an increase in the world's population and change in its composition. From a certain point of view, one may say that the former phenomenon is less dramatic that the latter, although the problem of providing food and work for 6 billions and a half people is not of secondary importance. However, it is change in the composition of the population that is most problematic, and especially so for the more industrialized countries, where the old age dependency ratio (population aged 65 and over as a percentage of the 15–64 aged population) is a clear indicator of progressive aging and changes in the labor market. People aged between 15 and 64 are conventionally considered to be those who can assume the burden of the goods and services necessary for life. It is likewise considered that after 65 people tend to leave the labor market, becoming consumers and no longer the producers of goods and services.

Considering the planet as a whole in the period 2000 to 2050 (see figure 5.1), in 2000 there was one person aged over 64 for every 10 persons of working age (15–64), but in 2050 there will be one for every four.

And the phenomenon will not be uniform. The USA, whose population will increase by 50 percent in the same period (estimate by the US Census Bureau, 2005), will see its old dependency ratio increase from one over-64 for every five persons of working age to one for every three. But the Europe of 25 will be in an even worse situation: in 2000 there was one over-64 for every four persons of working age, while by 2050 the ratio will have increased to 1:2. The trend will be even more pronounced in Japan, where the increase will be from 1:4 to 3:4.

In other words, many countries will face unprecedented changes in their labor forces: The elderly (conventionally people aged over 64) will be able to maintain their life-quality either by remaining longer in the labor market or by relying on welfare systems subject to increasing strain by the ratio between the active and inactive population. Matters will be different for the recently industrialized or developing countries. Nevertheless, even countries currently experiencing extraordinary acceleration in their economic growth will not diverge greatly from the trend described. For example China, whose population will increase by 12 percent between 2000 and 2050, will quadruple its old dependency ratio, from 1:10 to 4:10, in the same period. The same applies to Brazil, whose population will grow

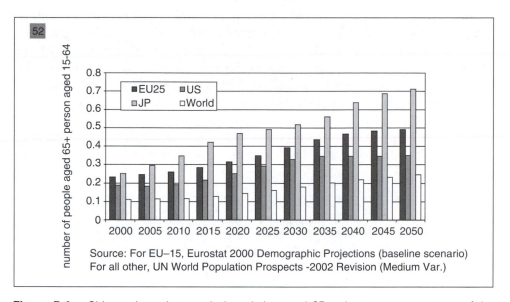

number of people aged 65+ person aged 15–64

Source: For EU–15, Eurostat 2000 Demographic Projections (baseline scenario)
For all other, UN World Population Prospects -2002 Revision (Medium Var.)

Figure 5.1: Old age dependency ratio (population aged 65 and over as a percentage of the 15–64 population): data and forecast 2000 to 2050 (Commission of the European Communities, 2004)

by 27 percent in the period 2000 to 2050, and whose old dependency ratio will quadruple from 8 : 100 to 35 : 100.

Ironically, after many years of attempts to reduce the burden of work on the elderly (for example with welfare policies and early retirement), the problem now seems to be how the elderly can be brought back into or retained in the labor market.

What will be the consequences for the living standards and life-quality of individuals? In its report on "The social situation in the EU 2004," the European Commission provides a worrying description of the demographic situation:

> The enlarged Union will still be marked by accelerated ageing in less than a decade . . . as fertility has been very low in the new Member States for more than a decade. Migration from the East to the West of the Union is expected to be moderate . . . but immigration into the Union, including the new CEE Member States, remains likely to increase . . . still – in stark contrast to the US – the EU population will be stagnating and shrinking. (pp. 13–14)

Life expectancy at birth (that is, the mean number of years that a newborn child can expect to live if subjected throughout her/his life to current mortality conditions) between 1960 and 2001 increased for the EU-15 population from 72.9 to 81.6 years.

Infant mortality falls, medicine cures more diseases, and people live longer, but the aging process has effects on the jobs and the labor market that older people are confronted with. One can see, for instance, that the employment rate of older workers (employed persons aged 55–64 as a percentage of the population in the same age group) was 40.1 in 2002 (EU-15). Note that in the same year the general employment rate (persons aged 15–64) was 64.3, which was one and a half times more.

Finally, a longitudinal picture (figure 5.2) very clearly shows the effects of aging patterns across the EU. There is a dramatic difference between the years

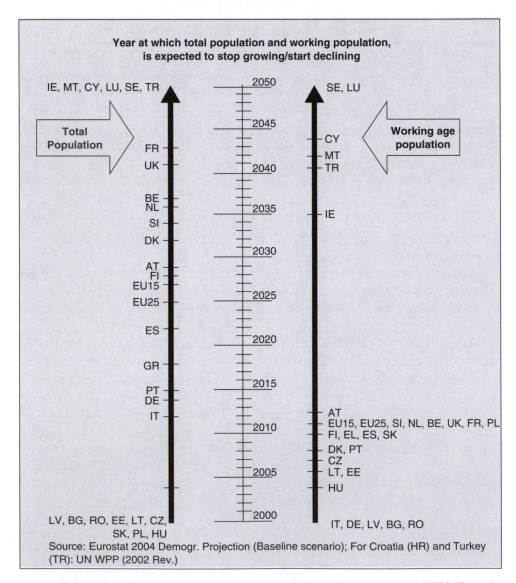

Figure 5.2: Total population and working age population in Europe 2000 to 2050 (Commission of the European Communities, 2004)

at which the total population and the working age population are expected to stop growing and start declining. For instance, the total population (EU-15) is expected to stop growing in 2027, while the working age population is expected to start declining in 2011, many years before (Commission of the EC, 2005). The figure shows that some countries are in an extremely difficult situation. In France, for example, growth of the active population will have halted by 2011, but the total population will continue to grow until 2043. There will therefore be a period of around 30 years in which either the weight of the economy will rest upon a declining number of 15- to 64-year-olds or the over-64s will have to be kept in work (how, where?).

This is the general scenario with its unprecedented problems. Never in the history of mankind has economic development been separate from demographic growth. But today it is precisely this challenge that confronts Europe. Among the various strategies devised by the Commission, some specifically concern the late work career: greater flexibility (organizational, temporal, occupational), more investments in lifelong learning, and greater value set on the experience of older workers.

The challenge is made even more complex by the fact that successive cohorts of older workers may differ greatly from each other – not only from country to country (one thinks, for example, of a largely private welfare system like that of the USA, and a largely public one like those of many European countries) but also within the same country. The majority of today's older European workers are about to retire with adequate economic protection (thanks to welfare benefits), but this cannot be said of today's 30-year-olds, whose incomes when they retire will depend to a much greater extent on their ability to save during their working lives. In other words, being an older worker today and in thirty years' time may be very different.

The challenge concerns many of the issues examined in this chapter, although it is not confined to workers and workplaces but extends throughout the entire life cycle. Because the success of individual strategies in the labor market also depends on general socio-economic conditions, the figures cited above should be borne in mind. In the language of psychology, they signal that the task awaiting older workers in the proximate future will be particularly difficult. It will require especially close attention to be paid to developing human resources; discovering how to attenuate the negative effects of possible failures on motivation and self-efficacy; and striking a balance between the abilities and knowledge of older workers and the demands of an increasingly diversified and exigent labor market.

Aging in Organizations

The problem of aging in workplaces can be examined from various points of view. A model which seeks to explain the reciprocal relationship between older workers and their organizational context has been recently developed by Farr,

Tesluk, and Klein (1998) and reprised by Farr and Ringseis (2002). The model has a multiple layers structure (using the metaphor of the onion), at the center of which is the older worker who interacts with diverse contextual factors: the immediate work environment (age norms; stereotypes; organizational structure); organizational policies and practices (training and development; retirement policies); and organizational strategies.

It is not possible here to fully discuss the complex system of relations theorized by Farr and colleagues. Proposed instead are some of its insights concerning the characteristics of older workers (abilities and performance), the organizational context (stereotypes and discrimination), and human resources management policies (training and development). The purpose is not to conduct a complete survey of research on the relation between the older worker and the organizational context, but rather to offer answers (certainly partial) to the following questions concerning the older worker and work organizations. How can an efficacious presence of older workers in work organizations be ensured? What management instruments (training, job design, reward systems) can work organizations use to handle the growing number of mature workers? How can work organizations prevent the discrimination and victimization due to prejudice about the productive capacities of older workers? How should training schemes be structured so that they meet vocational training needs in the late career?

Performance

The performance and cognitive skills of the elderly compared with young people have been much researched in psychology. Warr (2001) summarizes the main results as regards physical attributes, cognitive abilities, knowledge, personality traits, and motives in relation to the work behavior of old people. Unfortunately, the large body of results obtained by basic research can be used only in part to determine the relationship between age and performance in real work settings. They derive largely from laboratory research involving subjects of advanced age (sometimes over 70) and not part of the working population – as in the case of research on attention and working memory (Greller & Simpson, 1999). However, some studies have been conducted with subjects of working age. Laboratory experiments seem to show that certain complex cognitive skills decline with age (Hoyer, 1998). Longitudinal data confirm the weakening of fluid intelligence (the ability to identify relations, draw inferences, understand the connections between facts and objects, and comprehend their implications) even among subjects aged under 65. A more general finding indicates a modest decline in inductive reasoning and spatial orientation towards the age of 60, although there are marked interindividual differences and a more pronounced deterioration of these mental abilities in more advanced age groups. Older people may encounter difficulties when performing activities which require rapid reaction times and the processing of complex information. Decline in the functions of the working memory may also affect relatively younger subjects (from 60 upwards), especially when they undertake particularly complex activities with overlapping demands ("complexity effect") (Hansson, DeKoekkoek, Neece, & Patterson, 1997; Warr, 2001). In short, laboratory research shows that the poorer and slower mental processing observed at older ages only occurs when tasks are complex and place considerable demands upon the person. Age differences are greater when psychological resources are more strongly challenged (Warr, 2001, p. 6).

The performance of older workers in work settings has also been the subject of field studies. Almost 20 years ago, Waldman and Avolio (1986) and McEvoy and Cascio (1989) conducted meta-analyses on the matter. In both cases, the average general correlation between age and work performance was estimated as being close to zero, with extreme variability of the results obtained by the research. This singular unevenness of the results does not allow to draw reliable and valid conclusions on the quality of the work performance of more elderly compared with younger workers. In general, Warr (2001) concludes that work performance is on average constant despite some cognitive limitations at older ages. Furthermore, even when cognitive decrements are found, it has been shown that their magnitude is reduced by a variety of interventions (training; counseling; organizational aids) (Farr & Ringseis, 2002, p. 35).

How can this contradiction of laboratory results be explained? The decline with age of certain cognitive skills found in the laboratory – where the role of experience is deliberately excluded – may be off-set by the acquired cognitive strategies and domain-specific knowledge which constitute the strengths of the expert worker. For example, research on decision-making finds that younger managers perform better quantitatively (larger number of decisions taken, more intensive information search, greater activism in goal achievement) than do older managers. But the latter are better able to handle the interpersonal relations connected with the decision-making process, to assess the quality of information, and to adapt solutions to external conditions (Warr, 2001). In short, older workers do have deficits in performance, but those deficits are not substantial and other aspects of performance may compensate for them (Greller and Simpson, 1999). A key component of this compensation is the knowledge (declarative and procedural) that more elderly people usually possess to a greater extent than younger ones.

According to Warr (1994; 1999), this compensation process can be understood more thoroughly if a model centered on various aspects of work (see box 5.2) is used. Although the operationalization of the demands of particular jobs in terms of process and product abilities in Warr's model seems rather difficult, data from research on car-driving show that there is age-related decline in abilities like vision or reaction time, but there is no evidence of age-related increases in crash frequency, when controlling for the number of drivers of a given age (Wegman & McGee, 2004, on US Department of Transportation 1999 data).

Box 5.2: Warr's model

In order to understand the complex relation between age and work performance, Warr (1994; 1999) proposes that the problem should be addressed in function of various types of work activity. He suggests a four-category classification produced by cross-referencing two polar features of work: (i) do task requirements exceed basic capacities known to decline with age? (ii) is performance enhanced by experience?

Type A. Activities requiring basic capacities in which performance benefits from experience. The accumulation of experience produces positive effects: these activities have a substantial technical component and require considerable social and interpersonal skills. Consider for example a commercial representative working in a sector with limited innovation. It is likely that his work performance will improve with age.

Type B. Activities requiring few basic capacities, which decline with age, and where experience is unimportant. Work is routine and nonproblematic and requires little skill. Mental processes are relatively simple. An example is the work of a warehouseman, where there is no connection between age and performance: the worker's efficiency is independent of his age.

Type C. Activities requiring basic capacities, which may decline with age, and a significant amount of experience. There is no direct relation between age and performance because the worker is able to "compensate": that is, he may be slower in processing information, but experience provides him with everyday strategies that he can use to handle tasks more efficiently. For example, as a manager grows older, he may be less rapid in taking decisions; but experience enables him to manage the effects of those decisions with his role partners.

Type D. There is a negative relation between age and work performance. In this case, productivity does not benefit from experience, while age-deteriorating basic skills are predominant. This category comprises jobs involving the constant and rapid processing of information, speed in psychomotor reactions or great physical effort – as exemplified by call center operators.

Park (1994) analyses four different hypothetical models intended to explain the persistence of efficient performance among old workers. These models are based on various forms of compensation.

The first model (maintenance hypothesis) presumes that the occupations of elderly workers are selected for them. Elderly workers are usually placed (by choice or following instructions by their superiors) in jobs that make few cognitive demands on them and involve familiar and repetitive tasks. It is therefore unlikely that elderly workers will be required to do work beyond their capabilities: as a consequence, any deterioration in their cognitive resources will not be reflected in their performance. In this case, the compensation process is not cognitive-behavioral but social and productive. The result of the allocation and management of human resources is a balancing between the capacities and resources of older workers, on the one hand, and the demands of their work on the other.

The second model rests on the notion of "experience." Notwithstanding the deterioration of cognitive skills that allegedly takes place in advanced age, people of greater maturity are able to deploy their accumulated skills and knowledge to perform just as well as their younger counterparts. This explanation incorporates a model of compensation couched in behavioral terms. The processes and activities undertaken by individuals on a continuous and long-term basis may develop execution mechanisms which counter possible decline in the basic cognitive skills.

The third model supposes that complex knowledge structures (for example, the expertise accumulated in specific settings) may increase with age, and that these structures off-set deterioration in certain cognitive processes. This type of compensation concerns the development of different skills and structures of intelligence (fluid versus crystallized) as workers age.

The fourth model takes account of the fact that, with experience, the elderly enhance the opportunity for environmental support in counteracting cognitive decline. In this case, the compensation involves not only mental processes but also changes in the interaction with the environment. The model assumes that the advancement of age and the accumulation of experience are matched by greater access to environmental support, collaboration and assistance – and also by a greater willingness to utilize such forms of external help.

Stereotypes and discrimination

Research findings do not support the hypothesis that age is accompanied by a homogeneous, linear and irreversible decline in work skills. However, there are numerous prejudices and stereotypes about the productivity and efficiency of elderly workers. These negative age stereotypes may strongly influence decisions by human resources managers as regards selection, job assignment, and rewards systems (Greller & Stroh, 1995). They affect the work transitions of elderly workers by engendering low mobility and low employability, higher risks of dismissal during retrenchment, and difficult reemployment (Boerlijst et al., 1998). They condition the career development of older people because they reduce opportunities for training and development, and thus cause career plateauing (Greller & Simpson, 1999). Recently, however, legal issues concerning age discrimination in employment has led in the European and North American countries to revision of management policies on elderly workers and attempts to valorize them as an organizational resource. Potentially, this may also attenuate negative stereotypes and discrimination. Chiu, Chan, Snape, and Redman (2001) report that stereotypes of older workers are less widespread in organizations which more robustly implement policies to reduce age discrimination and to promote equal opportunities.

Anecdotally, numerous stereotypes expressed by managers and employers in regard to older workers can be cited. Given that these are stereotypes, they not surprisingly often contradict each other. In some cases, elderly workers are described as less productive, poor in health and fitness, less well-trained, less flexible and less motivated than younger workers. In others they are regarded as more loyal, more reliable, more expert, and wiser than young people. Empirical findings seem to confirm the existence of these stereotypes. Warr and Pennington (1994) interviewed more than 1000 UK personnel managers and found that they considered elderly workers (aged over 40) to be more reluctant to accept new technologies, resistant to change, less able to learn, and less interested in training. Positive stereotypes instead depict over-40s as conscientious, thinking more before acting, working better in teams, and interpersonally skilled. A survey of 774 US human resources managers by Peterson and Spiker (2005) found that they regarded older workers as having lower turnover, higher levels of commitment, as much ability to acquire new skills, less absenteeism, and greater reliability.

Chiu et al. (2001) confirm the hypothesis that the presence of negative stereotypes is associated with discrimination *vis-à-vis* training (it is a better investment to train younger workers rather than older workers), promotion (advancement opportunities should be reserved for young people), retention of older workers (in the case of crises, young workers should be the first to be reemployed), and the willingness to work with older workers (preference to work with younger people).

Besides description and diffusion of stereotypes and discriminatory practices, interesting studies on ageism (the systematic stereotyping and unfavorable treatment of people because of their age) have been produced by social cognition and social identity theorists.

The contact hypothesis – the idea that frequent interactions with older workers may reduce negative beliefs because these are inaccurate stereotypes refutable by direct experience – has been confirmed by Hassell and Perrewe (1995) and by Chiu et al. (2001). Frequency of contact negatively moderates the relationship between age and beliefs. Finkelstein, Burke and Raju (1995) and Finkelstein and Burke (1998) have tested hypotheses on age discrimination in employment. The former study, a meta-analysis, confirmed hypotheses on (i) in-group bias: younger people tend to rate older workers less positively on job qualifications and potential for development (a hypothesis also confirmed by Chiu et al., 2001); (ii) job information: judgments are generally more favorable to younger workers than older workers when less relevant information is provided; (iii) salience: younger workers are preferred to older workers when judgments are comparative rather than absolute. In the second study, which was experiment-based, the authors contacted 324 managers and asked them to evaluate two hypothetical job applicants: one younger (28 years old) and one older (59). The managers perceived the older worker as less economically valuable to their organization, and also as less interpersonally skilled. Again in the domain of social identity theory, Tougas, Lagagé, de la Sablonnière, and Kocum (2004) examined the potential psychosocial consequences of stereotypes concerning older workers. The authors asked a sample of more than 100 neo-pensioners (persons who have just retired) whether they had experienced feelings of relative deprivation (negative and invidious comparison with younger workers).Their conclusions was that the more subjects described their recent work experience in terms of current stereotypes applied to elderly workers (negative self-image), the more they experienced feelings of personal relative deprivation. A negative social identity has been found to be negatively associated with self-esteem. Moreover, negative comparisons and feelings of relative deprivation affect life satisfaction during retirement.

Training

It is widely believed that training (i.e. the updating of technological skills and the acquisition of new skills) is one of the best means to increase employability and development potential in the late career. On the other hand, there is a danger that older workers will be excluded from training because it is mainly intended for younger members of the work organization (Farr et al., 1998; Farr & Ringseis, 2002; Sterns & Miklos, 1995). From the neoclassical economic perspective, the costs of retraining older workers may be comparatively higher, and the return more limited, than for younger workers (Greller & Simpson, 1999, p. 314). But it is especially in the field of training and development that one finds subtle forms of ageism and discrimination against older workers. The sort of vicious circle described by Park (1994) may arise: human resources managers may decide to allocate elderly workers to tasks inferior in terms of performance content. This allocation may lead to an underutilization of skills which in its turn may accentuate the psychophysical decline associated with age. Likewise, if an elderly worker is unable gradually and constantly to increase his/her stock of skills and experience, s/he may subsequently find it more difficult to acquire new skills – especially complex ones unrelated to fields in which s/he has already had experience (Warr, 1998). Moreover, as shown by a recent meta-analysis (Colquitt, LePine, & Noe, 2000), there may be a progressive deterioration in the motivation to engage in training and development, and also in the level of self-efficacy. The psychophysical decline connected with aging is summed up as a decline socially induced by a lack of stimuli and the poverty of the work setting.

In fact, research on training provision for older workers (Belbin & Belbin, 1972; Schooler, Caplan, & Oates, 1998; Warr & Birdi, 1998) has shown that even persons of advanced age can benefit from training schemes. The findings, usually collected in a pre-post training perspective, are as follows: acquisition of complex mnemonic skills; significant learning even in unfamiliar areas (use of software); maintenance of already-acquired skills if supported by the work practice. In parallel, problems have been found in the speed of learning and in adaptation to the training setting (Warr, 2001). A meta-analysis by Kubeck, Delp, Haslett, and McDaniel (1996) found that older trainees had lower mastery of training material and took longer to complete the training program than younger

---

Box 5.3:   Training programs for older workers

Little is still known about the ideal form that the training of elderly workers should take. However some guidelines can be defined, albeit in rather summary form. Organizations should increase their awareness of the difficult and specific nature of the relationship between elderly workers and the training process. They should make greater efforts to analyze training needs and design appropriate responses. Training programs should take greater account of workers' backgrounds, their personal histories, the skills that they already possess, their current needs, attitudes to work and training, and their ability to respond positively to different training methods. Three guiding principles should be borne in mind: (i) *familiarity*, so that training programs reflect skills and knowledge that the trainees already possess; (ii) *organization*, so that information and materials are organized to match the characteristics of the elderly worker; (iii) *time*, so that the program is structured to reflect the usually slower learning pace of older persons (Sterns and Miklos, 1995). These various aspects can be summarized in the following features which training programs for the elderly should possess (Belbin & Belbin, 1972; Farr et al., 1998; Forteza & Prieto, 1989; Park, 1994; Warr, 2001):

- they should encourage active learning by using methods which enable the trainees themselves to discover knowledge, relations and processes, avoiding lectures and memorization as much as possible;

---

trainees. The differences were smaller in the field sample than in the laboratory. Moreover, more elderly subjects placed less trust in training activities and felt greater anxiety about the situation of guided learning.

Besides these difficulties connected with the aging process, there is a cohort effect which exposes the elderly to the risk of obsolescence. Workers in older age groups have below-average levels of schooling; scant familiarity with information technology; marked difficulties in acquiring languages and codes widespread among younger cohorts; and reluctance to use multimedia forms of knowledge transmission. These problems and difficulties due to aging combine with specific social features of the cohorts of workers now entering the final stage of their careers.

The Late Career

We saw at the beginning of the chapter that "late career" is a concept that can be applied in different ways to different individuals. In other words, some careers are later than others.

This means that, although the subjective experience of being a "late career worker" has many similarities from one worker to another, there are also important differences in when and how the tasks typical of the late career are tackled.

These tasks can be divided into three groups for the purpose of analysis: (i) those related to the job (being a worker with specific knowledge, skills, abilities

- they should consist of modules organized cumulatively so that the trainees are able to check their progress and obtain frequent feedback on their learning;

- they should stimulate the ability to "learn how to learn," an ability rather rare among elderly people who have not taken part in educational and training activities for some time;

- they should relate the new skills as closely as possible to those already possessed by trainees, highlighting similarities between their current work and the work that they will have to perform in the future;

- they should encourage open learning with temporal control over learning by the trainees.

Also to be emphasized is that work organizations should create a general organizational climate which encourages older workers to develop their skills (Sterns & Miklos, 1995). A positive climate for learning is evidenced by support and encouragement from supervisors and management, by the introduction of skill-based pay programs in which wage levels are linked to competences acquired in training, and by the availability of time, despite productivity pressure, for older workers to attend training courses.

and duties in the late career); (ii) those related to the organizational role (being a member of the organizational unit, performing an organizational role); and (iii) those related to the social role (being an individual in the late career phase of the life course: personal and social identity, relationships with family and friends).

As for the job-related tasks, the late career requires that the worker must still be able to meet the demands of the job. As we have seen, there is no reason to believe that older workers are per se less productive. Nevertheless, since labor market and workplaces tend to be more and more demanding, particular attention should be paid to complying with requirements in terms of knowledge, skills, abilities, and flexibility demands. As Luke (2000) points out, managing the older worker well requires managerial skills; but also important is the worker's ability to recognize his/her strengths and weaknesses.

As regards the tasks relative to the role in the organization, it is important to be aware of the stereotypes and prejudices regarding older workers. As we have seen, these may be entrenched, making the late career difficult and hampering the transition from full membership of the organization to exit from it. As in every transition, success depends closely on the resources available to the individual: on what s/he knows, on what s/he can do, and on whether s/he can rely on others for help with what s/he does not know or cannot do. This has been shown by studies on obsolescence (Pazy, 1994) – defined as the discrepancy between the demands of a particular work task and the knowledge and skill of the person performing it. Whilst one might think that older workers are at greater risk of obsolescence, it emerges from research (Pazy, 1996) that obsolescence and a lack of updated skills depend more on weak and organizationally marginal career positions than on age.

The availability of these resources largely depends on the person's previous work history. A great deal of research has confirmed the predictive power of the previous work situation on the forms and outcomes of late career management. For example, Schooler, Mulatu, and Oates (2004) followed up the well-known studies by Kohn and Schooler (1983) on occupational socialization by reinterviewing the same subjects 20 years later in 1994–5. They found that, even after so much time, doing intellectually demanding, self-directed work increases an individual's intellectual functioning. In other words, being exposed to cognitive demands within complex environments stimulates the growth of intellectual functioning.

Of course, the quality of working life matters as well. Wegman and McGee (2004) cite the results of the broadest study conducted to date on the work capacity of older workers: an 11-year follow-up carried out between 1981 and 1992 by the Finnish Institute of Occupational Health. The results showed that the 1981 score on a "work ability index" (combining objective measures of health status, such as the number of sick days within the past year, and more subjective measures, such as estimations of present work ability in relation to physical and mental work demands) was a strong predictor of retirement on a disability pension in 1992 or death: the poorer the index, the higher the risk of such an adverse outcome.

The link to health and well-being is important. For example, health status has greatly increased in current cohorts of older workers; but improved health care has enabled some persons with previously severe diseases to survive to adulthood and participate in the workforce. One can expect that future cohorts of older workers will require special consideration if they are confronted with health-at-risk jobs and workplaces.

Finally, as far as transition between social roles is concerned, studies on the lifecycle and life course (Rutter & Rutter, 1992) have shown that these involve aspects of personal and social identity. The resources available to the individual are of especial importance in this case: the more radical the transition (e.g., rapid, not freely chosen, not prepared for, not supported by the close social network), the more difficult it becomes. The poorer the resources (absence of control, poor self-efficacy, perception of imbalance between goal and personal skill, problematic family or health situation), the more difficult the transition. These variables have been frequently studied in regard to plans for retirement. Decision-making processes on how and when to retire are the main source of empirical data with which to test hypotheses about late career management by older workers. The following section sets out the main research results.

Preparation for retirement

The older worker's experience of work and life is marked by a process of preparing for retirement, the salient features of which have been described by Ekerdt (1998) and Talaga and Beehr (1989). On approaching the age of 50 – a phase usually well before retirement – people already begin to organize their jobs and lives with a view to their future retirement. During this phase of remote anticipation, the conception of work, the attitude towards retirement, and the level of organizational commitment and investment change according to individual expectations about when to stop work. Individuals develop socially structured convictions relative to the timing of retirement: indeed, a temporal representation of the "right" time to retire is formed by social norms, contractual provisions, interpersonal exchanges, organizational rules, and the person's self-diagnosis of the speed of his/her aging process. For example, Ekerdt (1998) used data on a representative sample of the population of the United States aged between 51 and 61 (Health and Retirement Study) to show that the majority of interviewees had a precise idea of the "normal" age at which to retire – between 62 and 65 years old, although some replies ranged from 55 to 70 years old.

Hence, the later career is characterized by a path of personal development and change leading up to exit from the labor market. This path is conditioned by individual factors (expectations, intentions, plans, motives) and social ones (contractual constraints and obligations, the law in force, incentive policies). But it is also affected by even minor events in the person's work experience and organizational life (Hoyer, 1998). A significant influence is exerted by interaction with work colleagues and their opinions on the right time to retire. Another factor is the assessment made by superiors of the older person's performance at work. Also important is the self-diagnosis by which the older worker compares his/her current performance with that of the past and looks for signs of obsolescence in his/her stock of skills. Minor accidents, banal errors, lapses of memory, ironic comments about aging by colleagues may condition the late career and help construct an exit path for workers who consider themselves "normatively" of an age when they can retire.

The theoretical analysis of early retirement by Feldman (1994) also takes this perspective on individual development and change. Feldman stresses the active role of people who can voluntarily decide to take advantage of early retirement schemes. The issues in this case are why people decide to retire and the factors (individual, financial, social, familial) responsible for the decision. Feldman stresses that early retirement does not mark the definitive end of a retiree's career, only the conclusion of his/her main work career. In many cases, retirees continue to work, given that pension entitlement increasingly occurs at a stage of the life-course when people are still highly active and mentally and physically efficient. Retirees may consequently look for work which is less remunerative but also less psychologically demanding and less fatiguing than their previous jobs. The question is therefore why workers retire early from their main jobs in order to take up what is known as "bridge employment" (see box 5.4).

Box 5.4:   Bridge employment

Research has shown that a significant proportion of retirees take up various forms of "secondary work" – part-time jobs, work in the hidden economy, self-employment, temporary work – after they quit their main jobs and before they definitively retire.

Bridge employment has a crucial role in the late careers of many workers. It enables them to disengage from their main occupation but still remain in the labor market and to preserve a temporal structuring even after early retirement. It gives also them a sense of continuity that may mitigate the negative effects of the social isolation, reduced income, and rolelessness that frequently follow retirement (Davis, 2003).

Empirical research has identified the following factors as inducing early retirees to enter bridge employment:

1. financial problems: low-income retirees take up bridge employment in order to supplement their pensions (Weckerle & Schultz,1999; Kim & Feldman, 2000).

2. work commitment: the more a person is committed to work, the more s/he finds bridge employment attractive.

3. possibility of a "second career," for example in business: Davis (2003) reports that bridge employment is attractive to people with a stronger entrepreneurial orientation.

In conclusion, bridge employment is not just an instrumental strategy. It may also satisfy intrinsic motives and satisfy the person's desire to valorize skills acquired during his/her main career.

Box 5.5:   Retirement options exercise

Consider two European "older" workers, Luigi and Maria. Both are middle-range civil servants. Both are 60 years old. Both live in a medium-sized town in northern Italy. Their pensions (when they retire in a few years' time) will amount to more or less 75 percent of their current salaries. These are the similarities between Luigi and Maria. Now the differences:

	Luigi	Maria
Family	His wife works. She owns a shop. He has two children, both of whom left home some years ago.	She has a husband and two children, both of whom have left home. Her husband is a middle manager in a private corporation.

Social relations	He is a member of a cycling club and regularly takes part in amateur races. He often socializes with friends at the bar or club.	She has little time for social relations. She helps her daughter with the granddaughter, which is demanding of her time. She likes her place of work, where she has made solid friendships.
Economic situation	He owns his own home. He has some small investments: he has two flats and some "safe" shares.	She owns her own home. She does not have large financial resources. Her only income is her salary, as for her husband.
Acitvities outside work	He has no particular pastimes apart from cycling.	None in particular
Health	Good	Good

Now, imagine that both Luigi and Maria are asked to think about their future lives as retirees. What can you say about their feelings and anticipated behaviors?

How do they feel when they think about retirement?	He has ambivalent feelings. On the one hand he likes his work. On the other, he finds it difficult to keep up with the numerous chang es of recent years (NT, new laws and rules, more flexibility demanded). He is not entirely unworried – after so many years of routine it is difficult to change – but he thinks that he will adapt in the end. He thinks that he will have more time for himself.	She is a little worried. She likes her work and it is important for her. It gives her independence and offers a network of social relations. She would like to be more financially secure: she fears that her family's standard of living may be reduced.

Summary

This chapter has demonstrated that the presence of elderly workers in workplaces is a major issue for human resources management and career development. Various socio-economic indicators signal that the problem is bound to become

Continued

crucial over the next few decades in Europe, as well as in the other countries of mature capitalism.

The chapter has surveyed numerous studies conducted in the area of work psychology and organizational analysis to examine the situation of the working elderly and their problems. Attention has focused in particular on performance, motivation, training, career management, stereotypes, and discrimination.

The chapter has also shown that perhaps the most promising approach addresses the question in terms of the management (individual and organizational) of the late career: how people redefine their work commitment, their life-projects in the last stage of their careers, and their preparation for retirement; and how organizations handle, and in certain cases seek to enhance, this particular type of human resource.

It has been stressed that better understanding of this process (and therefore more efficacious action) requires a multidisciplinary approach where the main concern of the psychology of work is to study the strategies with which people handle their late careers.

Further Reading

Schooler, C., Mulatu, M. S., & Oates, G. (2004). Occupational self-direction, intellectual functioning, and self-directed orientation in older workers: Findings and implications for individuals and societies. *American Journal of Sociology*, *110*, 161—97. An interesting account of the interweaving between the psychological and sociological approaches.

Boerlijst, J. G., Munnichs, J. M. A., & van den Heijden, B. I. J. M. (1998). The "older worker" in the organization. In P. J. D. Drenth, H. Thierry, & C. J. de Wolff (Eds.), *Handbook of work and organizational psychology* (pp. 183–214). Hove: Psychology Press. A classic of the psychology of work, which sets out many important aspects of the "older worker" issue.

Commission of the European Communities. The social situation in the EU 2004. http://europa.eu.int/comm/employment_social/social_situation/docs/SSR2004_en.pdf. A site which provides important information on how the European countries are addressing, with what similarities and differences, changes in the labor market.

Greller, M. M., & Simpson, P. (1999). In search of late career: A review of contemporary social science research applicable to the understanding of late career. *Human Research Management Review*, *9*, 309–47. A detailed survey of recent empirical studies on the late career which combine the psychology and organization studies approaches.

Job Stress and Occupational Health

Pascale Le Blanc, Jan de Jonge, and Wilmar Schaufeli

6

Overview

This chapter focuses on job stress in relation to employee physical and psychological health. We begin with an outline of job stress as a social problem, followed by a discussion of the main perspectives on (job) stress, including eustress ("good" stress), and of the potential role of individual differences variables in the stress process. In the next section, an integrative process model of job stress is presented that will be used as a frame of reference in the remaining part of the chapter, followed by a discussion of several prominent and new models on job stress and health. Finally, an overview of organizational and individual interventions to reduce job stress is given.

1 Job Stress as a Social Problem

Job stress is a major concern in all developing and industrialized countries, affecting not only employees whose health is at stake but also organizations and society as a whole. The workplace has changed dramatically due to globalization of economic activities, increased utilization of information and communication technology, growing diversity in the workplace (e.g., more women, older, and higher educated people, as well as increased migration, particularly between the EU Member States), flexible work arrangements, and changed organizational work patterns (e.g., Just in Time management) (European Foundation for the Improvement of Living and Working Conditions [EFILWC], 2005; Landsbergis, 2003). The impact of the global economy has also led to an increase in knowledge- and service-based organizations. One of the most striking developments, however, is the changing nature of work itself and increased workloads. New jobs (e.g., software consultant, process-operator, and cad-cam designer) and new types of companies (e.g., call centers) have arisen (De Jonge & Kompier, 1997).

Nowadays, for many employees, work poses primarily mental and emotional demands instead of physical ones.

According to recent figures, the prevalence of job stress is high. For instance, in the 2000 European Working Conditions Survey (EWCS), job stress was found to be the second most common job-related health problem across the EU Member States (28 percent) (European Foundation for the Improvement of Living and Working Conditions [EFILWC], 2005). Moreover, job stress is related not only to psychological disorders but also to a number of physical ailments such as cardiovascular diseases (Belkiç et al., 2004), musculoskeletal diseases (such as RSI, e.g., Ariëns et al., 2001), chronic low back pain (Hogendoorn, van Poppel, Koes & Bouter, 2000), and to absenteeism from work (Houtman et al., 1999). Finally, it should be noted that in addition to the direct costs due to work disability and sickness absence, there are also "hidden" consequences of job stress for organizations, e.g., more problems, conflicts, disturbed relations and turnover, and losses in the domain of image, corporate values, and productivity/quality of services (e.g., Gaillard, 2003; Schabracq, Maassen van den Brink, Groot, Janssen, & Houkes, 2000).

Prevalence rates of job stress not only are high, but also rising continuously. In Britain, an immense growth of stress-related absenteeism was observed across a 25-year period: from 1955 to 1979 absenteeism due to "nervousness, debility and headache" increased by 528 percent! (Hingley & Cooper, 1986). In The Netherlands, in 1967 when the Disability Security Act was introduced, mental disorders only accounted for 11 percent of workers' disability claims, whereas in 2002, 37 percent of disability claims were based on mental disorders.

Needless to say, the expenditures on job stress are huge. On the average, in the European Union about 10 percent of the Gross Domestic Product (GDP) is spent on the consequences of job stress (Cartwright & Cooper, 1996).

These immense costs have led to stronger legislation with regard to psychosocial work conditions and sickness absence. At the level of the European Union (EU), various countries have introduced legislation to improve the health and safety of employees in their work environment. Moreover, quite recently, the EU social partners signed a framework agreement for employers and employees aimed at preventing, identifying, and combating job stress (European Foundation for the Improvement of Living and Working Conditions [EFILWC], 2005). Modern European and national legislation emphasizes: (1) a broad and positive health concept; i.e. instead of solely combating ill-health, health, safety, and well-being at work are promoted; (2) a comprehensive approach, integrating health, safety and well-being at work; (3) active involvement and joint responsibility of employer and employee; (4) self-regulation by providing a supportive environment, for instance, by institutionalizing Occupational Health and Safety Services (see also De Gier, 1995).

Thus, job stress is a major and rising concern in industrialized countries and it seems that the level of job stress has increased alarmingly in the past decades. This is illustrated by increasing stress related absenteeism and work incapacity rates, as well as by rising associated costs.

2   What is Job Stress?

The original meaning of the term "stress" is derived from engineering. By analogy with physical force, it refers to external pressure that is exerted on a person, which in turn results in tension or "strain" (Kahn & Byosiere, 1992). Within certain limits, people are able to deal with this pressure and adapt to the situation, and to recover when the stressful period is over. However, in everyday language as well as in the scientific literature, the term "stress" is used to refer to the accompanying state of tension, and to the negative consequences of this state, as well as the cause. As there is little agreement as to how exactly "stress" should be defined, there is no general theory of stress. One of the main reasons for this lack of agreement lies in the large number of disciplines with different perspectives involved in stress research, such as biology, psychology, sociology, occupational medicine, and epidemiology. Nevertheless, most researchers in the field of stress do agree that three different meanings of the term stress can be distinguished (e.g., Cooper & Payne, 1988; Kahn & Byosiere, 1992; Kasl, 1987; Semmer, 2003): stress as a stimulus, stress as a response, and stress as a mediational process between stressor (stimulus) and reaction (response). Each of these perspectives is discussed below, with a focus on *job-related* stress.

Job stress as a stimulus: Job demands and job resources

In the domain of job stress, stressful stimuli can be categorized under two broad main categories: job demands and (lack of) job resources (cf. Frese & Zapf, 1994; Schaufeli & Bakker, 2004). Job demands refer to the degree to which the work environment contains stimuli that require sustained cognitive, emotional and/or physical effort (cf. Jones & Fletcher, 1996), and include workload, emotional labor and physical exertion. Other, more general demands are bullying, role conflicts, role ambiguity, and work-home conflicts. Job resources can be broadly conceptualized as a kind of energetic reservoir tapped when the individual has to cope with stressful stimuli (cf. Hobfoll, 1989; 2002). Examples of job resources are job autonomy, job variety and workplace social support. In general, individuals – when confronted with job stress – strive to minimize net loss of resources. In addition, when workers are not confronted with job demands, they strive to develop resource surpluses in order to offset the possibility of future loss ("energy accumulating behavior"; cf., Hobfoll, 1989). However, employing resources for coping purposes could be stressful in itself. Schönpflug (1985), for instance, showed that employment of resources in the coping process often depletes these resources.

Job demands and job resources may comprise cognitive, emotional and/or physical components. Three types of job demand can be distinguished: (1) cognitive demands that impinge primarily on the processes involved in information processing (Hockey, 2000); (2) emotional demands such as emotional labor, which refer primarily to the effort needed to deal with organizationally desired emotions during interpersonal transactions (Morris & Feldman, 1996); and (3) physical demands that are primarily associated with the musculo-skeletal system (i.e. sensomotor and physical aspects of behavior; cf. Hockey, 2000). Similarly, job resources may have a cognitive-informational component (e.g., colleagues providing information), an emotional component (e.g., colleagues providing sympathy and affection), and a physical component such as instrumental help of colleagues or ergonomic aids (cf. Cohen & Wills, 1985; Cutrona & Russell, 1990).

Job stress as a response: Job-related strain

In psychophysiology and occupational medicine, stress is viewed as a psychological and/or physiological *response* of the organism to some kind of threat. This notion of stress is based on Selye's (1956) classical General Adaptation Syndrome (GAS): exposure to a noxious stimulus triggers a complex of nonspecific physiological reactions that are intended to protect the individual against harmful consequences. The GAS consists of three stages: the alarm reaction (mobilization by means of physiological and hormonal changes), the resistance stage (optimal adaptation by activating appropriate systems), and exhaustion (depletion of adaptation energy). Although the GAS may be adaptive initially, negative consequences such as fatigue, tissue damage and high blood pressure may occur if the individual is not able to cope with the stressful stimulus and the stress reactions persist over longer periods of time. As stated above, it is assumed that different types of stressful stimuli trigger the same, nonspecific, response pattern, and that an individual's thoughts and emotions do not influence the type of response. However, these assumptions have proven to be untenable, as numerous studies have demonstrated that different types of physiological and hormonal reactions may occur, depending on the nature and interpretation of the stimulus and accompanying emotions (see e.g., Frankenhaeuser & Gardell, 1976; Frankenhaeuser, 1978).

Stress reactions (strains) can be expressed in different ways. They can be classified in five different clusters: (1) affective, (2) cognitive, (3) physical, (4) behavioral, and (5) motivational. In addition, three levels of expression, related to individual, interpersonal and organizational foci can be distinguished. In table 6.1, an overview of different types of stress reactions on each of the three different foci is presented.

Of course, stress reactions can differ in their intensity. Sometimes, the negative effects of stressors can easily be overcome by recreation and relaxation. However, in case of prolonged exposure to stressful stimuli, the individual may not able to reduce his or her (physiological) state of stress, and high activation levels are sustained (Ursin, 1986). This can in turn give rise to chronic physical (e.g., coronary heart disease; Siegrist, 1996) and/or psychological stress complaints (e.g., burnout; Maslach & Jackson, 1986; Schaufeli & Enzmann, 1998).

Table 6.1: Possible stress symptoms at the individual, interpersonal, and organizational level

Type/Level	Individual	Interpersonal	Organizational
Affective	anxiety tension anger depressed mood apathy	irritability being oversensitive	job dissatisfaction
Cognitive	helpless-/powerlessness cognitive impairments difficulties in decision making	hostility suspicion projection	cynicism about work role not feeling appreciated distrust in peers, supervisors and management
Physical	physical distress (headache, nausea, etc.) psychosomatic disorders (gastric- intestinal disorders, coronary diseases etc.) impairment of immune system changes in hormone levels		
Behavioural	hyperactivity impulsivity increased consumption of stimulants (caffeine, tobacco) and illicit drugs over- and under eating	violent outbursts aggressive behaviour interpersonal conflicts social isolation/withdrawal aggressive behaviour	poor work performance declined productivity tardiness turnover increased sick leave poor time management
Motivational	loss of zeal loss of enthusiasm disillusionment disappointment boredom demoralisation	loss of interest in others indifference discouragement	loss of work motivation resistance to go to work dampening of work initiative low morale

Job stress as a mediational process

Whereas both the stimulus approach and the response approach of stress emphasize directly measurable factors (characteristics of the psychosocial environment and measurable stress reactions, respectively), this approach focuses on the *cognitive, evaluative and motivational processes* that intervene between the stressful stimulus and the reaction (response). According to the mediational approach, stress reactions are a result of the interaction between person and environment. Potentially stressful stimuli may lead to different types of stress reactions in different individuals, depending on their cognitive evaluations (appraisals) of the situation (Lazarus & Folkman, 1984) and the resources they have at their disposal to cope with the stressful situation.

Latack and Havlovic (1992) developed a conceptual framework for coping with job stress. In this framework, a distinction is made between the focus of coping and the method of coping. The focus of coping can be problem-oriented or emotion-oriented. Problem-oriented coping refers to efforts aimed at altering the transaction between person and environment. For instance, it may include behaviors like seeking help or increasing efforts to counter the threat. Emotion-oriented coping, on the other hand, is defined as efforts aimed at regulating the emotions of a person (e.g., cognitive strategies like avoidance and relaxation techniques). With respect to the method of coping, two dimensions are distinguished. First, coping behavior can be observable (overt) or not observable (covert). Second, each of these two types of coping behavior can either be aimed at control or at escape. When the focus and/or method of coping do not match the stressor at hand, feelings of stress will be sustained or even intensified. Basically, active ways of coping (e.g., control coping) are to be preferred to passive ones such as escape coping (e.g., De Rijk, Le Blanc, Schaufeli, & De Jonge, 1998), provided the situation allows it.

In the preceding paragraphs, a static (stimulus or response) versus a more dynamic, interactionist, perspective (mediational process) on (job) stress was presented. Though the mediational approach has paved the way for a more theoretical view of the (job) stress process, a key disadvantage is that it is very difficult to disentangle the occurrence of an event, its cognitive evaluation and the individual's reaction to it. Within Work and Organizational Psychology, it is recommended to use all three perspectives to encompass the richness of the job stress process. For that very reason, job stress is defined as an experienced incongruence between job demands and job or individual resources that is accompanied by cognitive, emotional, physical or behavioral symptoms.

The other side of the coin: "good" stress and work engagement

From the outset, the very nature of stress has been debated: is it "bad" or does "good" stress exist as well? Originally, Selye (1956) defined stress as a nonspecific biological response to a stressor, meaning that stress in itself is neither bad nor good. He claimed that depending upon conditions "distress" (from the Latin *dis* or bad, like in disease) or "eustress" (from the Greek *eu* or good, like in euphoria) might occur. Despite this early distinction between good and bad, "stress" became the scientific and colloquial term for distress, whereas the conceptual development and empirical research on eustress was limited. However, eustress can be reconceptualized as a positive response to a cognitively appraised stressor. For instance, being accountable for a multimillion Euro project might be appraised as a threat to one's reputation because many things could go wrong, or it may be appraised as a challenge because it provides an opportunity to move one's career ahead. The former case would lead to distress, whereas in the latter case eustress might result. Indeed, researchers have found at least two differential physiological response patterns associated with positive and negative appraisals of a given situation (Nelson & Simmons, 2004). Thus it seems that rather than a nonspecific biological response pattern, as originally hypothesized by Selye, two such patterns exist that are associated with negative (distress) and positive (eustress) cognitive appraisals.

A new psychological movement has emerged recently that (re)emphasized psychology should cover the entire range of human behavior instead of being almost exclusively concerned with disease, damage, disability, and dysfunctioning (Seligman & Csikszentmihalyi, 2000). Positive Psychology – as this movement is called – seeks to study human resilience and flourishing. In a similar vein, an Occupational Health Psychology is developing that includes the entire spectrum of employee health and well-being, ranging from ill-health, unwell-being and poor functioning to positive health, well-being and optimal functioning (Schaufeli, 2005). This development coincides with major changes in modern organizations that expect their employees to be proactive and show initiative, collaborate smoothly with others in teams, take responsibility for their own professional development, and to be committed to high quality performance. Clearly, this cannot be achieved with a work force that is "healthy" in the traditional sense, that is, with employees who are merely symptom free. Instead of just "doing one's job," employees are nowadays expected "to go the extra mile." Thus, engaged employees are needed. But what exactly is work engagement, how can it be conceptualized?

Work engagement is considered to be the positive opposite of burnout; that is, contrary to those who suffer from burnout, engaged employees have a sense of energetic and effective connection with their work activities. More specifically, work engagement is defined as a positive, fulfilling, work-related state of mind that is characterized by vigor, dedication, and absorption (Schaufeli, Salanova, González-Romá, & Bakker, 2002). Vigor is characterized by high levels of energy and mental resilience while working, the willingness to invest effort in one's work, and persistence even in the face of difficulties. Dedication refers to being strongly involved in one's work, and experiencing a sense of significance, enthusiasm, inspiration, pride, and challenge. Absorption is characterized by being fully concentrated and happily engrossed in one's work, whereby time passes quickly and one has difficulties with detaching oneself from work. Being fully absorbed in one's work comes close to what has been called flow, a state of optimal experience that is characterized by focused attention, clear mind, mind and body unison, effortless concentration, complete control, loss of self-consciousness, distortion of time, and intrinsic enjoyment (Csikszentmihalyi, 1990). However, typically, flow is a more complex concept that includes many aspects and refers to rather particular, short-term peak experiences instead of a more pervasive and persistent state of mind, as is the case with engagement.

In-depth interviews showed that engaged employees are active agents, who take initiative at work, and generate their own positive feedback loops, they keep looking for new challenges in their jobs, and when they feel no longer challenged they change jobs (Schaufeli, Taris, Le Blanc, Peeters, Bakker, & De Jonge, 2001). Also, because of their involvement they are committed to performing at a high quality level, which usually generates positive feedback from their supervisors (e.g., praise, promotion, salary increases, fringe benefits) as well as from their customers (e.g., appreciation, gratitude, satisfaction). Furthermore, the values of engaged employees seem to match quite well with those of the organization they work for, and they also seem to be engaged in other activities outside their work. Finally, engaged employees are not addicted to their work as they enjoy other things outside work and, unlike workaholics, they do not work hard because of a strong and irresistible inner drive, but because of the fun of it.

Engagement is particularly related to the availability of job resources such as job control, social support, task variety, performance feedback, training facilities, and career opportunities. Possible consequences of engagement that have been identified are: positive job attitudes, (job satisfaction, work involvement, and organizational commitment) good health (low levels of anxiety, depression, and physical complaints), extrarole behavior, and individual work performance (quality of service, academic performance) and business-unit performance (profitability, productivity). It seems that an upward spiral exists in the sense that job resources and personal resources (notably efficacy beliefs) increase positive work outcomes via work engagement. In their turn, these positive outcomes and high levels of engagement seem to have a positive impact on both types of resources. These, and other more recent empirical findings on work engagement are described in greater detail in Schaufeli and Salanova (2007).

Individual differences and job stress

As people differ in the probability of encountering stressors, in their appraisal of stressors, and in their way of coping with stressors, associations between job stressors and strains may not hold for everyone in the same way (Spector, 2002). Research indicates that job stressors have negative effects on the health of all workers, although these may be more severe for some and less severe for others. Individual characteristics, such as age, gender, level of education, values, and personality, may influence one's coping abilities; they may interact with job stressors and either exacerbate or alleviate their effects. Three main categories of individual difference variables (cf. Parkes, 1994; Payne, 1988; Warr, 1987) can be distinguished:

1. *genetic characteristics* (like gender, constitution, and physique);
2. *acquired characteristics* (e.g., education, social class, and skills);
3. *dispositional characteristics* (such as coping styles, preferences, and type A/B behavior).

Space does not allow a complete description of all three categories. In this chapter, we will therefore restrict ourselves to the category of individual difference variables that stands out in the literature as being potentially relevant in the job stress process: dispositional characteristics (e.g., Parkes, 1994; Spector & O'Connell, 1994).

Some job stress studies have shown that the relationship between a certain job stressor and a certain strain reaction mainly, or even exclusively, occurs in employees with particular dispositional characteristics (e.g., Parkes, 1994; Warr, 1987). For example, a study among Intensive Care Unit (ICU) nurses by De Rijk et al. (1998) showed that the increase in job strain due to high job demands was attenuated by high levels of job control only for nurses high in active coping. In other words, job control acted as a stress buffer only for those nurses who are inclined to use it as a coping resource. In a study among Japanese managers, Shimazu, Shimazu, and Odahara (2005) found that psychological distress was lowest among managers with high levels of co-worker support combined with high levels of active coping, indicating that active coping can only be effective in reducing distress in working situations where job resources are present. Certain people are prone to becoming overcommitted to their job, which will have negative consequences for their health. Empirical support for this idea has been found in a study by Bakker, Killmer, Siegrist, and Schaufeli (2000), who showed that burnout was particularly prevalent among those nurses who experienced an imbalance between efforts invested in and rewards obtained from their jobs and who were overcommitted.

However, it remains unclear at what point in time the individual difference variables influence the job stress process. For instance, do they change the objective-subjective stressor relationship, or do they affect the perceptions of job stress as related to affective, cognitive, physical and behavioral outcomes? Moreover, it should also be noted that physical and psychological characteristics, such as physical fitness or a high level of optimism, may not only act as precursors or buffers in the development of stress reactions, but may also change as a result of these effects. For example, if workers are able to deal with job stressors at work, they will be more experienced and self-confident in overcoming similar situations the next time they have to face them (European Foundation for the Improvement of Living and Working Conditions [EFILWC], 2005).

3 Theoretical Models of Job Stress

Many different models focusing on job stress have been illuminated in the literature, and most of them are connected with our process-model that is presented in Figure 6.1. This process-model is based upon insights gained from several theoretical models and empirical studies concerning job stress and health, and integrates much of what has been outlined before.

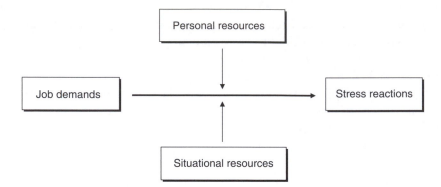

Figure 6.1: A process model of job stress

    According to this process-model, different types of demands (i.e., stressors) can result in different types of stress reactions. Moreover, the relationship between demands and stress reactions may be moderated by a) personal resources (e.g., coping styles), and b) situational resources such as job autonomy or workplace social support. The different components of our process-model will be elaborated in the next paragraph by discussing central themes in current theories on job stress.

    In this section we discuss several theoretical models on job stress, viz. the Vitamin Model, the Demand–Control–Support Model, and the Effort–Reward Imbalance Model. Furthermore, we discuss two recently developed models, viz. the Job Demands–Resources Model and the Demand-Induced Strain Compensation Model.

Vitamin Model

The most general job stress model was developed at the Institute for Social Research (ISR) of the University of Michigan (hence the designation "ISR" or "Michigan Model"; cf. Kahn & Byosiere, 1992). The Michigan Model assumes a general causal sequence from organizational characteristics via stressors leading to stress reactions and illness. Its successor is the Person–Environment (P–E) Fit Model, which is based on the premise that the interaction between environmental variables and relevant properties of a person determines job-related stress reactions. Based upon these two initial stress models, Warr (1987) developed in the 1980s his framework of mental health, referred to as the Vitamin Model (VM). The central idea underlying the VM is that mental health is affected by environmental psychological features, such as job characteristics, in a way that is analogous to the effects that vitamins are supposed to have on our physical health. Warr's framework has three principal parts:

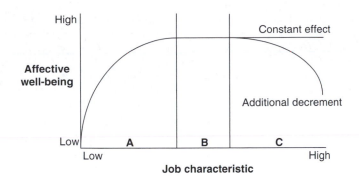

Figure 6.2: The Vitamin Model

1. Job characteristics are grouped into nine categories that relate differently to mental health outcomes according to the type of "vitamin" they represent;
2. A three-axial model of affective well-being, a core aspect of mental health, is postulated;
3. It is assumed that persons and situations interact in the prediction of mental health.

Warr (1987) draws an analogy between the way in which vitamins act on the human body and the effects of job characteristics on mental health. Following this line of reasoning, De Jonge and Schaufeli (1998) refer to Warr's vitamins as "psychological work vitamins."

Generally, as figure 6.2 shows, the absence of certain job characteristics impairs mental health, whereas their presence initially has a beneficial effect on employee mental health (segment A). Beyond a certain required level, vitamin intake no longer has any positive effects: a plateau has been reached and the level of mental health remains constant (segment B). The next segment shows that further increase of job characteristics may either produce a "constant effect" (denoted by CE) or may be harmful and impair mental health (denoted by AD or "additional decrement"). According to Warr (1987, 1994), which of the two effects will occur depends on the particular job characteristic.

Warr (1987, 1994) identified nine job features that may act as determinants of job-related mental health (see table 6.2). Warr assumes that six job characteristics (e.g., opportunities for control and variety) have curvilinear effects (U-shaped). The lack of such features or an excess of such features will affect mental health negatively. For example, the negative impact of excessively high levels of job control has been identified in laboratory as well as occupational studies (e.g., Burger, 1989; De Jonge, Schaufeli, & Furda, 1995). The remaining three job characteristics (i.e., physical security, availability of money, and valued social position) are supposed to follow a linear pattern: the higher such a job characteristic, the higher the level of mental health will be. Warr (1998) noted, however,

Table 6.2: The nine job characteristics of the Vitamin Model (cf. Warr, 1994)

CE Job Characteristics	*AD Job Characteristics*
– availability of money	– opportunity for control
– physical security	– opportunity for skill use
– valued social position	– externally generated goals
	– variety
	– environmental clarity
	– opportunity for interpersonal contact
CE: Constant Effect	*AD: Additional Decrement*

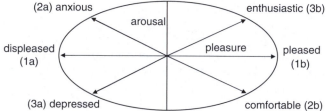

Figure 6.3: Job-related affective well-being

that it is improbable that the latter associations are purely linear. For instance, it seems plausible that an increase in income will have greater benefits at low income levels than at extremely high income levels. In other words, increased levels are desirable until a certain plateau has been reached. In addition, there is considerable evidence that younger employees have greatest need for income increase, whereas older employees consider income increase as relatively less important (e.g., Birdi, Warr, & Oswald, 1995).

A principal indicator of *job-related* mental health in psychological research is affective well-being. In order to measure affective well-being empirically Warr (1994) proposed three dimensions: displeasure-to-pleasure, anxiety-to-comfort, and depression-to-enthusiasm (see figure 6.3). Job-related affective well-being has most commonly been studied by measures of job satisfaction, job-related anxiety or tension, and by measures of occupational burnout and depression.

Finally, the interaction between persons and situations will be discussed. Essentially, the VM is situation-centered in that it focuses on the association between job characteristics and mental health. However, there are undoubtedly differences between people in the nature of those associations (Warr, 1994). Therefore, three categories of individual characteristics are viewed as possible moderators of the effects of job characteristics on mental health: *values* (e.g., preferences and motives), *abilities* (like intellectual and psychomotor skills) and *baseline mental health* (i.e., dispositions like negative affectivity).

Moderating effects are expected especially in the case of a so-called "matching" individual characteristic (Warr, 1994). In that respect, individual characteristics that match particular job characteristics will cause a stronger moderating effect than those that lack this matching property. Job autonomy may serve as an example: a matching individual characteristic might be the value "preference for autonomy." It is assumed that the preference for autonomy moderates (i.e. changes) the relationship between job autonomy and, for instance, job satisfaction (cf. Warr, 1987). In case of low preference for autonomy the relationship between autonomy and satisfaction will be zero (or even negative), whereas in case of high preference for autonomy the relationship between the two variables will be positive.

In recent years, a few cross-sectional studies have investigated the patterns proposed by the VM (e.g., De Jonge & Schaufeli, 1998; Jeurissen & Nyklícek, 2001; Xie & Johns, 1995; Warr, 1990). To summarize results were mixed and inconclusive. Job demands and job control, for instance, seem to be curvilinearly related to some aspects of employee mental health in the way that is predicted by the model, whereas the effect of workplace social support does not follow the model. Furthermore, all studies have failed to take account of the possible multi-faceted ways in which the nine job characteristics may affect job-related well-being. Added to this, longitudinal studies have not been reported yet, which means that causal orders in associations still have to be proved. Finally, there has been no empirical evidence for the interactions between individual and job characteristics as related to employee health *within* the VM.

Demand–Control–Support Model

Since the 1980s, the Demand–Control (DC) Model has dominated the empirical research on job stress and health. The model was introduced by Karasek in 1979 and further developed and tested by Karasek and Theorell (Karasek & Theorell, 1990; Theorell & Karasek, 1996). In 1988, Johnson and Hall elaborated the DC Model with the dimension of *workplace social support*. This expanded model was called the Demand–Control–Support (DCS) Model. In order to understand the principles of both models, we will first discuss the DC Model.

The DC Model depicted in figure 6.4 draws upon two research traditions, namely the occupational stress tradition (e.g., Michigan Model, Kahn, 1981) and the job redesign tradition (e.g., Hackman & Oldham, 1980). In both research traditions, attempts were made to relate job characteristics to employee health. The occupational stress tradition focused on "stressors" at work, such as high workload, role conflict, and role ambiguity (e.g., French & Kahn, 1962). The job redesign tradition focused mainly on job control, as its primary aim was to inform the (re)design of jobs in order to increase motivation, satisfaction, and performance at work.

For that reason, the DC Model postulates that the primary sources of stress lie within two basic job characteristics: *psychological job demands* and *job decision latitude*. According to the model, the jobs most likely to show extreme job-related stress reactions (like exhaustion and cardiovascular diseases) are those that

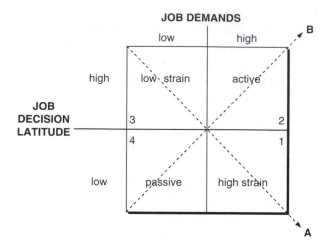

Figure 6.4:   The Job Demand–Control Model

combine high demands and low decision latitude. This combination is labeled *high strain* (quadrant 1). There is also an opposite situation termed *low strain*; that is, jobs in which job demands are low and worker's decision latitude is high (quadrant 3). In this situation the model predicts lower than average levels of stress reactions.

The second important assumption of the model is that motivation, learning and personal growth will occur in situations where both job demands and decision latitude are high (i.e., *active jobs*; quadrant 2). This assumption is closely related to what might be called "good stress" since most job stressors are translated into direct action (i.e., effective problem solving) with too few stressors left to cause job-related stress (cf. Karasek et al., 1998; Selye, 1956). The opposite of this situation is formed by *passive jobs*, in which skills and abilities may atrophy (quadrant 4). This situation resembles the "learned helplessness" phenomenon (cf. Lennerlöf, 1988). In short, psychological demands and decision latitude affect two psychological mechanisms, reflected by diagonal A and B in figure 6.4. The first mechanism influences the (adverse) health of the employee (diagonal A), while the other influences the work motivation and the learning behavior of the employee (diagonal B).

The assumption that more or less job decision latitude can translate (high) job demands into either positive or negative effects on employee health and well-being has often been operationalized as an *interaction effect* between job demands and job decision latitude. An interaction effect means that the total effect of high demands and low control is larger than the sum of the separate effects of high demands and low control on employee well-being.

The elaborated DCS Model (figure 6.5) was developed to examine the joint effects of three instead of two basic characteristics of the work organization, viz. job demands, job control and workplace social support. In this extended model,

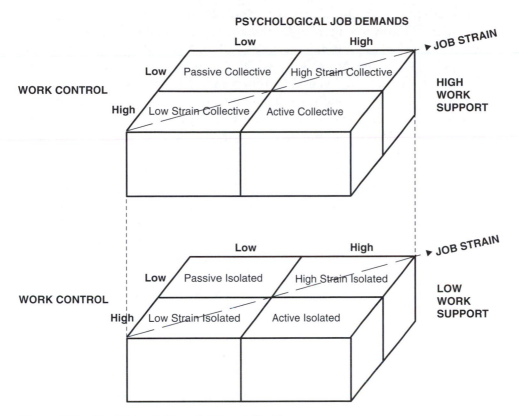

Figure 6.5: The Demand–Control–Support Model

both the strain and activity assumption are split up into *isolated* and *collective* conditions, and the processes are consequently redefined. In that respect, it is for instance assumed that the most unfavorable effects are expected for a combination of high demands, low decision latitude and low social support. This combination is sometimes called *iso-strain* (cf. Johnson & Hall, 1988). Workplace social support is assumed to buffer psychological strain depending on the degree of social and emotional integration, help and trust between supervisors, colleagues, etc.

Two major conclusions can be drawn from the studies using and evaluating the two models (De Jonge & Kompier, 1997; Van der Doef & Maes, 1998, 1999). The first conclusion is that large (mostly epidemiological and population-based) studies offer the most support for the model, and for the strain assumption in particular. The second conclusion is that the interaction assumption that particularly the combination of psychological demands, decision latitude and social support involves stronger responses (such as more physical symptoms or more work motivation) is not often supported. It is more often the case that the three components separately have an impact on the outcome variables, than that they reinforce each other in this respect (so-called synergistic effects).

Obviously, the strength of the DCS Model lies in its simplicity and practical implications. However a number of theoretical and methodological problems remain to be solved (e.g., Jones & Fletcher, 1996; Kasl, 1996; Kristensen, 1996; Van Vegchel, De Jonge, & Landsbergis, 2005). Firstly, for instance, the conceptualization, operationalization and measurement of the basic dimensions should be elaborated further. Secondly, there is no unanimous preference for a particular type of interaction term to test the model, which logically has also led to different empirical results. This is suprising as DC theory should drive the particular interaction term to be tested, because different theoretical meanings imply different mathematical formulations of such a term. Thirdly, being a situation-centered model, the issue of objective vs. subjective measurement of job characteristics has been neglected thus far. More specifically, the model focuses on characteristics of the work situation, but these are usually determined with the use of self-report questionnaires and the subsequent risk of common method variance. Effects of job demands and job resources on stress outcomes are very likely to be overestimated due to such a common method bias. Lastly, many studies have failed to take into account individual differences (like locus of control and coping styles).

Effort–Reward Imbalance Model

The Model of Effort–Reward Imbalance at work (e.g., Siegrist, 1996; Peter & Siegrist, 1997) has a more sociological focus and shifts from the concept of job control to the reward structure of work.

In the Effort–Reward Imbalance (ERI) Model, the work role of an employee is considered a basic tool to link important self-regulatory functions (i.e., self-esteem and self-efficacy) with the societal structure of opportunities and rewards (see Figure 6.6). Essentially, the model is based upon the principle of reciprocity: high effort spent at work in combination with low reward obtained in turn may cause a state of emotional distress and sympathetic arousal with an inclination to cardiovascular risks.

Effort is evaluated as two components: extrinsic effort or *job demands* (like time pressure, responsibility and physical demands), and intrinsic effort or *overcommitment*. The latter is regarded as a specific personal pattern of coping with

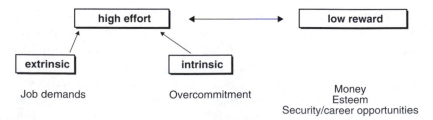

Figure 6.6:   The Effort–Reward Imbalance Model

job demands and of eliciting rewards that is relatively stable over time, and that may prevent people from accurately assessing cost-gain relations. Overcommitment is assessed by using four dimensions of coping behavior (i.e., need for approval, competitiveness and latent hostility, impatience and disproportionate irritability, and inability to withdraw from work obligations), which are combined to form one latent factor. According to Peter, Geissler, and Siegrist (1998) rewards are distributed to employees in three different ways: *money* (i.e., adequate salary), *esteem* (e.g., respect and support), and *security/career opportunities* (e.g., promotion prospects, job security and status consistency).

The combination of high effort and low reward at work has been found to be a risk factor for cardiovascular health, sickness absence as well as self-reported symptoms (for reviews, see Tsutsumi & Kawakami, 2004; Van Vegchel, De Jonge, Bosma, & Schaufeli, 2005).

Although the ERI Model looks very promising in the research domain of job stress and health, several preliminary comments have to be made (see also Kasl, 1996; Siegrist, 1996). First, it seems inconsistent to make a clear distinction between extrinsic and intrinsic efforts, but no clear distinction between extrinsic and intrinsic rewards. Intrinsic rewards, however, seem to be part of the overcommitment construct (i.e., need for approval). Second, one might question the extent to which the overcommitment construct is a stable trait and to what extent it is related to the work environment. For instance, will some employees experience more stress because of their character, or do some job characteristics evoke overcommitment? Third, the term *status inconsistency* is used to describe a misfit between occupation and education in both directions. In the model, both directions reflect low reward or low status control, which is not completely consistent with the work and organization psychology literature that indicates only an excess of education over occupational status as a risk factor. Fourth, because the model encompasses a broad social context, it is remarkable that little attention has been paid so far to the relationship between work and family life as an environmental factor of possible relevance ("work–home interference"). Finally, a last comment concerns the dynamic nature of the ERI Model. Longitudinal studies are clearly needed in order to investigate the time-dependent, causal and accumulating effects for both effort and reward in the prediction of health outcomes.

The Job Demands–Resources Model

Introduced by Demerouti and colleagues in 2001, the Job Demands–Resources (JDR) Model has gained popularity since with a lot of empirical studies applying the model to various occupational groups. The JDR Model has been designed to encapsulate job demands and resources unique to various occupations. Each occupation may have specific risk factors associated with job stress, but the JDR Model provides an overarching framework of burnout and engagement that can be applied to various occupational settings, irrespective of the particular demands and resources involved (Bakker, Demerouti, & Euwema, 2005). The choice for

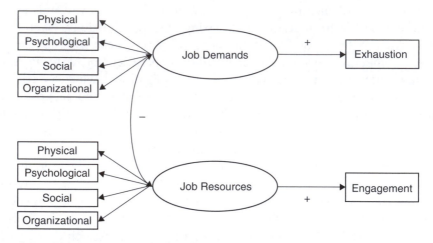

Figure 6.7:   The Job Demands–Resources Model

demands or resources is determined by empirical data analysis (e.g., confirmatory factor analysis), rather than theory. The model hypothesizes that job demands and resources are negatively related and that high job resources may reduce the negative impact that job demands may have on the individual. In addition, Demerouti et al. (2001) predict that job demands are primarily associated with exhaustion (the energy depletion process) while job resources are primarily and inversely associated with disengagement (the motivation depletion process; see figure 6.7).

The *original* JDR model concentrated on the unique contribution of demands and resources (main effects) in the prediction of burnout and engagement (Demerouti et al., 2001; Halbesleben & Buckley, 2004). Recently however, the interaction between them has been more explicitly tested as a buffer function of resources between demands and stress reactions.

At a global level, and in line with the assumptions of the model, most empirical studies provide strong evidence that working conditions (demands and resources) evoke two distinct processes, (1) the energy/erosion/health impairment process that links job demands with burnout; and (2) the motivational enhancement process that links job resources with engagement (Cotton, Dollard, & De Jonge, 2006). Moreover, the majority of job resources were capable of buffering the impact of job demands on employee well-being (burnout and to a lesser extent engagement). So, the combination of high job demands and low resources resulted in comparatively more feelings of exhaustion than would be expected on the basis of main effects alone (Bakker, Demerouti, Taris, Schaufeli, & Schreurs, 2003). In their systematic review of 20 JDR studies, Cotton et al. (2006) concluded that - given the newness of the model – the development of its theory has not been as clearly defined as the more traditional DC or ERI Models. Furthermore, because of the predominantly cross-sectional nature of the studies (85 percent of the studies included in the review were cross-sectional), common method variance may have influenced the results. While the studies conducted so far suggest causality, conclusions about the direction of effects can *not* be drawn. Finally, the potential for positive research bias; that is, a greater percentage of studies in agreement with the model being published and the fact that a large percentage of articles have yet to be peer-reviewed (50 percent of articles in the review were unpublished), needs to be considered with the appropriate level of caution. Notwithstanding, the JDR's broader, holistic framework – as compared to the restrictive nature of the DC and ERI Models – seems to be better able to capture the complexities across different work environments and in this way accounts for such promising support for the interaction hypothesis.

The Demand-Induced Strain Compensation Model

In light of the conceptual and practical limitations of the DC and ERI models De Jonge and Dormann (2003) developed a new model of job stress. This model, the so-called Demand-Induced Strain Compensation (DISC) Model, tries to unify principles that are common to both models, and thus create a more cohesive theoretical model of job stress (see figure 6.8).

The DISC Model is premised on four key principles. Firstly, De Jonge and Dormann (2003) emphasize the need to recognize the multidimensionality of concepts. They observe that job demands, job resources, and job-related strains each contain cognitive, emotional, and physical elements. Secondly, the Triple Match Principle (TMP) was developed. The TMP proposes that the strongest, interactive relationships between demands and resources are observed when demands *and* resources *and* strains are based on qualitatively identical dimensions. For instance, emotional support by colleagues is most likely to moderate (i.e., mitigate) the relationship between emotional demands (e.g., irate customers) and emotional exhaustion. The TMP suggests not only that stressors and resources should match (cf. Cohen & Wills, 1985), or that resources should match strains (cf. Frese, 1999), but also that stressors should match strains. For instance, insolent customers are more likely to cause emotional disorders than physical complaints. Thirdly, the compensation principle proposes that the negative effects of job demands can be counteracted through the availability and activation of job resources. It is also predicted that job resources from within the same domain as the job demands (i.e., cognitive, emotional, or physical) will produce a greater likelihood of counteracting the negative effects of job demands. The fourth principle of the DISC Model is that of balance. It is theorized that the optimal conditions for active learning, growth, and creativity exist where a balanced mixture of (high) job demands and corresponding job resources occurs. For instance, employee creativity may occur if an employee has a lot of job control in facing high mental demands.

While a body of empirical evidence for the DISC Model has not been established in the job stress literature due to its recent development, De Jonge and

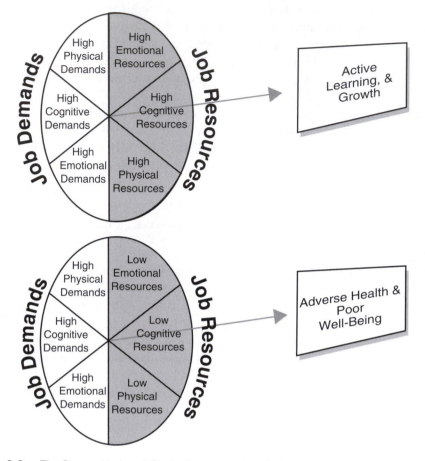

Figure 6.8:   The Demand-Induced Strain Compensation Model

Dormann (2004; 2005) presented evidence for the assumptions in the model. Belgian, German and Dutch studies conducted to test the principles of the DISC Model show that results have been supportive. More specifically, 8 out of 11 DISC studies (i.e., 73 percent) showed evidence for the TMP (cf. De Jonge & Dormann, 2005). For instance, two two-wave panel surveys among 280 and 267 health care workers showed robust support for the TMP (De Jonge & Dormann, 2006). The likelihood of finding moderating effects was linearly related to the degree of match, with 33.3 percent of all tested interactions becoming significant when there was a triple-match, 16.7 percent significant interactions when testing for so-called double-matches, and 0.0 percent when there was no match. Findings were most consistent if there was an emotional match or a physical match.

   In conclusion, job stress research may benefit from the idea that job demands and job resources do not interact randomly in the prediction of health and per-formance outcomes. Rather, it is the idea of *common match* (i.e., job demands and job resources should match) and the idea of *extended match* (job demands and job resources should also match job-related strain), both reflected in the *Triple Match Principle*, that merit attention in future job stress research.

By clarifying the relationships between different types of job characteristics and health, the above models have given some indications of interventions that can be used to prevent or reduce job stress. In the final section of this chapter, a systematic overview of different types of interventions is presented and discussed.

4 Interventions to Prevent or Reduce Job Stress

Job stress interventions may focus on three levels:

- *The organization.* By changing the work situation through organization-based interventions, the source of the problem is tackled and the employee's negative reaction is reduced.
- *The individual/organization interface.* By increasing the employee's resistance to specific job stressors, his or her vulnerability decreases.
- *The individual.* By learning to cope better with stress in general, the individual prevents negative psychological effects of job stressors.

In addition, job stress interventions may serve five purposes:

- *Identification* (i.e. early detection of job stressors and stress reactions)
- *Primary prevention* (i.e. reduction of job stressors)
- *Secondary prevention* (i.e. altering the ways employees respond to job stressors)
- *Treatment* (i.e. healing those who suffer severely from job stress)
- *Rehabilitation*[1] (i.e. planned return to the previous job)

Levels and purposes of job stress interventions may be combined into a classification table that constitutes a framework for discussing various approaches (see Table 6.3; for more elaborate recent reviews see: Kompier & Kristensen, 2000; Murphy, 2003; Semmer, 2003; Quick, Quick, Nelson. & Hurrell 1997).

Interventions primarily aimed at the organization

Instead of a prime target, reducing job stress is a mere byproduct of organization-based interventions. Usually, such interventions are primarily aimed at improving efficiency or effectiveness. Organization based interventions focus on: (1) diagnosis (i.e., job stress audits, cf. Zapf, Becholdt, & Dormann, in press); (2) removal or reduction of stressors (i.e., improve workload, job content and the work environment (job enlargement, job enrichment, job rotation), role clarification, better time scheduling, communication, decision-making, conflict

Table 6.3: Overview of job stress interventions

Focus/Purpose	Identification	Primary prevention	Secondary prevention	Treatment	Rehabilitation
Organization	job stress audit	improving work content and environment time scheduling management development corporate fitness and wellness programmes career management	anticipatory socialization communication, decision making, and conflict management organizational development	institutionalization of occupational health and safety services employee assistance programmes	outplacement
Individual/ Organization	personal screening	time management interpersonal skills training promoting a realistic image of the job balancing work and private life	peer-support groups coaching and consultation career planning	specialized counselling and psychotherapy	individual guidance and assistance
Individual	self-monitoring	didactic stress management promoting a healthy life style	cognitive-behavioural techniques relaxation		

management, and Organizational Development); (3) improvement of fit between the employee and the organization (i.e., career management, anticipatory socialization, Management Development, and outplacement); (4) institutionalization of procedures and services (i.e., corporate fitness and wellness programs, enrichment of Occupational Health and Safety Services, and Employee Assistance Programs).

In Europe, *the institutionalization of Occupational Health and Safety Services* has been facilitated by the introduction of new occupational health and safety legislation. OHSS's play an indirect role in reducing job stress in at least three ways: (1) by regularly carrying out stress audits and personal screenings; (2) by offering a specialized individual counselling and rehabilitation service for employees with work-related mental problems; (3) by expert consultation in occupational medicine, safety engineering, human factors and occupational psychology.

Employee Assistance Programs (EAPs) are worksite-based programs to assist in the identification and resolution of productivity problems associated with employees impaired by personal concerns including health, marital, family, financial, alcohol, drug, legal, emotional, stress, or other personal concerns which may adversely affect employee job performance (Lee & Gray, 1994). The ultimate concern of EAPs is with prevention, identification, and treating personal problems that adversely affect job performance.

Interventions primarily aimed at the individual/organizational interface

This type of interventions seeks to (1) increase awareness (i.e. personal screening); (2) improve individual coping skills (i.e. time-management, interpersonal skills training, promoting a realistic image of the job, and balancing work and private life); (3) provide emotional and instrumental support at work (i.e. peer-support groups, coaching, and career planning); (4) cure target complaints by intensive treatment (i.e. specialized counseling and psychotherapy); (5) rehabilitate employees (i.e. individual guidance and assistance).

Interventions primarily aimed at the individual

Most individual level interventions are well established and have a long and successful history in clinical or health psychology. Principally, individual strategies are aimed towards: (1) increasing the individual's awareness (i.e., self-monitoring and didactic stress management); or (2) reducing negative arousal (i.e., promoting a healthy lifestyle, cognitive-behavioral techniques, and relaxation).

Self-monitoring assumes that by explicitly focusing on the signs and symptoms of distress the individual's self-awareness is increased ("know thyself"). A powerful self-monitoring technique is to keep a stress diary; a personal record or log of stress symptoms and related events.

Didactic stress management refers to all kinds of information about job stress that is provided with the intention to increase awareness and to improve self-care.

For instance, workbooks are available with tips, tricks, and exercises that teach how to deal with job stress (e.g., Fontana, 1989; Schabracq & Cooper, 2001).

Promoting a healthy lifestyle includes regular physical exercise, proper nutrition, weight control, no smoking, enough sleep, and periods of rest for relaxation and recharge during the workday and thereafter. Many of these elements are part of corporate fitness and wellness programs. Of these approaches, physical exercise is perhaps the most powerful antidote to stress (McDonald & Hodgdon, 1991; Salmon, 2001).

Relaxation is considered to be a universal remedy to stress. Therefore, it is the cornerstone of virtually every stress-management program, often in combination with *cognitive-behavioral techniques* (Murphy, 2003). The goal of relaxation is to teach the aroused individual how to produce voluntarily a positive, alternate physiological response, a state in which (s)he deliberately eliminates the undesirable physiological effects of stress.

Despite their importance, relatively few sound empirical studies have been conducted on interventions aimed at preventing and/or reducing job stress. Therefore, it's difficult to compare the effectiveness of each of these types of interventions. However, on the basis of eleven European case studies, Kompier and Cooper (1999) concluded that interventions that are (a) comprehensive, i.e. addressing both individual and organizational factors, (b) use a stepwise approach (preparation, analysis, choice of measures, implementation, and evaluation), (c) involve workers centrally in the process (by considering them as "experts" with respect to their own working conditions and ways to improve them), (d) are context-specific, i.e. based on an accurate assessment of risk factors and/or risk groups, and (e) have top management support hold the greatest promise for effective prevention and/or reduction of stress at work.

Summary

Job stress is a scientific as well as a social problem. From a scientific point of view it may seem somewhat disappointing that after more than 30 years of intensive research a "grand, unifying theory of job stress" is still not within reach. However, the feasibility of one overarching framework can be seriously questioned, as job demands (stressors) are constantly and rapidly changing due to social developments. Over the past decennia, the nature of job demands (stressors) has shifted from purely physical to mental and emotional demands, which has important implications for job stress and thus for the theoretical models describing it. Therefore, the models that have been discussed in this chapter should be considered complementary rather than mutually exclusive. Nevertheless, future job stress research may benefit from the idea – as outlined by the Demands Induced Strain Compensation Model – that job demands and job resources do not interact randomly in the prediction of job-related strains. Rather, it is the idea of matching (job demands and job resources match job-related strain) that merits attention in future job stress research.

Unfortunately, there is still a gap between theoretical knowledge and practical implications. It seems most realistic to pursue an eclectic approach to job stress, in which possible solutions to stress-related problems are derived from one or several models of job stress that best fit the problem at hand. However, all models do make clear that job stress interventions should be targeted primarily to the source of many of the problems, i.e. the stressful working situation. For reasons of "fine tuning," these work-oriented interventions may be supplemented by measures aimed at the individual worker. As mentioned above, this point of view is also supported by modern labor legislation in many Western countries.

Discussion Points

Which job stress model is your personal favorite, and what are the key hypotheses? Explain why this model is especially suitable to apply to everyday practice in organizations.

Which level of implementation seems to be most effective for job stress interventions?

Key Studies

Van der Doef, M., & Maes, S. (1999). The Job Demand–Control(–Support) model and psychological well being: A review of 20 years of empirical research. *Work and Stress, 13*, 87–114. A state-of-the-art review of empirical research on the JDC(S) model in relation to psychological well-being.

Van Vegchel, N., De Jonge, J., Bosma, H., & Schaufeli, W. (2005). Reviewing the Effort–Reward Imbalance model: Drawing up the balance of 45 empirical studies. *Social Science & Medicine, 60*, 1117–31. A state-of-the-art review of empirical research on the ERI model.

Further Reading

Kahn, R. L., & Byosiere, P. (1992). Stress in organizations. In M. D. Dunette and L. M. Hough (Eds.), *Handbook of industrial and organizational psychology (volume 3)* (pp. 571–650). Palo Alto, CA: Consulting Psychologists Press. Chapter that gives a clear overview of what job stress is and how it "works."

Karasek, R. A., & Theorell, T. (1990). *Healthy work: Stress, productivity and the reconstruction of working life.* New York: Basic Books. Book that describes the development of the JDC(S) model and its practical implications.

Schabracq, M. J., Winnubst, J. A. M., & Cooper, C. L. (Eds.) (2003). *The handbook of work and health psychology, second edition.* Chichester: John Wiley & Sons. Recent overview of the theoretical state of the art in occupational health psychology.

Siegrist, J. (1996). Adverse health effects of high-effort/low reward conditions. *Journal of Occupational Health Psychology, 1*, 27–41. Article that describes and empirically illustrates the basic ideas of the ERI model.

Note

1 Please note that by definition rehabilitation goes beyond the purely individual level in the sense that it inevitably takes into account the employee's relation with the organization. Therefore, the box in the lower right corner of 6.4 is empty. Moreover, since we focus on job related problems, a general discussion of psychotherapy and counselling is beyond the scope of this book. Accordingly, the individual-treatment box also remains empty.

Research Close-Up 1

Schaufeli, W. B., & Bakker, A. B. (2004). Job demands, job resources and their relationship with burnout and engagement: A multi-sample study. *Journal of Organizational Behavior, 25*, 293–315.

Introduction

Previous research has identified several causes and consequences of burnout. More particularly, specific job demands and lacking job resources may act as causes, whereas health problems and withdrawal from the organization may be consequences of burnout. With the introduction of work engagement in occupational health psychology, two questions arise: (1) is work engagement indeed the positive "opposite" of burnout – i.e., are both concepts negatively related? (2) are the causes and consequences of burnout inversely related to work engagement – e.g., is the presence of resources related to work engagement? The study of Schaufeli and Bakker tested a model in which burnout mediates the relationship between job demands and health problems,

whereas work engagement mediates the relationship between job resources and turnover intention. In addition several cross-links were hypothesized (see figure 6.9).

Participants

A multisample approach was used that included employee samples from: (1) an insurance company (N = 381); (2) an Occupational Health and Safety Service (N = 202); (3) a pension fund company (N = 507); and (4) a home-care institution (N = 608). Response rates ranged from 47 percent to 66 percent.

Design and procedure

A cross-sectional field study was carried out. After informative meetings with representatives of the management, personnel department and workers–councils, employees received paper-and-pencil questionnaires and return envelopes at their work. After filling out the questionnaire, they could post it in a special box at their departments.

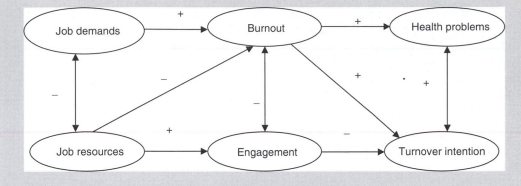

Figure 6.9: Factors affecting burnout, and their interrelationship

Burnout and work engagement were measured with the Maslach Burnout Inventory and the Utrecht Work Engagement scale, respectively. Job demands included quantitative (i.e. work overload) and qualitative (i.e. emotional) demands. Job resources included performance feedback, social support from colleagues, and supervisory coaching. Like perceived health problems and turnover intentions, the demands and resources were measured with validated multi-item scales.

The relationship between burnout and engagement (research question 1) was studied with confirmatory factor analyses. The hypothesized model (research question 2) was tested using structural equation modeling. Data analysis was carried out simultaneously across all four samples.

Results

As expected, burnout and work engagement were negatively related. However, the pattern of relationships slightly differed from what was expected. Instead of loading on burnout together with exhaustion and cynicism, lack of professional efficacy loaded on engagement (with vigor, dedication, and absorption). The hypothesized model fitted to the data of all four samples, albeit after some minor respecifications. Moreover, the relationships between the variables in the model were invariant – i.e. of similar size – across sample 1, 2, and 3. Additional analyses revealed that the direct paths form job demands to health problems and from job resources to turnover intention were *not* significant. This indicates that burnout and work engagement play a mediating role in the energy depletion process and the motivational process, respectively.

Discussion

The study demonstrated, across various independent samples, that burnout and work engagement are indeed each other's opposites. However, one burnout dimension – lack of professional efficacy – loaded unexpectedly on work engagement. Most likely this is caused by the fact that this dimension is measured with *positively* framed items that are inverted in order to assess *lack* of professional efficacy. The hypothesized model fitted the data of all four samples and the path coefficients were similar in three of the four samples – with the home-care

Continued

sample as the exception. Subsequent analyses revealed that it couldn't be ruled out that sample bias might have played a role – that is, the home-care sample largely consists of part-time working women. The major contribution of this study is that it suggests that two interlinked processes seem to be at work: (1) a process of energy depletion that is driven by high demands and lacking resources and which via burnout might result in health problems; (2) a motivational process that is driven by job resources and which via work engagement might result in commitment to the organization (i.e. low intention to leave). Since this study used a cross-sectional design, future longitudinal research should replicate these findings.

Research Close-Up 2

Dormann, C., & Zapf, D. (2004). Customer-related social stressors and burnout. *Journal of Occupational Health Psychology*, 9(1), 61–82.

Introduction

The rapid growth of service jobs has led to an increase in customer-related social stressors. Though nearly all studies on burnout implicitly assume that burnout is primarily caused by stressful employee–customer interactions, only a couple of studies have addressed this empirically. This research study of Dormann and Zapf is unique in a sense that (1) they developed a new instrument assessing different forms of customer-related social stressors (CSS), (2) they related this instrument to emotional dissonance (i.e., a key component of emotion work), and (3) they investigated the unique contribution of both CSS and emotional dissonance in the prediction of burnout.

Participants

The sample was composed of three different occupations, i.e. flight attendants, travel agency employees, and sales clerks. To assess CSS, the employees should have at least a moderate amount of direct contact to each customer. In total 591 respondents were recruited to participate in the current study (approx. 55 percent response rate). Seventy-eight percent were female.

Design and procedure

The design can be labeled a cross-sectional survey, as no factors were manipulated, and data were gathered once. Paper-and-pencil questionnaires were distributed and picked up by the researchers. With the exception of the flight attendants, people were allowed to complete the questionnaire during working hours.

Measures

Measures were derived from existing and new scales, such as a well-validated German instrument for stress-oriented task analysis (Zapf, Becholdt, & Dormann, in press) as well as the German version of the Maslach Burnout Inventory (Büssing & Perrar, 1992). New scales assessing different types of customer-related social stressors (CSS) were developed based on a couple of semi-structured interviews held with employees in shoe stores, and travel agencies, and with flight attendants.

Data analysis

The structure of the new instruments was analyzed by means of factor analysis. In addition, to test the associations between CSS, emotional dissonance and burnout, regression analyses were conducted using structural equation modeling.

Results

Firstly, factor analyses on the newly developed CSS instrument showed four themes: disproportionate customer expectations, customer verbal aggression, disliked customers, and ambiguous customer expectations. Secondly, data showed that the CSS scales and emotional dissonance were not mutually redundant: the CSS scales were able to explain variance in the customer interaction beyond the effects of emotional dissonance. Finally, the four CSS scales and emotional dissonance were able to predict burnout beyond a variety of control variables such as relevant job stressors (e.g., concentration demands) and job resources such as job control and social support by supervisors or colleagues.

Discussion

This study investigated employee–customer interactions from a job stress perspective. It revealed four constructs and corresponding measures to assess stressors in employee–customer interactions. These four scales showed acceptable psychometric properties. Moreover, the newly developed scales were also related to emotional dissonance, a key component of emotion work. Both the customer-related social stressors (CSS) and emotional dissonance were able to predict employee burnout, but CSS are a bit superior in this prediction. Limitations of the current study are its cross-sectional nature, which precludes causal inferences. In addition, there may still be other kinds of CSS, as the authors may not have covered their full range. Finally, the CSS scales should be tested further across different service occupations, and preferably in different languages and cultures. Future studies should continue accumulating knowledge about customer-related social stressors in the service sector, as they seem to be important antecedents of burnout in these jobs.

PART II

WORKING WITH TECHNOLOGY

Photo © Dominic Burke

Design and Use of Work Technology

Jan Noyes

7

Overview

This chapter considers the design and use of work technology from a human perspective. If we adopt a system's approach, the human element can be viewed as a system in its own right alongside the hardware, software, workplace, environment and other components. The area of study of human–system interactions is known as ergonomics or human factors, and these are defined and overviewed in conjunction with the influence of computers in the workplace and accompanying issues of usability and sociotechnical theory. One of the key decisions in system design concerns allocation of function, that is, the sharing of tasks between humans and machines, and the chapter covers the many influences in deciding whether a human or a machine should carry out a particular task or job. Finally, human error and mental representations and the role they play in the design and use of work technology are considered.

Developments in Technology

It is always hard to believe we are part of living history. Yet in my lifetime and over a short span of 30 years from when I was an undergraduate, work technology has changed beyond recognition. In the 1970s, all student essays were handwritten apart from the final year project, when either a professional typist or a portable typewriter had to be located. Mistakes were difficult to correct, and copious correcting fluid was needed. Adding text often resulted in typing subsequent pages or parts of them, and typing the page numbers was always the very last job, because again, adding a single page meant manually erasing and typing in the numbers of all the following pages. Library searches meant just that – a visit to the library to locate and photocopy relevant material. Computer programs

(Fortran IV in my case) required a set of punch cards, which were deposited at the Computer Centre, run on the mainframe computer overnight, and the result collected the following day. Usually, the program did not work, so the process had to be repeated again (and again). A further ritual for undergraduates in halls of residence was the weekly phone call home, which usually involved a long wait in a queue at a pay phone. We then returned to our rooms to listen to our vinyl long playing (LP) records.

Today, at my university, typed coursework is the norm. Undergraduates have access to 24 hour computer rooms, and most have a laptop or personal computer (PC). Editing text on the screen is now very straightforward with the use of "cut and paste" and other more sophisticated facilities such as "track changes" and macros. The introduction of the Internet in the early 1990s (Berners Lee, Cailliau, Luotonen, Nielsen, & Secret, 1994) has revolutionized how we search for material as electronic journals begin to replace their hard copy versions. There is now little need to move from my PC as I communicate via email and intranet systems, and use computer, statistical and bibliographic packages. These now operate in real-time, and feedback of input is immediate. Always with me is my mobile phone and often an MP3 player for listening to music.

The changes in the academic environment mirror those in other workplaces. Computers and databases are now part of most organizations: for example, 89% of European Union enterprises in 2004 had access to the Internet and this percentage increased in 2005 (see Eurostat Yearbook, 2005). The skills base has changed: in the 1960s and 1970s, the people who worked with computers were highly trained specialists. Likewise, the typists using the QWERTY keyboard were trained professionals, who had spent many months perfecting their skills. Today, most people who access the Internet have had no formal training; we attempt to "pick it up as we go along." We also are becoming increasingly physically static as the PC provides the point of focus for all our office-type activities. There is now little need to move off-screen as we search, communicate, write, edit, form-fill, create spreadsheets, book holidays, make travel arrangements, etc. using the one source. This has health and safety implications as we spend considerable periods of time "locked" into our PCs and focusing on display screens. Although the computer has far greater functionality than the typewriter, another change has occurred in the portability of electronic objects. In the 1970s, the telephone and the record player were relatively fixed objects; today, we can carry the equivalent objects with us, and are able to use them in most geographical locations.

This chapter is about the design and use of work technology. It considers how the area has developed over the last century with the growth in computers and related technologies, and the influence of ergonomics/human factors. Three key aspects of system design and use from a user perspective are usability, allocation of function, and human error. These are each considered within the backdrop of a system's approach.

Design and Use of Work Technology

The role of ergonomics

Humans have always used tools; the design of our hands with their opposable thumbs allowed us to make and use basic implements. This aspect of our physiology is one of the primary reasons why we have been able to design and develop so many objects in our environment. These have become progressively more technologically complex, for example, the steam engine, the phonograph, and the telephone in the eighteenth and nineteenth centuries. However, it was not until the Second World War that technological advances in the area of computing were made.

Between the First and Second World Wars, there was a shift in approach: the former had been fought primarily in the trenches (similar to the many wars preceding this time), while the latter began to utilize aircraft and the air space. The need to develop fighter aircraft and to move quickly through the design and development process to system implementation meant a number of mistakes were inevitably made. For example, the Douglas escape hatch for parachutists to exit the airborne plane had been designed on the ground without allowing enough clearance for the person plus parachute. It was not until the final phases of the design process when a person was attempting to jump from the plane that this was realized. In retrospect, this is an obvious mistake and one wonders how it could have been made. But, imagine a pressurized environment, and perhaps personnel working on a problem which involved a job, sky-diving, about which they are not familiar, and with no opportunity to see or talk with the parachutists, then this begins to make sense.

Given this scenario and many others described in Noyes (2001), it is perhaps not surprising that the formal study of human–machine interactions was channeled into the formation of a society after the Second World War. Hence, ergonomics came into prominence during the war years "in relation to equipment for the fighting services" (Editorial, 1957, p. 1). In 1949, the UK Ergonomics Research Society was formed (Edholm & Murrell, 1973). Around the same time, the US was forming the Human Factors Society. A decade later, the International Ergonomics Association was formed; it includes 42 federated Ergonomics societies from around the world.

The word, ergonomics, arises from the Greek, *ergon*, meaning work, and *nomos*, meaning natural laws; thus, ergonomics translates to the "natural laws of work." Essentially, it is the study of human–machine interactions with the emphasis being on designing for the human first and foremost, and not the machine (technology). It, thus, provides a good starting point in terms of considering work technology. The term is not new. Indeed, it has a long history, and was used as long ago as 1857 by Wojciech Jastrzebowski in his treatise entitled *An outline of ergonomics, Or the science of work* (Karwowski, 1991).

Initially, there was some resistance to the term, since it was considered ugly, incomprehensible, and easily confused with economics (Welford, 1976). This may help explain why initially the US adopted the term, human factors. Although most people in the field regard the descriptors as synonymous, ergonomics is often seen as focusing more on the physical aspects of human–machine interactions, while human factors is more concerned with the cognitive attributes. It should be noted that in 1994, the Human Factors Society became the Human Factors and Ergonomics Society; thus, both terms are now included in their name. Over the last few years, the term, cognitive ergonomics, has become increasingly popular as the cognitive issues merit separate attention from the physical and biological aspects.

In summary, ergonomics/human factors is the study of human–machine interactions. It has gained prominence and importance with the increasing use of technology, for example, space program activities in the 1950s and '60s, and computers with their transition from exclusive to more inclusive use in the 1980s and '90s.

The influence of computers

Computers and their associated computing functions have been a significant influence in the design and use of work technology. Although modern computers stem from the "analytical engine" designed by Charles Babbage in the nineteenth century, their rapid development has been post-Second World War. It is probably more than chance that this coincides with the development and growth of the discipline of ergonomics. Some milestones in the development of ergonomics and computers are summarized in table 7.1.

Table 7.1: Some milestones in the development of ergonomics and computer technologies

1937–53:	The first generation of computers.
1949:	Formation of the UK Ergonomics (Research) Society.
1953:	Formation of Gesellschaft für Arbeitswissenschaft.
1954–62:	The second generation of computers.
1957:	Formation of the US Human Factors Society.
1959:	Formation of the International Ergonomics Association.
1961:	Formation of Società Italiana di Ergonomia.
1962:	Formation of Nederlandse Vereniging voor Ergonomie.
1963:	Formation of La Société d'Ergonomie de Langue Française.
1963–72:	The third generation of computers.
1964:	Formation of La Asociación Española de Ergonomía.
1969:	Formation of the Nordic Ergonomics Society.
1972–84:	The fourth generation of computers.
1978:	Launch of the first personal computer.
1984–90:	The fifth generation of computers.
1984:	First international conference on human–computer interaction.
1988:	Formation of the Hellenic Ergonomics Society.
1990:	Formation of the World Wide Web.
1990– :	The sixth generation of computers.

The first electronic digital computers were large and cumbersome, and would fill a whole room (with a second room needed to keep the computer parts cool) (Evans, 1983). A significant point in their development was the transistor in 1948 and the so-called second generation of computers was formed. This was followed by the integrated circuit in 1964 (the third generation) and large-scale integration in the 1970s (the fourth generation of computers). Digital as opposed to mechanical or analogue computers now dominated the marketplace. The fifth generation lasted approximately from 1984 to 1990, with the aim to "solve complex problems which demand expertise and powers of reasoning when tackled by humans" (Hunt & Shelley, 1988, p. 164). However, providing computers with the capability to solve higher order problems in a similar manner to humans was a complex problem. The current development, where we are now, is the sixth generation; these are the computers with the high-tech central processing units capable of processing several instructions at once. They operate at high speeds, and require little physical space.

The development of computers since the Second World War has been immense. Since 1945, power, scalability, and economic considerations have driven computing developments, and together, these have influenced activities in the workplace. These advances have influenced the growth of computers, which in turn have had an impact on working practices. Table 7.2 summarizes some of the key changes. In the workplace, the increased functionality provided by modern computers has led to their greater use. It can be seen from the vignette at the start of the chapter that in a mere 30 years, academic working practices have radically changed. All the people involved with computers in the 1970s from the programmers to the data processors and keyboard operators were specialists. Today, we still have highly qualified people with programming skills, but the vast majority of computer users have received no formal training. Changes in the hardware and software initiated and facilitated this increasing and ubiquitous computer use. Mobile phones and music devices have mirrored these changes; technological advances in terms of scalability, power and economics have contributed to their development and increasing use.

Table 7.2: Key changes in computer use and related activities

People:	Move from relatively small numbers of specialists to large numbers of inclusive users.
Systems:	Increase in processing power, speed of operation, memory capabilities.
	Decrease in costs, size, turnaround times.
Computer hardware:	Move from large mainframes to portable laptops.
Computer software:	Move from specialist to inclusive programs.

The move from generalist to specialist users has had a major impact on the usability of human–machine interactions. Given the large numbers of the population accessing computers and technology, and their lack of formal training, the design of the interface, and in particular, its usability, has become an important consideration.

Usability

The concept of usability emerged in the early 1980s. One of the first individuals to draw attention to the concept was Emeritus Professor Brian Shackel in 1981; he has since been named "the father of usability" by the human–computer interaction community. In 1986, Shackel refined his earlier 1981 definition of usability, and suggested that in order for a system to be usable, it must meet the Learnability, Effectiveness, Attitude, Flexibility (LEAF) criteria (Shackel, 1981; 1986). He defined each of these four operational criteria and provided measures for each of them. These are shown in table 7.3. What is particular significant about Shackel's work is that he provided a quantitative measure for usability.

Table 7.3:   Definitions and measures for the LEAF criteria (Shackel, 1986)

Learnability (i.e. users must be able to learn to use the system after a certain amount of training)

Measures:

- within some specified time from installation and start of user training
- based upon some specific amount of training and user support
- within some specified relearning time (for intermittent users)

Effectiveness (i.e. a predefined proportion of target users must be able to use the system in a number of environments, within a certain time and error limits)

Measures:

- at better than some required level of performance (measured in terms of speed and errors)
- by some required percentage of the specified range of target users
- within some required proportion of the range of usage environments

Attitude (i.e. the engendering of positive attitudes towards using the system by the majority)

Measures:

- within acceptable levels of human cost in terms of tiredness
- discomfort, frustration and personal effort

Flexibility (i.e. user performance must not degrade by more than a certain percentage across tasks and environments)

Measures:

- allowing adaptation to some specified percentage variation in tasks and/or environments beyond those first specified

Prior to this, people had talked about user-friendly systems, but no one had attempted to measure it. (For this reason, usability experts now consider that user-friendly is a term used by those who have little understanding of usability.)

Shackel's work on usability spurred others to refine and redefine the definition and measures. Booth (1989) pointed out that a system could score highly on learnability, effectiveness and attitude, but still be unusable if users could not attain their chosen goals. Hence, he amended the LEAF acronym to include usefulness in place of flexibility. Eason (1984) focused on applying usability in a work environment. He developed a causal framework based on independent (user characteristics, system functions, task characteristics) and dependent variables (user reaction). These led to either a positive (i.e. good task–system match, continued user learning) or negative outcome (i.e. restricted or non-use). Eason highlighted the acid test of usability – whether or not users use the system. If users perceive that usability is inadequate or lacking, and there is an alternative means of task completion, they will take this route and not use the system. Nielsen (1993) viewed usability in terms of acceptability. He accepted Shackel and others' focus on learnability, efficiency, ease of use, and subjective considerations, but suggested that acceptability was a key aspect. This included both social and practical acceptability issues. Jordan (1998) extended the usability concept to include system potential and reusability. System potential refers to the optimal performance achievable with specific tasks while reusability concerns the level of performance attainable when a user returns to carrying out a task after a period of non-use. Recent work on usability has moved to focus on the affective characteristics (e.g. the role which emotions have in human–computer interactions), and the quality (enjoyment) of the users' perceptions of their interactions with the system (see Picard, 1997).

Usability is an important aspect of system use, and has been given much prominence in the ergonomics and human–computer literature. It has been defined by the International Organization for Standardization (ISO 9241; 1997): "the usability of a product is the degree to which specific users can achieve specific goals within a particular environment: effectively, efficiently, comfortably, and in an acceptable manner." It can be seen that the ISO definition of usability is an interesting mix of the work of Shackel, Eason, Booth, and Nielsen.

Given the practical emphasis of usability, as indicated by LEAF for example, it can be readily measured. (See an evaluation of a mobile learning organizer by Corlett, Sharples, Bull, & Chan, 2005). Accordingly, a number of questionnaires and checklists have been developed specifically to measure usability; some examples are given in table 7.4.

Although we now have a greater understanding of usability, and how to design products and evaluate them from this viewpoint, there is still a lot of work to do. Take, websites, for example. Many of these have been designed without usability in mind, and the user is subject to crowded pages, changing banners, small (hard to read) text, whilst struggling to find the information they require. Scant

Table 7.4: Assessing usability: some examples

SUS (System Usability Scale: Brooke, 1986),
QUIS (Questionnaire for User Interface Satisfaction: Chin, Diehl, & Norman, 1988),
CUSI (Computer User Satisfaction Inventory: Kirakowski & Corbett, 1988),
SUMI (Software Usability Measurement Inventory: Kirakowski & Corbett, 1993),
FACE (Fast Audit based on Cognitive Ergonomics: Hulzebosch & Jameson, 1996),
MUSiC (Measuring Usability of Software in Context: Macleod, Bowden, Bevan, &
  Curson, 1997),
WAMMI (ebsite Analysis and MeasureMent Inventory: Kirakowski & Cierlik, 1998).
MUMMS (Measuring the Usability of Multi-Media Systems: Human Factors Research
  Group at http://www.ucc.ie/hfrg/). This is a new multimedia version of the SUMI
  (developed by the same group of people).

attention is often paid to the disabled user: for example, the visually impaired person who may need larger text or the user who needs to print the page. Ahlstrom and Allendoerfer (2004) evaluated good (and not-so-good) usability characteristics of websites, and have generated a number of guidelines from this work.

The work on usability embodies the principles of ergonomics, that is, consideration of human–computer/machine interactions from a user perspective. Thus, key to this concept is user-centered design, that is, systems and workplaces are designed primarily from the perspective of the user. This is in contrast to a technology-centered or an organization-centered design approach (Stanney, Maxey, & Salvendy, 1997). Here, the dominant feature would result in the system being designed from this perspective.

A systems approach

When considering the design and use of work technology, a systems approach regards each of the components in the situation as systems in their own right. This would also extend to include the human using the technology. Hence, it is not unusual to hear mention of the "human system." In a system approach, the human is considered as yet another resource, which needs to be optimized, in order to ensure the goals of the whole operation are being met. The overall system's approach has also been termed "macro-ergonomics" (Hendricks, 1997).

The system's approach has a long history, which dates from the post Second World War years and the incorporation of technology into the workplace. In the 1950s, the term, sociotechnical systems, was used to demonstrate the need to give equal weighting to social and technical factors (Trist & Bamforth, 1951; Emery, 1959). Take, for example, designing a system where bottles needed to be filled and then packed. Glass bottling plants are noisy as the bottles move along the production line. They are also dangerous as bottles splinter and the glass shatters. Technically, there is a need to keep the line running and operations efficient. A social analysis would focus on social factors, for example, interpersonal communications between the workers. High noise levels may impinge upon workers communicating with each other, and yet, verbal communications may be an important element given the safety issues relating to this working environment. Therefore, some sort of compromise may have to be reached between the technical aspects of the bottling plant design and the needs and requirements of the workers.

Prior to the sociotechnical systems approach, the emphasis had tended to be on the design of the workplace from the point of view of the technology. During the industrial revolution of the nineteenth century, the human had been the expendable bit in the system; if a worker was injured or killed, there was always another available to fill their place. In the heavy industries of coal, steel, and iron, health and safety regulations were scant in comparison to today's legislation. The approach taken at this time was one of "FMJ – fitting the Man to the job." This is an anathema to the ergonomic approach of "FJM – fitting the job to the Man" (Rodger & Cavanagh, 1962).

The late Albert Cherns (1976; 1987) was well-known for his work on sociotechnical theory. In order to provide a flavor of some of his recommendations, table 7.5 lists some with specific reference to the bottling plant example.

Table 7.5: Sociotechnical theory applied to a bottling plant

1. Worker roles should be multifunctional and multiskilled, that is, workers should not be required to carry out the same task on the bottling production line.
2. Redesign should be continuous, that is, all systems are dynamic and undergoing changes; therefore workers' tasks should be continually reviewed as the technical aspects change.
3. Methods of working should be minimally specified, that is, leave workers some autonomy to decide how best to work the plant.
4. Resources should be available to those authorized to access them, that is, another example of giving the workers autonomy and trust.
5. Disruptions to the work processes for example unavoidable delays/breakdowns product changes should be handling at source, that is, as close to the plant as possible. This keeps workers informed and again gives them some autonomy.

Within the system's approach is a further layer of analysis since systems can be considered from a number of different perspectives. Noyes and Baber (1999), for example, adopted a four-level description, namely, physical, operational, social, and environmental (and abbreviated to POSE). Thus, the design of the systems comprising a particular work situation could be considered from these four aspects. If we take, as an example, a computer system, we can consider this in terms of its physical characteristics, for example, the hardware comprising the motherboard circuitry, microchips, the keyboard and mouse, display screen, printer, and perhaps other input/output devices and peripherals. Operational descriptions would include the software from the machine code to the compilers and various computer programs and packages. The social description would

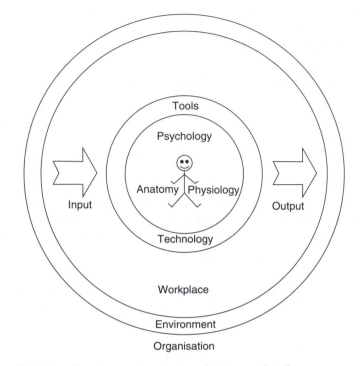

Figure 7.1: Overview of system components and the many interfaces

include the extent to which the computer allows various goals to be achieved, and engenders social interactions while the environmental level would include the workplace and organization in which the particular system is being used.

The POSE descriptions could also be applied to the human system. Physical characteristics include the anthropometry, biomechanics and physiology of the human, while the operational stem from the cognitive aspects. These include the higher order processes such as thinking, decision-making, problem-solving, and creativity. The social aspect is perhaps easier to describe for the human than the computer system since humans are regarded as "social animals." It would include the social activities relating to the human, for example, the effects of group interactions and team-working. This could also be extended to include the organization. Finally, the environmental factors relate to the specific workplace/environment in which the human is operating.

These component systems all lie within the overall system, and hence, they have a number of interfaces with each other. It can be seen in figure 7.1 that a key interface is the human–machine/technology interface. Certainly, human–computer interaction has attracted the most interest in the workplace and research literature. This is due to the increasing use of computers and computer-related technologies as already highlighted, and is evident from the rise in interest in human–computer interaction and associated publications, for example, usability.

Allocation of function

When designing systems, one of the key decisions concerns which parts of the task are to be carried out by the technology and which by the human. This has become known as "allocation of function." It was defined by Sharit (1997) as the sharing of tasks between the humans and machines in a system, and is viewed as being the core of the design and use of technology (Clegg, Gray, & Waterson, 2000).

Clegg et al. (2000, p. 240) stated that allocation of function was an "outdated term." This was because it does not have an obvious meaning; this opaqueness was due to the word, function. Clegg et al. suggested replacing the term with "sociotechnical allocation" (STA). The benefit of using STA for allocation of function is that it includes reference to the social/organizational issues. This is important as people have a need to work, and this consideration may not fit with a classic allocation of function approach. Take, for example, toll-collecting to cross a bridge or leave a car park. This task can be totally automated with coins or magnetic strips, or carried out manually by an attendant. One consideration might therefore be the creation of a job for a human. An alternate solution, which happens with a suspension bridge in Bristol, UK, is to have automatic barrier operation apart from in the rush hour. When the traffic is heavy, the tolls are collected manually and the barriers remain raised.

In the post-Second World War years, the trend was to automate as much as possible of the system operations. As Bainbridge (1987, p. 271) pointed out "the classic aim of automation is to replace human manual control." Tasks, which could not be automated, were allocated to the humans. This "left-over approach" had a number of drawbacks; the most obvious one being that the human was then left to do the tasks which were impossible for the machine. Correspondingly, complex tasks for the technology would also prove to be difficult for the human operator.

This so-called "left-over approach" was superseded by the "compensatory approach," which was based on the work of Paul Fitts (Fitts, 1951). He considered a number of functions or activities in terms of human and machines. This later became known as the MABA–MABA ("men are better at–machines are better at") list (Moray, 1999). An example of a Fitts list is given in Table 6.

The Fitts' list has become well-known in the allocation of function arena. However, as Sheridan (2000, p. 203) noted, people have referred to Fitts list as "a kind of gospel" for allocation of function. It is not thought to have been Fitts intention for the list to be considered in this way or to be viewed and used as a scientific basis for allocating tasks to humans and machines. Implicit in MABA–MABA is that humans and machines need to be compared at some level, and this also has to be questioned. With this in mind, table 7.7 presents some of the shortcomings of the list approach.

Although the dominant philosophy in allocation of function up until the 1970s was to automate as much as possible, this has not been the case since then. More

Table 7.6: Example of a Fitts' List approach

Function	Humans	Machines
Speed	Can work fast for short bursts, limited reaction times, comparatively slow, for example, measured in seconds	Can work fast for long periods of time, much faster reaction times, for example, up to the speed of light
Accuracy	Can be extremely accurate, but again difficult to sustain over periods of time	Can maintain high standards of accuracy over long periods of time
Repetitive actions	Soon tire, subject to learning, fatigue and boredom	Excellent at repeating actions in a consistent manner
Attention span	Poor, especially when required to sustain attention over long periods	Not an issue – if programmed to monitor, will continue to do this *ad infinitum*
Perceptual skills	Excellent especially at pattern detection and interpretation	Poor (unable, for example, to carry out simple tasks such as edge detection)
Memory	Selective, impressive in that unprompted instant retrieval of items is possible, not always reliable, versatile and innovative	Completely reliable in that all items stored in memory can be quickly accessed, limited (but extremely large) capacity, formal structure
Decision-making	Tend to use heuristics ("rules of thumb"), good at inductive reasoning when need to draw on past experience	Rule-based approach, good at deductive reasoning, poor in new situations
Intelligence	Excellent	Limited

Source: Noyes (2001).

Table 7.7: Some shortcomings of the "list" approach to allocation of function

1. Some functions have to be performed by humans because machines cannot do them, and *vice versa*.
2. There will be some functions where allocation is not obvious, that is, they might be carried out by humans or machines or both.
3. It implies that tasks which machines do well need to be assigned to them leaving the remainder for the humans.
4. Direct comparison of attributes suggests that machines and people have opposite capacities. Obviously, this is not the case.
5. Some functions must always be performed by the human operator, for example, abort control.
6. Some functions may be allocated to the humans in order to make their jobs more interesting.
7. Technology changes faster than the Lists.
8. It does not cover all the reasons why the human may be allocated a "machine" function.
9. Being skilled at a task is only one facet/dimension.
10. Humans have a need to work and feel valued.
11. They are also unique in that they have an emotional component.
12. Humans may have a preference to interact with other humans rather than machines.

Source: Noyes (2001).

recently, a complementary approach has taken precedence. Here, humans and machines are viewed in a symbiotic relationship where they work in conjunction and cooperation with each other. There is a need for flexibility in allocation of function, and the complementary approach allows for this. However, allocation of function/STA is a particularly difficult problem in the design and use of work technology, and there are no straightforward solutions.

One of the major problems is that design is a pluralistic activity with lots of stakeholders with knowledge and expertise. Accordingly, no one person fully understands all the processes, perspectives, etc. Clegg et al. (2000) argued that a lot of attention has been paid to job design and work organization, but relatively little to allocation of function. They viewed the latter as central to the design of systems, and therefore, it should not be overlooked as they thought was currently the case. In terms of a solution, they suggested that the emphasis should shift from working out how to find ways of engaging end-users in design to locating a way of getting the stakeholders and individuals involved in the design and working with the users in the design process. Fuld (1997) provided many practical methods and concrete ways (e.g., design principles, criteria, checklists, good practice) for dealing with the large number of people involved in the design process.

A further breakthrough might arise from having a flexible system where jobs and tasks move between humans and machines. Highly automated systems are designed to overcome human weaknesses, for example, humans are inconsistent, unreliable, and tire easily, but Clegg et al. (2000) argued that this flexibility and ability to adapt may in fact be the reason why highly automated systems work. Norman (1998) summed this up by stating that it all depends whether a human or machine-centered approach is taken. In a machine approach, humans are the weak link, for example, inconsistent, unreliable, etc., but when taking a human-centered approach, humans are viewed in a positive light. Their so-called weaknesses then become strengths as they adapt and modify their behavior to the situation. The key here would be to know under what circumstances work should be allocated to humans and under which circumstances it should be allocated to machines. Kaber and Endsley (2004), for example, developed a taxonomy with 10 levels of automation ranging from manual control to full automation for four different human/computer tasks (monitoring, generating, selecting, implementing). This provides a starting point for allocation of function in a dynamic control task. However, they suggested that situation awareness, workload, and trust/confidence in the system would also be relevant human performance indices for helping decide about function allocation. Further, account should be taken of normal and abnormal (i.e. failure) conditions.

Operation under normal or abnormal situations raises an important point with regard to allocation of function and its success. Take, for example, flying an aircraft. The avionics systems with their capability of being able to monitor and make adjustments to the flight path in milliseconds are far superior to humans, who are temporally limited by the time taken in cognitive processing and the physical length of their nervous system when making a response. In terms of allocation of function, controlling the plane under normal conditions by the computer systems is thus far superior. However, this may change under abnormal conditions, when the human is able to use past experience and knowledge as well as inductive reasoning to diagnose and rectify a problem.

Allocation of function is a difficult and complex problem, which may be why it has elicited so much interest and discussion. An underlying theme relates to human error. One of the reasons why the compensatory approach replaced the left-over approach concerned the human making errors. Logically, if the most difficult tasks for the machines are going to be left for humans to carry out, then these are likely to become sources of error. Implicit in the "automate as much as possible" approach is the need to keep the human away from the system and thus, prevent the opportunity for making errors. Thus, the concept of error-resistant systems was developed in the 1970s and 1980s with systems being designed on the principle of the human operator not making errors. As with the compensatory approach, the error-resistant philosophy has been replaced now with error-tolerance. Today, advanced and complex technological systems are designed in the knowledge that human behavior will result in unintended and unwanted actions.

Human error

Humans make errors. Most of these are inconsequential and amount to nothing, and some, the so-called near miss errors, can be beneficial. Experiencing a near miss situation, for example, driving a car and realizing a particular piece of road is poor for overtaking, means that we often learn and avoid that situation next time around. Hence, nearly making an error becomes a positive event in that it prevents us making the error on a later occasion. A few errors will lead to disastrous results, although accident analyses indicate that very rarely is one error the cause of an accident. Accidents nearly always have many causes. Some of these will happen at the time of the accident and some will have been "in the system" for a period of time. Reason (1990) using a medical analogy referred to these as resident pathogens. Examples might include an organization having a poor safety reporting culture. This in itself may not be a problem, but it is when combined with other situations. When the car ferry, the Herald of Free Enterprise, capsized in the English Channel in March 1987 with considerable loss of life, there were a number of factors feeding into that situation. One of these was the poor safety culture onboard the cross-channel ferries at that time, and the view that if "it's not my job, I won't do it," even when the safety of the passengers and crew was at stake.

Many organizations especially those which have a safety element, for example, transport and medicine, are highly concerned about human making errors. Errors can arise because of internal and external performance shaping factors. The former relates to the individual and would include factors such as low motivation to complete the task correctly, tiredness, inexperience, etc. External factors relate to the design and characteristics of the technology, the workplace, the environment and the organization. It is generally accepted that more errors arise due to external than internal performance shaping factors. The concept of system design induced errors has existed since the 1980s, where it is thought the human makes errors because of the poor design of a particular system. For example, on the civil flight deck, identical switches positioned side by side but with different functions can easily be confused.

One view of why people make errors concerns mental representations or models. When we use an object, we build up a mental representation of how it works. Errors will arise when the user's mental representation of how something works does not match the designers'. For example, when I learn to drive a car, I build a mental representation of how I think the vehicle is working. This may be very crude, and even inaccurate, but it allows me to maneuver and drive the car with some degree of success. It may fail however, if I have serious mechanical problems which need rectification. If my mental representation or model of how the car is operating is very different from the designers and auto-engineers, this will create problems for me. These mental representations evolve inductively as the user interacts with the system and are thought to be an important part of safe operation.

There are many ways to address the issue of error in organizations. Error-tolerant systems which allow the person to make and then retract a possible mistake are one approach. Techniques such as built-in redundancy of actions, graceful degradation of systems, and reversion back-ups, to name but a few, can all be employed. Open reporting systems are also useful in that they allow the organization to work out where the errors are occurring. Employees are asked to report mistakes which they have made in the knowledge that no action will be taken against them. However, if unreported mistakes are subsequently discovered, action will be taken against the person involved. Finally, recruitment and training have a role to place in shaping people's performance in the workplace.

Summary

When considering the design and use of work technology, humans are forever present from the very beginnings to the very end of the process. The development of computers and associated technologies has had a major influence on both work and home practices. This is evident from the growth of ergonomics and the work on usability; however, some difficult issues still remain. One of these is allocation of function and how best to distribute the jobs and tasks between humans and machines. The continuing possibilities associated with automation and more complex technologies mean that this issue has not been resolved. Likewise, the design of error-tolerant systems poses a similar challenge for the next decade.

Discussion Points

What are the basic premises for the assessment of usability?
How can allocation of function be achieved?

Key Studies

Shackel, B. (1986). Ergonomics in design for usability. In M. D. Harrison and A. F. Monk (Eds.), *Proceedings of the 2nd conference of the BCS HCI Specialist Group*. Cambridge, UK: Cambridge University Press.

Sheridan, T. B. (2000). Function allocation: Algorithm, alchemy or apostasy? *International Journal of Human–Computer Studies*, 52, 203–16.

Further Reading

Jordan, P. W. (1998). *An introduction to usability*. London: Taylor & Francis. This book provides a good introductory text to usability, as the title suggests, and covers concepts and definitions of usability, principles of design, and advantages and disadvantages of methods for usability evaluation.

Noyes, J. M. (2001). *Designing for humans*. Chichester, UK: Psychology Press. This book was written to address the ergonomics/human factors requirements of the British Psychological Society Master's syllabus for Occupational Psychology, and provides good coverage of human–machine interaction and the design of environments at work.

Noyes, J. M. (2004). The human factors toolkit. In C. Sandom and R. S. Harvey (Eds.), *Human factors for engineers* (pp. 57–79). London: IEE. This chapter provides an up-to-date overview of ergonomics/human factors tools and methods.

Special Issue on Allocation of function: *International Journal of Human–Computer Studies*, 2000, 52. This special issue comprises 10 papers compiled by leading researchers in the area of allocation of function.

Research Close-Up

Bainbridge, L. (1987). Ironies of automation. In J. Rasmussen, K. Duncan, & J. Leplat (Eds.), *New Technology and Human Error*. Chichester, UK: John Wiley & Sons.

Introduction

Irony can be defined as an outcome which is the direct opposite of what might be expected. The automation of systems results in the replacement of manual control activities carried out by the human being conducted automatically. However, one of the ironies is that humans still have a primary role in system operation. They design, develop, supervise, adjust, maintain and decommission the systems. Therefore, it is not possible to separate humans from the automation. Further, the designer may view the operator as unreliable and inefficient, and so should be eliminated from the system. There are two ironies to this. One, designer errors may be a major source of operating problems, and two, the designer who tries to eliminate the operator still leaves the human to do the tasks which the automation cannot.

There are two categories of task left for the operator in an automated task: monitoring of systems activities, and engaging in remedial actions when the automation fails, for example, calling a more experienced person or taking over. Manual control skills are needed to take over and stabilize the process, and fault diagnosis and subsequent actions, for example, shutdown or recovery, require cognitive skills.

One irony is that the automatic control system has been installed because it can do the job better than the human operator, and yet, the human is being asked to monitor that it is working effectively. In complex modes of system operation, the knowledge required may be considerable, and may only be acquired with specialist training. A further difficulty is that if decisions can be fully specified, then a computer may be able to make them more quickly taking into account more dimensions and criteria than a human can. However, it is not possible in real time that the computer is following the rules correctly. Therefore, the human operator can only monitor the system's decisions at some meta-level to decide if they are appropriate. This becomes impossible to do when the system is making decisions because human judgment and intuitive reasoning are not deemed adequate in this context.

A further aspect relates to operator attitudes. Operators often prefer to work in manual mode; this allows them to acquire and maintain their skills, and there are obvious advantages when system breakdowns occur. The alternative to the system operating in manual mode results in the operator having a monitoring role. This deskilling is often difficult for workers, and can lead to ironies of incongruous pay differentials, where deskilled workers have higher pay levels largely unrelated to job content.

Approaches to solutions

Monitoring

In low probability event monitoring, the operator(s) must be given artificial assistance, for example, alarms, displays showing target values and tolerances. Decisions made by the system should be carried out at a rate which the operator can follow. This is suggested even when this is not the most efficient method technically.

Working storage

When shutdown is simple and low cost, it should be carried out automatically. Manual shutdown may be useful when the system can be safely shut down for a few minutes to allow the operators some thinking time to work out what is happening and what to do. Problems arise when this is not possible and the system needs to be stabilized, for example, an aircraft in the air. For very fast failures (within a few seconds), online working storage would be useless. Reliable automatic response is needed in this situation; if this is not possible, the system should not be built as the costs of failure are unacceptable.

Continued

Long-term knowledge

It can be important to maintain manual skills. This can be achieved by including a manual session in every shift and/or frequent simulator practice. However, unknown faults cannot be simulated. Training must therefore be concerned with general strategies rather than specific responses. The irony is that it may be that it is the most successful automated systems with rare need for manual intervention, which may need the most investment in terms of training.

Man–computer collaboration

Methods of man–computer collaboration need to be further developed. Humans will always have a substantial involvement with automated systems and a "Fitts list" approach is not enough.

Instructions and advice

It is inappropriate for the human to receive instructions from the computer; if this is the case, the computer could readily activate a more reliable, other computer.

Mitigating human error

There are a number of machine possibilities for counteracting human error. These range from simple hardware interlocks to complex online computation. It is probably most appropriate to place "checks" on the actions of the operator.

Software generated displays

Soft displays offer many possibilities in terms of matching operator skill levels. It is recognized that operator skill levels will not fall on a simple continuum, and working under time pressure brings a special set of problems.

Reducing human workload

Computers can help reduce human workload by simplifying the operator's decisions or taking over some of the decision making. The operators' perception of the computers' capabilities is an important consideration. Studies have shown that when loads are light, people are content to let the computers do the work, but when loads are heavy, human operators took over from the computers. Hence, computer aiding is a multidimensional problem.

Conclusion

Humans can be impressive problem solvers particularly when not under time pressure. The irony is that automation does not remove the underlying difficulties: resolution of these will require greater technological ingenuity than classic automation.

Demanding Work, Technology, and Human Performance

8

Andrew J. Tattersall and
G. Robert J. Hockey

Overview

The primary requirement of all work is that employees carry out set tasks. The quality of performance on these tasks has a major and obvious significance for productivity, but also for outcomes such as safety, personal health, and well-being. Increasingly, appraisals of personal performance are used as the main criterion of employees' effectiveness and motivation, underpinning recognition and reward schemes. It is therefore important to understand how the achievement of satisfactory performance levels may be compromised by the conditions under which we work.

Work environments vary considerably. Some jobs (nursing, teaching, air traffic control, social work) are recognized as being demanding in a very general way, while others (computer operators, lorry driving, forestry work, accountancy) make more specific demands on employees. In some job roles, such as those in large offices, factories, and call centers, the flow of work is determined largely by managers and supervisors. In others (hospitals, schools, and universities) there may be more individual control over how tasks are conducted. Some employees work in air-conditioned, sound-attenuated offices. Others have a constant background of loud unpredictable noises, or highly variable levels of heat and cold, all of which can affect the efficiency of work (Broadbent, 1971; Hockey, 1986; Poulton, 1970). Some people work in large groups, as in open plan offices or factory assembly lines; others largely on their own. There are also differences in the scheduling of work. The expectation of 24-hour services and the desire for flexible working have meant an inevitable extension of the working day well beyond the traditional boundaries of a nine-to-five working day (which, at the beginning of the twenty-first century, now describes the schedule of only around a third of UK employees). Many have to work shifts, including nights, which usually means losing sleep and having severely curtailed lives outside of work.

In addition to these differences between the conditions of work, it is also clear that the nature of work itself has changed considerably, even over the past 20 or 30 years. The widespread introduction and acceptance of computer systems at all levels of employment has meant a reduction in physical demands and a corresponding incease in mental demands, not only in office-type work environments, but across most types of job. This may be seen as part of a long-continuing process of the increasing automation of human work since the industrial revolution (e.g., Chmiel 1998; McLoughlin & Clark, 1994), in which, in succession, the need to use physical power, then specific task functions, and finally information and control have been removed from the human and provided instead by machine-based systems. McLoughlin and Clark (1994) propose that the net effect of technological change is that the nature of work has shifted from physical towards mental labor.

With this context of predominantly mentally demanding work in mind, the present chapter considers the impact on the performance of human operators of the threat posed by high levels of workload and environmental stress, and the develoment of costs such as high effort and fatigue in individuals in their attempts to manage such conditions. Recent approaches to such problems (see Hockey, Gaillard, & Burov, 2003) have used the broad label of "operator functional state," implying an adaptive, transactional basis for the relationship between individuals and the environment. It also assumes that individuals have choices about how to interpret and deal with environmental factors that threaten performance goals (an assumption which, of course, applies equally to nonwork activities), and that different strategies give rise to distinctive patterns of performance and costs.

Workload

First, what do we mean by the term "workload"? Although commonly used in discussions about work, most people would find it difficult to give a clear definition. Some might talk about simply being busy or having too many things to do. Others may give a specific example – meeting a deadline, such as preparing a presentation. Yet others may focus on the experience of time pressure, the effort to plan and think about the work, concern over the quality of the work, or emotional outcomes such as anxiety, dissatisfaction or depression. Essentially, workload needs to be understood as a multidimensional construct (Damos, 1991; Gopher & Donchin, 1986), not defined by objective level of demand or task difficulty alone. To understand the full extent of the implications of the interaction between people and their work we need to consider not only objective task and environmental demands, but also the functional state of individuals, the resources available to them to support their efforts and their task goals.

Managing the costs of work

A simple definition, but one which captures the essence of the problem, is that workload can be conceptualized as the costs that human operators incur in performing tasks (Kramer, 1991). Although rather broad, such a view emphasizes the negative consequences of workload, resulting from demands that are too high, or even too low, and contributing not only to strain but to boredom and inattention. Costs may be observed in terms of performance, bodily state, well-being, safety, and even health. Managing workload may incur costs even under normal operating conditions. What this definition does not address is the transactional nature of workload (e.g., Gopher & Donchin, 1986; Hockey, 1993, 2005). If performance on a demanding task is below the level set by either the operator or their manager, we cannot assume that the operator is "overloaded," and cannot work harder to achieve these goals. An alternative is that they may not be sufficiently motivated to maintain the high level of effort required for satisfactory performance, for example due to a lack of awareness of the importance of the operating goals, or the result of protecting resources for dealing with future events. Suboptimal levels of individual physiological or emotional state caused by illness or environmental conditions may also result in impaired performance.

The central theoretical element of this approach is that effective work requires people to make decisions about how to manage their environment. What are their priorities for task and other goals? How willing (and able) are they to make a sustained effort to maintain required performance standards under difficult circumstances? In work situations, operators may compensate for increases in task demands by increasing the amount of effort invested in the task (Kahneman, 1973; Norman & Bobrow, 1975). In such cases, observed performance levels may remain constant while the operator experiences increased workload in the form of subjective strain. Conversely, a reduction in the level of performance may occur either because operators cannot maintain the level of effort expenditure required, or because they lower their criteria for adequate performance.

High levels of workload and difficult work conditions are typically associated with the experience of strain. However, this does not appear to be caused by direct activation of physiological mechanisms by stressors. Rather, the perception of threat to performance gives rise to tension through a disturbance of the relationship between goals and actions, that needs to be resolved by appropriate coping activity (Hockey, 2005; Hockey & Hamilton, 1983; Schönpflug, 1983). Specifically, if the goal is important enough, this means using a high effort mode of response to overcome the problem and preserve performance. The treatment of performance in this chapter recognizes the intimate relationship between the required outcomes of work and the adaptive, self-regulatory processes underlying all human–environmental interaction.

It is clear that humans are required to satisfy many different goals at different times. This means that switches between goals over time are not only common, but necessary features of work (see Hockey, 2005). At times, however, there is a need to focus on a specific task, allowing for (a) important goals to be maintained over long periods, and (b) behavior to continue to be adjusted (speeded up, made more accurate) in response any detected discrepancy. If maintaining goal orientation involves overcoming natural tendencies to switch to other goals, this ought to be reflected in costs of regulatory activity, and this is supported by research on coping and behavior control (Cohen, Evans, Krantz, & Stokols, 1986; Frankenhaeuser, 1986; Hockey, 1997, 2005; Schönpflug, 1983). Attempts to maintain performance standards under difficult or demanding conditions is effortful, and involves increased activity of bodily systems involved in stress and response to challenge. Coping with stress at work attracts costs, not only when it fails, but when it succeeds in resolving disruptions in planning and goal-oriented performance.

Performance protection

One of the most surprising findings of research on human performance under environmental demand is that the effectiveness of primary task actions is typically very high (Hockey, 1993, 1997, 2002; Kahneman, 1971, 1973): key performance aspects may be said to be *protected*. This is particularly true of tasks based on classical industrial activities, such as vigilance (monitoring and inspection activities), tracking (manual control of all kinds), and sequential responding (underlying the kind of complex perceptual motor skills found in many office tasks). Where decrements are found, they are usually not serious, have minimal practical implications, and are actively managed. In general, the management of performance under stress and high demand may be said to exhibit a "graceful degradation" (Navon & Gopher, 1979), rather than a catastrophic collapse.

One intriguing observation is that, where decrements do occur, they are more likely to be in laboratory studies than in real-life work situations. Although the reasons for this have not been formally studied, it is likely to be because of the greater motivation and commitment to performance protection in real life tasks (Hockey, 2005). Unlike laboratory tasks, the real-life context of work encourages the maintenance of task goals, and the use of sustained levels of effort, if required. Because work tasks are usually carried out well within the capacity of the individual (no one works flat out all the time – if at all), there is usually spare capacity to respond to increased demands, within the "effort budget."

The role of regulatory processes in the transactions between people and working environments is a central feature in the compensatory control model developed by Hockey and colleagues (e.g., Hockey, 1993, 1997; Hockey & Hamilton, 1983; Hockey, Briner, Tattersall, & Wiethoff, 1989; Hockey, Wastell & Sauer, 1998), developed to account for these observations of minimal decrement under high demand. A key feature is that performance protection typically involves an increase in effort, observable through its impact on physiological activation processes. For example, Lundberg & Frankenhaeuser (1978) found that increases in adrenaline and effort occurred when performance was protected under noise, but not when performance was impaired. We do not have space here for a detailed presentation of this framework, but it will be helpful to summarize the main points, as they relate to workload management issues.

Modes of Workload Management

The central feature of the compensatory model is the identification of three kinds of workload management strategy: engaged, disengaged and strain, characterized by distinctive patterns of trade-off between performance protection and costs (table 8.1). We first discuss these in relation to the model, then consider implications for differences in workload management observed in the workplace.

Engaged

Engagement involves the application of direct (high effort) coping within the limits of planned effort expenditure. Increased effort allows performance to be protected under demands from unexpected difficulties, periods of time pressure or additional stress conditions, but the engaged mode is generally manageable, since it is allows periods of routine activity, and does not exceed the individual's capabilities. It may be considered a standard feature of any complex mental work, especially where employees are actively involved in their task and "working well." It corresponds to Frankenhaeuser's (1986) description of "challenge" situations ("effort without distress"), and is characterized by feelings of enthusiasm and elation – of having had a "good day." It also involves increases in catecholamines (adrenaline and noradrenaline), but not cortisol. Regulatory problems occur primarily when external demands are greater than expected, so that they exceed current levels of effort. There is evidence that subjective limits for maximum effort expenditure are relatively conservative, even for physical tasks (Holding, 1983), so that increases beyond the set "maximum" are possible. Nevertheless, operating

Table 8.1:   Patterns of demand management under stress

Mode	Coping States	Performance	Psychophysiological state*
Engaged	Effort without distress	High	Increased A/NA; reduced C; High alertness
Disengaged	Distress without effort	Unacceptable	Little change, except where criticism or guilt involved (increased C, anxiety, depression)
Strain	Effort with distress	Acceptable	Increased A/NA/C; Increased anxiety/fatigue; Spill-over after work

* A = adrenaline, NA = noradrenaline, C = cortisol.

at a very high level for any length of time is likely to be uncomfortable, and impose considerable strain, giving rise to fatigue (Hockey et al., 1989; Hockey & Meijman, 1998). Two control options are available in such circumstances, referred to here as the disengaged and strain patterns.

Disengaged

The disengaged mode involves a reduced commitment to work goals. It may be achieved by reducing required levels of accuracy or speed, by adopting strategies which make less of a demand on limited resources such as working memory, or by neglecting secondary activities. In some cases, individuals may disengage completely from task goals, especially when an attempt at direct coping has little effect (Schultz & Schönpflug, 1982). This would be unusual (though not unheard of) in work contexts, though it is a common adaptive response in less constrained leisure activities. It corresponds to Frankenhaeuser's (1986) "distress without effort" mode of coping, with low levels of catecholamines, but high levels of cortisol, and anxious and depressed feelings. While such a strategy helps to combat stress from work overload, it may have unfortunate side effects. Apart from the reduced performance on the job, there may be a detrimental impact on job-related mental health. Employees may feel depressed or worried that they have not done as much work as they should, or concerned that they may have to make up the shortfall the next day. This is not a problem for the occasional use of such strategies (e.g., to combat sudden fatigue), but may lead to major problems if indirect coping was employed on a regular basis.

Strain

The strain mode is perhaps the most interesting from the point of view of work stress and adaptive behavior. It is characterized as a striving or struggle to overcome environmental demands in order to maintain task goals. It is assumed that striving effectively increases resources by drawing on the energy mobilization capabilities of the system (Kahneman, 1973). Considered as a voluntary process, striving demonstrates a willingness to sustain an aversive strain state, corresponding to Frankenhaeuser's "effort with distress." At the end of a high-strain work day employees feel tense and weary, and have increased levels of both catecholamines and cortisol. There are also likely to be spill-over effects in the period following work, affecting the ability to relax or sleep. Cropley & Millward (2004), for example, found that high-strain teachers took longer to disengage from work-related issues than low-strain teachers, finding it more difficult to stop ruminating or thinking about work or future work-related tasks.

Workload management options in the workplace

How might modes of workload management relate to everyday work contexts? Employees who generally adopt direct coping strategies as a way of managing unfavorable environmental conditions at work will be more likely to protect performance goals. They will tend to be more effective overall, completing work on time, preventing major problems developing in work situations, and maintaining a high level of quality in their output. On the other hand, they will also be more prone to any of the costs that such strategies attract (discussed in detail in the next section). For example, we may expect to see more evidence of neglect of minor work activities and cutting corners. We may also expect them to suffer more from the consequences of sustained active coping in terms of physiological and psychological strain. Although not very much is known about the effects of adopting a direct demand management style over a prolonged period, it seems likely that health status may be compromised. Problems may manifest themselves in increased incidence of minor symptoms, such as headaches, colds or indigestion, in problems of winding down after work, or in reduced well-being. It may also give rise to more serious longer-term problems, such as coronary heart disease or gastrointestinal disorders (Karasek & Theorell, 1990). In contrast, individuals with a generally indirect style of managing demands are less prone to such problems, since they maintain a more relaxed approach to their work: "If I can't get as much done, it doesn't really matter. The world's not going to end because of it. I'm not going to bust a gut to finish the work tonight." In many ways, this has to be seen as a healthy, balanced view of work in relation to the broader goals of life. However, it may sometimes lead to psychological problems, particularly those associated with a sense of failure and loss of self-esteem. Failing to complete tasks on time, at least when it happens frequently, will result in conflicts with supervisors and colleagues, and increase the emotional demands of the work environment.

Of course, some individuals appear to be able to work effectively under high demand without any obvious signs of strain. Others suffer strain effects if they make even a minimal effort to maintain work goals under stress. People may differ in various ways, apart from their general predisposition for coping directly or indirectly. These include their overall level of ability, their skill in managing stress, their orientation towards work goals (how strongly they value them), their capacity for effort expenditure, and so on. Stress tolerance is frequently cited as a reason why some people work effectively without apparent costs, but, from the control theory perspective, this may itself have at least two components: (1) a greater range of tolerance for the discrepancy between achieved and desired output (not making adjustments as a result of every small discrepancy), and (2) a more directed use of regulatory effort when it is used. Such people are efficient in managing environmental stress in the sense that they know both when and how to change their behavior, so as to stay on track without excessive effort or unnecessary tweaking. There may also be an additional effect of job skill. Being good at your job means that you can do tasks with less effort anyway, effectively increasing your reserve capacity for coping when problems arise.

Perhaps the main requirement for effective work management is "situational flexibility." Some situations respond well to active engagement. These are controllable problems, where secondary appraisal (Lazarus & Folkman, 1984) reveals the availability of suitable strategies for dealing with them. Yet, we may not wish to use this mode of coping all the time; for example, when we feel hungry, or tired from earlier coping, or have a headache. Other situations may not be controllable at all; nurses have to accept that people in their care will sometimes die, no matter how hard they try to prevent it. Process operators sometimes have to reduce production goals, in order to carry out maintenance checks. Most academics feel a need to operate occasionally as if their lives depended on getting a document finished, and all people recognize that need to work hard to get really important things done (both in and out of work): at the same time, we all have to accept that some tasks will just have to wait their turn – we can't do everything at once. The body and its energetical systems are designed for high level, responsive action – but only when "emergency conditions" apply. By its very nature, such a mechanism is not designed for regular or normal functioning. If overused it is likely to become less effective, and may lead to chronic psychological impairment, as in the phenomenon of burnout (Demerouti, Bakker, Nachreiner, & Schaufeli, 2001).

A "best practice" work management strategy may be to maintain a balance of engaged and disengaged modes (and the various shades of involvement in between), preserving the extreme active mode for special occasions and adopting less urgent responses to problems that really cannot be considered emergencies. This does not mean that one should cease to be conscientious in one's approach to work. Rather, it means redefining conscientiousness to include concern for oneself and one's health and well-being. This will provide the basis of both short-term enjoyment of work, and enhanced long term health for both the individual and the organization.

Effects of Automation

One of the strongest influences on workload is the extent to which work has been automated. Automation has been widely introduced in industrial and other processes, with the aims of producing safe, reliable, and efficient systems, and of reducing the load on the human operator. Early forms of automation were designed to reduce physical demands, replacing the need for human muscular effort by the use of hydraulic or electrical power. More recent developments have increasingly removed the need for human involvement in sensing and decision/control activity. Probably the single most influential factor in this is the remarkable advancement in computer technology. The sophistication, flexibility, availability and scope for domains of application of computers have increased dramatically in the last two decades, while the costs of implementation have fallen. It is perhaps not surprising that system designers have sought increasingly to introduce sophistication into the design of automation. In the final section of this chapter we examine the extent to which automation can influence the impact of workload on the effectiveness of operator performance.

The impact of automation on work

Wickens and Hollands (2000) proposed three fundamental reasons for automation. First, there is no alternative to automation in situations which may be hazardous or dangerous to humans or which humans cannot perform. Some diving operations, for example, may utilize remote or automated systems. The handling of toxic materials in chemical or nuclear plants may require the use of robots or complex control systems. Second, humans may not be able to perform some tasks efficiently because of high levels of workload. The use of autopilots during particular phases of flight provides an extremely useful function. Third, automation may aid or even enhance performance in tasks in which human operators may demonstrate limitations, perhaps in memory or attention. Radar advance warning systems can provide early warning of approaching aircraft or those in the vicinity. In this case, automation assists the operator by providing a better presentation of information for air traffic control.

Although we usually talk of automation as the replacement of human operations by a machine or computer, there are many different types of automation. Sheridan (1980) discussed ten levels which vary in the degree to which the human has a role in task performance and system functioning. In practice, however, although it is relatively easy to automate fully many existing tasks carried out by humans, it has proved to be much more difficult to develop new systems in which some task components are automated within human–machine systems. There is certainly now the opportunity to provide more support for human operators by providing appropriate decision-making facilities and by allowing more flexible "allocation of control" between human and automated parts of the system. Hockey, Briner, Tattersall, and Wiethoff (1989) argued that operator controllability could be enhanced by providing the operator with options relating to the use of automatic systems to aid the execution of work tasks.

However, it is now clear that automation may pose a number of problems for the human operator (Bainbridge, 1987; Hockey & Maule, 1995; Parasuraman & Riley 1997; Sarter, Woods, & Billings, 1997; Wiener, 1988). Thoughtless design may simply require the operator to perform those functions or tasks that have been unable to be automated. Even if this is not the case, there may be difficulties with operator control and skill development and maintenance. Having to control the system indirectly ("out-of-the-loop") can lead to feelings of loss of control and situation awareness, anxiety and frustration, and to impaired performance (e.g., Bainbridge, 1987; Wiener, 1985). A reduction in the use of control skills in general operations may lead to an impairment in performance when such skills are required in critical situations or following system breakdowns. It is also clear that automation does not always lead to improved performance and reduced workload (Danaher, 1980). Workload may increase under "clumsy" automation (Wiener, 1985). Metzger and Parasuraman (2005) reported improved performance and lowered workload of air traffic controllers when supported by an automated decision aid that was operating reliably. When it was less reliable, performance at detecting potential collisions was better with manual control than with automation.

Allocation of function

A key element in achieving desirable levels of safety and effectiveness is the selection of the appropriate type and degree of automation. This includes making a decision about which tasks should be allocated to the operator and which to the automated part of the system. Traditionally, task allocation has been based either on principles such as Fitts' list (Fitts, 1951; Kantowitz & Sorkin, 1987; see also chapter 7 by Noyes in this book), or simply on technological and economic constraints. Price (1985) evaluated the potential of such lists for current system design and although they provide useful suggestions for designers, they do not tend to take into account the expectations and preferences of human operators.

One solution to the problem of task allocation is offered by the recent development of *adaptive automation*. This refers to the flexible allocation of tasks or functions between the operator and the system in human–machine systems, based on some form of adaptation of the system to the individual's level of skill or current state. Such systems differ from fully automated systems and those wholly under the control of a human operator in that some or all of the task elements have the potential to be carried out by either the operator or the system itself. In comparison to more traditional automated systems in which tasks are rigidly allocated between the human and the computer, this form of adaptive control appears to have many benefits (Parasuraman & Mouloua, 1996; Rouse, 1981, 1988): workload may be maintained at a relatively constant level; system resources can be used more efficiently; it is more acceptable to operators than static automation; and, because operators have a flexible role, they will be more likely to maintain involvement and understanding of the system's state and functioning. This should lead to an enhancement of situation awareness and also prevent decay of manual control and problem-solving skills which may be required in breakdown or emergency situations (Lockhart, Strub, Hawley, & Tapia, 1993).

Shifts of control between operator and computer can be based on either explicit or implicit allocation (Tattersall & Fairclough, 2003). In the explicit mode the operator decides which tasks to carry out, and which to delegate to the computer. This is popular with operators, and also has the advantage of eliminating redundant actions by either the human or computer. Explicit allocation has been found to be effective, compared to static allocation, though only at high levels of mental workload (Tattersall & Morgan, 1997). There may also be other problems: 25 percent of operators chose never to use the opportunity to use automation; the decision to manage and allocate tasks, or to perform those under manual control, may actually increase overall workload; the operator may not always be aware of performance decrements, so not utilize the system's resources fully (Rieger & Greenstein, 1982). Although most system operators prefer explicit task allocation, implicit control has been shown to be superior in terms of overall system performance (Greenstein, Arnaut, & Revesman, 1986; Morris, Rouse, & Ward, 1988). However, it is relatively difficult to implement. Implicit control of task automation may be achieved by several means: (a) monitoring real-time performance and adapting automation according to explicit criteria which define acceptable and unacceptable regions of performance, (b) operator performance models which combine information about current system state and operator behavior to predict and automatically avoid adverse system states in the future, and (c) monitoring real-time psychophysiological signals to describe the functional state of the operator, i.e. when the presence of fatigue or stress compromises operators' capability to perform to a required or desirable standard.

The use of biocybernetics to invoke adaptive automation shows increasing potential (Fairclough & Venables, 2004, 2006; Fairclough, Venables, & Tattersall, 2005a, 2005b; Hockey et al., 2006; Prinzel, Scerbo, Freeman, & Mikulka, 1995). Physiological signals reflecting relevant brain (and autonomic) activity may act as markers of the individual's workload or strain, so that detection of such states within the course of an operational session may predict a breakdown of competence in the human element of the system. To counter this threat, markers of strain may be used as an input into an adaptive control system to trigger a shift of control from human to computer, returning control when recovery has been detected. One of the problems with the use of EEG signals to implement adaptive automation is that the present state of EEG recording technology offers few application possibilities outside laboratory or clinical environments. However, the rapid progress of current developments in wearable computers or *smart clothing* (e.g., Picard & Healey, 1997) may make this a more realistic possibility within the next decade or so.

Identifying Performance Decrement under High Workload and Strain

In this section we consider the detailed techniques that can be used to identify the consequences of workload management options for individuals and organizations and allow us to assess both short-term (acute) effects and the longer-term consequences for both performance and well-being. These might involve the use of performance measures of both primary and secondary tasks (defined in terms of level of priority and relevance to overall task goals), and measures of both subjective and physiological costs. An effective methodology would require the use of several of these methods in harness, since similar changes in performance may have different origins. For example, impaired primary task performance may be caused by current task overload, loss of task priorities, preexisting fatigue, reduced motivation, and so on. Measurement of at least primary task, secondary task and some measure of costs is required to disambiguate these explanations.

Recognition of the possibility of trade-off between task goals and other (nontask) goals is central to an understanding of performance changes under stress and high workload. Thus primary task decrements are regarded as only one of a number of techniques for detecting differential demands of tasks (e.g., Damos, 1991; O'Donnell & Eggemeier, 1986; Hancock & Meshkati, 1988). Effects of high workload can also be observed indirectly, through secondary task performance, strategy changes, after effects, subjective reactions and physiological changes. These effects (or costs) are referred to by Hockey (1997, 2005) as latent decrements, since their effects may often be masked because of performance protection. However, they imply a reduced capacity for further adaptive response (e.g., to unexpected events or emergencies), and leave a smaller safety margin for response. In this section we identify the markers of decrement in demanding work under the threat of disruption from both high workload and stress.

Primary task decrements

In most jobs some tasks are primary (central and afforded high priority), while others may be considered as secondary, having less impact on overall task goals. Under many conditions it is clear that primary task goals can be satisfactorily maintained, either by reconfiguration of remaining resources (allowing occasional errors or delays to occur in secondary tasks), or by the recruitment of additional resources. Where primary task errors do occur, they may sometimes be easy to obtain; for example, measuring a pilot's deviation from appropriate levels of speed and flight path during take off or landing. However, in other situations, such as air traffic control, teaching, or nursing it is difficult to generate a simple measure of an individual's level of performance (e.g., speed, accuracy, or errors and slips of action). Suitable measures are thus not easily transferable from one situation to another. More often the problem is that effects of workload may be underestimated, either because primary task measures may not be immediately sensitive to the effects of changes in task load or working procedures; or as a result of performance protection – the compensatory effort that operators typically apply to cope with additional demands. Thus, only a crude indication may be obtained of the cumulative effect of sustained and high task demands on primary task measures.

Secondary task decrements

Secondary task measures may be more sensitive to changes in workload or stress than primary task measures, because performance on secondary, less important, tasks is less likely to be protected. Secondary task decrements are commonly observed in workload paradigms, and provide an indirect measure of increasing load on primary tasks. Examples of widely-used secondary tasks include memory search, choice reaction time, time estimation and mental arithmetic (O'Donnell & Eggemeier, 1986; Wickens & Hollands, 2000). However, unless the allocation of information processing resources to the two tasks is controlled, it can be difficult to interpret such effects. Careful design of tasks is necessary to prevent intrusion or structural interference with the primary task. That is, the introduction of the secondary task should not result in primary task decrements simply because the operator is required to make similar manual control actions at the same time or monitor two physically distinct displays at once. Used appropriately, they have the potential to be both sensitive and diagnostic.

One of the best-documented forms of secondary task decrement under stress is the narrowing (or funneling) of attention found in spatially complex tasks. For example, Hockey (1970) found that a central pursuit tracking task was unaffected by noise, while detection of peripheral signals was impaired. Such effects have been found under both laboratory and field conditions, and for a wide range of environmental conditions – e.g., noise, anxiety associated with deep sea diving, threat of shock, fatigue (see Baddeley, 1972; Broadbent, 1971; Hockey, 1979).

To overcome problems of intrusiveness, it is sometimes possible to use tasks that are already part of the system being evaluated. Such embedded tasks (Shingledecker, 1987) might involve measuring response times to certain communications, signals or events. Some jobs (e.g., medical monitoring) require regular checks to be made of the status of certain parts of the system. In other occupations it is more difficult to incorporate or devise such tasks. An effective alternative to real life tasks is to use simulations, where embedded tasks can be designed into the system. For example, Hockey et al. (1998) found effects of sleep deprivation on two embedded tasks (responding to alarms, and checking system values) where the primary control task of maintaining system variables within limits showed no sign of impairment.

Strategy changes

While primary task measures may not show impairment, it may sometimes be possible to detect a shift to a simpler or less demanding strategy. For example, more time can be allocated to important elements by reducing the time spent on fringe activities. Strategic changes may also involve a shift to less resource-intensive modes of task control, reducing dependency on demanding processes such as working memory. It has been known for some time that under periods of difficulty or stress, process operators may abandon the open-loop control characteristic of skilled performance (where sequences of actions are carried out without waiting for feedback) in favor of a simpler closed loop (feedback-based) mode (Bainbridge, 1978; Umbers, 1979). Open-loop strategies involve a greater degree of planning and require a broader understanding of system processes. Air traffic controllers, also, have been found to vary their strategies according to task demand, taking fewer variables into account with increasing traffic load (Sperandio, 1978). Similarly, Bainbridge (1974) found that process operators under time pressure used faster but less accurate methods of finding data values. Chmiel, Totterdell, and Folkard (1995) found that following one night's sleep loss and several hours performing an adaptive control task, performance quality could be maintained but the work was carried out more slowly, particularly towards the end of a 1.5 hr work session. In the simulation study mentioned above (Hockey et al., 1998), sleep-deprived operators engaged less in monitoring system parameters, which help in the anticipation of developing problems, and relied more on correcting the system by all-or-nothing manual interventions, triggered by alarms whenever parameters went slightly out of range.

Strategy changes under stress have been most thoroughly studied by Schönpflüg and his colleagues (e.g., Schönpflug, 1983; Shultz & Schönpflug, 1982), in an innovative series of studies making use of simulated work environments, such as clerical work (checking bills, stock-keeping, etc.). When students carried out these tasks under time pressure or loud noise, they were observed to make more frequent checks of computerized directories containing information about stock holdings and unit prices. Whereas under normal conditions they typically held the information in memory while making several decisions, under stress they tended to check the lists repeatedly before making each decision. Reducing their reliance on the vulnerable memory system under stress helped participants to minimize decision errors, but the task took longer to carry out.

After-effects

A third performance-based method for assessing latent degradation through performance measures is to present additional tasks at the end of the work period (Broadbent, 1979; Cohen, 1980; Holding, 1983). Given its long-recognized importance, work fatigue has been studied extensively since the early days of psychology. On the view proposed here, fatigue results from sustained expenditure of mental effort, and should be revealed by post work tests. Nevertheless, the search for a sensitive test of the carry-over effect of sustained mental work to the performance of new tasks has proved elusive. Major research programs in the intensive postwar period of research on fatigue failed to find any marked effects on postwork tests such as tracking or multiple-choice reaction time from periods of up to 60 hours continuous work. Holding (1983) showed that there are methodological difficulties in the analysis of this apparently straightforward problem. Subjects in such experiments appear able to work harder (make more effort) for brief periods to respond to the challenge of the new test, effectively compensating for any reduction in capacity. When tired subjects were provided with alternative ways of carrying out the postwork test they were more likely to choose one requiring low effort, even though it entailed more risk of error. More recent studies have confirmed this effect. Meijman, Mulder, van Dormelen, and Cremer (1992) found driving examiners invested less effort (both subjective and physiological) in performing cognitive tasks following working days with higher levels of demand. A study comparing the effects of working and nonworking days in city bus drivers reported by Aasman, Wijers, Mulder, and Mulder (1988) found less efficient and effective task performance to be associated with increasing workload. The same effect has also been observed in laboratory studies of simulated work (Schellekens, Sijtsma, Vegter, & Meijman, 2000). Hockey and Earle

(2006) reported reduced persistence on an information search task after high workload/effort, though only under conditions of low control during the normal work period (being made to follow a particular task schedule, as opposed to being able to choose one's own).

Subjective costs

In comparison to other ways of measuring latent decrement, subjective or self report measures are relatively easy to employ. The notion that we can simply ask operators about their perceived levels of task demands, or stress, or effort is appealing, as well as having high face validity. Within the workload literature a number of subjective workload assessment techniques have been developed (see Eggemeier & Wilson, 1991 for a comprehensive review). Most widely used are the Cooper–Harper scale (Cooper & Harper, 1969; Wierwille & Casali, 1983), the NASA Task Load Index (TLX) (Hart & Staveland, 1988), and the Subjective Workload Assessment Technique (SWAT) (Reid & Nygren, 1988). The Cooper–Harper scale produces general workload ratings on a 1–10 scale. The other two assess perceived workload on a number of dimensions. SWAT asks for ratings on three indicators (mental effort, time load, and psychological stress), while TLX assesses workload using six scales (temporal demand, mental demand, mental effort, frustration, physical demand, and performance; Hart & Staveland, 1988). The Dundee Stress State Questionnaire (see Matthews, 2002) provides measures of loss of task engagement, distress and worry. Hockey and colleagues (e.g., Hockey, Payne, & Rick, 1996; Hockey et al., 1998) have modified Warr's (1990) scale of job well-being to assess three dimensions of task-related strain (anxiety, fatigue, and effort).

An issue is that many subjective ratings are obtained after task completion, rather than as events are experienced. Rehmann, Stein, and Rosenberg (1983) have argued that concurrent workload evaluation is more accurate than post-task ratings, although Moroney, Biers, and Eggemeier (1995) suggest that delays of up to 15 minutes do not tend to have a significant impact on the reliability of ratings, unless intervening tasks take place. Measuring workload during, rather than after task performance, has the advantage in complex tasks involving multiple elements or phases, of relating ratings more directly to specific phases and changing task demands. An example is the Instantaneous Self Assessment technique (ISA) which was originally designed for use in air traffic control settings and appears to be a relatively sensitive measure of workload (Tattersall & Foord, 1996). It provides a simple estimate of global workload on a five-point scale. Hockey and his colleagues (e.g., Hockey et al., 1998; Hockey, Nickel, Roberts, Mahfouf, & Linkens, 2006) have used single visual analogue scales embedded within a task simulation.

Psychophysiological costs

Physiological processes have long been identified as potential markers of mental effort or workload. The underlying assumption behind their use is that as more

Table 8.2: Summary of the capability of different broad categories of workload assessment technique to satisfy different requirements for use

Measure Type	Intrusiveness	Sensitivity	Diagnosticity	Applicability	Acceptability
Performance					
Primary task	not a problem	high when relevant data available	low	depends on availability of suitable data	no obvious problems
Secondary task	possible problems	high	high	may require training and extra equipment	possible distraction but generally acceptable
Strategy changes	not a problem	high when relevant data available	medium-high	suitable analytic toold and data required	no obvious problems
After effects	not a problem	can be high	low – global index of fatigue	minimal requirements	may be resistance because of additional task
Subjective					
Post-task	generally not a problem	high – may depend on length of task	low-medium	minimal requirements	no problems
Instantaneous	potentially intrusive	high	can be high – depends on task structure	equipment usually required	no problems
Physiological					
EEG	not usually a problem	high	depends on measure	extensive equipment and analysis requirements	not generally problematical
ECG	not a problem	high	low-medium	extensive equipment and analysis requirements	not generally problematical

effort is devoted to the task there will be increased activation in psychophysiological functioning associated with both central and autonomic nervous systems. Measures of cardiac and brain function are the most well researched and frequently used techniques, but other physiological processes have been examined, including respiration, eyeblinks, and pupil dilation. There is no space to summarize these findings in detail here: the reader is referred to reviews by, e.g., Byrne and Parasuraman (1996), Jorna (1992), Kramer (1991), and Wilson and Eggemeier (1991).

Effects on sensitive physiological mechanisms may be observed as the costs of maintaining performance on the primary task under high levels of workload or stress. The effort required to deal with increased demands involves increased activation of physiological systems involved in "emergency" reactions, such as sympathetic and musculoskeletal responses and neuroendocrine stress patterns (e.g. Frankenhaeuser, 1986; Ursin, Baade, & Levine, 1978). There are also likely to be effects on mood states reflecting the affective response to emergency and sustained coping effort. Increased levels of catecholamine excretion accompanied by lower levels of cortisol excretion and anxiety have been shown to be associated with active processing strategies linked with effort investment and increases in subjective perceptions of task control. On the other hand, increased cortisol and noradrenaline excretions are found under conditions associated with lowered control and increased distress (Frankenhaeuser, 1986). Using different measures, Steptoe (1983) observed increased physiological activation, indicated by higher levels of blood pressure and heart rate, when subjects were engaged in effortful problem-solving or activity in a controllable situation. Noise has also been found to increase heart rate and blood pressure in tasks where no performance decrement occurred (Carter & Beh, 1989; Veldman, 1992).

Unfortunately, there are few studies within real work contexts. This may be because of the difficulty of obtaining psychophysiological measures under such circumstances. However, a field study by Rissler and Jacobson (1987) found increases in adrenaline and cognitive effort in the absence of performance decrements during an intense period of organizational change. Such effects illustrate the role of compensatory regulation in the protection of performance. In general the above effects indicate that the regulation of effort is at least partially under the control of the individual, rather than being an automatic feature of task or environmental conditions.

Requirements for Effective Workload Assessment

Workload measurement techniques are not equally effective or appropriate for all situations. Techniques vary in their sensitivity to changes in demand, ability to distinguish different kinds of demand, and suitability or relevance to that situation. The factors involved are summarized briefly in table 8.2. The sensitivity of methods to different levels of primary task load is the most critical aspect of workload measurement (Eggemeier, 1988). It relates to whether the technique is able to detect changes resulting from increases in task demands. A low level of sensitivity will not allow effective discrimination to be made between different conditions or systems under evaluation. Diagnosticity is concerned with the extent to which the technique is able to distinguish between different types of task demands and to identify the particular components within complex tasks that result in difficulty. This is particularly useful when assessing the introduction of a new piece of equipment or a change in the way that a task is performed as solutions to problematic task elements might be identified, such as provision of further training or other support, or manipulation of the characteristics or timing of the problematic tasks. Generally, diagnosticity has not been found to be easily achieved, though secondary task methods may sometimes prove useful.

Workload assessment measures should also be practicable and acceptable to the workers being studied, not too difficult to apply in the workplace and, if possible, produce results that can be generalized to other, similar situations. Importantly, the technique should not be intrusive, to the extent that it disrupts the performance of the primary work task. The more obvious form of intrusion could result from the use of particular equipment or the application of a technique which requires the primary work task to be halted or interrupted whilst measures are taken. Perhaps less obvious is the potential for certain methods, particularly secondary-task methodology, to compete for certain processing resources with the primary work task. If safety is a major concern, as it is in many application domains such as in air traffic control, space operations and medical intensive care work, then clearly workload assessment techniques that may degrade performance should not be used. In all cases, the operational procedures should be standardized as much as possible. Finally, it almost goes without saying that measures must also be valid and reliable, and measure what they are claimed to measure in an accurate and consistent manner.

Summary

The patterns of performance observed under stress and high demand can be seen to reflect the adaptive response of the broader motivational control system to the ever-changing balance of goal priorities and environmental flux. While primary performance is often maintained under high workload and stress, this compensatory activity typically results in disruption to secondary or auxiliary components of the integrated system performance, and to increases in effort. These may represent a source of latent degradation, increasing the risk of breakdown on the primary task under critical conditions; unpredictable surges of task load, changes of task priorities, or the requirement to sustain control under emergencies. The effects of individual differences in workload management or effort regulation strategies will

Continued

determine the extent to which decrements are observed in work performance. The consequences of dealing with heavy work demands may therefore be measurable only in the form of tradeoffs between performance and other domains of individual activity, and longitudinal sampling of performance as well as subjective and physiological measures may well be required. It is argued that appropriate design of the task environment should address issues associated with workload management, so that potential decrements in individual performance and associated organizational problems are avoided. Some aspects of automation appear able to support workload management, notably the adoption of adaptive task allocation methods, where appropriate.

The experience of workload is thus unlikely to depend simply on external demands, but rather on the interaction between demands, the strategies adopted by an operator to deal with them, and the desired trade-off between level of performance and costs. Such effects are neither simple nor inevitable, but it is clear that the patterns of decrement (and costs) observed depend very much on both the individual and the particular situation. Through effective job and work design, it may be possible to capitalize on key elements of workload management processes that will benefit both individuals and work organizations.

Discussion Points

Why are measures of task demand alone insufficient for the effective prediction of the subjective experience of workload?

Discuss the role of cognitive and energetical factors in the management of effective performance.

Key Studies

Fairclough, S. H., & Venables, L. (2006). Prediction of subjective states from psychophysiology: a multivariate approach. *Biological Psychology, 71*, 100–10.

Hockey, G. R. J., & Earle, F. (2006). Control over the scheduling of simulated office work reduces the impact of workload on mental fatigue and task performance. *Journal of Experimental Psychology: Applied, 12*, 50–65.

Tattersall, A. J., & Hockey, G. R. J. (1995). Level of operator control and changes in heart rate variability during simulated flight maintenance. *Human Factors, 37*, 682–98.

Further Reading

Hockey, G. R. J. (1997). Compensatory control in the regulation of human performance under stress and high workload: A cognitive-energetical framework. *Biological Psychology, 45*, 73–93.

Hockey, G. R. J. (2005). Operator functional state: The prediction of breakdown in human performance. In J. Duncan, P. McLeod, & L. Phillips (Eds.), *Speed, Control and Age: In Honour of Patrick Rabbitt*. Oxford: Oxford University Press.

Hockey, G. R. J., Gaillard, A. W. K., & Burov, O. (Eds) (2003). *Operator Functional State: The Assessment and Prediction of Human*

Performance Degradation in Complex Tasks.
Amsterdam: IOS Press.
Parasuraman, R., & Mouloua. M. (Eds.) (1996).
Automation and Human Performance.
Hillsdale, NJ: Lawrence Erlbaum.

Stanton, N. A., Salmon, P. M., Walker,
G. H., Baber, C., & Jenkins, D. P. (2005).
Human Factors Methods. Aldershot:
Ashgate.

Research Close-Up

Hockey, G. R. J., & Earle, F. (2006).
Control over the scheduling of simulated
office work reduces the impact of workload
on mental fatigue and task performance.
Journal of Experimental Psychology: Applied,
12, 50–65. (Of the two experiments reported
only the second is discussed in detail
here.)

Introduction

Two experiments tested the hypothesis that
the impact of workload on task-induced
mental fatigue is reduced when employees
have control over the scheduling of work
tasks. Research using questionnaire methods
had suggested that effects of workload on all
kinds of strain states (including fatigue, psychological stress, and even illness) may be
reduced under conditions that permit the use
of high levels of personal control (where
employees may decide the order, timing and
methods used to carry out assigned tasks).
This was tested formally under laboratory
conditions of simulated office work, allowing
both performance and subjective state to
be assessed. Since Hockey's compensatory
control theory predicted that performance of
high-priority tasks would be preferentially
protected under adverse conditions, moderating effects of control were expected to be
more evident for less critical tasks.

Participants

The two separate studies employed a total
of 104 participants (experiment 1: 20 office

staff and 20 postgraduate students; experiment 2: 64 undergraduate and postgraduate
students).

Design and procedure

Participants worked through a set of simulated office tasks for an unbroken period of
two hours. These included: primary tasks, to
be completed during the session (e.g., entering student addresses into a spreadsheet);
secondary tasks, to be done when time permitted (proofreading and data entry), and
one-off tasks using yellow pages and train
schedules. Since Hockey & Earle were also
interested in after-effects of fatigue, they
included a surprise postwork task, asking
participants to check travel websites for suitable hotels.

   Matched pairs of participants were
assigned to conditions of either high or low
control, with a yoking procedure to equate
actual work sequences. High-control
members of each pair could decide the order
and timing of individual tasks, while yoked
low-control participants had to follow the
fixed sequences chosen by their counterparts. For the critical experiment 2, different
groups of pairs were instructed to work at
either 80 percent (low workload) or 120
percent (high workload) of their baseline
work rate.

Results

As expected, performance of primary tasks
was stable under all conditions. However,

consistent with the hypothesis, the impact of workload was reduced under high control for both subjective fatigue and most secondary tasks. Participants who had control over their schedule reported much lower levels of fatigue than the low-control group at the end of the two-hour period. They also showed greater increases in errors on the low-priority tasks, and reduced persistence in searching for the best hotel in the postwork task.

Discussion

Allowing people to organize their own work schedules appears not only to reduce feelings of fatigue during periods of intensive work, but also to reduce their vulnerability to increased errors and reduced productivity. There are also likely to be hidden benefits of high control. The findings showed that tired participants were able to protect important work from the effects of fatigue, though less important work suffered as a result. However, the increased fatigue generated under low control may carry over to subsequent tasks, and, if not allowed to dissipate (in the absence of sufficient break time), cause a more generalized breakdown across all task activities during subsequent work sessions.

Telework

Noel Sheehy

Overview

Teleworking, or telecommuting as it is referred to in North America, is an alternative way to organize work that integrates two sources of competitive advantage: an organization's human resources and its ability to access the benefits of advances in information and communication technologies (ICTs). While there is no generally accepted definition of telework most characterizations refer to the use of ICTs to enable employees to complete some or all of their work activities from varied and remote locations. The term is sometimes used to embrace telemanufacturing – a highly decentralized manufacturing system that capitalizes on the availability of technology to support the management of standardized, autonomous, cooperative elements (Abdel-Maleck, Wolf, & Guyot, 1998). Although teleworking is a relatively new phenomenon the systematic practice of "putting out" work to employees based in their homes is not. For example it was an important part of textile production in England in the fifteenth century but the Industrial Revolution significantly reduced its presence in favor of centralized factory-based production (Dangler, 1986). Modern interest in the potential of telework commenced in the early 1970s. The convergence of advances in communications and information technologies facilitated the growth of telework as an organizational work structure and there have been significant increases in the number of teleworkers during the last 15 years (Apgar, 1998; Hill, Miller, Weiner and Colihan, 1998). Although mutually germane, studies of virtual communities, computer supported cooperative work and telework generally have not informed each other (Wellman et al., 1996).

Telework: Definition and Development

A common definition of teleworking has yet to be agreed (see Sullivan, 2003, for a range of definitions). It comprises different elements of technology and location, which in different combinations lead to a range of work types. The different types of work are performed by people with different personal (e.g., gender, education) and occupational backgrounds (Haddon & Brynin, 2005). In broad terms telework has been represented or modelled in two main ways. One model of teleworking (Model 1) imagines a woman tied to the home by the needs of her family while undertaking routine, repetitive work for which she is underpaid by unscrupulous employers. According to this model teleworkers, especially those working from home, are some of the most disadvantaged groups in the labor market. A completely different model (Model 2) presents teleworkers as semiprofessional or professional workers with the opportunity to exercise choice over their employment options and the potential to access a range of well-paid jobs. Model 2 is often portrayed as the future of work. Many of the debates surrounding the nature and future of telework, including the extent of teleworking, have their origins in the contradictions inherent in these models. A useful way of accommodating both models is to regard them as referring to groups occupying different positions in the production process (Felstead, Jewson, Phizacklea and Walters, 2001). Model 1 teleworkers are those who work from home by selling their labor directly to clients or end-users and these are in a very different position from Model 2 teleworkers who receive a salary in exchange for their work. Felstead et al. have shown that the debate between Model 1 and Model 2 scenarios is simplistic and fails to discriminate adequately between different categories of teleworker.

In the absence of a common definition estimates of the numbers engaged in teleworking and growth forecasts vary greatly. In the UK the Labor Force Survey defines teleworkers as people who do some paid or unpaid work in their own home and who use both a computer and a telephone. It includes people who: mainly work from home in their main job, "teleworker homeworkers"; work from home in various locations but use their home as a base, "homebased teleworkers"; and do not usually work at home or use home as a base but did so for at least one day a week, "occasional teleworkers." A technologically narrower definition refers to those for whom both a computer and a telephone are essential for them to be able to perform their job. The Statistical Indicators Benchmarking the Information Society (SIBIS, 2003) consortium defines a home-based teleworker as a person who works from home and transfers work results electronically. Three subcategories are identified: permanent teleworkers (spending more than one full day per week and at least 75 percent of their working time at home); alternating teleworkers (spending more than one full day per week working at home, but less than 75 percent of their working time); and supplementary teleworkers (spending working time at home, but less than one full day per week).

Some forecasts suggested that telework will involve 90 million people worldwide by 2030 (Wilkes, Frolick, & Urwiler, 1994). In the UK the Department for Transport (2002) predicted an annual growth in teleworker numbers of 9 percent over the following 15 years with the biggest increase amongst occasional employee teleworkers. Such forecasts should be treated cautiously: there have been variations in the traditional profile of teleworkers which suggest that the underlying determinants are poorly understood (Gillespie & Richardson, 2000). For example, a 2002 survey of teleworkers in Southern California indicated that the majority were male with smaller households (Safirova & Walls, 2005) whereas the traditional profile characterizes the majority of teleworkers as women with partners and children (Popuri & Bhat, 2003). Eight million North Americans were thought to be working from their homes in 1993 (Bredin, 1996) whereas estimates for 1997 put the number somewhere between 11.1 million (Hill et al., 1998) and 40 million (Apgar, 1998). The SIBIS consortium provides "league tables" for Europe and the US on "eWork." The SIBIS (2003) survey indicated that the Netherlands (26 percent), Finland (22 percent), Denmark (22 percent) and Sweden (19 percent) have the highest proportions of teleworkers within their employed populations. The UK, Switzerland and Germany (all 17 percent) and Austria (14 percent) also had proportions of teleworkers above the EU 15 country average of 13 percent. Italy (9 percent), France (6 percent), Spain (4.9 percent) and Portugal (2.6 percent) had lower proportion of teleworkers.

Raghuram et al. (2001) surveyed the extent of flexible work practices in 4,876 companies distributed across Europe. Their findings are broadly consistent with predictions derived from Hofstede's (1991) conceptualization of national cultures and suggest that differences between countries are due to cultural factors. For example, compared to southern European countries Nordic countries prioritize support for large rural areas, promote an egalitarian work ethic and highly value the discretion of employees. In addition, the governments in the Nordic countries prioritize childbirth and childcare services while offering opportunities for mothers to remain in the labor market. Telework is regarded as an opportunity for mothers to continue employment.

The propagation of teleworking involves two primary agents – employers and employees. Almost all of the focus has been on modeling the decision-making of the employee although there have been some studies of the employer's decision (e.g., Yen, Mahmassani, & Herman, 1994) and a few have considered both the employee's and the employer's decisions (e.g., Sullivan, Mahmassani, & Yen, 1993). One of the most theoretically sophisticated approaches has been articulated by Salomon (1998) and summarized in figure 9.1.

According to the model a decision to telework is the product of four blocks of factors: Environmental, Individual (unobserved), Constraints and Observed Behavior. An individual (employer or employee) is understood to act within an Environment (Block 1) characterized by physical, economic, social/cultural and technological attributes. The unobtrusive decision-making mechanism of the individual is concealed from the researcher and represented by the "Black Box" (Block 2). The Black Box includes a range of behavioral processes (e.g., attitude, life style, decision making processes) that can be measured indirectly for, example through attitude and preference surveys. The third block represents the Observed Behavior which is more readily measurable, for example by identifying actual instances of teleworking. The relationship between the observed behavior and unobserved processes (the Black Box) is not a direct one because an employee

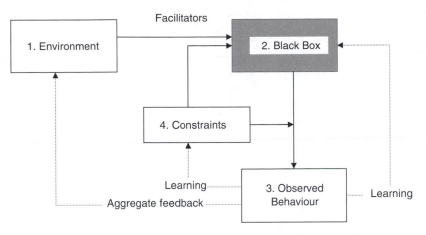

Figure 9.1: Behavioral model of teleworking (simplified from Salomon, 1998)

or employer might, for example, have a strong preference to telework but find that they are unable to realize their preferred option. Constraints (Block 4) are thus part of the explanatory model. Some studies have pointed to the gendered nature of some of the constraints (Wilson & Greenhill, 2004). Women tend to access teleworking opportunities following joint negotiations with their supervisor whereas men are more likely to take a decision to telework without reference to their line manager (Tremblay, 2003). The model incorporates two types of feedback mechanism. The first, at the individual level, affects future telework behavior on the basis of past experience. The second is the cumulative change of the environment, resulting from changes in peoples' working behavior.

Several empirical tests of the model have been undertaken. For example, Mokhtarian and Salomon (1996) examined the nature and distribution of constraints on individuals and found that the majority (88 percent) of people they surveyed regarded teleworking as a "preferred impossible alternative." Their analysis underscores the importance of considering constraints in analysis of seemingly desired technological-based enhancements to the organization of work. More generally the model is a useful conceptual framework for organizing the major factors, and their key interrelationships, implicated in the propagation of telework.

A complementary framework has been developed by Hunton and Harmon (2004) whose Telework Behavior Model (TBM) addresses the interaction of various psychological effects, individual consequences, and organizational outcomes. The TBM focusers on the motivation to work and is grounded in expectancy theory (Vroom, 1964):

$$\text{Motivation} = \text{Expectancy} \times \text{Instrumentality} \times \text{Valence}$$

Applied to teleworking, expectancy refers to an employee's belief that they possess the requisite skills to perform well as a teleworker. Instrumentality relates to the

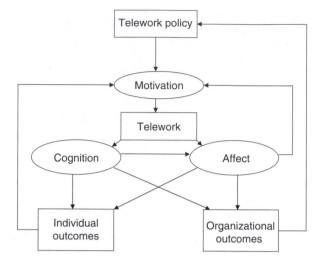

Figure 9.2: Telework behavior model (simplified from Hunton & Harmon, 2004)

employee's beliefs that their performance as a teleworker will produce the outcomes they wish. Valence refers to an employee's subjective expected value of
the desired outcome. Figure 9.2 describes the main components of the model.

The model indicates how an organization's policy sets the parameters for
teleworking: what kinds of job might be teleworked and under what terms and
conditions. Various individual motivational factors (as represented by expectancy
theory) guide employees' decisions to telework or not, and how frequently they
would prefer to telework. For example, several studies have given prominence to
the gendered nature of motivations to telework, suggesting that whereas women
tend to use telework to better satisfy family and domestic demands, men tend to
"overwork" by extending the time they commit to their employer (Sullivan and
Lewis, 2001).

According to Hutton and Harmon's model the experience of telework will
lead to a range of cognitive outcomes such as the extent to which it affords
opportunities to concentrate on complex or long-duration tasks. Affect outcomes
refers to factors such as one's job satisfaction as a teleworker and the experience
of the work–home interface. The telework experience will also have a wide range
of positive and negative outcomes at the level of the individual (e.g., potential
social isolation, reduced need to commute to work) and the organization (e.g.,
reduced overheads, loss of managerial control). Emotional reactions to the experience of telework, as well as a range of individual outcomes, feedback to motivations to telework. For example, home based telework is generally regarded by
workers as having a positive effect on their health, although potential problems
arising from poor work station design and long work hours can cause them to
review the attractiveness of the mode of work and to revise their motivations to
continue (Montreuil & Lippel, 2003).

Organizational outcomes feedback to and inform telework policy. For example, telework has often been linked with the prospect of productivity gains but the experience of some knowledge-based industries suggests that employees may work harder without delivering tangible productivity gains, which is why they may offer teleworking without encouraging uptake (Westfall, 2004). Surveys of managers have indicated that telework is believed to alter a wide range of organizational competences some of which can have beneficial effects on the resource based (e.g., more autonomous, self-motivated employees), some of which may be negative (e.g., teleworkers who identify less with the organization) (Illegems & Verbeke, 2004). Using a combination of methods (analysis of emails, in-depth interviews, and direct observation), Dambrin (2004) has shown that telework reduces formal communication between employees and their direct managers thereby reducing the importance of professional and social status and increasing employees' autonomy towards their manager. Essentially managers have a reduced range of devices to control teleworkers and rely mainly on management by objectives (Van Sell & Jacobs, 1994); and teleworkers come to feel that their professional relationship with their managers is largely defined by this alone. Hunton and Harmon have not empirically tested their model but, like that developed by Salomon (1998), it provides a useful conceptual framework for identifying that major forces that drive the adoption of telework and highlights the main interactions that need to be taken into account.

The evidence relating to the impact of teleworking on job satisfaction is not consistent. Some studies have suggested that teleworking leads to enhanced job satisfaction (e.g., McCloskey & Igbaria, 1998) whereas others indicate that teleworking can diminish job satisfaction (e.g., Chapman, Sheehy, Heywood, Dooley, & Collins, 1995; Cooper & Kurland, 2002). Golden and Veiga (2005) appear to have explained the contradiction. They contend there may be a curvilinear, inverted U-shaped relationship between the extent of teleworking and job satisfaction. Using an anonymous and confidential web-based survey of 321 employees in a very large (40,000 employees) organization they found that job satisfaction initially increases as the extent of teleworking rises; however, at higher levels of teleworking it starts to level off and decrease somewhat. Their findings (replicated by Golden, 2006) suggest that increases in job satisfaction at lower levels of teleworking are relatively substantial in comparison with those at higher levels. However, because their study was correlational it is not possible to conclude that teleworking leads to increases in job satisfaction, only that the degree to which employees initially telework is related to their level of job satisfaction.

Environmental Drives

Teleworking has often been regarded as carrying additional environmental benefits and seen as an important element in solving congestion-related transportation problems (Mokhtarian & Sato, 1994). Although in theory teleworking should reduce reliance on private and public transport, practice indicates that most teleworkers prefer to spend some time, usually at least one or two days each week, in conventional office environments (Gareis & Kordey, 1999). Thus, early predictions of significant changes in settlement patterns and commuting behavior (Niles, 1994) have not yet been realized. Surveys conducted in the 1990s indicated that the majority of teleworking companies in the UK were based in the Greater London area (Huws, 1993) and throughout Europe teleworking companies were overrepresented in large cities relative to large town and more rural areas. These trends suggest that in the medium to long term telework may be associated with an increase in private car use rather than large-scale reductions in traffic volumes and that to some extent telework simply redistributes environmental impacts rather than reduces them (Gareis & Kordey, 1999; Kitou & Horvath, 2003). Nonetheless, following formalization of a corporate-wide telecommuting policy in 1992, estimates based on interviews with a sample of 1,238 AT&T managers in 2000 showed that the total number of travel miles avoided in 2000 was 110,000; 5.1 million gallons of petrol was saved; and 48,000 tons of carbon dioxide emissions were avoided (Atkyns, Blazek, Roitz, & AT&T, 2002).

The development of various teleworking practices does not automatically confer environmental and social benefits. Heinonen and Kuosa (2005) considered four potential futures for telework based on the primacy of information security, the preeminence of consumerism, significant developments in intelligent engineering (e.g., applications of artificial intelligence to engineering processes), and the prominence of social networking and social cohesion. All four models pointed to a common set of issues for the future:

Telework should be thought of as part of an environmentally sensitive lifestyle.
Teleworkers should avoid half or partial telework days.
Teleworkers should avoid car driving on telework days for other purposes.
Teleworkers should not move farther away from the office simply because of the opportunity to telework.

Incentives to Telework

From a management perspective telework has been considered to have benefits in terms of downsizing, delayering, business process reengineering, the shift to a core/periphery organizational model, growth in interorganizational networks and increased productivity (Chapman et al., 1995; Daniels, Lamond, & Standen, 2000). It also has the potential to allow employers to access a broader pool of geographically dispersed employees who are not required to live within commuting distance of a central office (Wilkes et al., 1994; Donaldson & Weiss, 1998;

Hill et al., 1998; Watson Fritz, Narasimhan, & Rhee, 1998). Telework also has the potential to increase social inclusion, for example by allowing people with a range of sensory or motor impairments to enter the labor market, provided appropriate interfaces can be developed (Pieper & Hermsdorf, 1997). Employees who have been on extended leave of absence through illness and who are offered modified work (e.g., parts of their original job) are twice as likely to return to work than those who are not offered such an arrangement (Krause, Dasinger, & Neuhauser, 1998) and telework has been promoted as an obvious approach to reintegrating employees. Potential benefits to employees include general improvements to quality of life by removing the need to commute daily to and from work, greater control in maintaining a home-life balance, as well as enhanced job satisfaction (Chapman et al., 1995). The general research picture has consistently shown that telework tends to increase job performance and productivity (DiMartino & Wirth, 1990; Kurland & Bailey, 1999) although it also has the potential to lead to less synergy, weaker communication networks among workers and diminished organizational culture all of which have the potential to decrease job performance (Bailey & Kurland, 2002).

The projected growth in teleworking and the emphasis on its potential within the management literature contrasts with surveys indicating a general reluctance to engage in teleworking. One survey of a large number of organizations in EU member states indicated that 76 percent of companies who responded neither practiced telework, nor were interested in promoting it (EcaTT, 2000). A survey of 66 managers of market services businesses in Tokyo indicated that 70 percent had serious concerns about teleworking, principally because the additional responsibilities that would fall on managers to ensure its success were perceived to be too great (Hamsa & Miura, 2001). A similar picture has been reported in Spain (Pérez et al., 2002). Several studies have identified concerns about the security of information stored in remote locations (Sturgeon, 1996). If employees who work remotely do not have a strong awareness of security, then a lack of concern for safe data handling might lead to a failure to make regular systems backups. There is some evidence to suggest that managers' reluctance to adopt teleworking is not shared by their employees. A survey of 1,200 Dutch employees found that the majority regarded their work as suitable for teleworking whereas most of their employers believed that levels of interest in teleworking were so low it was unnecessary to develop policy in this area.

An important motivator to engage in telework concerns the perceived opportunities to better balance work and family commitments. Some studies have suggested that teleworking is particularly attractive to couples with family obligations (Yap & Tang, 1990). Ironically, the increased work–life balance that telework affords can result in increased stress for teleworkers who may find it difficult to manage competing demands at the work–home interface (Salomon & Salomon, 1984). For example, they can find it difficult to manage work–home boundaries when family members fail to appreciate that their presence in the home does not mean they can be continually interrupted in their work. The spillover of work into the home environment has meant that telework has come to be associated with the concepts of blurred boundaries and role blurring (Hill, Hawkins, & Brent, 1996). However, there have been relatively few studies of employees' perceptions of the role and boundary blurring associated with teleworking from home. Desrochers, Hilton, and Larwood (2005) have suggested that highly integrated work–family domains tend to have blurred boundaries. To test their hypothesis they developed the Work–Family Integration Blurring Scale (WFIBS) using a sample of 100 business professors raising children in two-parent families. They found moderately high correlations between scores on the WFIBS and the number of hours worked at home and on campus, the number of work–family transitions made when working at home, the presence of distractions when working at home, and the level of work–family conflict. The characteristics of the sample make it difficult to generalize the findings to other occupational groups although the development of the WFIBS means that it is possible to measure boundary blurring and its associations with the benefits and costs of a range of work–family arrangements.

A large study of IBM employees compared the effect of three work venues (traditional office, $n = 4,316$, virtual office, $n = 767$, and home office, $n = 441$) on several aspects of work (job performance, job motivation, job retention, workload success, and career opportunity) and personal/family (work/life balance and personal/family success). The evidence suggests that the influence of the virtual office is mostly positive on aspects of work but somewhat negative on aspects of personal/family life. The influence of the home office appears to be mostly positive on both work and personal/family life. The influence of the traditional office is mostly negative on aspects of both work and personal/family life (Hill, Ferris, & Mätinson, 2003).

Overall, teleworkers job performance and career choices are likely to depend on their ability to cope with the demands of their work and their home life. In general interrole conflict, such as work–family conflict, has been found to impact negatively on a range of work and personal outcomes. Teleworkers who can adopt strategies to proactively adapt their job responsibilities in response to the changes associated with their new way of working, and achieve successful personal work outcomes, are likely to flourish thereby providing contingent benefits to their employers. Self-efficacy is likely to be particularly important in determining the likely success of teleworking. According to self-efficacy theory, people judge their ability to successfully cope with new challenges when presented with environmental demands and thereby develop context-specific self-efficacy beliefs (Bandura, 1997). In other words, unless people believe that they can bring about desired outcomes by their actions they have little incentive to act or to persevere in the face of difficulties. Raghuram, Wiesenfeld, and Garud (2003) surveyed 723 participants in a large multinational telecommunications organization based in North America. Self-efficacy was measured by the way employees responded to questions such as "When telecommuting . . . if something looks too complicated, I will not even bother to try it." They found a positive correlation between tele-workers' self-efficacy and both behavioral strategies (i.e. those who agreed with statements such as "I begin my day by setting my performance goals") and work outcomes (i.e. those who agreed with statements such as "All in all, I am satisfied with telecommuting"). They also found that women were more vigilant in how they structured their workday compared to men, a difference which may be accounted for by the fact women may be more familiar with managing the simul-taneous demands imposed by work and by home. One practical implication of their findings is that self-efficacy can be raised through training interventions (e.g., Gist & Mitchell, 1992), by managing interpersonal expectations (Eden, 1993) and though enhanced supervisory trust (Staples, Hulland, & Higgins, 1999).

Those high in self-efficacy are likely to be particularly successful teleworkers. Are there other individual characteristics linked to successful teleworking? Workman, Kahnweiler and Bommer (2003) surveyed 552 full-time teleworkers and found that those who can best accommodate uncertainty, solitary work, and minimal organizational structure tend to be more strongly committed to telework than colleagues who cannot adapt to these features. They also found that people who prefer group interaction, such as brainstorming, expressed stronger commit-ments to their virtual team-mates than those who do not like this kind of interac-tion. However, their study used a cross-sectional rather than a longitudinal design and one cannot be certain that factors such as tolerance for ambiguity, a preference for solitary work and minimal structure motivated people to choose to become teleworkers. Other, as yet unidentified factors may have interacted with the experience of teleworking such that those most committed to this way of working tend to manifest those characteristics identified by Workman et al.

Barriers to Telework

A number of disadvantages associated with telework are considered to act as bar-riers to its uptake. From a manager's perspective there can be drawbacks to the reduced levels of supervisory control associated with telework (Nunes, 2005) and there are significant practical challenges in organizing team work and generating team commitment among dispersed employees who may not meet one another on a regular basis.

From an employee's perspective opportunities to interact with co-workers were believed to be substantially diminished leading to increased social isolation and lower levels of organizational identification and commitment to the work team (Chapman et al., 1995; Becker & Sims, 2001). However, some of the earliest empirical studies contradicted that belief: in some circumstances teleworkers did not communicate more frequently on-line with co-workers or supervisors than similarly occupied non-teleworkers (Kinsman, 1987), although teleworkers were found to have less postal and person-to-person contact (Olszewski & Mokhtarian, 1994). Early studies indicated that teleworking is associated with more structured and formalized communication with supervisors and, to a lesser extent, with co-workers (Huws, Korte, & Robinson, 1990). The somewhat simplistic picture given in early studies of telework has been superseded by more conceptually sophisticated analyses. For example, Wiesenfeld, Raghuram, & Garud (2001) examined organizational identification among a sample of 250 mandatory tele-workers (they were required to telework) in the sales division of a large technol-ogy organization. They found that workers' need for affiliation (the desire for social contact or belongingness) and the work-based social support they experi-enced were countervailing forces associated with stronger organizational identi-fication. Moreover, employees' perceptions of the work-based social support they receive moderated the association between their need for affiliation and the degree to which they identified with their organization. Thus, when work-based social support is high, even workers with lower need for affiliation may strongly identify with the organization.

It is important to bear in mind that social isolation is a highly subjective expe-rience and varies according to the teleworker's role, attitudes towards the tech-nology they use for their work and their personal circumstances (Simpson, Daws, Pini, & Wood, 2003). The professional isolation of teleworkers is linked to employee development activities such as interpersonal networking, informal learning, and mentoring (Cooper & Kurland, 2002). The degree to which tele-workers feel professionally isolated depends upon the extent to which develop-ment activities are valued within the organization as well as the extent to which they fail to avail of these opportunities.

Several studies in different cultures have identified the prospect of social isola-tion as a stressor that can act as a deterrent to participation in teleworking. These studies also suggest that the majority would only be willing to telework on a part-time basis – typically 1–3 days per week – in order to address this problem (Yap & Tang, 1990; Teo, Lim, & Wai, 1998). The likelihood that staff will leave an organization is suggested by attitudinal surveys indicating that, on the one hand, teleworkers regard themselves as highly skilled and see the prospects of securing alternative employment as generally good; and on the other as being less likely to secure promotion relative to peers who enjoy a more conspicuous presence in offices (Teo et al., 1998; Bentley & Yoong, 2000).

In general, the adoption of telework, regardless of the task and persons involved, is more likely to succeed if training and support procedures are well-designed and applied (Spinks and Wood, 1996). Companies with employee training programs perceive lower barriers to telework adoption (Perez et al., 2002).

Figure 9.3 summarizes the main *perceived* benefits and barriers to teleworking. It is important to emphasize that the quality and quantity of empirical evidence supporting this summary is variable.

Benefits for the organization	Disadvantages for the organization
Reduced office overheads	Increased ICT costs
Productivity gains	Need to restructure business processes
Lower absenteeism	Increases in errors linked to lower supervision
Increased employee flexibility	Motivating and retaining employees
Management by objectives	Maintaining teamwork ethos
Benefits for the employee	Disadvantages for the employee
Increased work flexibility	Difficulties managing work–home interface
Increased autonomy	Increased social isolation
Promotes autonomy	Diminished career prospects
Reduced commuting costs	Propensity to become a "workaholic"
Fewer interruptions from colleagues	Problems with work–home boundary

Figure 9.3:   Perceived benefits and disadvantages of telework

The "Teleworkability" of Work

Whereas two thirds of employees in European Union member states carry out activities that would seem to be suitable for telework at least 1 day per week only one third of companies practice telework, and the number of teleworkers per organization is relatively low (SIBIS, 2003). The discrepancy between employers' and employees' interests in teleworking can be explained in part by the suitability of the job – the extent to which it is "teleworkable" (Pérez et al., 2002; Peters et al., 2004). Several attempts have been made to compile lists of occupational categories that are potentially suitable. However, focusing on occupational categories is overly restrictive: Teleworkability is a multivariate construct and several factors need to be taken into account including location independency, task interdependency, task scheduling autonomy, and supervisory position, i.e. having a managerial job (Mokhtarian & Bagley, 2000). Other approaches are based on the idea that a job may be more teleworkable if it involves a relatively large number of "long duration" tasks, or several tasks that can be clustered into 1 or 2 days per week (Nilles, 1998). Surprisingly few studies relate teleworking to the degree of reliance on ICTs, or to jobs that were created by ICTs. Sheehy and Gallagher (1996) have argued a case for thinking about the teleworkability of an organization in terms of its "human bandwidth" requirements. Greater bandwidth is more costly and an organization needs to make a decision about how much bandwidth it needs for its purposes and what the cost implications will be. For some organizations (e.g., those offering certain types of financial services, data-processing facilities, etc.) narrower bandwidth such as telephones and elementary email services would be fit for the purpose. It would be wasteful to provide broadband audiovisual teleconferencing facilities to its employees. However, the activities and objectives of other organizations (e.g., those offering complex design solutions to engineering problems) may require more expensive broad bandwidth technology to support the kinds of virtual face-to-face meetings design teams require in order to work through the challenges they confront. Organizations with broad bandwidth communications requirements may find it more difficult to implement telework because of the cost implications. Such organizations would be ill-advised to opt for cheaper, narrow-band ICTs because of the increased risk of providing workers with technology that does not allow them to do their work properly. Moreover, investing in more costly ICTs can have benefits for an organization. In one of a very few longitudinal studies of teleworking Venkatesh and Johnson (2002) compared the impact of a traditional desktop metaphor (requiring lesser band width) with a virtual reality interface (greater band width) designed to enhance social richness and telepresence for workers. Over a year-long period they found that use of the virtual reality interface was associated with stronger motivation to telework and higher sustained use of the system.

A related notion concerns the degree to which an organization is populated with tasks requiring extended periods of concentrated activity. Offices can be noisy, busy places where employess can find it difficult to escape the interruptions of coworkers. Teleworking can offer employees an opportunity to escape the noise that continually detracts from the quality of their work. Evidence supporting this suggestion comes from a UK survey of 62 manager professionals who telework: the majority considered teleworking to offer opportunities to complete cognitively demanding long-duration tasks (Clear & Dickson, 2005). Similar findings have been reported in North America (Bélanger, 1999).

An example of an attempt to position studies of teleworkers within a theoretical framework has considered what types of people are likely to respond well to telework and membership of virtual teams. Using Sternberg's (1997) thinking styles framework Workman et al. (2003) examined the effects of cognitive style on employees "commitment to the telework function and to the virtual team, and whether the functionality of the media moderates those effects. They found that certain combinations of cognitive styles and media functionality contribute to commitment to the telework function and to virtual teams. Specifically, "richer" technology (broad-band ICT with greater functionality) is likely to facilitate commitment to telework and to virtual teams than will narrow-band technology media, for conservative cognitive styles (prefers structure, familiarity and convention). ICT with greater functionality was also found to improve commitment to telework for local cognitive styles (requires concrete detail) and commitment to the virtual team for employees who prefer working in groups.

Perceived restrictions concerning the availability of resources and opportunities are known to affect intention to engage in teleworking and actual practice (Handy & Mokhtarian, 1995). Peters et al. (2004) have agued that the preponderance of empirical evidence (much of it based on case studies and relatively small samples) suggests that employees' willingness to participate in teleworking is related to three major issues: opportunity, preference and practice. In other words they sough to answer three questions: Which employees are given an opportunity to telework? Which employees prefer to telework? Which employees engage in telework? They used four clusters of theoretically relevant variables to answer these questions. These clusters relate to characteristics of the employees' organization, features of the job, the nature of employees' family circumstances and individual characteristics (e.g., age, gender). Their study represents an improvement over earlier surveys in two main respects: it was based on a large ($n = 849$) representative sample of the (Dutch) labor force, and multivariate statistical analysis was used to explore the relationships among the key variables (previous studies have tended to limit analysis to bivariate measures of association). They found that opportunity was largely depended on organizational and job characteristics. For example, organizations with more than one business center were more likely to offer opportunities to telework and to prefer their employees to telework. However the actual number of business centers did not have an impact on telework practice. The size of the organization was *unrelated* to opportunity, preference or practice. With regard to job characteristics: employees in a managerial position were more likely to be given an opportunity to telework, although it had no effect on preferences and practices. Family circumstances were unrelated to telework opportunities and telework practices. However, family circumstances did affect telework preferences but not in the anticipated direction. The managerial literature contends that telework may be particularly attractive to employees with significant family commitments. However, Peters et al. found that the greater the number of children in the household the weaker the preference to telework. Contrary to the management literature, and some European and North American surveys, gender was unrelated to opportunity, preference or practice. Also unexpectedly partly disabled employees were not offered more opportunities to telework (even though they indicated a preference to telework) and they did not engage in teleworking more often.

Conclusions and Future Directions

Much of the early research on telework has been programmatic, predictive, or descriptive. From the outset there was a general presumption that the convergence of advances in communication and information technologies would largely determine the future organization of work and the skills profiles of employees and managers. However, the growth of teleworking has been influenced by a range of social, economic and environmental factors that are largely unrelated to the functionality of the technology. The main drivers have to do with pressures to downsize, increase flexibility, minimize overheads and reduce environmental impacts. The emphasis has gradually moved away from a position based on technological determinism to one concerned with the interplay between the organization of work, the nature of the work–life balance, the functionality of available technology and the environmental implications of teleworking.

Most of the literature on telework exists in a theoretical vacuum (although there have been a small number of notable exceptions, e.g., Hunton & Harmon, 2004) and has been guided by the discourse in the management literature which offers arguments for the adoption of telework, conjectures on potential barriers and advice on how to avoid those pitfalls that have been identified through both successful and problematic case studies. There have been few linkages between the empirical surveys of telework practice and established theories of work and organization.

Most studies of telework have adopted quantitative methodologies and relatively few have been based on rigorous qualitative methods. Some of the conceptual advantages of applying qualitative methods are illustrated in Steward's (2000) analysis of concepts on time in telework and conventional environments. Steward (2000) emphasizes the importance of the distinction between linear time and event related time. Linear time is measured by clocks and calendars whereas event-related time is understood in terms of the sequencing of tasks, the duration of regular tasks and the usual speed at which they are completed. Telework time in normally thought of in linear terms as reflected in questions such as "how long do teleworkers spend working compared to office-based staff?" It may be the case that home-based teleworking should increasingly be understood as event-related and therefore different from the linear time of the conventional office. In a small-scale study Steward (2000) found that teleworkers do not necessarily work more flexibly during conventional office hours but they tend to work in the evenings and on weekends. More importantly, teleworkers tend to recalculate time in terms of an "*optimally productive hour*." This has important implications for future research: telework time should not be framed in relation to conventional office time.

Summary

Most of the empirical literature has focused on answering the questions "what is teleworking" and "who teleworks?," and on characterizing a range of attitudinal, motivational and social psychological attributes. However, the concept of social capital is important here. Within an organizational context social capital comprises the relationships and networks of relationships that are created and maintained by its members. More formally, social capital has been defined "as the sum of the actual and potential resources embedded within, available through and derived from the network of relationships possessed by an individual or social unit" (Nahapiet & Ghoshal, 1998, p. 243). Understanding the role of social capital and its link to performance in telework contexts has important implications for the outcomes of individuals and organizations. An organization's social capital exists in its networks of social relationships and these provide a valuable resource for organizational innovation. If telework reduces opportunities for formal and informal interpersonal interactions it can undermine an organization's social capital and threaten its sustainability. Telework therefore has the potential both to enhance and adversely affect individual and organizational performance.

Discussion Points

In general the advantages of teleworking outweigh the disadvantages.

Many employees choose to telework in order to escape the pressure of conventional, office-based work.

The environmental benefits of teleworking are relatively insignificant.

Telework arrangements can fundamentally change the way in which teleworkers communicate with their superiors, their subordinates, their colleagues and their clients.

What precautions might be taken to reduce the sense of social isolation that teleworkers may experience?

Further Reading

Bailey, D. E., & Kurland, N. B. (2002). A review of telework research: Findings, new directions, and lessons for the study of modern work. *Journal of Organizational Behavior, 23*, 383–400.

Ellison, N. B. (2004). *Telework and social change: How technology is reshaping the boundaries between home and work*. New York: Greenwood Press.

Kowalski, K. B., & Swanson, J. A. (2005). Critical success factors in developing teleworking programs. *Benchmarking: An International Journal, 12*, 236–49.

Leslie, H., & Malcolm, B. (2005). The character of telework and the characteristics of teleworkers. *New Technology, Work and Employment, 20*, 34–46.

Research Close-Up

Workman, M., & Bommer, W. (2004). Redesigning computer call center work: A longitudinal field experiment. *Journal of Organizational Behavior, 25*, 317–37.

Employers make constant efforts to improve the quality of the teleworking experience. Social isolation and a sense of not being part of a team have been addressed through the development of satellite offices which have come to be referred to as call centers, support centers, or help desks. The emergence of these group-based work environments has been particularly apparent in technology-oriented jobs where workers provide hardware and software support, and where the technology-oriented demands placed on employees are further complicated by customer-service demands. While the work environment is strongly problem-oriented it can be highly repetitive and emotionally demanding: employees must deal with the details of technical queries while simultaneously inducing a sense of satisfaction in their emotionally charged callers. Managerial efforts to solve these problems have focused on: job redesigns that align personal motivations with organizational objectives; or the utilization of high-involvement work processes; or autonomous team-based work. Alignment job redesign focuses on removing motivational barriers from the job and addresses deficits in skill variety, task identity, individual-level

Continued

autonomy, and individual-level feedback. High involvement work processes provide mechanisms for enhancing collaborative effort through the sharing of knowledge and expertise, for example through peer teaching. Autonomous team-based work is concerned with replacing traditional group management with a cooperative of inter-dependent peers whole collectively take responsibility for their organizational structure, processes and performance.

Aim

The aim of the study was to examine how three interventions based on alignment job design (AJD), high-involvement work processes (HIWP), and autonomous work teams (AWT) affected job attitudes, with particular attention to whether a person's high preference for group work moderated the success of the interventions.

Hypotheses:

Hypothesis 1a: Alignment job redesign will increase employee job satisfaction.

Hypothesis 1b: Alignment job redesign will increase employee commitment.

Hypothesis 2a: High-involvement work processes will increase employee job satisfaction.

Hypothesis 2b: High-involvement work processes will increase employee commitment.

Although HIWP may enhance job satisfaction and commitment, these effects may not accrue equally to all employees. Team-based work involves greater collaboration and cooperation with colleagues than individual-centered work. The propensity team members have toward group work as opposed to individual work may affect both their attitudes and commitment as interdependence in their work requirements increases. Thus:

Hypothesis 2c: Improvements in job satisfaction associated with HIWP will be moderated by group work orientation – more group-oriented employees will enjoy greater improvements in satisfaction and commitment than will less group-oriented employees.

Hypothesis 2d: Improvements in job satisfaction associated with HIWP will be moderated by group work orientation – more group-oriented employees will enjoy greater improvements in satisfaction and commitment than will less group-oriented employees.

As team autonomy increases, the level of interactions among members and their involvement with the team often increase quite significantly. Thus:

Hypothesis 3a: Autonomous work teams will increase employee job satisfaction.

Hypothesis 3b: Autonomous work teams will increase employee commitment.

Autonomous team-based work requires close collaboration about work and work structures. It follows that the extent of a worker's orientation towards the team may influence their job attitudes. In particular employees with strong group work orientations may welcome AWTs as an opportunity to collaborate more closely with co-workers. Thus:

Hypothesis 3c: The improvement in job satisfaction associated with AWT will be moderated by an employee's work orientation – more group-oriented workers will show greater gains in job satisfaction than will less group-oriented employees.

Hypothesis 3d: The improvement in commitment associated with AWT will be moderated by an employee's work orientation – more group-oriented workers will show greater gains in job satisfaction than will less group-oriented employees.

Sample

This field study was of a large international computer company's call center and all of its members, 159 employees, participated in the study.

Procedure

The 149 support specialists were randomly assigned to one of four interventions: 35 specialists were randomly assigned to the AJD group intervention, 35 were randomly assigned to the AWT group intervention, which was further subdivided and randomly assigned into 5 teams of 7 support specialists. Forty-three employees were randomly assigned to the HIWP group intervention, which were subdivided randomly into 7 teams. Thirty-six employees were assigned to a control group (i.e., their work was unchanged).

Measures

Job satisfaction and organizational commitment were measured before the interventions commenced and six months later.

Results

Hypotheses 1a and 1b concerned the efficacy of alignment job redesign. Hypothesis 1a was supported but Hypothesis 1b was not. Those who received receiving the AJD intervention had increased job satisfaction (compared to the control group), whereas the effect on their commitment was not significant.

Hypotheses 2a and 2b concerned the efficacy of HIWP was the results showed that those who received this intervention scored significantly higher on job satisfaction and organizational commitment compared to the control group.

Hypothesis 3a suggested that employees who were part of the autonomous work team intervention would show improved job satisfaction and Hypothesis 3b predicted gains in organizational commitment. Neither hypothesis was supported.

When call center workers had high preference for group work, their job satisfaction responded more positively to the autonomous teams intervention than did colleagues with low team orientation. This finding supported Hypothesis 3c but not difference was found for organizational commitment and Hypothesis 3d was not supported.

Discussion

High-involvement work processes produced the greatest gains in job satisfaction and organizational commitment. A particular strength of the study is its ecological validity

Continued

– the interventions were conducted in a commercial call center. However gains in ecological validity can limit the generalizability of findings. It would be important to determine whether similar findings would be observed in a wide range of call centers. In addition it is usually not possible to isolate different work groups in a real working environment and, in this study, there was evidence of some degree of intervention "leakage" across groups: some employees exchanged information about their new working arrangements and made comparative evaluations as the study was proceeding. Future studies should also consider long terms impacts on productivity as well as job satisfaction and organizational commitment.

10

Virtual Team-Working and Collaboration Technology

Matti Vartiainen and J. H. Erik Andriessen

Overview

Due to the increasing decentralization and globalization, many organizations have introduced distributed groups and teams, often called "virtual teams." Virtual teams are components of distributed organizations, whose members work apart for a joint goal and mainly communicate and collaborate via information and communication technologies (ICT). The key feature of "virtuality" is the use of ICT technologies to enable communication and collaboration, in addition to the geographical distance of employees and their workplaces from each other. By definition, in a fully virtual organization, all the communication and collaboration takes place through collaboration technologies without meeting face to face. In practice, most distributed groups and teams are virtual to varying degrees. On the organizational level, many terms have been used to refer to this type of organization, such as a "virtual organization," "a dispersed or distributed organization," "a network organization," and "a telework organization."

The structure of this chapter is as follows. The first section deals with the reasons for introducing distributed groups and teams, their prevalence and conceptual background. The second section describes the characteristics and types of virtual teams. A systemic view to explore groups and teams is provided. A three-factor model to explain the type and outcomes of groups and teams is presented. The analysis of differences, both between distributed and conventional teams, and between various types of distributed teams, shows that the main types of nonconventional groups and teams are: distributed, virtual and mobile groups and teams. Next, the need and usefulness of available collaboration technologies are discussed. The bases to select them are described. In the final section, some managerial issues are discussed. The managerial tasks are located in a general phase-model of a group's lifecycle.

Virtual Work

Members of virtual teams are geographically distributed and coordinate their activities predominantly with electronic collaboration technologies, such as email, teleconferencing, and videoconferencing (Jarvenpaa & Leidner, 1998; Lipnack & Stamps, 2000; Maznevski & Chudoba, 2000; Martins, Gilson, & Maynard, 2004; Powell, Piccoli, & Ives, 2004; Hertel, Geister, & Konradt, 2005). Distributed virtual teams are a response to changes that require organizations and their processes and structures to become more flexible and adaptive: globalized or nationwide business needs; utilization of developments in mobile and wireless information and communication technologies, the potential of mutual learning and creativity; attraction and retention of key workers (Andriessen & Vartiainen, 2006).

Gareis, Lilischkis, and Mentrup (2006) report that 13 percent of the workforce did individualized telework (i.e., all kinds of work and work arrangements carried out outside a main office but related to it; Olson & Primps, 1984, and see chapter 9 by Sheehy in this book) in Europe in 2002, i.e. around 21 millions employees in the age group 15–64 years. Switzerland was the leader among the countries in the survey, followed by Finland, the USA, Germany, and Italy. The penetration in eastern and central Europe was much lower, although Estonia and Slovenia had impressively high figures.

Gareis et al. (2006) also estimated the extent to which the EU labor force is involved in distributed, i.e. virtual, teamwork. For this, a very basic definition was used which included everybody who regularly uses email or the internet to communicate with work contacts located at other business sites, either in other organizations or at other sites of the same organization. More than every third worker in the EU15 appeared to be involved in regular telecooperation, if defined in that way – about three times as many as there are teleworkers.

A virtual organization can be defined as consisting of employees or teams working apart but towards a joint goal, mainly collaborating via information and communication technologies (ICT). In a fully virtual organization, all the communication and collaboration takes place through ICT. Relative to the traditional organization, relationships in the virtual organization are more geographically distributed, more asynchronous, more multicultural, and more likely to extend outside the firm.

There is also literature that uses the concept of "virtual enterprise," referring to a network of legally independent companies that acts as one organization *vis-à-vis* a client (e.g., Goranson, 1999). Thus, virtual organizational structures can be classified into levels of networks, companies, projects, teams, and dyads (Jackson, 1999; Hyötyläinen, 2000).

Virtual teams are groups of people who work interdependently with a shared purpose across space and time, using technology to communicate and collaborate (Jarvenpaa & Laidner, 1998; Lipnack & Stamps, 2000). Members may come

from different organizations (Martins et al., 2004). Virtuality is a team characteristic referring to the degree of use of collaboration technologies, which is often
related to the degree of geographical distribution.

Characteristics and Types of Distributed Teams

Virtual teams can have many forms, because they operate in a variety of environments with different purposes, contexts, and internal regulative processes (e.g.,
Bell & Kozlowski, 2002). The purpose of this section is to provide a framework
for the analysis and description of virtual teams as work systems.

A systemic view of teams

Distributed virtual work units always have some purpose for their activity, which
expresses itself as the motives for and objectives of actions (see figure 10.1). Three
intertwined and partly embedded factors influence the type and outcomes of
virtual teams (Vartiainen, 2006). First, task complexity, whether a team has
to execute mainly routine tasks or creative tasks. Second, contextual complexity,
the kind of physical, virtual, and mental/social environments in which work is
done. Third, the internal mechanisms and tools needed to regulate actions, relations and boundaries between subjects, objects, tasks, and the environment. As
Ashby's law of requisite variety says (Ashby, 1958), the greater the variety in an
environment of a system, the greater the variety should be within the system to
adapt properly to its environment. Simple tasks in a simple setting require only
relatively simple regulatory activities, complex tasks in a complex context require
more regulation or at least more energy and support. These factors result in
positive and negative performance and well-being outcomes, and are discussed
next.

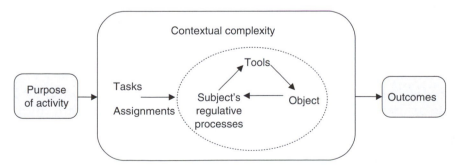

Figure 10.1:   The factors influencing the type and functionality of work systems (Vartiainen, 2006, p. 27)

Complexity of tasks   The first factor, "complexity of tasks," consists of two main features: (1) the mental requirements for task execution, and (2) interdependence of tasks. Task complexity has critical implications for the structure and processes of virtual teams as well as many leadership implications.

Mental requirements for tasks vary from routine task execution to problem-solving and creative tasks (Andriessen, 2003). The interdependence of tasks is shown as external and internal coupling (Bell & Kozlowski, 2002, pp. 18–20) of tasks to their environments. Tasks at the less complex end of the continuum require only weak and asynchronous member linkages, i.e. minimal collaboration and information sharing among team members. Simple tasks require less coordination and their competence requirements are lower than in the case of complex tasks. Complex tasks are more dynamic and involve tightly coupled external linkages. They are highly coupled temporally, with demanding pacing requirements for intrateam processes and for the team's interface with the external context. Tasks are challenging, requiring synchronous collaboration and intensive information sharing.

Contextual complexity: Embedded spaces and working places   The concept of "ba" (Nonaka et al., 2000)[1] concerns shared contexts. It is useful for differentiating various spaces in collaborative work. *Ba* refers to a shared context in which knowledge is shared, created, and utilized by those who interact and communicate there. *Ba* does not just mean a physical space, but a specific time and space that integrates layers of spaces. The concept of *Ba* unifies the *physical space*, such as an office, the *virtual space*, such as email, and the *mental or social space*, such as common experiences, ideas, values, and ideals shared by people with common goals as a working context.

Physical places. The physical environments that employees use for working are divided into five categories: (1) home, (2) the main workplace ("office"), (3) moving places, such as cars, trains, planes, and ships, (4) a customer's, partner's and employer's other premises ("other workplaces"), and (5) hotels and cafés etc. ("third workplaces") (Vartiainen et al., 2007). Usually some or even all places are used for working. This type of working in many places is called multilocational work (Lilischkis, 2003).

The use of physical places can be described by different indicators, such as their distance from each other (near–far), their number (one–many), and the frequency with which they are changed (seldom–often).

A *virtual place* refers to an electronic working environment or virtual working space. The internet and intranet provide a platform for working places for both simple communication tools, such as email, and complex ones, such as collaborative working environments, which integrate several tools like email, audio-conferencing, videoconferencing, group calendar, chat, document management like wiki and presence awareness.

A *mental/social place* refers to cognitive constructs, thoughts, beliefs, ideas, and mental states that employees share. Creating and forming joint mental spaces

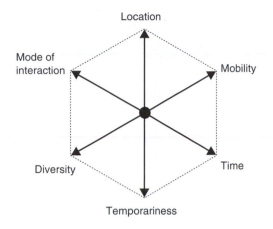

Figure 10.2: The physical, and virtual, characteristics of teamwork contexts

requires communication and collaboration, such as exchanging ideas in face-to-face or virtual dialogues.

Characteristics of contextual complexity The second factor, "complexity of context," influencing team outcomes is described by six "objective" requirement characteristics (figure 10.2). The characteristics are related to the *ba* as spaces to work in the following manner: location (geographical distance, mobility) and time (asynchrony, temporariness) characterize the use of physical space; interaction (mediatedness) indicates the requirements of virtual space; diversity (differences in team members' backgrounds) shows the potential social relations between people as the basis of mental and social space. The six characteristics are:

* *Location*: employees work face-to-face in the same location, or they or some of them are geographically dispersed in different places. For example, some of the team members or teams in a large project are working in one location and others are distributed to work at two other sites.
* *Mobility*: some team members may also be physically mobile and change their workplaces continuously, while others stay in a fixed place, working mainly in one location.
* *Time*: employees work asynchronously or synchronously either in different or same time zones. In addition, they work only for one team or project or divide their time between several teams and projects, doing a part-time job in them.
* *Temporariness*: the collaboration of team members may be permanent or only temporary. Most teams are project teams, which have a start and an end to their life cycle.

- *Diversity*: the composition of groups may vary according to the background and individual characteristics of their members, i.e. their age, education, gender, nationality, ethnical background, religion, language, style, and temperament may vary to a greater or lesser extent.
- *Mode of interaction*: communication and collaboration take place directly face-to-face or are mediated by various media and technological systems.

The value of the six characteristics varies from low to high. The higher the value is, the higher are the demands of the job. The middle spot reflects a situation in which all the team members are similar in their backgrounds and are working together face-to-face simultaneously at the same place and time on a permanent basis. An example is a traditional co-located work group such as a group of assembly workers around a production line. At the other extreme are teams in which all members work on temporary basis in different places and time zones, move a lot, and all have different educational and cultural background. An example is a global, virtual marketing team and a new product design team. The higher the demands, the more developed intrateam processes and regulation are needed for successful performance.

Work requirements and intrateam processes   Research on the development of *socio-emotional processes* in virtual teams has focused on relationship building in general, and on team cohesion and trust. Relationship building includes interaction processes designed to increase feelings of inclusiveness or belonging to the team that are hypothesized to foster cohesion and trust. *Task processes* occur as team members work together to accomplish a task or goal. The research on task processes has focused on communication, coordination and task–technology–structure fit, i.e. the fit between various technologies available to virtual teams and the tasks they are called upon to execute.

Marks, Mathieu, and Zaccaro (2001; see Martins et al., 2004) classify team processes into planning processes, action processes, and interpersonal processes. Planning processes include, for example, mission analysis, goal-setting, and strategy formulation. Action processes occur during the performance of group tasks, such as communication, participation, coordination, and monitoring of the group's progress. Interpersonal processes include, for example, conflict, tone of interaction, trust, cohesion, affect, and social integration.

In distributed virtual teams, getting to know each other's individual characteristics and "life space" is more difficult than in co-located groups. The clarity of common goals and tasks, or of each others' roles and accountability may be vague. Additionally, knowledge about the practices of communication and information sharing and the availability of technologies for communication and collaboration may differ. All this may influence intragroup processes such as cooperation and collaboration, trust, and cohesion. It is inevitable that knowledge sharing and mutual learning become more complicated when the task and context complexities increase.

In all, the major activities in any cooperative settings can be ordered into five basic categories of interaction processes (Andriessen, 2003, pp. 7–8). The performance and well-being outcomes of a group depend on the quality of and on the mutual fit of these processes:

Interpersonal exchange processes:
• Communication, i.e. exchanging signals and using communication tools. Communication has a special status in that it is basic to the other task and group oriented processes.

Task-oriented processes:
• Cooperation, i.e. working together, co-decision-making, co-editing, etc.
• Coordination, i.e. adjusting the work of the group members; this includes leadership.
• Information sharing and learning, i.e. exchanging (sharing) and developing information, views and knowledge.

Group-oriented processes:
• Social interaction, i.e. group maintenance activities, developing trust and cohesion, conflict handling, reflection.

Team outcomes Martins et al. (2004) and Powell et al. (2004) summarize empirical studies of the effects of work requirements and intrateam processes on member performance and satisfaction outcomes in virtual teams. When considering *performance*, it has been found consistently that virtual interaction increases the amount of time required to accomplish tasks. Some reasons offered for the increased time are firstly the fact that typing and using ICT technology takes longer time than face-to-face discussions, and secondly that asynchronous communication is slower than synchronous communication. The findings for the effects on performance quality are mixed. Several researchers have found no differences in performance quality between virtual and face-to-face teams, while others have found that face-to-face teams outperform virtual teams. On the other hand, there are findings, which show that virtual teams produce better work, make more effective decisions, generate more unique and high quality ideas, and report their solutions as being more original. Martins et al. (2004) show that these inconsistent results can be explained with factors such as *task type*, e.g., in negotiation and intellectually requiring tasks face-to-face teams perform better, *time spent working in a group*, e.g., groups evolve, learn and become experienced, and *social context*, e.g., cooperation and communication openness improves team performance. Powell et al. (2004, p. 13) for their part summarize factors contributing to the successful performance of a virtual team: training, strategy/goal-setting, developing shared language, team building, team cohesiveness, communication, coordination and commitment of the team, the appropriate task–technology fit, and competitive and collaborative conflict behaviors.

Mixed results on *satisfaction outcomes* have emerged from the comparison of traditional and virtual teams, with some studies detecting no differences while others found traditional team members more satisfied than virtual team members (Powell et al., 2004). According to Martins et al. (2004) satisfaction appears to be dependent on the nature of the task and on team composition. One study found that traditional team members started out more satisfied, but virtual team members' satisfaction levels rose throughout the year (Powell et al., 2004). Teams using electronic chat have reported higher levels of frustration. However, for decision-making tasks, members of virtual groups reported to be more satisfied with the group process. Similarly, members of electronic brainstorming teams have been found to be more satisfied than their face-to-face counterparts. Finally, all-female virtual teams tend to report higher levels of satisfaction than all-male virtual teams.

Hertel et al. (2005, pp. 71–2) name as potential advantages of high virtuality at the individual level "higher flexibility and time control together with higher responsibilities, work motivation, and empowerment of the team members. Challenges on the other hand are feelings of isolation and decreased interpersonal contact, increased chances of misunderstandings and conflict escalation, and increased opportunities of role ambiguity and role conflicts due to commitments to different work-units."

Differences in team types

The existence of different types of virtual teams is related to differences in group tasks and working contexts and differences in processes, with which teams regulate their activities. Below, the characteristics of task and contextual complexities are used to show the differences both between conventional and distributed teams and between various types of distributed virtual teams.

Distributed versus conventional teams Distributed and conventional teams are not distinguished by task complexity; variation in task demands: membership of other groups or projects, how temporary team members are, or how diverse the team. Three remaining characteristics make the difference, however, more visible. These are: *geographical distance*, i.e. crossing spatial boundaries, *mode of interaction*, i.e. the way information, data and personal communication are exchanged (Bell & Kozlowski, 2002, pp. 21–2), and *physical mobility* of team members.

Team types: Geographical distance Members of distributed teams may work in the same building but in different rooms and on different floors, in different buildings, towns or in other countries and continents. Usually some team members are located in distant places while others work in the main office.

A classic study (Allen, 1977) measuring the frequency of communication of 512 individuals in 7 organizations over 6 months showed that working at a distance of 30 meters does not differ from working 3,000 kilometers apart in terms of communication frequency! Even a small distance matters!

Team types: Mode of interaction   ICT is used both as a means of communication and collaboration and as a collective memory to collect, store, access, and utilize knowledge. The number and variety of communication and collaboration tools, the purposes for which they are used, and their frequency of use indicate roughly the complexity of communication between team members. The central dilemma is: to what extent are electronic media and communication and collaboration tools able to replace face-to-face communication with all its richness? Research on virtual teams shows that effective virtual teams are able to change their behavior and to adapt to changes in the organization/social environment, team structures and technology (Powell et al., 2004).

Team types: Physical mobility   *Physical mobility* as a contextual complexity characteristic can be evaluated in the following manner. First, how many places do team or project members visit because of their job? Secondly, how often do they change locations? Thirdly, what is the type of their physical mobility? The types can be described by using the five categories distinguished by Lilischkis (2003): "On-site movers," "Yo-yos," "Pendulums," "Nomads," and "Carriers." This classification is parallel to a dimension from micro-mobility to macro-mobility (Schaffers, 2005). Moving on-site in the same building or in nearby buildings and areas is called *micro-mobility* or *campus mobility*. Moving regularly between many places, e.g., the pendulums who go up and down between their home and work, and the Yo-Yos who occasionally visit other places, or the Nomads who do so most of their time, is called *multimobility*. And moving all the time between different sites, such as a truck driver (a "carrier"), is called *full or total mobility*. The more workplaces there are to visit, and the more distant they are from each other, the higher the contextual complexity related to location is.

Geographical distance, physical mobility and a mediated mode of interaction are the main characteristics that make distributed virtual teams different from conventional groups and teams.

Differences between distributed teams   Distributed teams vary as well. At one end, there are distributed teams that possess multiple characteristics of conventional work groups, such as all members are working in fixed places, though they are distributed. At the other end, there are the "ideal types" or prototypical global, highly mobile virtual teams and projects, such as management, marketing and sales teams and new product design teams, whose members are constantly moving and may never meet each other face-to-face.

In practice, teams and projects are only seldom fully distributed and "virtual" in the meaning of being at the extreme ends of the six dimensions (figure 10.2). The six characteristics of contextual complexity are closely related to and dependent on each other: a change in one of them results in changes in others or in

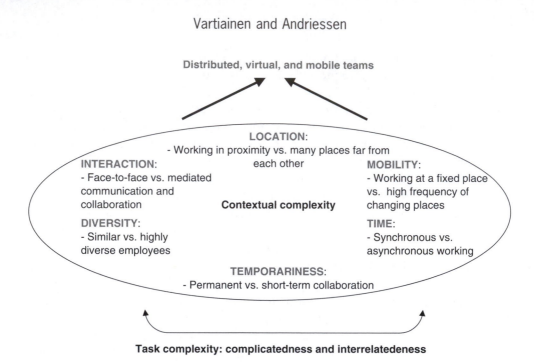

Figure 10.3: Characteristics that distinguish conventional, distributed, virtual, and mobile teams (modified from Bell & Kozlowski, 2002, p. 30)

all of them. For example, the greater the physical mobility of an employee is, the more likely (s)he is to meet people from diverse backgrounds.

In addition to variation in spatial distance, media use and mobility of team members, distributed virtual teams may vary in the three other characteristics of contextual complexity: time synchronicity, temporariness and diversity. The combinations of these characteristics yield many possible types of distributed teams (figure 10.3) one of them being a fully virtual team. They will be discussed next.

Time as a contextual complexity factor manifests itself in many issues and especially in the degree of synchronous and asynchronous distributed working time. Certain synchronous technologies such as videoconferencing are required in case of real time cooperating, whereas emails and other messages allow for greater temporal distribution. The complexity of tasks and task interdependence are related to synchronous or asynchronous working as Bell and Kozlowski (2002, pp. 30–1) underline. When a task is complex, the need for real-time communication increases and more interaction follows.

The following indicators and questions are used to clarify the role of time as a contextual characteristic. First, how much time is used for work in different places, Second, what is the ratio of move-time to time used in different workplaces? Third, are the team members simultaneously working on the same document? Fourth, what is the number of team members working in different time zones? Fifth, how many employees are available at the same time? For example, in global teams some team members may still be sleeping while others are working.

Temporariness is also an aspect of time and a complexity factor. Most teams exist only temporarily, varying from a couple of weeks to some years. People join and leave and belong to several teams and projects. When the number of projects that a team member has increases, more adaptation is required to a variety of team situations. Finally has a team's work or a project just started or is it about to end? For example, the cohesion of the group is usually smaller in the beginning of a project than at its end phase.

Diversity refers to differences in individual characteristics in distributed teams, and includes native language, nationality, educational background, sex, religion, ethnical background and age. Employees can also be diverse in their personality characteristics, emotions, temperament, styles, attitudes, knowledge and competencies. Diversity is the root for similarity or dissimilarity of mental and social spaces of team members, for example team members' perceptions of time or time visions differ and have influence on the team's dynamics and performance (Saunders et al., 2004). Powell et al. (2004) summarize that cultural differences appear to lead to coordination difficulties and create obstacles to effective communication. However, the negative effects may be mitigated by an effort to actively understand and accept the differences.

The more distributed an organization is, the higher the probability is that one will collaborate with different people. Mobility of employees increases this probability. In addition, customers, suppliers, and other interest groups are often involved in collaboration.

Conventional, distributed, virtual, and mobile teams   Conventional groups and teams are co-located, communicating face-to-face and working towards a joint goal here and now. The main types of nonconventional teams are: (1) distributed, (2) virtual, and (3) mobile virtual teams. Team members working in different locations and their geographical distance from each other make a distributed team. A team becomes virtual when group members communicate and collaborate with each other from different locations via electrical media. Physical mobility of group members adds a new feature to distributed work. Mobile, virtual teams are always distributed, but not all distributed, virtual teams are mobile (see figure 10.4).

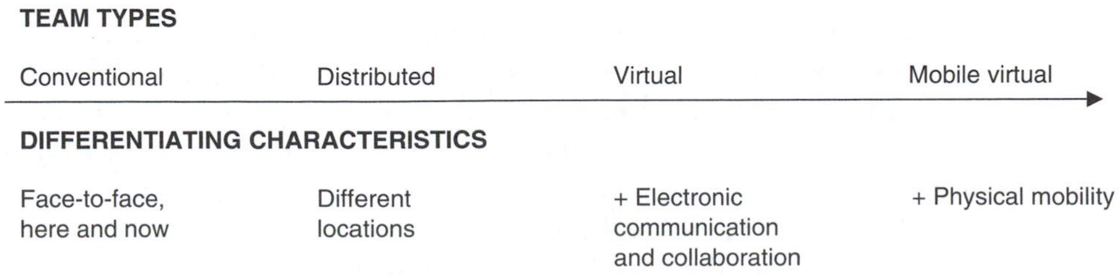

TEAM TYPES

Conventional	Distributed	Virtual	Mobile virtual

DIFFERENTIATING CHARACTERISTICS

Face-to-face, here and now	Different locations	+ Electronic communication and collaboration	+ Physical mobility

Figure 10.4:   The types of groups and teams by increasing contextual complexity

Collaboration Technologies

The Principle of Task–Context–Process–Technology Fit assumes that the choice of technology and the optimal outcome of the work system depend on the tasks to be done, the places where the work is done and the quality of team processes. The rules of thumb are: Firstly, the more common the goal and the more interdependent the tasks are, the more coordination is needed and the larger the role for collaborative technology. Secondly, the more complex the tasks are and the more turbulent the environment is, the more there is need for high quality communication. And thirdly, the need for coordination and collaboration tools depends on the experiences of employees with virtual work and on the degree to which group members know and trust each other, based on earlier experiences. In the latter case, people are able to communicate with fewer cues from each other than those who work together for the first time.

Content of tasks and collaboration

Cooperative Tasks   Powell et al. (2004) report findings that face-to-face meetings are best suited for ambiguous tasks, managing conflicts, managing external resources, brainstorming, and for setting strategic directions. Electronic communication for its part is supposed to be best used for structured tasks such as routine analysis and monitoring project status. Hertel et al. (2005, p. 77), on the other hand, conclude in their review that teams with high virtuality seem to have some advantages compared to face-to-face teams for generating tasks, e.g., brainstorming, but difficulties for decision tasks in particular. However, when teams have more time to adjust to new technologies and to develop stable work routines, the disadvantages of high virtuality may diminish or even reverse. Powell et al. (2004) also report studies showing that virtual teams without access to synchronous communication are able to overcome many limitations by adapting to and learning to use the available technologies, by developing shared language, and by changing team structures.

Requirements of context   The selection for tools of communication and collaboration depends especially on the three characteristics of work context: *location* (same vs. different), *mobility* (fixed place vs. changing place), and *time* (synchronous vs. asynchronous, permanent vs. temporary). The longer the distance between team members and the higher the number of working locations, the higher is the need of mediated interaction, and consequently, the need for technological support. As in traditional organizations, people in distributed organizations perform many of their tasks asynchronously in solitude, while at the same time a part of their tasks requires real-time cooperation, i.e. informing, exchanging information and knowledge, and joint decision-making.

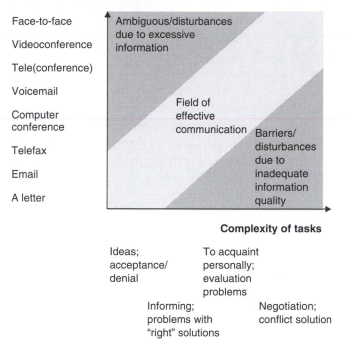

Figure 10.5: The media richness model (Daft & Lengel, 1984; Picot et al., 2001; see Meyer et al., 2001, p. 14)

Quality of communication The capacity of communication channels to transfer content-*rich information* is central for effective communication in any work. Factors involved are *content* for working, *awareness* of other participants, *Speed or timeliness*, and *volume*, i.e. the need for large amounts of information.

Originally Lengel (1983; see also Daft & Lengel, 1984) argued that communication media used in organizations determine the richness of information processed (figure 10.5). Communication media were proposed to fit along a 5-step continuum including face-to-face discussion, phone calls, letters, written documents, and numeric documents. The proposed explanation was that the media differ in (1) feedback capability, (2) communication channels utilized, (3) source and (4) language. Face-to-face was said to be richest because it provides immediate feedback with which understanding can be checked and interpretations corrected. Face-to-face also allows the simultaneous observation of multiple cues, such as body language, facial expression and tone of voice. Face-to-face information also is of a personal nature and utilizes natural language, which is high in variety. According to the model, the most effective communication is found by combining different media to meet the demands of the tasks and information quality.

Figure 10.5 illustrates the notions that performing a complex task, e.g., negotiating, through a simple medium such as email is *ineffective*, while performing a simple task, e.g., sending simple data through a rich medium such as video-conferencing is *inefficient*. There is, however, a danger that the model simplifies strongly the possibilities of different media to transmit complicated messages as well as the capacity of individuals and teams to adapt and overcome the limits of media. The media richness model has been criticized by saying that the fit between task and medium is not a one-to-one relation but falls within quite a wide band of good fit. For example, within this band, performance can be made more fluent by increasing competencies of people via training and education, recruiting new competent people, rotating tasks between employees, restructuring tasks, and by changing the working environment (Andriessen, 2003, pp. 79–80).

Presence and awareness   From the viewpoint of an employee, the challenges of distributed collaborations are, especially, related to two issues: what are his or her competencies and what are the resources of technology to create the *feelings of social presence and awareness* of others?

Lobard and Ditton (1997) define "presence" as the perceptual illusion of nonmediation. An "illusion of nonmediation" occurs when a person fails to perceive or acknowledge the existence of a medium in his/her communication environment and responds as (s)he would if the medium were not there. To those who study communication in organizations, presence is the extent to which interpersonal relations are perceived as sociable, warm, sensitive, personal or intimate when communication is mediated.

Social presence theory (Short, Williams, & Christie, 1976) and media richness theory (Rice, 1992) were developed to better match communication media and organizational tasks to maximize efficiency and satisfaction. Communication media are said to differ in the extent to which they "(a) can overcome various communication constraints of time, location permanence, distribution, and distance, (b) transmit the social, symbolic, and nonverbal cues of human communication; and (c) convey equivocal information" (Rice, 1992, p. 452). A shared physical space, such as an open plan office, provides a rich social environment for employees, which makes it possible to be aware of others' tasks, activities, locations, intentions, and feelings. This awareness helps a team to work efficiently if close communication and collaboration are needed. However, often tasks of individual workers do not require maximal richness and its cues may be perceived as disturbances and interruptions decreasing efficiency and satisfaction.

In co-located teams, the rich face-to-face interaction afforded by shared physical workspaces allows people to maintain real-time knowledge about others' interaction with the task environment. Gutwin, Greenberg, and Roseman (1996) call this "workspace awareness" as a part of the glue that allows groups to collaborate effectively. In real-time collaboration environments that provide a shared virtual space for collaboration, the possibilities for interaction are impoverished.

Steinfield, Jang, and Pfaff (1999; see Gutwin et al., 1996) expand the notion of awareness to knowledge about a project as a whole. They define awareness as occurring "when group members possess knowledge about the current status and actions of the various components (including people) in a collaborative system." They distinguish five types of awareness:

1. Activity awareness: knowledge about project related activities of group members, both during and between meetings; activities between meetings may be found reported in asynchronous groupware system.
2. Availability awareness: knowing the physical availability of group members; e.g., through active badges, certain features of video systems or of chat box systems.
3. Process awareness: knowing the state of affairs of the primary work process, for instance through a workflow management system.
4. Environment awareness: knowledge about outside events that may have implications for the group.
5. Perspective awareness: knowing background information to make sense of other people's actions.

Available collaboration technology and its usefulness

Collaboration environments are necessary elements among the support systems for virtual organizations. In this context the concepts of "groupware" and "Computer Supported Collaborative Work" are relevant. Borghoff and Schlichter (2000) note that these terms can be traced back to the early 1980's. They define groupware as follows (Borghoff & Schlichter, 2000, p. 94): "Groupware are computer-based systems that support groups of people in a common task (or goal) and that provide an interface to a shared environment." Groupware systems are characterized by their high values for the common task and the shared environment (figure 10.6). An email system provides hardly any shared environment, while an e-learning environment does so to a high degree. Borghoff and Schlichter specify as integral requirements of groupware that group members must not be isolated, that they must be informed explicitly about each others' existence, and that modifications must be mutually reported. Therefore, a traditional text system does not convert into a groupware simply by allowing several users sequential reading or writing access to the same document, as they note.

How should we categorize the available technologies for virtual organizations? Available ICT systems can be grouped into two broad categories: (a) *communication technologies* for exchange of information and knowledge, and (b) *collaboration technologies* or knowledge support or organization memory technologies to create, store and utilize information and knowledge for co-workers.

From the technological viewpoint, technologies can be categorized, on the one hand, into those allowing synchronous, real-time communication and to those allowing asynchronous, non-real-time communication, and, on the other

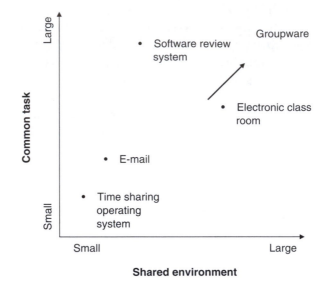

Figure 10.6: Ranges for the dimension common task and shared environment (Borghoff & Schlichter, 2000, p. 95)

hand, into those supporting face-to-face communication. These can be realized through the companies' own intranet and via the internet. Increasingly today and especially in the future, wired technologies are replaced by less-wired, mobile technologies.

Andriessen (2003) presents a taxonomy of collaboration technologies (table 10.1) by combining five types of interaction processes and three types of working: A. asynchronous, B. synchronous, and C. face-to-face. These tools support various kinds of collaboration and functions.

Today we have more and more collaboration environments that integrate and fuse diverse tools. The typical combination of "off-the-shelve" collaboration technologies consists of a smart phone, tele- and videoconference, email, and some web tools. Mobile devices provide one of the easiest ways to communicate. Smartphones themselves integrate the functionalities of a mobile phone, personal digital assistant or other applications, for example, a calender, browser, email, audio conferencing, chat, and document reading.

Managing Virtual Teams

Working in distributed organizations challenges the traditional models of team building and management. For example, Henry and Hartzler (1998: see Hertel et al., 2005) point to three main challenges that may be magnified by distance. One is the danger of losing focus of a team, losing sight of the purpose and specific

Table 10.1: Types of collaboration technology (modified from Andriessen, 2003, p. 12)

	A. Support between encounters: asynchronous communication different place/ different time	B. Support for synchronous electronic encounters different place / same time	C. Support for synchronous face-to-face meetings same place / same time
Communication systems	• Fax • email • voice-mail • text chat	• telephone/mobile phone • teleconference • video-conference • instant message/ chat, e.g. skype	• face-to-face
Information sharing systems	• websites • file- and application-sharing systems • bulletin boards, Internet forums • wikis	• teleconsultation systems • co-browser	• presentation systems
Coordination systems	• group-calendar • shared planning • shared workflow management systems • event manager • subgroup spaces	• notification systems, e.g. active batch	• command and control centre support systems
Co-operation systems	• document co-authoring	• shared CAD, whiteboard, word processor, spreadsheet • electronic brainstorming systems	• group decision support systems (meeting support systems, e.g. agenda, voting)
Social encounter systems	• weblog • community technologies and services	• media spaces • virtual reality • virtual presence	

mission of the work. Time should be invested to achieve a real and shared sense of clarity concerning vision, strategy, goals, and objectives, as well as building a project plan, doing resource analysis and defining responsibilities. The second challenge concerns the possibility of misunderstandings and conflicts. Tools to help developing teams' values and operating principles, for example an operating agreement, might help in avoiding possible difficulties. The third challenge deals with managing the synergy of a dispersed team. Virtual teams find this often difficult because of their dispersed locations. Developing communication is the key for creating synergy, keeping the team together, and moving forwards.

Models of virtual team building

There are several models available to build dispersed organizational units in addition to the traditional forming–storming–norming–performing–adjourning model (Tuckman & Jensen, 1977; see also chapter 14 by West in this book). The linear models of development have been countered by claiming that the development of a group varies according to the type of the group, and may proceed in iterative cycles, and that there are many possible sequences through which groups may develop. Some phase models deal especially with virtual teams (e.g., Lipnack & Stamps, 2000; Duarte & Snyder, 2001; Hertel et al., 2005).

Lipnack and Stamps (2000) use the metaphor of an airplane's flight. According to them, there are two periods of predictable turbulence: *takeoff*, the launch moment for teams, and *landing*, the test period for the team's work. Launch follows a sometimes lengthy *start-up* period, which includes a relatively short but intense period of producing a plan and defining leadership. During start-up people assess and gather information, speak out and test ideas. During *performance*, activities accelerate, tasks are undertaken and results accumulate. Work is then tested before acceptance, and delivered to customers. Lipnack and Stamps (2000) recommend managers spend time in the first two phases (start-up, takeoff). Mistakes, mistrust, unexpressed viewpoints, and unresolved conflicts too easily become parts of operating norms. Lack of clarity around goals, tasks, and leadership disturb the team in the performance phase. Failure to establish criteria and measures for results ensures problems during the testing phase.

Duarte and Snyder (2001; see also McGrath, 1991) divide the stages of their model of virtual team development into the realms of task and social dynamics. The goal of well-managed *task dynamics* is productivity. The goal of well-managed *social dynamics* is a feeling of team unity and satisfaction.

The four stages associated with *task dynamics* are as follows (Duarte & Snyder, 2001, p. 182; see also McGrath, 1991):

1. *Inception*. This stage involves the generation of ideas related to defining the goals of a team, how the goals might be accomplished, and overall plans to achieve them.
2. *Problem-solving*. This stage involves choosing the correct means by which to address issues and solve technical problems. Issues and problems can have knowable and "correct" answers or can be unique, with no existing answers.
3. *Conflict resolution*. This stage involves the resolution of conflicts that emerge from different points of view. Team members may have different approaches

to technical problems. Conflicts also can be the results of different cultural, functional, and organizational perspectives.

4. *Execution*. This stage involves performing the team's work and overcoming organizational barriers that inhibit performance. Barriers include power struggles between functions, issues of ownership over the final product, and conflict over allocation of resources.

Social dynamics parallel the task dynamics and include the following stages (Duarte & Snyder, 2001, 184–5):

1. *Interaction and inclusion*. Team members define their individual contributions to the team and begin to interact as a group to develop the team's charter and work plans.
2. *Position status and role definition*. Team members interact to define or redefine their roles and status in relation to one another. The focus may be on their roles as experts or as organizational representatives. It may be on their personal or expert status in relation to other members, particularly in determining the solutions to problems.
3. *Allocation of resources and power*. The team addresses issues regarding the allocation of resources and power that result from the team's activities or from particular approaches to problems. This stage can be contentious if the team contains members from many different stakeholder groups.
4. *Interaction and participation*. This stage involves participation and interaction among team members in performing work and in overcoming barriers that inhibit team productivity.

Duarte and Snyder (2001) note that when virtual teams are addressing simple and prescriptive tasks, they may be able to move from stage 1 to stage 4 after a minimal planning period. More complicated patterns are likely to occur in teams that have complex tasks in adaptive environments or in teams that have a number of team members with diverse interests.

Team building in practice

Next, a rough model with some guidelines is provided for virtual team building. The model has the general stages of forming, maintaining and completing of any group or team (figure 10.7). As there are varieties of distributed virtual teams arising from the different purposes and contexts where they live in, managing the structure and the composition of a team, and group process creates various demands for team leaders. Therefore, there is no "one-best-way," but a number of "good" principles and procedures to follow.

Forming by agreeing   The first task of a team leader is to do some preparations and map starting conditions and resources by, for example, consulting other

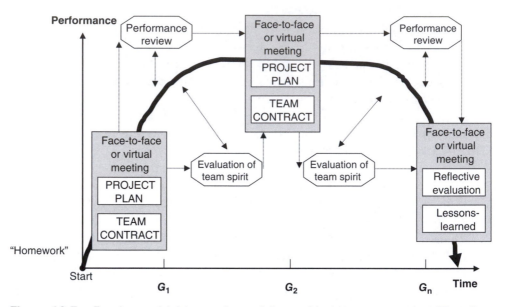

Figure 10.7: Forming, maintaining, and completing a virtual team or a project ($G_1 - G_n$ = subgoals)

experienced managers, or referring to reviews from similar, former virtual projects. The second task is to define the assignment, goals, tasks and composition of the team. Other issues to consider beforehand by a team manager are the reward system, available collaborative technologies, and the training to work virtually.

Almost all authors on virtual team management agree that at the start all members should meet each other face to face. Face-to-face discussion allows each member to express his or her views on what the team's core purpose and objectives are, thus clarifying early on where time and energy will be focused (Fisher & Fisher, 2001). A face-to-face meeting is needed for building the operating principles covering both task ("project plan") and social dynamics ("team contract"). Operating principles have two main contents: one, the project plan, is for setting vision, mission, strategy, goals and tasks of a team, the other, the team contract, is for fixing the rules, norms and procedures to follow.

Maintaining by communicating There are several managerial topics to pay attention to during team performance: type of leadership, regulation of communication, maintenance of motivation and emotion and team knowledge management (Hertel et al., 2005). Fisher and Fisher (2001) advise both task and team process facilitation during the performance phase. It is a danger that the technical or task aspects of work are focused on more heavily than the social or process side. When working virtually, i.e. without actual face-to-face interaction, a social structure and familiarity of a team must be built. For example, to get to know each other everybody may place his or her photo on the project's website and add information about his or her personal background. Some companies have an organization wide "yellow paper" system, where all this information is already available. Cultural sensitivity is also needed because what may be acceptable in Finland may not be so in China, and vice versa.

What kind of leadership fits with virtual work? Hertel's et al. (2005, pp. 80–1) review proposes three *leadership* approaches that differ in the degree of autonomy of team members: electronic performance monitoring (EPM), management by objectives (MBO) and self-managing teams. When leading from a distance, traditional management by controlling is not possible, thus EPM is not suitable for virtual teamwork. Instead, principles of delegation are more promising since they address the challenges of distributed work by shifting managerial functions to the team members. Fisher and Fisher (2001) suggest leaders address only what the constraints or limitations are and leave the determination of what and how work is done up to the team.

Trust, team identification and cohesion, and satisfaction of the team members are crucial motivational and emotional processes to maintain. In virtual teams it is, however, more difficult to implement common goals, feelings of anonymity and low social control may lead to social loafing, self-efficacy is more difficult to maintain due to reduced feedback, and trust is more difficult to build (see Hertel et al., 2005).

Hertel et al. (2005) provide several guidelines to increase motivation and trust: clarifying team goals, identifying and giving feedback on the importance of team members' contributions and on the progress of team task to increase personal awareness, providing constructive and supportive feedback to increase feelings of self-efficacy, and providing opportunities for informal communication to increase trust. Team identification and cohesion seem to be related to managers' ability to clarify team goals, roles and norms. Opportunities for a face-to-face meeting at the beginning of teamwork, non-job-related communication and constructive conflict management are related to high team member satisfaction. Fisher and Fisher (2001) recommend that when setting operative guidelines, statements have to be formulated about how conflicts will initially be handled and what to do when the parties involved cannot reach a resolution, e.g., do they bring in a manager or other third party to facilitate.

Many virtual teams have a temporary composition; members leave, new members join, and members divide their time between several teams. New team members should be integrated effectively. A new member should be acquainted with the project plan and the team contract. There should be personal contact with a newcomer from the leader.

Completing by learning   Teams have their lifecycle and every project has its end. Virtual teams have often a transient structure so that some of their members leave the team earlier than others. Teams often "melt" away. However, it is important to collect lessons learnt. This is the time for a face-to-face meeting for reflection and evaluation, for making reviews and accumulating experiences. The results of post-mortem reviews are very beneficial for new, starting distributed projects. Therefore, it is desirable to create documentation concerning the project's progress and best practices.

Summary

In this chapter, we have overviewed distributed virtual and mobile groups and teams as basic work units in distributed organizations and discussed about their prevalence and characteristics. The new types of work like mobile work and virtual teams are increasingly used in working life. Virtuality was defined as a team characteristic referring to the use of ICT technologies for communication and collaboration, to overcome the barriers of time, space and organizational borders of distributed teams. Conventional groups and teams differ from distributed, virtual and mobile teams especially in three characteristics: geographical distance of their members, time differences and mode of interaction. Conventional groups and teams are co-located, communicating face-to-face and working towards a joint goal here and now. Team members working in different locations form a distributed team. A distributed team becomes virtual when group members communicate and collaborate with each other via electronic media. Physical mobility of group members adds a new feature to distributed work. Mobile, virtual teams are always distributed, but not all distributed, virtual teams are mobile. The role of collaboration technologies is to support communication. Rich and versatile communication is the requisite for cooperation, coordination, information sharing and learning, and social interaction of team members. The final topic in the chapter was the managerial implication of virtual working. It was shown that management and new leadership are not only needed but also possible in virtual organizations.

Discussion Points

The characteristics of global virtual teams influence the communication between team members. What are these characteristics and how do they influence communication and collaboration?

You are a newly selected product design manager in a distributed team. Your team's members come from different parts of the world. What are your main challenges as team leader and how can you deal with these challenges?

You have been collaborating with other students while doing your course assignments. What kind of technologies have you used in your communication? Where these tools adequate or could you have done better with other tools?

Key Studies

1. Meyerson, D., Weick, K. E., & Kramer, R. M. (1996). Swift trust and temporary groups. In K. M. Kramer & T. R. Tyler (Eds.), *Trust in organizations* (pp. 166–95). Thousand Oaks, CA: Sage. The article presents the concept "swift" trust for temporary groups.
2. Majchrzak, A., Rice, R. E., Malhotra, A., & King, N. (2000). Technology adaptation adoption: The case of a computer-supported inter-organizational virtual team. *MIS Quarterly*, 24, 569–600. The adaptation and use of new technologies is dependent on several systemic factors.
3. Fiol, C. M., & O'Connor, E. J. (2005). Identification in face-to-face, hybrid and pure virtual teams: Untangling the contradictions. *Organization Science*, 16, 19–32.

Further Reading

Andriessen, J. H. E., & Vartiainen, M. (Eds.) (2006). *Mobile virtual work. A new paradigm?* Heidelberg: Springer.

Hertel, G., Geister, S., & Konradt, U. (2005). Managing virtual teams: A review of current empirical research. *Human Resource Management Review*, 15, 69–95.

Hinds, P. J., & Kiesler, S. (Eds.) (2002). *Distributed work*. Cambridge, MA: MIT Press.

Martins, L. L., Gilson, L. L., & Maynard, M. T. (2004). Virtual teams: What do we know and where do we go from here? *Journal of Management*, 30, 805–35.

Note

1 "Ba" roughly means "place." The concept was originally proposed by the Japanese philosopher Kitaro Nishida (in *An inquiry into the good*, 1921) and further developed by H. Shimizu (Ba-principle: New logic for real-time emergence of information, *Holonics, 5(1)* (1995), 67–79) (see Nonaka et al., 2000, p. 14).

Research Close-Up

Jarvenpaa, S. L., Knoll, K., & Leidner, D. E. (1998). Is anybody out there? Antecedents of trust in global virtual teams. *Journal of Management Information Systems*, *14(4)*, 29–64.

Introduction

The focus of this study was to explore the antecedents of trust in a global virtual-team setting. Trust has been considered critical in any new organizational arrangements where the traditional social controls based on authority give way to self-direction and self-control. Trust is even more essential in global virtual teams where members physically remain in different countries, interact primarily through the use of collaboration technologies, and rarely if ever see each other in person. In global context, the question is how to develop trust and how it is developing? First, the global virtual context renders other forms of social control, such as direct supervision, inoperable. Second,

Continued

other factors known to contribute to social control and coordination, such as geographical proximity, similarity in backgrounds, and experience, are often absent. This study explored the effects of factors that have been identified as sources of trust in traditional face-to-face relationships. The baseline hypothesis was: in a global team, team trust is a function of other team members' perceived ability, i.e. perceived competence of a trustee; integrity, i.e. adherence of a trustee to principles thought to make him or her dependable and reliable; benevolence, i.e. a belief that a trustee feels interpersonal care and concern and is willing to do good to the trustor, as well as of the members' own propensity to trust, i.e. a general personality trait that conveys a general expectation of how trusting one should be.

Method

Participants

Seventy-five teams, consisting of 4 to 6 members residing in different continents and countries, interacted and worked together for 8 weeks. The students came from 28 universities around the world. Of these students, 350 students sent at least one message to their teammates. The teams had the following characteristics: (1) each member of a team resided on a different continent or subcontinent of the world, (2) each team had a mix of students from low- and high-context culture.

Design and procedure

The teams were charged with completing three tasks during eight weeks time: two team-building exercises and a final project. The students' course grade and the 600-dollar reward were based on the successful completion of the final project. The first two tasks encouraged participants to exchange information about themselves that would be relevant for assessing one another's project-related skills (ability), their motivations for contributing to the team effort (benevolence), and their work/study habits believed to be compatible with a successful effort (integrity). The third assignment, the final project, asked the teams to propose a www site providing a new service of offering to an organization called ISWorld Net. The students had 4 weeks to complete this project. Students communicated solely through electronic means. The host institution established a www site to ensure the same information to students, e.g., schedule, advice for virtual collaborators, and a bulletin board. The following data was collected: the students' mail messages sent to the "team address," first electronic survey was sent after the first month, and the second survey was sent following the deadline for the completed final project. The items of the surveys measured benevolence, ability, integrity, trustworthiness, trust and propensity to trust.

Results

The two-week trust-building exercises did have a significant effect on the team members' perceptions of other team members' ability, integrity, and benevolence. However, they did not have a direct effect on trust. In the early phases of teamwork, team trust was predicted strongest by perceptions of other team members' integrity, and weakest by perceptions of their benevolence. The effect of other members' perceived ability of trust decreased over time. The members' own propensity to trust had a significant, though unchanging, effect on trust. In the end, a model of "swift" trust in global virtual team was presented.

Discussion

The antecedents commonly associated with trust in face-to-face dyadic relationships were found to predict trust in the virtual team context. A number of behavioral strategies were identified that appeared to distinguish the highest-trust teams from the lowest-trust teams. The strategies suggest the presence of swift trust. The paper proposes a preliminary model of trust for global virtual teams.

Organizations, Technology, and Safety

11

Nik Chmiel

Overview

Safety at work has received increasing political and research interest in recent years with the realization that simply providing technological safeguards and safety procedures is not the answer to reducing accidents at work. It is in the interests of organizations and governments to reduce accidents at work since not only are people harmed but organizational functioning and costs are affected too. This chapter first considers accident statistics from around the world, but with particular emphasis on Europe, and then discusses the limitations inherent in accident reports as a means to understand the organizational and individual contributions to accident causation. Thereafter case study and survey approaches to investigating the relationships between organizations, technology and accidents, and organizations and individual behaviors are introduced. Management approaches to safety have been a key focus for investigation over the last few years and concepts such as safety climate have become central to understanding the role organizations can play in safety at work.

International and National Accident Statistics

Recent estimates by Hämäläinen, Takala, and Saarela (2006) for the year 1998 indicated almost 350,000 fatalities at work worldwide, and over 260 million occupational accidents leading to more than 3 days away from work. Estimated accident rates were lowest in Established Market Economies (EME: the EU15, USA, Canada, Japan, and Australasia). It may be no coincidence that EMEs mostly have comprehensive accident prevention programs and include occupational safety management as part of their legislation. However, they also have more workers in the service sector where accident rates are lower.

Within the EU15 Spain and Italy had the highest accident and fatality rates and the UK and Netherlands the lowest. Most EU15 accident and fatality rates were lower than those in the USA or Canada. In Europe the EU15 estimated average accident rate for 1998 was less than half that of countries further to the east. Recent data produced from the 2005 European Working Conditions Survey (EWCS) show 25 percent of workers in the EU15 considered their health and safety to be at risk because of their work, whereas in the 10 new member states that joined in 2004 the figure was 40 percent.

Direct comparison of accident data across countries is problematic because different countries have different accident reporting systems, hence the use of estimates. For example some countries record accidents that lead to one or more days away from work whereas others record those leading to more than three days away. This point has been recognized in the European Union in relation to national reporting schemes with the result an initiative aimed at accident reporting harmonization across member states (Jacinto & Aspinwall, 2004). Member states still have the flexibility of using other variables and/or classification schemes for the production of their own national statistics.

Organizations and Legislation

In Europe laws around health and safety at work vary from country to country in their range and scope. Health and Safety Law in the UK places a duty on the employer to protect and keep employees informed about health and safety by: Making the workplace safe; Ensuring plant and machinery are safe; Ensuring that safe systems of work are set and followed; Ensuring articles and substances are moved, stored, and used safely; Providing adequate welfare facilities; Providing information, instruction, training, and supervision necessary for health and safety; and Assessing the risks to health and safety. The employee has a responsibility to look after themselves and others by: Taking reasonable care; Cooperating with their employer; Correctly using work equipment; and Not interfering with anything provided for employee health and safety. In short employees must act to protect themselves and others, comply with safety procedures and regulations, and not sabotage health and safety provision.

Accident reporting

In the UK employers, the self-employed, and those in control of work premises are required by law to report to appropriate national agencies: deaths; major injuries; accidents resulting in over 3 days away from work; diseases; dangerous occurrences; and gas incidents. Major injuries encompass: fractures (other than to fingers, thumbs, or toes); amputation; dislocation of the shoulder, hip, knee, or spine; loss of sight (temporary or permanent); chemical or hot metal burn or any penetrating injury to the eye; injury resulting in unconsciousness or requiring resuscitation or admittance to hospital for more than 24 hours (from e.g. electric shock, asphyxia, exposure to harmful substance); any other injury leading to hypothermia, heat-induced illness or unconsciousness; or acute illness requiring medical treatment, or where there is reason to believe that this resulted from exposure to a biological agent or its toxins or infected material. An over-3-day injury is one which is not "major" but results in the injured person being away from work OR unable to do their full range of normal duties for more than three days.

The basis for UK legislation was passed into law with the Health and Safety at Work Act 1974 and several further regulations were added subsequently to implement a European Commission directive (see Lewis & Sargeant, 2007, for details). The act reflected an emphasis towards workplace safety, dominant in that era, related to hazard identification and hazard control through risk awareness, training, design of technology and instigation of working procedures, rules and regulations aimed at lessening risk. More recent expert opinion on the challenges in improving workplace safety in addition highlight factors related to organizations, their operation and cooperation, and their management. The European Agency for Health and Safety at Work report on "New trends in accident prevention due to the changing world of work" (De Beeck & Van Heuverswyn, 2002) suggested modern work and its influence on accident prevention would involve more free-market, privatization and downsizing, changes in technology, changes in working hours, work pace, and workload, a growth of subcontracting, more service work, an increase in part-time jobs, temporary work, more women, an aging workforce and greater globalization and integration of work.

Changing perspectives on workplace safety have been reflected in what Hale and Hovden (1998) have proposed are three ages to the scientific study of safety. The first age was concerned with "technical measures to guard machinery, stop explosions and prevent structures collapsing" and lasted from the nineteenth century until after 1945. The second age, initiated between the two world wars, witnessed research into prevention measures based on personnel selection, training, and motivation, often referenced to theories of accident proneness. Hale and Hovden indicate that the technical and individual-based approaches merged in the 1960s and 70s with developments in ergonomics and probabilistic risk analysis, and the study of human error as a field of inquiry. They go on to identify the 1990s as well into the third age of safety, characterized as focused on management systems. Thus understanding the contribution of organizations to accidents in a systematic way is a relatively recent line of research.

Organizations and Accidents

Organizational contributions to accidents and safety at work have been investigated through several means, including: accident reporting schemes; expert views; case studies of system disasters and serious accidents, and organizational surveys. Each perspective has its own strengths and weaknesses but they all rely on the reporting of accidents and incidents in one way or another.

Accident reporting systems

Constraints in the way data are collated at the national level may only allow limited understanding of the causes behind the accident figures. Jacinto and Aspinwall (2004) reinforce this point by noting that although Spain has developed a particularly detailed accident report form for both serious and fatal accidents due to machines, involving an extensive questionnaire for assessing technical and working environment causal factors, other underlying human and organizational causes would not be thoroughly assessed.

However, could more detailed reporting schemes within organizations allow for better causal analysis and hence prevention of accidents? It is an attractive proposition that safety at work should be understood through the very thing that safety measures are designed to avoid. Brown, for example asserts that: "reporting accidents is the only practical way of evaluating system safety under real operating conditions, and of identifying factors which may be contributing to accident causation" (1990, p. 755).

Brown (1990) proposed that to be useful accident reporting systems should: highlight primary safety improvements; capture antecedent behavior; avoid subjectivity; avoid apportioning blame; detail task and system demands; collect data on all accidents regardless of their consequences; and detail the nature, severity and causes of accidental injury. These ideals are difficult to achieve in practice. Inter alia, accidents are frequently underreported and antecedent behaviors not captured.

There is a strong possibility that workplace accidents are under-reported. At the national-level comparison between the two main sources of UK accident data, the Labour Force Survey and official reports (RIDDOR), suggest that employers may report less than half of the non-fatal injuries that they should. Under-reporting is recognized as problematic in the EU as a whole (Jacinto & Aspinwall, 2004). Legislation does not require that minor injuries to be reported nationally.

The reporting of injuries may depend to some extent on how severe they are. Chmiel (2005) reported that a comparison of recorded and self-reported minor injuries revealed a large discrepancy, a ratio of approximately $1:11$, in a study in the UK chemical processing sector. Weddle (1996) reported that of hospital environmental service workers who recalled having been injured in the previous year 39 percent had not reported one or more injuries, and that the most frequently cited reason for not reporting was that the injury had seemed too minor, even though roughly 64 percent of unreported injuries required medical care and 44 percent resulted in lost work time. The next most common reason involved not wanting to appear careless to a supervisor.

Organizational factors also affect reporting. Clarke (1998) investigated via questionnaire the reasons behind intentions to report incidents among 128 British Rail Train drivers from three different railway areas. Intention *not* to report was predicted by drivers' beliefs that managers would take no notice of reports; and the interaction between views that incidents were just part of a days work and nothing would get done. Clarke concluded that incident reporting was most influenced by drivers' perceptions of managers' reactions to reports. Reason (1997) identified common features affecting reporting of incidents in successful schemes run by two safety-conscious organizations: British Airways in the UK and NASA in the USA. The common features were: confidentiality in reporting; ease of reporting; separation of agency for collecting reports and that responsible for discipline; rapid, accessible, intelligent feedback to employees; and indemnity against disciplinary action as far as is practicable.

In terms of antecedent behaviors Van der Schaaf and Kanse (2004) observed, despite a positive culture for reporting accidents, that self-recovered errors were not reported because they were not recognized by employees as important to understanding accident causation. More generally voicing views and concerns over safety and communicating to others on safety issues appears related to a number of organizational factors such as job characteristics and the quality of exchanges between leaders and their employees (Hofmann, Morgeson, & Gerras, 2003; Turner, Chmiel, & Walls, 2005).

In addition to the problem of under-reporting, Sheehy and Chapman (1987) observed that accident reporting systems had, by and large, grown to meet specific organizational, medical and legal needs, often failed to elicit ergonomic information, contained crude subdivisions of accidents (e.g., burns, falls, lost time) and, tellingly, reflected implicit theories of accident causation by only collecting information thought to be relevant. Further, and crucially, they pointed out that accident reports: "cannot begin to cater for the complexity of emotional responses associated with the occurrence, prevention, and investigation of accidents" (1987, p. 203).

As a means of understanding safety at work, particularly from a psychological and organizational perspective, accident-reporting schemes have considerable limitations, both in principle and in practice. To be of use for these purposes accidents require considerably more analysis and interpretation than typically provided for in organizational reporting schemes. Case studies of serious accidents and survey investigations of accidents including minor injuries have provided many more insights into the nature of accident causation.

Case studies of system disasters and serious accidents

Case studies demonstrate that large-scale systems accidents can be readily described and analyzed as resulting from a combination of managerial, technical, and design failures, as well as human behavior in the form of violations and errors. Six case studies focusing on latent failures are reported by Reason (1990) ranging across technological systems from chemical production (the Bhopal catastrophe in India), space exploration (the Challenger shuttle disaster in the USA) to transport (the Kings Cross Fire in London and the sinking of the ferry *Herald of Free Enterprise* in Europe) all show similar features. The analysis from the Chernobyl disaster in the Ukraine (then in the USSR) is a good example. On April 26, 1986, at 01:24, two explosions blew off the 1,000-tonne concrete cap sealing Chernobyl-4 nuclear reactor. More than 30 lives were lost. As a result there was widespread contamination 400 square miles around plant. The plume of radioactive material spread through the atmosphere over Scandinavia and western Europe, as far as the Hebridean islands off the northwest coast of Scotland. The explosions occurred as a result of a test to investigate whether the "coast-down" capacity of a turbine generator could power the "emergency core cooling system" for a few minutes. Reason (1990) describes the core features in his analysis of the disaster: The quality of test plan was afterwards assessed as poor, including the section on safety measures; Authority for the plan to proceed was given without formal approval of the Safety Technical Group; The principle testers were from Moscow, and the person in charge was not a specialist in reactor plants; The "emergency core cooling system" was disconnected as part of the test plan, 5 minutes later the plant was asked by the local Kiev controller to continue supplying the grid with electricity which it did at approximately 50 percent of full power; The "emergency core cooling system" was not reconnected – indicative of lax observation of safety procedures; Operating below 20 percent of full power was known to be dangerous; The reactor was released from the grid 9 hours later and operators continued to reduce power, omitting to enter a "hold power" order, leading to very low power, eventually stabilized at 7 percent. Reason concludes the test should have been abandoned at this point but was not. Instead other plant defenses were removed in order to continue the test, resulting in the explosions.

Reason (1990) suggested that the human contributions to complex system breakdowns were a function of active and latent failures. Active failures were unsafe acts, either cognitive errors or violations of safety rules. Latent failures consisted of several categories: Fallible managerial decisions; Line management deficiencies; Psychological precursors to unsafe acts; and inadequate defenses (against unsafe acts). The key idea was that latent failure and active errors combined to cause major accidents, even though the precise nature of the errors and failures was unique to each disaster.

A recent case study by Lawton and Ward (2005) demonstrates the interaction of active error and latent failure contributions. In 1999 two trains collided just outside Paddington Station, near Ladbroke Grove in London, UK. Thirty-one people were killed and more than 400 injured. The immediate "cause" was a Signal Passed at Danger (SPAD), i.e. the driver of one train went through a red light. A report on the accident, several hundred pages long, was compiled in 2000 by Lord Cullen. Lawton and Ward used witness statements and the Cullen report in an analysis of contributory factors from a systems perspective. The main features of the disaster identified by Lawton and Ward were: Driver cognitive error (it was likely the driver who went through the red light expected a green signal – a finding in other investigations of SPADs); The driver had only recently trained and had no experience of the signal he went through; Evidence suggested that the driver was unaware of his error, and could have misread the signal; There was a new track layout designed to allow more train throughput, leading to a very complex driving task; The signal itself was poorly sited, creating viewing problems; The signal had a history of being passed at danger (8 SPADs had been reported between 1993 and 1998) leading Lord Cullen to include in his report the calculation that there was an 86 percent chance in each year of a SPAD at this signal; Drivers were not made aware of SPAD histories along their routes; Training methods were considered suspect, especially with regard to route handling. A result of this and other train crashes led to 295 recommendations, targeted by the UK Health and Safety Executive (HSE) and monitored and approved by the Health and Safety Commission (HSC). Safety leadership and management were subject to 25 recommendations; and training, skills, competence, and behavior 41 recommendations.

A feature of case studies of accident analyses is that they are retrospective: an accident is investigated using a particular framework and it may not be easy to identify and categorize the safety behaviors involved and their causal links to organizational factors (Rasmussen, 1990). The approach has produced many interesting insights but one obvious limitation is that the framework used guides what the investigator is looking for.

Survey approaches to understanding organizational accident involvement

Hale and Hovden characterized the third age of safety as focused on management systems, and the literature, to the 1980s at least, as "accumulated common sense and as general management principles applied to the specific field of safety" (1998, p. 130) rather than science. Thus understanding the contribution of organizations to accidents in a systematic way is a relatively recent line of research. Expert views formed the basis for early studies, but these have been followed by more empirical investigation based on questionnaires focused on management practices and values.

Expert views   Zohar (1980) developed a concept of safety climate corresponding to experts' views that has been influential since. His starting point was the view that climate measures be based on "perceptions held by employees about aspects of their organizational environment, summarized over individual employees" (1980, p. 96). Through a literature review with the purpose "to define organizational characteristics that differentiate between high versus low accident-rate companies" (1980, p. 97), he identified companies with good accident records as having several features: managements demonstrated a commitment to safety (for example, top management was involved in routine safety activities, safety was given high priority at company meetings and in production scheduling, and safety officers had a higher status); safety training was given importance; open communication and frequent contact between management and workers was higher; there was good housekeeping, for instance through orderly plant operations and use of safety devices; safety promotion was through guidance and counseling rather than enforcement and admonition, and included individual praise or recognition for safe performance, and; low accident companies had a stable workforce, with less turnover and older workers.

Zohar (1980) developed a questionnaire to measure these organizational aspects through workforce perceptions. Eight dimensions were identified: importance of safety training programs; management attitudes to safety; effects of safe conduct on promotion; level of risk in the workplace; pace of work demands related to safety; status of the safety officer; the effects of safe conduct on social status, and; status of the safety committee. The questionnaire was given to a stratified Israeli sample of production workers in metal fabrication, food processing, chemicals, and textiles factories. Variance in individual scores within factories was found to be significantly smaller than variance between factories, thus supporting the idea that each factory could be considered to have a safety climate representing a fairly homogeneous set of shared perceptions among employees. Four experienced safety inspectors ranked factories according to their safety practices and accident-prevention programs. The textiles and three other factories could not be ranked. However, the agreement between the rankings for the remainder and their safety climate scores was high (metal and chemicals) to moderate (food processing), providing support for the validity of the safety climate questionnaire.

Subsequent research on organizational safety climate concentrated on the number and nature of the dimensions involved, but has not lead to a universal consensus (Brown & Holmes, 1986; Cooper & Philips, 2004; Dedobbeleer & Beland, 1991; Mueller, DaSilva, Townsend, & Tetrick, 1999, cited in Wiegmann, Zhang, & von Thaden, 2001). A key aspect of safety climate that emerged from analyses of safety climate dimensions is management's relationship to safety, and in particular the perception that management is committed to safety. This factor was seen as a central component of most safety climate measures (Flin, Mearns, O'Connor, & Bryden, 2000). The whole notion of what constitutes a safety culture or climate within an organization can be quite involved (see Guldenmund, 2000, for an extended discussion).

Griffin and Neal (2000), using perspectives from both general organizational climate and specific types of climate, proposed that climate be considered as a higher-order factor comprised of more specific first-order factors, and that these reflect perceptions of safety-related policies, procedures and rewards. The higher-order factor reflects the extent to which employees believe that safety is valued within the organization, which appears akin to management commitment to safety (Zohar & Luria, 2005). In contrast, Griffin and Neal argued ratings of risk, affective reactions to safety issues, normative beliefs about safety, and self-reports of safety behavior, should not be considered to be perceptions of safety climate. Griffin and Neal acknowledged that there was no clear agreement about what first order factors constituted the higher order factor (see research close-up) but they suggested that in "determining the overall impact of safety climate on safety outcomes, a higher order factor of safety climate will be most appropriate" (2000, p. 348). Taking a similar view, and using items covering the range of activities outlined in the British Standards Institute's (2000) safety management code to measure safety climate, Zohar and Luria (2005) showed a significant association between organizational safety climate scores and organizational safety as measured through a safety audit procedure carried out by a senior safety inspector and three observers. The audit did not include accident outcomes.

Salminen, Saari, Saarela, and Rasanen (1993) analyzed interviews with injured workers, foremen, and co-workers involved in serious accidents in Southern Finland. Their results suggested that the need to save time, work to tight schedules, and a lack of caution had a greater influence on accidents than the foremen, co-workers, customers, or wage system. In addition, accident risk was significantly greater for subcontractors.

Empirical studies   A key question is whether organizational practices, identified through expert views and otherwise, are actually associated with safety outcomes, particularly accidents.

Shannon, Mayr, and Haines (1997) reviewed ten studies that included at least 20 workplaces with factors in at least two studies that were consistently associated with injury rates (represented by worker's compensation rates, that is, the frequency of claims for injury-related compensation), a measure which ignores injury severity. Organizational factors associated with injury outcomes could be grouped under management style and culture (including empowerment of the workforce and good relations between management and workforce), organizational philosophy on health and safety (including delegation of safety activities, training, and an active role in health and safety of top management), good housekeeping, and safety controls on machinery. Shannon et al. (1997) noted, however, that the strength of their conclusions was limited by the nature of the studies: response rates were modest, several studies had not been published in peer review journals, most studies did not report their power to detect important associations, quantitative pooling of the data was not possible, and different sets of variables were studied, using different questionnaires.

Kaminski (2001) investigated performance-based pay, temporary employees, hours worked per week, amount of formal training per year, whether any employees were in teams, and the percentage of employees who worked on a production line in 86 USA manufacturing firms of more than 50 employees. In her analysis, Kaminski controlled for unionization and, interestingly, for industry injury rate on the basis that some industries are more hazardous than others. Performance-based pay was positively associated with injuries. Hours per week, training, and team-working were negative predictors of injury rate.

Vredenburgh (2002) reported on 62 hospitals in the US healthcare sector. She examined the relationship between rewards for reporting safety hazards, safety training, selecting those with a good safety record, communication/feedback on incidents and unsafe behaviors, worker participation in safety decisions, and management commitment to safety. As a whole, the management practices accounted for 16.5 percent of the variance in safety outcome (a combination of injury frequency over three years weighted by expert-rated severity of outcome) in her sample, and that the only practice that predicted the safety outcome was hiring practices related to safety.

Hoonakker et al. (2005) looked at the longitudinal effect of safety initiatives on an objective measure of safety performance related to company claims for injuries in the construction industry in the USA. Safety performance was measured at two time points four years apart. Of the 209 companies that responded, most were "small-size" employing less than 20 people with nearly half of them employing less than five people. Safety initiatives were measured by a set of questions (Does your company have a written policy on safety? Is there a safety committee in your company? Is there a required safety training program for new employees? Do you have regularly scheduled safety meetings?). The authors found that while larger companies generally had safety initiatives in place, less than 20 percent of small-size companies had any kind of safety initiatives. Companies reporting regularly scheduled safety meetings at time one, compared to those companies that did not, had better safety performance four years later. The results for the other initiatives were non-significant.

Zacharatos, Barling, and Iverson (2005) identified ten practices and defined them collectively as constituting a high performance work system (HPWS). The practices were employment security, selective hiring, extensive training, self-managed teams and decentralized decision-making, reduced status distinctions, information sharing, compensation contingent on safe performance, transformational leadership, high quality work, and measurement of management practices. In their study, human resource directors in 138 (of 1,471 who were approached) manufacturing organizations completed questions about the extent to which they thought a practice existed in their organizations, and estimated the percentage of employees to which a high commitment practice applied. Practices were combined into a single index measuring a HPWS. HR directors further reported the number of lost-time injuries and number of days lost due to eight specific types of injuries ranging from fractures to superficial wounds. The HPWS index predicted an additional 8 percent of the variance in lost-time injuries after controlling for the nature, size and age of the organizations.

Recently, Probst, Brubaker, and Barsotti (2006) reported on 38 contractor companies working on a large construction project in the USA. Rather than examining specific practices they used a global measure of safety climate. Their findings showed that companies with a weak safety climate had many more recordable injuries compared to those with a strong climate.

A summary of organizational-level analysis is that a number of organizational aspects could be related to safety outcomes but this is mainly based on expert opinion and experience. Some management practices have been linked empirically with safety outcome, but the results are suggestive rather than conclusive, and indicate they may only explain a very modest amount of the variance in injuries.

Safety climate has been associated with expert ratings of safety, and, although only recently, injury rate.

Workgroups and accidents

In an extension from organizations to teams within organizations, Hoffman and Stetzer (1996) found that safety climate – as measured using Dedobbeleer and Beland's (1991) scales, but analyzed using individual perceptions aggregated to the group level – was negatively correlated with group-level major accidents. Zohar (2000) further conceptualized the notion of a group safety climate related to supervisory practices and developed two scales to measure it. The action scale referred to overt supervisory reaction to subordinates' conduct and the initiation of action concerning safety issues. The expectation scale referred to noncommensurate task facets, mostly related to safety versus productivity. Zohar found that both action and expectation scales added significant prediction to group-level micro-accident rate once risk was controlled for. Micro-accidents were defined as on-the-job behavior-dependent minor injuries requiring medical attention, but not incurring any lost work-days. Wallace, Popp, and Mondore (2006), studying delivery drivers from a large multinational shipping and transportation company, found supervisory safety climate, measured with a combination of expectation and action scales, predicted driving accidents harming equipment or people. Where supervisors have changed their practices in relation to safety the result has been significantly lower injury rates, improvements in safety-related behaviors, and increases in workgroup safety climate scores (Zohar, 2002; Zohar & Luria, 2003). Neal and Griffin (2006) showed in one Australian hospital that group safety climate significantly predicted later participation in safety-related activities, but not compliance with safety procedures. Interestingly, although they found associations between group safety climate and accidents in one of the years they studied, the effect was non-significant in another year. They found that safety climate did not predict later accidents, although they noted that the power to detect effects at the group level in their study was low.

In sum, the concept of a workgroup climate for safety appears fruitful for understanding accident outcomes, and it may mediate organizational safety climate (Zohar & Luria, 2005). Supervisors appear to play a major role in workgroup climate. It will be interesting to see in future research whether other organizational players, for example co-workers, are also influential and whether group-level accidents are caused by similar antecedents to individual injuries (see Chmiel, in press, for further discussion).

Individuals and accidents

Case studies An accident to a single individual can also be analyzed through considering the combination of active and latent errors outlined above for systems disasters. Wagenaar, Hudson, and Reason (1990) presented an example of a maintenance operator in a transformer station who was tragically killed by touching a wire carrying 10,000 volts. The man had returned early from a coffee break and mistaken which of two adjacent transformers (each in a separate block) he had been working on earlier in the day (the transformers were not clearly marked). He then violated the procedure for safely opening a locked door guarding the transformer. The correct procedure involved walking back some way to an electrical switch that would open the door only if the power to the transformer had been turned off. Rather than walk back the operator opened the door by pushing his arm through a fence and opening the lock from the inside with a screwdriver, entering the block and touching the high voltage wire. Operators regularly opened locked doors in this way.

Wagenaar et al. analyzed this accident through reference to a general accident causation scenario "which describes how all accidents originate" (1990, p. 274). The last event in the scenario is the accident, and they are always caused by unsafe acts (which meant that whether the act was deliberate or not the accident could have been prevented by elimination of some preceding action). Defenses stand between unsafe acts and accidents. If an accident occurs the defenses must have been breached or were inadequate. Unsafe acts have their immediate origins in psychological precursors and these were argued to be elicited by the physical and organizational environment. These influences were called general failure types (GFTs). GFTs are created by management decisions (1990, pp. 274–5). Thus in terms of defenses, no alarm was triggered when a fence was opened with the power still on, and there was no automatic power shut-down. The unsafe acts were that the door was opened with a screwdriver, and the wire touched without a power check. Psychological precursors were confusion between the transformer cells, and the habitual response to violate procedures. GFTs comprised: labeling of cells that was ambiguous; a physical distance from cells to power switches that was too far; an alarm system wrongly designed; wrong habits not corrected by supervisors; and insufficient time to finish the job. Management decisions allowed an out-of-date design not to be replaced, and maintenance staff to be reduced.

Wagenaar, Hudson, and Reason defined a limited number of General Failure Types (GFTs) based on features of an operation that have been wrong for some time, but remain unrecognized as problematic until implicated in an accident, and which promote cognitive precursors to unsafe acts. The types were defined "somewhat arbitrarily, but after reading and analyzing hundreds of accident scenarios" (1990, p. 287). The GFTs were grouped into 3 broad categories: Physical Environment, that included design failures, missing defenses, hardware defects, negligent housekeeping, and error-enforcing conditions (i.e. design takes no account of its use under extreme time pressure, or by unqualified personnel); Human Behavior, including poor procedures (bad planning, insufficient control) and defective training (e.g., lack of training in specific expertise so people act as novices-safety awareness training is usually insufficient); and Management, including organizational failures (e.g., safety not treated as an important goal), incompatible goals (e.g. production trade-offs with safety), and lack of communication (leading to absence of information). Wagenaar, Groeneweg, Hudson, and Reason (1994) refined the types to include failures in maintenance, giving 11 types where the "frequencies of occurrence of failures in the eleven classes are essentially independent" (1994, p. 2001).

Surveys Survey approaches have shown associations between a number of organizational and job factors and injury. Training, job characteristics, leadership, supervisor and co-worker support, and role overload appear important. Oliver, Cheyne, Tomas, and Cox (2002), using data from 525 Spanish workers from a wide range of industrial sectors, found support for direct links between organizational involvement in safety and accidents and near misses. Organizational involvement included indicators of safety management and policy, supervisors' safety support and behavior, and co-workers safety support and behavior. Barling, Kelloway, and Iverson (2003) found a combination of extent of training received, task variety, and autonomy predicted occupational injury directly, and through job satisfaction. Zacharatos, Barling, and Iverson (2005) found a composite high performance work systems (HPSW) index correlated with first-aid injuries. Iverson and Erwin (1997), in a sample of blue-collar production and assembly workers, found supervisory and co-worker support predicted whether a worker had been injured or not in the 12 months following the survey.

Safety climate appears important at the individual level as well as at the organizational and workgroup levels. When measured at the individual-level safety climate is referred to as perceived safety climate. In a study of young Canadians, mainly in the service sector, Barling, Loughlin, and Kelloway (2002) showed a direct link between perceived safety climate and self-reported frequency of injury involvement. They also reported significant links between transformational leadership and safety climate, and role overload and safety climate. Kelloway, Mullen, and Francis (2006) extended these findings showing that safety-specific transformational leadership and passive leadership predicted injuries, and safety climate. In their structural model, leadership styles had effects directly on safety climate, and indirectly through safety consciousness, and safety climate related to injuries through safety events. Chmiel (2005), in a study of UK chemical production workers, found that perceived safety climate and job control predicted involvement in minor injury outcomes. Zacharatos, Barling, and Iverson (2005) found employees' perceptions of the extent to which high performance work systems (HPWS) practices had been adopted by their organization were related to safety climate. When self-reported injuries were combined with near misses safety climate was significantly directly related to safety outcome, and to what the authors called personal safety orientation, which consisted of items relating to safety motivation, knowledge and behavior.

Safety Behavior and Accidents

A notable observation from the analysis of accidents is that some kind of human behavior is almost always implicated (Reason, 1990). The conceptual problem is how behaviors should be classified, since the precise nature of behaviors linked to accidents is usually specific to the accident situation.

Reason (1990) proposed the classification of all unsafe behaviors into two broad categories within the framework of purposeful activity related to safety: Unintended acts in relation to planned actions and their goal; and Intended acts. Unintended actions are further broken down into slips and lapses, and intended actions into mistakes and violations. An attraction of Reason's conceptualization is that slips, lapses, and mistakes are explicitly related to cognitive functioning. Slips and lapses are defined as errors that result from some failure in the execution and/or storage of an action sequence, regardless of whether the plan that guided them was adequate to achieve its objective. Mistakes, on the other hand, are defined as deficiencies or failures in the judgmental and/or inferential processes involved in the selection of an objective, or in how to achieve it, irrespective of whether the actions necessary to realize the objective run according to plan.

Reason further related errors to a hierarchy of performance levels developed by Rasmussen over several years (e.g., Rasmussen & Jensen,1974; Rasmussen, 1986). Rasmussen studied, initially, workers engaged in fault-finding in electronic components using a verbal protocol technique, asking workers to explain what they were doing during their task. Rasmussen classified activity relevant to industrial settings in terms of skill, rule or knowledge-based performance levels. The levels reflect decreasing familiarity with the activity and situation. The skill-based level is concerned with routine actions in a highly familiar operating environment involving largely automatic cognitive (perceptual-motor) processing. At the other extreme, knowledge-based performance is required in novel situations and circumstances, and is dependent on effortful problem-solving and reasoning to work out and decide on a course of action. Rule-based performance also involves problem-solving but where a situation or set of circumstances has been encountered before, and where the action is governed by the selection and use of stored rules of the form IF [situation] THEN [action] rather than a direct automatic response. Slips and lapses are deemed errors at the skill-based level and are associated with attentional and memory failures. Mistakes are refined into two types: rule-based and knowledge-based. Rule-based errors are associated with problem-solving activities involving the misapplication of good rules, or the application of bad rules. Knowledge-based errors are associated with the limitations of human ability to solve problems and reason with new and unfamiliar circumstances.

The analysis above provides a plausible reason for considering cognitive errors as suitable behavioral building blocks for accident analysis. However some interesting questions for identification and measurement are raised by it. A key question is whether an independent analyst of an accident can classify behaviors reliably (see Rasmussen, 1990 for a discussion of the issues involved)? Reason (1990) documented examples of slips, lapses, and mistakes from incidents in the nuclear power industry. For example at the Davis-Besse plant in the USA, an operator, wanting to start the steam and feedwater rupture control system manually, inadvertently pressed the wrong two buttons on the control panel (a slip). Wagenaar and Groeneweg (1987) analyzed Dutch shipping reports of 100 accidents at sea. The accidents all resulted from several behavioral events, frequently from two or more people, and had multiple causes. Nonetheless the authors could attribute in a principled way individual human error behavior in 93 percent of the accidents that involved failures of reasoning and cognitive rule following. Similarly Salminen and Tallberg (1996) found that human error could be implicated in a majority (more than 80 percent) of 99 serious accidents investigated in Finland.

Violations, in contrast to errors, are not seen as breakdowns in normal cognitive processing, but as deliberate flouting of safety procedures and rules. "While errors may be defined in relation to the cognitive processes of the individual, violations can only be described with regard to a social context in which behavior is governed by operating procedures, codes of practice, rules and the like . . . violations can be defined as deliberate – but not necessarily reprehensible – deviations from those practices deemed necessary (by designers, managers and regulatory agencies) to maintain the safe operation of a potentially hazardous system" (Reason, 1990, p. 195). Violations are therefore "knowing" departures from specified safety rules and procedures. It is possible of course to violate rules unwittingly through ignorance of the rules, and these have been called "unintentional violations" but "to all intents and purposes should be regarded as errors" (Reason, Parker, & Lawton, 1998).

Reason (1990) identified as of greatest interest a category of "deliberate but nonmalevolent infringements" and distinguished therein between routine and exceptional violations. Routine violations were "largely habitual, forming part of an individual's behavioral repertoire." Exceptional violations were "singular violations occurring in a particular set of circumstances." Somewhat confusingly Reason, Parker, and Lawton (1998) subsequently suggested three major categories of "routinized" violation had been distinguished: routine, optimizing, and situational. Routine violations typically involved corner-cutting – taking a path of least effort. Optimizing violations involved optimizing nonfunctional goals ahead of safety, for example the enjoyment of speeding when driving. These two categories were linked to the attainment of personal goals. Situational violations involved seeing violations as essential "to get the job done," e.g. because of organizational failings related to the work environment or equipment.

Some support for the kind of division above is provided by Lawton (1998). She investigated the views of 36 UK railway personnel as to the motives for noncompliance behind violations of rules related to risks in shunting operations. Out of 14 endorsed reasons the most common were to do with the violations being seen as: a quicker way of working; due to time pressure; due to high workload; and due to inexperience. Least common were reasons connected to psychological gratification: that is violations being seen as exciting or macho ways to work. Other reasons included management turning a blind eye, a belief that skill means a violation is still a safe way to work, a belief that the rule is impossible to work to, and the belief that violation is necessary due to design of the railway sidings where shunters work.

Reason, Parker, and Lawton (1998) proposed also that "Recognizing a situation as hazardous and/or a rule as inappropriate is likely to lead to the adoption of self-protective behavior." and hence a violation under certain circumstances. Where the adoption of precautions is voluntary, health belief models emphasize the role of risk perception (e.g., Weinstein, 1988), however different factors predict risk-taking at work compared to nonwork domains (Soane and Chmiel, 2005). At work there is some reason to think that risk appraisal is not closely linked to compliance, some people intend to comply with rules without thinking they are at risk (Soane and Chmiel, 1999) and some people violate rules despite appreciating the risk, but believing they can use their skill to deal with it (Lawton,1998). In terms of whether people act by appraising risk the analysis of many accidents at work suggests that conscious appraisal of risk is rarely undertaken (Wagenaar, 1992).

Psychometric analyses of what employees say they do in relation to compliance with safety procedures (i.e. the opposite of violations) support a categorization referenced to behaviors rather than their potential underlying psychology. In the chemical industry Chmiel (2005) found two factors he labeled "bending rules" and "working safely." Bending rules referred to taking shortcuts to complete work. Working safely included items referring to the use of personal protective equipment. DeJoy, Searcy, Murphy, and Gershon (2000) found 2 factors they called compliance with personal protective equipment (PPE) and general compliance (GP). The items used were specific to the nurses' activities in relation to HIV treatment.

In addition to compliance measures other forms of behavior related to safety have been advanced (see Chmiel, in press, for further discussion of their nature and validity). Griffin and Neal (2000) proposed safety participation, Hofmann, Morgeson, and Gerras (2003) and Turner, Chmiel, and Walls (2005) investigated safety role definitions, and Cheyne, Cox, Oliver, and Tomas (1998) used involvement in safety activities. Together these measures could be thought of as safety citizenship behaviors.

Burke, Sarpy, Tesluk, and Smith-Crowe (2002) proposed a model of general safety performance. They produced four factors related to "typical coworker" performance from the responses of nuclear hazardous waste disposal workers. The factors were described as using personal protective equipment, engaging in work practices to reduce risk, communicating health and safety information, and exercising employee rights and responsibilities.

In a recent meta-analysis Clarke (2006) summarized the situation with respect to the relationships between safety compliance, safety participation, and accidents. She was able to include only nine studies relating safety compliance to accident outcomes, and only three studies relating safety participation to such criteria. Clarke found that, overall, the relationships between safety performance and accidents and injuries were valid and generalizable, but the effect sizes were small, with that for safety participation stronger than for safety compliance. Remember though that system defenses mean unsafe behaviors do not always result in an injury.

A framework of the categories related to behavior involved in the causes of accidents was proposed by Dejoy (1986) who outlined three categories: Predisposing, Enabling, and Reinforcing. Predisposing factors are personal characteristics such as beliefs, attitudes, values, and perceptions that affect self-protective behavior, for example personal skepticism. Enabling factors are characteristics of the work environment or system that promote or block safe behavior, for example training and knowledge. Reinforcing factors refer to actual or expected rewards or punishment as a consequence of the behavior, for example management support. Dejoy et al. (2000) investigated a range of variables including predisposing or personal attributes such as attitudes toward HIV patients, risk-seeking tendencies, and knowledge of HIV and its transmission, They found no effect of these variables on compliance with PPE, although the predisposing factors did predict general compliance. The only effects on compliance with PPE were availability of PPE, job hindrances, priority given to safety, formal and informal feedback. Interestingly there was no effect of a safety climate measure related to management commitment. Parker, Axtell, and Turner (2001) found supervisor support predicted later safety behavior.

More generally the General Accident Causation Scenario detailed above (Wagenaar et al., 1990) suggests unsafe behavior is a function of psychological precursors that in turn are made potent by organizational factors (GFTs). Griffin and Neal (2000) used theories of individual performance and organizational climate to develop a model relating safety climate to behavior through safety motivation, knowledge and skill (see research close-up). Support for the model has come from other studies too (Neal, Griffin, & Hart, 2000; Neal & Griffin, 2006).

Recently Clarke (2006) has contrasted perceptual, attitudinal and dispositional approaches to accident involvement in the workplace. Her conclusions were that safety perceptions (i.e. the basis for safety climate) had greater predictive utility than attitudes, but that one aspect of personality (agreeableness) had greater utility than either. Another aspect of personality studied in the safety context is locus of control. Locus of control (Rotter,1966) ranges from internal to external. Those who are internal expect their actions to affect what happens to them and others. Externals believe they have little influence on events. Jones and Wuebker (1985) developed a Safety Locus of Control scale and demonstrated that people in lower risk groups were more internally oriented. Wuebker (1986) further reported that externally oriented employees appeared to have more accidents. A problem in interpreting the relationship between personality (and indeed other factors) and accident involvement is that such analyses almost never control for accident exposure: i.e. the opportunity to have an accident given the behavior (Hodge & Richardson, 1985). Opportunity is a function of the hazardousness of the situation a person is in, and self-evidently workplaces differ: deep-sea diving is a more hazardous occupation than office work. Thus it is entirely plausible that different types of people select themselves into different types of jobs, for example sensation-seekers might prefer deep-sea diving over office work, and hence an association between personality characteristics and accidents may be observed because of it.

Summary

The study of safety at work has been advanced in recent years by the investigation of links from management approaches to accidents and safety-related behaviors. In particular the concept of safety climate has proved useful. Survey designs have been able to extend and build on the insights produced through case studies.

Discussion Points

Is the concept of safety climate enough to explain safety at work?
How far should management approaches to safety be complemented by individual responsibility for unsafe behavior?

Key Studies

1. Zohar, D. (1980). Safety climate in industrial organisations: Theoretical and applied implications. *Journal of Applied Psychology*, 65, 96–102. The article that defined contemporary views of safety climate, and that continues to inform the concept.
2. Wagenaar, W. A., & Groeneweg, J. (1987). Accidents at sea: Multiple causes and impossible consequences. *International Journal of Man–Machine Studies*, 27, 587–98. An elegant and sharp classification and analysis of the nature and operation of cognitive error.
3. Hofmann, D. A., & Stetzer, A. (1996). A cross-level investigation of factors influenc-ing unsafe behaviors and accidents. *Personnel Psychology*, 49, 307–39. An excellent, although demanding, article that examines the cross-level influences of group safety climate on individual-level outcomes.
4. Neal, A., & Griffin, M. A. (2006). A study of the lagged relationships among safety climate, safety motivation, safety behavior, and accidents at the individual and group levels. *Journal of Applied Psychology*, 91, 946–53. An interesting and important account of antecedents to safety participation and compliance.

Further Reading

1. Reason, J. T. (1990). *Human error*. Cambridge: Cambridge University Press. This is a seminal book on cognitive error particularly, and the notion that organizational factors and individual error behavior combine to produce serious accidents.
2. Feyer, A.-M., & Williamson, A. (Eds.) (1998). *Occupational injury: Risk, prevention and intervention*. London: Taylor & Francis. A collection of many interesting chapters including several on safety interventions.

3. Chmiel, N. (in press). Modern work and safety. In K. Naswall, J. Hellgren, & M. Sverke (Eds.), *The individual in the changing world of work*. Cambridge: Cambridge University Press. A book chapter that concentrates on survey approaches to safety at work in the context of challenges due to the changing nature of work.

Research Close-Up

Griffin, M. A., & Neal, N. (2000). Perceptions of safety at work: A framework for linking safety climate to safety performance, knowledge, and motivation. *Journal of Occupational Health Psychology*, 5, 347–58.

Background

Griffin and Neal were interested in how safety climate as measured through employee perceptions was related to safety behaviors. Using perspectives from both general organizational climate and specific types of climate they proposed that climate be considered as a higher-order factor comprised of more specific first-order factors. The first order factors reflect perceptions of safety-related policies, procedures and rewards, and the higher-order factor reflects the extent to which employees believe that safety is valued within the organization. In contrast, ratings of risk, affective reactions to safety issues, normative beliefs about safety, and self-reports of safety behavior, should not be considered to be perceptions of safety climate. Griffin and Neal acknowledged that there was no clear agreement about what first order factors constituted the higher order factor. They used four subscales in their study one: manager values toward safety; effectiveness of safety inspections; extent of safety training; and safety communication, and five in their study two: manager values toward safety; safety communication; thoroughness of safety practices; effectiveness of training for safety; and adequacy of safety equipment. Griffin and Neal used a model of performance that distinguished components, determinants and antecedents of performance. Components describe the actual behaviors that individuals perform at work and two were advanced: safety compliance and safety participation. Determinants represent proximal causes of variability in performance and they argued only include knowledge, skill, and motivation. Antecedents represent distal causes of variability in performance and influence performance through their effects on knowledge, skill and motivation. Griffin and Neal argued that safety climate should be classified as an antecedent, and safety performance may be mediated by safety motivation and safety knowledge.

Method

Two studies were reported. Study one was based on archival survey data produced from 1,403 employees in seven Australian manufacturing and mining organizations, but only included a determinant measure of safety knowledge. Study two was conducted in three Australian manufacturing organizations where 381 employees responded to a survey. Knowledge and motivation were measured. Thus a specific measure of skill was not used in either study. A more comprehensive examination of their proposed model was possible in study two compared to study one, so this is the study presented in more detail here.

In addition to the safety climate subscales already mentioned safety knowledge was measured by 4 items (alpha = 0.84) and safety motivation was split into compliance motivation measured by 3 items (alpha = 0.80) and participation motivation measured by 3 items (alpha = 0.81). Safety compliance was assessed by 2 items (alpha = 0.56) and safety participation by 3 items (alpha = 0.73).

Results

Confirmatory factor analyses demonstrated the viability of the measurement model for the factors used in the study. Interestingly the higher order factor model (where five subscales indicated safety climate), while giving an acceptable fit, was less good than a ten factor solution (with no higher order factor), a similar result was also found in study one. Overall structural equation modeling supported the proposed mediational model. The higher order factor of safety climate acted through safety knowledge and compliance and participation motivation on safety compliance and safety participation behaviors. Interestingly safety knowledge had direct paths to safety compliance and participation as did compliance motivation, but participation motivation had a direct path only to safety participation. However, the link between safety compliance motivation and safety participation was negative.

Discussion

Griffin and Neal concluded that their studies had provided general support for their proposed framework, and in particular for their distinctions between antecedents, determinants and performance, suggesting it was meaningful to distinguish between safety activities as part of the job (safety compliance), and safety activities that support the broader organizational context (safety participation). However they also pointed out that two aspects of their model were not supported: First the negative link between safety compliance motivation and safety participation was unexpected, although consistent with resource allocation models of performance that proposed goal-oriented task motivation can reduce participation in contextual behaviors; second safety knowledge was not related to safety participation in study one, although it was in study two.

PART III

ORGANIZATIONS AT WORK

Staffing the Organization: An Introduction to Personnel Selection and Assessment

Neil Anderson, Jesus Salgado, Sonja Schinkel, and Nicole Cunningham-Snell

12

Overview

Selection and assessment processes represent the "barrier to entry" for individuals into any work organization. As an applied field of both research and practice in Work and Organizational Psychology and Human Resource Management (HRM), employee selection methods and techniques have a long history of research interest in European countries and in North America and any introductory chapter can only realistically provide a selective overview of the major findings and the crucial trends in the professional practice of employee selection. Nevertheless, the synergy between robust research and effective practice in selection is emphasized throughout this chapter, as is the fact that selection procedures constitute the initial HRM procedure encountered by applicants and will therefore determine the subsequent pool of human talent available to an organization. Selection processes are thus of vital importance: they establish future employer–employee relationships; they represent the initial and determining HRM practice under the control of employer organizations; and they can have substantial effects on the reputation of any organization where large numbers of applicants are involved.

The chapter starts with the "*systems view*" of recruitment and selection highlighting stages in the process. Thereafter we overview two fundamentally different theoretical perspectives of selection, the "*predictivist perspective*" emphasized in North American texts, and the "*constructivist perspective*" more commonly found in European research and reviews. In the third section we discuss the validity and popularity of a range of different selection methods and techniques. Finally, we explore the candidates' perspective in selection and highlight in conclusion that both parties interpret information over a multi-stage process and reach outcome decisions, and that organizations need to be increasingly mindful of the impact of their procedures upon applicants.

Table 12.1: Recruiter and applicant perspectives during different selection phases

	Perspectives	
	Recruiter	*Applicant*
Phase I Recruitment	• Establishing recruitment needs and methods • Conducting job analyses • Advertising and choices	• Job search and self-evaluation • Whether or not to apply to certain organizations • Whether recruitment materials (brochure, materials, application form) encourage an application
Phase II Prescreening	• Deciding how to cope with potentially large numbers of applicants • Designing prescreening methods that are valid, fair, and cost-effective	• Surviving prescreening processes with only a limited input • Forming impressions of the organization based upon prescreening experiences • Deciding whether to remain in the selection process
Phase III Assessment	• Performing accurate, in-depth assessments on applicants • Reaching accurate and fair outcome decisions on all applicants • Communicating selection decisions and giving feedback if necessary	• Self-presenting as favorably as possible • Eliciting information on the job, work group and organization as a prospective employer • Deciding whether or not to accept any job offer
Phase IV Induction	• Transforming newly hired applicants into fully effective job performers • Determining early training and development needs	• Acclimatizing to the job, the work group, and the wider organization • Getting to know colleagues, job relevant information, and how the job is really performed day-to-day

The Recruitment and Selection Process

An important characteristic of most recruitment and selection procedures is that they involve several stages which occur over time where both organizations and applicants make suitability decisions – the organization whether the applicant is suitable for the job; the applicant whether the job and organization may be suitable for him or her. In table 12.1 we summarize likely differences in perspective between applicants and recruiters at different stages in the selection process to highlight that the contact between the two is likely to develop with each party having different perspectives, views of the other, and vested interests.

Figure 12.1 summarizes in some detail the four-phase process of selection: Recruitment, prescreening, assessment, and induction. This process usually includes an initial recognition of the need for new staff, then recruitment advertising, followed by prescreening applicants, then final selection decisions and induction of new employees into the organization. This figure is reasonably self-explanatory in terms of the critical objectives and key activities at each phase. The advantage of taking such a "systems view" of selection is that it provides a holistic overview of the entire process (see Cook, 1998, or Schmitt & Chan, 1998 for more detailed discussions). The day-to-day mechanics of the process are not our principal concern here; more important is to note two pertinent issues: *bilateral decision-making* and *validation feedback loops*. First, decisions are made by both the recruiter and the candidate at several points in the process (see decision-making stages in figure 12.1), supporting the perspective that both parties make decisions over whether to accept a working relationship with each other. At the initial stage of any recruitment process, both the organization and the candidate will be considering possible employment options for the future. Second, the systems view highlights the importance of the validation feedback loop. In larger-scale selection processes, where numerous recruitment decisions are reached over a period of time, the crucial question from the organization's perspective is "*how accurate are these decisions in selecting individuals who subsequently turn out to be effective job performers?*" Validation feedback loops recycle information on the effectiveness of selection decisions into the selection process at different stages in order to modify and improve the procedure. Selection accuracy can be determined by a *contingency table* and the *correlation coefficient* between selection ratings and subsequent job performance ratings. Having overviewed the main phases of the recruitment process, we now move on to describe the use of contingency tables and correlations in determining selection accuracy.

Contingency tables

Figure 12.2 illustrates the contingency table for a fairly typical selection scenario. The distribution of data points (marked by X's in the table) represents the cross-tabulation between an individuals' selection rating and the evaluation of their subsequent job performance. Note that:

Valid Positives – are individuals rated above the cut-off in selection who, it transpires subsequently, are rated as effective job performers (i.e. above cut-off).

Valid Negatives – are individuals rated below the cut-off in selection who, if they had been taken on, would have subsequently been rated as ineffective job performers (i.e. below cut-off).

False Positives – are individuals rated above the cut-off in selection who, it transpires subsequently, are rated as ineffective job performers (i.e. below cut-off).

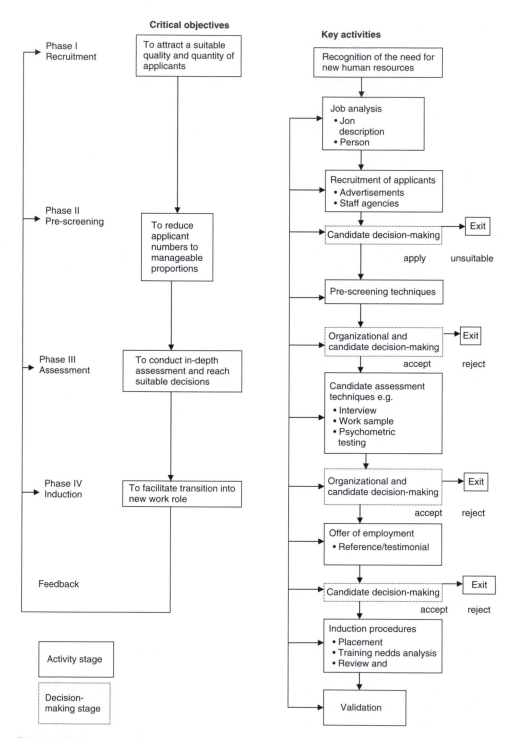

Figure 12.1: A four-phase process model of selection and assessment

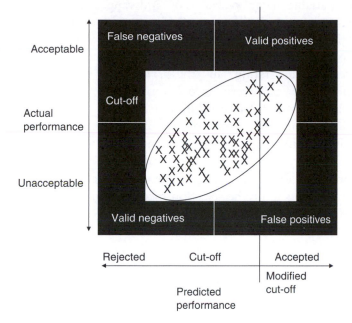

Figure 12.2: Contingency table

False Negatives – are individuals rated below the cut-off in selection who, if they had been taken on, would have subsequently been rated as effective job performers (i.e. above cut-off).

Clearly any organization seeks to both minimize false negatives and false positives while also maximizing valid positives and valid negatives. In reality, it is the false positives who may be seen by recruiters to be most costly as an organization actually employs these individuals whom, it transpires, do not perform the job to satisfactory standards. For false positives then, the "selection failure" is highly visible, whereas individuals in the false negative category have been rejected without having had the chance to prove that they could have been effective job performers. Theoretically, an organization could increase the selection method cut-off to the modified level shown in figure 12.2 in an attempt to eliminate all false positives. Unfortunately, as can be seen, this would have two deleterious effects: (a) rejecting a considerable number of valid positives, and (b) rendering only very few individuals as acceptable ($n = 6$ or 7 individuals above the modified cut-off), hence risking not meeting recruitment targets. So, in practice it is rarely possible to completely eliminate all false negatives and false positives. It can be said, then, that selection is not an exact science but is more about maximizing correct outcome decisions (Cook, 1998).

Correlation coefficients

A more statistically robust way of determining selection accuracy is by using the correlation coefficient. This is a statistical measure which assesses the association between two variables (symbolized as r) and ranges from $r = -1.00$ (perfect negative relationship) through $r = 0.00$ (no relationship) to $r = +1.00$ (perfect positive relationship). *Criterion-related validity* studies assess the magnitude of the correlation coefficient between the "*predictor*" in selection (e.g., psychological test score, interview rating) and the "*criterion*" (usually a rating of job or training performance) to determine decision-making accuracy. In the example from figure 12.2, the correlation coefficient between the selection method and subsequent job performance would be approximately $r = +0.3$ to $+0.4$. That is, applicants who obtain higher predictor ratings tend to obtain higher criterion scores, and conversely, applicants with lower predictor ratings tend to have lower criterion scores. Of course, in principle, the closer the correlation coefficient to $r = +1.0$, the more accurate the selection method, but in reality it is unlikely to exceed $r = +0.5$ (see for instance Schmitt & Chan, 1998).

Criterion-related validity

The contingency table and correlation coefficient provide methods for determining the criterion-related validity of selection. Hence, criterion-related validity is concerned with the extent to which future performance on the job is predicted accurately at selection. Two main types of criterion-related validity can be distinguished: *concurrent validity* and *predictive validity* (see figure 12.4). First, concurrent validation provides criterion-related validity results within a short timeframe by obtaining selection and criterion ratings from job incumbents already working for the organization. However, there are a number of disadvantages with this design: First, unlike job applicants, existing employees may be less motivated to give their best performance (Cronbach, 1970); second, existing employees represent a preselected group and are unlikely to accurately represent the potential applicants. Third, unlike a group of applicants, job incumbents may obtain similar ratings on the predictor and criterion scores since weak applicants would have been rejected and poor job performers would be unlikely to remain in the organization for any length of time. It is therefore likely that the scores from job incumbents will have a *restriction of range*, in other words, they will not represent the full spread of scores that might have been generated from candidates. The restriction of range lowers the magnitude of the correlation coefficient between predictor and criterion scores, but this can be corrected for by statistical procedures (see for instance Cook, 1998, or Guion, 1997).

The second approach to criterion-related validity is predictive validation. This approach uses a longitudinal (over time) design by obtaining criterion ratings from successful candidates after a period of employment with the organization. However, in order to identify the true relationship between selection and job performance, measures are required from applicants with the full range of predictor scores. Clearly though, few organizations are prepared to hire applicants with low predictor scores, so information is usually only available on a narrow band of candidates who score above the selection cut-off. Again, this results in a *restric-*

tion of range in the distribution of predictor variables, which lowers the magnitude of the correlation coefficient. As with concurrent studies, this restriction of range can be corrected for by statistical procedures (see for instance Cook, 1998).

Meta-analysis and validity generalization

The most important advance in our understanding of the accuracy of selection procedures over the last three decades has been the publication of Schmidt and Hunter's 1977 article and the subsequent refinements of psychometric meta-analysis and validity generalization techniques (see Hunter & Schmidt, 1990, 2004). Previous to 1977, work psychologists assumed that a new validity study was needed every time a personnel selection procedure (e.g., test, interview, assessment center, and so on) was used in a new setting even though the selection methods, job vacancies, organization, and criterion were essentially identical. Psychometric meta-analysis allows many individual validation studies reporting relational statistics (e.g., correlation coefficient) between a selection procedure and an organizational criterion of performance (e.g., supervisory ratings, training proficiency, counterproductive behaviors at work, productivity) to be combined and summarized in a single overarching operational average coefficient for the procedure. In the typical validity generalization study, the observed validity is corrected for criterion unreliability and range restriction in the predictor in order to obtain an operational mean validity. Furthermore, the observed variance within the studies contributing to the meta-analysis is corrected for sampling error variance, variance due to the predictor and criterion unreliability as well as the variance due to the range restriction. Consequently, in the typical validity generalization study, two estimates are of interest: the operational validity and the corrected standard deviation of the operational validity. These two estimates serve to create the 90 percent credibility value, which is the validity value for 90 percent of cases.

Schmidt and Hunter (1998) summarized the findings of 85 years of original studies, thus permitting quite definitive conclusions to be drawn over the criterion-related validity of various methods. Figure 12.3 summarizes these and other meta-analysis findings along with the popularity of different selection methods. Figure 12.3 presents some interesting and perplexing findings. The most valid methods are not necessarily the most widely used in organizations.

The criterion problem

A final word of caution on criterion-related validity is required. For some types of job, objective and independent measures of performance are virtually impossible to obtain. This is especially the case for service-related jobs where no physical output is involved (e.g., social workers, police officers, university lecturers). Often it is problematic to obtain an unbiased rating of performance. A supervisor may,

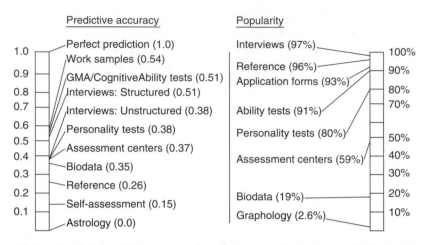

Figure 12.3: Predictive validity compared against popularity (Anderson & Cunningham-Snell, 2000)

for example, be prone to various errors such as personal-liking bias, or over-estimating performance when they were personally involved in the selection decision (known as *criterion contamination*). Collectively, these difficulties are known as the "criterion problem", the crucial point is that "measures" of performance will almost always be imperfect or biased in some way.

Choosing selection methods

When choosing between different selection methods, it is necessary to consider not only criterion-related validity, but also alternative forms of validity, *reliability*, and potential *adverse impact*. Three additional types of validity should be examined: construct validity, content validity, and face validity as illustrated in figure 12.4. First, an examination of construct validity is necessary since many selection constructs are abstract (e.g., "analytical ability") and can only be inferred indirectly from behavior during selection techniques. Second, consideration should be given to content validity to ensure that the selection method adequately samples all the competencies required in the job. However, the changing nature of many contemporary job roles makes this requirement increasingly difficult to fulfil (Herriot & Anderson, 1997; Frese, ch. 18 in this book). Finally, face validity should also be examined; if applicants do not perceive the selection method to be relevant to the job then they may not perform at their optimum level.

Another important requirement is that a selection method is reliable. *Reliability* is the extent to which the selection technique is consistent and free from random variation. Three approaches to measuring the reliability of a selection

1. *Predictive Validity* – the extent to which selection scores predict future job performance. Successful applicants are tracked through the selection process and after a period of employment with the organization, a subsequent measure of performance is obtained. The selection and criterion ratings are correlated.
2. *Concurrent Validity* – the extent to which selection scores predict current performance. Selection techniques are administered to existing job incumbents and correlated with ratings of job performance taken over the same time period.
3. *Construct Validity* – the extent to which selection accurately measures the constructs or dimensions it was designed to assess. The selection method is correlated with another method which is known to accurately reflect the construct.
4. *Content Validity* – the extent to which the selection process adequately samples all the important dimensions of the job. This requires a thorough examination of the job description and job specification.
5. *Face Validity* – the extent to which the applicant perceives the selection method to be relevant to the job.
6. *Parallel Reliability* – the measurement consistency. Each candidate completes two equivalent selection methods and the two scores are correlated.
7. *Test-Retest Reliability* – the measurement consistency. Candidates complete the same selection method at two time points. The two scores are then correlated.
8. *Split-Half Reliability* – the measurement consistency. Items from a measure are divided into two halves (e.g. odd-numbered versus even-numbered items) and the scores from each half correlated.

Figure 12.4: Types of validity and reliability

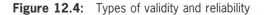

test are illustrated in figure 12.4. In practice though, there are difficulties associated with estimating reliability. Nevertheless, it is axiomatic that reliability is highly desirable and that an organization should be attempting to use selection methods that possess the highest level of reliability practicable.

Consideration must also be given to the potential *adverse impact* of selection techniques on minority groups protected by law. The negative consequences of adverse impact not only involve possible legal action, but also the failure to offer employment to candidates who will prove to be the more successful job performers. Across Europe and North America, countries have different legal approaches to dealing with discrimination. Perhaps the most stringent antidiscrimination legislation exists in the USA, where researchers and organizations have long been concerned over the potential negative effects of adverse impact and proven discrimination in legal cases brought against employer organizations by disgruntled, unsuccessful applicants (e.g., Schmitt & Chan, 1998).

Unfair discrimination may occur either directly or indirectly. *Direct discrimination* involves the conscious decision to reject certain applicants on the basis of irrelevant criteria, such as race or sex. *Indirect discrimination* is usually unintentional, arising when the selection method turns out to be favorable to one particular group, despite similar treatment for all groups. Antidiscrimination research has tended to define selection fairness with fairness being measured statistically, as pertaining only to minority groups, purely in terms of the selection outcome and not the process (Hough, Oswald, & Ployhart, 2001). In the final part of this

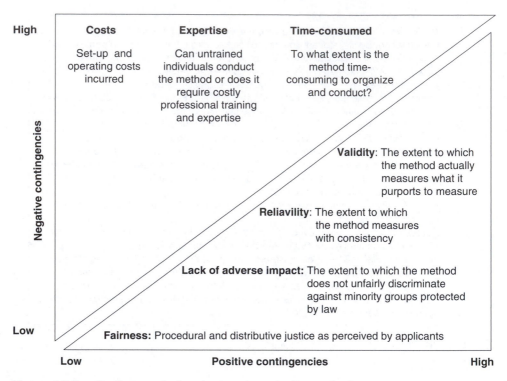

Figure 12.5: Contingency factors in choosing selection methods

chapter we overview research findings into applicant perceptions of the fairness of selection processes.

We have highlighted that a number of vitally important factors or contingencies should influence an organization's choice between different selection methods. Figure 12.5 summarizes the main contingencies, but also represents the trade-off which is so often observed between the more valid, reliable and fair methods and their immediate cost, need for expertise, and time-consuming administration. Before we turn our attention to different selection techniques, it is important to note that no method is one hundred percent accurate all the time. Choices therefore have to be made between efficacy and administration costs. However, the results from *utility analyses*, which estimate the financial payback of more accurate selection to an organization (Cronbach & Glesser, 1965), demonstrate that substantial financial gains accrue using more valid and reliable methods (see Guion, 1997, or Cook, 1998, for instance).

Theoretical Perspectives on Selection

Two main theoretical traditions exist internationally toward selection processes and candidate assessment methods. While North American Industrial/Organizational (I/O) psychology has tended to emphasize almost exclusively the organizational perspective in selection decision-making, European W/O psychology has been more eclectic in its concerns over both organizational and candidate decisions which emerge from the selection process (e.g., Anderson, Lievens, van Dam, & Ryan, 2004; Borman, Hanson, & Hedge, 1997; Herriot & Anderson, 1997; Hough & Oswald, 2000). The North American *"predictivist perspective"* has dominated this area for many years (see for instance Schmitt, 1976, or Smith & Robertson, 1993) with thousands of published studies having adopted this perspective. More recently, acknowledgement has been given to the importance of the European approach, perhaps best termed the *"constructivist perspective"* (e.g., Herriot, 1989; Iles & Robertson, 1997; Schuler 1993). Each perspective is not mutually exclusive of course, or wholly attributable to either continent (e.g., Chan & Schmitt, 2004; Gilliland, 1993; Rynes, 1993; Salgado, 1999).

The predictivist perspective

In essence the predictivist perspective views the job as a given and stable entity into which the most suitable candidate needs to be recruited. *Person–job fit* is therefore of primary importance (e.g., Anderson et al., 2004; Cook, 1998). In this viewpoint the recruiter is responsible for a series of actions put forward in most traditional predictivist selection textbooks.

From the predictivist perspective, since the number of applicants usually exceeds the number of job vacancies (and sometimes far exceeds depending on the labor market conditions), it is the recruiting organization which is seen as making the vital decisions of who to shortlist, and eventually, who to appoint (e.g., Smith & Robertson, 1993). Selection methods are therefore referred to as "predictors" with the more accurate methods accounting for future job performance more fully than less accurate predictors. The applicant is seen as "subject" to selection methods for which control is vested squarely in the hands of the organization (e.g., Schmitt & Chan, 1998). Recently, however, doubts have been expressed over the ongoing viability of this perspective given widespread changes toward flexible forms of working and team-based work roles.

The constructivist perspective

As job roles become more flexible and as organizations become increasingly aware of the need to compete for the best candidates (e.g., Murphy, 1986), selection research from the constructivist perspective has gained momentum. This perspective emphasizes that candidates, as well as organizations, make decisions in selection. Several European authors have emphasized expectations between the organization and the potential employee build up and that both sides use their meetings during the process to construct a "viable psychological contract" (Herriot, 1989) which underpins their future working relationship (e.g., Dachler, 1994; Herriot, 1989). The psychological contract has been defined by Kotter

(1973, p. 92) as "*an implicit contract between an individual and his [or her] organization which specifies what each expect to give and receive from each other in their relationship.*" The constructivist perspective views selection as a series of social episodes providing an opportunity for both parties to explore whether a future working relationship would be viable. Selection therefore serves as an opportunity for information exchange and the development of mutual expectations and obligations (Herriot, 1989). For example, interactions between the applicant and organization during selection may affect the applicant's initial expectations and attitudes about the organization. The extent to which these expectations are confirmed will influence the adjustment of the new employee during socialization. This has been termed the "*socialization impact*" of selection (Anderson & Ostroff, 1997).

Hence from this perspective, selection not only aims to ensure person–job fit but also *person–organization fit* (that is the fit between the applicant's values and organizational culture), and *person–team fit* (that is the fit between the applicant's skills and attitudes and the climate of their immediate working group).

Selection Methods and Techniques

In this part of the chapter we consider prescreening and candidate assessment methods. For those needing a comprehensive treatment of these issues see Salgado, Viswesvaran, and Ones (2001). Here, we confine our comments to the most important observations regarding each technique.

Application forms, curriculum vitae, and biodata

Although application forms are very popular in the UK, there are cultural differences across Europe with standard application documents being more popular in Germany and curriculum vitaes being more prevalent in Denmark (Salgado & Anderson, 2002; Shackleton & Newell, 1997). Both these methods can be used to prescreen applicants in order to generate a short list to be invited to the next stage. To facilitate effective prescreening, an application form should ideally be designed according to the selection criteria and a systematic screening process adhered to. However, research into graduate recruitment suggests that the typical process is far from systematic (Knights & Raffo, 1990; Wingrove, Glendinning, & Herriot, 1984) and this can clearly impact negatively on the selection process in the longer term (Keenan, 1997; Salgado, 1999).

An alternative method for prescreening is to use *biodata*, information about a person's past life and work experience. Identification of valid biodata predictors usually involves establishing significant correlations between biographical data and criterion measures for a group of job incumbents. The significant items are then used as criteria for future selection decisions. Confirmatory validation studies are required to ensure that valid biodata items for job incumbents are also valid for actual job applicants (Keenan, 1997; Stokes, Hogan & Snell, 1993), but the evidence suggests that biodata has a good level of criterion-related validity (Reilly & Chao, 1982; Schmidt & Hunter, 1998; Schmitt, Gooding, Noe, & Kirsch, 1984). For example, Schmidt and Hunter (1998) report a mean corrected validity coefficient of 0.35 for biodata measures against the criteria of job performance. Despite its strong validity as an initial stage prescreening method, biodata is rarely used. This is probably due to the costs involved in setting up a properly designed biodata form along with the poor face validity of biodata as question items may have no obvious connection with the job. Indeed, a number of studies have identified that candidates react negatively to the use of biodata for selection purposes as they doubt its accuracy and usefulness (Robertson, Iles, Gratton, & Sharpley, 1991; Smither et al., 1993; Stone & Jones, 1997).

Realistic job previews

Realistic Job Previews (RJPs) provide applicants with literally a realistic preview of the job and sometimes the organization so as to give a "warts and all" picture of the vacancy being applied for (Wanous, Poland, Premack, & Davies, 1992). RJPs therefore assist self-selection out of the process if the applicant feels the job is unsuitable for them. Traditional RJPs focus on the requirements and nature of the job and the company, but Schneider, Kristof-Brown, Goldstein, and Smith (1997) recommend that future RJPs should also incorporate the firm's values to provide information on likely person–organization fit. The results from a meta-analysis which included 21 studies of RJP validity for eight different criterion measures (total N = 6,088), found that the average mean validity coefficients ranged from 0.02 to 0.34 (Premack & Wanous, 1985). These findings indicated that RJPs tended to lower initial job expectations while increasing self-selection and job survival. However, research indicates that RJPs do not necessarily reduce absolute levels of labor turnover, but rather the rate at which turnover occurs (Dean & Wanous, 1984).

Interviews

The interview, in all of its guises, remains the most popular method of candidate assessment across Europe (see figure 12.3). Applicants also tend to rate the interview highly (e.g., Anderson, 2003; Chan & Schmitt, 2004). Recent meta-analyses have found that interviews, especially structured interviews, are considerably more valid and reliable than earlier discursive reviews had suggested (e.g., Conway, Jako, & Goodman, 1995; Huffcutt & Arthur, 1994; McDaniel, Whetzel, Schmidt, & Maurer, 1994; Salgado & Moscoso, 2002; Schmidt & Hunter, 1998). Indeed, it has become an unfortunate part of human resource management folklore that the interview is fundamentally flawed, but has to remain a component of any selection process simply because it provides the best opportunity for a face-to-face meeting between the organization and the applicant. This received wisdom is widely believed amongst personnel practitioners, but the unambiguous results of all of the recent meta-analyses indicate that interviews can be almost as valid and reliable as other more costly selection methods (Anderson, 1997). In one meta-analysis which included 160 studies of interview validity (total N = 25,244), McDaniel et al. (1994) found that the average mean validity was 0.37 for all types of interview combined. But for structured interviews, the average validity was 0.44, whereas for unstructured interviews this coefficient dropped to 0.33. Schmidt & Hunter (1998) and others report similar findings. Clearly structured interviews are more valid and reliable than unstructured interviews.

But what exactly is meant by "structure" in the selection interview? Structured interview designs usually incorporate several of the following elements:

1. in-depth job analyses, commonly using critical incident techniques
2. standardized questions asked in the same order of all candidates
3. candidates' replies are rated on behaviorally anchored rating scales (BARS)
4. interviewer training to ensure that all interviewers understand and adhere to the standardized format
5. computation of the outcome evaluation via arithmetic combination of ratings on
6. job-relevant dimensions.

Recently, Salgado and Moscoso (2002) classified interviews into two types based on the content of the interview questions: conventional interviews and behavior interviews. Conventional interviews are typically composed of questions directed at checking credentials, descriptions of experience, and self-evaluative information. Behavior interviews include questions concerning job knowledge, job experience and behavior descriptions. Salgado and Moscoso's meta-analysis showed that conventional interviews assessed general mental ability, job experience, personality dimensions, and social skills, while behavior interviews mainly assessed job knowledge, job experience, and social skills. These findings showed conventional and behavior interviews to be two different types of interview.

Paradoxically, one of the reasons why the interview remains so popular is that it offers a flexible and unstructured opportunity for recruiters and candidates to exchange information (Dipboye, 1997; Herriot, 1989). The dilemma then is between maximizing predictive validity while simultaneously retaining sufficient flexibility. This has resulted in many organizations developing semi-structured formats which include elements of the highly structured approach but which leave some free time for more open discussion (Dipboye, 1997).

Cognitive ability tests

Psychometric tests are standardized measures designed to assess a specific construct, and can be divided into two main categories: cognitive ability tests and personality tests (e.g., Smith & Smith, 2005). Cognitive ability tests, or tests of general mental ability ("g" or GMA), measure general intelligence or specific aptitudes such as numerical, verbal, or spatial ability, while personality tests measure personality dimensions such as conscientiousness, extroversion, and so forth. For both categories, test administration is governed by fixed procedures and test results are typically interpreted by comparing an individual's score to data collected on previous samples who have taken the same test. There is variation across Europe in relation to the use of cognitive ability tests (Salgado & Anderson, 2002): They are more used in Belgium, Britain, the Netherlands, Portugal, and Spain than in France, Germany, Greece, Ireland, or Italy; also they are more frequently used in Europe than in the United States. Candidates respond moderately well to cognitive tests (Chan & Schmitt, 2004; Steiner & Gilliland, 1996), but tend to rate tests with concrete items as more job-related than abstract tests (Smither et al., 1993). Hence, organizations may generate higher performance from candidates by selecting ability tests which have high face validity.

Cognitive ability tests are generally based upon general mental ability, GMA or "g", and meta-analyses have demonstrated notably robust predictive validity for such tests (Bertua, Anderson, & Salgado, 2005; Hunter & Hunter, 1984; Levine, Sector, Menon, Narayanon, & Cannon-Bowers, 1996; Salgado & Anderson, 2002, 2003; Salgado, Anderson, Moscoso, Bertua, & de Fruyt, 2003; Salgado, Anderson, Moscoso, Bertua, de Fruyt, & Rolland, 2003; Schmitt, Gooding, Noe, & Kirsch, 1984). Hunter and Hunter (1984), using a database of 515 single studies ($n = 38,620$), conducted with the General Aptitude Test Battery (GATB), found an average operational validity of 0.45 for predicting job performance and of 0.54 for predicting training proficiency. They also found that GMA validity was moderated by job complexity.

In Europe, Salgado, Anderson and their colleagues have recently carried out several meta-analyses using studies conducted in Belgium, France, Germany, Ireland, the Netherlands, Norway, Spain, Sweden, and the United Kingdom (Salgado & Anderson, 2002, 2003; Salgado, Anderson, Moscoso, Bertua, & de Fruyt, 2003; Salgado, Anderson, Moscoso, Bertua, de Fruyt, & Rolland, 2003). The results showed that GMA tests were valid predictors across twelve occupational categories, including drivers, electricians, information clerks, engineers, managers, police, salesmen, typists, skilled workers, chemists, mechanics, and industrial apprentices. The average operational validity was 0.62 ($n = 9,554$) for predicting job performance and 0.54 (16,065) for predicting training proficiency. Salgado and Anderson (2003) also examined the validity of GMA across six European countries: France, Germany, Belgium, the Netherlands, Spain and the United Kingdom. The results were very similar for all the countries, with operational validity ranging from 0.56 to 0.68 for predicting job performance and from 0.58 to 0.65 for predicting training proficiency.

Salgado, Anderson, and their colleagues have also examined the differential validity of several specific cognitive abilities, including verbal, numerical, spatial-mechanical, perceptual, and memory. The results showed that the operational validity of these measures was smaller than the validity of GMA measures. In fact, the average validity of specific abilities for predicting job performance ranged from 0.35 to 0.56, while the validity of GMA was 0.62. In the case of training proficiency, the validity of specific abilities ranged from 0.25 to 0.48, while the validity of GMA measures was 0.54. Also examined was the incremental validity of specific abilities beyond GMA validity. They found that the incremental validity was practically nil for both job performance and training success.

GMA also predicts other organizational performance criteria. For example, Schmitt et al. (1984) showed that GMA predicts turnover (observed $r = 0.10$), grade point average (observed $r = 0.44$), promotions (observed $r = 0.28$), work samples (observed $r = 0.43$). Summarizing all these findings, it can be concluded that GMA tests are the best single predictors of performance for entry-level and indeed even for higher-level jobs (Schmidt & Hunter, 1998).

Personality tests

The use of personality tests for selection has become increasingly popular in Britain (Cook, 1998; Keenan, 1995; Ones & Anderson, 2002), although applicants tend to react somewhat less favorably to these tests than to cognitive ability tests (Chan & Schmitt, 2004; Smither et al., 1993; Steiner & Gilliland, 1996). Research into the structure of personality has converged upon the *Five Factor Model* (FFM) or "Big Five" model of personality, incorporating the following factors (e.g., Goldberg, 1993; Tupes & Christal, 1992):

1. Neuroticism (insecure, anxious, depressed versus emotionally stable)
2. Extroversion (sociable, assertive versus timid and reserved)
3. Openness to Experience (creative, curious, versus practical with narrow interests)
4. Agreeableness (likeable, co-operative versus antagonistic)
5. Conscientiousness (hardworking, dependable, versus lazy, disorganized).

The FFM has been supported by compelling research findings although there is an ongoing debate over its comprehensiveness (e.g., Cellar, Miller, Doverspike, & Klawsky, 1996; Hough, 1992).

Barrick and Mount (1991) hypothesized that conscientiousness and emotional stability would be valid predictors of job performance for all occupational groups. Furthermore, they hypothesized that extroversion and agreeableness would be predictive of job performance in occupations with frequent interpersonal interactions (e.g., sales and managerial occupations) and that openness to experience would be a valid predictor for training proficiency. Their results partially supported these hypotheses.

Subsequently Salgado (1997, 1998) examined the validity of the Big Five in the European Community. The results of Salgado's study essentially replicated the findings by Barrick and Mount.

Barrick, Mount, and Judge (2001) reanalyzed all the previous meta-analyses and conducted a second-order meta-analysis with all the primary meta-analyses carried out during the 1990s. Their main conclusion was that two personality dimensions, conscientiousness and emotional stability, were valid predictors of job performance for all occupational groups and that the other three personality dimensions were valid predictors for some jobs and some criteria. Therefore, the cumulated empirical evidence did not leave room for doubts about the relevance of the Big Five personality dimensions (and personality measures in general) as tools for personnel selection.

Three recent studies have added new information. Salgado (2002) showed that conscientiousness and agreeableness were predictors of counterproductive behaviors (i.e. deviant behaviors at work) and that the five dimensions predicted turnover. Salgado (2003) found conscientiousness and emotional stability measures based on the FFM to have higher validity than other measures. Hogan and Holland (2003) examined the validity of the Big Five to predict two types of organizational criteria, getting along and getting ahead, as they are conceptualized in the socioanalytic theory of personality. Getting along was defined as *"behavior that gains the approval of others, enhances cooperation, and serves to build and maintain relationships"* (Hogan & Holland, 2003, p. 103). Getting ahead was defined as *"behavior that produces results and advances an individual within the group and the group within its competition"* (Hogan & Holland, 2003, p. 103). For the getting along criterion, adjustment (emotional stability) showed a validity of 0.34, likeability (agreeableness) showed a validity of 0.23 and prudence (conscientiousness) showed a validity of 0.31. For the getting ahead criterion, adjustment produced a validity of 0.22, ambition (one of the subdimensions of extroversion) produced a validity of 0.26, and prudence produced a validity of 0.20.

Therefore, the conclusions of the cumulated research in the last 14 years is that personality measures conceptualized as the Big Five personality dimensions are important variables for predicting and explaining job performance and training proficiency and that they can be used confidently in personnel selection by practitioners.

Typically, personality measures are not used alone in personnel selection processes but also with other instruments, mainly GMA tests. The incremental validity of conscientiousness and emotional stability over and above GMA for predicting job performance and training proficiency was examined by Salgado (1998) using data from the European Community. Conscientiousness showed incremental validity over GMA of 11 percent and emotional stability of 10 percent. More recently, Salgado and De Fruyt (2005) have demonstrated that three personality dimensions showed incremental validity over GMA: conscientiousness, agreeableness and emotional stability. The first dimensions resulted in strong additions of explained variance beyond GMA, specifically 30.3 percent and 20.1 percent for conscientiousness and agreeableness, respectively. Emotional stability also added validity over GMA but the percentage was smaller, 9.07 percent. Therefore, the result for emotional stability is very similar to the one found by Salgado (1998) but the current estimate for conscientiousness is remarkably larger. With regard to the training proficiency criterion, three personality dimensions showed an important increment in the explained variance over GMA: conscientiousness, openness to experience, and extroversion. Agreeableness also showed added validity, but the size of the increment was modest. Conscientiousness, openness and extroversion showed incremental validity by 24.2 percent, 22.2 percent, and 18.0 percent respectively, and agreeableness added validity by 7.5 percent over GMA explained variance.

The results of these two last analyses suggest that a good option for the practitioner, in the majority of cases, is to combine GMA measures with measures of conscientiousness, emotional stability and agreeableness for predicting job performance and to combine GMA tests with measures of conscientiousness, extroversion and openness to predict training proficiency.

Work samples

Work samples involve identifying tasks representative of the job and using these to develop a representative short test resembling actual components of the job. For example, a typing test may be used as part of the selection process for a secretarial position. Not surprisingly therefore, applicants rate work sample tests highly positively, perceiving them as fair, valid, and job related (Chan & Schmitt, 2004; Ryan & Ployhart, 2000). Work sample tests also have highly acceptable predictive validity. The Schmidt and Hunter (1998) meta-analysis found an average mean validity coefficient of 0.54 for work samples. Again, perhaps not surprisingly, rating the applicant actually performing key tasks is an accurate means of evaluating their subsequent performance in jobs which require little further training before proficiency can be achieved by the individual.

Assessment centers

Assessment centers (ACs) involve a combination of the selection methods already discussed, commonly, work samples, ability tests, personality tests, and interviews. These are given to a group of candidates over the course of a day, or several days where candidates' behaviors are rated by a number of trained assessors along identified selection dimensions. Organizations may use ACs for selection, promotion and for development purposes. Across Europe, there are wide differences in the use of ACs for selection; they are more common, particularly in large organizations, in the UK, Belgium, Denmark and Germany, and less common in France, Switzerland, Spain, and Italy (Shackleton & Newell, 1997). Overall, applicants tend to favor assessment centers, probably due to their use of work samples and the opportunity that they provide to meet with assessors and to perform job-related exercises alongside other candidates (Anderson, Born, &

Cunningham-Snell, 2001; Iles & Robertson, 1997; Ryan & Ployhart, 2000). Thus, Schmitt and Chan (1998) define ACs as follows:

> an evaluation method or process rather than a physical location . . . includes a day or more of exercises . . . and discussions [that] are observed by various trained assessors. At the end of the exercises, the assessors or raters report their observations to each other and are asked to rate the candidates. (pp. 175–6)

The criterion-related validity of well-designed ACs is strong although higher validities are observed when predicting potential rather than actual performance (Gaugler, Rosenthal, Thornton, & Bentson, 1987; Schmidt & Hunter, 1998). In a meta-analysis by Gaugler et al. (1987) which included 12 validation studies of selection ACs (total $N = 3,198$), the mean validity coefficient for selection was 0.41. When assessment centers are used for promotion purposes, the validity is somewhat higher. The largest American meta-analysis published by Schmidt & Hunter (1998) reports a criterion-related validity coefficient of 0.37 for ACs, although this figure may somewhat underestimate their true validity against specific job performance dimensions (Cook, 1998).

Not every exercise measures every dimension in an AC. Rather, a *targeted matrix* is developed whereby certain exercises are designed to elicit behaviors by candidates relevant to some of the dimensions. Table 12.2 shows one example of such a targeted matrix with the exercises listed along the top horizontal axis and the dimensions evaluated listed in the first vertical column.

Table 12.2: Example of a targeted AC matrix

Dimensions	Interview	Written Analysis Exercise	Exercises Strategic Meeting	Leaderless Group Meeting
Adaptability	4	5		
Analysis		4		
Creativity		4		4
Interpersonal skills	5		4	
Initiative	4		3	
Judgment		4	4	4
Energy				5
Oral Communication				3
Persuasiveness		4	4	5
Planning/organizing		5	4	4
Sensitivity to others	3	4	4	
Tolerance for stress		4	5	
Work standards	5	5	4	5
Written communication		5		

Assessors rate candidates on a five-point scale in this particular matrix, note that a gap indicates that the exercise does not measure that particular dimension. Once all exercises are completed and rated, the assessors then need to meet to agree a final combined rating, the so-called "Overall Assessment Rating" or OAR. The OAR for the candidate shown in table 12.2 is likely to be a "4" and assuming that higher ratings represent stronger within-exercise performance, this candidate is likely therefore to be successful on this occasion.

Not surprisingly, ACs are usually far more expensive than say a test of cognitive ability or even a structured interview. Yet ACs may not be any more valid or reliable, but remain quite popular, especially for graduate and managerial selection.

References

References involve the assessment of an individual by a third party, for example the applicant's previous employer. The use of references is more common in the UK, Ireland, and Belgium than in France, Sweden, the Netherlands and Portugal (Shackleton & Newell, 1997). References may involve either an open-ended format or a structured format with questions developed from selection criteria. References may serve at least two purposes; first to confirm the accuracy of information provided by the applicant, and second, to obtain information on the applicant's previous work experience and performance (Smith & Robertson, 1993). However, the criterion related validity evidence for references is poor (see figure 12.3), suggesting that not too much reliance should be placed upon their content. Indeed, research suggests that references suffer from leniency errors, with few applicants given negative evaluations (Browning, 1968). References are therefore rarely used in the decision-making process, but are more likely to be used merely as a final check before any job offer is made.

Self Assessment

Self-assessment (SA) is an introspective, self-evaluation made by a candidate of his or her own strengths and weaknesses in relation to a given job role. SA is rarely used in selection and perhaps rightly so as the accuracy of SA in validation studies has provided inconsistent results (e.g., Byham, 1971; Schmitt, Ford, & Stults, 1986). In a meta-analysis of 3 studies (N = 545) incorporating validity coefficients with overall performance criteria, Reilly and Chao (1982) found the average weighted validity was 0.15. Problems associated with SA include leniency effect and poor reliability of ratings (see Cook, 1998).

Alternative methods: graphology and astrology

Graphology involves the interpretation of a sample of handwriting as a means of generating personality descriptions or behavioral predictions. This method is most common in French-speaking cultures (Shackleton & Newell, 1997).

However, even French candidates tend to rate this method negatively (Steiner & Gilliland, 1996) and the predictive validity evidence is extremely weak (see figure 12.3). Astrology is another "alternative" selection method, although it is very rarely used. Neither graphology nor astrology deserve to be part of any professionally respectable organization's selection procedures.

Theory versus practice in selection

Having overviewed the key research findings, it is important to note that these have not necessarily been translated into common practice by organizations in their day-to-day selection procedures (Anderson, 2005; Cook, 1998). Although surveys suggest that some elements of organizational selection procedures have improved (for instance the use of psychometric testing is more widespread), other evidence is far less optimistic. Many organizations fail to conduct proper job analyses, rely solely upon unstructured interviews, use inappropriate or even misuse psychometric tests, or perhaps most common of all, do not validate their selection procedures in order to verify effectiveness. The challenge, then, is for the findings from this research to be accepted by organizations and recruiters, and for their results to inform professional practice in employee selection (Anderson, 2005).

Applicant Reactions and Decision-Making in Selection

A recurrent theme in this chapter has been the acknowledgement of the increasing importance of the candidates' perspective in selection. Several studies and reviews suggest that candidates prefer methods which appear to be more job-relevant (Robertson, Iles, Gratton, & Sharpley 1991; Rynes, 1993), which are nonintrusive (Ryan & Sackett, 1987), which do not invade personal privacy and which in general seem to be fair and objective (Anderson, 2003; Rynes & Connerley, 1993). More recently, a number of frameworks for examining the social issues involved in selection have emerged, providing more detailed insight into the aetiology of the applicants' perspective (e.g., Arvey & Sackett, 1993; Gilliland, 1993; Schuler, 1993; Anderson et al., 2001).

Gilliland's (1993) Selection Fairness Model is notable in moving beyond a list of the likely determinants of fairness perceptions, towards developing a framework that is rooted in organizational justice theory. Organizational justice theory distinguishes between *procedural justice* and *distributive justice*, referring to the fairness of the selection process and to fairness of the hiring decision respectively. Procedural justice has been found to relate to, among others, achievement strivings, evaluation of the information source (Schroth & Shah, 2000), and negative affect (van den Bos, Vermunt, & Wilke, 1997). It consists of three components. Firstly, the formal characteristics component relates to the rules of job relatedness, opportunity to perform, reconsideration opportunity, and consistency of administration. The explanation component is related to the rules of feedback, selection information, and honesty. Finally, interpersonal treatment consists of interpersonal effectiveness, two-way communication, and propriety of questions (Gilliland, 1993). Consistent with organizational justice theory, Gilliland suggests that it is the combined satisfaction or violation of specific rules that produce overall evaluations of procedural and distributive fairness. In line with this idea, it was found that procedures that are perceived as fair in turn lead to higher fairness perceptions of the outcome, even when this outcome is a negative one (Greenberg, 1986).

Research indicates that candidates' reactions to selection justice can have an impact on three important outcomes (Gilliland, 1993): First, perceptions of justice influence applicants' reactions and decisions during hiring, for example the extent to which the candidate will recommend the organization to others (Gilliland, 1994; Smither et al., 1993) and intentions to withdraw from the procedure. Second, perceptions of fairness impinge upon candidates' attitudes and behaviors after hiring or rejecting, for example organizational commitment, intention to leave and work performance in case of hiring (Anderson & Ostroff; 1997; Gilliland & Honig, 1994; Konovsky & Cropanzano, 1991; Robertson, Iles, Gratton, & Sharpley, 1991) and recommendation and purchase intentions, and the decision of whether to pursue (discrimination) cases (Gilliland 1993). Third, perceived fairness influences applicants' well-being and self-perceptions, such as self-esteem and self-efficacy (Gilliland 1994; Robertson & Smith, 1989; Schinkel, Van Dierendonck, & Anderson, 2004).

The second premise that has received considerable attention in applicant reactions research is based on Weiner's (1985) attribution theory (Arvey, Strickland, Drauden, & Martin,1990; Kluger & Rothstein, 1993; Ployhart & Ryan, 1997). This theory pertains to the *attributions* people make for the causes of all kinds of events, which form the basis for a variety of expectations, intentions and behaviors (Ryan & Ployhart, 2000). According to attribution theory, all attributions people make fall into one of the three following dimensions: (1) locus, which concerns the question whether a certain cause is perceived to be due to factors internal to the person, (2) stability, referring to the extent to which the cause is seen as stable or unstable in the future, and (3) controllability, which pertains to the amount of control the individual has over the outcome (Weiner, 1985). Following this line of thinking, Ployhart and Harold (2004) developed the applicant attribution-reaction theory (AART), in which they state that applicants' affective, behavioral and cognitive reactions to selection (e.g., fairness and test perceptions, test performance and motivation) are caused by an attributional process. The focal tenet of the theory is that between objective events (e.g., treatment during selection procedure, hiring decision, explanation of hiring decision) and the formation of reactions, applicants engage in attributional processing of the causes for the particular selection outcome. In a selection situation, for instance, applicants who receive a rejection decision may not react negatively toward the organization if they believe the decision to be based on their own substandard performance. However, if a rejected applicant perceives the rejection as unfair (perceived to be caused by biased tests, unfair procedures, etc.) he or she might react more negatively. A third possibility is that the applicant perceives the negative decision as being caused by an external and uncontrollable factor, for example an extremely low selection ratio (Ployhart & Ryan, 1997, 1998; Ryan & Ployhart, 2000).

AART also explains the occurrence of a self-serving bias in applicant reactions. Applicants who are hired by an organization generally perceive the procedure and organization as fair, while those who are rejected arrive at the opposite conclusion. Thus, in keeping their self-perceptions intact, rejected applicants lower their perceptions of an organization. To reduce the chances of this bias, organizations may provide applicants with more information about the selection procedure and decision (Ployhart & Harold, 2004). For example, in a scenario study, Ployhart, Ryan, and Bennett (1999) found that providing rejected applicants with a specific explanation for a selection decision increased their procedural fairness perceptions. However, at what cost should organizational perceptions be protected? Whereas feedback about a negative selection decision is hypothesized to enable an applicant to build a more accurate self-image and to develop more realistic career goals (Robertson & Smith, 1989), it has been found to cause lowered self-perceptions and well-being as well (Fletcher, 1991; Schinkel, Van Dierendonck, & Anderson, 2004).

In sum, rejected applicants' self- and organizational perceptions might be two sides of the same coin: it may merely be possible to increase either at the expense of the other. It is axiomatic then, that selected as well as rejected applicants' reactions to selection should remain just as important a concern as validity, reliability or adverse impact (Iles & Robertson, 1997).

Summary

In this chapter we have overviewed some of the critical theoretical approaches, design principles, research findings, and practical ramifications of personnel selection. Our intention throughout has been to provide an introduction to the fast-moving field of research and day-to-day applied practice which today constitutes recruitment and selection. We have explicitly emphasized a "European" constructivist perspective by arguing that candidates, as well as organizations, reach decisions as a result of their experiences during selection. Ironically, by the time this introductory review is published it will be somewhat out-of-date; such is the pace and volume of current research and development in this area. Yet, despite this academic and consultancy-based research activity, some organizations remain blissfully unaware of the huge paybacks which can be gained from the application of modern, sophisticated selection system techniques. It is our hope that this chapter may stimulate readers to reconsider personnel selection in light of these research findings, many of which have appeared only over more recent years, and finally to apply some of the principles of a systems approach to real life organizational selection procedures.

Discussion Points

Given the huge payoffs of using more sophisticated methods for personnel selection, why do organizations continue to use methods that have been proven to lack validity or reliability?

Compare and contrast the organizational and applicant's perspective at different stages in the recruitment and selection process. Why may these not match and what might the implications of any such mismatch be?

Key Studies

Personnel Psychology (1990), *43*, 2: Special Issue. Project A; The US Army Selection and Classification Project.

Schmidt, F. L., & Hunter, J. E. (1998). The validity and utility of selection methods in personnel psychology: Practical and theoretical implications of 85 years of research findings. *Psychological Bulletin*, *124*, 262–74.

International Journal of Selection and Assessment (2000). (Jesús F. Salgado, Guest Editor), *8*, 3&4; (2001) *9*, 1&2 (Part 1 and Part II): Special issues on Personnel Selection at the Beginning of a New Millennium: A Global and International Perspective.

International Journal of Selection and Assessment (2002). (Deniz S. Ones, Guest Editor), *10*, 1&2: Double Special Issue on Counterproductive Behaviors at Work.

International Journal of Selection and Assessment (2003). (Chockalingam Viswesvaran, Guest Editor), *11*, 2&3: Double Special Issue on Role of Technology in Shaping the Future of Staffing and Assessment.

International Journal of Selection and Assessment (2004). (Neil Anderson, Guest Editor) *12*, 1 & 2: Double Special Issue on Applicant Reactions and Decision-Making in Selection.

Further Reading

1. General

Evers, A., Anderson, N., & Smit-Voskuyl, O. (Eds.) (2005). *The Blackwell handbook of selection*. Oxford: Blackwell.

Cook, M. (1998). *Personnel selection: Adding value through people*, 3rd edn. Chichester: Wiley.

Schmitt, N., & Chan, D. (1998). *Personnel selection: A theoretical approach*. Thousand Oaks, CA: Sage.

2. Specialized

Smith, M., & Smith, P. (2005). *Testing people at work*. Oxford: BPS/Blackwell.

Woodruffe, C. (1997). *Assessment centres: Identifying and developing competence*. London: Institute of Personnel Management.

3. Key Journals

International Journal of Selection and Assessment

Journal of Applied Psychology

Journal of Occupational and Organizational Psychology

Personnel Psychology

13

Leadership in Organizations

Felix C. Brodbeck

Overview

In this chapter leadership in organizations is defined and the reader is introduced into the goals and methods of the scientific study of leader attributes and leadership effectiveness. Core questions raised are: "How can we identify leaders?", "What outcome criteria define an effective leader?," "What are leaders doing?," "What personal attributes of leaders are effective?," "How important is the leadership context?," and "What makes the leadership process effective?"

Three major approaches are introduced: leader-oriented trait, skill, and behavior approaches; contingency approaches, where situational factors are taken into account which impact on the relationship between leader attributes and the leadership outcome; and process approaches where the role of the followers' perceptions about their leaders and cultural differences for leadership effectiveness are described and the relatively new concepts of transformational and charismatic leadership are introduced. Finally, how leadership unfolds as a social interactive process is characterized by power relationships and mutual influence between leaders and followers.

Leadership in Organizations

There are numerous definitions of leadership. Leadership research should be designed to provide information relevant to the entire range of definitions, so as not to predetermine the answers to the central questions about leadership: *How to identify leaders? What are leaders doing? What makes leadership effective?*

Therefore, let's start with a simple definition of leadership, which is *influencing others*. This understanding of leadership is the common denominator of the numerous definitions of leadership that have been proposed in the literature (e.g., Bass, 1990; Yukl, 2005). More specifically, leadership in organizations, which this chapter focuses on, means *having and being seen to have the ability to influence and enable others to contribute toward the success of their work unit or organization.* This more specific definition of business leadership emerged from discussions among leadership scholars and social scientist from more than 60 countries representing all major cultural regions in the world as part of the Global Leadership and Organizational Effectiveness (GLOBE) program (House et al., 2004; Chhokar, Brodbeck, & House, 2007).

Leadership in organizations can be performed via structures and tools, like reward systems, lines of authority, role and job descriptions, rules and legal systems and via people. This chapter focuses on leadership that involves *people*, those who lead (the leaders), those who are led (the followers), and the organizational and social contexts within which leadership processes are embedded (e.g., reward systems, role descriptions etc.) and in the social settings where leadership takes place (e.g., work groups, meetings, one-to-one interactions, face-to-face or virtually via information technology).

Leadership research has focused on the reasons why certain persons emerge as leaders, and how leaders are perceived by followers (*How to identify leaders?*), what behaviors and skills leaders exhibit (*What are leaders doing?*), and factors that determine how leadership enables followers to accomplish group and organizational objectives (*What makes leadership effective?*).

Outcome criteria of effective leadership

To test the value of leadership theories and practical guidelines it is important to precisely specify which criteria of leadership success a theory or model aims to explain or predict. There are basically three different classes of criteria by which leadership success has been systematically measured: *(1) the extent to which a leader influences others*, for example, their behavior, values and attitudes, or a team's climate, group norms or perceived group efficacy, *(2) the extent to which a leader influences performance related output*, for example, the followers' work performance, job satisfaction, turnover, accident rates, or sick leave days, or the quantity and quality of a work units' products and services, return on investments (ROI), responsiveness to change, or innovations made, and *(3) the amount of recognition that a leader receives by relevant others*, for example, the leaders' individual progress in terms of recognition and acceptance by others, as well as their income, gratifications, levels and speed of advancement, or their esteem within and outside their work units and organizations.

Approaches to the study of leadership

Three major approaches of leadership research can be distinguished on the basis of where the emphasis is placed for describing leadership and explaining leadership success:

1) leader-oriented approaches focus primarily on the personality characteristics, behaviors, behavioral styles and skills of leaders in order to distinguish leaders from nonleaders and to identify effective leaders,

2) contingency approaches focus on predicting the conditions under which certain leader characteristics and leadership behaviors are successful by incorporating relevant situational factors (e.g., characteristics of the organization, the task, the followers), and

3) process-oriented approaches address the social interactive nature of relationships between leaders and followers under various context conditions.

Leader-Oriented Approaches

Leader traits

From the beginning of leadership research up until about the 1960's most leadership research focused on personal characteristics of leaders (e.g., intelligence, temperament, motives, personal values) following the idea that "a leader is born – not made". The central assumption underlying these "Great-Man" approaches is that effective leaders can be differentiated from nonleaders or ineffective leaders on the basis of *personality traits*, which are defined as dispositions of a person which are relatively stable over time and across different situations. The objective was to characteristic successful leaders in terms of traits, and to use these as criteria for personnel selection.

In several reviews of the early empirical studies the average strength of relationships between personality traits and various criteria of leadership success were reported to be rather weak and no particular set of universally relevant leadership traits could be identified (Mann, 1959; Stogdill, 1948). Re-analyses of these reviews (e.g., House & Baetz, 1979; Lord, DeVader, & Alliger, 1986) and newer reviews summarizing subsequent research (e.g., Bass, 1990) came to more positive conclusions. It seems that leadership success criteria are related to certain leadership traits. For example, traits like high energy level and stress tolerance help managers to cope with the hectic pace of their job, the long hours, and the frequently encountered stressful interpersonal situations, and self-confidence (i.e. self efficacy, self-esteem), relates positively to advancement and being perceived as a charismatic leader (for a review about personality and leadership, see Judge, Bono, Ilies, & Gerhard, 2002).

More generally, in leadership trait approaches explanations are missing about how the link between personality traits and leadership effectiveness actually comes about.

Leadership skills

One research approach investigated so called *leadership skills* (i.e. the ability to perform certain leadership tasks in an effective manner) and their relationship to leadership effectiveness. In contrast to personality traits leadership skills can be shaped, learned and trained, at least to some degree. Note that there are some close relationships between personality traits, like intelligence, and certain skills, like abstract thinking.

Leadership skills have been classified into *technical skills* concerned with objects, processes and functional relationships, *conceptual skills* concerned with ideas and abstractions, and *interpersonal skills* concerned with people and groups. Studies of the relationship between potentially relevant leadership skills and leadership effectiveness show weak to moderate effect sizes (Yukl, 2005).

Overall, it can be stated that certain leadership traits and skills can increase the likelihood of leadership success but only to a limited extent. For developing more sound theories about how traits and skills affect leadership effectiveness, we need to understand how traits and skills are expressed. Here leadership behavior comes into the equation.

Leadership behavior

Leadership behavior has been more widely researched than any other aspect of leadership. Throughout the 1950s and 1960s descriptions of leadership behaviors and how they relate to the followers' perceptions, attitudes and performance were investigated by many research groups, mainly based in North America. The objective was to develop improved leadership models which could better explain leadership success than it was possible at that time on the basis of traits and skills. In a first step, attempts were made to bring some order into the manifold descriptive studies about leadership behaviors by using the concept of *leadership style* (i.e. general behavioral preferences of a leader, for example, autocratic, task oriented, or people oriented).

Two groups of researchers contributed influential studies about leadership behavior that have shaped our understanding of leadership behavior: the Ohio Group (e.g., Hemphill, Fleishman, Stogdill) and the Michigan Group (e.g., Likert, Katz). Independently from each other they came to very similar conclusions. Thus the findings of only one group are described in more detail here.

Researchers at Ohio State University sought to classify relevant aspects of leadership behaviors by assembling about 1,800 leader behavior descriptions that were subsequently reduced to about 150 items, the Leader Behavior Description Questionnaire (LBDQ), a hallmark in the history of leadership research. Factor analysis of the LBDQ produced two independent dimensions: *initiating structure* (*IS*, i.e. task-oriented behaviors) and *consideration* (*C*, i.e. people-oriented behaviors).

Many subsequent leadership models capitalized on these concepts of leadership behavior. The cumulated empirical evidence supports the assumption of a two-dimensional construct of leadership (for a review, cf. Bass, 1990). (See figure 13.1.)

In a widely cited study by Fleishman and Harris (1962), Consideration and Initiating Structure were shown to relate to employee grievance and turnover in

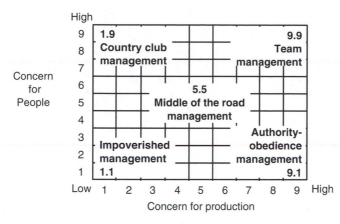

Figure 13.1: The two dimensions of leadership behavior (adapted from Blake, 1991, lecture slide)

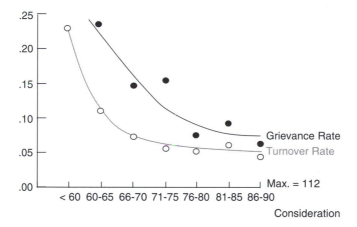

Figure 13.2a: Relationship between leadership consideration and indicators of followers' job satisfaction (adapted from Fleishman & Harris, 1962)

work groups (with $N = 57$ production foreman and their respective groups). Some of their results are depicted in figures 13.2a and 13.2b. Low consideration and high initiating structure go along with high grievances and turnover rates. The relationships are curvilinear, that is, there are certain critical levels beyond which increased consideration (>75 for turnover, >80 for grievance, see figure 13.2a) or decreased initiating structure (<40 for turnover, <35 for grievance, see figure 13.2b) have no noteworthy effects on grievance or turnover rates.

In a *meta-analysis* (Judge, Piccolo, & Ilies, 2004) of about 200 studies with about 300 samples and more than 400 different correlations both Consideration and Initiating Structure had moderately strong and nonzero relationships

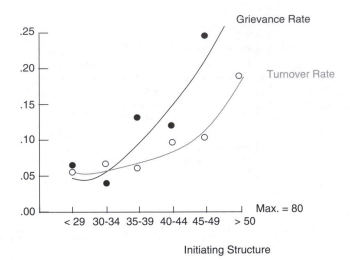

Figure 13.2b: Relationship between leadership initiating structure and indicators of followers job satisfaction (adapted from Fleishman & Harris, 1962)

Table 13.1: Relationship of consideration and initiating structure with leadership criteria

Leadership criteria	Consideration	Initiating Structure
Leader effectiveness	.39*	.28*
Leader job performance	.18*	.19*
Group / organizational performance	.23*	.23*
Follower satisfaction with leader	.68*	.27*
Follower motivation	.40*	.26*
Follower job satisfaction	.40*	.19*
Overall average correlation	.49*	.29*

Note: Entries are mean observed correlations based on a meta-analysis of about 400 correlation coefficients from about 200 studies with about 300 different samples (cf. Judge, Piccolo, & Ilies, 2004).

with various leadership outcomes (see table 13.1). However, as was also reported in earlier studies, Consideration appears to more strongly relate to leadership effectiveness criteria than Initiating Structure. Explaining this effect, Judge et al. (2004) note that task orientation (Initiating Structure) may be more susceptible to situational differences than people orientation (Consideration). For example, in some situations, task orientation is positively associated with job satisfaction in others it has negative effects (cf. Pierce & Newstrom, 2003).

A taxonomy of a variety of specific leadership behaviors was recently suggested by Yukl and associates (for an overview, cf. Yukl 2005) which distinguishes between *task behaviors* (e.g., clarifying role expectations), *relations behaviors* (e.g., mentoring) and *transformational behaviors* (e.g., empowering people to implement new strategies). From these studies it is evident that specific leadership behaviors seem to be better predictors of specific criteria of leadership effectiveness than the abstract dimensions which emerged in the Ohio and Michigan studies. For an example, cumulative empirical evidence speaks for "clarifying role expectations", in particular, the setting of specific, challenging but realistic goals, as strongly predicting leadership effectiveness on followers' motivation and task performance (Locke & Latham, 1990; Hertel & Wittchen, chapter 2 of this book).

A note of caution is in order here that applies to the empirical study of leaders' personality, skills, and behaviors. The commonly used cross-sectional studies, by which measures of personality etc. and performance are taken from a sample of leaders, supervisors, followers, and performance records at the same point in time, do not suffice to test causal hypotheses. With such a "correlative" design, the possibility remains that the true relationship works the other way around (for a review, cf. Korman, 1968). For example, people placed in a leadership position learn and develop skills, attitudes, and behaviors necessary to succeed (or just to survive), which can develop into relatively stable person characteristics and skills. Or, leaders show more consideration behavior toward followers who are already motivated and high performing (Greene, 1975). Or, third variables (e.g., mutual sympathy between leader and follower due to a match in personal values and back ground) may have an impact on both the leaders' behavior and the followers' behavior, in the same way. For example, mutual sympathy leads to more consideration on the leader's part and to higher performance on the follower's part.

Better approaches that allow more secure causal theories (that can also counter common method and common source bias effects) are longitudinal studies and quasi-experimental designs (cf. Cook, Campbell, & Peracchio, 1990). For example, McClelland (1965, 1985) presents a theory to account for the interaction between a leader's motivational dispositions and environmental factors. It has been tested with several longitudinal studies and is described in more detail in the Research Close-Up at the end of this chapter. Because McClelland's theory focuses on personality traits *and* takes situational factors into account, it can also be described as a contingency approach (see next section).

Leadership in Context: Contingency Approaches

Contingency approaches to the study of leadership effectiveness emphasize the role of factors other than the leader and how these moderate the relationship between leadership traits or behaviors and various criteria of leader effectiveness. From this perspective leader-oriented approaches can predict only a limited proportion of the variance in leadership effectiveness, because the effects of leadership traits and behaviors are likely to average out across different situations. Several theories have been proposed each of which stresses the importance of a particular array of situational factors and different leadership characteristics (for reviews, see Bass, 1990; Yukl, 2005). There is no unified theory from which the most critical situational factors or leadership characteristics can be derived. We therefore describe two of the more widely cited contingency theories (Fiedler's Contingency Theory, and House's Path–Goal Theory) in order to illustrate the basic principles. Thereafter we focus on the role of followers' perceptions, cultural differences and the leader–follower relationship as situational factors which are highly relevant for the leadership process.

Fiedler's contingency theory

Fiedler's (1967; 1972) theory was among the first in which the importance of situational variables for predicting leadership effectiveness was pointed out. The theory postulates three situational factors of importance to the control a leader can exert over a work unit: (a) *quality of leader–member relations* (e.g., collaborative, trusting, friendly versus not); (b) *power inherent in the leader's position* (e.g., the extent to which a leader can reward and punish, hire and fire), and (c) *task structure* (e.g., tasks can be spelled out, clear, and programmed versus vague, nebulous, and unstructured). Fiedler also uses the term "favorableness" of the situation, that is, the more favorable a situation is, the more control a leader can exert due to situational characteristics.

The leaders' overall effectiveness depends on the amount of control (defined by the above situational characteristics) they have *and* their own leadership motivation. They can be either predominantly task-motivated or predominantly relationship-motivated. Leadership motivation is measured by a questionnaire called "Esteem for the Least Preferred Co-worker" (LPC) in which leaders are asked to think of the person with whom they worked *least well* (see table 13.2). A leader who describes the least preferred co-worker in relatively favorable terms is motivated to maintain close relationships with others (in McClelland's terminology the respective leader would have a high need for affiliation, see the Research Close-Up). A leader, who uses negative terms, indicating that he or she strongly rejects someone whom he or she cannot work with, is basically motivated to accomplish tasks or to achieve high performance (high need for achievement, see the Research Close-Up).

In order to predict leadership effectiveness on the basis of a leader's motivation and situational factors, we need to know a little more about how the situational characteristics combine into overall more or less favorable situations. The combination of high versus low on each of the three situation characteristics gives us a $2 \times 2 \times 2 = 8$ celled taxonomy of situational configurations which descend in favorableness from left to right (high control, intermediate control, low control, see figure 13.3). The critical question is, "What kind of leadership is most effective in each of the eight situational classes? Fiedler reported results from 63 analyses with a total of 454 work units of various types (e.g., military crews, sports teams, management teams, boards of directors, problem solving groups). The correlations between leader LPC and work unit performance for each of the eight situational configurations are depicted in figure 13.3.

Table 13.2: Items of the least preferred co-worker measure (adapted from Fiedler, 1972)
Leadership Self-Assessment: Least Preferred Co-Worker (LPC) Scale

Instructions: This of the person with whom you can work least well. It does not have to be the person you like least well, but should be the person with whom you had the most difficulty in getting a job done. Describe this person by circling a number for each scale.

Pleasant	8	7	6	5	4	3	2	1	Unplasant
Friendly	8	7	6	5	4	3	2	1	Unfriendly
Rejecting	1	2	3	4	5	6	7	8	Accepting
Helpful	8	7	6	5	4	3	2	1	Frustrating
Unenthusiastic	1	2	3	4	5	6	7	8	Enthusiastic
Tense	1	2	3	4	5	6	7	8	Relazed
Distant	1	2	3	4	5	6	7	8	Close
Cold	1	2	3	4	5	6	7	8	Warm
Cooperative	8	7	6	5	4	3	2	1	Uncooperative
Supportive	8	7	6	5	4	3	2	1	Hostile
Boring	1	2	3	4	5	6	7	8	Interesting
Quarrelsome	1	2	3	4	5	6	7	8	Harmonious
Self-Assured	8	7	6	5	4	3	2	1	Hesitant
Efficient	8	7	6	5	4	3	2	1	Inefficient
Gloomy	1	2	3	4	5	6	7	8	Cheerful
Open	8	7	6	5	4	3	2	1	Guarded

• Your LPC score is the sum of the answers to all items. A score greater than 76 indicates *a relationship motivation*, and a score of less than 62 indicates *a task motivation*. A score of 58 to 63 places you in the intermediate range (*socio-independent*).

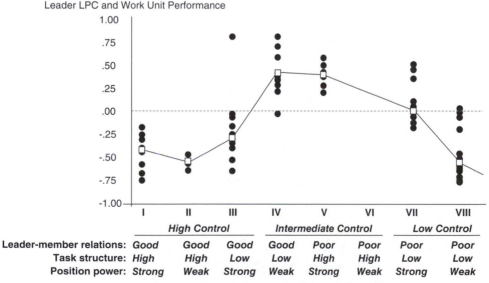

	I	II	III	IV	V	VI	VII	VIII
		High Control			Intermediate Control		Low Control	
Leader-member relations:	Good	Good	Good	Good	Poor	Poor	Poor	Poor
Task structure:	High	High	Low	Low	High	High	Low	Low
Position power:	Strong	Weak	Strong	Weak	Strong	Weak	Strong	Weak

Prediction of the Performance of Relationship- and Task-Motivated Leaders

Relationship-motivated HIGH LPC				Good	Good	Somewhat better	Somewhat better	
Task-motivated LOW LPC	Good	Good	Good					Good

Figure 13.3: Fiedler's contingency theory (adapted from Fiedler, 1972)

What can be seen in the upper part of figure 13.3, for example, is that the correlations between work unit performance and LPC score scatter around a Median of negative correlations for the situational configurations I, II, and III. These situations allow higher control, and high work unit performance is negatively linked with high LPC scores. In other words, a leader's higher task motivation (i.e. lower LPC) is linked with higher performance. On the bottom of figure 13.3 the predictions that result from Fiedler's study are shown.

Fiedler's model has been criticized for various reasons. Among others, the construct validity of its central variable (task versus relationship motivated leadership) was considered questionable due to its bipolar nature, contrasting with the two dimensions that emerged from the research on leadership behavior (Initiating Structure and Consideration). One could argue that Fiedler's leadership concept is motivational rather than behavioral in nature and therefore not comparable to the findings from the Ohio and the Michigan Groups. However this begs the question how the different leadership motivations exert influence over work units and their members if not via respective leadership behaviors, an aspect still not established. Moreover, Fiedler's concepts of relationship and task motivation overlap McClelland's work on leader motivations, where the Need for Affiliation and the Need for Achievement are seen as two distinct dimensions rather than as the two poles of a bipolar dimension.

Secondly, in Fiedler's theory the leaders' motivational orientations are seen as stable over time and across situations, which makes them comparable to personality traits. However, the LPC could be interpreted as measuring less stable *attitudes* of leaders toward their followers (Rice, 1978) rather than more stable personality traits or motivational dispositions.

Thirdly, Fiedler's concept of relationship motivation is likely to be confounded with one of the three situation characteristics, namely "quality of leader–follower relationships". That is, a leader who has a positive attitude toward followers is likely to actively establish or maintain favorable relationships with work unit members.

Although Fiedler's model is controversial, the general predictions made hold up fairly well, although most empirical evidence stems from laboratory rather than natural groups and some situations fit better than others (cf. Strube & Garcia, 1981; Peters, Hartke, & Pohlmann, 1985).

Path–goal theory

In contrast to Fiedler's theory, path–goal theory (House, 1971; House & Mitchell, 1974) focuses the process of motivation on part of the followers. It is rooted in expectancy theory (see Hertel et al., this book), a process theory of human motivation, which has been extended to the domain of leadership (e.g., by Nebeker & Mitchell, 1974). According to path–goal theory leaders are effective because their behavior impacts on, and should be adapted to, situational contingencies to maximize, subordinates' motivation and satisfaction. This is in contrast to Fiedler's theory from which follows that it is not the leader who should adapt or change, but rather the situational contingencies which should be changed to better fit the leader's motivational disposition.

In newer revisions of path–goal theory five classes of leadership behaviors are distinguished:

Clarifying behavior (e.g., clarifying rewards and punishments, performance goals, standards, and the means to achieve them) reduces role ambiguity and increases follower beliefs that effort in a certain direction will result in good performance and performance will be rewarded. It also clarifies expectations and increases the consistency of subordinate and organizational goals.

Work facilitation behavior (e.g., planning, scheduling, coordinating, guiding, coaching, counseling, and giving feedback) eliminates roadblocks and bottlenecks, provides resources, stimulates self-development and helps to delegate authority to subordinates.

Participative behavior (e.g., consulting with subordinates, incorporating subordinate opinions in decision-making) increases self-confidence and the personal value of job-related effort.

Supportive behavior (e.g., creating a friendly and psychologically supportive environment, displaying concern for subordinates' welfare) increases involvement with and commitment to work group and organizational goals.

Achievement-oriented behavior (e.g., setting high goals and seeking improvement, emphasizing excellence, showing confidence in subordinates stressing pride in work) increases subordinate confidence and the personal value of goal-directed effort.

Path–goal theory suggests that a leader's behavior motivates subordinates to the degree that it increases subordinates' goal attainment and clarifies the path to reach the goals set. The extent to which the above described leadership behavior is successful for motivating subordinates depends on two classes of contingency factors:

a) *Characteristics of the followers* (e.g., internal versus external locus of control, self-efficacy beliefs, their knowledge, skill and ability), which influence the degree to which the followers' see the leadership behavior shown to be a source of satisfaction or as instrumental to future satisfaction, and

b) *Characteristics of the environment* (e.g., task structure, formal authority system of the organization, primary work group), which are not within the control of the followers, but which are important to satisfy their needs or their ability to perform well.

An example of how path–goal theory works suggests the higher followers' self-efficacy beliefs about job performance are, the less they will view leader facilitation and coaching behaviors as acceptable. Thus these behaviors are less likely to result in follower's motivation and satisfaction when self-efficacy beliefs of the followers are strong (a moderation effect). Similar contingencies can be identified with environmental conditions. When goals and paths to desired goals are self-evident or immediately apparent for the follower (as with structured tasks, objective controls of formal authority systems, and clear group norms) not very much can be gained by leadership behavior that focuses on clarifying. This will be seen by subordinates as redundant or as imposing unnecessary close control which results in decreased satisfaction.

Despite inconclusive research results and some conceptual deficiencies (e.g., House, 1996; Wofford & Liska, 1993), path–goal theory provides a valuable conceptual framework for identifying situational factors relevant to leadership effectiveness which is based on theories about human motivation. Furthermore, path–goal theory has stimulated the development of new (and today well-known) leadership theories, which adopted the underlying idea that certain leadership behaviors are helpful and successful under certain circumstances. This idea was adopted, for example, in the Substitutes for Leadership theory (Kerr & Jermier, 1978), which proposes that certain conditions of structural leadership in an organization (e.g., personnel selection focuses on high ability, high expertise, and high need for independence among subordinates) substitute for personal leadership qualities, and thus, make certain leadership behaviors obsolete (e.g., clarifying) or require an overall different leadership approach. Another idea that path–goal theory has promoted in the study of leadership is that the followers and their characteristics matter in the leadership process to a large extent. Not only is their performance related behavior important but also their perceptions, cognitions, and beliefs about work related issues. These issues have been addressed in so called follower-focused theories.

Follower perceptions

Lord and Maher's (1991) implicit leadership theories are concerned with the cognitive processes of followers. Perception of just a few typical attributes of a leader (e.g., works 14 hours a day, meets many people, chairs many meetings) activates a leadership schemata (i.e. the cognitive representation of a leadership prototype) in the mind of the follower, on the basis of which further attributes are inferred from long-term memory (e.g., works on weekends, knows powerful people, controls the agenda of meetings, is successful in what he or she is doing). These inferred attributes have not actually been observed, but they are likely to come to mind, once the leadership schema is activated, and they are used to complete the picture of a particular leader held by a follower. And it is this complete picture of the leader to which the follower reacts.

Lord and Maher's model is viewed here as a contingency approach because it suggests that the better the match between a leader's characteristics or behaviors and the implicit leadership theories held by the perceivers (the followers), the more likely it is that the perceivers actually "see" an individual as a leader (or an excellent leader) and allow him or her to exert influence on them.

Implicit leadership theory points toward a problem with the assessment of leadership behavior through questionnaires such as the LBDQ, because it underlines the notion that such questionnaires do not measure actual leader behaviors but rather subjectively formed perceptions on part of the followers who fill in the LBDQ (Rush, Thomas, & Lord, 1977) whose perceptions are influenced by the implicit leadership theories they hold (cf. Eden & Leviathan, 1975).

Furthermore, from Lord and Maher's model, theoretical explanations have been derived that are relevant for different domains of contemporary leadership research, for example, the acceptance of female leaders or the effectiveness of leaders who cross cultural boundaries.

Acceptance of female leaders. It is known that women in leadership roles encounter difficulties in being accepted as leaders *and* as females. One explanation for these difficulties can be seen in the implicit leadership theories of their followers (and superiors), which do not match with their implicitly held concepts about gender roles and gender expectations. For an example, if a woman loudly commands a subordinate, she is more likely to be perceived as being overly stressed, incapable and helpless; her male counterpart who is doing the same, is more likely to be seen as decisive, resolute, and certain (cf. Morrison, White, & Van Velsor, 1987). Eagly, Makhijani, and Klonsky (1992) demonstrated using meta-analysis, that women in leadership positions are more negatively perceived than their male counterparts, when they show leadership behaviors that match the male stereotype of leadership (e.g., autocratic or directive leadership styles).

Cultural Differences. The GLOBE (Global Leadership and Organizational Behavior Effectiveness) program has collected data from Europe (cf. Brodbeck, Frese, & Javidan, 2002; Brodbeck et al., 2000) and also across more than 60 countries from all continents world-wide (cf. House et al., 2004; Chhokar, Brodbeck, & House, 2007). Findings show that implicit leadership theories of middle managers are intimately linked with the societal cultural values, norms and belief systems they grew up with (see figure 13.4, for Europe). In the cases of cross-cultural collaboration, joint ventures, or expatriate assignments, it can therefore be predicted that culturally endorsed differences in implicit leadership theories have a negative impact on the quality of leader–follower relationships, which is likely to result in performance losses, misunderstandings, loss of motivation and dissatisfaction on both sides (cf. House et al., 2004; Shaw, 1990).

Not all noteworthy and widely used contingency theories, like the normative model of decision-making (Vroom & Yetton, 1973; Vroom, 2000) or "situational leadership" (Hersey & Blanchard, 1988), can be described in sufficient detail here (for these and further examples, see Pierce & Newstrom, 2003). A basic message of contingency approaches is that leaders must be able to recognize, adapt or cope with different situational circumstances: otherwise they may lose their influence on followers. However, adaptation and coping do not mean

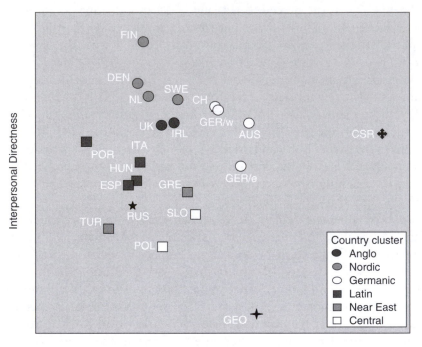

Figure 13.4:   Distribution of leadership prototypes in 22 European countries.
With multidimensional scaling, the 21 leadership scales measured by GLOBE are represented
in a two-dimensional space. The more interpersonal directness (top of the figure), the more
positively are symmetric leader–follower relationships seen in a country. The more autonomy
(righthand side of the figure), the more positively are leaders seen who display individualistic
behaviors. The coding denotes the membership of each country in respective cultural clusters
(Anglo, Nordic, Germanic, Latin European, Central European, and the Near East) which were
identified to significantly differ from each other on the basis of the literature about general
societal cultural values in these countries from 1950 to 2000. The leadership concepts held in
countries of the same region are located near to each other. Those from different cultural
regions are further away: This indicates that societal culture has an impact on the implicit leadership theories held by managers. (Adapted from Brodbeck et al., 2000.) AUS = Austria, CH =
Switzerland, CSR = Czech Republic, DEN = Denmark, FIN = Finland, GB = United Kingdom, GERw
= Germany, GERe = former East Germany, GEO = Georgia, GRE = Greece, HUN = Hungary, ITA
= Italy, IRL = Ireland, NL = Netherlands, POL = Poland, POR = Portugal, RUS = Russia, SLO =
Slovenia, SPA = Spain, SWE = Sweden, TUR = Turkey.

accepting situational factors as unchangeable conditions. Thus, we finally turn to
the power and influence processes by which leaders can introduce change.

Leader–member exchange (LMX) theory

Leader–member exchange theory (LMX) (Dansereau, Graen, & Haga, 1975;
Graen & Scandura, 1987) was one of the first leadership theories that focused

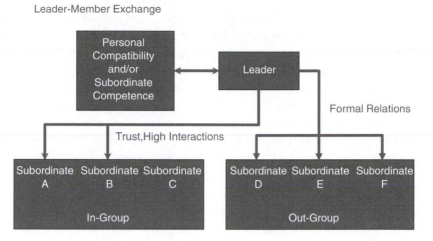

Figure 13.5: The differential quality of leader member relationships (LMX)

on the mutual influence between leaders and the led. In a first step the theory describes the quality of the relationship-based social exchange between leaders and members. Three "currencies of exchange" between follower and leader have been identified: *personal contribution* (i.e. perceived level of competencies and skill), *loyalty* (i.e. perceived level of being trustworthy and responsible), and *motivation* to take up ever more responsible tasks. Leaders differentiate their followers according to their competence, trustworthiness and motivation to assume ever more responsibility. Accordingly, the followers whom the leader perceives to display these attributes are perceived as "in-group" members and in exchange are given more attention, support and sensitivity by their leaders. The "out-group" members attract the more routine tasks and are part of more formal relationships with their leaders, who in return exert influence with formal authority (see figure 13.5).

In a second step, the theory describes that the relationship between leaders and followers develops in basically three phases over time (Graen & Scandura, 1987). In the beginning leaders and followers try to find out about their mutual interests, about each others motivation, attitudes, values, and potential resources for beneficial transactions. In the next phase, the context for exchange is developed by stepwise increasing mutual trust, loyalty, and respect. In some cases there is a third phase, in which the formerly exchange-based interest changes into a mutual commitment to a common task and to shared higher order goals or visions. In this phase, leadership is more a change process rather than a process of exchange (cf. transformational leadership versus transactional leadership, see further below).

Some leadership researchers have criticized LMX theory as only descriptive in nature, not allowing predictions about the effectiveness of leaders and work units on the basis of theory (e.g., Yukl & Van Fleet, 1990; but see also Howell & Hall-Merenda, 1999, who defended LMX as a normative theory, i.e. it prescribes which relationship qualities result in, for example, high performance). Another problematic aspect is the assumption that the leader categorizes followers as either "in-group" or "out-group" members. In early conceptions of the theory it was not made explicit whether this distinction was functional or dysfunctional for leadership effectiveness within work units. From a group dynamic perspective intergroup bias is seen as dysfunctional, hampering the collaboration between in-group and out-group members due to social categorization processes (cf. *social categorization theory*, Tajfel, 1978), resulting in in-group favoritism and out-group discrimination between leader and followers and also among respective subgroups of followers. Another argument was made by Yukl and Van Fleet (1990) who noted that out-group members, who tend to receive routine tasks and low attention by the leader, may become de-motivated, and thus don't identify with the task and the work, which reduces their commitment and their performance. From a theoretical viewpoint, these arguments mean that, a leader who succeeds in developing transformational relationships with more group members than just those who qualify as "in-group" members should be more successful in terms of work performance and satisfaction across the whole work unit than a leader who focuses solely on the naturally developing "in-group" members.

LMX is particularly relevant to leadership in groups because it establishes links between the relationship quality of group members with their leader and variables such as job satisfaction, performance ratings, turnover, and followers' decision influence, which have been empirically supported (e.g., Gerstner & Day, 1997). Furthermore, LMX draws our attention to the fact that the followers' ability, views, behaviors, and performance outcomes can shape the amount of consideration and initiating structure behavior exhibited toward them by the leader. That is, the causal arrow of social influence can also go in the opposite direction, from followers to the leader's behavior.

Transformational and Charismatic Leadership

A series of newer theories are concerned with how leadership changes people, their motivations, emotions, values, and aspirations, and how it changes structures, values, visions and the cultures of whole work units and organizations. These theories often analyze outstanding leaders (sometimes referred to as charismatic leaders) and how they influence others. To this group of theories belong, for example, theories of *transformational versus transactional leadership* (Bass, 1998; Bass & Avolio, 1993), the theory of *charismatic leadership* (House, 1977), the *attribution theory of charisma* (Conger & Kanungo, 1987; Conger, 1989) and the *self-concept theory of charismatic leadership* (Shamir, House, & Arthur, 1993).

The cited theories are similar to each other in several respects (cf. House & Podsakoff, 1994): (a) they compare characteristics of outstanding leaders with characteristics of ordinary or average leaders (similar to the method used by leadership trait and behavior approaches); (b) they use dependent measures that mainly reflect affective responses of followers (e.g., emotional bonding, motivation, self-esteem, confidence) and the classification of a manager as "outstanding leader" by others, in combination with the "bottom-line" criteria of leadership success, such as, work unit effectiveness (quality and quantity of products and services) and staff satisfaction; (c) they emphasize symbolic, visionary and inspirational leadership behaviors (some of them focus also the nonverbal behaviors of leaders); and (d) their basic propositions are related to the leadership process and how it brings about change. Outstanding leadership changes people, as well as whole work units and organizations, by emphasizing positive societal values and morally valuable goals thereby developing affective bonds and commitment to higher order goals on part of their followers (e.g., Shamir et al., 1993).

Bass (1998) reviews research on *transformational leadership*, a concept concerning leaders efforts to transform followers' attitudes and values, to activate their higher order motives and to stimulate them to transcend and implement the organizations' higher order goals by their self-interests and a proactive approach to their work. The four components of transformational leadership (idealized influence, inspirational motivation, intellectual stimulation and individualized consideration) are measured in the Multifactor Leadership Questionnaire (MLQ) and were found to be both empirically distinguishable and to relate to work unit effectiveness. Transformational leadership is often contrasted with transactional leadership which is based primarily on compliance and norms recognized through leader–follower exchanges, that is, reward and praise are given by the leader for task completion and loyalty given by the follower (i.e. contingent reward). In contrast, transformational leadership is about implementing change by changing people's values and behaviors.

Charismatic leadership is usually defined more narrowly than transformational leadership. It specifies an idolized leader's characteristics as perceived and attributed by followers. Behaviors typical of charismatic leaders are for example, the articulation of appealing visions, communication of high expectations and expression of high confidence in followers.

House (1977) proposed charismatic leaders have a high need for power, high self-confidence, excellent verbal skills, and a strong compassion for their own ideas. He argued that these characteristics motivate and enable a leader to convince others about their ideas. On the followers side, these and further characteristics (cf. Bass, 1998; Conger, 1989) promote trust, feelings of doing something important, self-confidence and the willingness to see the leader as a charismatic figure. For example, pointing out morally high standing ideals and values (i.e. *idealized influence*) helps followers to see their work as important and as contributing to higher order goals, for which they are willing to sacrifice personal goals and benefits. A leader who expresses confidence in the followers' abilities, and that they can achieve higher order goals (i.e. *inspirational motivation*), increases followers' self-confidence and self-efficacy beliefs which increases the likelihood that they exert more effort, show more perseverance in goal achievement, and have the confidence to engage in more challenging tasks. A leader looking to innovative ways for achieving higher-order goals impresses followers more than a conventional type of leader, thereby increasing the likelihood that the followers attribute exceptional and outstanding characteristics to the leader and thus are more willing to see her or him as a charismatic leader.

There is also a "dark side" to charismatic leadership. Leaders could: seek to induce commitment to narrow minded ideological goals or to themselves (instead of to organizational or societal goals); start glorious projects with often unrealistic premises; omit properly to invest in the implementation of their visions; and fail to develop competent successors (for a review see Conger, 1989).

There are situational factors that have an impact on the relationship between transformational/charismatic leadership and leadership effectiveness. For example, in situations of crisis, which impose feelings of uncertainty, anxiety, and stress, charismatic leadership is more effective than in stable situations (House, Spangler, & Woycke, 1991). Also the job itself can have a moderating influence on the relationship between transformational or charismatic leadership and leadership effectiveness. The more easily the link between a particular job and its importance for the achievement of higher order goals can be established (e.g. jobs that are perceived to be of particular relevance for society, as in politics, science, or medicine) the more influence can be exerted by transformational/charismatic leadership (cf. House, 1977).

The cumulated empirical evidence is in support of the distinction between transformational/charismatic leadership, on the one side, and transactive leadership, on the other side. Lowe, Kroeck, and Sivasubramaniam (1996) report a meta-analysis of 39 studies, which investigated relationships between the extent to which a leader is perceived as transformational/charismatic (measured by the Multifactor Leadership Questionaire, MLQ, Bass, 1998) and subjective and objective data about their followers' performance. Results show that transformational/charismatic leadership indeed relates more strongly to leadership effectiveness and to the above described forms of affective influence on followers than transactive leadership does.

In a recent meta-analysis, based on 626 correlations from 87 studies with more than 38,000 respondents, Judge and Piccolo (2004) revealed an overall validity of $r = 0.44$ for transformational leadership. Transactional leadership (i.e. contingent reward ($r = 0.39$) and laissez-faire leadership ($r = -0.37$) had the next highest overall relations. Surprisingly, there were several criteria for which contingent reward leadership had stronger relations than did transformational leadership. Furthermore, transformational leadership was strongly correlated with contingent reward ($r = 0.80$) and laissez-faire ($r = -0.65$) leadership.

Barling, Weber, and Kelloway (1996) report on a group of leaders trained to display inspirational and individual consideration leadership behavior (a control group of leaders was not trained). Several months later the followers of the trained leaders showed higher organizational commitment and better sales figures than the followers from the untrained leaders. In two laboratory experiments professional actors were trained to display transformational and transactional leadership behaviors (Howell & Frost, 1989). Results show that when the actors displayed transformational/charismatic behavior, their followers were more satisfied and performed better than when the actors displayed directive or people-oriented leadership behavior.

The theories of transformational and charismatic leadership combine and complement the previously described approaches in that they (a) propose leadership to be a process that is partially determined by a leader's traits and trainable behaviors and skills, (b) identify situational factors under which transformational charismatic leadership varies in effectiveness, (c) propose that charisma is partially based on leaders' characteristics and partially based on the attributions of followers and how they react to the leaders characteristics, and (d) propose that the followers responses are mediated by their emotions, which have not been looked at in previous approaches to the study of leadership. Furthermore, the theories have been tested with a whole variety of methods, including longitudinal studies, as well as field and laboratory experiments.

Still, several open research questions can be identified for these approaches. The commonly used instrument to measure transformational and transactional leadership (MLQ) has some drawbacks, for example, the scales for transformational leadership (idealized influence, inspirational motivation, intellectual stimulation and individualized consideration) are considerably intercorrelated indicating that the underlying concepts are empirically hardly distinguishable. This has made it difficult in the past to empirically distinguish the different leadership behaviors and the theoretically assumed different impacts these should have on the followers. Another critique is that the proportion of "outstanding leaders" is rather low in practice. Thus, it may be that theories apply to only a small proportion of highly visible charismatic leaders and less to the average manager or to more ordinary leaders in middle and lower management positions. A similar criticism was made of Fiedler's contingency model: leaders with sufficiently high or low LPC scores are seldom found, the majority scoring in the medium range. No predictions can be derived from Fiedler's theory for this population of leaders.

Leadership as Power and Influence Process

An introduction to leadership research would be incomplete without taking at least a glimpse at the role of power and the sharing of power in the leadership process. Power as a source of leadership influence has been analyzed from various angles. Some approaches classify the means by which leaders generate a power basis, others have identified the strategies and tactics used by leaders to acquire power and gain influence over others, and more recently newer concepts of power sharing describe leadership as a mutual influence process between leaders and followers or among team members who are equal in their power status.

Power bases

Power approaches seek to explain leadership effectiveness in terms of the amount and type of power possessed and exercised by leaders. The more power they have (or is attributed to them by followers) the more influence leaders can exert. A classic distinction of different forms of power was presented by French and Raven (1959, 1960): (a) *reward* and *coercive power* is the capability to offer incentives and to make use of organizational sanctions, (b) *legitimate power* is the organizational or positional power that is perceived to be rightful by all involved, (c) *expert power* derives from high experience, knowledge and ability which is useful to others, and (d) *referent power* exists when a person is referred to, or group norms are identified with, due to appealing personal qualities or values systems. These power bases have been complemented by others, for example, *informational power* which derives form the control over how information is distributed and the advantage gained through knowing before others know (cf. Yukl & Falbe, 1991).

Studies show that expert and referent power are overall positively related with employee satisfaction and performance. More specifically, Yukl (2005) describes three qualitatively different outcomes for the followers that result from employing different sources of power: *Commitment* is most likely to be associated with referent and expert power, *compliance* is most strongly associated with legitimate and reward power, and *resistance* with coercive power.

Influence tactics

The link between the use of power and behavioral approaches of leadership influence has been established by research about proactive *influence tactics* (i.e. specific types of behavior used to exercise influence), for example, rational persuasion, consultation, ingratiation, exchange, coalition building, or pressure. Altogether 11 such influence tactics were identified in a research program by Yukl and his colleagues (e.g., Yukl & Tracey, 1992) who developed the Influence Behavior Questionnaire (IBQ) on the basis of which multiscore feedback can be given to managers (for a review of this research, see Yukl, 2005, pp. 164 ff). Their studies revealed, for example, that pressure (the overall least effective tactic) is more often employed with one's own followers than with peers or superiors. Rational persuasion, ingratiation, and personal appeals (i.e. asking for support out of friendship) are most often used at the beginning of an interaction, whereas pressure, exchange (i.e. offering incentives, an exchange of favors, or offering willingness to reciprocate at a later time), and coalition building are employed when the previous strategies do not work. The overall most effective influence tactics are rational persuasion, consultation, and inspirational appeal (i.e. making an appeal to values and ideals or seeking to arouse the target person's emotions) whereas the overall least effective influence tactics are pressure, coalition building, and legitimating (i.e. establishing the legitimacy of a request or to verify the authority by referring to rules, policies, contracts or precedent).

Sharing power: team leadership

Last but not least, we take a look at the sharing of power in the form of team leadership, which becomes more and more important because of an increasing demand for multidisciplinary collaboration, interorganizational partnerships and work groups with diverse members (e.g., in age, gender, cultural back ground, experience, values and needs) where the hierarchical power differential is more ambiguous than in classic organizations.

Not very much is known yet about *team leadership* (sometime also termed *shared leadership*, e.g., Bradford & Cohen, 1984). It complements the concept of a singular leader who is usually more informed and more confident than other members of a work unit. Bradford and Cohen (1984), for example, contend that the predominant conception of a *heroic leader* undermines the principally positive effects of shared responsibility for leadership functions and empowerment of followers on leadership effectiveness.

With the concept of team leadership, the view is taken, that leadership in organizations is a reciprocal influence process (e.g., Smith, 1995) involving many people from various social sub-systems. Both terms, *team leadership* (e.g., Sivasubramaniam, Murry, Avolio, & Jung, 2002) and *shared leadership* (e.g., Pearce & Sims, 2000) denote a leadership concept according to which responsibility for leadership functions and the exercise of leadership behavior are shared by members of a group and the degree to which leadership is consensually perceived to be shared among group members is linked to group performance.

Some empirical evidence relating to team leadership has been recently published. For an example, West et al. (2003) investigated a sample of 3,447 employees from 283 multidisciplinary teams in various health care settings in the UK. They found that leadership clarity (i.e. team members' consensual perceptions of clarity of and no conflict over leadership roles within their teams) is associated with clear team objectives, high levels of participation among group members, high commitment to excellence and support for innovation. Their findings imply the need for theory that incorporates clarity and consistency of leadership within teams and related collaborative work contexts and not just an individual's leadership style or behavior in relation to the situation or to followers. Because shared and team leadership are very recent concepts, there is ample room for future research and theory development.

Summary

In this chapter different approaches to the study of leadership have been described: leadership traits, skills, behaviors, situational factors, followers' perspectives and reactions, as well as power, influence, and transformational processes of leadership. Although the current body of leadership research includes over 5000 studies and we know much more about leadership than is usually recognized, a general theory of leadership that integrates the different approaches is not available.

The world of work is dramatically changing. Organizations collaborate more and more across organizational, industrial and cultural boundaries. Power differentials become increasingly ambiguous, work units are becoming more diverse and more virtual, and power needs to be shared for performing increasingly complex tasks at work. Individual transitions across functions, disciplines, organizations, and countries are also more common today, which, among other things, implies life-long learning and development on part of employees. All these changes necessitate new forms of leadership as well as new approaches to the study of leadership.

Therefore, the prevailing "western" style leadership theories should be complemented by culture-specific and cross-cultural theories which are more appropriate for different societal cultures and for informing employees and leaders for a better management of a diverse work force. Leader and situation-oriented theories should be complemented by social psychological and multilevels approaches (e.g. about shared leadership). Leadership for the development of followers (e.g., via coaching) seems to be an underdeveloped area in the scientific research arena. Considering that employees are the most precious ingredient of modern organizations, we need leadership theory and practices that demonstrably enable them to make modern organizations more flexible, innovative, productive and human.

Discussion Points

"Leaders are born, not made" vs. "Leadership can be learned." Discuss the two perspectives by using leadership theories and evidence from empirical studies.

If you were a practicing manager, which of the many theories of leadership would you find most instructive and useful? Give reasons why.

Give examples of characters in Walt Disney's *Lion King* movie that have (a) reward power, (b) coercive power, (c) legitimate power, (d) expert power, (e) referent power, and (f) informational power. Discuss your results with others.

Key Studies

Lewin, K., Lippitt, R., & White, R. K. (1939). Patterns of aggressive behavior in experimentally created social climates. *Journal of Social Psychology, 10,* 271–99. Lewin and his students introduced the concept of leadership style and demonstrated different effects of different stiles (democratic, authoritarian, laissez-faire) on group climate and follower behavior.

House, R. J., Spangler, W. D., & Woycke, J. (1991). Personality and charisma in the US

Presidency: A psychological theory of leader effectiveness. *Administrative Science Quarterly*, *36*, 364–96. House and co-workers tested several propositions about the relationship between factors (crisis, leader motivation) and mechanisms (attribution of

followers) of charismatic leadership and leadership success on a unique sample of leaders – Presidents of the US – and an unprecedented array of qualitative and quantitative methods.

Further Readings

Bass, B. M. (1990). *Bass and Stogdill's handbook of leadership: Theory, research, and managerial applications.* New York: Free Press. An authoritative handbook of leadership theory with a comprehensive collection of research results.

Manktelow, J., Brodbeck, F. C., & Anand, N. (2006). *How to lead: Discover the leader within you.* Swindon, UK: Mind Tools. A self-directed leadership development course (printed and internet based) which includes many of the theories reviewed here. It provides self-assessments, reflective exercises, case studies, and coaching opportunities.

Pierce, J. L., & Newstrom, J. W. (2003). *Leaders and the leadership process* (3rd edn.). New York: McGraw-Hill. A good resource book with easy to read excerpts of classic papers which provides many tools for leadership self-assessment and exercises.

Yukl, G. (2005). *Leadership in organizations* (6th edn.). Upper Saddle River, NJ: Pearson/Prentice Hall. One of the most often cited leadership books. It reviews many leadership theories and related issues in detail.

Research Close-Up 1: McClelland's Leadership Motivation Theory

McClelland's leadership motivation theory postulates three unconscious motives which derive from individual need dispositions – the need for achievement, the need for power, and the need for affiliation. The respective motives can be measured by the projective Thematic Apperception Test (TAT), which assesses individual motivation indirectly. Individuals complete a set of unfinished stories and what they have written is content analyzed on the basis of which the relative strengths of each of the three unconscious motives is estimated (McClelland, 1980). Motives can be described as individual preferences for certain emotional states. Some people prefer situations in which performance is of particular relevance because they like the emotions that come

with achieving or having achieved performance goals (e.g., pride, fulfillment). Other people are mainly motivated by emotions that are associated with influencing others and thus prefer situations in which power can be exerted or gained. Again others are mainly motivated by the emotions they have while being together with others (e.g., feeling comfortable, loved), and thus, prefer situations in which they can be part of trusting relationships where they can satisfy their social needs.

The individual differences in behavior that result from motivational dispositions, derive for example, from the selective perception of situational characteristics (primarily those aspects of a situation are focused and reacted to that satisfy a dominant need),

Continued

the choice of situations (those situations which promise the satisfaction of a dominant need are approached, those which don't are neglected) and the habitual routines, knowledge, skills, and attitudes (KSAs) which result from experiencing many situations that are similar in motivational orientation. Motivational dispositions are relatively stable but can also be modified by training (e.g., the need for achievement can be changed, cf. McClelland & Winter, 1969).

The unconscious motivational dispositions are differently important for leadership success depending on the mix of situations that a leadership position provides. In leadership positions that mainly comprise situations where technical knowledge and performance matters and relevant feedback is available (e.g., farming, R&D, entrepreneurs) persons with high need for achievement should be most likely to succeed because they can satisfy their dominant need and employ their preferred KSAs. And indeed results from several studies are in support of this assumption. Leaders with high need for achievement are more successful in entrepreneurial positions that require technical performance than leaders in positions that are non-entrepreneurial or purely managerial without technical performance requirements (Meyer, Walker, & Litwin, 1961; McClelland, 1965). The theoretically optimal pattern of leaders' motives in technical professions, namely a high need for achievement, a medium power orientation and a medium need for affiliation, has been shown to related to economical success (e.g., for farmers, Singh & Gupta, 1977; R&D employees, Varga, 1975; for entrepreneurs, Chusmir & Azevedo, 1992).

In contrast, the theoretically optimal pattern of managerial motives in nontechnical (pure) managerial positions is a high (socialized) need for power and a low need for affiliation. This configuration has been termed a "leadership motive pattern" (LMP, McClelland, 1975). Results from several longitudinal studies show that the LMP indeed predicts economic success of leaders in purely managerial positions (Jacobs & McClelland, 1994; McClelland & Boyatzis, 1982; Winter, 1991).

Note that McClelland distinguishes between two different power motives, the personalized and the socialized power motive. Persons with a socialized power motive have a high degree of self-control and they satisfy their need for influencing others in a socially well adapted manner, that is, they influence others in order to pursue collectively valued goals or they use their power to support others to excel. In contrast, persons with a personalized power motive are less self-controlled (e.g., show emotional outbursts) and tend to dominate others for supporting their own goals rather than collective goals or the followers' developmental goals.

Purely managerial jobs which require no technical competencies satisfy high needs for power because the core job is to make decisions, to influence and to motivate *others* to perform well and less to self-motivate to perform well. Also, in these jobs it is sometimes necessary to make tough personnel decisions with negative consequences for the followers, which may be hampered if the need for affiliation were too high. By empirical research it could be shown, that the followers of leaders with a high (socialized) LMP report higher consciousness for their own responsibilities, more team spirit, and have a clearer understanding of their roles at work than followers of leaders with low LMP (McClelland & Burnham, 1976).

Effective Teams in Organizations

Michael A. West

Overview

Throughout history humans have worked in teams and they are ubiquitous in modern organizations. However, effective team work is more elusive. This chapter describes teams in modern organizations and explores the extent to which they contribute to organizational performance. The problems of working in teams are identified and solutions suggested. The chapter considers the stages of team development – forming, norming, storming, performing; leadership in teams and the importance of participative and supportive styles; conflict in teams and how interpersonal conflict can dramatically inhibit a team's performance; team decision-making and the many obstacles to teams in making wise decisions; and how organizations can support team-working by gearing their reward and communication systems around teams. The chapter also considers the effects of team member composition and explores the types of personalities that may be best for team-working; the team-working skills needed by teams; and the social skills that support effective team-working. The importance of interteam-working is stressed alongside consideration of the relationship between the team and the wider organization. Practical ways of developing good team-working are emphasized throughout the chapter.

What Are Teams and Why Are They Important?

The team rather than the individual is increasingly considered the basic building block of organizations and team-based working the modus operandi of organizations (West, Tjosvold, & Smith, 2003). There are numerous reasons for the extensive use of teams. In many work situations, tasks have simply become so complicated that their performance requires a combination of knowledge, skills and abilities that one person rarely possesses. Consequently, completing such tasks effectively requires that several people work in an interdependent fashion. Further, many organizations have become so much larger and/or more complex in their structures that activities must be closely coordinated, via teamwork, if organizational objectives are to be achieved (West & Markiewicz, 2003; West, Tjosvold, & Smith, 2003). But the use of teams to achieve our goals is hardly new.

There is a solid evolutionary basis to our tendency to form strong attachments and by extension to live and work in groups. Groups enable survival and reproduction (Ainsworth, 1989; Axelrod & Hamilton, 1981; Barash, 1977; Bowlby, 1969; Buss, 1990, 1991; Hogan, Jones, & Cheek, 1985; Moreland, 1987). By living and working in groups early humans could share food, easily find mates, and care for infants. They could hunt more effectively and defend themselves against their enemies. Individuals who did not readily join groups would be disadvantaged in comparison with group members as a consequence. And we see across all societies that when there is danger, illness or the darkness of night people have a desire to be with others, indicating the protection offered by group membership. "Over the course of evolution, the small group became the survival strategy developed by the human species" (Barchas, 1986).

However, there has been an extraordinary change in the design of work organizations in the last 200 years. Prior to around 1800, apart from the religious and the military, there were virtually no organizations bigger than around 30 people. Indeed, the vast majority were small groups of 6, 7, 8, or 9 people working together in small craft or agricultural groups. Since then, organizations have expanded rapidly to hundreds and thousands of employees. This has proved difficult with many people finding themselves alienated in large social structures that they struggle to identify with or to have a sense of belonging. How then can we recreate the basic form of human production in these large entities and enjoy the benefits of both team-working and economies of scale? In this chapter we will explore how to create effective teams.

Teams defined

Teams are a particular form of work group. They are groups of people who share responsibility for producing products or delivering services. They share overall work objectives and ideally have the necessary authority, autonomy and resources to achieve these objectives. The group is recognized by others in the organization as a team. Team members are dependent on each other to achieve the objectives and therefore have to work closely, interdependently and supportively to achieve the team's goals. Members have distinct and clear roles. Effective teams have as few members as necessary to perform the task and are ideally no larger than 6 to 8 members. Once the team goes above 6 to 8 members in size, problems of communication and coordination increase considerably.

Types of teams

There are multiple types of teams in organizations:

- Advice and involvement teams, e.g., management decision-making committees, quality control (QC) circles, staff involvement teams;

- Production and service teams, e.g., assembly teams; maintenance, construction, mining and commercial airline teams; departmental teams; sales and health-care teams;
- Project and development teams, e.g., research teams, new product development teams, software development teams;
- Action and negotiation teams, e.g., military combat units, healthcare surgical teams, and Trade Union negotiating teams.

Mohrman, Cohen, and Mohrman (1995) offer these reasons for implementing team-based working in organizations: Teams enable organizations to speedily develop and deliver products and services cost effectively, while retaining high quality; Most tasks in organizations simply cannot be performed by individuals working alone; Teams enable organizations to learn (and retain learning) more effectively since groups of people own knowledge rather than one individual and they learn from each other; Time is saved if activities, formally performed sequentially by individuals, can be performed concurrently by people working in teams; Innovation is promoted because of cross-fertilization of ideas; and Teams can integrate and link information in ways that an individual cannot.

Applebaum and Batt (1994) reviewed 12 large-scale surveys and 185 consultants' reports and academic case studies of managerial practices. They concluded that team-based working lead to improvements in organizational performance on measures of both efficiency and quality. Similarly, Cotton (1993) reviewed studies examining the effects of team-working on productivity, satisfaction, and absenteeism. He found 57 studies that reported improvements in productivity, seven that found no change, and five that reported productivity declines, following the implementation of autonomous teams (those teams with a large degree of autonomy in deciding how to perform their task). Macy and Izumi's (1993) investigated organizational change interventions involving 131 organizations using meta-analysis and found that the relationship between team-working and organizational effectiveness was strongly significant. The introduction of autonomous teams had the *strongest* effect size on overall company performance out of 18 different organizational interventions.

In healthcare organizations, team-working contributes to performance by reducing errors and improving the quality of patient care (Edmondson, 1996; Dawson, West, Scully, Beinart, Carpenter, & Smith, 2004; West & Borrill, 2005). Furthermore, these findings are not restricted to self report measures and soft outcomes such as team member satisfaction), but extend to patient deaths: West et al. (2002) examined the relationship between people management practices in hospitals and patient mortality and found a strong negative relationship between HRM practices and patient mortality. One of the three practices most strongly associated with mortality was team-working. Results showed that the higher the percentage of staff working in teams in hospitals, the lower the patient mortality. On average, in hospitals where over 60 percent of staff reportedly worked in formal teams, mortality was around 5 percent lower than would be expected.

Given these encouraging results, surely team-working should be the norm in every organization? The implementation of teams varies from a rigorous, thoughtful approach to developing teamwork in organizations to the use of the term "team" for any co-located group of people who happen to work in the same area of the building and who have tea and cakes together on a Friday morning. In recent studies of the UK National Health Service, 90 percent of a sample of over 200,000 employees reported working in teams. When asked whether: the teams had shared objectives; team members worked closely together to achieve these; they met regularly to review performance and how it could be improved; and they were less than 15 members in size – basic criteria for team-working – only 40 percent conformed to these criteria. What are the main reasons for ineffective team-working?

Barriers to effective team work

1   Teams without tasks   The only point of having a team is to get a job done, a task completed, a set of objectives met. Moreover, the tasks that teams perform should be tasks that are best performed by a team. Painting the hull of a super-tanker does not require painters to work interdependently and in close communication over decisions. Each of those involved in the painting simply needs to know which his or her bit of hull is. Navigating the tanker out of a port is likely to require teamwork as is doing a refit on the engines. Football teams have the name of team since members are required to work interdependently, to communicate constantly, to understand each other's roles, and to collectively implement a strategy in order to achieve their goals. Teams need team tasks to be of any value.

2   Teams without freedom and responsibility   Creating teams and then failing to give them the freedom and authority to make the decisions that allow them to accomplish their tasks in the most effective way is a little like teaching someone to ride a bicycle, giving them a fancy road racing bike and then telling them they can only ride it in their bedroom. Yet in many organizations teams are created but they are not given the power to make decisions, implement them and bring about radical change.

3   Unwieldy teams with the wrong members   Teams should be as small as possible to get the job done and no larger than about 6 to 8 people. Larger groupings are unlikely to be effective and, where larger groups are necessary, it is important to break them down into subgroups or subteams. It is increasingly difficult for team members to communicate with each other and to coordinate when teams begin to go above 8 members. Moreover, it is vital to ensure that teams have the members with the skills they need to get the job done, rather than those who happen to work in the location of the department in which the team is being formed. Imagine hiring only navigators to crew a ship and the reasoning becomes clear.

4   Organizations deeply structured around individual work   Teams are set up in many places in the organization but all of the systems are geared towards managing individuals. This is like deciding to plant seedlings in your garden but still preparing the bed as though you were growing potatoes. The seedlings are unlikely to survive. Creating team-based organizations means radically altering the structure, the support systems and the culture.

5   Team processes are neglected rather than developed   Bringing together a group of people and telling them to work as a team is unlikely to produce effective teamwork. How the team functions as a team is critical to its success. Teams must have clear objectives, meet regularly, engage in constructive debate about how best to serve customer/client needs, share information with each other, coordinate their work, support each other's ideas for new and improved ways of doing things, and constantly reflect on their performance and how it can be improved. It is the responsibility of team leaders and organizations to inculcate and nurture such team processes to enable effective team and team-based working.

6   Team dictators not leaders   Team leadership is very different from traditional supervision. Supervisors are often directive rather than facilitative and advice giving rather than seeking. They seek to determine rather than integrate views and play a directive rather than supportive role. The function of a leader of teams is very different – it is to ensure that the team profits optimally from its shared knowledge, experience, and skill.

7   Strong teams in conflict   Finally, even when effective teams have been developed there is a major threat to the effectiveness of team-based working. Cohesive, effective teams may become more competitive and discriminatory in relation to other teams precisely because they have been developed so effectively. So good team-based working ensures that norms of interteam cooperation are established from the beginning and reinforced throughout the process.

Understanding how to build effective teams requires us to understand that team processes vary according to the stage of their development and that their beginnings require particular consideration. Like any life form they develop and change, and what is significant at one point in their lives is replaced at other points by new influences. Whether it be humans, plants or planets, understanding them, requires an appreciation of their development.

The Stages of Team Development

The best-known and most widely used model of team development (Tuckman, 1965) suggests five stages: forming, storming, norming, performing, and adjourning.

Forming: There is often considerable anxiety at the forming stage. Team members ask testing questions which reflect their concern about roles – particularly the nature of the leadership role – and about the resources available to the team. Individuals within the team seek out information about other team members, particularly their backgrounds and experience in the type of work that the team will undertake. They are likely to be anxious about external expectations of the team, and to request information about rules and regulations that will affect the team's working methods. At this early stage, team members may be rather guarded in the information they divulge. Their early judgments of one another will therefore be based on limited information. The most important task at this stage is to ensure that team goals are clearly stated and agreed.

Storming: During the storming stage, conflict emerges between individuals and sub-groups. The choice, authority and/or competency of the leader are challenged, and individuals resist attempts by the leader to control team processes. Members question the value and feasibility of the team task. Hidden tensions surface during this stage. Individuals may react strongly and opinions may become polarized. This stage can also see an emerging honesty and openness within the team as they work through the conflicts. The team leader must build positively on this to gain shared commitment to the team goals, to build trust, begin the definition of team roles and to establish conflict resolution strategies for the team.

Norming: During norming, conflicts are resolved and the team begins to address the task with positive cooperation. Plans are made and work standards are established. Norms or agreed rules and ways of working emerge regarding team and individual behavior. Team members more readily communicate their views and feelings; networks for mutual support emerge. During this stage the team leader should allow the team to take more responsibility for its own planning and team processes, perhaps allowing team members to make mistakes and encouraging the team to reflect upon them. It is important to ensure that norms are established that meet the needs of the organization since teams could develop norms that are destructive to effective functioning (e.g., it's acceptable to be late or not to turn up for team meetings).

Performing: Team members begin to see successful outcomes as their energies focus constructively on the joint task. They settle into an effective team-working structure, within which individual members feel comfortable, and begin to work together more flexibly. The team leader can usually withdraw from day-to-day involvement, a change that is acknowledged and accepted by team members. At this stage, systems of regular review should be established to ensure that the team continues to be effective and responsive to its environment.

Adjourning: Not all teams go through the final adjourning stage as a team, but at various times of its life key members will leave or major projects will be completed or curtailed. It is important that the effects of such changes on the life of the team should be acknowledged: teams may revert to earlier stages of development depending on their levels of maturity, their stability and the scale of the change.

Not all teams will fit neatly into Tuckman's sequence. A team might go back and forth, revisiting stages to deal with them gradually at different levels. Team leaders can encourage teams by introducing an effective team-development process and ensuring that the team task is clear; that conflicts are processed with satisfactory (and ideally creative) consequences; that team members' roles are clear; that positive norms are established; that the team performs well; and that it disbands constructively and in a timely fashion when its task is complete.

What other factors influence effective team work?

Many researchers have been persuaded by the value of an input-process-output model for understanding teams – this distinguishes between the basic building blocks for the team – the task, the people, the organization (inputs); team processes (communication and decision-making for example) and the outputs (team performance – do they win?). Using this model we can map the key dimensions at team and organizational level that must be managed to ensure effective team functioning.

Inputs into the Team

The inputs into the team include the task the team must perform, the team members and the organizational and national/cultural context within which the team performs. A team works towards specific outcomes, e.g. a primary healthcare team (those teams that are the first point of contact for people seeking healthcare in the UK and other European countries) has the task of maintaining and improving a community's health. Teams also consist of diverse individuals, and team composition will clearly influence team effectiveness. The team works for and within an organization, and so will be affected by the interaction with the surrounding organizational context.

Input 1: The task

The task a group performs is a fundamental influence on the work group, defining its structural, process and functional requirements – the personnel needed, their roles, and how they should work together. A team is defined by the task it is required to perform.

The characteristics of a team task are:

* completeness (i.e., whole tasks)
* varied demands
* opportunities for social interaction

- autonomy
- opportunities for learning
- development possibilities for the task
- task significance – the importance of the task.

Gulowsen (1972) suggests the degree of autonomy of the work group can be assessed in relation to group influence over: The formulation of goals – what and how much it is expected to produce; Where to work and number of hours (when to work overtime and when to leave); Choice about further activities beyond the given task; Selection of production methods; Internal distribution of task responsibilities within the group; Membership of the group (who and how many people will work in the group); Leadership – whether there will be a leader and who will be the leader; and How to carry out individual tasks.

Input 2: Team Composition

How can we select the right team members and with the right mix? One general question is whether heterogeneity (or diversity) is advantageous or disadvantageous to groups and their members. Is it "better" to put together a group whose members are quite different from each other? Or is group functioning disadvantaged by such diversity? Both arguments have been made. Theoretically, it has been argued that heterogeneity will serve the group by providing a wide range of perspectives and, hence, performance enhancement. On the other hand, it is clear that heterogeneity (in age, cultural background, values, and beliefs) can increase team process difficulties (less clear communication, interpersonal challenges) and, hence, diminish performance. For the most part, the evidence suggests that diversity, when well managed through good team processes, leads to performance gains rather than losses in the long term (van Joshi & Jackson, 2003). However, initial performance is likely to be affected by process difficulties more than homogenous teams. Below, we consider some of these issues by exploring ability, then personality and the skills of teamwork.

Personality and ability

For individual jobs, general mental ability is one of the best predictors of job performance (Schmidt & Hunter, 1998, Anderson et al chapter this book). Not surprisingly, team members' overall ability predicts team performance. This was demonstrated in one study of military crews (Tziner & Eden, 1985) that showed people of high ability contributed most to performance when all the other crew members were also high in ability.

What of personality? The "Big Five" model of personality (Barrick & Mount, 1991) offers a robust personality model that we can use to analyze the mix of personality in teams and the effects on team performance. The model describes five dimensions of personality:

Openness to experience – Fantasy, actions, and ideas
Conscientiousness – Competence, order, and self-discipline
Extraversion – Positive emotions, gregariousness, and warmth
Agreeableness – Trust, straightforwardness, and tender-mindedness
Neuroticism – Anxiety, self-consciousness, and vulnerability

It is not surprising that certain personality dimensions are linked to effective team work, but what is enlightening is the discovery that the particular dimensions that emerge as important depend on the type of task. In interdependent teams where individual contributions to team success are easily recognized and rewarded, hardworking and dependable team members are most successful (Mount, Barrick, & Stewart, 1998). Other team members see these conscientious individuals as valued team members because they can be relied upon to perform their part of the work. Conscientiousness is particularly important in team settings because hierarchical control is reduced, so there is a need for self-discipline (Mount et al., 1998; Barrick et al., 1998). Such self-discipline is particularly important if team-based rewards are used in the organizations (i.e., compensation is based on performance of the entire team) because team member pay is dependent on the successful performance of each and every team member. Teams composed of conscientious team members perform at a high level, particularly on productivity and planning tasks.

However, teams with high levels of extraversion are better at decision-making than at planning and performance tasks, probably because their warmth and optimism helps them in persuading others to accept their decisions. For teams requiring creative decisions or innovation, openness rather than conscientiousness or extraversion are most important. In effect, the research evidence suggests that *teams composed of conscientious people with high levels of extraversion are likely to be most effective.* Having high levels of agreeableness in teams does not appear related to team performance but having any very disagreeable individual in a team undermines effectiveness. In teams requiring creative output, openness is also an important characteristic. It is best therefore to have teams whose members all score relatively high on measures of conscientiousness and extraversion (see for a review Allan & West, 2005).

Teamwork skills

When we create teams we should think beyond the relatively unchangeable aspects of people such as their personality and think more of their motivation, knowledge and skills for working in teams. This includes their preferences for working in teams; whether they have an individualist or collective approach to working with others; their basic social skills such as listening, speaking, and cooperating; and their team-working skills such as collaboration, concern for the team, and interpersonal awareness.

Social skills

Social skills include: Active listening skills – listening to what other people are saying and asking questions; Communication skills; Social perceptiveness – being aware of others' reactions and understanding why they react the way they do; Self monitoring – being sensitive to the effects of our behavior on others; Altruism – working to help colleagues; Warmth and cooperation; and Patience and tolerance – accepting criticism and dealing patiently with frustrations.

Such skills are likely to be particularly valuable to the performance of teams and could therefore be among the criteria for selecting team members (Peterson et al., 2001).

Knowledge, skills, and attitudes (KSAs) for teamwork

In teamwork settings, employees need the abilities to perform the job as individuals as well as the abilities to work effectively in a team because both are important for team performance (West & Allen, 1997). Stevens and Campion (1994; 1999) propose that effective team functioning depends on teamwork abilities, focusing on team members' knowledge of how to perform in teams that extend beyond the requirements for individual job performance. Based on the literature on team functioning, they identified two broad skill areas (interpersonal KSAs and self-management KSAs), consisting of a total of 14 specific KSA requirements for effective teamwork (see Table 1 below). Stevens and Campion (1994) developed a 35-item multiple-choice test in which respondents are presented with challenges they may face in the workplace and asked to identify the strategy they would most likely follow. They found that team members' scores on this test were significantly related to team performance in several studies (McDaniel, et al., 2001). Regardless of their task specialty or their preferred team role, there are certain attributes that *all* team members need to demonstrate if the team is to achieve its goal. We should create teams of people who have all or most of the KSAs described by Stevens and Campion and train all team members to develop these KSAs.

Input 3: Organizational Supports

We now describe the systems and practices that are required to ensure the effectiveness of team-based organizations. Broadly, team performance must be monitored and managed to ensure effectiveness, reward systems must be correctly aligned, selection and assessment procedures must take into account the skills required for effective team-working, and good team level communication systems

Table 14.1: Steven's and Campion's knowledge, skills, and abilities for team-working (Stevens & Campion, 1994; reprinted with permission)

I	**Interpersonal Team Member KSAs**		
A	Conflict resolution	1.	Fostering useful debate, while eliminating dysfunctional conflict
		2.	Matching the conflict management strategy to the cause and nature of the conflict
		3.	Using integrative (win–win) strategies rather than distributive (win–lose) strategies
B	Collaborative problem-solving	4.	Using an appropriate level of participation for any given problem
		5.	Avoiding obstacles to team problem solving (e.g. domination by some team members) by structuring how team members interact
C	Communication	6.	Employing communication that maximize an open flow
		7.	Using an open and supportive style of communication
		8.	Using active listening techniques
		9.	Paying attention to nonverbal messages
		10.	Warm greetings to other team members, engaging in appropriate small talk, etc.
II	**Self-Management Team KSAs**		
D	Goal-setting and performance management	11.	Setting specific, challenging and acceptable team goals
		12.	Monitoring, evaluating and providing feedback on performance
E	Planning and task coordination	13.	Coordinating and synchronizing tasks, activities and information
		14.	Establishing fair and balanced roles and workloads among team members

must reinforce the principles of team-based working. Perhaps most important for organizational success is the extent to which teams cooperate and support each other across team boundaries.

1   Climate for team-based working

Team-based working is a philosophy or attitude about the way in which organizations work, where decisions are made by teams rather than by individuals and at the closest possible point to the client or customer. It is vital therefore that there is a general commitment within the organization to this way of working and the existence of an organizational climate which nurtures and promotes the growth of team-based working.

Supportive and challenging environments are likely to sustain high levels of team performance and creativity, especially those which encourage risk taking and idea generation (West, 2002). Teams frequently have ideas for improving their workplaces, work functioning, processes, products and services. Where climates are characterized by distrust, poor communication, personal antipathies, limited individual autonomy and unclear goals, the implementation of these ideas is inhibited. The extent to which teams in the organization are encouraged to take time to review their objectives, strategies and processes; plan to make changes and then implement those changes, will also determine the effectiveness of the teams and their organizations. Such "reflexivity" is a positive predictor of both team and organizational innovation (West, 2002). And innovation in turn predicts organizational performance.

2   Appraisal and performance review systems

Team performance review   Considerable performance benefits result from the provision of clear, constructive feedback to teams, though this is often an area which team members report is neglected. Individuals get feedback on performance but team performance is rarely evaluated. In a team-based organization, attention is most appropriately focused on the development of performance criteria against which teams can be measured. Such team-based working performance criteria need to reach further than simply evaluating team output. Thus effectiveness criteria could include not only team performance, likely to be best defined and evaluated by the team's "customers," but the extent of team members' sustained identification with and commitment to their teams, the learning, development and satisfaction of team members, the introduction of new and improved ways of doing things by the team, or team innovation, and the cooperation with other teams and departments within the organization.

Goal setting   Perhaps the most powerful component of appraisal is goal setting (see Fletcher chapter this book) and this applies no less to teams. The overall direction of a team's work – its purpose – should be clearly articulated by the team leader or the senior management team. This purpose should link tightly to the overall purpose of the organization.

In keeping with the nature of team-based working, goal- setting works best if all team members are involved in the process. This involves these goal-setting steps:

- develop a shared understanding amongst all team members of the needs of their "customer" or "customers"; their customer/s may be the organization, another part of the organization or an external customer

- describe the overall goal or purpose of the team's activity (the team task)
- define outcomes that will enable the achievement of the goal
- identify performance indicators
- establish measurement processes.

Teams should have the opportunity to review their performance against targets, whether set internally or by others within the organization. This enables learning to take place which will enhance future team performance. It also prompts the review of team processes that will enable the team to grow and develop.

Individual performance review Individuals also require regular, constructive feedback about their performance if they are to grow and develop in their jobs. Team-based organizations do not replace individual performance management with team performance management. Rather, team performance reviews become the key focus which is augmented by individual performance review. Traditionally this has taken place via the annual appraisal or review interview in which the individual's manager gives feedback on the year's performance. However, as flatter structures lead to larger spans of control and each employee's contact network becomes wider, this is an ineffective means of giving an individual the feedback they need. Moreover, it is consistent with a team-based working philosophy that the team, rather than the individual's manager, should be the primary agent that appraises team members.

3   Reward systems

Reward systems can be focused on the following:

The individual Here individual performance is appraised and rewarded. This can include individual rewards for contribution to team-working where this is a specific target set for the individual. Performance related pay can reflect individual contributions to the team's performance as rated by other team members.

The team Here reward is related to the achievement of predetermined team goals. Reward may be distributed equally to each member of the team or it may be apportioned by senior management, by the team leader or in a manner determined by the team itself. It is important to note that where rewards are given equally to team members by an external party, this can lead to considerable resentment. Team members who do not pull their weight are seen as "free riders" and their failures lead to resentment and demotivation amongst other team members (Rutte, 2003). It is important therefore that the reward system for the team be seen as fair by its members, and this may involve some process by which team members themselves determine the distribution of the team rewards.

The organization   The performance of either the total organization or the business unit is reflected in rewards allocated to individuals or teams. Incorporating all elements (individual, team and organizational) provides a well-rounded reward system. However if the organization's aim is to introduce team-based working then there must be a strong emphasis on team performance factors and as much delegation of decisions regarding team reward distribution as possible.

4   Interteam processes

The strengths of team-based working in organizations are the involvement of all in contributing their skills and knowledge, in good collective decision-making and innovation. The fundamental weakness is the tendency of team-based organizations to be torn and damaged by competition, hostility and rivalry (sometimes called a "silo mentality") between teams, Richter, West & van Dick, (in press).

   The best team level strategy to reduce interteam bias in organizations is to increase the quantity and quality of interteam contact, for example by having the conflicting teams meet on a regular basis (Hewstone et al., 2002). Some experimental research suggests that overcoming problems of interteam bias when teams come into contact is *not* best achieved by having the teams work on a task together, but is better achieved by encouraging them to get to know each other on a personal level. In this light it is perhaps also not surprising that having friends who are members of the other team also reduces bias. Other research suggests that it is vital to encourage all team members to have strong identification and a sense of pride in their organization. A strong team and organizational identification (particularly amongst those who communicate or span the boundaries between teams) leads to more interteam cooperation and less competition and conflict.

Processes

In the previous section, we examined the inputs to team performance – how teams are formed and the context in which they operate. Now, we examine the way in which teams work. In order to accomplish a task, teams must be led, communicate, make decisions and work together cohesively. They will also generate a team climate which denotes the general atmosphere that the team works in. It is these processes that we concentrate upon here.

Process 1: Leadership

The team leader has three overall tasks to perform: to create the conditions that enable the team to do its job; to build and maintain the team as a performing unit; and to coach and support the team to success (see Hackman, 2002 for an extended exploration of these three tasks).

First, creating the right conditions means ensuring that the team has a clear task to perform (and one that is best done by a team) and making sure the team has the resources it needs to do its work. This means that sometimes the leader has to fight to ensure the team gets the necessary budget, accommodation, IT equipment, or other tools to do its job effectively.

Second, in order to build and maintain the team as a performing unit the leader must ensure that the team is composed of members with the necessary skills and abilities. The leader must also develop team processes that help the team to perform effectively by nurturing good decision-making, problem solving, conflict management and the development of new and improved ways of working together.

The third task of the team leader is to coach and support the team to success. The team leader has to learn to be sensitive to the mood of the team and to how well members are interacting and communicating with each other. The leader must pay attention to these processes and intervene to encourage more meetings between particular members, encourage more exchange of information, or shape a supportive approach to suggestions made by team members. The leader's task also includes helping team members develop their skills and abilities. This means taking time to review what it is they want to achieve, what skills each needs to develop, and creating learning opportunities for them (this could be formal training, visits to other organizations, or learning on the job).

Team leadership differs most clearly from traditional leadership in that the leader focuses on the team as a whole rather than on just the individuals, and shares responsibility for the team's functioning with the team.

Process 2: Participation

Being part of a team involves participating, which includes interacting, information sharing, influencing decision-making and creating a sense of safety.

i)   Interaction

In order for a group of individuals who share a common goal to be called a team they must have some minimal ongoing interaction, otherwise their efforts are essentially uncoordinated. Interaction during task performance provides an exchange of information, communication etc, which enables the team to coordinate individual member efforts to achieve their shared goals. In effect they learn to dance the dance of teamwork better, the more time they spend dancing together. Imagine the success of a football team that only met to play together once or twice a year, compared with a team that played together and discussed their performance every week.

ii)   Information sharing

Information in a team context is data which alters the understanding of the team as a whole and/or of individual team members. Monitoring information is essential for team effectiveness.

Within team settings the ideal medium is face to face except for routine messages. Of course, there is a temptation to avoid such direct communication since this may take up time. In general teams err on the side of electronic mail messages and communicate too little face to face. Yet the whole basis of teamwork is communication, coordination, cooperation and transfer of information in the richest possible form (see Vartiainen & Andriessen, chapter 10 in this book). Virtual teams are less effective and innovative than teams that are co-located (Agarwal, 2003). The richness of information transfer and the learning about teamwork are simply much greater among those working in co-located or face-to-face teams.

Process 3: Team Decision-Making

A principle assumption behind the structuring of organizational functioning into work teams is that teams will make better decisions than individual team members working alone. A good deal of research has shown that teams are subject to social processes which undermine their decision-making effectiveness:

i) Team members must take into account some of the hidden dangers of team decision-making. One is the powerful tendency for team members to focus on information all team members share before the discussion starts and to ignore new information that only one or two team members know about. Even when they introduce this information team members are likely to ignore it since it is not information they all already share. This is the *hidden profile* phenomenon and teams can avoid it by ensuring that members have clearly defined roles so that each is seen as a source of potentially unique and important information, that members listen carefully to colleagues' contributions in decision-making, and that leaders alert the team to information that is uniquely held by only one or two members (Stasser & Stewart, 1992).

ii) Team members are subject to *social conformity* effects causing them to withhold opinions and information contrary to the majority view – especially an organizationally-dominant view (Brown, 2000).

iii) The team may be *dominated* by particular individuals who take up disproportionate "air time" or argue so vigorously with the opinion of others that their own views prevail. It is noteworthy that "air time" and expertise are correlated in high-performing teams and uncorrelated in teams that perform poorly (Rogelberg et al., 1992).

iv) *Status and hierarchy* effects can cause some members' contributions to be valued and attended to disproportionately. When a senior executive is present in a meeting, his or her views are likely to have an undue influence on the outcome (Brown, 2000).

v) "*Group polarization*" refers to the tendency of work teams to make more extreme decisions than the average of individual members' opinions or decision. Team decisions tend to be either more risky or more conservative than the average of individuals members' opinions or decisions. Thus shifts in the extremity of decisions affecting the competitive strategy of an organization can occur simply as a result of team processes rather than for rational or well-judged reasons (Semini & Glendon, 1973; Walker & Main, 1973).

vi) In his study of failures in policy decisions, social psychologist Irving Janis, identified the phenomenon of "*groupthink*," whereby tightly-knit groups may err in their decision-making because they are more concerned with achieving agreement than with the quality of the decisions made (Janis, 1982). This can be especially threatening to organizational functioning where different departments see themselves as competing with one another, promoting "in-group" favoritism and groupthink.

vii) The *social loafing effect* is the tendency of individuals in teams to work less hard than they do when individual contributions can be identified and evaluated. In organizations, individuals may put less effort into achieving quality decisions in meetings, if they perceive that their contribution is hidden in overall team performance (Karau & Williams, 1993).

viii) The study of brainstorming groups shows that quantity and often quality of ideas produced by individuals working separately, are consistently superior to those produced by a group working together. This is due to a "*production-blocking*" effect. Individuals are inhibited from both thinking of new ideas and offering them aloud to the group by the competing verbalizations of others (Diehl & Stroebe, 1987).

In team settings, it is important that team members perceive a climate of interpersonal safety, free from the possibility of attack or threat. Where the team is perceived as unsafe, members behave cautiously and maintain a kind of anxious watchfulness in their work. For example, if team members in a customer service team feels they are being criticized constantly by colleagues, they will be unlikely to suggest new ways of providing customer services and offering ideas for improving team functioning. The individual member will also be unlikely to exercise their own initiative in improving the quality of support to customers. Each team member has a responsibility to promote safety. This involves encouraging others to offer their views and then supportively exploring those ideas. Trust in teams is vital to team members' preparedness to cooperate (Korsgaard et al., 2003).

In a revealing study on safety in teams, Edmondson (1996) found major differences between newly formed intensive care nursing teams in their management of medication errors. In some groups, members openly acknowledged and discussed their medication errors (giving too much or too little of a drug, or administering the wrong drug) and discussed ways to avoid their occurrence. In others, members kept information about errors to themselves. Learning about the causes of these errors, as a team, and devising innovations to prevent future errors were only possible in groups of the former type. In these groups there was a climate of safety developed partly by the leader. Edmondson gives an example of how, in one learning-oriented team, discussion of a recent error led to innovation in equipment. An intravenous medication pump was identified as a source of consistent errors and so was replaced by a different type of pump. She also gives the example of how failure to discuss errors and generate innovations led to costly failure in the Hubble telescope development project. Edmondson (1996; 1999) argues that learning and innovation will only take place where group members trust other members' intentions. Where this is the case, team members believe that well-intentioned action will not lead to punishment or rejection by the team. Edmondson argues that safety "is meant to suggest a realistic, learning oriented attitude about effort, error and change – not to imply a careless sense of permissiveness, nor an unrelentingly positive affect. Safety is not the same as comfort; in contrast, it is predicted to facilitate risk" (Edmondson, 1999, p. 14).

Process 4: Task Focus

Task focus refers to team members' preparedness to examine their team performance critically. Dean Tjosvold has coined the term "constructive controversy" to describe the conditions necessary for effective questioning within a team (Tjosvold, 1998).

Research evidence amassed by Tjosvold and others, suggests that when teams explore opposing opinions carefully and discuss them in a cooperative context, quality of decision-making and team effectiveness is dramatically increased (see also West, Tjosvold, & Smith, 2003).

> Controversy when discussed in a cooperative context promotes elaboration of views, the search for new information and ideas and the integration of apparently opposing positions. (Tjosvold, 1991)

Tjosvold believes that a lack of constructive controversy can lead to events like the Challenger space shuttle disaster, where engineers suppressed controversy over the fact that opinions differed about the appropriateness of flying the shuttle in cold weather. Tjosvold argues that there are three elements to controversy: elaborating positions, searching for understanding and integrating perspectives.

1. First, team members should carefully describe their positions, explaining how they have come to their decisions in relation to any particular issue within

the team. They should also indicate to what extent they are confident or uncertain about the positions they have adopted.

2. People with opposing viewpoints should seek out more information about others' positions and attempt to restate them as clearly as possible. There should be attempts to explore areas of common ground in opposing positions along with an emphasis on personal regard for individuals whose positions oppose their own. This process will lead to greater creativity and outcomes that are more productive.

3. Team members should encourage integration by working to resolve controversy based on the principle of excellence in decision-making. Team members should attempt to influence their colleagues towards a solution based on shared, rational understanding rather than attempted dominance. Finally, members should strive for consensus by combining team ideas wherever possible rather than using techniques to reduce controversy, such as majority voting. Strategies such as voting may merely postpone controversy.

Teams can encourage constructive controversy by: coaching team members to play with and combine diverse ideas; to explore all team members' views in an open-minded way, so that creative ideas emerge; having the team consider all team members' views and suggestions; considering all team members' views based on whether their proposals would improve the team's service to its clients; vigorous and supportive discussions of alternatives since such comprehensive decision-making encourages all team members to develop their critical thinking and to learn from each other in the course of teamwork.

Constructive controversy does not exist when there are competitive team climates. Team members can alert each other if they seem more interested in winning arguments than finding the best solutions. If team members publicly question their colleagues' competence, destructive arguments about team decisions erupt and quality of decision-making suffers. Team leaders should discourage such discussions and, if they feel there is a problem of competence, deal with these issues privately.

Team members should build cooperative team climates, characterized by trust, supportiveness, safety and a professional approach to work. Leaders can emphasize the team's shared goals because, when team members are aware of their shared goals, they work towards the same end. This unites them and enables them to use disagreement as a means to better quality decision-making. Leaders should also encourage team members to communicate their respect for each other's competence and commitment. In this way, they will feel that disagreements do not represent attacks on each other's ability and this will be clear to all.

As the team practices these creative, rigorous and open-minded approaches to making decisions and constructively using disagreements, members learn, grow, become more confident in their individual abilities and more skilled in the team dance together.

The team's dance will reflect the extent to which all team members engage, contribute and shape each other's views. All are open to others' reactions to their positions and to having their views shaped or changed by others within the team, regardless (for example) of their status in the team. The team is an arena in which all play, strive and contribute to shaping the team's direction in the interests of their shared vision. In a good sports team, team members talk to each other to encourage better team performance throughout the game.

Process 5: Team Conflicts

Conflict is not only endemic but, if it is constructive, desirable in teams (Deutsch, 1973). Constructive team conflict can be a source of excellence, quality, and creativity. At the same time we know that conflict in teams can be interpersonally destructive and lead to poor team performance or the break up of the team altogether (De Dreu & van de Vliert, 1997).

There are three types of conflict in teams. Conflict about the task (e.g., "which new product should we launch"); conflict about team processes (e.g., "It's your job to do that not mine"); and interpersonal conflict (e.g., "I think you are a rude and irritating person!") (De Dreu & Van Vianen, 2001; Jehn, 1997). In productive and creative teams, constructive task conflict is not only endemic but desirable (Tjosvold, 1998. Team diversity and differences of opinion about how best to meet customers' needs should be a source of excellence, quality and creativity. *But too much conflict (whether it is about the task or not) or conflict experienced as threatening and unpleasant by team members can destroy relationships and the effectiveness of the team.* What may be a comfortable level of debate for you, can be intensely uncomfortable for your colleagues. For example, the person who responds to your suggestion by saying "that's rubbish" may see this as robust and constructive exchange, but you may be insulted and hurt by the comment.

Process conflict ("that's your job not mine"; "I have a much heavier workload than she does and it's not fair") and interpersonal conflict undermine team effectiveness and the well being of team members whatever the level (De Dreu & Van Vianen, 2001). Conflict is especially damaging when it becomes personal, where team members attack one another or denigrate each other's skills, abilities or performance in some way. This is unhealthy both for the individuals concerned and for the team as a whole. All team members should decisively discourage such conflict and ensure that roles and responsibilities are sufficiently clear and fair that process conflict is rare.

Resolving Team Conflicts

How do we resolve conflicts? There are a five basic ways and only one of them is good. We can *avoid* the conflict. Neither side gets its needs met and the conflict is likely to arise in the future. We can give the other person what they want and *accommodate* them. The consequences are that they get what they want and I don't. I feel resentful and they expect me to accommodate them every time. We can *compete* to win against them at all costs and, if we do, their needs are not met and they are likely to harbor resentment that may manifest in the next conflict. *Compromise* sounds good but it means that neither of us get our needs fully met – still, it is a better solution than the other three. Or, we can *collaborate* to find a creative solution that meets both our needs. This is a "win–win" solution. It is ideal since both parties are happy and their relationship is stronger because of the successful conflict negotiation.

Team members may have genuine differences (strong political differences for example), but if team members are committed to a shared team vision, and have emotional maturity they will not allow these differences to interfere with team success. We don't need to vote for the same political party in order to work together successfully to catch a wildebeest. Moreover, there is some evidence that when team leaders intervene to try to resolve interpersonal difficulties between team members, the situation is usually made worse (De Dreu & Van Vianen, 2001). There is nothing wrong with agreeing to differ, as long as it does not interfere with the effectiveness of the team.

Summary

Team-working in modern organizations is complex and demanding because of the size and complexity of these organizations, the uncertainty and demands of their environments and the diversity of functions, peoples, and teams that make up the organization. For effectiveness and creativity to emerge from team work there must be strong team integration processes, good leadership and a high level of safety. This requires that members have the integration abilities to work effectively in teams; and that they develop a safe psychosocial climate and appropriate group processes. Moreover, given the diversity of composition of modern organizations, we have to learn how to make the most of this diversity. Indeed, emerging evidence suggests that when team members have positive attitudes to diversity this can lead to the creativity and productivity benefits that we require from teams. The other central challenge for organizations with a high level of team-working is developing strategies that ensure that teams work effectively together across boundaries rather than operating as silos. Effective group processes, good leadership, integration between teams and positive team member attitudes towards diversity create the conditions for team effectiveness in modern organizations, but crucially too, the well-being which is a consequence of effective human interaction in challenging and supportive environments.

Discussion Points

Why is team-working often so difficult in modern organizations and what can be done to improve it?

How can we best train people for working in teams prior to their entry into organizations?

Key Studies

Jackson, S. E., Brett, J. F., Sessa, V. I., Cooper, D. M., Julin, J. A., & Peyronnin, K. (1991). Some differences make a difference: Individual dissimilarity and group heterogeneity as correlates of recruitment, promotions and turnover. *Journal of Applied Psychology, 76,* 675–89. This paper reveals the importance of group composition and differences between team members upon a variety of processes and outcomes in groups.

Pritchard, R. D., Jones, S. D., Roth, P. L., Stuebing, K. K., & Ekeberg, S. E. (1988). Effects of group feedback, goal setting, and incentives on organizational productivity. *Journal of Applied Psychology, 73,* 337–58. This very important study reveals how we can dramatically alter a team's performance by using wise management devices to encourage excellent performance.

Further Reading

Hackman, J. R. (2002). *Leading teams: Setting the stage for great performances.* Cambridge, MA: Harvard Business School Press. Dedicated to leadership in teams, this book offers a readable and wise account of how to create effective teams.

Paulus, P. B., & Nijstad, B. A. (Eds.) (2003). *Group creativity: Innovation through collaboration.* Oxford: Oxford University Press. A good overview of how groups can be most creative and therefore how we can use teams to create new and improved products, processes and procedures.

Thompson, L., & Choi, H. S. (2006). *Creativity and innovation in organizational teams.* Mahwah, NJ: Lawrence Erlbaum. Creativity and innovation applied in organizational teams: cognitive processes, group dynamics and organizational influences on team creativity at work.

West, M. A. (2004). *Effective teamwork. Practical lessons from organizational research* (2nd edn.). Oxford: Blackwell. A practical overview of this area of research and theorizing.

Research Close-Up

Introduction

There is very little research exploring how teams engage with the rest of the organization within which they work. Psychologists have tended to focus on internal rather than external team processes. Deborah Ancona and David Caldwell (Ancona & Caldwell, 1992) explored how teams "bridge the boundaries," i.e., how teams interact with their organizations as a whole.

Methods

The researchers explored the patterns of groups' external activities by collecting qualitative data, including interviews with 38 product-team managers, daily logs maintained by all members of two product teams, and observation of the activities of those two teams. These methods enabled the researchers to describe a wide range of activities that groups use to carry out their complex tasks. In the second phase of the research (the "classification phase") they used quantitative data from 45 new-product teams, to group similar activities into independent clusters. Teams were classified by the types of external activities they engaged in.

Results and Discussion

By studying teams interacting with their organizations, Ancona and Caldwell identified three main strategies that teams use in managing their organizational environments:

a) Ambassadorial activities

These involve communicating with and influencing senior management in order to promote the team's profile and to give senior management a picture of the team as effective, committed and innovative. The aim of ambassadorial activities is also to secure organizational resources and protect the team from excessive interference.

b) Task coordinator activities

These aim at improving communication with other teams and departments. Rather than being characterized by vertical communication (as is the case with ambassadorial activity), task coordinator activities focus on coordination, negotiation and feedback horizontally, i.e., with departments and teams at the same organizational level. The aim is to manage workflow activities in a coordinated way through negotiation and via feedback with other departments and teams, in order to achieve effective performance.

In the case of, say, an oil company training team this would mean engaging in high levels of communication with functional departments in order to gain information about training needs. The training team would also negotiate with those other departments in order to specify training course prices, priorities and frequencies. By seeking constant feedback on the adequacy of the training they would also be in a better position to coordinate and negotiate in the future.

c) Scouting activities

These aim to provide the group with up-to-date information on market needs and requirements and on new technical developments. The aim of scouting activities is to be aware of changes occurring in the external environment of the team. One example comes from a research team established to examine the factors that contributed to the performance of manufacturing firms. One team member contacted other researchers on a regular basis to find out about new developments in the area, perused relevant journals to glean information about new methodologies, and consulted with academic contacts about related research. Such scouting activities provide a means of ensuring that a team is up-to-date with technical developments. This same team member also consulted with senior managers in other similar organizations to discover their principal questions about company performance in order to identify correctly market needs for the research.

Continued

Not all teams have a single dominant strategy for external activity within the organization. Some employ all three types of activities, while others focus on only one. Still others are isolationist, employing none of the strategies in any consistent way. Ancona and Caldwell found that team performance was not dependent upon the *level* of organizational communication that teams maintained. Far more important was the *type* of activities they engaged in. Ancona and Caldwell found that teams that engaged predominantly in scouting activities had poorer performance than other teams. Moreover, internal processes within the team tended to be unsatisfactory. Task and team cohesiveness were both lowest in teams that adopted predominantly scouting activity strategies. In contrast, teams that adopted a "comprehensive strategy" of a mix of ambassadorial, task coordinator, and scouting activities tended to have the highest performance, task process, and team cohesiveness scores.

In the short term, ambassadorial activities were associated with the best team performance, good task processes and high cohesiveness. But, over the long term, a combination of ambassadorial and task coordinator external activities appears best. Comprehensive strategy teams were the most effective overall, though they seemed to pay a price with low team cohesiveness compared with the pure ambassadorial strategy teams.

Isolationist teams tended to do badly, though unlike the scouting teams, they did have higher scores on internal task processes and cohesiveness. It may be that these teams concentrated so much on internal processes that they neglected important organizational cues and so performed less well. Teams that engaged predominantly in scouting seemed to make their work so complex that they were unable to perform effectively. By constantly seeking new approaches, they were unable to adopt a single team plan that took them forward over any period. They could not make clear decisions about work plans or processes and could not implement a plan. Continual exploration brought conflicting information, requiring complex internal interaction. As the difficulty of decision-making became greater, relationships within the teams suffered.

This research shows that, contrary to popular belief, it is not the amount of external communication that a team engages in which predicts successful team performance. Rather it is the *type* of external communication.

15

Strategic Management

Gerard P. Hodgkinson

Overview

In order to survive and prosper the rigors of a turbulent environment, organizations need to adjust their strategies and working practices, as and when required. However, a growing body of psychological theory and research at the interfaces of cognitive and work and organizational psychology and the interdisciplinary field of strategic management suggests that designing and implementing such adaptive processes is not as straightforward as popular writers on management have implied. This chapter considers why and how work and organizational psychologists are beginning to contribute new knowledge and practices to enhance the interrelated strategic management processes of analysis, choice and implementation, with a view to increasing the adaptive capabilities of the organization. The central message is that cognitive competence, defined as the ability of individuals and groups to formulate and adjust their mental models of the strategic situations confronting them, in an unbiased, timely fashion, is crucial to successful adaptation. The evidence base concerning a number of prominent tools that purport to help achieve this fundamental objective is critically evaluated.

Introduction

The recent and well publicized case of Marks and Spencer PLC dramatically illustrates what can happen when an organization fails to adapt in a timely fashion to a changing environment. During the early mid-1990s, the London-based retail giant enjoyed preeminent status on the high street of every major UK town and city and had done so for many years, with a significant and growing presence throughout continental Europe and beyond. A decade later, the organization was still struggling to recover from a major deficit situation, following an unprecedented decline in sales and concomitant loss of market share over a period that had lasted for more than 5 years.

Unfortunately, the Marks and Spencer story is by no means unique. Many organizations are currently experimenting with a range of new organizational forms and strategies (Bartlett & Ghoshal, 1993; Brown & Eisenhardt, 1997, 1998; Floyd & Wooldridge, 2000; Ghoshal & Bartlett, 1990; Nohria & Ghoshal, 1997) in an attempt to adapt to or manage competitive dynamics of a severity considered hitherto unprecedented by a number of leading commentators (see e.g., Zohar & Morgan, 1998). D'Avini (1994) has coined the term "hypercompetition" to characterize the increasingly typical organizational response to this state of affairs:

> The language and metaphors of today's managers make one point abundantly clear: they are experiencing the strongest and most disruptive competitive forces of their careers. Rather than a game, business has become war. Rather than an honorable fight with the best firm winning, the goal has become extermination of the enemy. CEOs from industries ranging from telecommunications to auto parts describe the competition they face as "brutal," "intense," "bitter" and "savage." In the words of Andrew Grove, the CEO of Intel, "only the paranoid survive" in a world of hypercompetition. Increasingly, managers are turning to academics and consultants to understand why the nature of competition is changing and for insights about how to compete in chaotic and disorderly times." (Ilinitch, Lewin, & D'Aveni, 1998, p. xxi)

While not all theorists agree with the increasing hypercompetition thesis (see e.g., McNamara, Vaaler, & Devers, 2003), there is no question that the capacity of work organizations to develop and change in the face of significant environmental turbulence is a major determinant of their longer-term survival and prosperity. However, the struggle at Marks and Spencer PLC to regain market supremacy illustrates the difficulties encountered when seeking to meet the challenges of such adversity in practice.

Varieties of Social Scientific Knowledge

Anderson, Herriot, and Hodgkinson (2001) have developed a basic fourfold typology of knowledge in an attempt to characterize the state of the science base underpinning the work and organizational psychology field. Contrasting research which is both highly rigorous and practically relevant (*Pragmatic Science*) with that which is highly rigorous but low in terms of relevance (*Pedantic Science*), from that which is low in terms of rigor but highly relevant (*Populavist Science*), and that which is neither rigorous nor relevant (*Puerile Science*), they have argued that in order for the work and organizational psychology profession to flourish, it is vital that its practices are informed by strong theory and research. Pragmatic Science has to be *the* way forward, because in the absence of a rigorous evidence base to underpin its practices, there is nothing inherently unique to differentiate the work and organizational psychology profession from other groups of professionals seeking to enhance productivity and well being in the workplace.

Fortunately, as the work reviewed in the previous chapters of this book demonstrates, considerable progress has been achieved by work and organizational psychologists in ensuring that the scientist-practitioner model, epitomized by Pragmatic Science, continues to be the hallmark of the profession. A range of psychological factors have been identified that impact on the productivity and well being of *individuals* and *groups* (e.g. stress, motivation, and team working) and numerous well founded interventions have been pioneered (e.g., reliable and valid personnel selection procedures, systematic approaches to training, and enriched job designs), i.e. enduring solutions for the enhancement of workplace effectiveness, backed by scientifically robust concepts, theories, and findings.

The positive situation outlined above, stands in marked contrast with what has been achieved by work and organizational psychologists with respect to the analysis and evaluation of solutions for addressing the fundamental problem of strategic adaptation confronting many modern day organizations. A number of groups are now offering a range of organizational development services directed toward this problem, ones that very clearly fall within the territory of the work and organizational psychology profession, but are doing so without the attendant background knowledge or training to critically evaluate the impact of their interventions and adjust their actions accordingly. Business bookshops are replete with works of the "how to do it" variety. Almost invariably, these tomes are written from a management perspective and comprise little more than a series of basic checklists of the actions to be taken, with no explanations offered as to *why* the techniques advocated are more or less appropriate and under what circumstances. Given the absence of strong theory in this area, backed by a suitably rigorous evidence base to support many of techniques in prominent use, perhaps it is not too unsurprising to learn that that fewer than 30 percent of organizational change initiatives are estimated to yield successful outcomes (Binney, 1992).

Paradoxically, the rise of Popularist Science in the organizational change and development literature presents a major opportunity for work and organizational psychology professionals. All too often, the profession has been viewed by senior managers as a highly technical, operational-level, specialist field that has little or nothing to contribute at a strategic-level (Anderson, 1998; Hodgkinson & Herriot, 2002). However, as the material reviewed in the remainder of this chapter will demonstrate, over the past 15–20 years or so, a body of work has begun to accumulate at the interfaces of cognitive and work and organizational psychology and the interdisciplinary field of strategic management that has laid the foundations to redress this major shortcoming, through the generation of new knowledge of a form that has the potential to enhance the adaptive capabilities of organizations at all levels, while breaking the vicious cycle of non-involvement in strategic decision-making that for too long has undermined the professional standing of work and organizational psychologists in the eyes of top management.

The Nature and Scope of Strategic Management

Arguably, strategic management is one of the most important but also one of the least understood areas of organizational life (Mintzberg, Ahlstrand, & Lampel, 1998). Whereas other areas of management deal with routinized, operationally specific issues and problems of a short-term nature, strategic management addresses organization-wide issues and problems of a fundamental nature. Strategic issues and problems, by definition, tend to be relatively ambiguous, complex, and surrounded by risk and uncertainty. According to Johnson and Scholes (1999, p. 10):

> Strategy is the direction and scope of an organization over the long term, which achieves advantage for the organization through its configuration of resources within a changing environment, to meet the needs of markets and to fulfil stakeholder expectations.

For analytical purposes they maintain that it is convenient to consider the concerns of strategic management as encompassing three major sets of issues: analysis, choice and implementation. Strategic analysis involves understanding the strategic position of the organization, its environment, resources, values and objectives. Strategic choice involves the formulation of possible courses of action/options, an evaluation of their suitability or fit, and the selection of the particular strategy to be followed. Finally, strategy implementation is concerned with the translation of strategy into action, resource planning, designing the organizational structure to carry through the strategy, and adapting the people and the systems used to manage the organization. In practice, analysis, choice and implementation can occur in parallel and breaking down the major component activities of the strategic management process in this way should not be taken to imply in any sense a linear progression. Indeed, as we shall see, once organizations embark upon a given course of action a number of the individual and social psychological processes discussed in previous chapters of this book (e.g. the adoption of cognitive heuristics and group think) can come into play, in ways that serve not only to limit the range of choices that might be considered possible at later stages, but also constrain the feasibility of particular actions in terms of their implementation; analysis, choice and implementation co-exist, in a dynamic interplay.

The psychological contribution

Such is the complex nature of strategy and strategic management that no one base discipline of the social sciences can adequately address the problems that fall within its purview. Within this field, researchers and practitioners alike must be able and willing to gain insights from a range of social science disciplines, in much the same way that the medical sciences draw upon biology, chemistry, physics and so on in order to refine theoretical and practical understanding. Consequently, isolating psychological contributions within the strategy field is potentially problematic. Ultimately, a broad range of social, economic, political, technical and financial factors determine the success or failure of an organization's strategy and, accordingly, a range of cross-disciplinary perspectives are required in order to make sense of this phenomenon, incorporating material from fields as diverse as economics, accounting and finance and sociology (see e.g., Johnson & Scholes, 1999; Mintzberg et al., 1998). However, as observed earlier, the discipline of psychology potentially has much to contribute to this vitally important, multidisciplinary endeavor and a sufficient volume of work has now accumulated to warrant the status of an emergent subfield: the psychology of strategic management (Hodgkinson, 2001a,b; Sparrow, 1994; Hodgkinson & Sparrow, 2002). In this chapter, a number of the major developments that have occurred within this specialty over recent years will be selectively outlined, in order to illustrate how scientifically sound psychological theory and research is leading to an enriched understanding of the strategic management process, thereby enhancing organizational effectiveness through the design of interventions to foster strategic competence.

Strategic competence: A cognitive perspective

Hodgkinson and Sparrow (2002) have argued that the many changes currently confronting organizations are placing unprecedented informational burdens upon those responsible for strategy formulation and implementation and that cognitive competence is thus becoming increasingly central to the adaptive capabilities of the organization. Strategic competence, as viewed from a cognitive perspective, demands that organizations are able to acquire, store, recall, interpret and act upon information with sufficient alacrity to be able to adjust to rapidly shifting environmental contingencies:

> In practice, this means being agile, open to the environment, capable of picking up those weak signals indicative of the need for change . . . In cases where strategic competence is highly developed, the organization is able to proactively develop new competencies and stake out new strategic territories. Conversely, where the organization fails to develop such strategic competence, it responds reactively in an ever-viscous circle, which at best enables it to defend its existing markets, products and/or services. (Hodgkinson & Sparrow, 2002, p. 3)

The range of issues that can be legitimately addressed from a psychological perspective is potentially as broad as the entire field of strategic management, covering all aspects of strategic analysis, choice and implementation, from an analysis of cognitive processes in the boardroom (e.g., Forbes & Milliken, 1999), to the nature and impact of the personality characteristics of the chief executive officer (CEO) and other organization members on organizational structure, strategy, and performance (e.g., Boone & De Brabander, 1993; Boone, De Brabander, & van Witteloostuijn, 1996; Hodgkinson, 1992, 1993; Miller & Toulouse, 1986), and the psychological impact of mergers and acquisitions (Cartwright, 2005; Cartwright & Cooper, 1990; Hogan & Overmyer-Day, 1994). Hence, the present chapter must be selective in its coverage.

Three interrelated streams of work will be outlined, which in complementary ways have highlighted the dangers cognitive bias and inertia in the processes of strategic analysis, choice and implementation and contributed to the development and evaluation of tools and techniques for intervening in these processes. As we shall see, in each case the basic notion of mental representations/mental models, grounded in schema theory (Bartlett, 1932), has proven highly insightful.

Mental Models of Competitor Definition in Strategic Analysis

A major objective of strategic analysis is to gain an understanding of the strategic position of the organization. To this end, in recent years a great deal of research attention has been devoted to an examination of the ways in which business competitors come to be defined and represented within the minds of strategic decision-makers:

> From a cognitive perspective, decision-makers act on a mental model of the environment. Thus any explanation for strategic responses to competitive pressures must ultimately take into consideration the mental models of competitive strategists . . . before competitive strategies can be formulated, decision-makers must have an image of who their rivals are and on what dimensions they will compete. Given the diverse range of organizational forms and decision-makers' limited capacity to process complex interorganizational cues, the task of defining "the competition" is both important and problematic. (Porac & Thomas, 1990, pp. 224–5)

Building on this fundamental insight, researchers have set out to systematically explore the structure and content of managers' mental representations of competition. This work has addressed two rather different sets of questions, at different levels of analysis.

Mental models of competitor definition at the interorganizational level of analysis

Strategic management researchers have long argued that neither industries nor individual firms constitute the most appropriate unit of analysis for conducting a strategic analysis of the competitive position of organizations. Rather, an intermediate level of analysis, known as the strategic group, is more informative, because within a given industry competing firms fall into discernible clusters, defined in terms of their overall similarity along the various dimensions (e.g. geographical scope, product range, pricing policy) that comprise the bases of competition (see e.g., Porter, 1980; McGee & Thomas, 1986). The main purpose of the economic theory underpinning the notion of strategic groups is to explain variations in the strategic behavior (conduct) and performance of firms within industries. According to this theory, once strategic groups have formed, the various players develop isolating mechanisms (barriers to entry and mobility) that serve to deter new entrants from stepping into the competitive arena and deter existing players from attempting to switch membership from one group to another (Caves & Porter, 1977). The theory of strategic groups predicts that *mobility barriers* enable significant between-groups performance differences to accrue, over and above differences within groups, due to the fact that these barriers afford stable advantages to particular groups at the expense of other groups within the same industry. Hence the concept of mobility barriers not only provides an explanation for intergroup performance differences, but also a conceptual basis for competitively positioning rival firms (Porter, 1981, p. 615). The upsurge of interest in cognitive approaches to the analysis competitor definition has arisen due to a growing dissatisfaction with this dominant economic explanation for what is essentially an economic, cognitive and social psychological process (see e.g., Hodgkinson, 1997a; Porac & Thomas, 1990, 1994; Peteraf & Shanley, 1997; Reger & Huff, 1993). Based on the foundational work of Weick (1979) and Berger and Luckmann (1967), over the past 15–20 years a growing body of psychological theory, centered on the notion of *competitive enactment* (Porac, Thomas, & Baden-Fuller, 1989; Porac & Thomas, 1990), has helped to address this shortcoming.

A major limitation of the predominantly economic approach of strategic groups theory is its inability to explain how or why competitive structures in industries come to develop in the first place, and on what basis particular strategies are chosen. Competitive enactment theory has illuminated a number of basic social and psychological mechanisms that might account for the social construction of competitive industry structures and the ways in which these structures come to undermine the adaptive capabilities of organizations over the longer term. Porac et al. (1989) coined the term "competitive enactment" as a basis for understanding the way in which strategists from rival firms come to share common conceptions of competition.

The structure → conduct → performance paradigm of industrial economics (Bain, 1956; Mason, 1957), upon which the theory of strategic groups is based, implies that the environment is an objective entity waiting to be discovered through the application of rational analytical techniques (cf. Porter, 1980). Moreover, sequential information processing models advanced by cognitive psychologists (e.g. Broadbent, 1958; Wickens, 1984) suggest that the reason subjective differences in perception occur is because the objective environment can only be partially comprehended by individuals, due to "limits on their knowledge and computational capabilities (bounded rationality)" (Simon, 1997, p. 20; see also Simon, 1955, 1956). Weick's (1979) concept of enactment challenges this limited view of the environment (which he terms "the perceived environment"), arguing that theories stressing the notion that reality is selectively perceived overemphasizes the object/subject relationship, at the expense of the idea that often the subject exerts considerable influence on the object, through active, constructive processes which impose meaning on "objective" features. In turn, these belief systems constrain the actions of the individuals and groups who created them, as if they were true, objective constraints.

The idea of *competitive* enactment was developed in the context of a relatively small scale, inductive study conducted in the Scottish knitwear industry. Based on interviews with various top-level managers from rival knitwear producers, Porac and his colleagues (1989) argued that although individuals' mental models of competition within a given organizational field are idiosyncratic at the outset, they converge over time, through processes of mutual enactment. Their study revealed an overwhelming tendency to disregard as competitors firms located outside the immediate vicinity of Scotland. Despite the fact that Scottish knitwear producers account for a mere 3 percent of the total amount of knitted outer-wear manufactured on a world-wide basis, only firms within the immediate locality, and who produced a similar range of goods to one another, using similar technological processes of production and common channels of distribution, were regarded as serious competition. According to Porac et al., these findings can be accounted for in terms of a basic social construction process in which a *group level mental model* came to define the boundaries of the competitive arena; that is, managers from rival firms within the locality developed a common understanding of the bases of competition, thereby providing them with a shared sense of strategic identity (see also Peteraf & Shanley, 1997). In turn, this has led individual firms to consider a relatively narrow range of strategic options.

More generally, Porac and his colleagues argue that such group level mental models come about because of a tendency for organizations to imitate one another, both directly and indirectly, an inevitability given that strategists from rival firms face similar technical and material problems with a finite number of solutions and exchange key information with one another through participation in common social networks (see also Lant & Baum, 1995; Porac et al., 1995; Reger & Huff, 1993). Building on these insights, Porac and Thomas (1990) have argued that these myopic views of the competitive arena can have deleterious effects on organizational behavior and effectiveness, leading to collective blind spots in competitor definition and inertia (see also Zajac & Bazerman, 1991).

Population ecologists (e.g., Hannan & Freeman, 1977, 1988) have demonstrated that "inertial forces" often prevent organizations from adapting to major environmental change. Drawing on this work, Porac and Thomas (1990) have argued that one possible source of such inflexibility might be the cognitive inertia arising from strategists' mental models of the competitive arena: discernible competitive structures and/or industry-wide conceptions of what it takes to compete successfully begin to emerge (cf. Spender, 1989) and strategists may become overly dependent on the shared mental model that has come to prevail, to the extent that dramatic changes to the competitive landscape may go undetected (or unheeded) until successful adaptation is no longer possible (see also Abrahamson & Formbrun, 1994). Left unchecked, such inertia can threaten the adaptive capabilities of the individual firm or entire subpopulations of firms, to the point of extinction.

Prospective longitudinal evidence in support of the cognitive inertia hypothesis (discussed later in this chapter, see the "Research Close-Up" at the end of the chapter) has been provided in a study of UK residential estate agents (Hodgkinson, 1997b, 2005), but more work along similar lines is badly needed (cf. Reger & Palmer, 1996). In general the bulk of studies investigating competitive enactment theory and related conceptions have employed cross-sectional designs and/or small samples of participants (for reviews see Hodgkinson & Sparrow, 2002; Hodgkinson, 2005).

Mental models of competitor definition at the intra-organizational-level of analysis

A second stream of work has rendered problematic one of the key assumptions underpinning competitive enactment theory and related approaches: the assumption of intra-organizational homogeneity in mental models of competitor definition. Research designs employed in the development and testing of cognitive enactment theory and related formulations have been predicated on the implicit assumption that sole informants can adequately represent the views of the wider organization (or at least the dominant coalition). However, a number of researchers (e.g. Bowman & Johnson, 1992; Daniels, Johnson, & de Chernatony, 1994; Hodgkinson & Johnson, 1994) have argued that a variety of intra-organizational social and political processes have been neglected in the development of this work, ones that might give rise to salient individual differences in competitor cognition. In turn, these cognitive differences could play a central role in the micro-processes of strategy formulation and implementation within firms.

Supporting the above alternative line of reasoning a number of studies have identified intra-organizational differences in mental models of competition (e.g., Bowman & Johnson, 1992; Calori, Johnson, & Sarnin, 1992; Daniels, Johnson, & de Chernatony, 1994; Hodgkinson & Johnson, 1994), thus confirming the need for more sophisticated research designs. Hodgkinson and Johnson (1994), for example, employed a "hierarchical taxonomic interview procedure" to elicit and compare managers' representations of competition in two UK grocery retail organizations, a quasi-national chain and a smaller, regionally based organization. Participants were first asked to identify what class of business they were in (e.g. "retailer") then enumerate the various subcategories (e.g. grocery retailer, electrical retailer, clothing retailer), proceeding in a top-down (i.e. superordinate–subordinate) and bottom-up (i.e. subordinate–super-ordinate) fashion, until all meaningful varieties of firm within their served markets had been identified. In both organizations a wide range of variations were identified in terms of structure and content of the representations, ranging from very basic representations comprising relatively few levels, categories and subcategories to exceedingly rich ones, characterized by numerous levels, categories and subcategories.

Ultimately, however, as recently argued by a number of theorists and researchers (cf. Hodgkinson, 2005; Porac, Ventresca, & Mishina, 2002; Porac & Thomas, 2002; Sutcliffe & Huber, 1998) these two streams of work need to be reconciled, if we are to develop a truly comprehensive understanding of the role played by mental models of competitive industry structures in strategy formulation and implementation. To this end, Daniels, Johnson and de Chernatony (2002) reported a study conducted in the UK financial services industry, which was designed in an attempt to ascertain the relative contributions of intra- and interorganizational factors as determinants of managerial representations of competitive industry structures. Theories emphasizing the primacy of interorganizational processes (e.g. Greve, 1998; Lant & Baum, 1995; Porac et al., 1989, 1995) suggest that managerial mental models within the same industry sector should move towards convergence at the level of the industry, strategic group, managerial function and seniority, whereas theories asserting the primacy of the competitive or task environment (e.g. Hodgkinson & Johnson, 1994; Starbuck, 1976) predict that mental models should diverge. Interestingly, the overall pattern of findings in Daniels et al.'s (2002) study suggests that neither explanation is inherently superior in the context of the particular industry setting in which they undertook their fieldwork. Whilst there is some evidence that the wider institutional environment exerts significant influence (primarily through convergence of mental models among middle managers across the industry as a whole) there is also evidence of significant task influences. In particular, a number of significant differences emerged across organizations, with greater differentiation among senior managers. The Daniels et al. (2002) study has brought together these hitherto largely disparate streams of theory and research within a unified framework. In exploring the relative contributions of intra- and interorganizational influences on managers' mental models of competition, it has undoubtedly broken new ground. Unfortunately, however, as I have argued elsewhere (Hodgkinson, 1997a, 2001a,b, 2002, 2005; Hodgkinson & Sparrow, 2002), the way in which representations of competitor definition were elicited in this and several other studies (e.g., Daniels et al., 1994; Hodgkinson & Johnson, 1994) is highly problematic. The majority of these studies have tended to use idiographic cognitive mapping techniques (often the repertory grid technique, Kelly, 1955) to elicit participants' representations. These techniques encourage participants to express their thoughts using their natural language, and thus are inherently unsuitable for exploring the extent of homogeneity and diversity in representations of competitor definition because, by their very nature, they tend to accentuate surface level differences in content and structure at the expense of deeper, underlying communalities (Hodgkinson, 1997a).

In contrast to Daniels et al. (2002), Hodgkinson (2005) revealed evidence of strong structural commonalities in participants' dimensional representations of competitor definition within and between organizations in the same industrial sector, which persisted in the face of significant shifts in the trading conditions confronting the organizations concerned (see research close up). Clearly there is a need now for further multi-informant, multi-organization investigations, using similarly sophisticated methods of data collection and analysis to those high-lighted in the Research Close-Up (at the end of this chapter), in order to refine our understanding the extent to which, under what circumstances, and over what timescale and with what effect, strategists' mental representations of competition converge, diverge, stabilize and change. Such work is a vital prerequisite for the development and validation of intervention techniques to help overcome the potential dangers of cognitive bias and inertia in competitive positioning analysis, exemplified by the case of Marks and Spencer PLC.

Heuristics and Biases in Strategic Choice

Another major body of theory and research that has led to the development of key insights into strategy formulation is drawn from the field of behavioral deci-sion-making (e.g. Fischhof, 1975; Fischhoff et al., 1977; Kahneman et al., 1982; Tversky & Kahnemen, 1974). Starting from the basic premise that decision-makers are subjected to the aforementioned constraints of bounded rationality, arising from fundamental limits to their knowledge and information processing capabilities, behavioral decision researchers (e.g. Kahneman, Slovic, & Tversky, 1982; Tversky & Kahneman, 1974) have amassed over many years an impressive volume of evidence demonstrating that in order to render the world manageable, decision-makers employ a variety of "rules of thumb," known as "heuristics." Heuristic processing strategies enable the decision-maker to cut through the welter of information bombarding them, by imposing a number of simplifying assumptions on the data.

Simon (1955, 1956) identified one such heuristic, known as "satisficing"; when faced with a number of choice alternatives, decision-makers select the first alternative that meets their minimum requirements, rather than choosing the best from all the alternatives on offer. Satisficing is much simpler in terms of its cogni-tive operations, thus placing fewer demands on scarce mental resources. Subse-quent research has identified other heuristics that, in common with satisficing, involve less mental effort (see, for example, Svenson, 1979; Payne, Bettman, & Johnson, 1993) and there is growing evidence to suggest that heuristic modes of reasoning underpin human judgment processes, particularly in the context of judgments involving the assessment of risk and uncertainty, as typical of strategic decision-making in organizations (for reviews see Das & Teng, 1999; Hodgkinson, 2001b; Maule & Hodgkinson, 2002, 2003).

Although the use of heuristics reduces the information processing requirements on the decision-maker, there are also risks involved, in that their deployment may lead to suboptimal outcomes. In the case of satisficing, for example, once an "acceptable" option is found, the search for and evaluation of additional potentially viable alternatives ceases. Consequently, "better" options that have not been considered at this juncture will be ignored.

A number of attendant biases associated with particular heuristics that might have a significant bearing on choice in strategic decision-making have been identified. Schwenk (1984), for example, identified three different phases of the strategic decision process ("goal formulation and problem identification," "alternative generation and evaluation," and "selection"). By analyzing documentary accounts of how actual strategic decisions were taken in practice, Schwenk argued different biases tend to come to the fore during different stages of the strategic decision process. Early on, when identifying the problem, individuals seek information that confirms their initial beliefs. When generating alternatives they use these beliefs to anchor or restrain their judgments. Feelings of personal responsibility can also lead to group convergence, in an attempt to diffuse such responsibility. The effectiveness of the initial judgment is affected by the representativeness of the analogies that they draw with other, similar situations. Consequently, some alternatives tend to be preferred from the outset, while others are discussed in negative terms. It is easy to then justify preferred alternatives on the basis that they do not involve cognitively demanding trade-offs. In the final evaluation stage of a group decision, managers use analogies to justify their point of view, but this can lead to an overestimation of the extent to which past experiences are applicable, partial descriptions of strategic alternatives, and the devaluation and dismissal of vitally important information by the group. The deployment of heuristics can also result in decision-makers being over-confident in their decisions and can create a misdirected search for certainty and a consequent *illusion of control* (Fischhoff, 1975; Fischhoff, Slovic, & Lichtenstein, 1977; Langer, 1975).

Framing bias

One other bias, known as the "framing bias," that might have a significant bearing on choice in strategic decision-making is illustrated in box 15.1. This bias arises when trivial changes to the way in which a decision problem is presented or "framed," emphasizing either the potential gains or the potential losses, lead to reversals of preference. The example presented in box 15.1 demonstrates the potentially powerful impact of framing on choice behavior, which can dramatically alter the way in which the expected outcomes associated with particular decision alternatives are evaluated. In general, decision-makers are risk averse when gains are highlighted and risk seeking when losses are highlighted (Kahneman & Tversky, 1979, 1984; Tversky & Kahneman, 1981).

Box 15.1:   Illustration of the framing bias

Consider the following problem:

A large car manufacturer has recently been hit with a number of economic difficulties, and it appears as if three plants need to be closed and 6,000 employees laid off. The vice president of production has been exploring alternative ways to avoid this crisis. She has developed two plans:

Plan A: This plan will save one of the 3 plants and 2,000 jobs.
Plan B: This plan has a 1/3 probability of saving all three plants and all 6,000 jobs, but has a 2/3 probability of saving no plants and no jobs.

Which plan would you select?
Now reconsider this problem, replacing choices A and B, above, with the following choices:

Plan C: This plan will result in the loss of two of the three plants and 4,000 jobs.
Plan D: This plan has a 2/3 probability of resulting in the loss of all three plants and all 6,000 jobs, but has a 1/3 probability of loosing no plants and no jobs.

Which plan would you select?
   An analysis of each pair of decision choices (Plans A and B versus Plans C and D) reveals that they are objectively identical (A is same as Plan C, and B is the same as Plan D). Nevertheless, when presented with the first pair of choices (Plans A and B), an overwhelming majority of individuals express a preference for Plan A, whereas Plan D becomes the favorite when presented with the second set of choices (Plans C and D).

Source: Bazerman, 1984, pp. 333–4.

Several laboratory and field studies have demonstrated that the framing bias is indeed likely to occur in the context of strategic decision-making (Bateman & Zeithaml, 1989a, 1989b). However there is evidence suggesting that more effortful thought prior to making decision choices can eliminate framing bias (e.g., Maule, 1995; Sieck & Yates, 1997). In studies to identify steps to minimize its effects (see e.g., Hodgkinson, Bown, Maule, Glaister, & Pearman, 1999; Hodgkinson & Maule, 2002; Hodgkinson, Maule, Bown, Pearman & Glaister, 2002) undergraduates and senior managers within a financial services organization, using a graphical version of a technique called causal cognitive mapping (Huff, 1990) depicted their causal beliefs concerning a decision scenario. In both cases, the application of causal mapping prior to choice eliminated the framing bias, providing supporting evidence for its efficacy as an intervention technique for use in practical settings.

Fast and frugal heuristics

Recently Gigerenzer and his colleagues (e.g., Gigernezer, Todd, and the ABC Group, 1999) have questioned the extent to which mainstream behavioral decision research such as that outlined above is *ecologically valid*, arguing that many experimental studies demonstrating the irrationality of human judgment are based on tasks involving probabilistic reasoning and other forms of abstract judgment far removed from the real-world environments to which humankind has readily adapted over many years. Based on a fundamentally different conception of bounded rationality, known as *ecological rationality* (Gigerenzer & Todd, 1999, p. 5), which emphasizes the adaptive capacities of heuristic processing, they have identified a whole new class of heuristics that make minimal computational demands on the decision-maker: *fast and frugal* heuristics. These heuristics do not involve probabilities and utilities, and are deployed in situations that require individuals to draw inferences with limited time and knowledge. Gigerenzer and his colleagues maintain that fast and frugal heuristics complement *satisficing heuristics*, as originally conceived by Simon (1955, 1956), i.e. heuristics for searching through available alternatives. Since fast and frugal heuristics and satisficing heuristics are adaptively matched to the real-life environment of the decision-maker, Gigernezer et al. argue that both are ecologically valid.

The potential power of fast and frugal heuristic processing to enhance decision-making has been demonstrated rather dramatically in the field of medicine. Breiman et al. (1993) devised a simple three-stage decision tree, involving basic dichotomous (yes/no) questions, to assess heart attack patients, rather than the monitoring and evaluation of 19 different cues. There is much to be gained by seeking to identify instances of such fast and frugal heuristics in the context of real-life organizational decision-making, with a view to enhancing the strategic choice process.

Cognitive Barriers to Strategy Implementation

The translation of strategy into action poses a number of significant psychological challenges in respect of the management of employees, not least in terms of the processes of adjustment that need to be sensitively handled in the face of major organizational development and change. It has been estimated that less than one in three change initiatives are successful, implying a need for a more careful sifting of the plethora of tools and techniques that purport to facilitate the management of change. Organizational development, the application of behavioral science concepts, theories, tools and techniques to the diagnosis of and intervention in work systems and organizations, with a view to better understanding the nature of change and transformation and implementing the insights derived from systematic research, is addressed by Peiro and Martinez-Tur in chapter 16 of this book. Much of the material covered in that chapter is highly relevant to the problems of strategy implementation, as highlighted by its contributors (see also Johnson, Scholes, & Whittington, 2005; Weick & Quinn, 1999). Rather than duplicate that material I shall highlight a couple of theoretical advances, paralleling developments in respect of strategy formulation outlined in earlier sections, that have the potential to contribute to an understanding of the role played by mental models in undermining organizational change initiatives, with a view to identifying practical steps that might be taken in order to help employees reframe their understanding of the realities confronting them, a vital prerequisite for the acceptance of change.

Challenges to organizational identity: the case of total quality management

Drawing upon three related cognitive self-concept theories, organizational identity theory (e.g., Albert & Whetten, 1985; Dutton & Dukerich, 1991), personal construct theory (e.g., Ginsberg, 1990; Kelly, 1955), and self-discrepancy theory (e.g. Higgins, 1987, 1989), Reger, Gustafson, DeMarie, and Mullane (1994) have argued that one of the primary reasons planned organizational change efforts, such as the introduction of total quality management (TQM) schemes, often fail is because employees' extant mental models, in which their most basic assumptions about the nature of the organization are encoded (Bartunek, 1984), fundamentally constrain their understanding of, and support for, the new initiative. In turn, this leads to a lack of cooperation. Reger et al. conclude that the cognitive literature in general points to the overall conclusion that inertial cognitive limitations are likely to be endemic whenever new ideas and practices are introduced in organizations. This is because ideas and practices that radically depart from well established schemas or frames will be actively resisted, especially when those new ideas and practices radically challenge the beliefs an individual holds about the organization's identity (see also Labianca et al., 2000).

As shown in figure 15.1, the probability of change acceptance by members of the organization is hypothesized to vary as a function of the size of the perceived

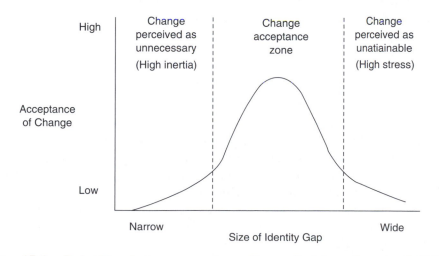

Figure 15.1: Probability of change acceptance (Reger, Gustafson, Demarie, & Mullane, 1994)

gap between their current conception of the organization's identity and that which would be required in the event the change initiative were to be fully embraced. In cases where the identity gap is perceived to be overly narrow, change will be considered to be unnecessary, a state of high inertia, whereas in cases where the gap is perceived to be overly wide, this will create undue stress, leading in turn to a rejection of the proposed changes, due to a sense that the required change is unattainable. Moderate levels of organizational stress, in contrast, as experienced when the degree of required change falls within the "change acceptance zone," will create negative affect of a magnitude that will stimulate the necessary actions to move the organization away from its subideal state, thereby restoring affective harmony.

The overall implications of this model for maximizing the probability of acceptance of the strategy to be implemented are that change agents should adopt "tectonic" tactics, i.e. the unfolding of a series of mid-range changes, when seeking to radically reposition the organization through major change initiatives such as TQM, rather than incremental or synoptic ones:

> The term tectonic is intended to evoke an earthquake metaphor. As pressure builds along a fault, seismologists hope for moderately powerful earthquakes – ones that are significant enough to overcome the inertia preventing the plates from moving, ones that will relieve stress building along the fault. Insignificant earthquakes, like incremental change in organizations, may cause rumblings, but they often do little or nothing to relieve the pressure. A *great* earthquake, analogous to synoptic change in organizations, relieves much of the stress, but it often results in major, undesirable destruction. (Reger et al., 1994, p. 577)

Viewed from this perspective, dramatic and incremental adjustments are best avoided. Unfortunately, despite the considerable potential of this theoretical formulation to enrich our understanding of employee resistance to organizational change and contribute to the enhancement of strategy implementation processes, its validity has yet to be subjected to empirical scrutiny.

Challenges to the psychological contract

The psychological contract constitutes the implicit, as opposed to the formal written, agreement between the individual employee and the wider organization concerning their mutual expectations and obligations (Argyris, 1960; Levinson, 1962). While early scholars recognized that the psychological contract is essentially perceptual and subjective in nature, in recent years there have a number of explicit calls to increase our understanding the dynamics of the employment relationship through an analysis of the sociocognitive processes underpinning contract formation and change (see e.g., Rousseau, 2001; Shore, Tetrick, Coyle-Shapiro, & Taylor, 2004).

In a somewhat similar vein to the arguments of Reger et al. (1994) in respect of the implementation of TQM systems, outlined above, Rousseau (2001) maintains that the psychological contract is encoded by members of the organization in the form a mental model or schema, which in turn provides the lens through which information concerning employer and employee actions will be interpreted and decisions made regarding the degree of investment and commitment on the part of each party to the employment relationship. In keeping with the above line of reasoning, Rousseau (2001) contends that in their earliest stages of development mental models of the psychological contract are relatively simple in nature, characterized by few concepts and linkages, becoming more complex and inflexible over time. Hence, at the preemployment stage, the mental models held by candidates and employers concerning their mutual expectations and perceived obligations are essentially of a skeletal form, encapsulating the basic beliefs acquired through prior socialization and employment experiences brought by each party into the negotiation arena. Preemployment schemas (or schemata) are necessarily incomplete because each party has gaps in their knowledge of one another. As negotiations proceed toward the offer of formal employment, however, Rousseau maintains that the schema of each party will contain greater numbers of concepts and linkages, acquired as a result of a series of information exchanges, and that these will become relatively fixed, serving as filters through which new information is screened in such a way that each party will find it increasingly difficult to revise their expectations and perceived obligations.

Like the above theoretical formulation advanced by Reger et al. (1994), Rousseau's (2001) cognitive perspective on the psychological contract has considerable potential to illuminate some of the sociocognitive mechanisms underpinning more and less successful attempts to manage strategic change. In particular, as observed by Sparrow and Cooper (2003), change initiatives are more likely to prove successful when the managers and supervisors responsible for their implementation are equipped with the skills to facilitate the necessary cognitive reframing of the employment relationship that must occur as a precursor to the acceptance of change; such reframing is more likely to occur when the employee is afforded the opportunity to embark upon a process of reflection and self-discovery. At this point in time, however, no studies within the psychological contract literature have sought to validate these claims, although work is presently underway to do so (Clarkson & Hodgkinson, 2004, 2005, 2007).

Summary

Strategic management is concerned with the longer-term direction and scope of the organization. Over the past two decades or so a considerable body of work has accumulated within this interdisciplinary field of study concerned with the application of basic concepts borrowed from cognitive and work and organizational psychology, in an attempt to refine our understanding of the strategic management

Continued

process. The concepts and theories outlined in this chapter imply a need for interventions for overcoming the dangers of cognitive bias and cognitive inertia, both of which have the potential to undermine all aspects of the strategic management process, from analysis and choice to implementation. In a world dominated by Popularist Science, the work and organizational psychology profession is confronted with a rare opportunity indeed to overcome the major obstacles that have rendered it strategically impotent, by bringing advanced research skills to bear on the analysis of fundamental cognitive processes that lie at the heart of the modern enterprise. A number of writers in popular works for managers have claimed that cognitive mapping techniques and related procedures such as scenario planning can enhance the strategic management process through the enrichment of decision-makers' mental models (see e.g., van der Heijden, 1996; van der Heijden et al., 2002). Meanwhile, recent theoretical advances and associated empirical evidence is beginning to accrue that seems to lend credence to this claim. Thus far, however, as observed by Mintzberg (1994), independent, critical scrutiny of strategic interventions based upon scenario-based techniques has been exceedingly rare (but see also Hodgkinson & Wright, 2002, 2006) and the time has now come to embark upon programmatic work to formally identify the precise mechanisms underpinning their effectiveness or otherwise. As the material surveyed in this chapter demonstrates, work and organizational psychologists are eminently placed to contribute to this endeavor.

Discussion Points

In what ways might the advancement of psychological theory and research on strategic management benefit the professional standing of work and organizational psychologists?

What do you consider to be the major challenges facing work and organizational psychologists in seeking to contribute to the science and practice of strategic management? Consider the implications of your analysis for the training and development of work and organizational psychology researchers and practitioners.

Key Studies

Hodgkinson, G. P. (2005). *Images of competitive space: A study of managerial and organizational strategic cognition.* Basingstoke, UK: Palgrave Macmillan. As discussed in the Research Close-Up below, this book reports in depth the findings of one of the largest ever longitudinal field studies of the nature and impact of individual and group mental models of competition on the development of business strategy at the individual, group, and industry levels of analysis, providing supporting evidence for a number of the key theoretical concepts reviewed in this chapter and powerfully demonstrating from a psychological standpoint why we need well-validated techniques to improve strategic thinking.

Porac, J. F., Thomas, H., & Baden-Fuller, C. (1989). Competitive groups as cognitive communities: The case of Scottish knitwear manufacturers. *Journal of Management Studies*, 26, 397–416. This seminal article reported early findings that laid the foundations of theory and research on mental models of competitor definition.

Further Reading

Hodgkinson, G. P., & Sparrow, P. R. (2002). *The competent organization: A psychological analysis of the strategic management process.* Buckingham, UK: Open University Press. This book provides a comprehensive overview of cognitively oriented theory and research on the psychology of strategic management.

Huff, A. S. (Ed.) (1990). *Mapping strategic thought.* Chichester: Wiley. This edited book of specially commissioned chapters laid the conceptual, theoretical, methodological, and empirical foundations of work on the psychology of strategic management and managerial and organizational cognition more generally.

Porac, J. F., & Thomas, H. (2002). Managing cognition and strategy: Issues, trends and future directions. In A. Pettigrew, H. Thomas, & R. Whittington (Eds.), *Handbook of strategy and management* (pp. 165–81). London: Sage. A useful overview, covering similar territory to the present chapter, from two of the field's leading contributors.

Walsh, J. P. (1995). Managerial and organizational cognition: Notes from a trip down memory lane. *Organization Science*, 6, 280–321. This highly influential article provides an authoritative overview of classic work on managerial and organizational cognition that has shaped cognitively oriented research in the field of strategic management and management and organization studies more generally.

Acknowledgments

The financial support of the UK ESRC/EPSRC Advanced Institute of Management Research (AIM) in the preparation of this chapter (under grant number RES-331-25-0028) is gratefully acknowledged.

Research Close-Up

Hodgkinson, G. P. (2005). *Images of competitive space: A study of managerial and organizational strategic cognition.* Basingstoke, UK: Palgrave Macmillan.

Introduction

The primary objective was to investigate three key issues that have yet to be resolved, given the limitations in previous work, as outlined in the chapter:

1. The extent to which measurable features of actors' mental models of competitor definition correlate in theoretically meaningful ways with measurable strategic behaviors and measurable features of the organization and its environment;

2. The extent to which and in what ways key actors within a given industry hold similar or diverse mental models of competitor definition;

Continued

3. The extent to which these mental models remain stable in line with the cognitive inertia hypothesis, or change contemporaneously with significant environmental shifts.

The study took place in the UK residential estate agency industry during the late 1980s – early 1990s, a highly appropriate setting because the key actors involved in house sales (e.g., valuers, negotiators, surveyors, and financial advisors) comprise a dense, highly interdependent interorganizational social network, i.e. spanning the boundaries of rival firms, mirroring the conditions in which belief convergence, as hypothesized by Porac et al.'s (1989) competitive enactment theory, is likely to occur. Furthermore, the timing of data collection was ideal for testing the cognitive inertia hypothesis (Porac & Thomas, 1990), because during the run up to data collection the industry had faced a series of major changes, not least the entrance of major financial services organizations (corporate players on a national scale) and a severe down turn occurred in the UK housing market just as the fieldwork began.

Research design and participants

A two-wave panel design was employed, in order to enable the comparison of mental models over time. Time 1 (T1) ran from mid-July 1989 to October 1989. Time 2 (T2) data were gathered over a comparable period which ran from September to December 1990.

Two hundred and eight individuals from 58 residential estate agency organizations in the north east midlands region of the UK returned completed questionnaires at T1. In all cases, the participants held positions that required them to possess insights into the competitive positioning strategy of their organization and its rivals in the execution of their duties.

Unfortunately, as is common in longitudinal research, many individuals who took part at T1 declined to continue their involvement in the study (or could not be traced at T2). A total of 114 of the original participants from 41 organizations took part in the second phase of the study, a sample attrition rate of 45.19 percent for individuals and 29.31 percent for participating organizations, respectively. However, extensive statistical tests revealed nothing to suggest that this sample attrition might have biased the findings in ways that would undermine the reliability or validity of the conclusions.

Procedure

In order to overcome the limitations of idiographic cognitive mapping procedures for investigating similarities and differences in participants' mental models of competitor definition (outlined in the main body of this chapter) a modified repertory grid approach was adopted. The competitor analysis questionnaire (CAQ) comprises a series of 21 bipolar attribute rating scales, or "constructs" in Kelly's (1955) terms (e.g., "quality of staff," "profitability," "financial resources," "amount of advertising"), which the participants used in order to evaluate their own business organization and some 19 competitors. The competitors were elicited by means of a standard list of categories, or "elements" in Kelly's (1955) terms (e.g., "my major competitor," "a solicitor agent," "an estate agent with a good reputation," "an inferior competitor"), thus ensuring that the research task was personally meaningful to the participants, yet controlled, systematic comparisons could be made at various levels of analysis.

The participants also completed a series of self-report instruments that assessed their background characteristics and behaviors (e.g. locus of control beliefs, the extent to which they scanned the business environment and whether they scanned the environment primarily for opportunities and/or threats), together with instruments designed to assess various structural, strategic and performance characteristics of their organizations.

Results

Responses to the CAQ were submitted to an advanced multivariate analysis technique known as weighted multidimensional scaling (Schiffman, Reynolds, & Young, 1981), or equivalently three-way scaling (Arabie, Carroll, & DeSarbo, 1987). This procedure revealed that a basic two-dimensional configuration derived from the full sample at T1, reflecting market power x quality, was sufficient to represent the participants' aggregate judgments, both conceptually and statistically. Further analyses of the data revealed strong commonalities in terms of the dimensional structure across organizational and functional subgroups, thus implying that in general, during the late 1980s, estate agency businesses located in the north east Midlands area of the UK enacted their competitive strategies within a two-dimensional arena, bounded by considerations of market power and quality. An examination of this configuration revealed a commonly held belief that the firms perceived as successful enjoyed greater power in the marketplace and offered a superior quality of service in comparison to their "less successful" counterparts.

Individual differences weights reflecting differences in the relative salience of the market power and quality dimensions at T1 and T2 were found to correlate meaningfully with responses to the various exogenous measures of organizational strategy, structure and performance and the background characteristics of the participants. The overall pattern emerging from these analyses suggested a self-perpetuating cycle may have been operating in this industry over the period of the study, in which the relatively strategically proactive organizations, typically the larger corporate financial services organizations, were differentially attending to the quality dimension relative to the market power dimension. Conversely, the strategically less proactive organizations (i.e. the smaller, local and regional players) were attending to the market power dimension at the relative expense of quality. Moreover, both the basic two-dimensional structure and the individual differences weights were found to remain highly stable over time, despite clear evidence of a major down turn in the marketplace from T1 to T2. Against the prevailing objective market conditions this image of competitive space was clearly an over simplification, fundamentally out of step with the performance realities of the organizations that were being held up as role models; the majority of the larger corporate estate agents were in deep financial distress during this period. Indeed, one such organization, the Prudential, eventually withdrew from the sector altogether, with accrued losses estimated in the region of £300 million.

Discussion

This study uncovered: (1) very clear evidence that there are indeed detectable empirical linkages between actors' mental models of competitor definition and a

Continued

number of exogenous variables of theoretical interest, reflecting key differences in the background characteristics of the participants, and their individual and organizational strategic behaviors and organizational performance; (2) high levels of structural convergence in the multidimensional scaling dimensional representations, with virtually no meaningful differences at the organizational and functional subgroup levels of analysis in terms of the number and nature of the dimensions characterizing the participants' judgments of competitor definition categories; and (3) high levels of stability in both the dimensionality of the representations and the relative salience of the dimensions in the face of significant changes in market conditions, all entirely in keeping with the predictions of extant theory derived from the work of Porac et al. (1989) and related formulations (e.g., Peteraf & Shanley, 1997; Porac & Thomas, 1990; Reger & Palmer, 1996). Overall, these findings provide a convincing demonstration of the deleterious role played by mental models of competitor definition in the evolution of the competitive behavior of groups of firms, powerfully illustrating from a psychological standpoint why we need well-validated techniques to improve strategic thinking.

Organizational Development and Change

José M. Peiró and Vicente Martínez-Tur

16

Overview

This chapter provides an introduction to the field of organizational change, focusing on organizational development and transformation. Four basic concepts are examined, exploring the specific features of each of them: organizational change, (re)design, development, and transformation. Next, general conditions facilitating possibilities for development and transformation are analyzed. These conditions refer to both the characteristics of external environment and internal dynamics within organizations. A case study, describing the creation of Patient Advice and Liaison Services in London, is also analyzed and interpreted considering conditions for change. In addition, theories about change are described, classifying them into "theories to explain change" and "intervention theories." The first type of theory focuses on the study of causal factors explaining change processes. Two of them (lifecycle and evolutionary) help to explain organizational development, while the other two (teleological and dialectical) extend the possibilities of change to organizational transformation. Thus, they differ in their conceptualization of the nature of organizational change. Regarding "intervention theories," four well-recognized theories are described: action-research, self-reflection, participation, and narrative-rhetorical intervention. Three contemporary methods of intervention are also analyzed (appreciative inquiry, large-group intervention, and organizational learning) as well as the differentiating roles of practitioners for organizational development and transformation. Finally, the AMIGO model is presented as a conceptual tool to understand organizations and guide organizational change.

Introduction

Psychologists and behavioral-science practitioners who advise, diagnose, and/or intervene in work systems and organizations must perforce understand processes of change, development, and transformation. Of course, they can participate in specific planned organizational changes, but understanding the nature of change is also necessary when other types of activities are carried out (e.g., personnel selection, training). For instance, when a practitioner aims to increase employees' motivation, he or she needs to anticipate the goals and purposes of the organization in order to establish behaviors that will be reinforced in the future and the manner in which employees' efforts will facilitate the required change of the organization.

Both superficial and deep changes can be continuously observed, describing one of the basic characteristics of work and organizations. This statement is, however, paradoxical. Despite its pervasiveness, people show a natural resistance towards change (Heller, 1998). We have a psychosocial need of security and stability in order to avoid uncertainty inherently associated with change, and subsequent tension and anxiety. In fact, society develops social institutions (e.g., family, government) to increase predictability and security feelings. Nevertheless, stability aspirations are unreal in an era where rapidly changing environments require organizations to anticipate and control changes, facilitating adaptation and survival. Environmental pressures derived from increasing competitiveness, globalization, and development of communication and information technologies, force organizations to manage and take advantage of organizational development and/or transformation.

This chapter introduces the subject of organizational change, especially forms of development and transformation. The following sections define the main concepts involved, discuss conditions for change, describe theories to explain change processes, review intervention theories and methods for development and transformation, and present the AMIGO model to understand organizations and to guide organizational change.

Concepts

Although this chapter focuses on development and transformation, it is necessary to refer to other topics in order to understand the nature of these types of organizational change. More specifically, we need to describe four concepts, establishing the main features of each of them. These concepts are: organizational change, (re)design, development, and transformation.

Organizational change, redesign, and development

Organizational change is the more general concept. It refers to "one type of events, is an empirical observation of difference in form, quality, or state over time in an organizational entity" (Van de Ven & Poole, 1995, p. 512). Thus, the confirmation of any difference over time in organizations can be considered as a change. Changes can be unintended and intended. Organizational (re)design, development, and transformation are three different types of intended change describing processes that vary in the manner and/or the content of the change.

The first differentiation to be described corresponds to the distinguishing characteristics of *organizational (re)design* and *organizational development*. These types of change differ in how (the manner) they act and the facets (content) of organizations they primarily focus. More specifically, redesign and development approaches differ in how they conceive organizations, change initiators, and organizational members. From the (re)design approach the *organization* is seen as a formal system where the problems should be solved by redesigning efforts (e.g., changing the distribution of tasks in the work system). When the organization has an inadequacy, it needs a concrete change to solve the specific problem. An example is Business Process Reengineering (BPR), analyzing and redesigning the workflow within and between enterprises. The complexity of the organization tends to be simplified, underestimating the role of social processes, informal forces, and knowledge of employees. The initiators of the redesign are the top managers of the organization with the expert recommendations of the consultant. They have the necessary expertise to make the change, using an empirical rational strategy where the general sequence of actions is as follows: diagnosis of problems – redesign and change – stability. Finally, it is assumed that people will accept the decisions based on expertise with a restricted participation in decision-making. This corresponds with a *classical view of human nature* where expertise pertain to consultants and top managers and where individual development needs at work are relatively neglected.

The conceptualization of the *organization* is different in the development approach. This approach views the organization as a very complex social system with formal and informal groups and, therefore, the goals of the change are not as concrete as those characterizing redesign. All employees have knowledge and competencies that could be used during the development process and, accordingly, they also are initiators of change. The consultant and top managers act as facilitators, collaborators, and co-learners with the rest of the organization. The different levels of the organization are involved in decision making and problem solving. People participate in the process of change because it is assumed that they have necessary knowledge and experience to facilitate organizational development. An *humanistic model* underlies this approach, assuming that people have individual development needs that could be satisfied at work establishing democratic decision-making at all levels of the organization.

Differences in conceptualization also influence consultant activities. Well known is the classification elaborated by Edgar Schein distinguishing between three kinds of consulting models: the "purchase of expertise model"; the "doctor–patient model," and the "process consultation model." In the "purchase of expertise model" there is a need of information or expertise that is not present at the organization. The consultant offers this information making a report and suggesting recommendations for action. In the "doctor–patient model" the organization detects problems and the consultant diagnoses the situation, identifies the causes of problems, and prescribes the actions to solve the problems. Finally, in the "process consultation model" the consultant cooperates with the

	Redesign	Development
Manner	-Initiating from formal system of the organisation -Top managers and consultants as responsibles of the change -Classical view of human nature	-Initiating from social system of the organization -Participation of all employees. Managers and consultants as facilitators -Humanistic view of human nature
Content	-Focus: hard factors -Outcome: operational efficiency	-Focus: soft factors -Outcome: operational efficiency + individual development and well-being at work

Figure 16.1:   Differences between redesign and development

leaders and groups of the organization in order to identify problems, constraints, and opportunities, formulating actions to improve the organization and achieve goals. In general, the first two categories correspond to the traditional expert model of consulting. It is intimately associated with the (re)design approach in organizations. In contrast, only the third category ("process consultation model") can be identified with the organizational development approach (French, Bell, & Zawacki, 2005; van der Vlist, 1998).

The (re)design and development approaches not only differ in how they act but also in the facets of the organization (content) they primarily focus on (figure 16.1). Because it is based on the diagnosis of specific problems, and because distance is taken by the consultant in order to analyze the organization, the (re)design approach tends to focus principally on the more visible and structural aspects of the organization (e.g., work-system, technology). These "hard" factors are usually central for redesign while social processes (e.g., communication, conflict resolution) are more secondary, at least initially. Nevertheless, and assuming interdependence between organizational facets, a change in structural or hard factors can lead to changes in social or "soft" factors.

The development approach is initially focused on changing social processes. Using group dynamics and assuming a participative, democratic, and problem-focused view, organizational development is a powerful change strategy that requires the involvement of the consultant in the internal and complex social processes of the organization, collaborating with leaders and members in order to increase effectiveness and individual development. Although organizational development is primarily interested in changing processes, this strategy can also result in structural changes. In other words, the open and democratic communication in the development approach offers opportunities to intervene in social processes of the organization (e.g., increasing participation) and in so doing, also change structures (French, Bell, & Zawacki, 2005; van der Vlist, 1998).

Another important distinction in content between (re)design and development approaches is the differential consideration of outcome or criteria variables. The (re)design approach focuses on operational efficiency, using expertise and establishing changes that aim to increase criteria such as profitability and market share. The development approach also take into account this type of criteria but outcomes involved in organizational development go beyond efficiency, including individual development and well-being at work (e.g., van der Vlist, 1998). Some scholars have criticized the vast majority of definitions (see Porras & Robertson, 1992, p. 723) and studies (see Armenakis & Bedeian, 1999, 304) for concentrating on operational efficiency, neglecting individual development. Nevertheless, humanistic and democratic values underlie organizational development and, therefore, the development approach should include aspects such as psychosocial well-being, self-actualization, and capabilities. From a European perspective, the consideration of individual development criteria is especially pertinent. Development has links with well-recognized European traditions such as the sociotechnical approaches of the Tavistock Institute in the UK. Also, action programs of the European Commission (e.g., growth and employment) aim to make compatible performance and quality of work life (see http://europa.eu.int/growthandjobs/index_en.htm).

Taking into account all these arguments, we consider that the definition by Porras and Robertson (1992) describes organizational development appropriately:

> Organizational development is a set of behavioral science-based theories, values, strategies, and techniques aimed at the planned change of the organizational work setting for the purpose of enhancing individual development and improving organizational performance, through the alteration of the organizational members' on-the-job behaviors. (p. 722)

Organizational development and organizational transformation

A second conceptual differentiation is needed between development and transformation. Organizational transformation is considered as a "second generation of organizational development" (Porras & Silvers, 1991) or as an extension of organizational development (French, Bell, & Zawacki, 2005), describing the more radical change of organizations. Traditional organizational development

---

Box 16.1:   Typology of outcomes

- Alpha: change in the levels of variables within a cultural paradigm without altering their configuration (e.g., an increment in job satisfaction).

- Beta: change in the meaning of variables within a cultural paradigm without altering their configuration (e.g., change in the importance attributed to criteria of performance evaluation).

- Gamma(A): reconfiguration of all variables within a cultural paradigm (e.g., change within the "production-driven" cultural paradigm from "cost containment" to "quality focus")

- Gamma(B): replacement of cultural paradigm with the addition of new variables (e.g., from a "production-driven" to a "customer-responsive" cultural system).

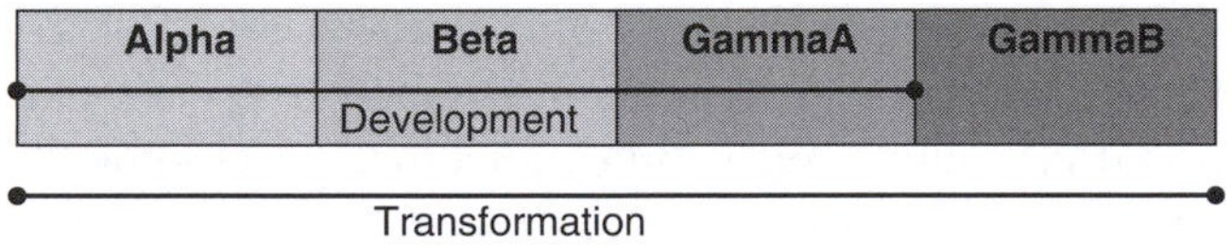

Alpha	Beta	GammaA	GammaB
	Development		

Transformation

Figure 16.2:   Development – transformation and outcomes

and transformation partially differ in the content of the change. Extending the typology of changes proposed by Golembiewski and colleagues, Porras and Silvers (1991) established four kinds of change to refer to the differential outcomes of organizational development and transformation: alpha, beta, gamma(A), and gamma(B). Definitions of these outcomes are shown in box 16.1.

The consideration of these types of change helps to differentiate between organizational development and transformation. Development is restricted to the first three types of change (alpha, beta, and gammaA), while transformation is directed to all types of change, including gammaB. Accordingly, the distinguishing characteristic of transformation is the change of the cultural paradigm of the organization (see figure 16.2).

Transformation is a radical change because the organizational cultural paradigm refers to the fundamental set of beliefs which describe the unquestioned assumptions about the organization. These assumptions reflect the "deeper causal aspects of how organizations function" (Schein, 1990), explaining other surface facets such as organizational climate, norms, and behaviors. If the cultural paradigm is changed the organization as a whole is transformed because all variables depend on the system of beliefs the organization members share as a collective. It is for this reason that transformation is also described as a revolutionary change that affects all parts of the organization simultaneously (e.g., McNulty & Ferlie, 2004). Organizational transformation requires more effort that organizational development because development uses the existing cultural paradigm to achieve desired convergent changes, while transformation needs a radical change of the essence of the organization. With this in mind, an intriguing question is to describe the conditions that make possible both development and transformation.

Conditions for change

During the last few decades there has been an increasing interest in radical organizational change or transformation (Carrero, Peiró, & Salanova, 2000). Although experiences of transformation can be found in 1960s and 1970s (e.g., with the creation of "autonomous work groups"), changes in the socio-economical context have been amplified since 1980s requiring deeper organizational changes. Increasing competition and globalization, generalization of information and communication technologies, customers demanding better products, and quality emphasis are changes that force organizations "to be transformed, not just tweaked" and, therefore, the old cultural paradigms or belief systems need to be modified, transforming organizations.

Two perspectives represent polarized positions related to the possibilities of transformation in organizations. Strategic management assumes that organizational transformation is possible, while for population ecology the cultural context constrains strategic transformation.

Strategic management assumes that managers have choice of action, playing a pivotal role in organizational change. However, other perspectives, such as population ecology, argue that the possibilities for strategic choices are very restricted. Organizations have a code established at the beginning of their lives – including norms, customs, and rituals – that determines the functioning of each organization. Immutable codes of industries and sectors (populations) need to be congruent with the characteristics of the external environment, assuming an environmental determinism where organizations that survive are those with the more congruent code. The congruence of the internal code refers to the fit extant between organizational norms, customs, and rituals, on the one hand, and environment, on the other. Three dimensions usually describe external environment (Boyd, 1990; Sharfman & Dean, 1991): *complexity* (e.g., technical complexity, diversity of products and services in the sector, geographical concentration of organizations); *dynamism* (e.g., instability of technologies and markets); and *resources availability* (e.g., competition and growth in the sector).

Studies demonstrate that radical change is difficult, but not impossible. McNulty and Ferlie (2004) describe a process of change in a UK National Health Service, evaluating the existence of important obstacles that limited the intended organizational transformation and concluding that only a "sedimented" or developmental change is possible. In contrast, Uhlenbruck, Meyer, and Hitt (2003) referred to companies located in Central and Eastern Europe with recent successful transformation processes.

In spite of difficulties some organizations are able to experience transformation. With this in mind, there is a need to explore the conditions for development and transformation. In their exciting article, Greenwood and Hinings (1996) reviewed the factors that explain the incidence of radical or transformational changes and also how quickly organizations can implement this type of change. Based on this effort, an analysis of conditions for change – not only for organizational transformation but also for development – is feasible, taking into account the central concept of cultural paradigm. Possibilities for change are based on the characteristics of the external context of the organization as well as on the internal dynamics.

Conditions of the external context

With respect to the external context, there are two relevant characteristics for change: *tight coupling* and *permeability*. Regarding tight coupling, sectors (e.g., hospitals, lodging services, sports facilities) in which specific organizations are located differ in the degree to which they have clearly legitimated organizational structures and systems – shared mechanisms and norms within the sector to orient organizational functioning (e.g., normative regulations) – and have highly articulated mechanisms to communicate and disseminate these structures and systems (e.g., ethics in professionals associations). Usually, mature sectors (e.g., medical services) have higher levels of tight coupling than less developed sectors (e.g., biotechnology). Sectors also differ in their permeability, the degree to which they are open to ideas from other sectors and, therefore, reflect dispositions to learn through the evaluation and use of other experiences. In general, tightly coupled and impermeable sectors reduce the rates of transformational change in their organizations, increasing the likelihood of convergent development changes only. The cultural paradigm of a specific organization tends to be very consolidated and resistant to change when it pertains to a tightly coupled and impermeable sector. In contrast, the cultural paradigm tends to be more disposed to transformation when the organization belongs to a weakly coupled and permeable sector.

Internal precipitating dynamics

In addition to the characteristics of the external context, there are intra-organizational dynamics that explain the acceptance or rejection of previous legitimated practices. Greenwood and Hinings distinguished between *precipitating dynamics* (interest dissatisfaction and value commitments) and *enabling dynamics* (power dependencies and capacity for action). Regarding precipitating dynamics, it is well-known that organizations have functionally differentiated groups holding different views about the purposes of the organization, actions to achieve goals, and evaluation criteria. Each coalition or group has a specific perception about the degree to which their own interests are satisfied within the organization. Taking into account that organizations differ in the size of groups or coalitions as well as in their position of advantage or disadvantage, *interest dissatisfaction* – defined as the degree to which interests of groups or coalitions are dissatisfied – vary from organization to organization, even in the same sector or market.

Given that groups could interpret a position of disadvantage as not linked to the dominant cultural paradigm, interest dissatisfaction is not sufficient to produce transformation, it is also necessary to include relationships between extant groups and the dominant culture of the organization in question. Following the review by Greenwood and Hinings (1996), *value commitments* can be defined as the patterns linking the dominant cultural paradigm to the position of advantage or disadvantage of groups or coalitions. Accordingly, four generic types of pattern can be established: (1) "status quo" commitment (all groups are committed to the dominant cultural paradigm); (2) indifferent commitment (groups are neither committed nor opposed to the dominant cultural paradigm); (3) competitive commitment (some groups prefer the dominant cultural paradigm, while other are committed to an alternative cultural paradigm); and (4) reformative commitment (all groups are opposed to the dominant cultural paradigm and they prefer an alternative). Patterns of competitive and reformative commitment facilitate organizational transformation, especially if interest dissatisfaction is high. In contrast, status quo and indifferent commitment only permits convergent changes with the dominant cultural paradigm (organizational development).

Internal enabling dynamics

The enablers of organizational transformation are *power dependencies* and *capacity for action* (enabling dynamics). Power dependencies refer to the pattern of power relationships existing in an organization, describing differences in the degree to which groups have power to promote changes congruent with their interests. Accordingly, development and transformation are only possible if groups with power promote changes. The established cultural paradigm determines the power dependencies, but market pressures (e.g., need to adapt to competitiveness) can change the power pattern of relationships within an organization.

The other enabler (capacity for action) refers to the ability to manage the process of change. This has three aspects: (a) understanding (the desired new situation); (b) managing (the process of change); and (c) having (the new skill and competencies to function in this situation). This is congruent with recent empirical evidence linking leadership to organizational change (e.g., Bommer, Rich, & Rubin, 2005). These authors observed that transformational leadership behaviors, including the display of supportive leader behavior, reduce employees' cynicism about organizational change. Transformational leadership can be considered as an indicator of capacity for action, helping to manage the process of change and reducing attitudinal obstacles. It is argued that employees are more likely to accept initiatives of leaders who care about them as individuals, especially in stressful situations. Employees who receive support from the leader are more disposed to accept the change message.

Type of change depends of the combination between value commitments and enablers. Transformation is only possible if enabler dynamics exist and alternative cultural paradigms are known and recognized (competitive or reformative value commitments). In contrast, when alternative cultural paradigms are not known and recognized (status quo and indifferent commitments) only convergent development is possible.

Intra-organizational dynamics can also explain the speed of change. Capacity for action accelerates the change because a clear understanding of the process, and of how to manage the change and act in the new situation exists. It increases feelings of security and the disposition of the organization to initiate development or transformation. In addition, a reformative commitment increases the speed in the case of an organizational transformation, while a competitive commitment leads to a more gradual transformation.

Organizational structure and change

The structure of an organization influences what type of change is more likely to occur. It is generally accepted that change is difficult in bureaucracies (see Bloodgood & Morrow, 2003). This type of structure is reliant on rules and regulations. Usually, bureaucratic organizations are located in mature and stable environments (e.g., public hospitals) characterized by clear and legitimated normative regulations (tight coupled) and low permeability. As Merton (1957) suggested, these organizations are conservative and rules are critical. Accordingly, it is reasonable to expect the status quo is reinforced by groups with power, decreasing capacity for action in these organizations. Conditions for radical change are, therefore, not generally present in bureaucratic structures and only convergent changes may be feasible and successful. The speed of any change will depend on the internal capacity for action extant in the organization in question.

In contrast, an inherent characteristic of the organic organization is its ability to adapt the structure to dynamic and uncertain environments (e.g., Lawrence & Lorsch, 1967). It assumes the existence of weakly coupled and permeable sectors, because legitimated and stable regulations hinder the dynamic adaptation of these organizations. Also, the organic structure requires the involvement of groups with power in change efforts, increasing the capacity for action. Conditions for radical change – and not only for convergent development – are present, and transformation is feasible. The speed of potential transformations will vary as a function of capacity for action and type of commitment. A combination of high capacity for action and reformative commitment increases both the likelihood of organizational transformation and speed of change.

An integrated model of conditions for change: a case study

Taking into account the previous discussion, a model to explain type of change (development versus transformation) and speed (gradual versus quickly) can be

	Development	Transformation
Quick	**Quick Development** -Tightly coupled and impermeable sector -Status quo or indifferent commitment -Enabling pattern of power dependencies -High capacity for action	**Quick Transformation** -Weakly coupled and permeable sector -Reformative commitment -Enabling pattern of power dependencies -High capacity for action
Gradual	**Gradual Development** Tightly coupled and impermeable sector -Status quo or indifferent commitment -Enabling pattern of power dependencies -Low capacity for action	**Gradual Transformation** -Weakly coupled and permeable sector -Competitive commitment -Enabling pattern of power dependencies -Low capacity for action

Figure 16.3: General conditions for change

elaborated (see figure 16.3), indicating general conditions for change. An enabling pattern of power dependencies – with powerful groups supporting change – is a general condition for all types of planned change. Type of context (e.g., permeability of the sector) and value commitments determine type of change. Finally, capacity for action and type of value commitment (the second only for transformation, distinguishing between reformative and competitive) explain variation in the speed of change.

There is a lack of empirical studies evaluating these conditions for change at the holistic level. However, there are case studies that illustrate change efforts congruent with the rationale of the model. An excellent example is the creation of Patient Advice Liaison Services (PALS) in London (see Buchanan, Abbott, Bentley, Lanceley, & Meyer, 2005). The National Health Service (NHS) initiated a 10-year "modernization" plan involving a cultural transformation to turn itself into a patient-centered organization. The development of PALS was considered as an experiment in user-driven change. Initially, PALS were conceptualized as instruments of transformation. These services were encouraged to solve customer problems on the spot or find a senior manager to negotiate resources and remove constraints. They were conceived as mechanisms to change the delivery of services and organizational culture. Buchanan et al. (2005) analyzed the development of PAL services in London recruiting six case studies and adopting a qualitative multimethod approach (semi-structured interviews, review of relevant documentation, and meetings). They observed that the promotion of substantive changes was inhibited, restricting the attributes of PALS to "repair and maintenance."

Using the factors involved in the integrated model of conditions for change (figure 16.3) and conclusions obtained by Buchanan and colleagues, an analysis and interpretation of PALS change efforts can be made. Although the National Health Service aims to obtain a cultural transformation through the creation of PAL Services, only restricted and very limited changes seem to be possible. Evidence indicates that conditions for transformation were not present in this case. First, Healthcare is a typical example of a mature, non-permeable, and tightly coupled sector with clearly legitimated and consolidated structures and systems (e.g., rules and regulations) that are communicated and disseminated, for instance through medical professional organizations. Second, a cultural change towards patient-centered organizations aims to reduce the privileged status of the medical staff. Probably, this group will be generally disposed to maintain their status quo, hindering transformation efforts. As Buchanan et al. (2005) pointed out, "even senior managers have difficulty processing change unless they can first persuade medical staff" (p. 326). Power dependencies reduce the magnitude of change, given that groups with power (medical staff) do not promote the change. Third, capacity for action is also restricted because the support and autonomy of managers are limited in a professional bureaucracy, such as the NHS, where the medical staff has been socialized through well-consolidated and disseminated structures and systems reinforced by professional associations.

Summarizing, Buchanan and colleagues concluded that PALS structures are isolated from management decision-making and, therefore, their power base is constrained and change efforts inhibited. In fact, relevant characteristics of the context where the PAL Service operates are: instability, boundary disputes, variable management support, resource limitations, and financial insecurity (Buchanan et al., 2005, p. 325).

Theories to Explain Change Processes

In addition to the general conditions for change, there is also a need to describe more refined theories of change processes related to development and transformation. This is the purpose of the present section. The theoretical development of the field describes a chaotic "potpourri" of approaches, and only the typology of theories of change processes by Van de Ven and Poole (1995) has contributed to order the topic. This typology is consolidated in the literature and it is accepted by scholars focused on organizational change (see Austin & Bartunek, 2003; Weick & Quinn, 1999). About 20 different theories were reviewed by Van de Ven and Poole, and these theories were grouped in four basic schools of thought. Two of them concentrate more on convergent development in organizations (Lifecycle Theory and Evolutionary Theory), while the other two are more appropriate in describing organizational transformation (Teleological Theory and Dialectical Theory).

Theories explaining organizational development

Lifecycle Theory. This theory uses the metaphor of organic growth to explain organizational development. It is assumed that organizations have a code or logical program that regulates the process of change. Organizations follow a sequence characterized by three aspects: (a) unitary (describing a single sequence of phases); (b) cumulative (aspects obtained in earlier phases are present in later phases); and (c) conjunctive (phases are intimately related describing a unique process of change). Progression is present given that the final state of the organization requires a historical sequence of previous phases. Each phase is necessary in order to initiate the following stage of the development. Of course, external context or environment influences organizational change, but this impact is only effective if it is congruent with the situation of the organization within its lifecycle.

Lifecycle models of organizational change have been frequently used in the 1970s and 1980s. Although the popularity of these models has declined during the last decade, there are efforts in describing organizational change that continue to use the principles of Lifecycle Theory (e.g., Cagliano, Acur, & Boer, 2005). *Entrepreneurship* and *punctuated equilibrium* are also models related to lifecycle of organizations. Regarding entrepreneurship, lifecycle is used to understand success and failure of new ventures. Punctuated equilibrium also uses lifecycle principles. It views organizational change as an incremental and extended development, only disturbed by short revolutionary periods.

Lifecycle Theory of change helps to understand organizational development but seems less useful when the purpose is to describe organizational transformation. Taking into account Lifecycle principles, organizational change is viewed as prescribed, prespecified development, with incremental changes characterized by predictability and stability of the cultural paradigm of the organization. Changes do not question the underlying dominant belief system and, therefore, Lifecycle Theory focuses on convergent organizational development.

Evolutionary Theory. In evolutionary theory development is viewed as cumulative changes in structural forms of populations of organizations within a sector or the society as a whole. Change is based on a continuous cycle of variation, selection, and retention. Variation refers to the creation of new organizational forms, assuming that this change emerges by chance. Selection reflects competition for resources existing in the external context or environment. Finally, retention describes forces that perpetuate and maintain the organizational form. Survival is based on the organizational ability to respond to environmental pressures. Once the new organizational form is created (variation) and it is adapted to its environment (selection), retention tends to maintain previous practices and forms. Changes are cumulative and recurrent, describing a probabilistic progression where the population or organization follows the prescribed dynamics.

The aforementioned *population ecology* perspective is based on evolutionary principles. This approach helps to understand and explain empirical changes in organizations (e.g., Burt, 2000). In addition, two more recent models of organizational change are inspired by these principles: *internal change routines* and *institutional change*. From internal change routines, it is assumed that variation, selection, and retention of routines are also present within each specific organization. Organizational routines tend to be more and more sophisticated as they are used, including modification routines. These routines permit the organization to adapt to changes maintaining stability over time. Organizational expertise of modification routines increases and similar changes can be initiated in the future. For instance, Amburgey, Kelly, and Barnett (1993) observed this pattern of change in the Finnish newspaper industry. Change actions are institutionalized and future organizational change is predictable and inertial. To some degree, these ideas underlie the other model of organizational change (institutional change), but focus the attention on the pressures of environment. It is argued that ideas, values, and beliefs of the environment explain organizational functioning. A strong institutional environment legitimates the type of change possible in organizations. Given that the environment institutionalizes and restricts a limited number of organizational actions (e.g., using normative regulations of professional associations), predictability and stability of type of change increase in order to adapt the organization to the pressures of the institutional environment.

Evolutionary Theory helps to understand organizational development but not transformation. It is assumed that only convergent change is possible maintaining and reinforcing previous actions congruent with the dominant cultural paradigm. Accordingly, organizational practices are institutionalized, formulating cumulative, recurrent, and predictable changes, and excluding divergent transformation efforts.

Theories explaining organizational transformation

Teleological Theory. This school of thought proposes that purposes or goals determine change. Congruent with this idea, change is viewed as purposeful and, therefore, organizations are able to formulate a final and desired state, to design and implement actions to achieve this state, and to monitor the process of change. Change emerges when organizational members perceive a discrepancy between their current actions and the desired goals. Although this theory recognizes environmental obstacles and resource constraints that limit the possibilities of action, creativity underlies Teleological Theory because it is assumed organizations are free to design their own purposes and actions. Accordingly, there is not a necessary sequence of stages describing how the organization will act.

The aforementioned *strategic management* perspective follows the principle of Teleological Theory, assuming that managers are able to change the organization and its environment. Two related models of organizational change also incorporate the rationale of this theory: *cognitive framing theories* and *theories of innovation*. Cognitive framing theories attribute importance to the role of the cognitive change managers are able to provoke in their organizations. They are forced to build a new conceptualization of the organization and its external context or environment, facilitating cognitive consensus about the need of a change among organizational members (see Hodgkinson, chapter 15 in this book). Regarding the other model of change, theories of innovation argue that change is based on individual creativity combined with the characteristics of the group and the organization. A complex multilevel approach is proposed where the creativity of the individual is interrelated to the opportunities and constraints for innovation existing in the group or team and the organization as a whole. For example, Oldham and Cummings (1996) presented empirical evidence congruent with this multilevel approach to innovation and creativity.

Because Teleological Theory excludes predetermined, congruent, and predictable sequences of change – emphasizing an active role for the organization to implement an envisioned and desired purpose – this theory goes beyond development, incorporating possibilities of transformation. Individuals (e.g., managers) can help to build a divergent and new cultural paradigm to adapt the organization to environmental pressures. Recently, Teleological Theory has obtained popularity among scholars (e.g., Bloodgood & Morrow, 2003). As Austin and Bartunek (2003) indicated, some topics are now central in research: the manner in which organizations accomplish their purposes; the role of managers; the cognitive processes involved in change; and change resistance. All these aspects of the Teleological Theory involve divergence with the past.

Dialectical Theory. This school of thought assumes a conceptualization of the world where opposing values and forces compete for domination and control. These conflicts can describe opposing interests between groups within a specific organization and/or conflicting interests between different organizations. The possibilities of change are determined by the balance of power existing in the parties of a conflict, following a Hegelian process of thesis and antithesis. Change only occurs when the opposing values and interests of an alternative group or coalition (antithesis) have sufficient power to challenge the values and interests of the dominant coalition or group (thesis), producing a new situation (synthesis).

At least two models of change follow the principles of the Dialectical Theory: *schematic change* and *communicative change theories.* Schematic change assumes that change requires a modification in the shared schemas (cognitive frameworks to provide meaning and structure to the information) of the organization. Organizations have schemas to interpret their internal functioning and external environments. Current schemas (thesis) should be compared with a new schema (antithesis) in order to provoke change to other frameworks to interpret the organization and its environment (synthesis). The modification of schemas is present in radical change or transformation, increasing the possibilities of adaptation to important changes in the environment (e.g., Kostera & Wicha, 1996).

The other models of dialectical change, communicative change theories, are based on social construction. They argue that change is possible by social interaction and using conversation and other forms of communication. When communication is used, different understandings about the organization are evinced, increasing the possibilities that a new synthesized view emerges and can be diffused (for an analysis of empirical studies using this model, see Grant, Michelson, Oswick, & Wailes, 2005).

As in the case of Teleological Theory, Dialectical Theories view change as a rupture with the past. Thus, organizational development, in terms of congruent, recurrent, and predetermined change, is not considered. In contrast, both schematic and communicative changes help to explain radical change or organizational transformation. Change and replacement of the dominant cultural paradigm require a modification in the manner in which organizations provide meaning and structure to the information (schemas) as well as new languages and concepts (communicative change).

Combination of theories in explaining change

Figure 16.4 shows the main distinguishing characteristics between theories about development, on the one hand, and theories about transformation, on the other, related to the conceptualization of change. Nevertheless, Van de Ven and Poole (1995) argued that the consideration of only one theoretical perspective of organizational change is incomplete and represented a partial view of a complex phenomenon. Accordingly, they argue it is "the interplay between different perspectives that helps one gain a more comprehensive understanding of organizational life" (p. 511). Confirming this proposition, some theoretical models use principles from different theories simultaneously. For example, the aforementioned punctuated equilibrium combines lifecycle principles with teleological aspects, viewing organizational change from an evolution-revolution framework with an extended period of incremental evolution interspersed with short revo-

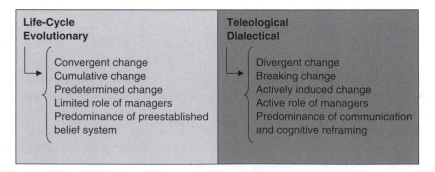

Figure 16.4:   Main differences between developmental and transformational theories in understanding change

lutionary events (see Austin & Bartunek, 2003). The combination of theories is, therefore, a challenge for scholars in order to explain organizational change more accurately.

Practice

One of the most important limitations in the area of organizational development and transformation is the division existing between practitioners and academics. Ideally, practice and research should be intimately interrelated, but there are important constraints in order to achieve collaboration and mutual reinforcement. For example, practitioners and academics have different goals. Academics aim to explain change processes, using theories described in the previous section, while practitioners aim to solve practical problems assuming theoretical models of implementation/intervention and using specific methods. Nevertheless, there are recent efforts to integrate research and practice (Austin & Bartunek, 2003). Based on this effort, the present section describes theories of intervention/implementation and methods, linking these topics to the theories to explain change processes. Also, differential strategies oriented to development versus transformation will be discussed.

Theories of intervention

Intervention theories refer to how actions provoke changes and what actions can be considered in order to achieve organizational development and transformation. Austin & Bartunek (2003) propose the existence of four approaches to intervention, using literature written for practitioners: *action-research, participation, self-reflection*, and *narrative-rhetorical intervention*. The main characteristics of these intervention theories and their links with theories of change processes are described below.

Action-Research. Original models of action-research focused on problem-solving actions in order to provoke changes that also contribute to theory. Typically, it includes six stages: (1) preliminary diagnosis; (2) data gathering from the organization; (3) data feedback to the organization; (4) data exploration by the organization; (5) action planning by the organization; and (6) action implementation by organizational members. More contemporary models of action-research also emphasize a direct comparison between action and theory. For example, *action learning* proposes that groups or teams try to understand social theories applying them to solve a real problem. In general, Action-Research approach is very adaptable, given that the process of research and action can be intentionally oriented to cope with different types of problems or situations. In fact, it can help to facilitate the different types of change described in the four theories used to explain change processes (lifecycle, evolutionary, teleological, and dialectical) (Austin & Bartunek, 2003) and, conversely, action-research can offer data and information contributing to advances in these theories.

Self-Reflection. Self reflection considers leaders to be central to organizational transformation. Leaders need to reflect while they are acting, responding to changing situations by creating new beliefs, values, and interests. Accordingly, leaders should be empowered to be change agents with a high level of responsibility for the change, and able to evaluate contradictions in the organization, change the cultural paradigm, and constantly question organizational assumptions. This empowerment is especially linked to the aforementioned Teleological theory of change processes. The leader is seen as a purposeful change agent, formulating desired final states and facilitating radical changes in organizations.

Participation. This intervention theory posits change is achieved using employees' participation. The role of participation in organizational change varies from a restricted view, assuming that employees will accept decisions if they participate in the decision making, to a more expanded and democratic system where employees contribute with their knowledge questioning organizational practices. To some degree, this extended participation is the complement of the leaders' self-reflection. Employees can collaborate in the creation of new beliefs, values, and interests, increasing their responsibility in problem solving and in the formulation and achievement of organizational desired purposes. Thus, there is a direct relation between expanded participation and the Teleological Theory of change processes.

Narrative-Rhetorical Intervention. This intervention theory assumes that persons partially create their organizational reality by recounting previous experiences and communicating future-oriented images of the organization that can be achieved by action. Different and controversial images of the future could be shared among organizational members to facilitate a consensus about the goals of the organization and their relationships with previous organizational experiences and future problems and opportunities. This intervention theory has direct connections with the Dialectical Theory of change processes, establishing opportunities for organizational transformation. In other words, new images of the organization could question previous assumptions, provoking radical changes.

In sum, although all theories of change processes could be considered given the adaptability of the action-research approach, intervention approaches are primarily linked to theories explaining transformation, especially Teleological Theory. It is possible practitioners overestimate the potential of organizational members to provoke significant and radical change, neglecting the impact of lifecycle and evolutionary principles. Also, environmental changes in the 1980s and beyond have reduced the emphasis on organizational development, increasing the interest in transformation.

Methods of intervention

It is not possible to list the large number of methods used for organizational development and transformation. Although there are approaches traditionally linked to organizational development, such as T-Group training and survey feedback (Peiró,

González-Romá, & Cañero, 1999; Van der Vlist, 1998), this section presents a short description of more contemporary methods (Austin & Bartunek, 2003).

Appreciative Inquiry. This is a recent and very popular method for intervention with three basic assumptions: (1) organizational members create their own reality by dialogue and enactment; (2) all organizations have positive elements; (3) change is promoted by creating consensus about positive elements of the organization, avoiding negative aspects and increasing the positive. Practitioners should be able to provoke positive future images within the organization.

Large-Group Interventions. At this moment, there is an great number of large-group methods of interventions (future search, real-time strategic change, open space technology, search conferences, participative design workshops, simu-real, workout, conference model, ICA strategic planning process) (e.g., Bunker & Alban, 1996), with two basic characteristics (Austin & Bartunek, 2003). First, it is assumed that thinking on future preferences is more motivating for employees than analyzing previous organizational problems. Accordingly, these methods are oriented to the desired purposes for the future. Secondly, they emphasize the participation of the organization as a whole or at least a large number of representatives. The contemporary popularity of large-group interventions is due to the prominence of organizational transformation, and it requires the participation of all levels of the organizations in the process of radical change.

Organizational Learning. There are different approaches to increase organizational learning. From developmental and transformational perspectives, all of them are based on the idea that organizations and their members are able to learn in order to improve and create new future scenarios. Taking into account the review by Austin and Bartunek (2003), learning can involve different objectives and procedures: (1) systems thinking (provoking the learning of the interdependencies existing in the organization and its environment); (2) personal mastery (promoting lifelong learning); (3) mental models (developing reflection, awareness, and test of personal and organizational assumptions); (4) building shared vision (developing shared images about the future); (5) team learning (promoting group interaction to increase individual insights through dialogue, discussion, and diagnosis of interaction patterns in teams that reduce learning); and (6) learning histories (learning from previous experiences about large organizational changes).

These three methods combine theories explaining organizational transformation (teleological theory and dialectical theory). In fact, they propose the consideration of future desired objectives (teleological) and the creation of the organization and new shared images of future through dialogue and enactment (dialectical).

Practitioner roles for development and transformation

Contemporary intervention theories (e.g., self-reflection) and methods (e.g., large-group interventions) tend to be more focused on transformation than on development, describing the prominence of radical change during the last few years. However, the use of intervention theories and methods is flexible, and they could be adapted to the content of the change. The focus on development or transformation also depends on the role of the practitioner or change agents (see Weick & Quinn, 1999). To facilitate organizational transformation and, therefore, a change in the cultural paradigm, the practitioner should be very effective in using language, speaking differently, presenting clearly and persistently a new schema with alternative beliefs and values, and demonstrating that a successful radical change is needed. In contrast, if the focus is on convergent organizational development the role of practitioner is partially different. Convergent and less ambitious changes could be planned but these changes can also be spontaneous and continuous within organizations (e.g., new individual actions). When convergent development is required, it increases the importance of the ability to make sense of planned and emerging changes congruent with the cultural paradigm, recognizing and making them more salient, reframing and redirecting continuous and convergent changes when it is necessary, and promoting a shared meaning and a common process of thinking.

At this moment, with the increasing interest in organizational transformation, the importance of incremental changes could be unfairly underestimated. Small and convergent continuous changes can prepare the organization for episodes of transformational change. Successful radical changes need to be attributed to transformational efforts but also to the connection with the past. Similarly to the necessary research efforts devoted to the integration of theories explaining processes of development and transformation, the challenge for practitioners is to be able to take advantage of both previous organizational development and potential radical change.

AMIGO: A Model to Guide Organizational Development and Transformation

To finish the present chapter, we present a short description of the AMIGO (Analysis, Management and Intervention Guidelines for Organizations) model (Peiró, 1999; 2000). This is a conceptual tool for organization intervention and management that helps to understand the facets and functioning of the organization, guiding organizational change efforts. Variables involved are classified into five blocks that are described below (see figure 16.5) (Peiró, 2000).

Paradigmatic and strategic facets. The first block corresponds to the paradigm of the organization, including culture, mission, and vision, and strategic facets related to the environment pressures and opportunities. It also takes into consideration the services and goods produced by the organization.

Hard facets. The second block includes four types of hard facets: economic resources and infrastructure; organizational structure; technology; and work system. The work system is the critical facet of the "hard" block. It is defined as

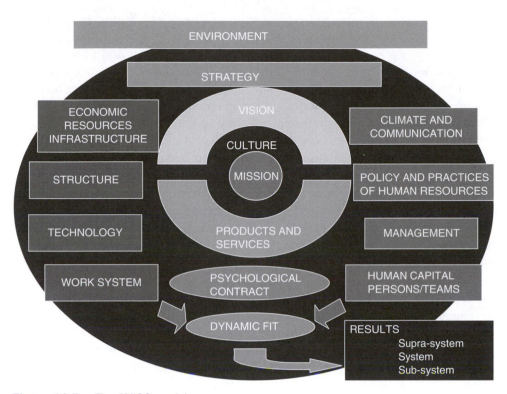

Figure 16.5: The AMIGO model

the set of arrangements to design, produce and sell the goods and services provided by the company, as well as to perform any other activities aiming to this end. The technology, the structure and the infrastructure and material resources of the organization are meant to contribute to the effective and efficient functioning and operation of the work system.

Soft facets. The third block corresponds to four types of soft organizational facets: communication and climate; policies and practices of human resource management; organizational management; and human capital (individuals and groups). In a parallel way to what it was presented in the previous block, human capital (individual and groups) is the central facet of the "soft" block. All the other soft facets should contribute to the best performance and development of this human capital.

Integrating facets. These facets involve two critical adjustments in organizations. First, adjustment between individuals and groups (human capital), on the one hand, and the work system of the organization, on the other. Because characteristics of persons are critical, this adjustment is essential for the production of goods and services, the achievement of organizational goals, and the fulfillment of the mission. Second, the psychological contract, describing mutual expectations of employees and employers about work conditions, performance, and other transactional and relational aspects, also plays an important role, extending the notion of dynamic fit between the individuals and teams and the work system to the fit between the individuals expectations and the values, human resources policies and practices, styles of management and many other facets of the organization. Promises and deals between employer and employees (individually and collective) play an important role in building the psychological contract which is one of the core facets in the model because it deals with the degree of integration between the organization and its members.

Organizational outcomes. Organizational outcomes are catalogued into three categories: outcomes for the supra-system (outcomes for the society as a whole, clients, etc.), for the system (outcomes related to the survival, improvement and development of the organization as a system), and for the sub-systems (compensation, satisfaction of interests and development of individuals and groups). Moreover these outcomes are to be considered in the short and the middle term and a balance between achieving ones while not impeding or hampering the others is important.

The model assumes interdependencies between the different facets of the organization. Modifications in one specific facet could lead to changes in other parts of the organization. It also assumes dynamism of the organization and change produces misfit between previous well fitted facets and then processes intended to find new congruence between facets are released. Different types of organizations are feasible if they show congruence among their parts or facets. Accordingly, there is not a better organizational form. In addition, the AMIGO model considers culture as central in order to define and understand organizations. Thus, under certain circumstances change is so radical and deep that the culture of the organization alters producing a *transformational change*. So, as they are defined in this chapter, different types of change are primarily focused on specific blocks of factors. *Organizational redesign* is centered on hard factors, although subsequent changes in soft factors most probably will be induced. In contrast, *organizational development* focuses change efforts on soft factors (e.g., communication) that can also influence hard factors. These two types of change are limited because they focus on specific facets of the organization and predominant culture is not changed. Only transformation provokes a radical change in the cultural paradigm through organizational learning. Because culture is the deeper causal factor involved in the organizational functioning as a whole, describing its beliefs' system, transformation tends to change all parts or the organizational simultaneously.

The model proposes that organizational change can be *reactive* or *proactive* (anticipatory). Reactive changes follow an *outside–inside* sequence in the relation between the organization and its environment. In other words, changes in the external environment create a need to change and organizations are forced to react and adapt their functioning to survive. In contrast, proactive changes are based on an *inside–outside* sequence where organizations are able to anticipate environmental changes, reorientate their functioning to be prepared for the future, and, to some degree, modify their own organizational environment.

Proactive changes are especially recommendable, given the interdependencies extant between the facets of organizations. However, changes in the environment often go first and afterwards organizations try to adapt. The AMIGO model provides a framework to better understand change patterns in organizations. Chambel, Peiró, and Pina (1999) studied retrospectively eight Portuguese ceramics companies and found that all of them experienced a largely reactive change ahead of market changes produced by the import of products from Asia. Seven out of the eight companies decided to initiate a strategy of cost reduction through investment in new technology and one decided to change their products and to go into a new market niche producing hand painted artistic ceramics. Those who incorporated new technology had to change their work system considerably. Some of the companies also carried out some restructuring and a few were acquired by or merged with another company. All these changes improved the performance of the eight companies, however this "redesign" approach to change showed several malfunctions of the soft facets. People was not well trained and prepared for the change, management – specially at the lower levels – had to change their roles and functions and in several cases supervisors had to be replaced with younger people with another profile. Human resources management policies and practices had to be revised. In fact, any change in one facet can influence the dynamic and complex equilibrium between facets underlying organizations. Special attention is due to the psychological contract between employees and employers (mutual expectations and perceived commitments) when changes are large, broad and fast. In fact, Chambel and Peiró (2003) – using the AMIGO model as framework – observed in this sample of ceramic companies violations of psychological contract mainly related to changes in human resources practices. In addition, employees who perceived that human resources practices violated their psychological contracts indicated lesser job satisfaction and greater turnover intentions than those who maintained their previous psychological contracts. Thus, caution and pro-action are necessary and adequate stages are required in planned changes.

In sum, the AMIGO model provides a framework to better analyze the different factors of an organization under a taxonomy that distinguishes paradigmatic–strategic, hard–soft, and integrative–outcome facets. Moreover, the analysis of the interrelationships and interdependence between facets provides a guide to identify either congruence or misfit between them. Finally, a dynamic consideration of the model suggests that any change in one or more facets can require changes in the others. The rationale of the model makes it possible to identify several patterns of change on the basis of whether the change starts in the environment or within the organization and thus, whether it is mainly proactive or reactive. This is a helpful heuristic model to guide the successive sequence of changes in the organization one an intervention or a change has been started in one or several facets.

Summary

This chapter focuses on organizational development and transformation. These approaches view the organization as a complex social system where the change is only possible with the participation of the different organizational levels and employees. Transformation is an extension of development. While development describes changes congruent with the dominant cultural paradigm of the organization, transformation is a more radical change including the replacement of culture. Subsequently, transformation requires certain types of external (weakly coupled and permeable sector) and internal (recognition of alternative cultural paradigms) conditions to be effective.

Four basic theories are established in the literature in understanding processes of development and transformation. Some theories focus on development (lifecycle and evolutionary) and others on transformation (teleological and dialectical). The first type of theories views change as convergent, cumulative, and predetermined. In contrast, the second conceive change as divergent, breaking, and actively induced.

There are also theories linked to practitioner efforts devoted to provoke changes. More specifically, four well-recognized intervention theories are described: action-research, self-reflection, participation, and narrative-rhetorical. Additionally, contemporary methods of intervention are presented: appreciative inquiry, large-group interventions, and organizational learning. Both intervention theories and methods tend to be more focused on transformation than on development, reflecting the contemporary trend towards radical changes. Nevertheless, methods are flexible and focus on development versus transformation also depends on practitioner role.

The chapter finishes with the description of the AMIGO model. This model represent the main facets of the organization, guiding change efforts and providing a framework to better understand different type of changes in organizations and their dynamics.

Discussion Points

You are examining if a specific organization presents conditions for transformation. What type of variables would you consider to diagnose the possibilities of transformation?

A client organization needs an ambitious transformation program. What combination of intervention approaches and methods would you use?

Key Studies

Henderson, L. J., and Mayo, E. (1936). The effects of social environment. *Journal of Industrial Hygiene and Toxicology*, 18, 401–6. This article describes two of the more influential experiments at the Haw- thorne Plant of the Western Electric Company, remarking the complexity and informal character of groups in under- standing, intervening, and changing the organizations.

Trist, E., and Bamforth, K. (1951). Some social and psychological consequences of the Long-wall method of goal-getting. *Human Relations, 4*, 1–38. This article describes one of the earlier studies on sociotechnical systems theory and quality of working life, emphasizing participation in groups and optimization of technical and social systems in order to understand and change organizations.

Further Reading

Carter, L., et al. (2005). *Best practices in leadership development and organization change*. San Francisco: Pfeiffer. This book describes 18 successful real experiences on organizational development and change, offering practical "how-to" advice on how implement organizational change.

French, W. L., et al. (2005). *Organization development and transformation*. New York: McGraw-Hill. The new of edition of this book describes classic elements about organizational development but also offers innovations and new directions, differentiating between development and transformation.

Rothwell, W. J., et al. (1995). *Practicing organization development. A guide for consultants*. San Francisco: Jossey-Bass/Pfeiffer. This book offers to consultants a practical guide to design and implement organizational development, with a comprehensive and systematic description of stages.

Sange, P., et al. (1995). *The dance of change*. New York: Doubleday. This is an intriguing book that discuss about the difficulties to implement changes, especially when these changes need to be extended over time, offering guides for practice.

Research Close-Up

Bommer, W. H., Rich, G. A., and Rubin, R. S. (2005). Changing attitudes about change: Longitudinal effects of transformational leader behavior on employee cynicism about organizational change. *Journal of Organizational Behavior, 26*, 733–53.

Introduction

The authors indicated that there is little empirical data about processes of change and the causal factors involved, while research efforts are traditionally concentrated on conceptual models, the context of change, and organizational effectiveness. For this reason, they aimed to study the impact of leader behaviors on employees' attitudes about change. It is generally recognized that employees tend to show some irrational resistance to change, but successful change efforts indicate that positive attitudes and acceptance of change are possible. Are leader behaviors explaining a reduction of employees' resistance to change? To respond to this question, the authors tested the relationship between transformational leader behaviors (e.g., providing intellectual stimulation) and employees' cynicism about change (describing the futility of change and a loss of faith on those who are responsible of the change), expecting that transformational behaviors reduce employees cynicism.

Participants

Participants were employees from three privately owned manufacturing firms: a textile manufacturer, an electronics refurbisher,

Continued

and a manufacturer of machined metal products. In time 1, 89 percent of the population (N = 877) of the three companies answered usable surveys, but the percentage of usable surveys reduced to 64 percent (N = 561) in time 2. Of these, 372 remained with their same supervisors. Given that the authors tested the aforementioned relationship using a longitudinal approach, the final sample consisted of 372 employees who maintained their same supervisors through two time periods.

Design and procedure

The authors designed and conducted a survey field study, with measures of transformational leader behaviors and cynicism about change as well as control variables such as structure, other leader behaviors, and attitudinal variables. The employee surveys were administered on-site at the manufacturing companies. The data were collected at two different time points to make a longitudinal test of proposed relationships, with time 2 occurring 9 months after time 1. In the five years prior to time 1, the three companies experienced changes related to growth, with an increment of hiring and professionalism.

Results

The results confirmed the hypothesis of the study. Perceptions of transformational leader behaviors in time 1 had a significant negative impact on employees' cynicism about change in time 2. This reduction of cynical attitudes over time was observed once the influence of cynicism in time 1 and control variables was considered in statistical analysis.

Discussion

The most important contribution of this research study is that change agents who engage in transformational leader behaviors reduce cynicism about change, decreasing resistance. Thus, transformational behaviors can be used in processes of selection and training of supervisors, especially when change events are anticipated.

Mergers and Acquisitions through Perspectives of Work and Organizational Psychology and Management

17

Handan Kepir Sinangil and
Asli Küçükaslan

Overview

Globalization, along with fierce competition and ever-changing economic circumstances, has been forcefully leading organizations towards structural change. Especially during the recent years, organizational downsizing, mergers, acquisitions, and the role of the human factor in strategic partnerships have formed some of the fundamental research topics.

Although research concerning mergers and acquisitions has dramatically increased during the last decades, historically its first application or "the first merger wave" dates back to the 1800s. Various studies have been published regarding this topic, yet the research conducted after 1970s started to emphasize the role of human resources in the success of organizational mergers and acquisitions.

What are Mergers and Acquisitions?

What is a "merger" and what an "acquisition"? The definition of a "merger" generally reflects the consolidation of two organizations into a single organization successfully. A merger is joining of two companies into one larger company. Mergers are commonly voluntary and involve stock swap or cash payment to the target. A merger results in a new company name (often combining the names of the original companies) and in new branding.

On the other hand an acquisition is the joining of two unequal companies where the large one is buying the small one and combining the two with the dominance of the acquirer company.

Borys and Jemison (1989) suggest that the concept of mergers refers to the aspect of business strategy and management dealing with the merging of different companies. Usually these occur in a friendly setting where officers in each company involved get together.

Doz and Hamel (1998) imply that mergers and acquisitions are the combinations that have the greatest implications for investment, control, integration requirements, structural and cultural issues, and human resource aspects.

Schuler and Jackson (2001, p. 240) define the difference between mergers and acquisitions as:

> in a merger, two companies get together and create a new entity. In an acquisition, one company buys another one and manages it consistent with the acquirer's needs . . .

Reasons for mergers and acquisitions

As we have emphasized, mergers and acquisitions are considered a strategic way of creating synergy in today's business world, but furthermore there are some other causes of mergers such as environmental, financial, managerial, legal, and technical, as shown in figure 17.1. It is also possible to expand on the causes of mergers and acquisitions with the items in table 17.1.

Table 17.1:   The main causes of mergers and acquisitions

Economic factors	• to decrease the production costs • to benefit from the economies of scale • to combine the supplementary resources
Managerial factors	• strengthening the competencies of management • synergy • growth • gaining more experience
Financial factors	• using the funds • low financial costs • increasing the worth of stakeholders • low risk
Marketing factors	• entering the new markets • developing the distribution channels • enhancing competitive advantage
Fiscal and Legal factors	• tax advantage • customs law • having valuable industrial rights
Technical factors	• developing and using higher technology • developing quality
Other factors	• psychological factors • political factors

Source: Aypar Topkara Uslu (1997). Strategic mergers as an important tool in internationalism, *Öneri Journal, 2(7)*, p. 22.

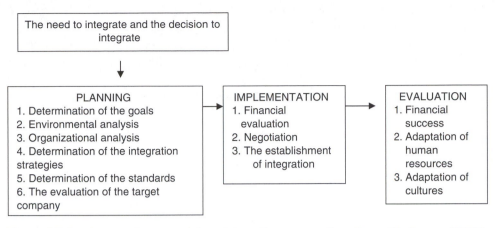

Figure 17.1:   A strategic approach to an integration process (from Beyza Oba Furman (1989). International mergers in the frame of strategic management. 3rd Congress of National Business Administration, Kapadokya, p. 292)

The critical processes of mergers and acquisitions

When mergers and acquisitions are examined strategically, it can be realized that the integration process is composed of 3 main stages. As figure 17.1 shows, those stages are as follows:

a.   Planning of integration
b.   Implementation stage
c.   Evaluation and result stage.

Planning of integration   Waalevijin and Segaar (1993, p. 24) refer to two main subjects that are considered during M&A planning:

• The determination and evaluation of the suitable company.
• The organization and consideration of the legal, financial, and technical issues.

M&A planning is certainly considered with a strategic approach. Since M&As are important strategies, those processes require a strategic planning process.

Implementation stage   In this stage, after the evaluation of the companies, financial evaluations are executed and the essential subjects are discussed through the negotiations. According to the result of the negotiations and compromise, the integration process comes out. Moreover, the proposals of merger or acquisition are discussed, the opinions of both sides are expressed and the last decisions are stated in this stage (Jemison & Sitkin, 1996).

Evaluation and result stage In this stage, the consistency of the integration process with the aims, strategies, policies and goals that are determined at the planning stage is controlled and the outcome information is checked by feedback (Butler, Ferris, & Napier, 1991). Hence, it can be looked over the integration process.

Butler et al. (1991, p. 199) list the substages existing in the evaluation stage as follows:

*   The evaluation of financial success.
*   The evaluation of the new organizational structure.
*   The evaluation of cultural consistency.
*   The evaluation of human resources systems and adaptation.

Scale and Scope of Merger and Acquisitions

From the end of the 1980s onwards, the increasing number of studies and publications regarding mergers and acquisitions has been surprising. The goal of mergers and acquisitions has been demonstrated as increasing the strength, efficiency and profit of an organization. However, the numbers point out that in many companies this goal has not been fully met, and moreover billions of dollars have been wasted in the endeavor. Many studies indicate that this loss is due to the failure in resolving managerial as well as employee related problems, rather than technological and economic issues. According to Terry and Callan (1998) employees generally show a strong resistance to the merging process. Some frequent aspects include, inter and intra group hostility and conduct, prejudice against the employees of the "other" company and pessimistic attitudes. In light of these, many merger and acquisition researchers point out that management has a responsibility regarding the preparation, transition and postpreparation stages.

On the other hand, Wang (1994) states that as a result of economic reforms and China's endeavors in "opening up to the world," established mergers and strategic partnerships have proved efficient. According to the statistics, in 1990 China formed 25.000 companies involving M&As. Eighty percent of these are part of the production sector, with the remaining ones functioning in various other sectors. Eighty-five percent of these partnerships are among the most successful and high performance establishments. The People's Republic of China has a Human Resources Management special law regarding organizational mergers and foreign partnerships. This law encompasses regulations regarding recruitment, selection, lay-offs and resignations, compensation, reward systems, employee insurance, discipline, and employee protection. Other than foreign partnerships and company mergers, Chinese companies employ various different human resources practices, attracting the attention of many researchers. In the studies conducted in 1990 and 1992, Wang has revealed that leadership style and decision making authority are crucial factors in maintaining the efficiency of partnerships, and that a country's culture and values also affect workplace behavior.

Created by the waves of globalization and expected increase in volume in the coming years, the mergers, acquisitions and foreign partnerships have to pay careful attention to the subsystems of the human factor, management and leadership in order to reach the goal of growth and increasing profits.

Mergers begin with people and end due to people. When reasons for the failure of organizational M&As are examined, neglect of human resources factors such as management, leadership styles, organizational culture, and strategic communication, has been found to be a major cause.

Management and leadership research point out that the managerial styles in organizations directly affect company performance and the turnover of labor. During the process of mergers and acquisitions, employees of the two organizations are faced with a different managerial style under equal or non-equal conditions (for example downsizing). The differences encountered by the employees are not only in the management/manager area. Individuals are also troubled by the challenges of new colleagues, communication styles, superior–subordinate relations, the physical environment, differences in mutual expectations and more changes resulting from the organizational culture.

Companies today need to grow fast, become efficient, profitable, flexible, adaptable, and have a dominant market position. Without these qualities, firms believe that it is virtually impossible to be competitive in today's global economy. In some industries such as insurance or banking, firms may enter new markets. In others such as pharmaceuticals or software technology, firms may work with smaller firms that have developed or are developing new products that they can manufacture and/or distribute more efficiently, while some of the firms focus on their own internal growth, leadership and development.

"Mergers and acquisitions are becoming a popular strategic option for organizations" (Schraeder & Self, 2003, p. 511). According to Buono, Bowditch, and Lewis (1985) and Cartwright and Cooper (1999), goals for this strategy converge around themes including growth, diversification, financial and managerial aspects and achieving economies of scale. As Marks and Mirvis (1998) pointed out, obtaining a global presence is also acknowledged as a motive for mergers or acquisitions.

Many of the largest and most successful global firms like DaimlerChrysler, Chase-J.P. Morgan, McKinsey-Envision, UBS-Paine Webber, Credit Sussie-DLJ, Celltech-Medeva, SKB-Glaxo, NationsBank-Bank of America, AOL-Time Warner, Pfizer-Warner Lambert, Nestlé-Purina, Deutsche Telekom-Voice Stream, and GE-Honeywell have been involved in M&A processes (Schuler & Jackson, 2001).

Mergers have become increasingly common in both North American and United Kingdom healthcare sectors in the past 20 years. Between 1996 and 2001 in the healthcare sector in England, 99 healthcare provider mergers were formalized among acute care, mental health, and community health services providers. (Fulopa et al., 2005)

An Evaluation Whether Mergers and Acquisitions Have Been Successful

The primary purpose of merging and acquiring new firms is usually to improve overall performance of the organization, or to attain certain economies of scale; and to achieve synergy effects between two business units that will increase their competitive advantage (Porter, 1985; Weber, 1996). Recent research indicates that most M&As have a negative impact on the economic performance of the organization. In fact, it is estimated that 60 to 80 percent of all mergers fail to achieve their financial and strategic goals (Appelbaum & Gandell, 2003).

Lasn (2005) states that at the end of 1990s, a rapid increase occurred in the amount and financial value of the mergers. Time Warner and American Online (AOL), DuPont, General Motors, General Electric, Citicorp and Travelers Group, SBS and Ameritech are examples of mergers established in the United States. Between 1997 and 1999 the financial value of mergers in the United States reached up 2.8 trillion dollars.

The same tendencies were observed in Europe as well, especially when European Union was established. In 1997, European Union companies actualized 7,100 mergers and acquisitions. The value of the mergers in 1999 was 1.5 trillion dollars and in 2000, 2 trillion dollars, and England was the champion of the year (Gedikkaya & Gürler, 1999).

Reasons for success

According to Schuler and Jackson (2001, p. 242), some of the major reasons for success in mergers and acquisitions include:

- Leadership
- Well-thought out goals and objectives
- Due diligence on hard (organizational structure, strategic management, managerial aspects etc.) and soft (organizational culture, communication, leadership, human resource aspects) issues
- Well-managed M&A team
- Successful learning from previous experience
- Planning for combination and solidification steps completed early
- Key talent retained
- Extensive and timely communications to all stakeholders.

Thus, while there are many reasons for success and failure in mergers and acquisitions, whether in North America, Europe, or Asia, at the core of many of them are organizational structure, culture, communication, and human resources issues.

Reasons for failure

As Doz and Hamel (cited in Schuler & Jackson, 2001, p. 241) imply, mergers and acquisitions fail for a variety of reasons and typical reasons for failure include:

- Expectations are unrealistic
- Hastily constructed strategy, poor planning, unskilled execution
- Failure/inability to unify behind a single macro-message
- Talent is lost or mismanaged
- Power and politics are the driving forces, rather than productive objectives
- Requires a high degree of synergy
- Culture clashes occur between the two entities
- Transition management fails
- The underestimation of transition costs
- Financial drain
- Focus of executives is distracted from the core business.

> As an example, it is believed the culture gap made DaimlerChrysler's postmarriage period of adjustment was more difficult than that of any other merger around. DaimlerChrysler believed that the two company cultures could simply be put in a blender and poured out as a new synergistic company. Cultural issues were all but ignored and seemed to be addressed by executives when making broad statements to the media regarding the differences in the two companies. Either Daimler and Chrysler did not fully recognize the implications of cultural differences or they chose to focus on the operational and business synergies hoping that culture would sort itself out. During the initial stages of the merger, Chrysler President indicated that Daimler intended to adopt Chrysler's product development methods which emphasized teamwork rather than individual-oriented work procedures. Chrysler in turn would adopt Daimler practices such as rigid adherence to timetables and their methodological approach to problem-solving. However, evidence of the lack of true sharing and cooperation was soon to emerge and could be demonstrated by Daimler executives' refusal to use Chrysler parts in Mercedes vehicles. (Schuler & Jackson, 2001, p. 242)

Although DaimlerChrysler is one company in name, the fact is that two separate operational headquarters were maintained: one in Michigan and other in Germany. Business operations continued to be separate. Daimler and Chrysler each had their own agenda focusing on different aspects of the automobile market, making one vision difficult to see (Schuler& Jackson, 2001).

The Factors Effecting the Success and Failure of M&As

In the light of the literature, human resources factors are considered as key elements in the success or failure of a merger or acquisition. This chapter combines three dimensions; as organizational structure, organizational culture and human resource issues. It will demonstrate how a properly implemented M&A will affect the final success or failure of an organization from work and organizational psychology and management perspectives.

The success of mergers and acquisitions is closely related to whether or not cultural integration is carried out successfully. However, cultural conflict is inevitable during the process of the assimilation of two different organizational cultures. Therefore, in order to decrease the impact of the cultural clash, primarily human resources managers and those managers responsible for the change have a major responsibility.

Corporate culture can be traced from the behaviors, attitudes, and relations both within and outside the organization. During the process of mergers, a new organization needs to be formed and also a new mutual culture has to be created. The impact of culture on organizational behavior is well known. In the mergers of corporations from different countries or different organizational cultures, potential problems gain priority, thus affecting negatively the time frame and success of the merger. According to Schein (1996), in every organization three different cultures exist unaware of each other's assumptions. Schein calls them the "operator culture," "engineer culture," and "upper-management culture." The frequent incompatibility of these three subcultures with each other prevents organizational learning. Due to such reasons, major problems arise during the process of organizational change. Regarding mergers and acquisitions, the situation gets even more confusing and the problems may sometimes get out of hand, resulting in unexpected turnover, aggressiveness, and harm to the work environment.

In order to reach the desired state of success in mergers and acquisitions, the type and level of cultural unification is essential. As the merging efforts spread, both companies' managers start to get to know and better understand each other's cultures. Therefore, in the preparation period before the merger, both companies' leaders have to determine the desired type and level of cultural assimilation.

The human factor in the organizational culture change

The cultural change process takes place at the individual and group level. At the first stage of the individual level, some employees, feeling that they will not be able to adapt to a diverse organization's norms, values and management style, quit their jobs. This condition can be observed not only in mergers and acquisitions, but also in all companies going through organizational change. This may also happen when the person who has longed worked for that organization believes that he/she is incompatible with a new technology (such as moving from a traditional accounting system to the computer) or a procedure that has changed the working conditions. In addition to the plight in mergers, similar problems arise when companies send managers and specialists to work temporarily for their foreign partners. Managers (expatriate) who are sent to work in other countries for six months or more, due to not being able to adapt to the culture, country or management, head back home with feelings of failure and low morale, thus causing the corporations where they worked, especially the ones in North America, huge amounts of material loss.

At the organizational level, in order to maintain cultural change, the buyer organization can choose to recruit employees and experts who are able to adapt to the new organizational culture's target goals, beliefs and values, and thus prefer to minimize the potential problems. Even though at first glance this approach appears costly, in the long run it brings great value to the organization. Changing employees' behavior, habits, and conducting training to foster open communication tend to make the adaptation process easier (Sinangil & Ones, 2001).

Cultural conflict and its prevention

Conflict that is present even at the foundation of all organizations becomes much more intense during mergers and acquisitions. In two different organizations, during the process of large-scale change and enculturation; conflict is inevitable since it is not only the organizational structure and managerial styles that undergo change, but also the way things are run, values, norms, languages (especially in mergers where two different languages are spoken) and habits.

Conflict experienced during the merging process has a negative impact upon the morale, motivation and thus performance of employees, leading eventually to huge financial losses as well as unwanted resignations (Marks & Mirvis, 1998). It could be possible to keep conflict to a minimum. As premerger process preparations take place, conducting meetings to bring together all employees and managers, sharing the current agenda of the merging process with employees such as its aim, goals, expectations and market share targets, will encourage participation and minimize the level of conflict.

One of the critical factors of success during the merger and acquisition process concerns human resources managers. Especially during the premerging period, the actions taken by these managers; such as starting up orientation programs and sharing new human resources strategies with employees, facilitate employees' adaptation to the new organizational culture.

Change management, leadership and strategic communication during the merging process

Mergers and acquisitions are organizational change processes. Some of the critical concepts in converting change to organizational development are management, leadership styles, employees' perception of change and strategic communication (Ashkanasy & Jackson, 2001).

Change management Despite all the preparations made before the merger, during the merger and acquisition process, the changes in organizational structure, its implementation and other tasks and functions may lead to uncertainty and chaos, even if short-lived. In such transition periods, in order to avoid the reduction of performance and to prevent unwanted resignations, managers and consultants have to implement crisis management to minimize problems and turn the organizational functioning back to normal. At this stage, the management approach adopted by organizational leaders is crucial. Research points out that, during transition periods, a participative managerial style, even though yielding results in a little longer time than autocratic management, leads to the strongest and most permanent results. Both before and after the merger, a management team made up of the upper management of both companies need to create synergy. The synergy created during the transition period as well as utilizing open communication, leads to a less stressful work environment and lower costs than expected (Ashkanasy & Jackson, 2001).

During the transition period, in order for change management to be successful, the necessary steps that need to be taken can be summarized as: restructuring the work processes in line with the company's goals; implementing an interactive communication approach between management and employees to foster mutual interaction; and creating and implementing a new shared organizational culture in line with both organizations' cultural values. Moreover, establishing and implementing a new human resources system in a shared value framework, utilizing both organizations' human resources systems, and application of trainings and personal development programs for all levels of managers necessitated by the new culture and its functions, all bring major benefits to the organization.

Leadership As a result of mergers and acquisitions, in order to carry out the corporate transition both successfully and efficiently, and also in order for employees to absorb the ongoing changes, leaders in the company take on essential tasks. Ensuring that employees have access to accurate information, gaining their trust and thus participation are only some of the roles leaders need to take on during a period of change. Following the merger and acquisition process, and during the transition to the target structure, the availability and presence of well-trusted leaders within the company is the first and the most critical step. During the merging phase, along with the leaders, all managers should also work as human resources managers and try to prevent the various possible problems that might arise during the transition period.

According to Marks and Mirvis (1998), the success or failure of mergers and acquisitions is affected by the chief executive officer's (who is in charge of the implementation of the merger) attitudes and personal characteristics, as well as the processes implemented by the employees. In other words, the CEO or general manager in charge of the merger takes on the role of the model leader as necessitated by the new organizational culture.

During the merging process, it is extremely crucial for leaders possessing these personal characteristics to lead the employees. Their mission includes identification of the new company's goals, and their announcement to all levels in the organization, thus enabling the employees to understand the new mission and vision of the company, removing their hesitations, giving them trust, and facilitating the company to reach its targets at the highest level.

Strategic communication in the process of mergers and acquisitions Where mergers and acquisitions are concerned, all employees face incredible amounts of tension due to the uncertainty of the dynamics and consequences of change, resulting in feelings of apprehension regarding the future of the organization. These kinds of negative thoughts at the individual level or reflecting upon the division or team, will lead to a decline in motivation followed by a loss of performance.

One of the most essential tools that a manager needs to utilize effectively in guiding his/her employees is communication. The change management process at the same time needs to entail continuous information gathering and sharing. Keeping up the communication with an encouraging attitude will reduce the uncertainty and anxiety of the employees and facilitate their participation.

According to Marks and Mirvis (1998), employees' anxiety and worries continue during the premerger, merger, and postmerger periods. Some questions and individual worries caused by them regarding the premerger period are: "Who is the other side?," "Who is in control of the new organization?," "What will happen to the supplementary benefits to the compensation?," "What will happen to the project I'm currently involved in?," "Will I get my promotion?," "Do I still have a job?," "Or else which department will I be assigned to?"

Some of the questions causing anxiety during the merger period are: "How are decisions taken?," "Who controls the methods that we implement?," "Will the best positions be acquired by the other side?" Similarly, after the merger takes place some of the potential questions troubling the minds of employees will be; "What is expected of me?," "Does my manager trust me?," "Do I trust my manager?"

The above-mentioned questions and the anxiety stemming from them is undoubtedly experienced both individually and in groups in organizations going through the merger and acquisition process. Where the necessity of strategic communication is devalued under these conditions, rumors and gossip carried by the grapevine are translated into unreal accusations. Unless all information is shared, this process will lead the key people in the organization to look for other jobs (leading to possible resignations), and even if they do not resign, they will perform below their usual capacity in a time where their highest input is called for.

The key concept in reducing all of these troubles is communication. Face-to-face communication that is well-timed and accurate in content, meetings where ideas can be exchanged, an unthreatening style, and an explanation of the overall process and goals will greatly lessen the declining morale, facilitate the employees in taking on their new roles, and thus prevent diminished performance. At this stage, the major duty of all group leaders from the CEO and the general managers to the first level managers is to foster face-to-face meetings rather than engaging in written communication. When supervisors engage in "mentoring" or "coaching" behavior, this leads to the formulation of shared resolutions regarding the problems arising from the merger process, thus enabling the workforce to deal with this situation experiencing minimum damage and reach the required performance.

Some crucial human resources applications regarding the merger and acquisition period

One of the most active departments in organizations during mergers and acquisitions is the human resources management department. The basic function of human resources ranges from compensation management to the maintenance of employer–employee relations leading to the development of both the organization and the employees as individuals. Due to these reasons, in order to prevent the possible problems resulting from the merger/acquisitions and to quickly adapt employees to the new circumstances and ensure their success, at the first stage, upper management should make strategic plans together with the human resources management to start the required applications. Research indicates that, 80 percent of the organizations employ the human resources management in the postmerger period, thus losing many of their key employees. It is also pointed out that only 3–5 percent of the organizations develop their strategies together with their human resources departments during the premerger period and thus resolve the issues regarding the merger and the internalization of the new culture without going through much trouble (Light, 2001).

In mergers, two separate organizations go through restructuring to form a single organization. Therefore, it is unavoidable that there'll be recruitment for some newly created positions, a change of places for some positions due to their closure or fusion, as well as repositioning and lay-offs.

In line with the new arrangements concerning the working conditions, the human resources plans need to be made to facilitate the success of human resources practices.

Selection and recruitment – lay-offs   During the process of mergers and acquisitions, the concept of "selection" covers both the recruitment of personnel from outside of the organization as well as the accommodation of the current employees and managers to the available positions. Therefore, selection and recruitment is a simultaneous process, and mostly takes the form of accommodation of employees.

In mergers and acquisitions, human resources frequently practice the accommodation of employees to various positions. Generally, corporations think of laying off only a small percentage of their workforce. They prefer to maintain their key employees, especially the ones who can add value to the new organization via their knowledge, skills and expertise and those who are ready to accept the new culture as well as being familiar with the old one. At this phase, in what proportion and for which positions the old employees will be accommodated by the buyer organization as well as the acquired one will be determined by the framework of managerial politics.

Tests and interviews are the most important tools in the decision of choosing the first time applicants for the various positions in the company. According to the requirements of the position, determined by the job description, evaluations are carried out based on skill and ability tests and those inventories objectively measuring personality characteristics. The benchmarking of the test results with the applicants' characteristics and interviews (which are subjective methods) will lead to accurate final decisions.

Performance evaluations and management   The application of performance evaluations twice a year after the merger is crucial in managers' discovery of problems among their teams of employees. Moreover, providing them with feedback will be beneficial in preventing possible problems and unwanted resignations. Instead of conducting an evaluation based on only the employee and his/her immediate superior, performance appraisals deriving form more than one source offer rich feedback to the employee and his/her management. As an example, in the 360-degree feedback approach, people rate themselves as well as being evaluated by colleagues (those making in similar positions), subordinates, immediate supervisors, and if available, by a customer. This approach, which has acquired widespread interest as an area of practice, provides feedback regarding employees' problems, needs, strengths, and potential for growth. Another benefit offered by this system is providing an integration between organizational and employee targets during mergers and acquisitions.

Training, orientation, and development programs   Traditionally organizations have been conducting formal or informal training programs for their employees. However, the need for training during the merger and acquisitions increases dramatically and becomes a priority. The transformation of two separate companies into one, re-allocation of targets, the changes in organizational structure, style of management and types of leadership, the emergence of new technologies and teamwork lead to the need for training.

At this stage, along with organizational and task-directed individual needs, a training needs analysis that will facilitate the development of group/team work has to be conducted. The organizations that are aware of the relationship between the company's growth and the employees' development carry out training programs after preparing a comprehensive needs analysis. As a result of the needs analyses completed at the first stage, the training applications follow in the second step. The third step entails the evaluation of the applied training programs.

In summary, the two crucial concepts regarding training are a systematic needs analysis to be conducted before the training, and a systematical evaluations to be conducted in the post-training period (for instance after 3 to 6 months). At this stage, the organization's responsibility is to create a work environment that will enable the trained workers and specialists to apply what they have learned and transfer their knowledge into performance.

After the merger and acquisition period is completed, orientation programs need to be conducted enabling the employees to adapt to the new organization and its culture in a short time.

Conclusion

In this chapter we discussed many wide-ranging questions regarding people, management, culture, and strategy, which have a direct effect upon the success of merger and acquisitions. In Bice's words, the upper management during the merging process can be likened to the "deck officer in *Titanic*" (cited in Buono & Bowditch, 1989). Whatever the style, they have to successfully start, manage, implement, and finalize the integration (acquisition, takeover, strategic partnership, etc.) process in the desired and planned way. Due to this, just like an adventure, they have to skillfully take care of the various troubles and other sensitive issues.

Lastly, regarding some of the problem-causing issues we've touched upon until now, the critical factors regarding the formation, maintenance of healthy integrations will be summarized, and some suggestions will be provided below:

- From the first stages of the integration, the human resources department has to work together with upper management and merger teams, and take an active role in the human resources applications, surfacing problems and communication with the employees during and following the transition period.
- The human resources department has to work with upper management to ensure that during the merger and acquisition process, the managers and employees of both companies have a positive outlook regarding the future.
- Every stage of the integration has been closely monitored; possible problems need to be identified in advance and immediately dealt with.
- During the integration, interactive and healthy communication has to be maintained at every level and involving every group, and rumors, gossip, and unwanted resignations need to be prevented.
- Encouraging employee participation during the integration process and taking their views and suggestions regarding the situation has an essential role in preventing resignations.

- The choice and training of those leaders responsible from the transition teams of the organization has a direct impact upon successful outcomes.
- The upper management has to define the vision of the new company formed as a result of the integration, and employees need to be given specific targets to fulfill this vision.
- The newly established organization as a result of the integration has to complete its human resources applications in the shortest time frame possible. Some of the possible applications are, terminating the employment of those resigned, retirement and referral procedures, and finalizing the new selection and recruitment transactions. Moreover, in order to prevent undesired resignations, certain activities need to be planned in order to retain the employees needed for key positions.
- Research regarding the training needs of the employees working in the new organization has to be quickly finalized and training programs and change management activities have to be given priority.
- Following the integration, performance evaluations for the newcomers have to be conducted after the first three or first six months, and those demonstrating outstanding success need to be rewarded to boost motivation.
- During the integration, communications with customers need to be emphasized and when necessary, applications may need to be conducted in line with their suggestions and reactions.

One frequent setback confronted during mergers and acquisitions is the withdrawal (handover to the newcomers) of the upper management, who have made the decision to start the integration process, and actively participated in its implementation, after the integration is over. However, approximately one year is needed for the growth and healthy functioning of a new culture.

Hunsaker and Cooms (cited in Cartwright & Cooper, 1999) summarize the emotional journey people go through during mergers and acquisitions as follows: When people first hear about the news of a merger & acquisition, the denial stage begins. The reaction here is: "This can't be true." The anxiety and fear at this stage emerges in the "When will it take place and what will happen to me" question. This is followed by the frustration stage, "Can't we acquire them?" Then frustration gives way to a nostalgic sadness, "Everything used to be better in the old days . . ." Then slowly comes acceptance, "Whatever has happened has happened." Then comes the relaxation stage, "It is better than I expected." Then things get more optimistic in time, "It is worth trying". Finally the interest stage is achieved by increasing the trust factor. Next is the likeability and enjoyment stage, where new opportunities are realized. Now, the employee has made up his/her mind, enjoys the new situation, and the adaptation stage is on. During all of these stages, rescuing the people from the "trauma" they're going through and motivating them is the task of managers and work and organizational psychologists as well as the specialists part of the human resources management.

Summary

From 1980s to today, the business world has witnessed an increase in mergers and acquisitions (M&As) between firms of different sizes and industry types. The primary purpose of merging and acquiring new firms is usually to improve overall performance of the organization, or to attain certain economies of scale; and to achieve synergy effect between two business units that will increase their competitive advantage. It is seen that companies aiming to grow in the emerging markets attempt to enter these markets by involving in mergers and acquisitions. However, it can be observed that such processes have either some difficulties or problems in certain dimensions (Siegel, 2000). These integrations face some important problems when reaching the aimed results and performance. One of the most important factors of failure is considered as the insufficient management of main processes. Moreover, some important problems occur as a result of inadequete applications of human resources. Thus, inconsistency among organizational processes influences the success of the new system.

We investigated a company which was involved in a merger process and analyzed critical factors of integration process. The results of the study has shown that, considering structural consistency, cultural adaptation and human resources aspects are important factors in attaining the expected goals. Consequently, structural, cultural and particularly human side of M&As seems to be crucial for creating synergetic results. In this respect, the fusion or integration of human resources, cultures and structures is required, and success becomes heavily dependent on the synergy of those.

Discussion Points

How far do you agree that failures of M&As result from the adaptation problems of organizational structures, cultures, and human resource aspects of both companies? Support your idea with illustrations.

Do mergers and acquisitions really have an impact on the leadership style, communication style, culture, and human resource systems of the company?

How do you think that the managers can make a difference to organizational effectiveness during and after M&A processes?

Key Studies

Buono, A.F., Bowditch, J.L., & Lewis, J.W. (1985). When Cultures Collide: The Anatomy of A Merger. Human Relations, Vol. 38, No. 5, p. 478.

Doz, Y.L., & Hamel, G. (1998). *Alliance advantage: The art of creating value through partnering*. Cambridge, MA: Harvard Business School Press.

Schuler, R., & Jackson, S. (2001). HR issues and activities in mergers and acquisitions. *European Management Journal, 19(3)*, 239–53.

Further Reading

Appelbaum, H. S., & Gandell, J. (2003). A cross method analysis of the impact of culture and communications upon a healthcare merger. *Journal of Management Development*, *22(5)*, 370–409.

Cartwright, S., & Cooper, C. L. (1999). *Managing mergers acquisitions and strategic alliances: Integrating people and culture*. Oxford: Butterworth-Heinemann.

Gugler, K., & Yurtoglu, B. B. (2004). The effects of mergers on company employment in the USA and Europe. *International Journal of Industrial Organization*, *22*, 481–502.

Katz, P. J., Simanek, A., & Townsend, B. J. (1997). Corporate mergers and acquisitions: One more wave to consider, *Business Horizons*, Jan.–Feb., 32–40.

Schraeder, M., & Self, D. R. (2003). Enhancing the success of mergers and acquisitions: An organizational culture perspective. *Management Decision*, *41(5)*, 511–22.

Siegel, H. P. (2000). Using peer mentors during periods of uncertainty. *Leadership & Organization Development Journal*, *21(5)*, 243–53.

Steensma, H., van Rijnsoever, R., & vander Feen, M. (2003). Mergers and changes in identification of workers: The social identity approach. In F. Avallone, H. K. Sinangil, & A. Caetano (Eds.), *Identity and diversity in organizations*. Milan: Guerini Studio, 57–63.

Walters, D., Halliday, M., & Glaser, S. (2002). Creating value in the new economy. *Management Decision*, *40(8)*, 775–81.

Research Close-Up

Sinangil & Kűçűkaslan (2005). Why mergers and acquisitions cannot create synergistic results: Challenges in the Turkish market. In F. Avallone, H. K. Sinangil, & A. Caetano (Eds.), *Synergy in Organizations and Society* (pp. 95–104). Milan: Guerini Studio.

Introduction

During the last two decades organizations are facing large "change" challenges. Particularly globalization has accelerated the change process. Various developments in the global business world led companies to develop new and different strategies in order to be able to survive and compete. One of the major strategies involves mergers and acquisitions (M&As). The purpose of merging and acquiring new firms is usually to improve the overall performance of the organization and to increase the competitive advantage. However, research indicates that 60–70 percent of M&As did not succeed in attaining their expected goals (Appelbaum & Gandell, 2003). The objective of this study is to investigate the reasons and problems which led to failure in mergers and acquisitions in Turkey.

Participants

The sample of the research was selected by investigating the official annual reports of M&As that were established in Turkey between 1984 and 2004. One hundred companies were asked to participate in the study, however the response rate was 40 percent. Forty national company representatives from diverse sectors (banking–insurance, automotive, petroleum, manufacturing, retail, tourism, media) participated.

Continued

Among the respondents, the average age was 44, 80 percent of the participants were male and 20 percent were female. The average tenure was 23 years and the average tenure in the current company was 11 years.

Design and procedure

This was an exploratory study as a part of qualitative research. The primary source of data was both semi-structured interviews and observations. The interview questions consisted of structural and cultural factors and essential human resource applications. Company visits were made during the ordinary daily workflow, which enabled direct observations.

Results

The content analysis of the data indicated that companies involved in M&A processes did not attain the expected success. The common reason was the weak adaptation of the M&A processes to the companies' systems. The interviews with managers indicate that common problems and dimensions regarding the integration were stated as: inconsistency of business & process characteristics of the companies, structural inconsistency, problems stemming from the integration of two different companies with culture and leadership style differences.

Also the managers mentioned that the company chosen for M&As should be well evaluated at the initial state of the mergers and acquisitions. Additionally although training programs were conducted, communication problems and conflict were the main problems either in operational or managerial issues. Such problems appear particularly when different cultures integrate. Finally one of the basic problems of the new emerged structure in post merger was the poor integration and coordination of human resources systems.

Discussion

The results of the study displayed the importance of human resources management systems in the success or failure of mergers and acquisitions. Schuler and Jackson (2001) state that for the success of M&As, the human resources departments in coordination with the top management of the two organizations should start the presentations for adjustment at premerger period. A transition team from the two organizations could be composed of eligible staff and work on the culture change and ensuring smooth adaptation to the new system.

PART IV

THEORY AND APPLICATION

The Changing Nature of Work

Michael Frese

18

Overview

Students at the university today will work in organizations and companies of the future. Thus, the question of changes of the nature of work is of paramount interest for students. There is no doubt that the world of work is changing. If a worker from the late part of the nineteenth century would be catapulted into a modern workplace, he or she would have difficulties understanding present-day work: Its speed, the emphasis on timeliness of production and service, the modern technology used, the cleanliness and safety of the workplace, the emphasis on customer satisfaction and quality, the modularity of the products, the nonmilitary nature of the organizations, the courtesy and at the same time distance in social relationships at work (including the relations towards women and foreigners), the speed with which product lines are changed, the international nature of production and the relations with other foreign companies, the internationality of the workforce (this can be easily taken from the writings of Marx (1932), Ford (1922), Licht (1983), or Taylor (1911)).

Work life has undergone tremendous changes within the last 100 years. One function of this chapter is to ask the question what kind of research will be required if work and organizational psychology will want to deal well with future problems. Thus, we would like to know: What changes will the next 50–100 years bring about?

Only two answers are certain: First, most probably we shall make erroneous forecasts; second, most likely some of the changes will appear much slower than we tend to think. As proof for the first statement, just think of the fact that at the time of writing this article, people had just barely become accustomed to the fact that the Eastern tigers (Thailand, South Korea, Hong Kong, etc.) were the inevitable bearers of the future markets, when the crisis in these countries led to a serious economic depression in these countries. All those forecasters who thought of these markets to be the most important ones in the future, turned out to be wrong (at least for a certain period).

As proof of the second statement, think of the fact, that in the beginning of the computer technological revolution (starting in earnest in the late 1970s with the advent of personal computing), it was estimated that human intelligence would soon be replaced by computer technology (e.g., Feigenbaum & McCorduck, 1984) and that a paperless office would develop. Neither of these two predictions have come to be true. However, there are developments in the direction of this forecast. In rule governed areas, computer supported decision support has become more commonplace (e.g., stock exchange, medicine, technical supplies, or logistics) and in specialized nonwork related areas, e.g., chess, computer intelligence has made tremendous gains. Similarly, there have been developments to use more and more data banks electronically although this did not lead or even approach the idea of a paperless office.

2 Prediction of the Future:
Methods and Perspectives

Most frequently, people tend to extrapolate from current trends. For example, in the 1960s, there were ample futurists who extrapolated the energy use into the future and predicted that all fossil energy would be depleted in the early part of the twenty-first century. In the meantime, new technology and the energy conservation movement, has helped us to conserve energy to a large extent; in addition new energy technologies have been developed. Thus, while we all have to use extrapolations to make predictions for the future, we should be cautious, to also describe the counterforces to these extrapolations.

Catastrophy and chaos theory (Gleick, 1987) and system perspectives (Buckley, 1968) have emphasized two issues: First, that some small developments may have enormous effects even at another place. The fact that Hitler was rejected to be a student in an art school may have led him to become a politician with enormous consequences. Small causes may have large effects that are difficult to foresee. Second, there are countermovements by systems which work against certain trends that appear obvious. A good example is the effect of the computer revolution in the office. In contrast to strong savings projected by the computer industry, there were essentially no saving. However, the quality standards for written and oral presentations increased: just think of the fancy multicolored overheads or the near professional printing quality of reports common today which were out of reach 20 years ago for most office workers. Thus, the system (in this case office work) did not lead to savings, as anticipated, but to higher quality reports.

In addition, there are two limiting conditions for changes that are inherent in every system. First, organizations are conservative (Katz & Kahn, 1978). New technology research has shown that the potential of new technology is usually not realized at once. At any one time, the organization uses an evolutionary approach and changes the work situation only a bit (the evolutionary approach: Pomfrett, Olphert, & Eason, 1985). Therefore, the changes are usually much smaller than one would imagine (Agervold, 1987; Frese & Zapf, 1987; Kling, 1980).

Another system characteristic that leads to inherent conservatism is human nature (Nicholson, 1998). As Nicholson shows in this important article, any attempt to reduce hierarchies in organizations may produce countertendencies by which hierarchies develop even when "nonhierarchical structures" are advocated. Human nature may tend to reintroduce hierarchies even if they are counterproductive.

A further approach to attempt to understand the future of work is to empirically research jobs at the cutting edge of new technology and new organization. The best model for such jobs are software designers because they work with very new technology and most new and interesting organizational approaches have been attempted there. We shall report some of the findings on this profession.

The scenario approach has also been used to forecast the future. It asks the question, which alternative scenarios are plausible and how then alternative trajectories of developments are developed based on these scenarios. For example, what happens to future workplaces in Europe if the influence labor unions collapses across Europe in the same way as it did in the United Kingdom? Or what happens to workplaces in West European when East Europe is integrated into the European Union? This is a plausible approach that helps to make the prerequisites of our predictions more explicit.

These introductory statements were supposed to make us sufficiently humble with regard to predictions of the future. Having said all of this, we shall now venture into looking at potential trends at the workplace, potential counterforces and potential consequences. Our emphasis in each case will be on what issues of work and organizational psychology will become more important to deal with potential (new) problems.

3   Trends that Describe the Job of the Future and Consequences for Work and Organizational Psychology

Important edited volumes have made the task of summarizing the literature on the future of work easier (Ilgen & Pulakos, 1999; Patterson, 2001). The following points constitute a fair summary of the trends discussed in the literature (cf. e.g., Bridges, 1995; Howard, 1995; Rifkin, 1995; Storey, 1994):

* Dissolution of the unity of work in space and time
* Changing job and career concepts

- Faster rate of innovation
- Increase of complexity of work
- Personal initiative versus adaptability to the new workplace
- Global competition
- Both larger and smaller units will develop
- More team work
- Reduced supervision
- Increase of cultural diversity.

We will discuss these trends below.

3.1   Dissolution of the unity of work in time and space

With the advent of the internet and computer based work, it has been possible to overcome restrictions imposed by time and space to work together. For example, I have once written a paper with two American colleagues whom I had never met before; we communicated only via email. Some car designers already work on a 24-hour schedule: When the designers in Tokyo stop working, the European designer takes over. When they stop their shift in the evening, the American colleagues continue where the Europeans have left off. At the consulting firm Accenture in Paris, people do not have their individual offices any longer but they get assigned an office whenever they need one. Within minutes, their individual filing cabinet is rolled into this office and their own telephone number and email connection is built up. A final example of a virtual office is Pacific Bell Directory that had a special contract with a hotel chain, built up their own offices there and asked its salespeople to work from hotel rooms (using a modem and phones as tools to be related to the main office) (Goves, 1995; Wigand, Picot, & Reichwald, 1997). Somewhat dated statistics from the US show that telecommunication is used by 11 million workers (Cascio, 1998). Obviously, telecommunication is a broad concept that includes the use of email but also sophisticated GroupWare with concurrent videoconferencing.

Thus, there are enormous potentials in the fact that one does not need to be at one's office any more to be able to work together. People using telecommuting seem to like it and prefer it to working in an office; they even argue that they have fewer distractions and work more productively (Cascio, 1998; Chapman, Sheehy, Heywood, Dooley, & Collins, 1995). Productivity was enhanced between 2 to 40 percent through telework (Chapman, et al., 1995). However, these positive effects have been recorded up to this point only in situations where people volunteer for participation in telework (Chapman, et al., 1995). This may change when people who do not like to participate in telework are forced into it.

Lest the reader thinks that telework is extremely widespread, let me hasten to add that there are many reasons that hinder the quick and widespread use of telework. Some forms of work pose legal requirements that make it difficult to use telework. For example, many bank and insurance jobs cannot legally be done from home because privacy cannot be ensured in the homes of the teleworkers (this is certainly more important in Europe with its strict privacy laws than in other parts of the world). Similarly, many managers and business owners want to *see* their employees work with their own eyes. Many organizations do not like to invest into an uncertain technology and assume that it will be difficult to keep up organizational commitment. On the other hand, certain political decisions have made it necessary to invest in telework, for example, the decision by Germany to distribute the capital across two cities (Bonn and Berlin) has led to a push in information technology to deal with distributed decision making across these two cities (Schmidt & Wolf, 1997). In all, there is little doubt that telework has been growing, that it has been profitable where used, and that it will continue to grow in the future.

A new area of psychological inquiry has developed – computer-supported cooperative work, which looks at distributive cognitions and evaluates computer tools that support cooperative work (Finholt & Teasley, 1998). Distributed cognition implies that the ideas, thoughts, and manipulations of objects are distributed among the group members (often based on knowledge that only one member of the group really has and needs to share with others). Shared mental models may help in good problem solutions. Similarly, the way we use objects is often based on distributive cognitions, including the use of ShareWare – a software that is supposed to support cooperative work.

Obviously there are important implications for work and organizational psychology that derive from the "dissolution of the unity of time and space at work" that accompanies telework.

- First, there are problems of coordination. How can the organization make sure that everybody knows his or her tasks? Tasks that require fine-grained communication are better done in face to face than in computer-mediated groups (Straus & McGrath, 1994).
- Second, how do organizations overcome the problem of reduced organizational commitment? Telework reduces the chances to feel that one belongs to the organization (Chapman et al., 1995). Of particular difficulty is to develop a common culture in virtual organizations.
- Third, the communication patterns change when communicating via the computer (at least to a certain extent). There is a large literature in this area which we do not need to summarize here. There is some evidence that communication becomes more democratic because status differences cannot be conveyed as vividly via the computer than in face to face communication (Kiesler, Siegel, & McGuire, 1984).
- Fourth, how can a culture of telecommunication be developed and furthered? At the moment, there is evidence that people use rougher and less sophisticated language when typing something into a computer.
- Fifth, there is an overabundance of information in today's telecommunication systems. Obviously, a large amount of what one receives is not really relevant.

How can these systems help to differentiate uninformative garbage from information that is really needed?

- Sixth, in which phase of their work do projects get better or worse support through some type of computer-based groupwork support?

3.2   Change of job and career concepts

Some authors have argued that the notion of jobs as we know it will evaporate (Bridges, 1995; Rifkin, 1995). First, there is a clear reduction of jobs in the traditional production and service industries. With every reengineering attempt, the number of blue- and white-collar workers is reduced tremendously. Louisville Capital Holding reduced its backoffice staff from 1,900 to 1,100 while increasing business by 25 percent after reengineering (Bridges, 1995).

Second, technological innovation leads to a reduction of personnel. For example, cashier jobs (the third largest clerical group in the US) will be cut by 10 to 15 percent by new scanning equipment (Rifkin, 1995); in Britain, there are already some stores that do not employ cashiers and people scan and pay themselves; this trend will probably be increased by electronic shopping.

Third, temporary and project work increases. A symbol of this is that temporary employment agencies have the highest increase in sales and number of employees (Bridges, 1995). More and more companies are outsourcing, employing people only on a project basis, or they are even reducing the company to a virtual company consisting of a network of small-scale entrepreneurs.

Fourth, modern companies change the job concept. For example, Phillips introduced the idea of an umbrella contract. People are frequently assigned to projects and not to jobs any longer. For example, Microsoft has no regular working hours, people are accountable to their project team which is again accountable to the larger project. When a project ends, employees move on to another project (Bridges, 1995). "The dejobbed system lacks the normal kind of 'edges' that tell workers when they have done a normal, satisfactory job. Since they are expected to do *anything necessary* to accomplish the expected results, they are no longer protected by the boundaries of a job" (Bridges, 1995, p. 42).

All of this makes the concept of employability so attractive (van Dam, 2004). Every employee has to be quite interested to develop his or her skills. Employees will be less dependent upon one company. Projects will be selected by different characteristics than today. For example, one will attempt to participate in projects that allow one to develop one's skills and that make it possible to work with new technology or new procedures in one's area. Continuous development of one's professionalism will become more important.

From a work and organizational psychology perspective, this has positive consequences. Traditional jobs have been designed from a Tayloristic perspective. Tayloristic jobs have tended to take away the authority from the people; they were given to the supervisor, the bureaucracy, the assembly line, etc. In contrast, these newer jobs for professionals will make it necessary to develop one's skills to a higher degree and will decrease the division of labor typical of Taylorism.

On the other hand, there will be spouts of unemployment much more regularly than in traditional jobs in which one stays with one company and continues to work in one job or where one's career was made within one company. Moreover, loss of jobs in large companies and the emphasis on project work and networks make it necessary to develop more entrepreneurial spirit and to have more entrepreneurs. This is particularly important in Europe which has fewer entrepreneurs than other areas of the world (such as North America or developing countries). For example, the GEM study found that Europe had between 3.5 and 8 percent of the population showing some entrepreneurial activity, while the US was near 11 percent (Reynolds, Bygrave, Autio, Cox, & Hay, 2002).

Obviously, employees cannot keep up a high degree of commitment to and identification with one company if they know that they will work in different projects in different companies in a few years. Thus, commitment will be largely to the content of the project, the project group. It is likely that commitment will also grow with one's professional group (e.g., being a civil engineer or a psychologist) because the (continuous) development of one's professionalism is important. Employability implies a certain degree of professionalism.

Since people compete both in the internal company and in the external market for new projects and contracts, they have to behave much more entrepreneurial (even if they are employed). They have to decide which strategies to use, which markets they want to target (e.g., which market niches within the company), how they want to market themselves, etc. For example, it will be much more important to ask the question, whether a student of work and organizational psychology has chosen a research program that has obvious practical and scientific relevance in the future. Obviously, these are difficult tasks that need to be tackled as part of professional life which increase the requirements on cognitive and social skills.

Individuals will have to think of market issues even when they have a stable employer. They will have to make strategic decisions, e.g., whether or not they want to participate in a certain project or whether they want to orient themselves towards a certain market segment (a certain area of expertise). They also have to market themselves both within their profession, within their company, and across relevant segments across companies (and even across countries to a certain extent). Individuals will have to network to a larger extent than is typical today. Complex decisions have to be made that are risky. Thus, good feedback has to be proactively sought and flexible adjustments of one's orientations and skills will be much more necessary. These are all topics, that need to be supported by a higher degree of knowledge from work and organizational psychology.

Since these decisions need to be made by the individual himself and cannot be delegated to the company any longer, the individual has to show more personal initiative (Frese & Fay, 2001); and this includes individuals' decisions to participate in some form of training. Much of training will be in the form of self-training, because the company will not be responsible in the same way for continuing education. Companies may help in developing trainings to increase proactive and personal initiative in developing careers (Raabe, Frese, & Beehr, 2007).

One additional problem is that one needs to do get good career advice not only at the start of one's career but throughout one's life time. Career changes may appear more frequently than today. The integration of one's career with one's private life may be enhanced under those circumstances. At least the traditional division between work and leisure may become less strong than it is today. Given the facts, that project work is more dominant, that there are more transitional periods between projects, and that one works more from home through electronic means, there may be a development to combine work and leisure to a higher degree again (remember, the division between work and leisure did not exist in farming).

3.3   Faster rate of innovation

There will be more pressure to innovate because of pressures of a global market and because the time to create new products from new knowledge becomes shorter. Hamel and Prahalad (1994) have argued that the competition between firms will be more and more on opportunity shares (shares in future markets with products that may not exist yet). This is of particular importance for European countries which have fallen back against the US and Japan in terms of innovativeness and patents.

There are various implications for work and organizational psychology.

First, we need good models of individual and group innovation since they are necessary to support innovatory behavior. There tend to be two types of models. One is related to the creative element of innovation. A good model for group innovation (West, Garrod, & Carletta, 1997; West & Anderson, 1996) showed the importance of group reflexivity and support for innovation. For individuals, this perspective was developed for example by Oldham and Cummings (1996). Another approach relates innovation to personal initiative: To achieve innovation, one has to have a good idea; but in addition it is also necessary to implement the idea which necessitates to show personal initiative (Frese & Fay, 2001; Frese, Teng, & Wijnen, 1999).

Second, it makes sense to differentiate between process (how to produce) and product innovation; different psychological processes may apply to these two types of innovation. Even more important is the differentiation between different parts of the innovation process. Both West and Amabile have suggested appropriate process models of the innovation process (Amabile, 1988; West, 2002). For example, financial resources may be detrimental in the creativity phase, but have positive effects on the implementation phase of an innovative product.

Third, work and organizational psychology can contribute to helping people to learn faster. We will have to change how we do training. The traditional training literature has rightfully argued that it is necessary to do a task analysis first; however, our change of work perspective in this chapter implies that tasks will change so quickly that it will be difficult to train for specific tasks but that one needs meta-skills. This poses a dilemma: We know that it is very difficult to train general skills because transfer is difficult to areas one does not know well (Baldwin & Ford, 1988). We need to learn much more about how to develop transferable skills. The most probable starting point is to train for self-regulation (Karoly, 1993). Self-regulation is particularly important because whenever we have to regulate our regulation (e.g., boost our motivation to approach a new situation with curiosity when we really do not want to), self-regulatory processes apply.

Another starting point is to teach people to train themselves (or at least to feel responsible for their own training needs). One of the more important situations that may trigger a learning approach may be the occurrence of errors and problems (Keith & Frese, 2005). However, it is likely that people will only start to learn from an error if they do not feel anxious about making errors and do not feel the need to cover them up (Rybowiak, Garst, Frese, & Batinic, 1999).

This leads us to a point of organizational learning. The organizational culture itself must support learning. New strands of research are required here; one important issue is the error culture which determines whether people feel at ease to discuss errors, and, thereby, learn from them. It has been shown that companies with a mastery-oriented error culture are more profitable than those with a timid error culture (van Dyck, Frese, Baer, & Sonnentag, 2005). A learning organization needs to support curiosity: there needs to be a certain safety to explore (West et al., 1977) and general uncertainty avoidance needs to be low. At the moment, we know too little about cultural processes, including processes of national culture, such as uncertainty avoidance (Shane, 1993; Tung, Walls, & Frese, 2007).

Organizations can only succeed as learning organizations if they drive and support curiosity among their members. Thus, everything that increases curiosity will also increase innovation. This means that companies like 3M, that force its employees to spend a certain amount of time, dreaming up new products or ideas, will in the last analysis do the right thing. On the other hand, companies tend to decrease time pockets that can be used for such curious pursuit of ideas with the introduction of better (and tighter) organizations of production and even research and development. Thus, at some point in time, innovation may be hindered by the very effectiveness of the organization.

3.4 Increase of complexity of work

While there is little effect of new technology *per se* (Frese & Zapf, 1987; Kern & Schumann, 1984), changes in work organization interacting with new technology will make work intellectually more demanding (Chmiel, 1998; Kern & Schumann, 1984; Womack, Jones, & Roos, 1990). Moreover, since the rate of change is increasing, this implies that new knowledge has to be acquired rather constantly.

The factors that contribute to an increase of work complexity are production for small niches, customization, and customer orientation. Most car companies already work on a principle of demand with each car being specified individually and separately. Complexity of work also increases because of increasing environmental turbulence and ever more rapidly developing fashions and global changes.

The most important implications for work and organizational psychology are in the following areas:

- First, what can be done for unskilled workers? Complex work presupposes a high degree of intelligence and training (Ree & Caretta, 1998). Thus, jobs for the unskilled will become scarcer and scarcer. Since worldwide competition will increase and since modern technology makes it possible that work that was once given to unskilled workers in the industrialized world is now given to people in the developing world. This produces serious problems in the industrialized world, a continuously unemployed lower class with a welfare mentality, high crime rate, social unrest, and widespread dissatisfaction. We do not yet have a solution, but work and organizational psychologists need to develop one. This may imply to search for job characteristics that do not need a high degree of cognitive ability and it may mean that those jobs may have to be economically subsidized in some way. It may also be useful to develop improved and fine-tuned concepts of training for this group of people.

  Politically, there have been two approaches to this problem: Thatcherism attempted to reduce the wages for this group to a large extent (making them comparable to the third world and, thus, competitive again). Social democracy attempted to keep up the wages of this group of people; however, to induce companies to employ them, they had to subsidize those jobs; moreover, the trend has been to force those people into work again, who for some reason have motivational problems (e.g., in Denmark).

- Second, a similar problem occurs for not so socially competent people. The increase in customer orientation makes it necessary to employ people with good social skills. While social skills can be more easily learned than cognitive abilities, the problem persists what to do with people who have difficulties to learn the appropriate customer-oriented skills.

- Third, in general self-esteem and self-efficacy become much more important because they help to get going even with complex tasks.

- Fourth, intellectual work becomes more dominant. At the moment, most of our job analysis or appraisal methods are geared towards nonintellectual work. This makes it important to concentrate more on intellectual regulation of work (Frese & Zapf, 1994).

3.5   Personal initiative versus adaptability to new work

There is some debate which strategy should be suggested to employees to deal with the changing job concept. Some scholars have suggested that employees need to develop a certain degree of adaptability which is characterized by the factors of handling emergencies and stress, creative problem-solving, dealing with uncertain situations, learning, interpersonal, cultural, and physically-oriented adaptability (Pulakos, Arad, Donovan, & Plamondon, 2000). The contrasting position does not deny that there are pressures to adapt in modern workplaces but that employees should be counseled to develop initiative and actually use opportunities to adapt the workplace to one's own preferences, working styles, and proactive thoughts. This position is heavily influenced by proactive approaches at work, be it personal initiative (Frese & Fay, 2001), or finding a voice, in the sense of influencing conditions at work (LePine & Van Dyne, 2001). It would probably pay off to look at moderators of work and organizational characteristics to determine which of the two employee strategies has the best long-term effects.

3.6 Global competition

There is no doubt that there is a more global competition today than in the past and it is highly probable that this trend will increase. In the 1960s, 7 percent of the US economy was exposed to international competition while in the 1980s this number climbed to above 70 percent (Gwynne, 1992). Global competition will not only reign on the company level but more and more also on the individual level. With better communication networks, software developers in India compete for work with software developers in Holland or Switzerland. The most fiersome competitors of German and French construction workers are Polish workers who work as small-scale entrepreneurs in Europe, selling their labor power. In order to be able to hold out against this competition, the highly paid workers of the West have to improve their skills, have to be more active, show more initiative, be more reliable, and be more up-to-date than their competitors (who will usually earn less than citizens of the highly developed countries of the West).

Important implications for work and organizational psychology are:

- First, since peoples' ideas and attitudes become more important to increase productivity, the development of work and organizational psychology itself becomes a factor that will determine whether or not a society will be able to compete globally.
- Second, companies have to become more imaginative in how to stimulate self-reliance and initiative (Frese, 1997). Without active cooperation and individual self-starting and long-term involvement in the company, the company will not be able to compete well.
- Third, a high degree of employee initiative is particularly important when companies have to deal with turbulence and changes. Since globalization increases the amount of turbulence in company's environment, companies have to learn to react flexibly to them.

- Fourth, international cooperation will become more important. The most obvious issue for work and organizational psychology is that there will be a higher need for cross-cultural management. This implies that managers need to have skills to negotiate, lead, organize, and plan across cultures. There will be more international project work (particularly across European countries), there will be more internationally assigned managers who have to deal with living in cultures other than their own. All of these factors need the expertise of work and organizational psychology.
- Fifth, it is much more difficult for smaller companies to make use of globalization. Partly this is a function of the thought patterns of small-scale entrepreneurs who may not even think about the chances of international activities. Work and organizational psychologists may help to overcome thought barriers here.
- Sixth, globalization leads to a reduction of the power of the labor unions. While labor unions may have contributed to a certain degree of inflexibility, they have also helped to increase the degree of procedural and distributive justice in companies. Thus, other groups will have to take care of justice issues in the organizations. Also, the stability of the employer–employee relations may be negatively affected by the lack of a clear and historically powerful representation of employees.

3.7   Development of larger and smaller units

There is a curious polarization appearing in the world of organizations: On the one hand, organization are becoming bigger and bigger, forever increasing in size through mergers and acquisitions. This is done in spite of the fact that most mergers and acquisitions do not lead to the expected positive effects and often have even negative ones (Hogan & Overmyer-Day, 1994). On the other hand, large units are consistently downsizing and decreasing in size (Kozlowski, Chao, Smith, & Hedlund, 1993) and more and more small start-up firms develop. Moreover, there is evidence that smaller units from 10 to 150 are more flexible, work better with each other, and show a higher degree of innovative potential (Simon, 1996; Nicholson, 1998). Organizations develop networks with each other instead of employing more and more people in their ranks. Of course, some companies attempt to be big and at the same time attempt to mimic the "small is beautiful" strategy of small-scale enterprises (e.g., the Swiss-Swedish firm of Avery Brown Bovery (ABB), which governs its total company with sales of $28 billion produced by 220,000 employees worldwide with only 140 people in their headquarters: *International Herald Tribune*, 1992).

It will be interesting to do more research on the issue of the size of a company. Most likely it will be necessary to develop a contingency theory. For example, those companies that rely on innovation, cohesion of employees, and good working climate, may be better when they are small. In contrast, those companies that thrive particularly on the economy of scale in supplies and supporting demands will tend to do better when they are big.

Another important issue is the development of small-scale entrepreneurs. Since the big companies often leave important niches that can be exploited by small-scale entrepreneurs. Moreover small business people produce more new jobs than big organizations and finally, many innovations are carried by small organizations. Organizational psychologists have been too frequently interested only in large organizations. A new research focus should look at the psychology of small-scale entrepreneurs and the organizational issues of small-scale businesses (Baum, Frese, & Baron, 2007).

3.8   More team work

Ever since Womack et al. (1990) showed that in Japan 69 percent of all car workers were working in groups, while the respective percentage was 17 percent in the US and not even 1 percent in Europe, introduction of group work has been an important aspect of productivity improvement. Team work is being introduced, particularly in Europe (Germany and Holland), often relating it to the tradition and experiences that had been made 15–20 years ago with semi-autonomous groups (Antoni, 1994; Parker, Wall, & Jackson, 1997). For example, at a big automobile company that I observed in detail, a lean production system similar to the Japanese experience was introduced. However, it was coupled with experiences that were made some years ago with semi-autonomous work groups. As it turned out, earlier experiences financed by the government had led to knowledge within the firm that made faster adaptation and use of Japanese principles of production more possible.

Team work will appear even more frequently in future job settings than at present. First, production responsibilities are increasingly given back to the shop floor (as is common to all new production concepts). Since, there are dependencies among the shop floor workers, self-regulated team decisions have to made. This implies that the team participants should know something about each other's work (therefore, there is a need for job rotation). Second, new production methods (like lean production) are geared towards reducing coordination costs by reducing the number of supervisors. Coordination is then done within production units (teams). Third, increasing complexity will increase the need for coordinated effort. Since highly complex decisions require the input from sources of different disciplines, there will be a higher need for interdisciplinary team work. Interdisciplinary work is difficult because one has to be able to talk about one's own discipline in ways that other people understand, has to learn to understand the basics of another discipline quickly, and has to learn to appreciate the different approaches taken by various disciplines (which is as difficult as cross-cultural learning at times; Baron, 1993). Often there will only be one person of each discipline in the group, so that reliance on this person's expertise is quite high. Finally, teams will have to react to environmental turbulence and local shop floor teams are better regulators of such turbulence (cf. the sociotechnical system approach of Emery & Trist, 1969).

One implication of a higher degree of team work is the higher need for good social and communication skills. One reason, why the concept of emotional intelligence (Goleman, 1995) was attractive to so many people may have something to do with the fact that it is required in team work. It is interesting that the automobile companies that invested in East Germany have selected even blue-collar workers by assessment centers in order to explicitly gauge the social skills of their newly employed blue-collar workers who are working in lean, team based, production systems.

Team training, team development measures may become much more important (remember, the teams are often assembled from scratch for each new project again). Thus, from the employees' point of view, it is important to integrate into the team quickly. From the employers' point of view, team development needs to be done to make the team function well within a shorter period of time.

Teams are not necessarily more efficient than individuals working separately. As a matter of fact, there is ample evidence that for creative tasks, this is not the case (Diehl & Stroebe, 1987). While certain tasks (e.g., interdisciplinary ones) require teams in spite of the loss of productivity in teams, these results suggest that the tendency to do team work, may be supplemented by countertendencies to increase individual work again.

3.9   Reduced supervision

Lean production (Womack et al., 1990) and other organizational techniques of restructuring have decreased the number of managers. Thus, a higher degree of responsibility for production and service is given to the shop floor again. Moreover, telework reduces the amount of direct supervision possible. Therefore, supervisors' functions change; they should not intervene directly into day to day affairs but should rather be mentors of the groups they supervise (Emery & Trist, 1969). Reduced supervision also reduces the outside structure of the job and makes shop floor initiative necessary.

The theory of leadership substitution (Kerr & Jermier, 1978) can help explain, how one can deal with this situation. Standardization, a high degree of professionalism, intrinsically satisfying tasks, and formalization all reduce the need for leadership (De Vries, Roe, & Tailleu, 2002).

Major problems remain: How can companies make sure that ethical behavior is upheld throughout the company when there is very little direct influence? Supervisors have often been the carriers of organizational knowledge – a function that is much more difficult to develop, if there is little knowledge of the concrete work done by the employees. Errors and negative error consequences may increase if there is little supervision. Impetus for change is sometimes carried forward by supervisors (and organizational changes are made possible because first line supervisors smooth the transition in various ways). The upkeep of organizational culture, holding up the symbols and values of the organization, and organizational socialization (Morrison, 1993) are other issues. All of these functions of supervisors need to be developed within future organizations with a leaner structure.

3.10   Increase of cultural diversity

Cultural diversity is on the rise. Even if European countries succeed attempt to reduce the influx of foreign workers, the European union itself makes it necessary that different nationalities work together in teams across the different European countries. In the US, more than 50 percent of workers will soon belong to minorities (e.g., Blacks, Hispanics) or be women. While there is more and more knowledge of dealing with cultural diversity, intercultural work often means that people from cultures have to work together that are deeply suspicious of each other for historical reasons (e.g., the Dutch and Germans or French and English) or cultural reasons (e.g., Muslims and Christians). This goes beyond understanding another culture and implies that one deals with prejudices and animosities.

An added factor is language – for example, when Europeans have to work together. This goes beyond the issue of which language is used in the meetings; some approaches are language dependent; concepts are used in a certain common cultural framework of understanding and their importance is often historically and culturally based. I have been to international meetings in Europe which were supposed to increase understanding for each other's approaches; however people went away with even more problems understanding what people from the other language group actually wanted to say and prejudices were enhanced rather than reduced.

Future research will have to look more deeply into issues of how one can overcome such biases and prejudices and how one can make diversity work well. An approach by (Van Knippenberg, De Dreu, & Homan, 2004) will be useful in this area. These authors differentiate between a categorization-elaboration model which is based on social psychology and maintains that people want to keep their identity and discriminate against those who are different. In contrast the elaboration of task-relevant information model implies that diversity improves the information that group participats get because people have different backgrounds. This approach may lead to better teamtrainings, better decision making concepts in diverse groups and better approaches to multicultural teams within Europe.

4   Software Developers as an Example of a Cutting-Edge Job

A good indicator of future trends in the workplace are jobs at the cutting edge of modern technology that can be empirically researched. Software design is such a job. In a careful study of the work situation of this profession, we have come to the conclusion that the following aspects are of primary importance in their jobs (Brodbeck & Frese, 1994; Frese & Hesse, 1993):

- a high degree of learning by oneself (e.g., new techniques and methods, etc.),
- a high degree of working in groups,
- a high degree of communication with co-workers,
- a high degree of interdisciplinary work (e.g., with customers who are experts in another area),
- a high degree to which the people determine themselves how they will solve problems.

These empirical observations reinforce the above-mentioned trends and they point again at the importance of self-reliance.

Summary

Most of the above mentioned trends increase the importance of self-reliance and initiative. Self-reliance implies that one is being able to rely on one's knowledge, skills, and motivation; it enables people to stay in this race with many changes. Personal initiative implies that a self-starting and proactive approach is taken. The paradigmatic profession using self-reliance and initiative is self-employment. More and more professions will increase the level of self-employment, largely because networks of self-employed will work together, larger units will mimic self-employment for its constituents (e.g., in profit centers), internal entrepreneurs (intrapreneurs) will be encouraged within the companies, people will have to participate in an internal market for their skills (mimicking the outside market and, thus, becoming similar to a small-scale entrepreneur). The respective changes in qualification requirements and in training needs are immense. However, anxiety and insecurity will also increase correspondingly. As happens frequently in radical change situations, there are losers and winners of this change. For this reason, work and organizational have to find ways of making it possible for potential losers to participate in these change processes and to deal with the requirements. Some of work and organizational psychology is already prepared for these issues, but much more research has to be done and the feasibility of practical approaches have to be tried out and evaluated. Most likely psychological processes will be generally perceived to be more important than up to this point. Thus, work and organizational psychology has to take up the challenge and work in issues of changing workplaces.

Obviously, as pointed out in the introductory comments, none of the changes will develop without provoking countermovements. For example, there will be attempts to reduce the pressures of globalization, there will be attempts to reduce the necessary qualifications and to enhance job security. There will be attempts to keep Tayloristic workplaces intact. We do not want to argue that there is a mechanistic development towards higher complexity, need for self-reliance and entrepreneurship. It is possible to hold the tide at least for some time. However, effort and energy will have to be expanded which would be better used to develop better methods of dealing the changes that are ahead of us in the world of work.

Discussion Points

What are likely trends in the future – which ones will appear? Discuss how likely they are in various workplaces.

If you want to do a study (e.g., as a thesis) in work and organizational psychology: Which areas would you work on, given that these areas will become more important in the future? Argue for the future importance of your area(s).

Creating Inclusive Organizations

Binna Kandola

19

Overview

This chapter looks at the most recent research into diversity and discrimination. Specifically it examines:

- The meaning of inclusion

- The psychology of bias

- Diversity faultlines

- Organizational discrimination

- External Factors which impact on an organization.

Inclusion

Inclusion is a term which appears alongside diversity in journals and especially corporate information. Often these terms are used interchangeably. This begs the question, "What is inclusion, and how does it differ from diversity?"

What is inclusion?

The application of the term "inclusion" to organizations appears a recent development. The term has its roots in two other fields, education and social policy.

The term inclusion has been used in educational establishments since the 1970s, for example in the case of educating all or most children in the same classroom, including children with physical, mental, and developmental disabilities (McBrien & Brandt, 1997). Booth et al. (2000) suggest inclusion is concerned not only with those with impairments or those who are categorized

414

as "having special educational needs. Inclusion involves restructuring the cultures, policies and practices in schools so that they respond to the diversity of students in their locality. Inclusion in Education is one aspect of inclusion in society."

"Social inclusion" was a term first used in France in 1974, in relation to policy-making. "Social Inclusion is the process by which efforts are made to ensure that everyone, regardless of their experiences and circumstances, can achieve their potential in life" (Britton & Casebourne, 2002). People's group belongingness (or level of inclusion) can be regarded as a specific but central aspect of people's group membership and may often be a prerequisite for social relationships and group memberships in everyday life (Van Prooijen, Van den Bos, & Wilke, 2004).

In Work and Organizational Psychology inclusion as a diversity strategy attempts to embrace and leverage all employee differences to benefit the organization. As a result, managing all workers well has become the focus of many corporate strategies. Inclusion opens the pathway for a variety of different individuals to marshal their personal resources to do what they do best. While there are commonalities or general themes in terms of what people experience as inclusion – feeling valued, respected, recognized, trusted, and that one is making a difference – not everyone experiences these in the same way (Ferdman & Davidson, 2002). Inclusion therefore could be defined as the degree to which individuals feel part of critical organizational processes (Mor-Barak & Cherin, 1998).

Several key themes emerge from the above:

* Inclusion involves all people
* Inclusion is active: Inclusion is described as a process or strategy by some of the definitions
* Inclusion is measured by how people feel: i.e. it results in people feeling involved
* Inclusion needs effort to be achieved: there is the sense that inclusion has to be worked at to be fulfilled.

How does inclusion differ from diversity?

The basic concept of managing diversity accepts that the workforce consists of a diverse population of people. The diversity consists of visible and non-visible differences which will include factors such as sex, age, background, race, disability, personality and workstyle. It is founded on the premises that harnessing these differences will create a productive environment in which everybody feels valued, where talents are being fully utilized and in which organizational goals are met. (Kandola & Fullerton, 1994)

This definition seems to incorporate the four key themes of inclusion. The major difference in definitions of diversity and inclusion is one of emphasis: diversity emphasizes difference more whereas inclusion does not, otherwise they are remarkably similar.

Psychology of Bias

The psychology of bias encompasses many different aspects. This section looks at social identity theory and social categorization theory, prejudice and in particular a concept referred to as Modern Prejudice, and stereotyping and its suppression.

Social identity and social categorization

We all have multiple identities which are both personal and related to groups. The basis of Social Identity Theory (SIT) (Tajfel & Turner, 1979), and its related theory, Social Categorization (SCT), is that we relate more comfortably with people who have the same social identity as ourselves and that we have a related, but opposing, bias against people we see as being different.

SIT proposes we want to feel positive about ourselves. A key factor in obtaining this positive sense of self is to relate to who we see as similar. This group is our ingroup. The ingroup is the group we feel most comfortable being a part of. Our ingroup reinforces its own positive image which in turn helps us to feel positive about ourselves. As we know the members of our ingroup well we also recognize individual differences and consequently we will be less prone to stereotyping (i.e. the ingroup differentiation effect). This is in contrast to how we behave toward outgroups, i.e. those whom we see as being different and with whom we believe we have little in common. Lack of knowledge and contact with these outgroups means we are more likely to see them as all being the same (i.e. the homogeneity effect).

How do we choose people who are like ourselves? Factors such as race and sex are, not surprisingly, used commonly to help us determine who are members or our ingroup. The ingroup members will also share our attitudes and beliefs and they serve to validate who we are by supporting our views of the world. Being part of an ingroup provides a sense of comfort, security and no less importantly, pride (Bochner, 1994).

SCT involves the comparison of oneself and one's ingroup with the outgroup. This reinforces these feelings of security and pride and creates a sense of superiority over the outgroup.

One important aspect is that this desire to create categories and to place people into ingroups and outgroups is a natural cognitive impulse (Allport, 1954; Bruner, 1957; Higgins, 1996) which helps us to reduce the complexities in the

Table 19.1: Impact of categorization

Ingroup	Outgroup
– Members individuated	– Seen as homogeneous
– Difference accepted	– Differences minimized
– Positive information remembered	– Less positive information
– Greater recall of contributions	– More likely to forget contribution
– Works hard for ingroup	– Won't put in so much effort
– Prepared to make sacrifices for ingroup	– Less prepared to offer support
• Feelings of:	• Feelings of:
– Trust	– Anxiety
– Worth	– Distrust
– Self-esteem	– Unfamiliarity
– Security	– Hostility
(Turner, 1985)	**(Inskoet, 2001)**
(Gaertner & Dovidio, 2000)	**(Stephan & Stephan, 1985)**

world. It helps us decide who we will interact with more, who we will choose to be with and also, those people whom we well seek to avoid.

This desire to reduce uncertainty and to enhance our own self-esteem creates the need to categorize. Outgroups though are not only different but this difference is also seen as a deficiency and is the basis of derogation and stereotyping. The most powerful categories are those based on race, sex, disability, and sexual orientation (Hogg & Terry, 2000; Tajfel & Turner, 1979; Williams & O'Reilly, 1998).

This process of putting people into crude boxes of "us" and "them" is seen as a precursor for prejudice and for discrimination against them. The impact of categorizing people is shown in table 19.1.

Consequences for organizations

It is clear that not only do SCT and SIT have implications for organizations, but also that the effects can quite clearly be seen (Hogg & Terry, 2000). For example, in a study in a law firm it was concluded that "social identity may link an organization's demographic composition with an individual's workplace experiences" (Ely, 1994). Women in firms with fewer senior women had more negative experiences at work including less support from women peers and lower perceptions about advancement. However, being underrepresented and being seen as an outgroup by the majority will not have the same effect on everyone. For example, with a group of MBA students women and ethnic minorities were underrepresented. However only ethnic minorities formed their own ingroups. The female students formed wider social friendships and so became part of an enlarged majority ingroup (Mehra, Kilduff, & Brass, 1998).

This leads to ideas of a social marking, or the status of particular groups (Sampson, 1999). For example, in an organization there may be Asian and African Caribbean minorities. If the mark for Asians is seen as being less negative than that for Afro-Caribbean people then it will be easier for the former group to establish broader networks and friendships than the latter. Asians, by being part of the white networks therefore, may well be able to achieve more in terms of opportunities given to them. The other side of this coin is that African Caribbean's will then be more likely to form a stronger ingroup of their own which in turn reinforces the view of the them held by the white group. It all in effect, becomes a vicious circle.

This has led some to suggest, therefore, that the processes described within SCT and SIT will have detrimental effects within organizations as diversity increases. Indeed, in some studies it has been found that in organizations with greater diversity it is white men who have benefited more. The argument goes something like this:

- The white male ingroup is the one that holds power in the organization
- This group has high self-esteem and is naturally comfortable with its position
- As diversity increases within the organization this group becomes increasingly uncertain about the people they are dealing with
- To cope with this uncertainly they provide opportunities and advancement to those that they feel more comfortable about, namely other members of the ingroup.

This has been called the "glass escalator" (Maume, 1999).

What is needed, therefore, are processes which create greater intergroup inclusion. The intergroup boundaries are important here, i.e. who we describe as "them." Our natural inclinations will lead us to provide resources, opportunities, support etc. to those who are like us.

While we have many aspects to our identities the ones that we engage with at any given moment in time will be determined by circumstances. At one moment the most relevant group could be the football team you support, (e.g., Aston Villa), your profession (e.g., psychologist), your nationality (e.g., British). Some group identities are more visible than others, in particular race and sex. If you are in a minority you may well be more aware of those groups over all others. If you are working in an environment where others define you in those terms, explicitly or implicitly then the degree of discomfort and the feelings of "otherness" would be increased.

Two approaches have been put forward to deal with being categorized in this way. One is decategorization and the other recategorization (Dovidio et al., 1998; Gaertner et al., 1989).

Decategorization is where you seek to get members of two discrete groups to see people as individuals rather than members of a group. Recategorization involves getting the groups to see themselves as one group rather than being separate. Of the two, recategorization has been seen to work the best. Decategorization leads to more positive feelings toward the former outgroup members but also leads to making your former ingroup less attractive. By implication, therefore, your self-esteem, one of the drivers for being in an ingroup, may well be reduced.

Recategorization, however, does seem to provide better results. You can imagine a strong team leader, for example, creating a unified team ethic. Everyone is part of the team, the team has clear goals and everyone has their own part to play. This suggests clarity of goals, purpose and direction, but it also suggests strong management skills including dealing with conflict, self-reflection and preparedness to learn. These are themes we will return to later.

Modern prejudice

Prejudice can be seen to have three components:

A – Affective, i.e. feelings and emotions
B – Behavioral, i.e. actions
C – Cognitive, i.e. thoughts.

The cognitive components have been discussed in the earlier section describing SIT and SCT.

Prejudice is commonly defined as "an unfair negative attitude toward a local group or a person perceived to be a member of that group. Like other attitudes, it provides a schema for interpreting the environment by signaling whether others in the environment are good or bad, thereby preparing people to take appropriate action. Prejudice may be reflected in general evaluative response and may also involve emotional reactions, such as anxiety or contempt" (Davidio & Hebl, 2005).

As with the SIT and SCT, prejudice and stereotyping are deemed to (Fiske, 1998):

• Be enduring
• Have an automatic aspect
• Have social utility
• Be mutable
• Be influenced by social structures.

So there is something which is natural about prejudice and stereotyping. Critically, however, they can be changed.

Prejudice does not have to be something that we are consciously aware of. For example we may not be aware that we are categorizing people. This happens automatically on some dimensions, particularly race, sex and age (Fiske, 1998).

This is not necessarily a bad thing. In a world in which we are receiving and processing huge amounts of information in any given day, it is sensible, if not natural, to have a schema which helps us to interpret the data quickly (Bargh & Chartrand, 1999; Jacoby, Lindsay, & Toth 1992). On many occasions our data processing will be done accurately. This leads us to have faith in our decisions and impulses. However, there are occasions where our perceptions will be faulty.

Data in the US shows that racial prejudice has declined over the last 30 years, to the extent that approximately only 10 percent of the population have openly negative attitudes towards black people (Brief & Barsky, 2000). The key word in that sentence is "openly," and that is the starting point for recent research into prejudice, often referred to as modern prejudice. Prejudice is not about to become extinct, instead, as Dovidio and Gaertner (1998), put it, it is a virus that has mutated.

Modern prejudice contends that a prejudiced individual will hold back from voicing their attitudes or acting upon them until the situation they are in enables them to do so. The modern racist (McConahay, 1986), for example, will have seemingly rational and justifiable reasons for their views, decisions and actions. The working environment today and the legal context in which organizations operate do not allow individuals to voice their prejudices whenever and wherever they want. However, given the right circumstances our prejudiced individual will behave in discriminating ways. By these means the individual can present an image to the world, and indeed to themselves, as being fair, impartial and objective (Brief et al., 2000).

Another form of prejudice is referred to as aversive prejudice. This refers to the way ingroup members will view the qualifications of people from the outgroup (Dovidio & Gaertner, 2000).

Aversive racism, in recruitment situations, refers to the way black applicants' qualifications are compared to white applicants. Where the qualification requirements are clear, little bias is observed. When the qualifications required are unclear, however, bias against black applicants occurs. As one psychologist notes, however, the common theme of all these new forms of prejudice is "the conflict between the denial of personal prejudice and underlying unconscious negative feelings and beliefs" (Brewer & Brown, 1998).

There is also positive prejudice which refers to acting positively towards your ingroup members without suggesting acting negatively towards any outgroup members.

Consequences for organizations

Aversive, modern and positive prejudice are important for organizations. They provide a way of moving on the discussion about prejudice and discrimination. Prejudice is typically seen as something crude i.e. deliberate and obvious acts designed to have negative impact on outgroup members. Modern prejudice acknowledges however that prejudicial acts may not be intentional. Nor will it necessarily be obvious as the person will only make prejudicial decisions when the circumstances appear favorable. In addition, it does not have to involve acts *against* members of the outgroups. Instead, they may be actions which are in *favor* of other ingroup members.

What can be done to reduce prejudice? The conclusions reached in the most famous and pioneering book on this subject, the Nature of Prejudice by Gordon Allport (1954), are still relevant over 50 years after it was written. His finding was that contact with the outgroup was the best way to reduce prejudice.

For contact to work best four conditions need to be met (Allport, 1954; Pettigrew, 1997, 1998):

- Equal status
- Common goals
- Cooperation instead of competition
- Support of authorities and institutions

Intergroup friendship is recorded as an ideal contact experience and one where all four of the above are satisfied. The results of studies are summarized in box 19.1.

These four conditions have been tested in hundreds of studies, examining different groups in different circumstances, and the results show overall that they are influential in reducing prejudice (Pettigrew & Tropp, 2004).

These studies have helped to refine the original conditions. For example, it is accepted that the quality of contact is more significant than amount of contact.

Box 19.1:   Conditions for reducing prejudice

- Contact with out-group under four conditions

    1.   equal status

    2.   common goals

    3.   cooperation

    4.   support of authorities and institutions

- Quality of contact is more important than amount of contact

- Importance of the contact. The more important the contact is seen to be the more attitude change can be expected.

- Inclusion of others into one's own self-concept.

- The nature of the expected outcome is important

- The more personal the contact the higher chance of reducing prejudice

Furthermore, the importance of the contact also has an impact in determining the extent to which prejudiced attitudes are changed.

Other research has highlighted the importance of our own self-concept, based on the self-expansion model (Aron & McLaughlin-Volpe, 2002). This proposes that self-expansion is something that drives our behavior. Close relationships help us to achieve self-expansion. We incorporate others' identities into our own and they do likewise. Through this we can gain additional resources and achieve other outcomes. Friends in particular are treated with empathy and share resources with one another.

The amount of contact you have with outgroup members has been shown not to differentiate between those who are prejudiced and those who are not, what mattered was the inclusion of outgroup friends and acquaintances with oneself.

Having contact with outgroup members or even knowing them is not sufficient to change biased attitudes. The ingroup member has to attach some importance to the relationship (Omoto & Borgida, 1988). When we feel something is important we tend to have more information on those topics and we try to ensure our opinions are accurate, and they are less susceptible to other influences, such as images in the media.

Overall, what does this mean to organizations? Well, given the overwhelming view that the contact hypothesis works, there seems little reason for organizations not to ensure that this happens. This is potentially a very valuable way forward for organizations to progress in terms of diversity. However, the nature of the solutions has yet to be determined exactly.

With many managers, particularly top and senior managers, it may well be that approaches which seek to tap into the self-expansion model would appear to be very relevant. There is a real recognition in many organizations now that leadership and management development are critical for them to survive and thrive, now and into the future.

Equally there is a recognition that self-reflection, self-insight, and self-analysis are needed to ensure that managers grow both personally and professionally.

Our diversity approaches can and should be exploiting this desire for self-expansion quite directly.

This means:

- Looking at our leadership development programs and ensuring that we are providing participants opportunities to meet with people who may be seen as typical outgroup members.
- Creating opportunities for contact with outgroup members ensuring that the optimal conditions are achieved.
- Finding tools where people can explore their own behavior toward outgroup members.
- Helping people to find ways of recategorizing their groups by showing them how their behaviors can be more inclusive

- Developing the skills of empathy as these appear to be central in many of the discussions about dissolving the intergroup boundaries.

Stereotypes

Discussion of bias and prejudice would be incomplete without a discussion on stereotypes.

A stereotype can be defined as "a generalization of beliefs about a group or its members that is unjustified because it reflects faulty thought processes or over-generalizations, factual incorrectness, inordinate rigidity, misattributions or rationalization for prejudiced attitudes or discriminatory behaviors" (Dovidio, Brigham, Johnson, & Gaertner, 1996).

It is not the intention here to go into detail about the essential nature of stereotyping (these are summed up in box 19.2). Instead we will explore some of the more recent research into stereotyping and the findings which tell us more about how they operate and the potential implications for counteracting them. In particular we examine:

- Emotional reactions
- Stereotype threat
- Self-fulfilling prophecies
- The impact of suppressing stereotypes
- Recent research into the brain.

Emotional reactions

Interesting work has been done looking at the emotional reactions that stereotypes generate. Society has rules not only in terms of how we should behave but also the emotions we should experience should someone violate those norms (Eagly & Karau, 2002). These emotions could range from being disgusted and angry to being sympathetic. If the emotion is particularly strong this will lead to avoidance behavior (Jones et al., 1984).

One study (Fiske, Cuddy, Glick, & Xu, 2002) found that stereotypes basically vary along two dimensions – competence and warmth. Where a group is seen as highly competent but cold (e.g., rich people), we feel envy. Those high in warmth and lower in competence (e.g., older people, disabled people) tend to generate sympathy and pity. A combination of low competence and low warmth (e.g., black people) will result in feelings of contempt.

Interestingly, if someone behaves in a way that is counter to the stereotype, even where the stereotype is a negative one, this can lead to even worse feelings towards them. For example, the stereotype for women is that they should not be career minded and self-promoting. In one study (Rudman, 1998), self-promoting women were rated more negatively than self-promoting men and more negatively than non-self-promoting women. As a result they were less likely

> ## Box 19.2:   Key features of stereotypes
>
> - Stereotypes are generalisations about a group or members of a group **(Dovidio et al., 1996)**
>
> - They influence how information about a group or group member is acquired, processed, shared and recalled **(von Hippel et al., 1995)**
>
> - They provide shortcuts to enable us to decide how we should interact with others **(Mackie et al., 1996)**
>
> - Stereotypes can guide the way we decide to find out about others i.e. we tend to look for information that confirms our stereotype – the confirmation orientation **(von Hippel et al., 1996)**
>
> - Once stereotyped, we tend to see out-group members as being the same, i.e. the out-group homogeneity effect **(Dovidio and Hebl, 2005)**
>
> - Personality traits are over-emphasised e.g. black people are lazy. These can be traits as they are part of each person and long lasting. In effect provide rationalisations for the treatment of people from those groups **(Dovidio & Hebl, 2005)**
>
> - Information that disconfirms a stereotype is more readily ignored or treated as an exception i.e. so the stereotype remains intact **(von Hippel et al., 1995)**
>
> - Stereotypes do not have to be negative but out-groups are more likely to be described negatively. **(Esses, Haddock and Zanna, 1993)**
>
> - Knowledge of a stereotype does not mean that a person believes it.

to be hired. So going against a negative stereotype can also produce a negative outcome for those individuals.

Self-fulfilling prophecies

One powerful and destructive effect of stereotyping lies in self-fulfilling prophecies where a negative stereotype leads to lower expectations that transmit to members of the target group, potentially leading to poor performance. For example, two groups sat a mathematics test. One group was told that typically women perform worse than men on that sort of test. The other group were not given that statement. In the former group women performed less well than men. Interestingly, African-American students performed less well on tests just by being asked to provide data on their ethnicity (Steele & Aronson, 1995).

Where there are few minorities in a particular role or organization, it is likely they will receive greater scrutiny and stereotyping, leading to feelings of isolation, exclusion, and threat, affecting performance which declines and so is another manifestation of the self-fulfilling prophecy (Thomas & Chrobot-Mason, 2005).

Stereotype threat

Stereotype threat is something that is felt by members of outgroups and likely to be experienced most strongly where the outgroup member is not only in a significant minority but is also aware of the stereotypes that attach to their group. They will then be under pressure to act in way which does not allow them to be judged in the stereotypical manner. This increased self-awareness and self-consciousness places extra strain on the person in that position and this impedes performance (Steele & Aronson, 1995).

Ingroup members do not have this extra cognitive load and consequently can put more of their effort into the task in hand rather than worrying about whether their behavior conforms to a stereotype (Cheryan & Bodenhausen, 2000).

In conditions where the stereotype threat has been reduced, if not removed, the performance of outgroups improves.

The role of the brain

Research with new technologies, particularly Magnetic Resonance Imaging (MRI), has highlighted the importance of the amygdala. One of its functions is to help us determine the level of threat we are likely to face in any given situation and consequently what action we need to take, (e.g., Adolphs, Tranel, Damasio, & Damasio, 1994). MRI research has shown that amygdalla responses are different when we see pictures of our ingroup members to those of an outgroup (Hart et al., 2000). Thus it is possible that people who do not appear to have biased attitudes on the surface may nevertheless have unconscious biases. It appears that if we have knowledge about particular outgroup stereotypes, a response will be activated (Fiske, 1998). This could lead to discriminating behavior but not necessarily. The amygdala not only identifies potential threats but also helps us moderate our emotional response and can filter these before they reach consciousness.

There are individual differences. Some people will be more prejudiced toward a particular outgroup member than others and the strength of the response therefore will be stronger than with less prejudiced individuals (Blair & Banaji, 1996; Fiske & Neubert, 1990; MaCrae et al., 1997).

Interestingly, depending on the circumstances, each of us can behave differently. We are more likely to think and behave in prejudiced ways when we are:

- having to process mentally different things at the same time i.e. the cognitive load is higher
- under pressure
- trying to reach closure
- drawing overall impressions of people.

All of these conditions increase the likelihood (Fiske, 1998) of us thinking and behaving in a prejudiced way.

The good news is that it appears possible to overcome these effects. For example, by:

- asking people to look at others as individuals (i.e. to individuate)
- instructing people to be objective
- making them accountable to a third party
- creating situations where they and the outgroup member are mutually dependent on each other
- getting people to look for information that disconfirms or contradicts our stereotype (Wheeler & Fiske, 2005).

So while the research into the brain shows the extent to which we have automatic responses to others, it also shows that these responses are malleable and that by creating the right context we can moderate their effects.

Stereotype suppression

So overall, stereotypes are natural, often automatic, shaped by the society and the environment we live and work in and lead to distorted views of other people. Can they be suppressed?

One study (Dumon et al., 2003) looked at stereotypes of hairdressers i.e. that they are not very bright but they are sociable. Participants were told they were about to meet a hairdresser and they could choose questions from a list to ask them. One group were told that they could ask any of the questions, the other was told they could not ask questions based on the stereotypes of hairdressers. The good news is that the results showed that suppression of this stereotype led participants to ask a far wider set of questions than the control group. In effect, they appeared *not* to be looking for confirmatory evidence.

The bad news is that the evaluation the suppressors reached about the people they subsequently met were in fact more stereotyped. It appears that stereotype suppression led to more extreme stereotypical reactions.

Findings such as these have emerged from other studies. For example a group of people were asked to suppress stereotypes of skin heads (MaCrae et al., 1994). Participants then had to wait in a room for a while and on a chair were items suggesting they belonged to a skinhead. Participants who were from the stereotype suppression group sat further away than the control group.

This has been labeled the rebound effect and has potentially important consequences for organizations (Wegner, Schneider, Carter, & White, 1987).

In many organizations it is clearly unacceptable to make comments based on stereotyped judgments. This has led to environments where stereotypes are in effect being suppressed. This appears to be good, on the surface. However, this also could be creating a different set of problems. Suppressing a stereotype may in fact lead to an increased awareness of the stereotype when judgments have to be made about people.

Consequences for organizations

It is generally acknowledged that stereotyping occurs, although it may not necessarily be admitted by people. In many organizations discussions about stereotypes are not acceptable, and have been suppressed.

However, neither the issue nor the proposed solutions are as simple as that. Self-fulfilling prophecies and stereotyping threat can help us to understand what is occurring within organizations. Where individuals are in a minority they are more likely to be under extra scrutiny. This can have negative interesting effects when, for example, we look at performance management systems. It is likely that for people in a minority there will be an abundance of evidence to support evaluations that are made. We might be likely therefore to conclude that assessments reached are fair. What we need to look at also, however, is the extent of the scrutiny they appear to be under. Are the same levels of observations made for the ingroup? What we often also do not know is the expectation levels that managers have of their staff. Knowing this could provide us with evidence of the self-fulfilling prophecy effect.

We need also to be asking outgroup members about the knowledge of the stereotypes attached to their groups and the impact this has on their performance. No organization we know of has looked into these topics.

These results also show us that we need to explore different avenues for training and development within diversity. We need to find ways of enabling people to see their biases, to discuss them and to realize the effect it could be having on their decisions and actions.

Diversity Faultlines

This section discusses the new topics of diversity faultlines and, connected to that, the field of relational demography.

This section bridges the last, looking at prejudices, and the next one looking at organizational discrimination, as it seeks to locate what appear to be personal biases into an organizational and group context.

Faultlines

In its fullest sense diversity is about all the way in which a group or organization can be different. We are interested in work style as well as sex, personality as well as ethnicity, background and as well as age.

This obviously makes logical and practical sense. However, research shows that firstly, some demographic dimensions have greater impact on our perceptions and group relations than others, and secondly, that these are almost always used for categorizing purposes. Sex, race, age, and disability are some of the most significant. These we will call superordinate dimensions (Chatman et al., 1998: Cox, 1993).

The superordinate dimensions represent potential faultlines within any group (Lau & Murnigham, 1998). The term faultlines itself is intended as an analogy between geological faultlines that occur in the earth's crust and the social identity boundaries that can occur within organizations. Lau and Murnigham, define group faultlines as "hypothetical dividing lines that may split a group into sub-groups based on one or more attributes."

Where faultlines are identifiable and strong, problems are more likely to occur than not (Riordan et al., 2005). For example, imagine a group of new graduates in a team of auditors who are black, female, and in their early twenties. In the organization there are white male partners who have been in the firm for twenty plus years and who are middle aged. In this situation the subgroups divide completely on key dimensions – sex, race, and age. Millken and Martins (1996, pp. 414–15) noted, "Diversity in observable attributes have constantly been found to have negative effects on affective outcomes." They go on to say that this suggests "the possibility that deep seated prejudices some people hold against people who are different from themselves on race and gender (and other attributes) may be adding to the difficulty of interaction"

What the research also tells us is that conflict will be least when diversity in a work group is higher or when there is little or no diversity. In the former condition the subgroups will be smaller and more fragmented and so the faultlines are weaker. In the latter condition subgroups simply do not exist. It is reasonable to expect therefore, that organizations in the process of building up diversity should find greater conflict occurring (Riordan et al., 2005).

There are of course complexities in all of this. We have multiple identities that in practice can have an impact on how we perceive others and how we are perceived. Some parts of our identities bring certain privileges. For example, white women will have a certain degree of privilege owing to their color and ethnicity, but they will be denied other privileges due to their sex. If the white women appreciate and accept their privileged status then many will not identify with the issues confronted by black women. However, if they feel more the lack of privilege this will mean they connect more with the experiences of racial minorities.

Where a group is diverse with potentially strong faultlines, the effects can be mitigated by the personalities of the people involved. Where the minorities were more extravert, and the ingroup had high self-awareness, the effect of faultlines were not observed (Flyn et al., 2001).

So the experience of being in a minority will not be the same for all people. White males, white female, black males and black females will have different reactions to being in a minority. Similarly, there appears to be a relationship to positional and role status in the organization. The faultlines will not become so problematic if the group that people belong to is seen as being of high status.

Relational demography

Relational demography is a new but fascinating attempt to build theory around the dynamics of diversity within organizations. In particular it proposes that individuals are aware of and compare their demographic characteristics with those of others within the team, unit and organization. The level of similarity or difference between individuals will affect their attitudes and behaviors (Riordan & Shore, 2000; Williams & O'Reilly, 1998; Tsui, Eagan, & O'Reilly, 1992; Tsui & O'Reilly, 1989).

Its usefulness rests on the fact that it attempts to explain and even predict the impact diversity, or lack of it, will have on individuals.

Relational demography draws upon five theoretical strands.

- Similarity attraction
- Attraction–selection–attrition
- Social identity and social categorization
- Value in diversity
- Tokenism

Similarity attraction

People like to be with people who are like themselves (Lazersfeld & Merton, 1954; Hinds, Carley, Krackhardt, & Choley, 2000). This tendency, known as homophilia, occurs because people feel that they will understand their fellow group members more, will feel more comfortable being with them and consequently will feel increased trust. As we have already noted some demographic variables carry a lot more significance than others and these are used as a way of identifying people who are similar. Groups which are very different in terms of age, ethnicity and sex will have more obstacles to overcome than those which are similar.

Studies support the similarity attraction theory. In one study (Elvira & Cohen, 2001) in a large financial firm, it was predicted that there would be lower female turnover when there are more women at the same job level. This proved to be the case. Having more female peers led to lower female turnover and had far more effect than having women above and below them.

Attraction–selection–attrition

This is an extension of the similarity attraction theory and takes the personal desire to be with similar people and applies it to organizations. Attraction–selection–attrition (ASA) (Schneider, 1987) states that the mix of personalities, values and attitudes and interpersonal context are the key factors in determining organizational behavior. People who see themselves as similar to those in the organization will be attracted to it. This move toward homogeneity is heightened by organizations selecting people who are similar to those already in it.

Those who are dissimilar but get through the screening processes are more likely to feel uncomfortable in the organization and will then leave.

These processes may occur unconsciously but they are not random. The organization and those within it will attract and select people who are similar and it will serve to expel those who are different. The idea of organizational fit, which will be discussed further later, may be seen as an acceptable way of describing this process.

This model is one that can readily be seen in social groups. We choose to go toward people who are like us. Each social group has its own gate-keeping function. If people do not fit in with the social group they will leave and join another which shows the relevant demographic characteristics.

These ASA processes also cover access to power, information and opportunity within organizations. Informal social networks and friendship groups based on the ASA model determine who will have access to the relevant networks, mentoring, and senior level support (Riordan & Shore, 1997; Ibarra, 1995; Ragins, 1999; Thomas, 2001).

Social identity and social categorization

These have been covered in an earlier section, but the processes described by those theories are important aspects of relational demography.

Value in diversity

This describes studies which have looked at the conditions under which differences or dissimilarity might be beneficial, and is known as the value in diversity hypothesis (Ely & Thomas, 2001).

It would appear that:

- Functional background and diversity are useful characteristics to have for product innovation and for overall team effectiveness (Ancona & Caldwell, 1992)
- Product innovation is also enhanced by having people with different perspective with in the teams (Ely & Thomas, 2001; Williams & O'Reilly, 1998)
- Decision making can be better in culturally diverse teams. The open and frank discussions will eventually lead to greater effectiveness (Kirchmeyer & Cohen, 1992)
- Problem solving and generating solutions is better in diverse teams than homogeneous groups (Watson, Kumar, & Michaelson, 1993)
- Cooperation can be greater in very diverse groups compared to homogeneous groups (Cox, Lobel, & MacLeod, 1991).

Tokenism

Tokenism occurs where people are in a small minority, defined by being 15 percent or less. In these circumstances the people become tokens because they are not seen as individuals but instead as representatives or symbolic of a group.

In a seminal study examining the functioning of groups, Kanter (1977) found tokenism can affect performance. Being a token can affect performance in a number of ways (Pettigrew & Martin, 1987). Firstly, tokens may be stereotyped. Secondly, tokens may be subject to low expectations (cf. self-fulfilling prophecies) or unrealistically high expectations.

In addition, tokens can face dual pressures of having to work harder than others in order to be recognized but some will also not want to be seen as a threat so they try not to be too ambitious or too good.

Being a token, has negative consequences on individuals. Studies have shown that in America, black leaders working in white teams experience greater emotional difficulties including depression, anxiety, and lower self-esteem (Jackson, Thoits, & Taylor, 2005).

Tokens also are seen as having received preferential treatment and they experience negative consequences because of that (Pettigrew & Martin, 1987).

However, as the numbers of a group increase so the problems that groups experience can reduce, e.g., where women make up 20 percent or less of a workgroup, their performance ratings tend to be lower than men's. However, when the numbers increase to 50 percent or more, then their performance ratings tend to be better than those of males (Sackett et al., 1999).

Consequences for organizations

Relational demography is an exciting development of theory. It brings together many solid psychological concepts and theories and applies them to diversity. The overall description provides an explanation of many of the things that we see occurring in organizations. In other words it rings true. Now this is not sufficient to make a credible theory but it sure is a good start. It seems to be able to tell a good story which people can relate to.

Faultlines is a graphic way of describing the issues that individuals and organizations face. It is helpful because it does not attempt to hide from the fact that diversity does not always have beneficial consequences.

The other way that faultlines helps us is by recognizing that while people are different in many ways, some differences are noticed more than others and can create greater psychological responses.

Faultlines and relational demography are not just descriptive but they are also predictive. Studies on faultlines have demonstrated that they do occur in reality more often than not.

However, it also must be noted that where people have self-awareness or self-monitor, then the faultlines do not become apparent. So awareness and a willingness to adapt, accept feedback and to empathize can indeed mitigate the negative effects of greater diversity.

Organizational Discrimination

In this section, we will examine organizational discrimination. In the UK debate on this topic has been prompted by the report on the London Metropolitan Police's response to the murder of Stephen Lawrence, a black student.

The report pointed out many lapses in the reaction of police officers which led to action being taken very slowly. The report stated that there was a culture of institutional racism which created the conditions for officers to behave in this way.

Some people questioned whether institutional racism was just an invented concept.

The literature, however, reveals something different. It shows that organizations can have cultures where discriminatory and prejudiced behavior is more likely to occur.

Power and privilege

It is interesting how little these two topics are discussed within organizations and yet they appear central to much that is written about diversity in the literature.

Power

Social dominance theory indicates that all human social systems operate a caste system. The dominant (or hegemonic) group will strive to maintain its power and superior position in part through discrimination (Sidanius, Devereus, & Pratto, 2001). This will include the use of formal and informal processes.

Formal processes include retention and promotion criteria which may be subtly biased towards their ingroups.

Less formal processes will include social networks and through these networks mentors are sought and obtained.

Women and minorities will occupy more junior positions and where they achieve more seniority it will most likely be in areas less powerful within the organization (Ragins & Sundstrom, 1989).

This has a dual effect. Firstly, it limits these groups' access to power. Secondly, it can serve to reinforce stereotypes and prejudices. For example, a white male with prejudices will have these reinforced when he sees women and minorities occupying junior positions and white males occupying senior ones. Furthermore, some studies have found that where women are very underrepresented, they are not only considered by the men as not being a competitive threat but they are more likely to be competing with one another (Ely, 1994, 1995). In these situations, women were less likely to view senior women as role models "If getting to the top means being like her then I don't want it" is a comment that is heard frequently in our consultancy work.

As one commentator concludes: "The result of studies suggest that majority dominance, minority distinctiveness and limited access to organizational power and resources all contribute to individual and institutional discrimination."

However, where there is diversity at the top and throughout the organization, it is less likely to have people who rely on their stereotypes when dealing with others (Perry et al., 1994).

Privilege

If power is rarely discussed, then privilege is never discussed. A definition would be useful here.

Wildman (1996) defines privilege as the

> systematic conferral of benefit and advantage. Members of a privileged group gain this status by affiliation, conscious or not and chosen or not, to the dominant side of a power system . . . Affiliation with the dominant side of the power line is often defined as merit and worthiness. Characteristics and behaviors shared by those on the dominant side of the power line often delineate the societal norm.

This idea of privilege is probably noticed more by those who experience the lack of it, e.g., women and ethnic minorities, than those who have it e.g., white males.

The notion of privilege extends to everyday situations that we would normally pay very little attention to, for example, attending meetings with superiors. In this situation, a white male can expect to be confronted with people who are demographically, on some of the key faultlines, similar to himself. While meeting a senior manager may be nerve wracking, it may well be more stressful when you know you are demographically very different (McIntosh, 1993).

Privilege extends to other areas such as networking and mentors. Studies have found that ethnic minorities are more likely to have an ethnic minority mentor yet in terms of financial impact having an ethnic minority mentor was the same as having no mentor at all. In other words, having a white mentor is what counts (Dreher & Cox, 1997).

We need to recognize here that this privilege is unearned, undeserved and not merited. And yet those words – unearned, undeserved and not merited – run counter to any organization's values that we know of. Another effect of privilege is that despite being unearned, individuals with privilege will disassociate themselves from those without it. This can then lead to interpersonal discrimination including avoidance of people from those less privileged groups.

This, of course, leads us back to Social Identity Theory and Social Categorization Theory, i.e. where people seek to enhance their self-esteem and associate with groups where this can be achieved. Categorizing others, negatively we can also create a positive self-image of our own group and of ourselves. This can then help justify discriminatory behavior toward the outgroup.

Organizational culture

Organizational culture is seen as the most important cause of organizational discrimination. However, this is a big area and we need to concentrate on the individual elements of the culture further and in more detail.

Informal rules

Organizational culture determines "how individuals behave, what people pay attention to, how they respond to different situations and how they socialize with new members and exclude those who do not fit in" (Spataro, 2005).

Culture is not about formal policies necessarily but more about the informal control systems that operate. As they are informal; they are more subtle and difficult to pin down directly. In one study (Brief et al., 1995) with MBA students, it was found that their behaviors changed if it was known to them that the CEO thought discrimination against certain groups was a good thing. Organizations' formal policies will dictate what should occur and they will be quite explicit that people should be treated on merit. Formal procedures attempt to create "identity blind" (Konrad & Linnehan, 1995) processes but as the faultline research shows, this is practically impossible to achieve as some demographic characteristics have a very strong hold on our thoughts and actions.

Informal processes are critical in determining how people act. For example there may be regular instances of what would be called minor cases of discrimination. These may not be conscious nor do they have to include direct action. Instead, they may be things we do not do, like avoiding a group of people or not giving eye contact. People not only, for example, feel more comfortable with members of their own group (Pettigrew & Tropp, 2000), they are also more likely to be more disclosing, open and helpful. In addition, they are more likely to avoid contact with other groups (Dovidio & Gaertner, 1998). Avoidance may be based on a negative view but also some research has shown that avoidance can occur because people fear behaving inappropriately (Gaertner & Dovidio, 1986). These small actions and decisions may appear trivial taken in isolation but become considerable when aggregated. One study (Martell, Lane, & Ernrich, 1996) has shown that a 1 percent bias against women at an individual level translates into a 15 percent bias against recruiting women at a societal level. So these small incidents count.

A culture then can be determined by the way people act, what they consider important, what they chose to focus on. Some examples of what occurs in organizations include: regularly "scheduling evening meetings, recruiting and promoting people with high verbal fluency (e.g., polished English in presentations, input during meetings, self-confident speech patterns) and lack of wheelchair access" (Cox, 1994). In these examples it can be seen that a powerful ingroup is determining how the organization should be run, who should be included and who should be excluded.

A strong culture will be one where people are expected to conform to a clear set of norms and behaviors. Those people who are different may be expected to change and behave like the majority. The strength of the culture is important but not as important as you might think (Cox, 1994). Weak cultures are no better. Where people are allowed to do what they want you may well find much greater tolerance of prejudiced behavior. What is really required is a strong culture in which diversity and inclusion are considered important values.

The ideal culture would appear to be one with a strong set of guiding principles about the overall way people are expected to behave but with tolerance for individual differences.

Organizational learning

Argyris (1977) has identified two types of learning that are needed within organizations – reactive and reflective. Reactive learning is more appropriate for routine or repetitive issues. Reflective learning is more appropriate for complex, non-routine problems. For diversity and inclusion reflective learning is required. This means examining situations carefully, trying to see what occurred and the learning the lessons for the organization as a whole and not just for that specific occurrence.

Organizations have set ways of doing things – their routines, if you will. Seemingly effective routines will become accepted, and difficult to change. Inertia means routines are difficult to change even when cases of discrimination appear. An analysis of disability related court cases in the US (Wooten & James, 2005) has shown that one of the principal problems with regard to diversity and inclusion is that organizations treat discrimination as one-off events and so engage in reactive learning, i.e. trying to find a solution to that particular problem. Furthermore, the organization may not be prepared to accept that discriminatory behavior occurs and/or they do not want bad publicity. Such defensiveness means that incidents will be treated as isolated incidents. Wal-Mart had seven separate violations of the disability discrimination legislation in the US. It appeared to have treated each incident as a one-off. HR have a powerful role in examining discrimination cases to ensure that more reflective learning takes place (Wooten & James, 2005). The tendency to cover up embarrassing incidents is anti-learning (Argyris, 1990).

Window dressing

Another reason why organizations do not learn sufficiently is because they believe their own publicity, otherwise known as window dressing. This is, as the name suggests, a superficial commitment to diversity and inclusion.

Wal-Mart have been criticized for window dressing because although they incorporate disabled people into their advertisements, it has done little to prevent discrimination against disabled people (Wooten & James, 2005).

Organizations most likely to engage in window dressing from studies done in the US are voluntary organizations, government departments and agencies and retailers.

Organizational fit

This is a term that is used frequently in many organizations. As it is commonplace, carries a clear meaning and is accepted, it makes it a difficult concept to challenge.

Organizations with strong cultures typically perform better than those with weaker cultures. It makes sense therefore for the organization to attract people who will fit with its culture. Back to the attraction–selection–attrition model, part of Relational Demography: organizations will also attract people who feel they should fit and will remove those people who do not.

In situations where people are clearly qualified to do a job, you find that adverse impact is less prevalent. However, when you move into general management, the need for specific qualifications is not so apparent. Here you find adverse impact occurs (Dovidio & Gaertner, 2000). Women and minorities tend to lose out in such roles. Heilman (2001), suggests that the lack of women in senior levels in organizations is due to stereotypes that "result in devaluation of their performance, denial of credit to them for their successes and their penalization for being competent."

The same process affects disabled people, where the notation of "fit" includes an implicit aspect of "ableness" (Wooten & James, 2005).

Networks

It is often the case that when carrying out diversity audits that a key problem will be the "old boy network." The people making this observation will have difficulty pinning down exactly what this is or how this occurs, but they know it is happening.

The senior men in the organization will have little idea as to what this means due to a lack of concrete examples. It may even be denied as an issue. This may be because it is seen as an issue referring to golf days, gentlemen's clubs, drinks with the boys, i.e. overt actions. However, it appears to be far more subtle than this. It is not necessarily a bias against a particular group of people, more a bias for. The people we choose to talk to, the ones we impart information and knowledge to, the ones we give opportunities to, are what these networks are referring to (Krieger, 1998).

Related to the issue of networks is that of mentors. People who are the same as those in senior positions will be able to find mentors more often, more quickly (Gefland et al., 2005).

Where outgroup members have other outgroup members as their mentors, the results are often less favorable. Their mentors will often be less powerful, with few privileges and can be of less benefit to the mentee.

External Factors

Organizations do not exist in isolation. They are located in communities and are influenced by national customs, cultures, legal frameworks, and markets conditions.

National culture

In a seminal study, Hofstede, a Dutch anthropologist, found that national cultures could be differentiated on a number of dimensions, two of which are relevant to diversity: the extent to which a culture is individualistic or collectivist; and the way it views hierarchy, otherwise known as power distance.

Collectivist cultures prioritize collective goals over individual ones. These cultures emphasize unity and community. In individualistic cultures, the individual is most interested in their own achievement. Individual success is highlighted, praised and rewarded. The words used to describe the different end of the scale – unity, community on the one hand; individualism, pursuit of your own goals on the other – may lead you to think that as far as diversity is concerned a collectivist culture may be more beneficial. However, the opposite is true.

Research has shown that, compared to individualist cultures, collectivist ones show more ingroup bias. Collectivism extends to one's ingroup not to outgroups. The inter group boundaries will be more clearly defined (i.e. the faultlines). The powerful ingroups will be more likely to derogate the outgroups and will show far more favoritism to ingroup members. In such collectivist cultures this behavior will be more overtly apparent.

Individualist cultures recognize individual achievement and are more likely to recognize and reward success irrespective of the individual's perceived group membership.

Furthermore, those cultures which prefer a more hierarchical approach in the way they deal with their bosses should also display more resistance to diversity and inclusion because, as was noted earlier, bureaucratic organizations are less likely to be inclusive by nature. Bearing this in mind therefore it may be no surprise that the US, high on individualism and low on power distance, is taking the lead on diversity and inclusion.

Legislation

Organizations work within legal as well as cultural boundaries, and more and more countries within the developed world have some antidiscrimination legislation.

Clearly, having legislation is not enough. It needs to be effectively implemented and transgressors appropriately penalized. Where all three of these conditions apply there will clearly be an incentive for organizations to take action to ensure that they comply.

When dealing within a global environment therefore we should be able to predict those countries where organizations will be making more effort to eliminate overt discrimination.

It can often be a shock for people moving from one country with well-established antidiscrimination legislation moving to one where there is none, to experience the level of overt discrimination occurring.

Stakeholder impact

There are other stakeholders who can have an impact on organizations policies and practices. Stakeholders can include:

- Unions – to what extend do they consider diversity and inclusion issues?
- Customers – are their purchasing behaviors influenced by good or bad diversity and inclusion practice? Are customers are prepared to unite to boycott an organization?
- Government departments – when making procurement decisions etc, are diversity and inclusion practices considered as part of the criteria? In the US public authorities can use this particular lever with significant effect. There is little doubt that this will occur in the UK.
- Shareholders – do they see a relationship between diversity and inclusion and the value of their investments? Is it a concern? It should be noted that there is an increasing concern amongst fund managers and analysts about the way people are treated within organizations, such factors are becoming more important in predicting how an organization will perform.

Market conditions

When employment levels are high diversity issues come higher up on the agenda. The supply of good staff becomes less plentiful, competition for people intensifies and it is only natural that more effort will be placed on recruiting, selecting, and retaining good people. However during economic downturns, unemployment increases, the supply pool enlarges and diversity becomes less relevant.

Also, organizations are influenced by the behavior of their peers. If an organization is working in a sector where few others take diversity seriously, the expectation will be that this one will not make it a priority either. Peer group pressure works with leaders as much as anyone else.

Implications for organizations

The environment that an organization is located within can give us certain clues about the way it will respond to diversity and inclusion.

By examining the national culture, the legislative framework, stakeholder impact and market conditions we should be able to form hypotheses about how an organization will respond to diversity and inclusion. This creates problems for global organizations however. The intentions are to ensure that diversity and inclusion are taken seriously in all their operations. The external environment however will have a considerable bearing of what needs to be done.

There is a tendency for organizations to leave their local operations alone, to allow them to do their own thing. However, where the external pressures are less powerful, the internal pressures need to be stronger if any impact is to be achieved.

Research has also revealed that American female expatriates experience overt prejudice and discrimination from most nationals. The same is true for US minority expatriates.

We should also bear in mind the research on implicit bias discussed in an earlier section. Here it was found that many prejudices will be held in check because they will be seen as unacceptable. However, given the right circumstances they are more likely to be revealed. If a person with covert prejudices is moved to a position of power and status in another culture where most discrimination is not tolerated they may well also take the opportunity to behave in discriminatory ways.

Summary

There is much to consider in this review of the recent literature.
  Discrimination in organizations is a combination of:

- Individual biases and prejudices. Much of this will be natural reactions. However, we will also be taking these biases into the workplace and this will impact on how we relate to one another and the decisions we make.

- The organizational culture will determine the extent to which these prejudices play out at work. It is the informal rules which are more powerful here.

- External factors and pressures will also determine how seriously diversity will be taken.

What this review has revealed is if organizations want to create inclusive environments then these issues of personal bias and organizational discrimination need to be tackled.

Discrimination and prejudice are much more subtly expressed than before. Therefore we need different methods to reveal this and different solutions to tackle it.

A focus for attention has to be the leaders of the organization with obvious implications for their development. However, in addition to this we need to develop audit tools sensitive to the ways diversity and discrimination operate.

Discussion Points

Biases can affect us all, so consider what biases you think you have and how they may impact on your decision-making and behavior?

How do you think an organization may be biased? Among other factors consider attraction and selection of candidates, performance appraisal, and the language and behavior of leaders.

Roles and Methods of Work and Organizational Psychology Practitioners

20

Henry Honkanen and Ute Schmidt-Brasse

Overview

In this chapter we try to analyze and describe the professional field of work and organizational (w/o) psychologists. We correspondingly ask questions like: Where are w/o psychologists working? What does the profession and work of w/o psychology look like? What are the typical tasks and assignments offered to us? Who are our working partners? What are the typical roles we are playing, and what are the working models we are using? How can we meet the clients' requirements? Where do we find the practical tools and methods we apply? In responding to those questions and by providing some models and general thoughts this chapter may also stage some sort of contextual and explaining frames for the articles to follow in this book.

The chapter starts by looking at the knowledge base of the profession from two different angles – the contribution of science and the part of practice and professional community. We then turn to outline how we as w/o psychologists work in three different subfields of our discipline, i.e. work psychology, organizational psychology, and personnel psychology. We then analyze more closely the multidisciplinary nature of developing organizations, management, and human resources. Subsequently, we try to answer the questions how our work is generated and who our clients in organizations are before we go over our work process and give some examples of the typical methods and tools applied. We conclude the chapter delineating typical roles we are playing in our work and defining the competences, skills and ethical conduct required if claiming to be a proper and respectable professional in work and organizational psychology.

The Basis of the Profession

Whom are we writing about?

W/o psychology practitioners work in social contexts – with someone or for someone, sometimes employed in organizations like industrial enterprises or service providers or in nonprofit organizations, sometimes as freelancers in bigger consulting firms or on their own, sometimes for the whole organization, sometimes for parts of organizations, sometimes for individual clients. They work as Human Resources or personnel managers or as in-house specialists, as process consultants, trainers, coaches etc. In most of these settings – internally as externally – they predominantly work as or in the sense of consultants trying to help and support clients in an interactive, appreciative, and consistent way and materializing their "help for self-help" motto in order to transfer their interventions into routine and to make their clients self-dependent and qualified to deal with their tasks, projects, issues on their own and without further external follow-up.

The role of science

The work of a practitioner w/o-psychologist generally is based on two pillars, similar to the work of any other psychologist: (1) on the science of psychology, and (2) on the proven professional practice.

First, work of the practitioner rests upon the science of psychology or more specifically on the discipline of w/o psychology. Our scientific training enables us to think critically and to differentiate between the "scientific" and the "non-scientific." This is an essential competence because in the world of work and organizations we find all kinds of emerging and disappearing management fads and consulting products.

Thus, working science-based means that all we are doing and saying as w/o psychologists should be reasonably justifiable from a scientific point of view. Following this principle sometimes turns out to be challenging because psychology as a science does not offer wisdoms beyond doubts and absolute truths – as it does not give us the one generally applicable and comprehensive theory that explains all. But being conscious of these limitations, the science of psychology still provides us a steadily growing range of elaborate knowledge and proven experience in order to support and help our clients reliably.

The important question is how the knowledge base of our profession is generated or created. According to Hodgkinson et al. (2001) there are two different approaches to knowledge production and meaning construction (see also Hodgkinson & Herriot, 2002). The first approach stresses theoretical and methodological rigor and is based on traditional scientific inquiry, the second looks out for practical relevance and rests upon pragmatically solving problems. In the problem-solving approach, knowledge typically is generated by various stakeholders and multidisciplinary teams in the context of application; the working methods and procedures are rather creative and diffuse than disciplined and directly repeatable; it can be hard to trace the results back or to explain them with hindsight, and they are usually more context-specific than easily generalized. The transferable learnings are more likely to be of a procedural nature than outcome-centered. Actually, Hodgkinson et al. perceive that over recent years the w/o psychology science possibly has too much and too one-sidedly preferred the first – strongly empirical, methodologically rigorous – to the second – application-oriented, socially relevant – approach. They note that many of our nonpsychological competitors, such as management consultants, HR professionals, or accountants otherwise have adopted and pursued a hands-on problem-solving approach (with the result flourishing business). However, the danger is to generate quasi-populist and over-simple solutions for complex problems.

Of course, to be successful we need both these approaches – the question is how to find the proper balance between them. For the academic side, Hodgkinson et al. suggest some sort of "Pragmatic Science" producing knowledge that is both valid and of practical relevance and "determined far more than it is at present by the needs of the users of research." This seems to directly mirror and fit in with the kind of "Scientific Pragmatism" of the practitioners' problem-solving approach which looks at the incurring operational and practical issues, purposes, and context first and then looks out for applicable scientific concepts and evaluation methods as a basis and prerequisite for responsible w/o psychologist practitioner professionalism. This hands-on approach may also generate interesting onsets for further w/o psychological research.

In fact the situation does not look ideal in the field of management either. According to Kieser (2002) management science, the consultancy system, and the client (the management system) live a highly autonomous life of their own. There is a dire need to dismantle communication barriers between clients and consultants. In addition, science should move towards increasing its attractiveness as a learning agent for organizations.

The role of practice

The second pillar the work of w/o-psychologist is based on are state-of-the-art practices accepted by the professionals working in the field. This "community of practice" is influential in various ways. Many of the skills or competencies needed in the work of a practitioner psychologist are developed and acquired through work experience alone. Especially so-called tacit knowledge can only be transferred through social means and in a social context, i.e. by the practitioner being involved in the profession in the field and exchanging information with peer experts. This rather pragmatic problem-solving approach influences the development and creation of professional practice a great deal.

The professional community also creates, maintains, and controls the norms and codes (see later on) all practitioners should follow. It keeps up the unique identity of the profession, too. The separate professional identity of w/o psychologists has formed and become much clearer over the last 15 years: When defining our identity as w/o psychologists we need not only consider the difference regarding other areas of psychology but also with respect to other professions working in the field of work, organizations, and management. In many cases, as practitioners, we cannot restrict our working approach purely to our own discipline but we have to be ready to cooperate and cope with other disciplines and professions as well, such as business, economics, engineering, pedagogy, sociology, or medicine.

Ideally we could claim that the science of w/o psychology be a universal and context-free discipline, although certainly the subjects of research often depend on the context. However, the communities of practice inevitably are context-dependent. There are cultural differences – even in Europe we will easily find different practices and ways of thinking and doing that vary from one country or region to another. In addition, the profession is bound to historical, economical, political, or societal contexts. Next, the work of the practitioner w/o psychologists is greatly defined by the market forces and by technical progress. We are expected to satisfy our clients' needs – whatever they are or however they are defined – the boundary being our code of ethics.

Actually, there are many dynamic factors (scientific and societal) influencing the formation of practices in the field of w/o psychology. Thus our profession is continually evolving and progressing. This is simultaneously very confusing, exciting, and inspiring. That's the real essence and empowering challenge of our work as w/o psychologists.

Different Views of our Fields of Work

Three main fields of the discipline and profession: the ENOP Model

What do work and organizational psychologists do? The area of practice can be divided into three main fields which are defined in the so-called ENOP model (ENOP 2005) as follows:

- work psychology
- organizational psychology
- personnel psychology.

In the field of work psychology the typical areas are issues such as job analysis, work design, ergonomics, occupational safety and health issues, coping with stress as well as the issues of well-being and work. This approach emphasizes the development of the work system as such, the relationship of the individual and the work setting (e.g. the man–machine interface) and enhancing performance at work. Work psychologists locate and analyze those points in the work process that are ineffective or causing too much stress and try to find better ways of achieving the same or even increased output. They redesign the tasks so that jobs are more motivating and offer opportunities to learn and improve. Their target can also be to eliminate the possibility of human error and accidents from the work process.

In the field of organizational psychology the typical areas of interest roughly are organizational development and change from vision work to downsizing decisions, management, and leadership as well as intrapreneurship, group work, and team development as well as cross-departmental client orientation. Psychologists work as organizational development consultants carrying out organizational diagnostics by using e.g. climate surveys. They support change management projects by facilitating the process and the involvement of people and helping them to cope with new situations. They build up models of more effective communication in organizations, mediate common understanding of leadership and cooperation, or act as a catalyst in conflict situations.

In the field of personnel psychology (or human resources psychology) the focus of interest is on the individual and his or her performance and development in the organization. The typical areas are personnel selection and assessment, vocational guidance and counseling, career management, outplacement, performance appraisal, rewarding, training, and coaching. When selecting new employees the organization can appoint a psychologist to assess the candidates by using psychological tests or interview techniques. W/o psychologists also plan and carry out assessments and appraisals linked with performance management or competence development programs. W/o psychologists as trainers or coaches develop the interpersonal skills (e.g. leadership or group work skills) of the employees or help them discover their own talents and strengths, find their goals, and elaborate the best way how to get there.

In practice, these tasks and fields often are interwoven with each other. When developing some work processes we easily face many issues at an individual level. But perhaps we also have to find out about requirements of work and to assess the present capacity of workers to perform adequately. Additionally, we might be faced with a gap in their knowledge and skills or even with health or safety problems which impair their performance. Another example of multiple issues could be developing work motivation. In the area of work psychology we could use job rotation as means of maintaining motivation. As an organizational psychologist we could develop teamwork so that people are more empowered. And in the field of personnel psychology we could support people in the development of their competences and guide them on a more energizing career path.

A systemic view of a w/o psychologist's work

The above-mentioned fields – work, organization, and personnel – represent three different system levels of organizational life. Another way to analyze the work of a w/o-psychologist is presented in table 20.1. Here we identify three main target areas of organizational, developmental, or change work. For example, within developmental work, a consultant can try to influence one or more of the following areas:

- the "*hardware*" of the organization: including structure, business processes, technology, the task and the work system of the organization,
- the "*peopleware*" of the organization: including the whole workforce through-out the organization – human resources, its management and competence development,
- the "*software*" of the organization: including the social processes of the organization, how change is managed, leadership, culture, values, or conflict management.

As we see in table 20.1, a mixture of professionals is working in the field of organizational development representing different disciplines. Management consultants dominate many of the areas at the "hardware" level – usually their background is engineering or economics. However, w/o psychologists are able to contribute a lot to the area of work-processes or organizational design or when developing the work environment.

The area of "peopleware" covers many of the core issues of w/o psychology. In this field w/o psychologists could play a dominant part. Nevertheless, they are in strong competition with other influential professions such as HR professionals and experts who have their background in economics, educational science, pedagogy, other behavioral sciences, or even healthcare. Especially in the area of training we see a varied background.

Professionally, the area of "software" is the most diverse one and consequently is subject to the hardest competition between the different approaches and disciplines. The issues of social processes are congruent to the core issues of social psychology and this is why w/o psychologists feel they are able to contribute a lot – we might even claim ownership of many of the questions. However, especially in the areas of organizational change and leadership, anyone involved in management, in whatever way, claims to be an expert. Here w/o psychologists play an important role as agents of change, work place counselors, team builders, OD or process consultants, but so do many other professionals, too.

A managerial view to w/o psychology: using the St. Gallen Management Model as a taxonomic frame

In terms of management we can look at the three "-wares" as similar to the "pillars," one of the two perspectives which in the St. Gallen Model of Management (Bleicher, 1991, 1994; figure 20.1) are interlinked in a matrix built of:

- three "pillars" of management: Structure (organization of structure and procedures), Policies (goals, visions), and Culture (behavior, communication), representing and organizing the problem fields of managerial activity and of
- three "levels" of management: the normative, the strategic, and the operative management level. The normative level looks at the purpose and defines

Table 20.1: The types of organization developmental and consulting work (adapted from Honkanen, 1999)

System level	The target of development or change	The content of typical developmental or consultant work	The type of experts, consultants, or change agents involved
Hardware	• THE STRUCTURE AND BUSINESS PROCESSES	strategic management, organizational design, task structure, business process improvement, management systems	– management consultants – experts on business economics – production engineers – organization design experts
	• THE TASK AND THE WORK SYSTEM	the developing of work settings and work environment, safety on work, health in work	– experts on work-study and ergonomics – work psychologists
Peopleware	• HUMAN RESOURCES	HRM, resource planning, recruiting, career management, appraisals, occupational health	– recruiting and personnel assessment consultants – career counselors – HR-managers
	• COMPETENCIES	HRD, training, educational programs	– training institutions, trainers, coaches – HRD-managers
Software	• CHANGE IN THE ORGANIZATION	the change processes, participative change management, learning organization	– experts on organization theory and change management – action researchers – on-the-job counselors – experts on group dynamics and team development
	• LEADERSHIP, VALUES, CULTURE, CONFLICTS	developing interaction, social processes, problem solving skills, the well-being of people	– organization psychologists – OD-consultants and change agents – process consultants – work place counsellors

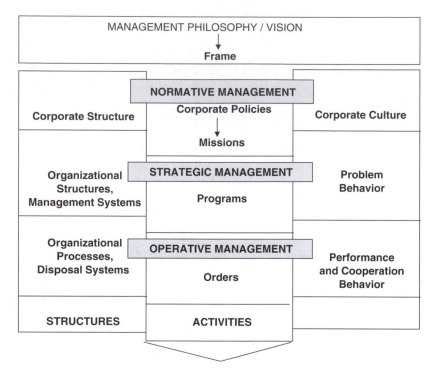

Figure 20.1: Development of the enterprise (picture adapted from Bleicher, 1994)

corporate goals in the context of society and economy. It procures sense and identity internally as well as externally and lays the ground for all activities of the management. Strategic management derives its reference parameters from the normative level, develops programs how to achieve goals, defines structures and systems to be effective and helpful, and cares for success securing behavior. Normative and strategic management are materialized by operational conversion into down-to-earth performance, financial, informational, and social processes. To cut a long story short: Whereas normative and strategic management configure and design = build the conceptual frame operative management as day-to-day business concept-driven fulfils and controls the corporate development.

The "pillars" and "levels" are related to each other, they depend on each other, and they are driving each other in two directions:

- Vertically, the pillars stress the problem fields of managerial activity (structure, policies, or culture) and point to the consistent line through the different levels of generalization: one topic percolating down from normative to strategic to operative level, one deriving out of the other and thus integrating conception and materialization.

- Horizontally, the management levels (normative, strategic, and operative) clamp together and integrate the activities across the problem fields of management on the different levels thus avoiding problem-egoistic solutions and interventions and safeguarding a systemic and comprehensive managerial view and development.

This model adds a systematic taxonomy of abstraction of tasks in an organization to our description and shows how and where on these (hierarchical) levels to pigeonhole the different management tasks.

Accordingly, the model defines the levels on which w/o psychologists are delivering added value to their clients. Actually, w/o psychology practitioners are working on all levels mentioned: On the normative level, where structure, policies, and culture are influenced and defined on a relatively general and comprehensive corporate tone – w/o psychologists as methods specialists e.g. facilitate processes to find and formulate missions or company guidelines with respect to corporate culture. On the strategic level they help to e.g. develop concrete and achievable goals and strategies and construct fitting instruments and tools to percolate those goals and strategies down through all hierarchical levels. On the operative level, w/o psychologists e.g. take all actions needed and commissioned in the life of the organization to work with the given or evolving structures, they accompany current operational activities, and they train, coach, and monitor concrete behavioral topics – be it with groups or be it with individuals.

Diversity of w/o psychological work

What can we learn from this multiformity of the w/o psychology arena?

The first finding is that the wide spectrum of our profession is demanding. It is impossible to be an expert in all areas, issues or applications – even in the domain of w/o psychology itself. We are bound to specialize.

The second finding is that dealing with work, organization, and personnel is a multidisciplinary business. Even if we could draw upon certain issues and areas as belonging to the academic discipline called w/o-psychology, there is no realistic way for practitioners to claim an ownership or monopoly to this knowledge. Other professions involved are using the knowledge of their own disciplines, but simultaneously are making borrowings from w/o psychological knowledge integrating them in their work. As psychologists we should do the same: Prop up ourselves on our own discipline and utilize the knowledge base of others, too. But there are limits to expand one's expertise and we should responsibly observe where those limitations and boundaries are. Consequently we learn: There is the inevitable need to work and cooperate interdisciplinarily.

A third finding suggests that w/o psychology practitioners depend in a way on their clients. That is why they must dive into the world of management with its context of society and economy and try to understand the logic of managers. They have to respect and support or improve their clients' processes, systemic relations, conditions, and interfaces, should scrutinize the level on which work is done in order to adjust their interventions, and observe the added value they are expected to bring up.

Working Process and Methods

How is our work generated?

Where do our commissions come from? How are the developmental tasks defined and methods chosen? In the introductory considerations we have already made the point that w/o psychologists are expected to satisfy their clients' needs. That means that w/o psychology practitioners – as internal and external consultants – and managers are complementary partners in their working fields. As a fact, consultants and their clients, e.g. the managers are initially independent, autonomous systems with their own realities. In order to arrive at a suitable consulting relation these systems must become interconnected (Gehringer & Pawlik, 2000).

We can describe management work as a series of tasks and functions that can be performed both in larger organizations and in smaller teams. These different process- and action-oriented tasks can be seen to form a sort of problem-solving wheel or management cycle (see the outer cycle in figure 20.2). In order to survive, every organization or team should keep this cycle running without disturbance. However, there are various factors that may prevent the smooth and frictionless flow of operations along the cycle. The constraints may comprise e.g.: a communication mismatch, a break in information flow, too complex an environment to be understood, poor performance, difficulties in management decision-making, or for example lack of management skills. If the managers and employees were able to accomplish all their tasks and solve all the problems by themselves, there would not be any need to ask for help from a consultant or w/o psychologist. But they often are confronted with new and complex or time-eating challenging situations demanding knowledge, skills, resources, time, or motivation which they do not possess or do not have the possibility or capacity to procure or acquire in time. These are the situations where a need arises to make use of an expert or an additional hand.

In a sense the tasks and roles of consultants and managers do not differ greatly from each other. In fact, the link between consultancy and management work should be self-evident: consulting is a service function, the objective of which is to support the fluent performance of different management functions in the organization. However, in practice linking these two areas can be of utmost difficulty.

Figure 20.2 illustrates one possibility how the interconnection could ideally look like. The developmental or consulting cycle drawn in the centre of the

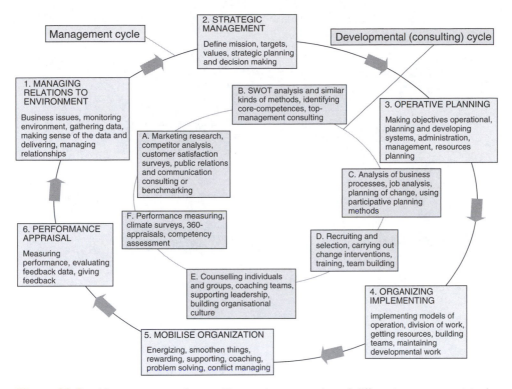

Figure 20.2: Management and consulting cycles: examples of different management tasks and developmental or consulting methods compared (adapted from Honkanen, 2006)

management cycle describes different services and methods the consultant uses in order to support the functioning of the management task in question. The idea is that the management cycle and the developmental cycle optimally should run in synchronization. However, in practice, these cycles many times live a life of their own. Managers ask for services and methods that do not fit the problem in hand. Alternatively, consultants offer solutions and models that reveal their poor understanding of what the client really needs. We often hear that even HR departments are blamed for developing services which managers (and employees) do not really need or that they do not support the organization in achieving its goals but strive for their own ones. What is to be done to resolve this problem?

It is obvious that mutual information about goals, common elaboration of decisions and tasks, and perfect adjustment of means and processes are badly needed in order to synchronize flow of performance of both, managers and consultants, and to generate sustainable results for the organization. That is why it is necessary to follow a systematic way of delivering the work of – internal and external – w/o psychologists.

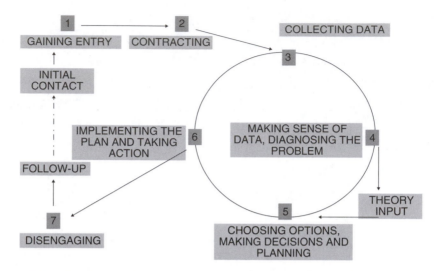

Figure 20.3: The phases of consulting process (Cockman et al., 1999)

The phases of consulting work

Whenever we work with someone to help solve a problem we are beginning a process that starts and ends somewhere. In the area of change management we can find descriptions of change processes and their different phases, for example the famous Lewin three-phase model: unfreeze, move, refreeze. In the field of the OD the process is usually described as follows (Senior, 2002): diagnose current situation, develop a vision for change, gain commitment to the vision, develop an action plan, implement the change, assess and reinforce change. We present in figure 20.3 a model constructed by Cockman et al. (1999).

When a w/o psychologist starts to work with a client (be it an individual, a team, or an organization) he or she first faces the questions of making an initial contact, establishing the working relationship and contracting with the client (phases 1 and 2). These phases define who are our clients, what do they need and whether we might be able to help them. We may e.g. carry out different kinds of need or requirement analyzes. The essential data and comprehensive understanding mainly are generated by discussing and negotiating with the client (and the respective employees). Additionally, systematic interviews or surveys or field observation can be used as well as exploiting all data available from the client's organization. In contracting, the most important issues will usually arise in the area of the so called psychological contract, i.e. the tacit set of expectations of the w/o psychologist and the client about what each will give and receive in the relationship. Trials to make these expectations fully explicit often prove difficult and according to Schein (1999) are not very feasible or fruitful because of remaining "black holes" and the ever changing reality when we move on.

In the diagnostic phases (3 and 4) we may apply a number of different methods, tools, and approaches to collect the data. For example we can deploy psychological tests to assess employees or climate surveys to explore the satisfaction of the personnel in general. Additionally, we can engage our clients to use the diagnostic tools by themselves or to analyze the results. In any case, it is crucial to choose the appropriate tools and ways to collect the data because the quality of data influences and directs our interpretations and judgments essentially – and stating a wrong diagnosis could be fatal. However, the client does not always need to know the full "objective or absolute true" – sometimes this could even do harm. Much more important is that the data and the interpretations help the client to move forward.

To move from the diagnostics to plan the changes (phase 5) can require that the data are checked, analyzed, interpreted, and organized according to some theoretical model. Here we will of course use the knowledge base produced by w/o psychology – theories, models, and research results. This may be materialized e.g. by using coaching, training, or educational programs.

Sometimes the consulting contract ends at phase 5: the client needs the w/o psychologist or the consultant only to help with data collecting, diagnostics, and planning future development. However, when we proceed to implementing change (phase 6) we will move to an area of consulting which demands quite different skills and methods than the earlier phases. According to Cockman et al. (1999) our job then consists of monitoring, mentoring, encouraging, supporting, confronting, opening doors, counseling, training. A successful w/o psychologist will need interpersonal skills and tools to handle issues like group dynamics, attitude change, resistance to change, adult learning.

Every consulting work and helping relationship finally has an end and there comes the time to let go. Disengaging (phase 7) is an important phase for both the client and the consultant which too often is accomplished poorly. However, people vitally need to "say goodbye" – possibly by a farewell rite – and to be released from the project and consultant/client to be free for the next step or project. Nevertheless, there remains a need for evaluation of results. Follow-up meetings may be useful in order to help the client maintain or advance the implementations and – also for the consultant – to learn for the next loop.

The Cockman model displays the ideal consulting procedure but in many occasions the service of the w/o psychologist is used narrowly only to accomplish the diagnostic work (phases 3 and 4) or alternately to provide limited training (between phases 4 and 5). Far too often our expertise is not utilized in the implementation phase, or the consultant's work ends with implementing the plan (beginning of phase 6). Transferring the analytic outcomes or the training contents into daily life and routine building (end of phase 6) are almost ever left to internal consultants – if there are any. Otherwise this part of phase 6 very often will not take place – with the sad result that many endeavors of participants of interventions and of internal as well as external consultants will fade away after some time. In the majority of cases there is no interest, time, and money for following up the results and evaluating them – this is vastly astonishing because on the other hand there is a considerable demand for cost-cutting and controlling in the Personnel and Organization Development scene. The phase which almost never is incorporated in a project is that of accomplishing properly the disengaging work (phase 7). However, the mission of any w/o psychologist would be to participate and contribute in all phases of the consulting cycle.

The Different Roles and Working Models

The continuum of roles

Different tasks often require different approaches from w/o psychologists. Accordingly, Schein (1999) describes three consulting approaches which in each case embody different goals, accesses, and outcomes:

- "telling and selling" or the expertise model – the consultant selling information and professional expertise
- "check," the doctor-patient or the analyst model – the consultant diagnosing and prescribing his or her "medicine" in a kind of physician–patient relation
- "help," the process consultation or the facilitator model – the consultant providing process consultation and monitoring.

It is possible for one w/o psychologist to act successfully in more than one of these roles but often he/she will possess one "chocolate side" where she/he is most authentic and most effective. The display of more than one of those approaches in one and the same project by one and the same consultant may also irritate the clients because each of these accesses asks for a special complementary behavior on the opposite, the client's side. In such cases it is advisable to either call in an additional consultant or to behave in such a "clear" way that it is unmistakable from which position the consultant is acting right now. For example the consultant could have adopted the role of the expert and has told facts and provided instructions and directions to the client. Thus the client is expecting to get this kind of answers also in the future. It is very hard for the consultant (and for the client) to take suddenly the role of the facilitator, who doesn't give straight answers anymore but makes counterquestions and tries to get the client use his/her own brain.

Naturally, this is also true for the roles of consultants in the slightly different, more differentiated, and descriptive order scheme Wohlgemuth (1991) offers. (See also figure 20.4.) With regard to the client's self-determination vs. heteronomy when solving problems he arrays the roles on a scale between the poles of "firefighter" and "neutral third." The following short features reveal the differences for consultants and clients in the five roles displayed:

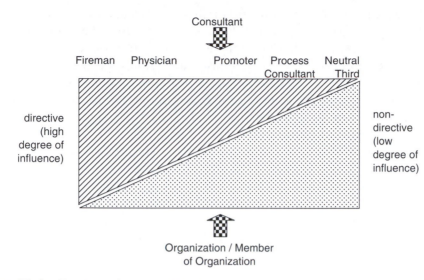

Figure 20.4: Typology of consultants' roles

- "Firefighter"
  The role of firefighter is directed towards the quickest possible dealing with acute problems. Due to their expertise firefighters are endowed with high-level authority. During the consultation process the client largely takes the role of supernumerary and surrenders initiative to act to the consultant.
- "Physician"
  The w/o psychologist works on the lines of the physician's role: Based on their diagnosis physicians administer a specific medicine. The patients only need to retrace the problem solving process as far as they are ready or able to. Experience has it that the patients will only swallow the medicine if they fully accept the physician's authority or if the medicine responds their prejudices.
- "Promoter"
  Unlike the role of physician the role of promoter is quite distinct: Discrete steps in the development process will not be heteronomously fixed by the consultant but will be effected by the organization, i.e. as far as possible by those people concerned. The promoter needs not confine himself purely to his methods competence though. Instead, along to his empowering facilitation, he or she may actively contribute some minor textual part to the development of procedural or structural solutions by suggesting alternatives. Decisions are completely reserved to the client.
- "Process consultant"
  Compared to the promoter the process consultant is a mere specialist for procedures in personal and organizational development processes. He or she acts even less directive than the promoter refraining from actively contribut-

ing any contents. W/o psychologists as process consultants restrict themselves to helping their clients to identify basic values, processes, behavioral patterns, and their impacts. This is to conjointly create the ground to find hidden alternatives, to decide more consciously, to be more open towards innovations. There is an intensive promotion of learning processes attached to that in order to increase the ability of the organization to analyze their developmental process on their own and to fix their next steps themselves.

- "Neutral third"
  The neutral third acts as a kind of catalyzer. He makes his impact by just being present and by mirroring the structure of cases of conflict and by "controlling" the communication between the parties so that solutions become visible. This role is some sort of outlier in the usual professional business consultation because there is quasi no influence by the consultant at all but may become valuable in (conflict) coaching contexts.

It is apparent that the self-competence of clients is increasing when the influence of the consultant is decreasing and converging the goal of w/o psychological consulting: to provide "help for self-help." The choice of role, though, depends

1. on the state of the client or system asking for help – he may be beginning or unsure or not ready to act so that he needs closer guidance or even a temporary substitute (firefighter or physician) or he is "adult" and knowledgeable and ready to act but seeks somebody to facilitate or accompany a process or project as someone not directly concerned (promoter or process consultant).
2. on the task or commission assigned, e.g.: Does the client just need additional factual expertise he is lacking and/or is there no possibility or desire to acquire this knowledge in due time himself, then the adequate solution may be the roles of firefighter or physician. Does the client need somebody to support him and/or his employees to cope with a process or problem, who makes them access their task in a different way than before and open up for new ideas, or who helps them resolve a conflict the roles of promoter or process consultant will be more appropriate. The "Neutral Third" in most cases will above all act out in coaching situations or when people just need a kind of catalyzer.

Traditionally engineers and natural scientists (for example) tend to be "firefighters" and "physicians," economists often act as "physicians" and "promoters," w/o psychologists prefer the "promoter" and "process consultant" approaches. The last two roles often are subsumed in the role of "facilitator" (in Germany: "Moderator") which is not included in the systematics of Wohlgemuth.

When weighting the future importance of these different roles some key developments can be observed:. First; expert vs. facilitator: There seems to be a tendency to move away from the expert role to adopting a more facilitator-like mode of working (Schein, 1999). Second, advising vs. doing: There is a pressure for consultants to take responsibility to act (do) instead of merely advise clients (Czerniawska, 1999). A third important dimension is internal vs. external.

Internal or external consultant

If we look at the roles displayed we very often have the impression that the one or the other role would fit better or worse into or would have more or less impact on the organizational framework of a special company or in a given situation. Sometimes clients would rather prefer somebody external to import fresh and best practice or even "shocking" knowledge from "outdoors" or show an unknown face or use somebody external as a scapegoat, sometimes it might be better to softly and knowledgeably (context and conditions) evolve the little seeds which have been sown.

In this context, it is often discussed whether an external consultant actually is able to take effect in a system. The "cons" mentioned are: external w/o psychology practitioners do not know the micropolitics affecting the system, they are not familiar with the circumstances and backgrounds of the company, they thus need valuable and expensive preparation time and possibly are not available quickly enough when needed. A series of big companies by these concerns felt – among other things – caused to build up their own internal pools of consultants. Paradoxically, a number of these pools have long since mutated to lines of business of their own selling their expertise gained in their own enterprise to "external" clients (in Germany e.g. "Siemens Management Consulting," "Telekom Training," "Volkswagen Coaching GmbH"). They are now capitalizing on the arguments in favor of external consultants. Here are the "pros": Because of their greater "distance" the external w/o psychology practitioners often gain more acceptance and still "see the wood for trees." "People stop questioning inefficient use of resources, time, or people because it has 'always' been that way. Much of what happens becomes so familiar that it becomes invisible" (LaMarsh, 1995). From experience, a tandem of both, an internal and an external consultant, would be a good and synergetic solution in change times.

Inside organizations HR professionals are typical examples of internal consultants. The role of HR people has changed considerably during the past 20 years: there is a paradigmatic shift from so called personnel management to human resources management, HRM (Mabey et al., 1998). This shift implies that for example HR people in progressive companies are supposed to not only administer their employees but also to play a strategic partner role in their work (Ulrich, 1997). Recently, Kahnweiler, and Kahnweiler (2005) have enumerated as repertoire of possible HR roles: helper, guide, collaborator, feedback provider, trainer, model, process observer, expert advisor, and director.

In order to gain the advantages and avoid the disadvantages of both, the internal and the external w/o psychologist, clients sometimes tend to team up an external and an internal consultant – a solution which often works out quite successfully provided that they are willing to work as partners and to avail themselves of the possible synergies. These may consist of the external consultant contributing latest state-of-the-art knowledge and benchmarks from other commissions and a certain freedom and distance from inner constraints while the internal consultant brings in his factual, procedural, cultural corporate knowledge and acts as the familiar link to the everyday life in the company. This way the participants of an intervention will get the flavor of the "Big Wide World" administered with the flavor of "That's us."

This does not relativize that it is imperative for internal and external w/o psychologists like for all other consultants: Because they in (especially long-term) consulting processes in the views of the clients become part of their world, they must understand "to be in the relation and in the same time to stay objective" (Hackney & Cormier, 1993).

Competences and Ethics in the Profession

What is needed to become a competent work and organizational psychologist? According to Roe (2002) there are two ways to look at this question: the input and output models. The first, the input model, looks at the education route that provides the right to call oneself a psychologist or a w/o psychologist. In the field of w/o psychology the ENOP model (ENOP, 2005) is an attempt to set minimum standards and a reference frame any university curriculum in Europe should match with in order to guarantee a comparable quality of education. With the second, the output model, we can look at the competences that psychologists are expected to display in order to perform their role properly.

Primary competences

When defining the competences any w/o psychologist should be able to demonstrate we can take as a reference model those competences defined in the European Diploma in Psychology (EuroPsy, 2003/2005). The model includes 20 primary competences which are grouped into six categories which relate to professional roles.

1. *Goal specification.* Interacting with the client in order to define the goals of the service to be provided. The primary competences are the mastery of need analysis and goal setting. For example, a psychologist is able to gather relevant information about the client's developmental needs and to negotiate and agree with the client about the goals to be achieved. This requires customer orientation. We may have the best knowledge and technical skills but these are useless if we cannot match them with the needs of the client.

2. *Assessment.* Establishing relevant characteristics of individuals, groups, organizations, and situations by means of appropriate methods. The primary competences are the mastery of carrying out assessments by means of e.g. testing, interviewing, observation, surveys in different organizational contexts. We can call these features diagnostic skills.

3. *Development.* Developing services or products on the basis of w/o-psychological theory and methods for the use of clients or w/o psychologists or other consultants. The primary competences are the mastery of service definition, requirement analysis, service design, service testing, and evaluation. It is important that we understand how our services help organizations and employees to perform better – where real value is actually added.

4. *Intervention.* Identifying, preparing, and carrying out interventions which are appropriate for achieving the fixed goals, using the results of assessment and developmental activities. The primary competences are the mastery of intervention planning, direct person-oriented intervention, indirect intervention, and service implementation. In our developmental work we are capable to use different tools, methods, or technologies. The mastery of different intervention tools is essential, but not enough. We should also be able to cope with changes and use the tools in different contexts and varying situations.

5. *Evaluation.* Establishing the adequacy of interventions in terms of adherence to the intervention plan and the achievement of set goals. The primary competences are the mastery of evaluation planning, measurement, and analysis. Continuous learning and development are based on feedback and the reflection of our experiences.

6. *Communication.* Providing information to clients in a way that is adequate to fulfil the clients' needs and expectations. The primary competences are the mastery of giving feedback and report writing. Good communication skills are the cornerstone of being a successful change agent.

According to the EuroPsy model a psychologist should gain each of these competences within a particular professional context. For example a w/o psychologist-to-be must demonstrate that he or she can master these competences adequately and independently in the field of w/o psychology.

Essential skills for change agents

The competences defined by the EuroPsy model give us a basic and generic framework to understand what is needed in the profession. We can describe the competences and skills needed in different professional contexts even more detailed by looking at three levels on which the work of w/o psychologists should be build up: theory, behavior, and professional competence (Heintel, 1992). For this purpose we can ask the following questions: What should I know (level of theory)? What should I be like (level of behavior)? What should I be able to cope with (level of professional competence/expertise)?

For example, when acting as an organization consultant or a change agent Cockman et al. (1999) define the basic skills as follows: knowing ourselves, communication skills, problem solving skills, team building, dealing with people's feelings, and dealing with our own feelings. Knowing ourselves means that we are aware of our strengths and weaknesses and are able to understand our limits as a practitioner to provide services or to use certain tools and methods. Dealing with feelings means that we are able to recognize our own and other people's feelings during our consulting work. We should have skills to cope with those feelings and handle them in an appropriate way and to keep our professional orientation and operative functioning also during confused, chaotic situations where a lot of emotions are expressed.

Many of the described skills above still require the fundamental qualities Rogers (1957, p. 95) has postulated for the behavioral level half a century ago:

- *Congruence and Authenticity*
  means: coincidence of thinking, feeling, and acting. Whatever we as w/o psychologists do or say must accord to our thoughts and feelings and get across full commitment – otherwise it will take dishonest, imposed, and fetched effects. This presupposes us to be aware of our own thoughts and feelings and having psychological insight in our own inner life.
- *Appreciation and Acceptance*
  means: taking the advice-seeking party seriously and with positive inclination. Clients will only be at ease, open up, accept advice, or collaborate when they feel emotionally appreciated like they are and whatever strengths and weaknesses or problems they have.
- *Empathy and Sensitive Understanding*
  means: willingness and ability to understand other human beings. We need the genuine readiness to empathize and antennas to realize the inner reference frames of the vis-à-vis including emotional components and connotations in order to help and support our clients successfully. This again calls for good command of our own motives and effective control of our perception and for watching out not to get entangled emotionally in business situations.

Special requirements for the interculturally working w/o psychology practitioner

Of course, all what has been discussed about competences and skills before, is valid for internationally working w/o psychologists, too. However, some issues are getting more prominent (Schmidt-Brasse, 2006).

As a matter of fact current knowledge, methods, and procedures are a sine qua non especially on the international floor. Those employers or clients who commission an intercultural order very often do this more consciously and under higher pressure than under normal conditions. Because of the raised complexity of the situation clients more than ever rely on the appointed w/o psychologists' expertise. Additionally, competition in the international field is even sharper and more differentiated due to the variety of applicants from different countries.

For sustainable results the consultant should have a motive to go abroad which surpasses adventuresomeness, flippant enchantment of differentness, and undifferentiated perception of challenges. Such an attitude probably will not "survive" the phases of cultural shock and disillusion inevitably following the initial "honeymoon." Trompenaars et al. (1998) expect more positive effects when consultants recognize that "we are in the business of creating wealth and value, not just for ourselves, but for those who live in different cultural worlds. We need to share the values of buying, selling, of joint venturing, of working in partnership."

Working in an intercultural context with diverse cultures and different views to functional, structural, and personal management processes means striving for successfully providing appropriate suggestions to cope with management problems determined by culture. In doing so managers and experts "need not only produce analytic expertise and command of foreign languages but they must adjust their behavior to intercultural standards which allow for successful action in a heteroculturally coined surrounding" (Rothlauf, 1999). Lippitt (1986) states that "each cross-cultural consulting predominantly depends on how far the consultant respects different views and how far the consultant is open, honest, and ready to learn." Thus, Bergemann and Sourisseaux (2003) list the following requirements regarding intercultural qualification of consultants:

- as to the consultant: ability to cope with stress, ability to find out culture-bound possibilities contributing to satisfaction, ability to cope with alienation and isolation (clear awareness of identity), mobility, holistic culture-comprehensive thinking, ethical awareness.
- as to interaction with others: ability to develop lasting interpersonal relations with members of foreign cultures, ability to communicate interculturally.
- as to adjusting and fitting into the environment: ability to interpret heterocultural behavioral patterns, ability to cognitively adjust to heterocultural schemes of assessment.

To sum up: The term "intercultural action competence" signalizes that intercultural competence inheres an action-controlling function. Action comprises all human behavior which does not appear by reflex, but is performed goal-oriented, expectation-controlled, planned, and largely consciously.

However, to cope or deal with clients and their problems and feelings is not purely the matter of skills or competences. We also need to hold the appropriate attitudes and values, and here we touch the sphere of ethics.

The importance of professional ethics and safeguarding quality

On account of the deep going impact on human beings, enterprises, and their social and ecological environment, practitioners in w/o psychology must execute their consulting endeavors responsibly and sustainably with regard to resources of all kinds. We must be ready to be assessed by professional standards, be it rather informally by self-obligation, by being coached, or by benchmarking with peer colleagues or be it officially by the yardsticks of professional associations or other norms – also in the international context.

Almost every community of practice in Europe, usually the local Psychological Association, maintains an ethical code of conduct which normally covers a range of topics. The European Federation of Psychologists' Associations (EFPA 1995) has published an ethical meta-code where the most crucial principles are categorized into four main categories:

- respect for the individual's rights and dignity
- professional qualifications
- responsibility
- professional integrity.

According to these principles, we are bound to respect people's self-determination and when working with people or administering interventions we have to make sure that all individuals are participating voluntarily. Additionally, we must withstand the temptation to answer luring questions of employers/clients asked about participants of interventions without their permission and transparency to those.

We are bound to carefully avoid misusing our professional knowledge and causing harm. Information that is intended as confidential should not be reported forward. Professional integrity means that we act openly and do not hide away relevant information from our client. We express ourselves with clarity. In organizational life we take a neutral and impartial professional role and we resist predisposition by any attempts of influence that are not proper.

Furthermore, we are responsible for the quality of our own work by continually developing our competences looking out for and into new developments in scientific and professional knowledge of our field and neighbor disciplines. This means that we safeguard quality by keeping up-to-date with literature and intervention methods, by attending events where fresh knowledge and experience are shared and elaborated, and by trying not only to consume but to contribute actively. There is yet another aspect to quality, too: We are aware of the special requirements of our profession regarding stability, emotional strength and remaining true towards ourselves, the dangers of burning out or throwing our weight about, of feeling blue or playing the go-getter etc. We therefore should subject us to cooperative intervision and coaching and ask for critical feedback.

We should be well aware of the limits of our professional qualifications and look out for complementation and addition of expertise if needed, be it by peer w/o colleagues, by colleagues from other fields of psychology, or by experts from neighboring sciences.

Summary

Work and organizational psychology practitioners live and act in a world of tantalizing and in parallel exciting ambiguity. Clearly, the conduct of the w/o-psychology profession is based both on scientific knowledge and practical experience. We badly need both approaches – in reality however, joining these two fields and maintaining a balance between them can prove challenging. Further, developing organizations is the aim of a number of other professions as well. We may experience them as competitors but on the other hand we need them and their expertise. We must realize that – if we want to be successful – we are bound to adopt a genuine interdisciplinary attitude. Third, as practitioners our work always is complementarily connected with the organizational management system. The objectives of our work are generated and our clients are defined by that management system. That's why it is vitally important for us to properly understand the organizational context we are working in while in parallel mentally staying out of the system. Forth, there is a wide range of different working models, methods, and tools to be utilized when acting as a consultant in organizations. Choosing the right tools is a skill as such. Applying a systemic viewpoint keeps us on the map. But mastering methods is not enough. We must also succeed in choosing the adequate role mode for a given working situation.

In order to cope with those ambiguities and the questions, challenges, and chances behind in a professional way, a set of competences is helpful the most important of which unquestionably – in our view – are self-awareness, client-orientation, fairness, up-to-date knowledge and skills, and a high-level ethical standard. These help us fulfil the cornerstone aim of our profession as a work and organizational psychologist (and this is the fifth ambiguity): providing help for self-help, as a consultant making ourselves redundant.

Discussion Points

Consider how a w/o psychologist could best contribute to the development of an organization in comparison to a professional from another field.

Analyze what kind of role you typically adopt when trying to help somebody else (in everyday life and for example in situations of training, homework, group work or conflicts).

Key Studies

Bamberg, E., Hänel, K., & Schmidt, J. (2006). Beratung – counseling – consulting. *Anforderungen und Kompetenzentwicklung bei der Organisationsberatung.* Göttingen: Hogrefe.

Further Reading

Cockman, P., Evans, B., & Reynolds, P. (1999). *Consulting for real people, a client-centered approach for change agents and leaders*. London: McGraw-Hill.

Lippitt, G., & Lippitt, R. (1986). *The Consulting Process in Action* (2nd edn.). San Francisco: Jossey-Bass/Pfeiffer.

Schein, E. H. (1999). *Process consultation revised, Building the helping relationship*. Reading: Addison-Wesley.

Case Study A

The Benefits of Ongoing Stress Risk Assessment: A Law Enforcement Case Study

Ivan Robertson, Susannah Robertson, and Chris Lewis

Background

Project goal

The City of London Police Force is responsible for policing the square mile that is the financial hub of the UK. Top policing priorities are antiterrorism and combating economic crime. The Force employs approximately 1,100 police officers and staff and is committed to ensuring they experience a working environment that supports them to provide a world-class policing service to those that work in the City and the much smaller number of people who live there.

In 2003, the Force commissioned Robertson Cooper Limited to carry out a "quality of working life" audit. As the prevention and management of stress is central to maintaining and improving quality of working life, Robertson Cooper was requested to evaluate the impact of interventions put in place following the audit by conducting a reassessment two years later.

Project structure and agreement process

After a series of meetings with the client's Health and Safety coordi-nator, it was decided that the structure of the project should involve the initial use of a formal stress risk assessment instrument with follow up discussion groups. The output of these would provide the basis for Robertson Cooper proposing a number of tailored recommendations, developed in consultation with Force representatives. These would be considered by a special working party with representatives from across the Force. The recommendations would then be formulated into an action plan for the Force to prioritize, take forward and integrate with other change initiatives. (Stage One.)

After a two-year period the assessment would be repeated using the same instrument. The aims being to assess the impact of the actions implemented and to suggest any necessary changes in continuing to take the action plan forward. This evaluative stage of the stress risk assessment process is ongoing. (Stage Two.)

Theoretical and Practical Issues

The theoretical problem

It is sometimes difficult to convince organizations of the existence of stress, and that its assessment is valid. This can negatively impact on "quality of working life."

The implication of this is significant. It flies in the face of the demonstrated link between productivity and "quality of life" in terms of the way we experience "well-being" (Cropanzo & Wright, 1999, 2001). Peak performance depends on maintaining a fine balance between too much pressure and too little. While this is a multi-faceted issue, the end result is best described as "motivated well-being." To fully understand and utilize this concept, Robertson Cooper have taken established principles from performance management, leadership, development and selection and combined them with aspects of well-being such as stress management and work-life balance.

Stress is the major workplace hazard according to a UK report by the Trades Union Council (TUC, 2000) survey of 9,000 safety representatives. The TUC report, *Focus On Health and Safety*, showed stress to be the number one concern for 2 out of 3 safety representatives (66 percent) and the main concern across almost all industrial sectors. A number of other surveys show that their concerns are well founded. The Industrial Society Survey (2001) showed that 91 percent of the 492 human resource and personnel professionals questioned believed stress to be a problem in their organization. Thirty six percent indicated that it was a significant problem and 5 percent indicated that it was a serious problem. According to research by the Health and Safety Executive (O'Driscoll & Cooper , 1996), 1 in 5 people are suffering from high levels of work-related stress.

The cost of stress is high for the individual victims, their organizations and for the economy. For the individual, stress can result in irritability, depressive mood, back and chest pains, high blood pressure, gastrointestinal disturbances and miscellaneous minor illnesses such as gum, mouth and tooth trouble, shortness of breath and headaches. Stressed individuals will often indulge in a range of harmful behaviors such as excessive drinking, smoking and over or under eating. Prolonged stress will ultimately lead to long-term health problems including coronary heart disease and mental illness.

At the organizational level, stress manifests itself through high absenteeism, poor quality control, reduced morale, poor performance and high labour turnover. The monetary cost is phenomenal: The HSE estimate that in the UK, stress-related illness is responsible for the loss of 6.5 million working days each year, costing employers around GB£370 million and society as a whole as much as GB£3.75 billion.

This means that preventing and managing stress is essential for good employee health and motivated well-being and therefore, for organizational effectiveness and productivity.

The practical solution
As the formal assessment of "quality of working life" requires a rigorously developed tool that

measures the different components of stress, this project was well served by the use of Robertson Cooper's validated instrument "ASSET."

ASSET has been designed as an initial screening tool to help organizations assess the risk of stress in their workforce. It measures potential exposure to stress in respect of a range of common workplace stressors. It also provides important information on current levels of physical health, psychological well-being, and organizational commitment and provides data to which the organization can be compared. It presents an effective means of assessing and monitoring stress levels and directing organization attention and resources to areas of potential risk.

ASSET is based upon a large body of academic and empirical research and has been developed using rigorous psychometric methods. It has been specifically developed to meet the organizational needs of its users and is designed for maximum practicality. It is designed to survey the level of stress in an organization; examine the extent to which groups or departments in the organization are differentially affected by stress and identify the sources of pressure for each group within the organization as well as across the organization as a whole. ASSET also provides extensive normative data with which an organization's profile can be compared. This includes for example, norms relating to the general working population, the public sector, the Police Service and specific functions within the Police Service.

The ASSET questionnaire has three core sections. The first measures "perceptions of the job" and relates to eight known workplace stressors, e.g. work life balance, control, overload, etc. The second measures "attitudes towards the organization" and considers employee perceptions of commitment both to and from the organization. The third section asks about perceptions of physical health and psychological well-being. There is also a supplementary section that is concerned with stress-relevant biographical data. The collation of this data also enables the organization to breakdown the results by different organizational groups, e.g. department, pay scale, location, etc.

Discussion groups were carried out following the ASSET survey in order to explore in more depth some of the issues highlighted by specific staff groups. The discussions were also focused around generating realistic solutions and key priorities for change. This method was utilized in order to increase perceptions of involvement and consultation and to help ensure that subsequent recommendations were practical and appropriate for those concerned.

A particular benefit of using ASSET is that Force representatives have access to its sophisticated online reporting software allowing them to interrogate the results from both of the audits themselves. Trained Force representatives are able to investigate the results for specific subgroups, change the comparison groups used and drill down to identify specific areas of concern. This functionality provides a powerful management information tool for the Force.

Action and Outcome

Project activities
At Stage One, all employees of the City of London Police were asked to complete a "pencil and paper" version of ASSET. These were delivered, in sealed envelopes, to a point of contact within the organization and subsequently distributed to each employee. Each participant was supplied with a pre-paid envelope to return their completed survey to Robertson Cooper. This method ensured the anonymity of participants. A response rate of 33 percent was achieved.

Discussion groups were set up in the stress "hotspot" areas identified by the ASSET survey results, i.e. areas of the Force where higher than average stress levels were reported. Employees were then invited to attend the discussion groups on a voluntary basis.

The results from the ASSET survey and the outcomes from the discussion groups were integrated and the overall findings along with initial recommendations were presented to the Force's special working party. The recommendations were then formulated into an action plan for the Force to prioritize, take forward and integrate with other change initiatives.

Results
The recommendations ranged from being quite broad to very specific. At the time of writing, the key actions undertaken by the Force as a result of the audit are as follows:

- Consideration of resources available to front line staff by the Resource Allocation Group. This is now an ongoing monitoring task.
- As part of the process of reviewing and improving performance management, a new round of Personal Development Reviews (PDRs) was undertaken and the quality of completed PDR documentation was reviewed and related to role profiles. In addition, the criteria for special merit awards were reviewed.
- In an effort to improve opportunities for staff to participate in feedback and consultation exercises, a "Promote Staff Suggestion" scheme was put in place.
- The Force sought to make best use of all means of communication in order to improve the management of change. This included for example a new intranet design and a Management of Information policy. In addition, a policy on maintaining roles so that project leaders remain with projects regardless of tenure was agreed on, in order to ensure change initiatives are followed through to completion.
- Workplace bullying policy was prepared in consultation with

Corporation of London. In addition, mentoring and welfare services were heavily promoted and appropriate training was set up to coincide with the launch of the bullying policy.

- A flexible working pilot initiative was run at one of the Force's Divisions and a flexible working policy was prepared in conjunction with the Health management Policy.

A number of other key actions are partially implemented and ongoing, such as:

- Extending Occupational Health/Welfare initiatives to encompass stress management through training or self-help groups.
- Staff reward scheme (to include merit certificates, commendations, bonuses etc) in draft format.
- Continuing generation of ideas for new consultation mechanisms.
- Considering introduction of change management training for line managers.
- Considering the provision of training to assist staff coping with change (linked to asserting influence).

Evaluation
This is Stage Two of the project. The Force acknowledged the importance of engaging with the action plan and demonstrated a commitment to moving forward in a structured and considered

way in order to realize bottom line benefits in terms of Policing performance and effectiveness.

Stage Two took place in September 2005 and was again a Force-wide initiative. Members of staff were invited to complete the ASSET survey on line, as email and internet provision within the Force had moved on significantly since the first audit. Moving over to the electronic completion method led to substantial cost savings for the Force, as well as much more efficient data collection and reporting of the survey results. Participants responded by accessing the ASSET website and submitting their completed survey online. As with the first audit, participants remained anonymous. The response rate achieved second time around was 46 percent.

The opportunities for benchmarking of the data collected from the second audit were extensive. Not only was Robertson Cooper able to compare the Force's results to the general working population and a large database of responses from other Police personnel, but a detailed comparison of the results from the first and second audits was also undertaken.

The headline finding was that in terms of the outcomes of stress (perceptions of health and organizational commitment) and the sources of pressure (e.g. overload, working relationships, resources and communication etc) measured by ASSET, the results were overwhelmingly positive in relation to the findings from the 2003 audit.

For example, significant improvements in perceptions of physical health and psychological well-being were identified, as well as significant increases in organizational commitment. All of the sources of pressure measured by ASSET were reported to be significantly less concerning to employees when assessed in 2005 relative to 2003. Most notably, perceptions of work life balance, job security, aspects of the job and pay and benefits had all improved. In terms of comparisons to other Police Forces, City of London Police respondents generally reported better health, stronger organizational commitment and less concern around the sources of pressure, than is typical of Police service personnel.

The findings from the second audit indicate that the actions undertaken by the Force following the first audit have clearly had a positive impact on employee well-being. While it's not possible to specifically attribute the improvements solely to the interventions put in place, there is a compelling case for suggesting that they have had a positive impact. It is clear to see the aspects of workplace stress that the different interventions have impacted on, e.g. the work done on resource allocation is likely to have improved staff perceptions of the availability of resources. Similarly, the efforts to improve staff consultation are likely to have impacted on perceptions of control and influence.

While a positive picture of "quality of working life" across the Force was revealed in the 2005 audit, specific stress "hotspot" areas were also identified. These included the Control room/Call center, Criminal Justice Unit, Traffic/Road Policing and Specialist Crime Operations. Further follow up discussion groups were carried out with staff from a number of the "hotspot" areas to explore the issues raised. Identification of the "hotspot" areas, along with additional qualitative information to flesh out the issues, will allow the Force to pin point where to target further effort and resources.

What Would You Do Differently Next Time?

Clearly, the improved level of technology available would now mean that the use of "pencil and paper" methods would not be used. However, some consideration of how to raise the electronic response rate significantly higher would be worthwhile.

While the impact of this project has notably improved "quality of working life" it would have been beneficial to have designed-in clearer links with explicit performance indicators. This would have reduced ambiguity at the evaluation stage.

Case Study B

Designing Technology for Work and Home Applications

Juergen Sauer and Bruno
Ruettinger

Background

Project goals

The goal of the project was to design marketable environmentally friendly technical systems and to create and apply methods and tools that support their development. This was done in close collaboration with manufacturers and a number of research teams from different disciplines, such as occupational psychology, engineering and computer science. The present chapter will be chiefly concerned with the contribution of psychology to this goal.

The contribution of psychology in the present project mainly stems from two fields: ergonomics and consumer psychology. While ergonomics focused on improving the design of the technical systems with a particular emphasis on the criterion of environmental friendliness, consumer psychology was concerned with user perceptions of the product and aimed to assess the attractiveness of different product features for users. The close collaboration of these two fields is crucial because it is insufficient if good ergonomic design merely improves the environmental friendliness of technical systems but these systems are not attractive to consumers. In that case,

they would not sell in sufficiently large numbers at the expense of less environmentally friendly systems.

The technical systems examined in the course of the project were used in work contexts (e.g., floor scrubber) as well as in the domestic domain (e.g., kettle). Some of these may be considered dual-domain systems (e.g., vacuum cleaner). The systems analyzed are of low or medium complexity, which makes them distinct from highly complex systems (e.g., aircraft, nuclear power plants) that generally dominate research in industrial ergonomics. The focus on environmental friendliness (e.g., energy and water consumption) as an important design criterion gives this project a new angle since this aspect has rarely been explicitly examined in ergonomics. However, it may have played a role hitherto as a subsidiary efficiency indicator in system design (e.g., petrol consumption for cockpit design). The contribution of psychology to that end is considered to be very important since analyses have demonstrated showed that, on average, about 80 percent of the environmental impact of energy-driven consumer products occurs during product utilization phase (i.e. during user–product interaction), as opposed to preceding and subsequent phases of the product life cycle, such as production or disposal

471

(Wenzel, Hausschild, & Alting, 1997).

Project structure and agreement process

During the course of the project, the psychology research team worked with several manufacturing companies to improve ergonomic design and marketability of their systems. This included a manufacturer of cleaning equipment (e.g., floor scrubber, high pressure washer) and the makers of electrical body care products (e.g., hair drier) as the main collaborators.

The process of agreement for carrying out the project comprised two main steps. First, a project team was formed before a formal agreement was reached. Over a time period of several months, shared interests between the research group and the industrial collaborator were identified. This involved in some cases the completion of pilot studies to give the collaborator an indication of the kind of support that can be given by the research team. After extensive discussions of the project plan, it was subsequently specified in writing, including milestones and deliverables of each collaborator. Second, the project plan was submitted to a public funding body that employed two chief criteria for funding the work: (a) the scientific value of the proposal and (b) to what extent scientific knowledge can be transferred to industry to improve their competitive edge. The costs incurring in the research institutions were covered by the funding body while the industrial collaborator covered their own expenses. An important deliverable to be provided by the collaborator was to develop and make available various prototypes for human factors testing.

Theoretical and Practical Issues

Role of theory

While the project clearly had an applied focus, the work benefited from the use of several theories and models of the research literature. For example, action theory (Frese & Zapf, 1994) was employed for carrying out analyses of user tasks. Furthermore, models of information processing (e.g., Rogers, Lamson, & Rousseau, 2000) were used for the design of effective on-product information. To provide a third example, resource models were employed to explain changes in user behavior under varying cognitive-energetical demands (e.g., "variable state activation theory" from Hockey, 1997). The use of all these theories and models provided helpful support for the research team in guiding the project work.

Special project skills

In order to successfully complete the project with the industrial collaborators, a number of skills were found to be very helpful during project completion. (1) It was important to provide illustrative examples to demonstrate the contribution of work psychology since in engineering-driven manufacturing companies the possible contribution of psychology to the design process may not be that evident. (2) It was also important to be able to adopt the perspective of the organization, which was driven by market- and cost-orientation. The use of scientific empirical studies had to be justified in terms of their incurring cost with regard to time and financial resources.

Action and Outcome

Project activities
The activities within the project were mainly concerned with the design and development of new products or the modification of existing products. During the course of the project, 9 different technical systems were examined (e.g., high pressure washer, central heating system). While some of the project work was carried out inside the organization of the industrial collaborators (e.g., interviews and surveys), most of the project work focused on the user and the context of technology usage (e.g., by simulating usage context in human factors laboratory of research team or by completing field studies in work setting of system operators) rather than taking place in the organizational context of the manufacturer.

When working on ergonomic system improvements, the typical methodological approach adopted comprised five steps. First, an analysis of the human–system interaction was carried out, employing methods such as observation, interviews and question-

naires (e.g., user of central heating system was interviewed). Second, the data collected permitted the identification of problems in human–system interaction that led to nonoptimal product usage with regard to environmental friendliness (e.g., behaviors were reported that resulted in excessive energy consumption). Third, based on the problems identified in human–system interaction, design modifications were developed to improve environmentally friendly system use (e.g., interface for heating system was developed that provided better user support). Fourth, these measures were empirically tested in lab and field studies to evaluate their effectiveness (e.g., interface was tested with prospective users). Fifth, based on the results of these tests, recommendations for system designers were given (e.g., to provide an efficiency index of system operation).

Results
The project identified several impediments to environmentally friendly behavior, such as habits, lack of motivation and, in some cases, insufficient knowledge. For example, habitual behavior patterns play an important role for user–technology interaction if it involves the use of simple systems that are used very frequently. This applies in particular to the domestic domain because technical systems are of lower complexity than at work.

The project also demonstrated the effectiveness of a number of

Table B1: Estimated effectiveness of measures to deal with different causes of nonoptimal user behavior (high***, medium**, low*)

	Habits	Lack of knowledge	Lack of motivation
Static on-product information	*	**	*
Dynamic feedback	**	***	*
Enhanced controls design	**	**	*
Automation	***	**	***

design modifications in dealing with these impediments by improving environmentally friendly behavior. Interestingly, the different design measures (e.g., static on-product information, dynamic feedback about system state, enhanced control design, automation of functions) had differential effects depending on the underlying cause of the problem. For example, lack of knowledge may be dealt with by on-product information or dynamic feedback whereas these measures may not be helpful if the cause was lack of motivation to show environmentally friendly behavior. Table B1 provides a summary of the overall effectiveness of design measures as a function of the underlying causes of environmentally damaging behavior.

The kind of work carried out in the project is illustrated with an example from vacuum cleaner design, in which knowledge deficits and undesirable habits have been identified as the cause of non-ecological user behavior. Technical analyses of our collaborating engineers have revealed that a motor power level of around 750 W is most efficient for performance of a vacuum cleaner, with increases in motor power

above that level providing at best marginal gains in suction performance. At the same time, a manufacturer produced a vacuum cleaner with that level of power but it was unsuccessful on the market because consumers were not convinced (i.e. they had insufficient knowledge) that the 750 W model was equal to a 1500 W model with regard to suction performance. This illustrates the obvious conflict between fulfilling the criterion of environmental friendliness (i.e. energy consumption of around 750 W) and, at the same time, market demands (i.e. the higher the motor power, the more attractive the appliance). Following in-depth analyses of user behavior, a solution to this conflict was to provide the user with a powerful model as requested but which was equipped with an automated power control function. Automation was implemented in the form of an auto reset function, which meant that the power control was reset to its most efficient level (around 750 W) every time the appliance was switched off. This is the same principle as the default setting for volume control of a TV-set, which is reset to its default level every time the appliance is switched off.

The reset function allowed users to select higher power level if they wished to do so (i.e. it was a form of automation that did not constrain actions of the user) but empirical testing revealed that nearly half of the users did not override the automation (Sauer, Wiese, & Rüttinger, 2004). Overall, the results of that experiment provided clear evidence that this design modification was effective in improving environmental friendliness of the appliance while maintaining its attractiveness to consumers. It reiterates the point that automation is highly effective in dealing with knowledge deficits but also stresses the importance to provide the user with sufficient decision latitude to choose settings that may be nonoptimal in terms of operational efficiency but may meet the personal need for control and for a powerful appliance.

Finally, some methodological effects observed during the empirical work are referred to. It was found that these influenced the estimated effectiveness of design measures (e.g., Sauer & Ruettinger, 2004). Generally, in scenarios of high fidelity (e.g., a field study using a fully operational prototype) the effects of design modifications (e.g., providing on-product information) were found to be much weaker than in lower-fidelity scenarios (e.g., laboratory study with a paper mock-up) on ecological user behavior. This does not suggest that lab-based studies are not suitable but rather that a correction needs to be made in order to make an accurate assessment of the effect size in the real world.

Practical constraints

A few practical constraints were encountered during the completion of the project. First, industrial collaborators often provided several contact persons (e.g., because they were responsible for different products). While this was very helpful because an expert for each area was available, the drawback was that it slowed down the decision-making process because of the larger number of people involved. Second, the time schedules of BSc and MSc students who were also involved in the project work did not always coincide with the required time schedule of the project. This sometimes required modifications of the project plan.

Evaluation

Evaluations were carried out at several levels to determine whether the project goals have been met. (1) According to the goals of the projects, technological devices were evaluated with regard to several already existing criteria, such as usability, marketability and environmental friendliness. At a more specific level, this included aspects like error tolerance, pleasure in product operation, and energy consumption. (2) A further evaluation criterion concerned the satisfaction of the industrial collaborator with work progress and project results. This was achieved during regular project meetings. (3) An additional evaluation criterion referred to the knowledge transfer from academic institutions into industry and vice versa. For example, this concerned the question whether work activities of the research team would be continued by the industrial collaborator after the termination of the project (e.g., human factor testing).

What Would You Do Differently Next Time?

A number of lessons have been learnt from this project. (1) In the next project of this kind, we would aim to achieve a stronger centralization of responsibility on the side of the industrial collaborator. (2) Furthermore, there should be a stronger outcome orientation rather than a methodological orientation, with the latter being perhaps more typical for academic work. This should already be specified in the project planning stage in that tangible deliverables are specified (e.g., checklists, newly built prototypes, list of design recommendations). (3) There should be a stronger involvement of the industrial collaborators in evaluation research to ensure a stronger knowledge transfer from the academic institutions to industry. This may also involve running training courses in the collaborating organization. (4) A more precise definition of the researcher's role at the beginning of project may be helpful. It needs to be made clearer that the researcher is not always able to provide instant answers to all problem situations encountered by using his/her expert knowledge. The completion of empirical tests is often required to provide answers.

Case Study C

Designing a Longitudinal Study to Monitor the Perceptions of the First Recruits to the Police Service of Northern Ireland

Micaela McGinley and
Kerri McDonnell

Background

Organizational context and agreeing the project

In-house occupational (work and organizational) psychologists, working for the Police Service of Northern Ireland (PSNI), designed and carried out this assignment. The PSNI officially came into existence on November 4, 2001. On this date, and for the first time ever, the new police recruits joining the organization were drawn equally from the Protestant and Roman Catholic communities. The organization as a whole was subject to an unparalleled exercise in police reform with the success of the change process being seen as vital not only for the delivery of effective and impartial policing in Northern Ireland, but also instrumental in ensuring the success of the wider peace process.

Two months before the arrival of the first PSNI recruits, occupational psychologists received a telephone request from the Police College to assist in developing a "training evaluation" process. The request came from the senior officer responsible for delivering the intensive, 21-week initial training to the new officers. To scope out the precise organizational need, psychologists consulted extensively with a variety of internal and external stakeholders and reviewed strategic documents and previous evaluations. Key questions we asked at this stage included "What are we evaluating?" "Who is the evaluation for?" "How will the information from the evaluation be used both inside and outside the PSNI?" The key outcome from this important stage was a decision that psychology could play a key role in evaluating the success of the new arrangements. However, we decided that our specialist resource would be best maximized not by carrying out a simple training evaluation process (adequate feedback and evaluation mechanisms were already in place for the university-accredited, initial police training program) but by designing and implementing a more strategically-focused study that would inform a wider range of organizational processes over a substantial and critical period of time in the organization's history.

Project goals

We sought and obtained approval from the PSNI Director of Human

Resources for a program of longitudinal research that would monitor the perceptions of new officers towards key aspects of life in PSNI over the first three years of their service. The specific goals for the project were to:

- Explore the extent to which new recruits are *committed* to the PSNI organization, its values and goals, and are motivated to work to achieve these goals.
- Assess recruits' *satisfaction* levels with key components of the job itself and the training provided.
- Measure recruits perceptions of the *learning climate* that exists within the organization.
- Assess recruits' perceptions of how the organization manages and promotes *diversity* in working practices and service provision.
- Monitor any significant *changes in attitudes over time* as the new recruits leave the training college and become attached to District Command Units.
- Monitor any significant *differences in attitudes due to demographic variables* such as age, gender and community background.
- Monitor and explore reasons for any *voluntary turnover* that may arise among the new recruits.

Before the project started, the precise terms of reference for the study were clearly written down in a Project Specification docu-ment. This document captured the project aim, goals, methodology, timescales, costs, project team as well as the outputs or deliverables from the study. The specification served a vital role in clarifying our own thinking. It also provided a clear and agreed frame of reference that helped to keep us on track throughout the project.

Theoretical and Practical Issues

Starting off with a blank sheet, the design of this study was challenging but also extremely stimulating and rewarding. The challenge lay in the sheer quantity of theory and tools available from the world of work psychology that we could potentially bring to bear on the design. For example, the vast literature and tools on how to measure job satisfaction and employee motivation; the varying approaches to diagnosing organizational climate and culture; the extensive literature on optimizing and evaluating adult and on-the-job learning, not to mention the enormous and very helpful literature on planned models of organizational change.

While we clearly required a broad understanding of the organizational development literature, arguably even more important was our ability to map these psychological tools and theory against the exact needs and circumstances of PSNI at that particular point in time. To do this, meant that we needed more than just our psychology training. We also required a sound understanding of policing, some knowledge of the police reform process and an awareness of wider political and stakeholder interests in understanding the outcomes of our study and ultimately gaining an insight into the experiences of the first PSNI recruits. We would reinforce a vital point here – an occupational psychologist needs to know the actual business s/he is operating in!

The key areas that we finally settled on as holding most promise for PSNI, were theories of job satisfaction and organizational commitment; models of good practice in promoting diversity in organizations, and the concept of the learning organization. Each of these areas offered us a valuable lens for exploring and measuring new officers' experiences over time and would help us to answer key questions of relevance to the organization.

While it was very important to know our options in terms of the available tools and theoretical concepts, other skills were also important in making this study a reality and a success. These included skills in research design and planning; a commitment to independent and robust evaluation drawing defensible conclusions based on firm evidence; courage of our convictions and a willingness to deliver both positive and difficult messages for the organization; endless energy in gathering copious amounts of data, analyzing it and communicating the results to an increas-

ingly wider and more diverse audience over time. The latter was particularly important given our role as internal psychologists. As time progressed, interesting new work assignments inevitably came our way. It was important to accommodate these requests and to shape and influence new applications for psychology within PSNI, while remaining wedded to the vision of the longitudinal study and what it was trying to achieve. This had significant implications for our team resources and long-term work planning processes.

Action and Outcome

Project design and activities
The project design included the collection of both questionnaire and interview data at four different points in the recruits' early careers. The sample comprised the first six intakes of officers who joined PSNI between November 2001 and May 2002 (N = 297). Questionnaire data was collected from the entire sample and supplemented, at each intervention point, with in-depth data from interviews with a subsample of 21 officers. The data-gathering and reporting cycle took place between late 2001 and late 2004.

The questionnaire contained a combination of previously published scales and especially written items designed to measure:

- Perceptions of the learning climate in PSNI
- Feelings of job satisfaction

- Levels of organizational commitment
- Attitudes to diversity and how it is managed and promoted within PSNI.

As the officers progressed outside of the training college and moved into their first operational postings, new issues emerged and we expanded the questionnaire to explore these, while retaining the same core items to allow for comparisons over time.

Questionnaire data was analyzed using the Statistical Package for the Social Sciences (SPSS). Differences in officers' views were explored by gender, age, community background and a variety of other demographic variables. Variations in group responses over time were also analyzed. The qualitative data from the interviews was analyzed using content analysis procedures to identify recurring themes and to provide context and depth to the questionnaire findings. At each intervention stage in the study, both interim and final outputs were produced. The interim findings highlighted emerging issues for management to be aware of at that stage in the process. The emphasis was on providing early and informative feedback in a timely manner. The final report provided a full and comprehensive analysis of the full stage results based on the complete data set and also contained detailed recommendations for action. This reporting structure was important as there was typically a six-month time lag between collecting data from the first and

sixth intakes at each intervention stage.

Evaluation

This project represented a significant achievement for the Human Resource Department and the organization as a whole. It demonstrated a willingness on the part of PSNI to open itself up to internal critique and evaluation at a turbulent time in its history, when it was already subject to extensive, external oversight. The results of the study demonstrated largely positive results with high levels of job satisfaction and commitment among recruits from all sides of the religious divide in Northern Ireland. Notwithstanding this, critical issues and problems were identified at each stage and the study provided officers with a powerful voice to lobby for change. As a result, key improvements were made to the manner in which new officers were received in their stations; to the initial training and assessment processes; and to the methods by which contentious, diversity issues were aired and discussed within the organization. For example, as a result of the study's findings, Police Commanders were encouraged to set up proper induction procedures for their new officers upon their arrival at their stations. Commanders were also encouraged to allow the new recruits to observe important Performance Accountability Meetings during which the Police Commander was held to account by a senior officer for overall police performance in his/her district. This was based on direct feedback from the student officers and their identification of factors that would help them to perform their own role more effectively.

The study was very well received both internally and externally. Over time, the project reports were disseminated to an increasingly wider and more diverse audience and often accompanied by oral presentations and practical workshops designed to facilitate practical action upon the results. We generated positive publicity externally through delivering conference presentations and media interviews on the findings. The Office of the Oversight Commission, which was set up as part of the political agreement to independently monitor police reform, consistently welcomed and tracked the course of the study's findings.

As well as documenting officers' views and effecting immediate changes to their work environment, the study also provides a valuable baseline data set to inform future organizational development initiatives in the police service. Moreover, it provides a rich historical database outlining how the first officers to the PSNI perceived their early policing experiences.

What Would You Do Differently Next Time?

This study was ambitious in its scale and scope. The volume of data gathered, at times, threatened to swamp the small research team of two psychologists. With hindsight, we feel that a better balance could be achieved between the time spent on data-gathering and analysis activities and the time devoted to actually disseminating and acting upon the findings. We feel the latter is crucially important. In redesigning a similar survey, we would consider a design model based on less data and we would double the amount of time allocated to communicating the findings.

We would also research innovative methods upfront for guarding against survey fatigue in organizations and ensuring proactive ownership and action upon results. A common problem we faced was a perception that psychologists, as the evaluators, should own the action points. However, to be truly effective, the actions and recommendations need to be owned by managers and senior officers with the necessary influence and resources to make things happen. A clearer specification upfront of the key customers for each stage of the study and allocation of responsibility for generating and monitoring implementation of the study recommendations would be useful. In reality, however, we appreciate that this is a complex area and a variety of dynamic and ongoing approaches are required to facilitate continuous improvements arising from employee surveys. Small, but significant, actions can help. These include investing time and energy into really "marketing" your findings internally and externally as well as employing professional assistance to present the outputs using novel, summary report formats and snappy graphics.

Longitudinal research poses particular issues and complexities. We were highly fortunate in retaining the majority of our sample over time, as most people tend to join the police and see it as a job for life. However, we would design the study differently in the future. In this study, we consistently tracked six intakes of officer (N = 297) over four points in time. A lot of the information we gathered from the latter intakes (intakes 4 to 6) at each stage was redundant in terms of yielding new issues for the organization. In future, a more productive design would be to track a smaller number of intakes over time and then to come back and add entirely new intakes to the study (e.g. intakes 1 to 3 plus intakes 15 to 18, rather than intakes 1 through to 6). This way, and using the same resources, we could see if things have improved as a result of earlier recommendations and action points. We could also see if new issues are emerging for officers recruited in a slightly later time period.

Other important learning from the study includes the importance of providing regular feedback to the study participants; constantly communicating with internal project sponsors and seeking their continual input and support and fine-tuning of skills in statistical analysis in order to maximize important organizational messages that can be extracted from the data.

The things that we would definitely retain in future studies included the combined emphasis on qualitative and quantitative data-gathering approaches. We would also maintain a firm commitment to both formative and summative evaluation practice wherein the data is used not only to describe a particular situation (summative) but also to try and make things better (formative). Our project reporting structure of interim and final outputs greatly helped to facilitate this.

Finally, in terms of reflections on learning, we feel that exploring possible collaborative partnerships with a research institution or university in future could open exciting possibilities for conducting such research in a new manner.

In summary, we feel this project offers a good example of occupational psychology being applied in a proactive manner to advance organizational change. It provides an illustration of how psychologists can not only react and respond to organizational events but can actually be instrumental in shaping and influencing key organizational processes and in helping to promote an organizational culture of openness and continuous improvement.

References

Aasman, J., Wijers, A. A., Mulder, G., & Mulder, L. J. M. (1988). Measuring mental fatigue in normal daily working routines. In P. A. Hancock & N. Meshkati (Eds.), *Human mental workload*. Amsterdam: North Holland.

Abdel-Maleck, L., Wolf, C., & Guyot, P. D. (1998). Telemanufacturing: a flexible manufacturing solution. *International Journal of Production Economics*, *56–7*, 1–12.

Abrahamson, E., & Fombrun, C. J. (1994). Macrocultures: Determinants and consequences. *Academy of Management Review*, *19*, 728–55.

Adams, J. S. (1965). Inequity in social exchange. In L. Berkowitz (Ed.), *Advances in experimental social psychology* (Vol. 2, pp. 267–99). New York: Academic Press.

Adolphs, R., Tranel, D., Damasio, H., & Damasio, A. (1994). Impaired recognition of emotion in facial expressions following bilateral damage to the human amygdala. *Nature*, *372*, 669–72.

Agarwal, R. (2003). Teamwork in the netcentric organization. In M. A. West, D. Tjosvold, & K. G. Smith (Eds.), *International handbook of organizational teamwork and cooperative working* (pp. 443–62). Chichester, UK: Wiley.

Agervold, M. (1987). New technology in the office: Attitudes and consequences. *Work & Stress*, *1*, 143–53.

Ahlstrom, V., & Allendoerfer, K. (2004). *Web-based portal computer–human interface guidelines* (DOT/FAA/CT–TN04/23). Atlantic City International Airport, NJ: Federal Aviation Administration William J. Hughes Technical Center.

Aiman-Smith, L., & Green, S. G. (2002). Implementing new manufacturing technology: The related effects of technology characteristics and user learning activities. *Academy of Management Journal*, *45*, 421–30.

Ainsworth, M. D. S. (1989). Attachment beyond infancy. *American Psychologist*, *44*, 709–16.

Albert, S., & Whetten, D. (1985). Organizational identity. In L. L. Cummings & B. M. Staw (Eds.), *Research in organizational behavior* (Vol. 7, pp. 263–95). Greenwich, CT: JAI Press.

Allan, N. J., & West, M. A. (2005). Selection for teams. In A. Evers, N. Anderson, & O. Voskuijl (Eds.), *The Blackwell handbook of personnel selection* (pp. 476–94). Oxford: Blackwell Publishing.

Allen, T. D., Russell, J. E. A., Poteet, M. L., & Dobbins, G. H. (1999). Learning and the development factors related to perceptions of job content and hierarchical plateauing. *Journal of Organizational Behavior, 20*, 1113–37.

Allen, T. J. (1977). *Managing the flow of technology*. Cambridge, MA: MIT Press.

Alliger, G. M., Tannenbaum, S. I., Bennett, W. J., Traver, H., & Shotland, A. (1997). A meta-analysis of the relations among training criteria. *Personnel Psychology, 50*, 341–58.

Allport, G. (1954). *The nature of prejudice*. Reading, MA: Addison-Wesley.

Amabile, T. M. (1988). A model of creativity and innovation in organizations. *Research in Organizational Behavior, 10*, 123–76.

Ambrose, M. L., & Kulik, C. T. (1999). Old friends, new faces: Motivation research in the 1990s. *Journal of Management, 25(3)*, 231–92.

Amburgey, T. L., Kelly, D., & Barnett, W. P. (1993). Resetting the clock: The dynamics of organisational change and failure. *Administrative Science Quarterly, 38*, 51–73.

Ancona, D. F., & Caldwell, D. F. (1992). Demography and design: Predictors of new product team performance. *Organisation Science, 3*, 321–41.

Anderson, N. (1997). The validity and adverse impact of selection interviews: A rejoiner to Wood. *Selection and Development Review, 13(5)*, 13–7.

Anderson, N. (1998). The practitioner–researcher divide in work and organizational psychology. *The Occupational Psychologist, 34*, pp. 7–16.

Anderson, N. (2003). Applicant and recruiter reactions to new technology in selection: A critical review and agenda for future research. *International Journal of Selection and Assessment, 11*, 121–36.

Anderson, N. (2005). Relationships between practice and research in personnel selection: Does the left hand know what the right hand is doing? In A. Evers, N. Anderson, & O. Smit-Voskuyl, (eds.), *The Blackwell handbook of selection*, Oxford: Blackwell.

Anderson, N., Born, M., & Cunningham-Snell, N. (2001). Recruitment and selection: Applicant perspectives and outcomes, in N. Anderson, D. Ones, H. K. Sinangil, & C. Viswesvaran (eds.), *Handbook of industrial, work, and organizational psychology*, Vol. 1. London: Sage.

Anderson, N., & Conningham-Snell, N. (2000). Personnel Selection. In N. Chmiel (Ed.), *Introduction to work and organizational psychology. A European perspective* Oxford: Blackwell.

Anderson, N., Herriot, P., & Hodgkinson, G. P. (2001). The practitioner–researcher divide in industrial, work and organizational (IWO). Psychology: where are we now and where do we go from here? *Journal of Occupational and Organizational Psychology, 74*, 391–411.

Anderson, N., Lievens, F., van Dam, K., & Ryan A. M. (2004). Future perspectives on employee selection: Key directions for future research and practice. *Applied Psychology: An International Review, 53*, 487–501.

Anderson, N., & Ostroff, C. (1997). Selection as socialisation. In N. Anderson & P. Herriot (Eds.), *International handbook of selection and assessment*. Chichester, UK: Wiley.

Andriessen, J. H. Erik (2003). *Working with groupware. Understanding and evaluating collaboration technology*. London: Springer.

Andriessen, J. H. Erik, & Vartiainen, M. (eds.) (2006). *Mobile virtual work. A new paradigm?* Springer: Heidelberg.

Annett, J., & Duncan, D. (1967). Task analysis and training design. *Occupational Psychology, 41*, 211–21.

Antoni, C. (1996). *Teilautonome Arbeitsgruppen*. Weinheim: Psychologie Verlags Union.

Apgar, M. (1998). The alternative workplace: Changing where and how people work. *Harvard Business* Review, *76*, 121–35.

Appelbaum, H. S., & Gandell, J. (2003), A cross method analysis of the impact of culture and communications upon a health care merger. *Journal of Management Development*, *22(5)*, 370–409.

Applebaum, E., & Batt, R. (1994). *The new American workplace*. Ithaca, NY: ILR Press.

Arabie, P., Carroll, J. D., & DeSarbo, W. S. (1987). *Three-way scaling and clustering*. Sage University Paper Series on Quantitative Applications in the Social Sciences, 07–065. London: Sage.

Argyris, C. (1960). *Understanding organizational behavior*. Homewood, IL: Dorsey Press.

Argyris, C. (1977). Double loop learning in organisations. *Harvard Business Review*, *55*, 115–25.

Argyris, C. (1990). Overcoming organisational defences. Boston, MA: Allyn & Bacon.

Ariëns, G. A. M., Bongers, P. M., Hogendoorn, W. E., Houtman, I. L. D., van der Wal, G., & van Mechelen, W. (2001). High quantitative job demands and low co-worker support as risk factors for neck pain: results of a prospective cohort study. *Spine*, *26*, 1896–1903.

Armenakis, A. A., & Bedeian, A. G. (1999). Organisational change: A review of theory and research in the 1990s. *Journal of Management*, *25*, 293–315.

Arnold, J. (1997a). *Managing careers into the 21st century*. London: Paul Chapman Publishing.

Arnold, J. (1997b). The psychology of careers in organizations. In C. L. Cooper & I. T. Robertson (Eds.), *International Review of Industrial and Organizational Psychology* (Vol. 12, pp. 1–37). Chichester, UK: John Wiley, & Sons, Chirchester.

Aron, A., & McLaughlin-Volpe, T. (2002). Including others in the self. In C. Sedikides & M. B. Brewer (Eds.), *Individual self, relational self, collective self* (pp. 89–108). Philadelphia: Psychology Press.

Arthur, M. B., Hall, D. T., & Lawrence, B. S. (1989). Generating new directions in career theory: the case for a transdisciplinary approach. In M. B. Arthur, D. T. Hall, & B. S. Lawrence (Eds.), *Handbook of career theory* (pp. 7–25). Cambridge: Cambridge University Press.

Arthur, M. B., Inkson, K., & Pringle, J. K. (1999). *The new careers: Individual action and economic change*. London: Sage.

Arthur, M. B., & Rousseau, D. M. (1996). *The boundaryless career: A new employment principle for a new organizational era*. New York: Oxford University Press.

Arthur, W. J., Bennett, W. J., Edens, P. S., & Bell, S. T. (2003). Effectiveness of training in organizations: A meta-analysis of design and evaluation features. *Journal of Applied Psychology*, *88*, 234–45.

Arvey, R. D., & Sackett, P. R. (1993). Fairness in selection: Current developments and perspectives. In N. Schmitt & W. Borman (Eds.), *Personnel selection in organizations*. San Francisco: Jossey Bass.

Arvey, R. D., Strickland, W., Drauden, G., & Martin, C. (1990). Motivational components of test taking. *Personnel Psychology*, *43*, 695–716.

Ash, R. A. (1988). Job analysis in the world of work. In S. Gael (Ed.), *The job analysis handbook for business, industry and government* (Vol. 1, pp. 3–13). New York: Wiley.

Ashby, W. R. (1958). Requisite variety and its implications for the control of complex systems. *Cybernetica, 1,* 83–99.

Ashkanasy, N., & Jackson, C. R. A. (2001). Organizational culture and climate. In N. Anderson, D. S. Ones, H. K. Sinangil, & C. Viswesvaran (Eds.), *Handbook of industrial, work and organizational psychology* (Vol. 2, pp. 398–415). London: Sage.

Atkyns, R., Blazek, M., Roitz, J., & AT&T. (2002). Measurement of environmental impacts of telework adoption amidst change in complex organizations. *Resources, Conservation and Recycling, 36,* 267–85.

Austin, J. R., & Bartunek, J. M. (2003). Theories and practices of organisational development. In W. C. Borman & R. J. Klimoski (Eds.), *Handbook of psychology* (Vol. 12, pp. 309–32). Hoboken, NJ: John Wiley.

Axelrod, R., & Hamilton, W. D. (1981). The evolution of cooperation. *Science,* 211, 1390–6.

Baddeley, A. D. (1972). Selective attention and performance in dangerous environments. *British Journal of Psychology, 63,* 537–46.

Bailey, C., & Fletcher, C. (2002). The impact of multiple source feedback on management development: Findings from a longitudinal study. *Journal of Organizational Behaviour, 23,* 853–67.

Bailey, D. E., & Kurland, N. B. (2002). A review of telework research: findings, new directions, and lessons for the study of modern work. *Journal of Organizational Behavior, 23,* 383–400.

Bailyn, L. (2004). Time in careers – careers in time. *Human Relations, 57,* 1507–21.

Bain, J. S. (1956). *Barriers to new competition.* Cambridge, MA: Harvard University Press.

Bainbridge, L. (1974). Analysis of verbal protocols from a process control task. In E. Edwards & F. P. Lees (Eds.), *The human operator in process control.* London: Taylor & Francis.

Bainbridge, L. (1978). The process controller. In W. T. Singleton (Ed.), *Analysis of practical skills, vol 1: The study of real skills.* Baltimore: University Park Press.

Bainbridge, L. (1987). Ironies of automation. In J. Rasmussen, K. Duncan, & J. Leplat (Eds.), *New technology and human error.* London: John Wiley.

Bakker, A. B., Demerouti, E., & Euwema, M. C. (2005). Job resources buffer the impact of job demands on burnout. *Journal of Occupational Health Psychology, 10(2),* 17–180.

Bakker, A, B., Demerouti, E., Taris, T. W., Schaufeli, W. B., & Schreurs, P. J. G. (2003). A multigroup analysis of the Job Demands–Resources Model in four home care organizations. *International Journal of Stress Management, 10(1),* 16–38.

Bakker, A. B., Killmer, C. H., Siegrist, J., & Schaufeli, W. B. (2000). Effort–Reward Imbalance and burnout among nurses. *Journal of Advanced Nursing, 31,* 884–91.

Baldwin, T. T., & Ford, J. K. (1988). Transfer of training: A review and directions for future research. Personnel Psychology. *Personnel Psychology, 41,* 63–105.

Baldwin, T. T., & Magjuka, R. J. (1997). Training as an organizational episode: Pretraining influences on trainee motivation. In J. K. Ford, S. W. J. Kozlowski, K. Kraiger, E. Salas & M. S. Teachout (Eds.), *Improving training effectiveness in organizations* (Vol. 99–127). Mahwah, NJ: Lawrence Erlbaum.

Bandura, A. (1977). *Social learning theory.* New York: General Learning Press.

Bandura, A. (1986). *Social foundations of thought and action: A social cognitive theory.*

Bandura, A. (1991). Social cognitive theory of self-regulation. *Organizational Behavior and Human Decision Processes*, *50*, 248–87.

Bandura, A. (1997). *Self-efficacy: The exercise of control*. New York: W. H. Freeman.

Bandura, A., & Cervone, C. (1983). Self-evaluative and self-efficacy mechanisms governing the motivational effects of goal systems. *Journal of Personality and Social Psychology*, *45*, 1017–28.

Bandura, A., & Locke, E. A. (2003). Negative self-efficacy and goal effects revisited. *Journal of Applied Psychology*, *88*, 87–99.

Barash, D. P. (1977). *Sociobiology and behavior*. New York: Elsevier.

Barchas, P. (1986). A sociophysiological orientation to small groups. In E. Lawler (Ed.), *Advances in group processes: Vol. 3.* (pp. 209–46). Greenwich, CT: JAI Press.

Bargh, J. A., & Chartrand, T. L. (1999). The unbearable automaticity of being. *American Psychologist*, *54*, 462–79.

Barley, S. R. (1989). Careers, identities, and institutions: The legacy of the Chicago school of sociology. In M. B. Arthur, D. T. Hall, & B. S. Lawrence (Eds.), *Handbook of career theory*. Cambridge: Cambridge University Press, pp. 41–65.

Barling, J., Kelloway, E. K., & Iverson, R. D. (2003). High-quality work, job satisfaction, and occupational injuries. *Journal of Applied Psychology*, *88*, 276–83.

Barling, J., Loughlin, C., & Kelloway, E. K. (2002). Development and test of a model linking safety specific transformational leadership and occupational safety. *Journal of Applied Psychology*, *87*, 488–96.

Barling, J., Weber, T., & Kelloway, E. K. (1996). Effects of transformational leadership training on attitudinal and financial outcomes: A field experiment. *Journal of Applied Psychology*, *81*, 827–32.

Baron, J. (1993). Why teach thinking? – An essay. *Applied Psychology: An International Review*, *42*, 191–213.

Barrick, M. R., & Mount, M. K. (1991). The big five personality dimensions and job performance: A meta-analysis. *Personnel Psychology*, *44*, 1–26.

Barrick, M. R., Mount, M. K., & Judge, T. (2001). Personality and performance at the beginning of the new millennium: What do we know and where do we go next? *International Journal of Selection and Assessment*, *9*, 9–30.

Bartlett, C. A., & Ghoshal, S. (1993). Beyond the M-form: Toward a managerial theory of the firm. *Strategic Management Journal*, *14(special issue)*, 23–46.

Bartlett, F. C. (1932). *Remembering: A study in experimental and social psychology*. London: Cambridge University Press.

Bartram, D. (2005). The Great Eight Competencies: A criterion-centric approach to validation. *Journal of Applied Psychology*, *90*, 1185–203.

Bartram, D., & Brown, A. (2005, Jan.). Generating competency profiles from job descriptions. In *Proceedings of the BPS Occupational Psychology Conference*, Chesford Grange (pp. 63–7). Leicester, UK: BPS.

Bartunek, J. M. (1984). Changing interpretive schemes and organizational restructuring: the example of a religious order. *Administrative Science Quarterly*, *29*, 355–72.

Bass, B. M. (1990). *Bass and Stogdill's handbook of leadership: Theory, research, and managerial applications* (3rd edn.). New York: Free Press.

Bass, B. M. (1998). *Transformational Leadership*. Mahwah NJ: Erlbaum.

Bass, B. M., & Avolio, B. J. (1993). Transformational leadership: A response to critique. In M. M. Chemers & R. Ayman (Eds.), *Leadership theory and research* (pp. 49–80). San Diego: Academic Press.

Bateman, T. S., & Zeithaml, C. P. (1989a). The psychological context of strategic decisions: a model and convergent experimental findings. *Strategic Management Journal, 10*, 59–74.

Bateman, T. S., & Zeithaml, C. P. (1989b). The psychological context of strategic decisions: a test of relevance to practitioners. *Strategic Management Journal, 10*, 587–92.

Baum, J. R., Frese, M., & Baron, R. A. (Eds.) (2007). *The Psychology of Entrepreneurship*. Mahwah, NJ: Lawrence Erlbaum.

Baumeister, R. F., & Leary, M. R. (1995). The need to belong: Desire for interpersonal attachments as a fundamental human motivation. *Psychological Bulletin, 117*, 497–529.

Bazerman, M. H. (1984). The relevance of Kahneman and Tversky's concept of framing to organizational behavior. *Journal of Management, 10*, 333–43.

Becker, F., & Sims, W. (2001). *Offices that work: Balancing communication, flexibility and cost*. Ithaca, NY: Cornell University Press.

Beier, M. E., & Ackerman, P. L. (2005). Age, ability, and the role of prior knowledge on the acquisition of new domain knowledge: Promising results in a real-world learning environment. *Psychology and Aging, 20*, 341–55.

Bélanger, F. (1999). Workers' propensity to telecommute: an empirical study. *Information and Management, 35*, 139–53.

Belbin, E., & Belbin, R. M. (1972). *Problems in adult retraining*. London: Heinemann.

Belkiç, K., Landsbergis, P., Schnall, P., Baker, D., Theorell, T., Siegrist, J., Peter, R., & Karasek, R. (2004). Psychosocial factors: Review of empirical data among men. In P. L. Schnall, K. Belkiç, P. Landsbergis, & D. Baker (Eds.), *The workplace and cardiovascular disease* (pp. 24–6). Philadelphia: Hanley & Belfus.

Bell, B. S., & Kozlowski, S. W. J. (2002). A typology of virtual teams. Implications for effective leadership. *Group & Organization Management, 27*, 14–49.

Bennett, J. B., Lehman, W. E. K., & Forst, J. K. (1999). Change, transfer climate, and customer orientation. *Group and Organization Management, 24*, 188–216.

Bergemann, N., & Sourisseaux, A. L. J. (2003). Internationale Personalauswahl. In N. Bergemann & A. L. J. Sourisseaux (Eds.), *Interkulturelles Management* (pp. 181–235). Berlin: Springer Verlag.

Berger, P. L., & Luckmann, T. (1967). *The social construction of reality*. Harmondsworth: Penguin.

Bergmann Lichtenstein, M. B., & Mendenhall, M. (2002). Non-linearity and responseability: emergent order in 21st century careers. *Human Relations, 55*, 5–32.

Bernardin, H. J., & Villanova, P. (1986). Performance Appraisal. In E. Locke (Ed.), *Generalizing from laboratory to field settings*. Lexington, MA.

Berners Lee, T., Cailliau, R., Luotonen, A., Nielsen, H. F., & Secret, A. (1994). The World Wide Web. *Communications of the ACM, 37(8)*, 76–82.

Bertua, C., Anderson, N., & Salgado, J. F. (2005). The predictive validity of cognitive ability tests: A U.K. meta-analysis. *Journal of Occupational and Organizational Psychology, 78*, 387–409.

Binney, G. (1992). *Making quality work: Lessons from Europe's leading companies.* London: Economist Intelligence Unit.

Birdi, K., Allan, C., & Warr, P. (1997). Correlates and perceived outcome of four types of employee development activity. *Journal of Applied Psychology, 82,* 845–57.

Birdi, K., Warr, P., & Oswald, A. (1995). Age differences in three components of employee well–being. *Applied Psychology, 44,* 345–73.

Blair, I. V., & Banaji, M. R (1996). Automatic and controlled processes in stereotype priming. *Journal of Personality and Social Psychology, 70,* 1142–63.

Bleicher, B. (1991). *Das Konzept Integriertes Management – Das St. Galler Management-Konzept.* Frankfurt/New York: Campus Verlag

Bleicher, K. (1994). *Normatives management. Politik, verfassung und philosophie des unternehmens.* Frankfurt/New York: Campus Verlag

Bloodgood, J. M., & Morrow, J. L. (2003). Strategic organizational change: Exploring the roles of environmental structure, internal conscious awareness and knowledge. *Journal of Management Studies, 40,* 1761–82.

Bochner, S. (1994). Culture shock. In W. J. Lonner & R. S. Malpass (Eds.), *Psychology and culture* (pp. 245–52). Needham Heights, MA: Allyn & Bacon.

Boerlijst, J. G., Munnichs, J. M. A., & van den Heijden, B. I. J. M. (1998). The "older worker" in the organization. In P. J. D. Drenth, H. Thierry, & C. J. de Wolff (Eds.), *Handbook of work and organizational psychology* (pp. 183–214). Hove: Psychology Press.

Bommer, W. H., Rich, G. A., & Rubin, R. S. (2005). Changing attitudes about change: Longitudinal effects of transformational leader behavior on employee cynicism about organisational change. *Journal of Organisational Behavior, 26,* 733–53.

Boone, C., & De Brabander, B. (1993). Generalized versus specific locus of control expectancies of chief executive officers. *Strategic Management Journal, 14,* 619–25.

Boone, C., De Brabander, B., & van Witteloostuijn, A. (1996). CEO locus of control and small firm performance: An integrative framework and empirical test. *Journal of Management Studies, 33,* 667–99.

Booth, P. A. (1989). *An Introduction to human–computer interaction.* Hove, UK: LEA.

Booth, T., Ainscow, M., Black-Hawkins, K., Vaughan, M., & Shaw, L. (2000). *Index for Inclusion. Developing learning and participation in schools.* Manchester: Centre for Studies in Inclusive Education.

Borghoff, U. M., & Schlichter, J. H. (2000). *Computer-supported cooperative work. Introduction to distributed applications.* Berlin: Springer.

Borman, W. C., Hanson, M. A., & Hedge, J. W. (1997). Personnel selection. *Annual Review of Psychology, 48,* 299–337.

Borys, B., & Jemison, D. B. (1989). Hybrid arrangements as strategic alliances: theoretical issues in organizational combinations. *Academy of Management Review, 14(2),* 234–49.

Bowlby, J. (1969). *Attachment and loss. Attachment, 1.* New York: Basic Books.

Bowman, C., & Johnson, G. (1992). Surfacing competitive strategies. *European Management Journal, 10,* 210–9.

Boyatzis, R. E. (1982). *The Competent Manager.* New York: Wiley.

Boyd, B. (1990). Corporate linkages and organizational environment: A test of the resource dependence model. *Strategic Management Journal, 36,* 343–56.

Bradford, D. L., & Cohen, A. R. (1984). *Managing for Excellence: The Guide to Developing High Performance Organizations.* John Wiley, New York NY.

Bredin, A. (1996). The Virtual Office Survival Handbook. New York: Wiley.

Breiman, L., Friedman, J. H., Oshen, R. A., & Stone, C. J. (1993). *Classification and regression trees.* New York: Chapman and Hall.

Brett, J. F., & VandeWalle, D. (1999). Goal orientation and goal content as predictors of performance in a training program. *Journal of Applied Psychology, 84,* 863–73.

Brewer, M. B., & Brown, R. J. (1990). Intergroup relations. In D. T. Gilbert, S. T. Fiske, & G. Lindzey (Eds.), *Handbook of social psychology* (Vol. 2, pp. 554–94). New York: McGraw-Hill.

Bridges, W. (1995). *Jobshift.* London: Allen & Unwin.

Brief, A. P., & Barsky, A. (2000). Establishing a climate for diversity: Inhibition of prejudice reactions in the workplace. In G. R. Ferris (Ed.), *Research in personnel and human resources management* (pp. 91–129). Greenwich, CT: JAI.

Brief, A. P., Buttram, R. T., Elliott, J. D., Reizenstein, R. M., & McCline, R. L. (1995). Releasing the beast: A study of compliance with order to use race as a selection criterion. *Journal of Social Issues, 51,* 177–93.

Brief, A. P., Dietz, J., Cohen, R. R., Pugh, S. D., & Vaslow, J. B. (2000). Just doing the business: Modern racism and obedience to authority as explanations for employment discrimination. *Organisational Behaviour and Human Decision Processes, 81,* 72–97.

Britton, L., & Casebourne, J. (2002). *Defining social exclusion.* Working Brief 136. London: Centre for Economic & Social Inclusion (www.cesi.org.uk).

Broadbent, D. E. (1958). *Perception and Communication.* London: Pergamon Press.

Broadbent, D. E. (1971). *Decision and Stress.* London: Academic Press.

Broadbent, D. E. (1979). Is a fatigue test now possible? *Ergonomics, 22,* 1277–90.

Brodbeck, F. C., & Frese, M. (Eds.) (••). *Produktivitaet und Qualitaet in Software–Projekten* (Productivity and quality of softwareprojects). Munich: Oldenbourg.

Brodbeck, F. C., Frese, M., Ackerblom, S., Audia, G., Bakacsi, G., et al. (2000). Cultural variation of leadership prototypes across 22 European countries. *Journal of Occupational and Organizational Psychology, 73,* 1–29.

Brodbeck, F. C., Frese, M., & Javidan, M. (2002). Leadership made in Germany: Low on compassion, high on performance. *Academy of Management Executive, 16(1),* 16–29.

Brooke, J. (1986). *The system usability scale.* Reading, UK: Digital Equipment Co. Ltd.

Brown, I. (1990). Accident Reporting and Analysis. In J. R. Wilson & E. N. Corlett (Eds.). *Evaluation of human work.* London: Taylor & Francis.

Brown, R. (2000). Group processes (2nd edn.). Oxford: Blackwell.

Brown, R. L., & Holmes, H. (1986). The use of a factor-analytic procedure for assessing the validity of an employee safety climate model. *Accident Analysis & Prevention, 18,* 445–70.

Brown, S., & Eisenhardt, K. M. (1997). The art of continuous change: Linking complexity theory and time-paced evolution in relentlessly shifting organizations. *Administrative Science Quarterly, 42,* 1–34.

Brown, S., & Eisenhardt, K. M. (1998). *Competing on the edge: Strategy as structured chaos*. Boston, MA: Harvard Business School Press.

Browning, R. C. (1968). Validity of reference ratings from previous employers. *Personnel Psychology*, *21*, 389–93.

Bruner, J. (1957). On perceptual readiness. *Psychological Review*, *64*, 123–52.

Brutus, S., Derayeh, M., Fletcher, C., Bailey, C., Velazquez, P., Shi, K., Simon, C., & Labath, V. (2006). Multisource feedback systems: A six-country comparative analysis. *International Journal of Human Resource Management*, In Press.

Buchanan, D., Abbott, S., Bentley, J., Lanceley, A., & Meyer, J. (2005). Let's be PALS: User-driven organizational change in healthcare. *British Journal of Management*, *16*, 315–28.

Buckley, W. (Ed.) (1968). *Modern systems research for the behavioral scientist*. Chicago: Aldine Publishing Co.

Bunker, B. B., & Alban, B. T. (1997). *Large-group interventions*. San Francisco: Jossey-Bass.

Buono, A. F., & Bowditch, •• (1989). *The human side of mergers and acquisitions: managing collisions between people, culture and organizations*. San Francisco: Jossey-Bass.

Burger, J. M. (1989). Negative reactions to increases in perceived personal control. *Journal of Personality and Social Psychology*, *56*, 246–56.

Burke, M. J., Sarpy, S. A., Tesluk, P. E., & Smith–Crowe, K. (2002). General safety performance: A test of a grounded theoretical model. *Personnel Psychology*, *55*, 429–57.

Burt, R. S. (2000). Decay functions. *Social Networks*, *22*, 1–28.

Buss, D. M. (1990). The evolution of anxiety and social exclusion. *Journal of Social and Clinical Psychology*, *9*, 196–210.

Buss, DM. (1991). Evolutionary personality psychology. *Annual Review of Psychology*, *42*, 459–91.

Butler, J. E., Ferris G. R., & Napier, N. K. (1991), *Planning for and managing mergers and acquisitions: strategy and human resources management*. Oklahoma: South Western Publishing Co.

Byham, W. C. (1971). The assessment centre as an aid in managerial development. *Training and Development Journal*, *25*, 10–22.

Byrne, D. (1971). *The attraction paradigm*. New York: Academic Press.

Byrne, E. A., & Parasuraman R. (1996). Psychophysiology and adaptive automation. *Biological Psychology*, *42*, 249–68.

Cagliano, R., Acur, N., & Boer, H. (2005). Patterns of change in manufacturing strategy configurations. *International Journal of Operations & Production Management*, *25*, 701–18.

Calori, R., Johnson, G., & Sarnin, P. (1992). French and British top managers' understanding of the structure and dynamics of their industries: A cognitive analysis and comparison. *British Journal of Management*, *3*, 61–78.

Cameron, J., Banko, K. M., & Pierce, W. D. (2001). Pervasive negative effects of rewards on intrinsic motivation. *The Behavior Analyst*, *24*, 1–44.

Campbell, D. J., Campbell, K. M., & Chia, H. B. (1998). Merit pay, performance appraisal and individual motivation; An analysis and alternative. *Human Resource Management*, *37*, 131–46.

Carrero, V., Peiró, J. M., & Salanova, M. (2000). Studying radical organizational innovation through grounded theory. *European Journal of Work and Organizational Psychology*, *9*, 489–514.

Carter, N. L., & Beh, H. C. (1989). The effect of intermittent noise on cardiovascular functioning during vigilance performance. *Psychophysiology*, *26*, 548–59.

Cartwright, S. (2005). Mergers and acquisitions: An update and appraisal. In G. P. Hodgkinson & J. K. Ford (Eds.), *International Review of Industrial and Organizational Psychology*, Vol. 20. Chichester, UK: Wiley.

Cartwright, S., & Cooper, C. L. (1990). The impact of mergers and acquisitions on people at work: Existing research and issues. *British Journal of Management*, *1*, 65–76.

Cartwright, S., & Cooper, C. L. (1999). *Managing mergers acquisitions and strategic alliances: Integrating people and culture*. Oxford, Butterworth-Heinneman.

Cartwright, S., & Cooper, C. L., (1996). Public policy and occupational health psychology in Europe. *Journal of Occupational Health Psychology*, *1*, 349–61.

Cascio, W. F. (1995). Whither industrial and organizational psychology in a changing world of work? *American Psychologist*, *50(11)*, 928–39.

Cascio, W. F. (1998). The virtual workplace: A reality now. *TIP (The Industrial Organizational Psychologist)*, *35*, 32–6.

Cassidy, T., & Lynn, R. (1989). A multifactorial approach to achievement motivation: The development of a comprehensive measure. *Journal of Occupational Psychology*, *62*, 301–12.

Caves, R. E., & Porter, M. E. (1977). From entry barriers to mobility barriers: Conjectural decisions and contrived deterrence to new competition. *Quarterly Journal of Economics*, *91*, 421–34.

Cellar, D. F., Miller, M. L., Doverspike, D. D., & Klawsky, J. D. (1996). Comparisons of factor structure and criterion–related validity coefficients for two measures of personality based on the five factor model. *Journal of Applied Psychology*, *81*, 694–704.

Chambel, M. J., & Peiró, J. M. (2003). Alteraciones en las prácticas de recursos humanos y violación del contrato psicológico: implicaciones para las actitudes y la intención de abandonar la organización de los empleados. *Arxius*, *8*, 105–201.

Chambel, M. J., Peiró, J. M., & Pina, F. X. (1999). El modelo AMIGO en el análisis del cambio estratégico en las organizaciones. Ocho estudios de casos realizados en pequeñas empresas del sector cerámico. *Trabajo y Seguridad Social del Centro de Estudios Financieros*, *50*, 199–240.

Chan, D., & Schmitt, N. (2004). An agenda for future research on applicant reactions to selection procedures: A construct-oriented approach. *International Journal of Selection and Assessment*, *12*, 9–23.

Chao, G. T. (1997). Unstructured training and development: The role of organizational socialization. In J. K. Ford, S. W. J. Kozlowski, K. Kraiger, E. Salas & M. S. Teachout (Eds.), *Improving training effectiveness in work organizations* (pp. 129–51). Mahwah, NJ: Erlbaum.

Chapman, A. J., Sheehy, N. P., Heywood, S., Dooley, B., & Collins, S. C. (1995). The organizational implications of teleworking. In C. L. Cooper & I. T. Robertson (Eds.), *International review of industrial and organizational psychology* (pp. 229–48). Chichester, UK: Wiley.

Charness, N., Kelley, C. L., Bosman, C. A., & Mottram, M. (2001). Word-processing training and retraining. Effects of adult age, experience, and interface. *Psychology and Aging*, *16*, 110–27.

Chatman, J. A., Polzer. J. T., Barsade, S. G., & Neale, M. A. (1998). Being different yet feeling similar: The influence of demographic composition and organisational culture on work processes and outcomes. *Administrative Science Quarterly*, *43*, 749–80.

Cherniss, C. (1995). *Beyond burnout: Helping teachers, nurses, therapists and lawyers recover from stress and disillusionment*. New York: Routledge.

Cherns, A. B. (1976). The principles of sociotechnical design. *Human Relations*, *29*, 783–92.

Cherns, A. B. (1987). Principles of sociotechnical design. *Human Relations*, *40*, 153–62.

Cheryan, S., & Bodenhausen, G. V. (2000). When stereotypes threaten intellectual performance: The psychological hazards of "model minority" status. *Psychological Science*, *11*, 399–402.

Cheyne, A., Cox, S., Oliver, A., & Tomas, J. M. (1998). Modelling safety climate in the prediction of safety activity. *Work & Stress*, *12*, 255–71.

Chhokar, J., Brodbeck, F. C., & House, R. (2007). *Culture and leadership across the world: The GLOBE Book of in–depth studies of 25 societies*. Mahwah, NJ: LEA Publishers.

Chin, J. P., Diehl, V. A., & Norman, K. L. (1988). Development of an instrument measuring user satisfaction of the human–computer interface. In *Proceedings of CHI '88* (pp. 213–18). New York: ACM.

Chiu, W. C. K., Chan, A. W., Snape, E., & Redman, T. (2001). Age stereotypes and discriminatory attitudes towards older workers: An east–west comparison. *Human Relations*, *54*, 629–61.

Chmiel, N. (1998). *Jobs, technology and people*. London: Routledge.

Chmiel, N. (2005). Promoting healthy work: Self-reported minor injuries, work characteristics, and safety behaviour. In C. Korunka & P. Hoffman (Eds.), *Change and Quality in Human Service Work*. Munich and Mering: Rainer Hampp. Verlag.

Chmiel, N. (in press). Modern work and safety. In K. Naswall, J. Hellgren, & M. Sverke (Eds.), *The individual in the changing world of work*. Cambridge: Cambridge University Press.

Chmiel, N., Totterdell, P., & Folkard, S. (1995). On adaptive control, sleep loss and fatigue. *Applied Cognitive Psychology*, *9*, 39–53.

Clark, A., Oswald, A., & Warr, P. (1996). Is job satisfaction U-shaped in age? *Journal of Occupational and Organizational Psychology*, *69*, 57–81.

Clarke, N. (2002). Job/work environment factors influencing training transfer within a human service agency: Some indicative support for Baldwin and Ford's transfer of climate construct. *International Journal of Training and Development*, *6*, 146–62.

Clarke, S. (1998). Organizational factors affecting the incident reporting of train drivers. *Work & Stress*, *12*, 6–16.

Clarke, S. (2006). Contrasting perceptual, attitudinal and dispositional approaches to accident involvement in the workplace. *Safety Science*, *44*, 537–50.

Clarke, S. (2006). The relationship between safety climate and safety performance: A meta-analytic review. *Journal of Occupational Health Psychology*, *11*, 315–27.

Clarkson, G. P., & Hodgkinson, G. P. (2004). *Sensemaking on the frontline: The key implications for call centre performance*. In A. Neely, M. Kennerley, & A. Walters (Eds.), *Performance measurement and management: Public and private*. Centre for Business Performance: Cranfield University.

Clarkson, G. P., & Hodgkinson, G. P. (2005). Introducing Cognizer™: A comprehensive computer package for the elicitation and analysis of cause maps. *Organizational Research Methods*, *8*, 317–41.

Clarkson, G. P., & Hodgkinson, G. P. (2007). *Making sense of workplace performance*. AIM Executive Briefing Series. London: ESRC/EPSRC Advanced Institute of Management Research.

Clear, F., & Dickson, K. (2005). Teleworking practice in small and medium–sized firms: management style and worker autonomy. *New Technology, Work and Employment*, *20*, 218–33.

Clegg, C. W., Gray, M. O., & Waterson, P. E. (2000). The "Charge of the Byte Brigade" and a socio-technical response. *International Journal of Human–Computer Studies*, *52*, 235–51.

Cleveland, J. N., & Murphy, K. R. (1992). Analyzing performance appraisal as goal–directed behavior. *Research in Personnel and Human Resources Management*, *10*, 121–85.

Cleveland, J. N., Shore, M. L., & Murphy, K. (1997). Person and context oriented perceptual age measures: Additional evidence of distinctiveness and usefulness. *Journal of Organizational Behavior*, *18*, 239–51.

Cockman, P., Evans, B., & Reynolds, P. (1999). *Consulting for real people, a client–centred approach for change agents and leaders*. London: McGraw-Hill.

Cohen, S. (1980). The aftereffects of stress on human performance and social behavior: A review of research and theory. *Psychological Bulletin*, *88*, 82–108.

Cohen, S., Evans, G. W., Krantz, D. S., & Stokols, D. (1986). *Behavior, health and environmental stress*. New York: Plenum.

Cohen, S., & Wills, T. A. (1985). Stress, social support and the buffering hypothesis. *Psychological Bulletin*, *98(2)*, 310–57.

Colquitt, J. A. (2001). On the dimensionality of organizational justice: a construct validation of a measure. *Journal of Applied Psychology*, *86*, 386–400.

Colquitt, J. A., LePine, J. A., & Noe, R. A. (2000). Toward an integrative theory of training motivation: a meta-analytic path analysis of 20 years of research. *Journal of Applied Psychology*, *85*, 678–707.

Commission of the European Community. (1999). Towards a Europe for all ages. Retrieved 2002, from http:\\europa.eu.int/comm/employment_social/soc–prot/ageing/com99–221/com221_en. pdf.

Conger, J. A. (1989). *The charismatic leader: Behind the mystique of exceptional leadership*. San Francisco, CA: Jossey-Bass.

Conger, J. A., & Kanungo, R. N. (1987). Toward a behavioral theory of charismatic leadership in organizational settings. *Academy of Management Review*, *12*, 637–47.

Conway, J. M., Jako, R. A., & Goodman, D. E. (1995). A meta-analysis of interrater and internal consistency reliability of employment interviews. *Journal of Applied Psychology*, *80*, 565–79.

Cook, M. (1998). *Personnel Selection*. Third Edition, Chichester, UK: Wiley.

Cook, T. D., Campbell, D. T., & Peracchio, L. (1990). Quasi experimentation. In M. D. Dunnette & L. M. Hough (Eds.), *Handbook of industrial and organizational psychology* (2. Aufl., Bd. 1, S. 491–576). Palo Alto: Consulting Psychologists Press.

Cooper, C., & Kurland, N. B. (2002). Telecommuting, professional isolation and employee development in public and private organizations. *Journal of Organizational Behavior, 23*, 511–32.

Cooper, C. L., & Payne, R. (Eds.) (1988). *Causes, coping and consequences of stress at work.* Chichester, UK: Wiley.

Cooper, G. E., & Harper, R. P. (1969). *The use of pilot rating in the evaluation of aircraft handling qualities.* Moffett Field, CA: NASA–Ames Research Center. Report No. NASA TN–D–5153.

Cooper, M. D., & Phillips, R. A. (2004). Exploratory analysis of the safety climate and safety behavior relationship. *Journal of Safety Research, 35*, 497–512.

Corlett, D., Sharples, M., Bull, S., & Chan, T. (2005). Evaluation of a mobile learning organiser for university students. *Journal of Computer Assisted Learning, 21*, 162–70.

Cotton, J. L. (1993). *Employee involvement: Methods for improving performance and work attitudes.* Newbury Park CA: Sage.

Cotton, S. J., Dollard, M. F., & Jonge, J. de (2006). *A review of the JD–R Model: A move towards wellness.* Manuscript submitted for publication.

Cox, T., Jr. (1994). *Cultural diversity in organisations: Theory, research and practice.* San Francisco: Berrett-Koehler

Cox, T., Lobel, S., & McLeod, P. (1991). Effects of ethnic group cultural differences on co-operative and competitive behaviour on a group task. *Academy of Management Journal, 34*, 827–47.

Cronbach, L. J. (1970). *Essentials of Psychological Testing.* New York: Harper & Row

Cronbach, L. J. & Glesser, G. C. (1965). *Psychological Tests and Personnel Decisions.* Urbana: University of Illinois Press

Cropanzo, R., & Wright, T. A. (1999). A 5–Year Study of Change in the Relationship Between Well–Being and Job Performance. *Consulting Psychology Journal: Practice and Research, 51(4)*, 252–62.

Cropanzo, R., & Wright, T. A. (2001). When a "happy" worker is really a "productive" worker. A review and further refinement of the happy–productive worker thesis. *Consulting Psychology Journal: Practice and Research, 53(3)*, 182–99.

Cropley, M., & Millward, L. J. (2004). Job strain and rumination about work issues during leisure time: a diary study. *European Journal of Work and Organizational Psychology, 12*, 195–207.

Crown, D. F., & Rosse, J. G. (1995). Yours, mine, and ours: Facilitating group productivity through the integration of individual and group goals. *Organizational Behavior and Human Decision Processes, 64*, 138–150

Csikszentmihalyi, M. (1990). *Flow: The psychology of optimal experience.* New York: Harper & Row.

Csikszentmihalyi, M., Abuhamdeh, S., & Nakamura, J. (2005). Flow. In Elliot, A. J., & Dweck, C. S. (Eds.), *Handbook of competence and motivation* (598–608). New York: Guilford press.

Csikszentmihalyi, M., & LeFevre, J. (1989). Optimal experience in work and leisure. *Journal of Personality and Social Psychology, 56*, 815–22.

Cutrona, C. E., & Russel, D. W. (1990). Type of social support and specific stress: Toward a theory of optimal matching. In B. R. Sarason, I. G. Sarason, & G. R. Pierce (Eds.), *Social support: an interactional view* (pp. 319–366). Ne w York: John Wiley.

Czaja, S. J., & Sharit, J. (1998). Ability–performance relationship as a function of age and task experience for a data entry task. *Journal of Applied Psychology, 4,* 332–51.

Czerniawska, F. (1999). *Management Consultancy in the 21st Century.* London: MacMillan Press.

D'Avini, R. A. I. (1994). *Hypercompetition.* New York: Free Press.

Dachler, M. P. (1994). A social–relational perspective of selection. Paper presented at the 23rd International Congress of Applied Psychology, Madrid, Spain, July, 1994.

Daft, R. L., & Lengel, R. H. (1984). Information richness: a new approach to managerial behaviour and organization design. *Research in Organizational Behavior, 6,* 191–233.

Dambrin, C. (2004). How does telework influence the management–employee relationship? *International Journal of Human Resource Development and Management, 4,* 358–74.

Damos, D. L. (Ed.) (1991). *Multiple–task Performance.* London: Taylor & Francis.

Danaher, J. W. (1980). Human error in ATC system Operations. *Human Factors, 22,* 535–45.

Dangler, J. F. (1986). Industrial homework in the modern world. *Contemporary Crises, 10,* 257–79.

Daniels, K., Johnson, G., & de Chernatony, L. (1994). Differences in managerial cognitions of competition. *British Journal of Management,* 5: S21–S29.

Daniels, K., Johnson, G., & de Chernatony, L. (2002). Task and institutional influences on managers' mental models of competition. *Organization Studies,* 23, 31–62.

Daniels, K., Lamond, D. A., & Standen, P. (2000). Managing Telework. Perspectives from Human Resource Management and Work Psychology, London: Thomson Learning.

Dansereau, F. Jr., Graen, G., & Haga, W. J. (1975). A vertical dyad linkage approach to leadership within formal organizations : A longitudinal investigation of the role making process. *Organizational Behavior and Human Performance, 13,* 46–78.

Das, T. K., & Teng, B.–S. (1999). Cognitive biases and strategic decision processes. *Journal of Management Studies, 36,* 757–78.

Davis, M. A. (2003). Factors related to bridge employment participation among private sector early retirees. *Journal of Vocational Behavior, 63,* 55–71.

Dawson, J. F., West, M. A., Scully, J. W., Beinart, S., Carpenter, M., & Smith, D. (2004). *Health Care Commission report of national findings NHS staff survey 2003.* London: Commission for Healthcare Audit Inspection.

De Beeck, R., & Van Heuverswyn, K. (2002). *New trends in accident prevention due to the changing world of work.* European Agency for Safety and Health at Work. Luxembourg: Office for Official Publications of the European Communities.

De Dreu, C. K. W., & Van de Vliert, E. (1997). *Using conflict in organizations.* London: Sage.

De Dreu, C. K. W., & Van Vianen, A. E. M. (2001). Responses to relationship conflict and team effectiveness. *Journal of Organizational Behavior, 22,* 309–28.

De Vries, R. E., Roe, R. A., & Tailleu, T. C. B. (2002). Need for leadership as a moderator of the relationships between leadership and individual outcomes. *The Leadership Quarterly, 13,* 121–37.

Dean, R. A., & Wanous, J. P. (1984). Effects of realistic job previews on hiring bank tellers. *Journal of Applied Psychology, 69,* 61–8.

Deci, E. L., Koestner, R., & Ryan, R. M. (1999). A meta-analytic review of experiments examining the effects of extrinsic rewards on intrinsic motivation. *Psychological Bulletin, 125,* 627–68.

Dedobeleer, N., & Beland, F. (1991). A Safety Climate Measure for Construction Sites. *Journal of Safety Research, 22,* 97–103.

Dejoy, D. (1986). A behavioural–diagnostic model for self-protective behaviour in the workplace. *Professional Safety, 31,* 26–30.

DeJoy, D. M., Searcy, C. A., Murphy, L. R., & Gershon, R. R. M. (2000). Behavioural–Diagnostic Analysis of Compliance With Universal Precautions Among Nurses. *Journal of Occupational Health Psychology, 5,* 127–41.

Demerouti, E., Bakker, A. B., Nachreiner, F., & Schaufeli, W. B. (2001). Job demands–resources model of burnout. *Journal of Applied Psychology, 86,* 499–512.

DeNisi, A. S. (1997). *Cognitive Approach to Performance Appraisal: A Programme of Research.* Routledge: London.

Desrochers, S., Hilton, J. M., & Larwood, L. (2005). Preliminary Validation of the Work–Family Integration–Blurring Scale. *Journal of Family Issues, 26,* 442–66.

Deutsch, M. (1973). *The resolution of conflict: Constructive and destructive processes.* New Haven, CT: Yale University Press.

Dick, P., & Jankowicz, A. D. (2001). A social constructionist account of police culture and its influence on the representation and progression of female officers: A repertory grid analysis in a UK police force. *Policing, 24(2),* 181–99.

Diehl, M., & Stroebe, W. (1987). Productivity loss in brainstorming groups: Toward the solution of a riddle. *Journal of Personality and Social Psychology, 53,* 497–509.

DiMartino, V., & Wirth, L. (1990). Telework: a new way of working and living. *International Labour Review, 129,* 529–54.

Dipboye, R. L. (1997). Structured selection Interviews: Why do they work? Why are they underutilized? In N. Anderson & P. Herriot (Eds.). *International Handbook of Selection and Assessment.* Chichester, UK: Wiley.

Donaldson, S. I., & Weiss, R. (1998). Health, well–being, and organizational effectiveness in the virtual workplace. In M. Igbaria & M. Tan (eds.) *The Virtual Workplace.* Hershey, PA: Idea Group Publishing, pp. 24–44.

Donovan, J. J. (2001). Work Motivation. In N. Anderson, D. Ones, H. Sinangil, & C. Viswesvaran (Eds.), *International Handbook of Industrial, Work and Organizational Psychology.* Sage: London.

Dovidio, J. F., Brigham, J. C., Johnson, B. T., & Gaertner, S. L. (1996). Stereotyping, prejudice and discrimination: Another look. In C. N. Macrae, C. Strangor, & M. Hewstone (Eds.), *Stereoypes and stereotyping* (pp. 276–319). New York: Guildford.

Dovidio, J. F., & Gaertner, S. L. (1998). On the nature of contemporary prejudice: The causes, consequences and challenges of aversive racism. In J. L. Eberhardt & S. T. Fiske (Eds.), *Confronting racism: The problem and the response* (pp. 3–32). New York: Sage.

Dovidio, J. F., & Gaertner, S. L. (2000). Aversive racism and selection decisions: 1989 and 1999 *Psychological Science, 11*, 319–23.

Dovidio, J. F., Gaertner, S. L., & Validzic, A. (1998). Intergroup bias: Status differentiation and a common ingroup identity. *Journal of Personality and Social Psychology, 75(1)*, 103–20.

Dovidio, J. F., & Hebl, M. R. (2005). Discrimination at the level of the individual: Cognitive and affective factors. In R. L. Dipboye & A. Colella (Eds.), *Discrimination at work* (pp. 11–35). Mahwah, NJ: Lawrence Erlbaum.

Doz, Y. L., & Hamel, G. (1998), *Alliance advantage: The art of creating value through partnering*, Boston, Harvard Business School Press.

Dreher, G. F., & Cox, T. H., Jr. (1997). Race, gender and opportunity: A study of compensation attainment and the establishment of mentoring relationships. *Journal of Applied Psychology, 81*, 297–305.

Drucker, P. F. (1955). *The Practice of Management*. London: Heinemann.

Duarte, D. L., & Snyder, N. T. (2001). *Mastering virtual teams. Strategies, tools, and techniques that succeed*. Jossey-Bass, San Francisco.

Dumon, M., Yzerbyt, V. Y., Snyder, M., Mathiiu, B., Comblin, C., & Scillet, N. (2003). Suppression and Hypotheses testing: Does suppressing stereotypes during interactions help to avoid confirmation biases? *European Journal of Social Psychology, 33*, 659–77.

Dunn, T. G., & Shriner, C. (1999). Deliberate practice in teaching: What teachers do for self-improvement. *Teaching and Teacher Education, 15*, 631–51.

Dutton, J. E., & Dukerich, J. M. (1991). Keeping an eye on the mirror: Image and identity in organizational adaptation. *Academy of Management Journal, 34*, 517–54.

Dweck, C. S., & Leggett, E. L. (1988). A social-cognitive approach to motivation and personality. *Psychological Review, 95*, 256–73.

Dye, D., & Silver, M. (1999). The origins of O*NET. In N. G. Peterson, M. D. Mumford, W. C. Borman, P. R. Jeanneret, & E. A. Fleishman (Eds.), *An occupational information system for the 21st century* (pp. 9–20). Washington, DC: American Psychological Association.

Eagly, A. H., & Karau, S. J. (2002). Role congruity theory of prejudice toward female leaders. *Psychological Review, 109*, 573–98.

Eagly, A. H., Makhijani, M. G., & Klonsky, B. G. (1992). Gender and the evaluation of leaders. *Psychological Bulletin, 111*, 3–22.

Eason, K. D. (1984). *Information technology and organisational change*. London: Taylor & Francis.

EcaTT (2000). Benchmarking progress on new ways of working and new forms of business across Europe. EcaTT Final Report August 2000, Empirica, Bonn (http://www.empirica.com/ecatt).

Eden, D. (1993). Interpersonal expectations in organizations. In P. D. Blanck (Ed.), *Interpersonal expectations: Theory, research, and applications* (pp. 154–78). New York: Cambridge University Press.

Eden, D., & Leviathan, M. (1975). Implicit leadership theory as a determinant of the factor structure underlying supervisory behavior scales. *Journal of Applied Psychology, 60*, 736–41.

Edholm, O. G., & Murrell, H. (1973). *The Ergonomics Society: A history 1949–1970* (London: Ergonomics Research Society). Winchester, UK: Warren & Sons, Ltd.

Edmondson, A. C. (1996). Learning from mistakes is easier said than done: Group and organizational influences on the detection and correction of human error. *Journal of Applied Behavioral Science*, *32(1)*, 5–28.

Edmondson, A. C. (1999). Psychological safety and learning behavior in work teams. *Administrative Science Quarterly*, *44*, 350–83.

EFPA. (1995). Guidance for the content of the Ethical Codes. Adopted by the General Assembly 1995, July 1 in Athens. European Federation of Psychologists' Associations (see http://www.efpa.be/start.php).

Eggemeier, F. T. (1988). Properties of workload assessment techniques. In P. A. Hancock & N. Meshkati (Eds.), *Human mental workload*. Amsterdam: North-Holland.

Eggemeier, F. T., & Wilson, G. F. (1991). Performance-based and subjective assessment of workload in multi-task environments. In D. L. Damos (Ed.), *Multipl-task performance*. London: Taylor & Francis.

Ekerdt, D. J. (1998). Workplace norms for the timing of retirement. In K. W. Schaie & C. Schooler (Eds.), *Impact of work on older adults*. New York: Springer.

Elvira, M. M., & Cohen, L. E. (2001). Location matters: A cross-level analysis of the effects of organizational sex composition on turnover. *Academy of Management Journal*, *44*, 591–605.

Ely, R. J. (1994). The effects of organizational demographics and social identity on relationships among professional women. *Administrative Science Quarterly*, *39*, 203–38.

Ely, R. J. (1995). The power of demography: Women's social construction of gender identity at work. *Academy of Management Journal*, *38*, 589–634.

Ely, R. J., & Thomas, D. A. (2001). Cultural diversity at work: The effects of diversity perspectives on work group processes and outcomes. *Administrative Science Quarterly*, *46*, 229–73.

Emery, F. E. (1959). *The characteristics of a socio-technical system*. Tavistock Document 527, London.

Emery, F. E., & Trist, E. L. (1969). Socio-technical systems. In F. E. Emery (Ed.), *Systems thinking*. London: Penguin.

ENOP (2005). European Curriculum in W&O Psychology Reference Model and Minimal Standards. Updated March 7th, 2005. European Network of Organizational and Work Psychologists (see: http://www.ucm.es/info/Psyap/enop/rmodel.html).

Erez, M., & Somech, A. (1996). Is group productivity loss the rule or the exception? Effects of culture and group-based motivation. *Academy of Management Journal*, *39*, 1513–37.

Ergonomics Research Society. (1957). Editorial. *Ergonomics*, *1*, 1–3.

Ericsson, K. A., Krampe, R. T., & Tesch–Römer, C. (1993). The role of deliberate practice in the acquisition of expert performance. *Psychological Review*, *100*, 363–406.

Esses, V. M., Haddock, G., & Zanna, M. P. (1993). Values, stereotypes and emotions as determinants of intergroup attitudes. In D. M. Mackie & D. L. Hamilton (Eds.), *Affect, cognition and stereotyping: Interactive processes in group perception* (pp. 137–66). San Diego: Academic Press.

European Foundation for the Improvement of Living and Working Conditions [EFILWC] (2005). *Work-related stress*. Dublin: European Foundation for the Improvement of Living and Working Conditions (available in electronic format only).

EuroPsy (2003/2005). The European Diploma in Psychology, a framework for education and training of psychologists in Europe. Version 2003/2005 published in the home page of EFPA, European Federation of Psychologists' Associations (see: http://www.efpa. be/start. php).

Eurostat Yearbook (2005). *Europe in figures* (ch. 5). Luxembourg: Office for Official Publications of the European Communities.

Evans, C. (1983). *The mighty micro: The impact of the computer revolution*. London: Victor Gollancz.

Evans, M. G., & Ondrack, D. A. (1991). The motivational potential of jobs: Is a multiplicative model necessary? *Psychological Reports, 69*, 659–72.

Facteau, J. D., Dobbins, G. H., Riussell, J. E. A., Ladd, R. T., & Kudisch, J. D. (1995). The influence of general perceptions of the training environment on pretraining motivation and perceived transfer. *Journal of Management, 21*, 1–25.

Fairclough, S. H., & Venables, L. (2004). Psychophysiological candidates for biocybernetic adaptation. In D. de Waard et al. (Eds.), *Human factors in design* (pp. 177–89). Shaker: The Netherlands.

Fairclough, S. H., & Venables, L. (2006). Prediction of subjective states from psychophysiology: a multivariate approach. *Biological Psychology, 71*, 100–10.

Fairclough, S. H., Venables, L., & Tattersall, A. J. (2005a). The influence of task demand and learning on the psychophysiological response. *International Journal of Psychophysiology, 56*, 171–84.

Fairclough, S. H., Venables, L., & Tattersall, A. J. (2005b). The use of autonomic measures for biocybernetic adaptation. *Psychophysiology, 42(Supplement 1)*, S25.

Farr, J. L., & Ringseis, E. L. (2002). The older worker in organizational context: Beyond the individual. In C. L. Cooper, & I. T. Robertson (Eds.), *International Review of Industrial and Organizational Psychology* (Vol. 17, pp. 31–76). Chichester, UK: John Wiley.

Farr, J. L., Tesluk, P. E., & Klein, S. R. (1998). Organizational structure of the workplace and the older worker. In K. W. Schaie & C. Schooler (Eds.), *Impact of work on older adults*. New York: Springer.

Feigenbaum, E. A., & McCorduck, P. (1984). *The fifth generation*. New York: Signet.

Feldman, D. C. (1994). The decision to retire early: A review and conceptualization. *Academy of Management Review, 19*, 285–311.

Felstead, A., Jewson,N., Phizacklea, A., & Walters, S, (2001). Working at home: statistical evidence for seven key hypotheses. *Work, Employment and Society, 15*, 215–331.

Ferdman, B. M., & Davidson, M. N. 2002. Inclusion: What can I and my organization do about it? *The Industrial-Organizational Psychologist, 39(4)*, 80–5.

Fiedler, F. E. (1967). *A theory of leadership effectiveness*. New York: McGraw-Hill.

Fiedler, F. E. (1972). How do you make leaders ore effective? New answers to an old puzzle. *Organizational Dynamics*, 1–18.

Fine, S. A. (1988). Functional job analysis. In S. Gael (Ed.), *The job analysis handbook for business, industry and government* (Vol. 2, pp. 1019–35). New York: Wiley.

Finholt, T. A., & Teasley, S. D. (1998). The need for psychology in research on computer–supported cooperative work. *Social Science Computer Review, 16*, 40–52.

Finkelstein, L. M., & Burke, M. J. (1998). Age stereotyping at work: the role of rater and contextual factors on evaluations of job applicants. *Journal of General Psychology, 125*, 317–45.

Finkelstein, L. M., Burke, M. J., & Raju, N. S. (1995). Age discrimination in simulated employment contexts: an integrative analysis. *Journal of Applied Psychology*, *80*, 652–63.

Fischhoff, B. (1975). Hindsight and foresight: The effect of outcome knowledge on judgement under uncertainty, *Journal of Experimental Psychology: Human Perception and Performance*, *1*, 288–99.

Fischhoff, B., Slovic, P., & Lichtenstein, S. (1977). Knowing with certainty: The appropriateness of extreme confidence. *Journal of Experimental Psychology: Human Perception and Performance*, *3*, 552–64.

Fisher, K., & Fisher, M. D. (2001). *The distance manager. A hands-on guide to managing off-site employees and virtual teams.* McGraw-Hill, New York.

Fiske, S. T. (1998). Stereotyping, prejudice and discrimination. In D. T. Gilbert, S. T. Fiske, & G. Lindzey (Eds.), *The handbook of social psychology* (4th edn., Vol. 2, pp. 357–411). New York: McGraw-Hill.

Fiske, S. T., Cuddy, A. J. C., Glick, P., & Xu, J. (2002). A model of (often mixed) stereotype content: Competence and warmth respectively follow from perceived status and competition. *Journal of Personality and Social Psychology*, *82*, 878–902.

Fiske, S. T., & Neubert, S. L. (1990). A continuum of impression formation, from category based to individuating processes: Influences of information and motivation on attention and interpretation. In M. P. Zanna (Ed.), *Advances in experimental social psychology* (Vol. 23, pp. 1–108). San Diego: Academic Press.

Fitts, P. M. (1951). *Human Engineering for an Effective Air Navigation and Traffic Control System.* Washington DC: National Research Council.

Flanagan, J. C. (1954). The Critical Incidents Technique. *Psychological Bulletin*, *51*, 327–58.

Fleishman, E. A., & Harris, E. F. (1962). Patterns of leadership behavior related to employee grievances and turnover. *Personnel Psychology*, *15*, 43–56.

Fleishman, E. A., & Mumford, M. D. 1988). Ability Requirements Scales. In S. Gael (Ed.), *The job analysis handbook for business, industry and government* (Vol. 2, pp. 917–35). New York: Wiley.

Fletcher, C. (1991). Candidates' reactions to assessment centers and their outcomes: A longitudinal study. *Journal of Occupational Psychology*, *64*, 117–27.

Fletcher, C. (2001). Performance appraisal and performance management: The developing research agenda. *Journal of Occupational and Organizational Psychology*, *74*, 473–87

Fletcher, C. (2002). Appraisal – An individual psychological analysis. In S. Sonnentag (Ed.), *The psychological management of individual performance: A handbook in the psychology of management in organisations.* London: Wiley.

Fletcher, C. (2004). *Appraisal and feedback.* London: Chartered Institute of Personnel & Development.

Fletcher, C., & Baldry, C. (1999). Multi-source feedback systems: A research perspective. In C. Cooper & I. T. Robertson (Eds.), *International review of organizational and industrial psychology* (Vol. 14). New York & London: Wiley.

Fletcher, C., & Williams, R. S. (1996). Performance management, job satisfaction and organisational commitment. *British Journal of Management*, *7*, 169–79.

Flin, R., Mearns, K., O'Connor, P., & Bryden, R. (2000). Measuring safety climate: Identifying the common features. *Safety Science*, *34*, 177–92.

Floyd, S. W., & Wooldridge, B. (2000). *Building strategy from the middle: Reconceptual-izing strategy process*. Thousand Oaks, CA: Sage.

Flynn, F. J., Chatman, J. A., & Spataro, S. E. (2001). Getting to know you: The influence of personality on impressions and performance of demographically different people in organizations. *Administrative Science Quarterly, 46*, 414–42.

Fontana, D. (1989). *Managing stress*. London: Routledge.

Forbes, D. P., & Milliken, F. J. (1999). Cognition and corporate governance: Understanding boards of directors as strategic decision-making groups. *Academy of Management Review, 24*, 489–505.

Ford, H. (1922). *My life and work*. Garden City, NJ: Doubleday, Page & Co.

Forteza, J. A., & Prieto, J. M. (1989). Aging and work behavior. In H. C. Triandis, M. D. Dunnette, & L. M. Hough (Eds.), *Handbook of industrial and organizational psychology*. Palo Alto: Consulting Psychologists Press.

Fossum, J. A., Arvey, R. D., Paradise, R. D., & Robbins, N. E. (1986). Modelling the skills obsolescence process: A psychological/economic integration. *Academy of Management Review, 11*, 362–74.

Fraccaroli, F., & Sarchielli, G. (2002). *È Tempo di Lavoro? Per una Psicologia dei Tempi Lavorativi*. CLUEB, Bologna.

Frankenhaeuser, M. (1978). Psychoneuroendocrine approaches to the study of emotion as related to stress and coping. In H. E. Howe & R. A. Dienstbier (Eds.), *Nebraska Symposium on motivation 1978* (pp. 123–61). Lincoln: University of Nebraska Press.

Frankenhaeuser, M. (1986). A psychobiological framework for research on human stress and coping. In M. H. Appley & R. Trumbull (Eds.), *Dynamics of stress: Physiological, psychological and social perspectives*. New York: Plenum.

Frankenhaeuser, M., & Gardell, B. (1976). Underload and overload in working life: Outline of a multidisciplinary approach. *Journal of Human Stress, 2*, 35–46.

French, J. R. P., & Raven, B. H. (1960). The bases of social power. In D. Cartwright & A. F. Zander (Eds.), *Group dynamics*. Evanston, IL: Row & Peterson.

French, W. L., Bell, C. H., & Zawacki, R. A. (2005). *Organisation development and transformation*. New York: McGraw-Hill.

Frese, M. (1995). Error management in training: Conceptual and empirical results. In C. Zucchermaglio, S. Bagnara, & S. U. Stucky (Eds.), *Organizational learning and technological change* (pp. 112–24). Berlin: Springer.

Frese, M. (1997). Dynamic self-reliance: An important concept for work. In C. L. Cooper & S. E. Jackson (Eds.), *Creating tomorrow's organizations* (pp. 399–416). Chichester, UK: Wiley.

Frese, M. (1999). Social support as a moderator of the relationship between work stressors and psychological dysfunctioning: A longitudinal study with objective measures. *Journal of Occupational Health Psychology, 4*, 179–92.

Frese, M., Brodbeck, F., Heinbokel, T., Mooser, C., Schleiffenbaum, E., & Thiemann, P. (1991). Errors in training computer skills: On the positive function of errors. *Human–Computer Interaction, 6*, 77–93.

Frese, M., & Fay, D. (2001). Personal Initiative (PI): A concept for work in the 21st century. *Research in Organizational Behavior, 23*, 133–88.

Frese, M., Fay, D., Hilburger, T., Leng, K., & Tag, A. (1997). The concept of personal initiative: Operationalization, reliability and validity in two German samples. *Journal of Occupational and Organizational Psychology, 70*, 139–61.

Frese, M., & Hesse, W. (1993). The work situation in software development – Results of an empirical study. *Software Engineering Notes, 18(3)*, A65–A72.

Frese, M., Teng, E., & Wijnen, C. J. D. (1999). Helping to improve suggestion systems: Predictors of giving suggestions in companies. *Journal of Organizational Behavior, 20*, 1139–55.

Frese, M., & Zapf, D. (1987). Die Einführung von neuen Techniken am Arbeitsplatz verändert Qualifikationsanforderungen, Handlungsspielraum und Stressoren kaum: Ergebnisse einer Längsschnittuntersuchung. *Zeitschrift für Arbeitswissenschaft, 41*, 7–14.

Frese, M., & Zapf, D. (1994). Action as the core of work psychology: A German approach. In H. C. Triandis, M. D. Dunnette, & L. M. Hough (Eds.), *Handbook of industrial and organizational psychology* (2nd edn., Vol. 4, pp. 271–340). Palo Alto, CA: Consulting Psychologists Press.

Frese. M. (Ed.) (1998). *Erfolgreiche Unternehmensgruender* (Successful business founders). Goettingen, Germany: Verlag fuer Angewandte Psychologie.

Fried, Y., & Ferris, G. R. (1987). The validity of the job characteristics model: A review and meta-analysis. *Personnel Psychology, 40*, 287–332.

Fuld, R. B. (1997). The fiction of function allocation, revisited. In E. Fallon, L. Bannon, & J. McCarthy (Eds.), *Proceedings of the 1ˢᵗ International Conference on Allocation of Function* (Vol. 1., pp. 17–30). Louisville, KY: IEA Press.

Fulopa, N., Protopsaltisb, G., Kingc, A., Allena, P., Hutchingsa, A., & Normanda, C. (2005). Changing organisations: A study of the context and processes of mergers of health care providers in England. *Social Science & Medicine, 60*, pp. 119–30.

Furman, B. O. (1989). International mergers in the frame of strategic management (In Turkish: "Stratejik Yönetim Çerçevesinde Uluslararası Birlesmeler"). 3rd Congress of National Business Administration, Kapadokya, 1989, p. 292.

Gaertner, S. L., & Dovidio, J. F. (2000). *Reducing intergroup bias: The common ingroup identity model.* Philadelphia: The Psychology Press.

Gaertner, S. L., Mann, J., Murrell, A., & Dovidio, J. F. (1989). The benefits of re-categorisation. *Journal of Personality and Social Psychology, 57(2)*, 239–49.

Gaillard, A. W. K. (2003). *Stress, productiviteit en gezondheid* (Stress, productivity and health) (2nd edn.). Amsterdam: Nieuwezijds

Gareis, K., & Kordey, N. (1999). Telework – An overview of likely impacts on traffic and settlement patterns. *Netcom, 13*, 265–86.

Gareis, K., Lilischkis, S., & Mentrup, A. (2006). Mapping the mobile eworkforce in Europe. In J. H. E. Andriessen & M. Vartiainen (Eds.), *Mobile virtual work. A new paradigm?* (pp. 45–69). Heidelberg: Springer.

Gaugler, B. B., Rosenthal, D. B., Thornton, G. C., & Bentson, C. (1987). Meta-analysis of assessment centre validity. *Journal of Applied Psychology, 72*, 493–511.

Gedikkaya, T., & Gürler, C. (1999). Mergers and acquisitions (In Turkish: "Birlesme ve Sat nalmalar"). Board of Foreign Affairs, Central Bank of Republic of Turkey, The Press Paper of Board of European Union Affairs, November 10, pp. 2–4.

Gehringer, J. & Pawlik, H. (2000). *Das Berater–Training. Kompetenz–Handbuch für verantwortliches und erfolgreiches Handeln.* Düsseldorf & Berlin: Metropolitan Verlag.

Gelfand, M. J., Nishi, L. H., Raver, J. L., & Schneider, B. (2005). Discrimination in organisations: An organisational-level systems perspective. In R. L. Dipboye & A.

Colella (Eds.), *Discrimination at work* (pp. 89–96). Mahwah, NJ: Lawrence Erlbaum.

Gerstner, C. R., & Day, D. V. (1997). Meta-analytic review of leader–member exchange theory: Correlates and construct issues. *Journal of Applied Psychology, 82,* 827–44.

Ghoshal, S., & Bartlett, C. A. (1990). The multinational corporation as a differentiated interorganizational network. *Academy of Management Review, 15,* 603–25.

Gier, E. de (1995). Occupational welfare in the European Community: Past, present, and future. In L. R. Murphy, J. J. Hurrell, S. L. Sauter, & G. P. Keita (Eds.), *Job stress interventions* (pp. 405–16). Washington DC: American Psychological Association.

Gigerenzer, G., & Todd, P. M. (1999). Fast and frugal heuristics: The adaptive toolbox. In G. Gigerenzer, P. M. Todd, & the ABC Research Group (Eds.), *Simple heuristics that make us smart.* New York: Oxford University Press.

Gigerenzer, G., Todd, P. M., & the ABC Research Group (Eds.) (1999). *Simple heuristics that make us smart.* New York: Oxford University Press.

Gillespie, A., & Richardson, R. (2000). Teleworking and the city – Myths of workplace transcendence and travel reduction. In J. O. Wheeler, Y. Aoyama, & B. Warf (Eds.), *Cities in the telecommunications age – The fracturing of geographies* (pp. 228–45). London: Routledge.

Gilliland, S. W. (1993). The perceived fairness of selection systems: An organizational justice perspective. *Academy of Management Review, 18,* 696–734.

Gilliland, S. W. (1994). Effects of procedural and distributive justice on reactions to a selection system. *Journal of Applied Psychology, 79,* 691–701.

Gilliland, S. W., & Honig, H. (1994, April). The perceived fairness of employee selection systems as a predictor of attitudes and self-concept. In S. W. Gilliland (Chair), *Selection from the applicant's perspective: Justice and employee selection procedures.* Symposium presented at the 9th annual conference of the Society for Industrial and Organizational Psychology, Nashville, TN.

Ginsberg, A. (1990). Connecting diversification to performance: a sociocognitive approach, *Academy of Management Review, 15(3),* 514–35.

Gioia, D. A., & Longenecker, C. O. (1994). Delving into the dark side: The politics of executive appraisal. *Organizational Dynamics, 22,* 47–58.

Gist, M. E., & Mitchell, T. R. (1992). Self-efficacy: A theoretical analysis of its determinants and malleability. *Academy of Management Review, 17,* 183–211.

Gist, M. E., Schwoerer, C. E., & Rosen, B. (1989). Effects of alternative training methods on self-efficacy and performance in computer software training. *Journal of Applied Psychology, 74,* 884–91.

Gleick, J. (1987). *Chaos: Making a new science.* New York: Viking Penguin.

Goffman, E. (1961). *Asylums.* New York: Anchor Books.

Goldberg, L. R. (1993). The structure of phenotypic personality traits. *American Psychologist, 48,* 26–34.

Golden, T. D. (2006). The role of relationships in understanding telecommuter satisfaction. *Journal of Organizational Behavior, 27,* 319–40.

Golden, T. D., & Veiga, J. F. (2005). The impact of extent of telecommuting on job satisfaction: Resolving inconsistent findings. *Journal of Management, 31,* 301–18.

Goleman, D. (1995). *Emotional intelligence.* New York: Bantam.

Gopher, D., & Donchin, E. (1986). Workload: An examination of the concept. In K. R. Boff, L. Kaufman, & J. P. Thomas (Eds.), *Handbook of perception and human performance, vol II: Cognitive processes and performance*. New York: Wiley.

Goranson, H. T. (1999). *The agile virtual enterprise cases, metrics, tools*. Westport, CT: Greenwood Press.

Gott, S. P., Hall, P., Pokorny, A., Dibble, E., & Glaser, R. (1993). A naturalistic study of transfer: Adaptive expertise in technical domains, *Transfer on trial: Intelligence, cognition, and instruction* (pp. 259–88). Norwood, NJ: Ablex.

Goves, M. (1995, April, 5). Welcome to the "virtual" office. *Jerusalem Post Money Magazine*, p. 10.

Graen, G. B., & Scandura, T. A. (1987). Toward a psychology of dyadic organizing. *Research in Organizational Behavior*, *9*, 175–208.

Grant, D., Michelson, G., Oswick, C., & Wailes, N. (2005). Guest editorial: Discourse and organizational change. *Journal of Organizational Change Management*, *18*, 6–15

Greenberg, J. (1986). Determinants of perceived fairness of performance evaluations. *Journal of Applied Psychology*, *71*, 340–2.

Greenberg, J. (1990). Employee theft as a reaction to underpayment inequity: The hidden costs of pay cuts. *Journal of Applied Psychology*, *75*, 561–8.

Greene, C. N. (1975). The reciprocal nature of influence between leader and subordinate. *Journal of Applied Psychology*, *60*, 187–93.

Greenstein, J. S., Arnaut, L. Y., & Revesman, M. E. (1986). An empirical comparison of model-based and explicit communication for dynamic human–computer task allocation. *International Journal of Man–Machine Studies*, *24*, 355–63.

Greenwood, R., & Hinings, C. R. (1996). Understanding radical organisational change: Bringing together the old and the new institutionalism. *Academy of Management Review*, *21*, 1022–54.

Greller, M. M., & Simpson, P. (1999). In search of late career: A review of contemporary social science research applicable to the understanding of late career. *Human Research Management Review*, *9*, 309–47.

Greller, M. M., & Stroh, L. K. (1995). Careers in midlife and beyond: A fallow field in need of substance. *Journal of Vocational Behavior*, *47*, 232–47.

Greve, H. R. (1998). Managerial cognition and the memetic adoption of market positions: what you see is what you do. *Strategic Management Journal*, *19*, 967–88.

Griffin, M. A., & Neal, N. (2000). Perceptions of safety at work: A framework for linking safety climate to safety performance, knowledge, and motivation. *Journal of Occupational Health Psychology*, *5*, 347–58.

Guerrero, S., & Sire, B. (2001). Motivation to train from the workers' perspective: Example of French companies. *International Journal of Human Resource Management*, *12*, 988–1004.

Guion, R. M. (1997). *Assessment, measurement, and prediction for personnel decisions*. London: Lawrence Erlbaum.

Guldenmund, F. W. (2000). The nature of safety culture: a review of theory and research. *Safety Science*, *34*, 215–57.

Gully, S. M., Payne, S. C., Koles, K. L. K., & Whiteman, J.-A. K. (2002). The impact of error training and individual differences on training outcomes: An attribute–treatment interaction perspective. *Journal of Applied Psychology*, *87*, 143–55.

Gulowsen, J. (1972). A measure of work group autonomy. In L. E. Davis & J. C. Taylor (Eds.), *Design of jobs* (pp. 374–390). Harmondsworth: Penguin.

Gutwin, C., Greenberg, S., & Roseman, M. (1996). Workspace awareness in real-time distributed groupware: Framework, widgets, and evaluation. In M. A. Sasse, R. J. Cunningham, & R. L. Winder (Eds.), *People and computer XI, Proceedings of HCI '96* (pp. 281–98) London: Springer.

Guzzo, R. A., Jette, R. D., & Katzell, R. A. (1985). The effects of psychologically based intervention programs on worker productivity: A meta-analysis. *Personnel Psychology*, *38*, 275–92.

Gwynne, S. C. (1992). *The long haul. Time*, Sept. 28, pp. 34–8.

Hacker, W. (1998). *Allgemeine Arbeitspsychologie: Psychische Regulation von Arbeitstätig-keiten* (General work psychology: Psychological regulation of work actions). Bern, Switzerland: Huber.

Hackman, J. R. (1987). Work design. In R. M. Steers & L. W. Porter (Eds.), *Motivation and work behavior* (4th Edn., pp. 467–92). New York: McGraw-Hill.

Hackman, J. R. (2002). *Leading teams: Setting the stage for great performances.* Cambridge, MA: Harvard Business School Press.

Hackman, J. R., & Lawler, E. E. (1971). Employee reactions to job characteristics. *Journal of Applied Psychology Monograph*, *55*, 259–86.

Hackman, J. R., & Oldham, G. R. (1976). Motivation through the design of work: Test of a theory. *Organizational Behavior and Human Performance*, *16*, 250–79.

Hackman, J. R., & Oldham, G. R. (1980). *Work redesign.* Reading, MA: Addison-Wesley.

Hackney, H., & Cormier, L. S. (1993) *Beratungsstrategien Beratungsziele.* Munich and Basel: Reinhardt Verlag

Haddon, L., & Brynin, M. (2005). The character of telework and the characteristics of teleworkers. *New Technology, Work and Employment*, *20*, 34–46.

Halbesleben, J. R. B., & Buckley, M. R. (2004). Burnout in organizational life. *Journal of Management*, *30(6)*, 859–79.

Hale, A. R., & Hovden, J. (1998). Management and culture: the third age of safety. A review of approaches to organizational aspects of safety, health, and environment. In A.-M. Feyer & A. Williamson (Eds.). *Occupational injury: Risk, prevention and inter-vention.* London: Taylor & Francis.

Hall, D. T. (2004). The protean career: A quarter-century journey. *Journal of Vocational Behavior*, *65*, 1–13.

Halliday, F. E. (1995). *England, a concise history.* London: Thames & Hudson.

Hämäläinen, P., Takala, J., & Saarela, K. L. (2006). Global estimates of occupational accidents. *Safety Science*, *44*, 137–56.

Hamel, G., & Prahalad, C. K. (1994). *Competing for the future.* Cambridge, MA: Harvard Business Review Press.

Hamsa, A. A. K., & Miura, M. (2001). Do managers favor for teleworking in Japan? Paper Presented at the 6th International ITF Workshop and Business Conference, 26–30 August, Tokyo.

Hancock, P. A., & Meshkati, N. (Eds.) (1988). *Human mental workload.* Amsterdam: North-Holland.

Handy, S. L., & Mokhtarian, P. (1995). Planning for telecommuting. Measurement and policy issues. *Journal of the American Planning Association*, *61*, 97–111.

Hannan, M., & Freeman, J. (1977). The population ecology of organizations. *American Journal of Sociology, 82,* 929–64.

Hannan, M., & Freeman, J. (1988). *Organizational ecology.* Cambridge, MA: Harvard University Press.

Hansson, R. O., DeKoekkoek, P. D., Neece, W. M., & Patterson, D. W. (1997). Successful aging at work: annual review, 1992–1996: The older worker and transitions to retirement. *Journal of Vocational Behavior, 51,* 202–33.

Harris, M. M., Smith, D. E., & Champagne, D. (1995). A field study of performance appraisal purpose: Research versus Administrative based ratings. *Personnel Psychology, 48,* 151–60.

Hart, A. J., Whalen, P. J., Shine, L. M., McInerney, S. C., Fischer, H., & Rauch, S. L. (2000). Differential response in the human amygdala to racial outgoup vs. ingroup face stimuli. *NeuroReport, 11,* 2351–5.

Hart, S. G., & Staveland, L. E. (1988). Development of a NASA TLX (Task Load Index): Results of empirical and theoretical research. In P. Hancock & N. Meshkati (Eds.), *Human mental workload.* Amsterdam: Elsevier.

Hassard, J. (1999). Images of time in work and organization. In S. R. Clegg & C. Hardy (Eds.), *Studying organizations.* London: Sage.

Hassell, B. L., & Perrewe, P. L. (1995). An examination of beliefs about older workers: Do stereotypes still exist? *Journal of Organizational Behavior, 16,* 457–68.

Havercamp, S. M., & Reiss, S. S. (2003). A comprehensive assessment of human strivings: Test–retest reliability and validity of the Reiss profile. *Journal of Personality Assessment, 81,* 123–32.

Heckhausen, H., & Gollwitzer, P. M. (1987). Thought contents and cognitive functioning in motivational versus volitional states of mind. *Motivation and Emotion, 11,* 101–20.

Heilman, M. E. (2001). Description and prescription: How gender stereotypes prevent women's ascent up the organisational ladder. *Journal of Social Issues, 57,* 657–74.

Heinonen, S., & Kuosa, T. (2005). Ecological realities of telework in four different futures: living, working and travelling in new knowledge-intensive communities. *Progress in Industrial Ecology – An International Journal, 2,* 329–57.

Heintel, P. Lässt sich Beratung erlernen? (1992). In R. Wimmer (Ed.), *Organisationsberatung* (pp. 345–76). Wiesbaden: Gabler–Verlag.

Heinz, W. R. (2003). From work trajectories to negotiated careers: The contingent work life course. In J. T. Mortimer & M. J. Shanahan (Eds.), *Handbook of the life course.* New York: Kluwer Academic Publishers.

Heller, F. (1998). The levers of organisational change: Facilitators and inhibitors. In P. J. D. Drenth, H. Thierry, & C. J. de Wolf (Eds.), *Handbook of work and organisational psychology* (Vol. 4, pp. 229–251).

Hendricks, H. W. (1997). Organizational change and macroergonomics. In G. Salvendy (Ed.), *Handbook of human factors and ergonomics.* London: Wiley.

Herriot, P. (1989). Selection as a social process. In M. Smith & I. T. Robertson (Eds.), *Advances in Staff Selection.* Chichester, UK: Wiley.

Herriot, P., & Anderson, N. (1997). Selecting for change: How will personnel and selection psychology survive? In N. Anderson & P. Herriot (Eds.), *International Handbook of Selection and Assessment.* Chichester, UK: Wiley.

Hersey, P., & Blanchard, K. H. (1988). *Management of Organizational Behavior: Utilizing Human Resources.* Englewood Cliffs, NJ: Prentice-Hall.

Hertel, G., Deter, C., & Konradt, U. (2003). Motivation gains in computer–mediated work groups. *Journal of Applied Social Psychology, 33*, 2080–2105.

Hertel, G., Geister, S., & Konradt, U. (2005). Managing Virtual Teams: A Review of Current Empirical Research. *Human Resource Management Review, 15*, 69–95.

Hertel, G., Konradt, U., & Orlikowski, B. (2004). Managing distance by interdependence: Goal setting, task interdependence, and team-based rewards in virtual teams. *European Journal of Work and Organizational Psychology, 13*, 1–28.

Herzberg, F. (1966). *Work and the nature of man*. Cleveland: World Publishing.

Herzberg, F., Mausner, B., & Snyderman, B. B. (1959). *The motivation to work*. New York: Wiley.

Hesketh, B. (1997). Dilemmas in training for transfer and retention. *Applied Psychology: An International Review, 46*, 317–86.

Hewstone, M., Rubin, M., & Willis, H. (2002). Intergroup bias. *Annual Reviews of Psychology, 53*, 575–604.

Higgins, E. T. (1987). Self-discrepancy: A theory relating self and affect. *Psychological Review, 94*, 319–40.

Higgins, E. T. (1989). Continuities and discontinuities in self-regulatory and self-evaluative processes: A developmental theory relating to self and affect. *Journal of Personality, 57*, 407–44.

Higgins, E. T. (1996). Knowledge activation: Accessibility, applicability and salience. In E. T. Higgins & A. W. Kruglanski (Eds.), *Social psychology: Handbook of basic principles* (pp. 133–68). New York: Guilford.

Hill, E. J., Ferris, M., & Mätinson, V. (2003). Does it matter where you work? A comparison of how three work venues (traditional office, virtual office, and home office). influence aspects of work and personal/family life. *Journal of Vocational Behavior, 63*, 220–41.

Hill, E. J., Hawkins, A. J., & Brent C. M. (1996). Work and family in the virtual office. *Family Relations, 45*, 293–301.

Hill, E. J., Miller, B. C., Weiner, S. P., & Colihan, J. (1998). Influences of the virtual office on aspects of work and work/life balance, *Personnel Psychology, 51*, 667–83.

Hinds, P. J., Carley, K. M., Krackhardt, D., & Wholey, D. (2000). Choosing work group members: Balancing similarity, competence, and familiarity. *Organizational Behavior and Human Decision Processes, 81*, 226–51.

Hingley, P., & Cooper, C. L. (1986). *Stress and the nurse manager*. London: John Wiley.

Hinsz, V. B., Kalnbach, L. R., & Lorentz, N. R. (1997). Using judgemental anchors to establish challenging self-set goals without jeopardizing commitment. *Organizational Behavior and Human Decision Processes, 71*, 287–308.

Hobfoll, S. E. (1989). Conservation of resources: A new attempt at conceptualising stress. *American Psychologist, 44*, 513–24.

Hobfoll, S. E. (2002). Social and psychological resources and adaptation. *Review of General Psychology, 6(4)*, 307–24.

Hockey, G. R. J. (1970). The effect of loud noide on attentional selectivity. *Quarterly Journal of Experimental Psychology, 22*, 28–36.

Hockey, G. R. J. (1979). Stress and the cognitive components of skilled performance. In V. Hamilton & D. M. Warburton (Eds.), *Human Stress and Cognition*. Chichester, UK: Wiley.

Hockey, G. R. J. (1986). Changes in operator efficiency as a function of environmental stress, fatigue and circadian rhythms. In K. R. Boff, L. Kauffman, & J. Thomas (Eds.), *Handbook of Perception and Human Performance, Vol II: Cognitive Processes and Performance*. New York: Wiley.

Hockey, G. R. J. (1993). Cognitive–energetical control mechanisms in the management of work demands and psychological health. In A. D. Baddeley & L. Weiskrantz (Eds.), *Attention, selection, awareness and control. A tribute to Donald Broadbent*. Oxford: Oxford University Press.

Hockey, G. R. J. (1997). Compensatory control in the regulation of human performance under stress and high workload: A cognitive-energetical framework. *Biological Psychology*, 45, 73–93.

Hockey, G. R. J. (2000). Work environments and performance. In N. Chmiel (Ed.), *Introduction to work and organizational psychology: A European perspective* (pp. 206–30). Malden, MA: Blackwell Publishers.

Hockey, G. R. J. (2005). Operator functional state: The prediction of breakdown in human performance. In J. Duncan, P. McLeod & L. Phillips (Eds.), *Speed, Control and Age: In Honour of Patrick Rabbitt*. Oxford: Oxford University Press.

Hockey, G. R. J., Briner, R. B., Tattersall, A. J., & Wiethoff, M. (1989). Assessing the impact of computer workload on operator stress: the role of system controllability. *Ergonomics*, 32, 1401–18.

Hockey, G. R. J., & Earle, F. (2006). Control over the scheduling of simulated office work reduces the impact of workload on mental fatigue and task performance. *Journal of Experimental Psychology: Applied*, 12, 50–65.

Hockey, G. R. J., Gaillard, A. W. K., & Burov, O. (Eds). (2003). *Operator Functional State: The Assessment and Prediction of Human Performance Degradation in Complex Tasks*. Amsterdam: IOS Press.

Hockey, G. R. J., & Hamilton, P. (1983). The cognitive patterning of stress states. In G. R. J. Hockey (Ed.), *Stress and fatigue in human performance*. Chichester, UK: Wiley.

Hockey, G. R. J., & Maule, A. J. (1995). Unscheduled manual interventions in automated process control. *Ergonomics*, 38, 2504–24.

Hockey, G. R. J., & Meijman, T. F. (1998). The construct of psychological fatigue: A theoretical and methodological analysis. *Proceedings of 3rd international conference on fatigue and transportation: Coping with the 24–hour society*, Fremantle, WA.

Hockey, G. R. J., Nickel, P., Roberts, A., Mahfouf, M., & Linkens, D. A. (2006). Implementing adaptive automation using on–line detection of high risk operator functional state. *Proceedings of ISSA 9th International Symposium*, Nice, France.

Hockey, G. R. J., Payne, R. L., & Rick, J. T. (1996). Intra–individual patterns of hormonal and affective adaptation to work demands: an n = 2 study of junior doctors. *Biological Psychology*, 42, 393–411.

Hockey, G. R. J., Wastell, D. G., & Sauer, J. (1998). Effects of sleep deprivation and user–interface on complex performance: a multilevel analysis of compensatory control. *Human Factors*, 40, 233–53.

Hodge, G. A., & Richardson, A. J. (1985). The Role of Accident Exposure in Transport System Safety Evaluations I: Intersection and Link Site Exposure. *Journal of Advanced Transportation*, 19, 179–213.

Hodgkinson, G. P. (1992). Development and validation of the strategic locus of control scale. *Strategic Management Journal*, 13, 311–7.

Hodgkinson, G. P. (1993). Doubts about the conceptual and empirical status of context–free and firm–specific control expectancies: A reply to Bonne and De Brabander. *Strategic Management Journal, 14,* 627–31.

Hodgkinson, G. P. (1997a). The cognitive analysis of competitive structures: A review and critique. *Human Relations, 50,* 625–54.

Hodgkinson, G. P. (1997b). Cognitive inertia in a turbulent market: The case of UK residential estate agents. *Journal of Management Studies, 34(6),* 921–45.

Hodgkinson, G. P. (2001a). The psychology of strategic management: Diversity and cognition revisited. In C. L. Cooper & I. T. Robertson (Eds.), *International Review of Industrial and Organizational Psychology Volume 16.* Chichester, UK: Wiley.

Hodgkinson, G. P. (2001b). Cognitive processes in strategic management: some emerging trends and future directions. In N. Anderson, D. S. Ones, H. K. Sinangil, & C. Viswesvaran (Eds.), *Handbook of Industrial, Work and Organizational Psychology – Volume 2: Organizational Psychology.* London: Sage.

Hodgkinson, G. P. (2002). Comparing managers' mental models of competition: Why self-report measures of belief similarity won't do. *Organization Studies, 23,* 63–72.

Hodgkinson, G. P. (2005). *Images of Competitive Space: A Study of Managerial and Organizational Cognition.* Basingstoke: Palgrave Macmillan.

Hodgkinson, G. P., & Herriot, P. (2002). The role of psychologists in enhancing organizational effectiveness. In I. T. Robertson, M. Callinan, & D. Bartram (Eds.), *Organizational effectiveness, the role of psychology.* Chichester, UK: John Wiley, 227–58.

Hodgkinson, G. P., & Johnson, G. (1994). Exploring the mental models of competitive strategists: The case for a processual approach. *Journal of Management Studies, 31,* 525–51.

Hodgkinson, G. P., & Maule, A. J. (2002). The individual in the strategy process: Insights from behavioural decision research and cognitive mapping. In A. S. Huff & M. Jenkins (Eds.), *Mapping Strategic Knowledge.* (pp. 196–219). London: Sage.

Hodgkinson, G. P., & Sparrow, P. R. (2002). *The Competent Organization: A Psychological Analysis of the Strategic Management Process.* Buckingham: Open University Press.

Hodgkinson, G. P., & Wright, G. (2002). Confronting strategic inertia in a top management team: Learning from failure. *Organization Studies, 23,* 949–77.

Hodgkinson, G. P., & Wright, G. (2006). Neither completing the practice turn, nor enriching the process tradition: Secondary misinterpretations of a case analysis reconsidered. *Organization Studies, 27,* 1895–01.

Hodgkinson, G. P., Bown, N. J., Maule, A. J., Glaister, K. W., & Pearman, A. D. (1999). Breaking the frame: an analysis of strategic cognition and decision making under uncertainty. *Strategic Management Journal, 20,* 977–85.

Hodgkinson, G. P., Herriot, P., Anderson, N. (2001). Re–aligning the Stakeholders in Management Research: Lessons from Industrial, Work and Organizational Psychology. In *British Journal of management,* Vol. 12, Special Issue, S41–S48 (2001).

Hodgkinson, G. P., Maule, A. J., Bown, N. J., Pearman, A. D., & Glaister, K. W. (2002). Further reflections on the elimination of framing bias in strategic decision making. *Strategic Management Journal, 23,* 1069–76.

Hodgkinson, H., & Hodgkinson, P. (2004). Rethinking the concept of community of practice in relation to schoolteachers' workplace learning. *International Journal of Training and Development, 8,* 21–31.

Hofmann, D. A., & Stetzer, A. (1996). A cross–level investigation of factors influencing unsafe behaviors and accidents. *Personnel Psychology*, *49*, 307–39.

Hofmann, D. A., Morgeson, F. P., & Gerras, S. J. (2003). Climate as a Moderator of the Relationship Between Leader–Member Exchange and Content Specific Citizenship: Safety Climate as an Exemplar. *Journal of Applied Psychology*, *88*, 170–8.

Hofstede, G. (1991). *Cultures and Organizations: Software of the Mind*. London: Harper Collins.

Hofstede, G. (1991). *Cultures and organizations: software of the mind*. London: McGraw-Hill.

Hogan, E. A., & Overmyer–Day, L. (1994). The psychology of mergers and acquisitions. In C. L. Cooper & I. T. Robertson (Eds.), *International Review of Industrial and Organizational Psychology*, Vol. 9. Chichester, UK: Wiley.

Hogan, E. A., & Overmyer–Day, L. (1994). The psychology of mergers and acquisitions. In C. L. Cooper & I. T. Robertson (Eds.), *International Review of Industrial and Organizational Psychology 1994* (pp. 247–281). Chichester, UK: Wiley.

Hogan, J., & Holland, B. (2003). Using theory to evaluate personality and job performance relations: A socioanalytic perspective. *Journal of Applied Psychology*, *88*, 100–12.

Hogan, R. Jones, W. H., & Cheek, J. M. (1985). Socioanalytic theory: An alternative to armadillo psychology. In B. R. Schlenker (Eds.). *The self and social life* (pp. 175–198). Newberry Park, CA: Sage.

Hogendoorn, W. E., van Poppel, M. N. M, Koes, B. W., & Bouter, L. M. (2000). Systematic review of psychosocial factors at work and private life as risk factors for back pain. *Spine*, *25*, 2114–25.

Hogg, M. A., & Terry, D. J. (2000). Social identity and self-categorization processes in organizational contexts. *Academy of Management Review*, *25*, 121–40.

Holding, D. H. (1983). Fatigue. In G. R. J. Hockey (Ed.), *Stress and Fatigue in Human Performance*. Chichester, UK: Wiley.

Holdsworth, R (1991). "Appraisal". In F. Neale (Ed.), *The Handbook of Performance Management*. Institute of Personnel Management: London.

Holland, J. L. (1997). *Making vocational choices* (3rd ed). Odessa: Psychological Assessment Resources.

Holman, D., Epitropaki, O., & Fernie, S. (2001). Understanding learning strategies in the workplace: A factor analytic invesitgation. *Journal of Occupational and Organizational Psychology*, *74*, 675–81.

Holman, D., & Wall, T. D. (2002). Work characteristics, learning–related outcomes, and strain. A test of competing direct effects, mediated, and moderated models. *Journal of Occupational Health Psychology*, *7*, 283–301.

Holman, D., Wall, T. D., Clegg, C. W., Sparrow, P., & Howard, A. (2003). *The new workplace: A guide to the human impact of modern working practices*. Chichester, UK: Wiley.

Honey, P. (1979). The repertory grid in action. *Industrial and Commercial Training*, *11(11)*, 452–9.

Honkanen, H. (1999). Organisaation kehittämismallien juurista tulevaisuuden haasteisiin (Organisation development models – history and future challenges). *Aikuiskasvatus*, *19(1)*, 16–22).

Honkanen, H. (2006). *Muutoksen agentit, muutoksen ohjaaminen ja johtaminen* (The Agents of Change, consulting and managing change). Helsinki: Edita Publishing.

Hoonakker, P., Loushine, T., Carayon, P., Kallman, J., Kapp, A., & Smith, M. J. (2005). The effect of safety initiatives on safety performance: A longitudinal study. *Applied Ergonomics*, *36*, 461–9.

Hough, L. M. (1992). The "Big Five" personality variables – construct confusion: Description versus prediction. *Human Performance*, *5*, 139–55.

Hough, L. M., & Oswald, F. L. (2000). Personnel selection: Looking toward the future – Remembering the past. *Annual Review of Psychology*, *51*, 631–64.

Hough, L. M., Oswald, F. L., & Ployhart, R. E. (2001). Determinants, detection and amelioration of adverse impact in personnel selection procedures: Issues, evidence, and lessons learned. *International Journal of Selection and Assessment*, *9*, 152–94.

House, R. J. (1971). A path–goal theory of leader effectiveness. *Administrative Science Quaterly*, *16*, 321–8.

House, R. J. (1977). A 1976 theory of charismatic leadership. In J. G. Hunt & L. L. Larson (Eds.), *Leadership: The cutting edge*. Carbondale, IL: Southern Illinois University Press.

House, R. J. (1996). Path–goal theory of leadership: Lessons, legacy, and a reformulated theory. *Leadership Quarterly*, *7*, 323–52.

House, R. J., & Baetz, M. L. (1979). Leadership: Some empirical generalizations and new research directions. In B. M. Staw (Ed.), *Research in Organizational Behavior*, *1*, 341–423.

House, R. J., & Mitchell, T. R. (1974). Path–goal theory of leadership. *Contemporary Business*, *3 (Fall)*, 81–98.

House, R. J., & Podsakoff, P. M. (1994). Leadership effectiveness: Past perspectives and future directions for research. In J. Greenberg (Ed.), *Organizational behavior: The state of the science* (S. 45–82). Hillsdale, NJ: Erlbaum.

House, R. J., Hanges, P. J., Javidan, M., Dorfman, P., Gupta, V., & GLOBE country co-investigators (2004). *Leadership, culture, and organizations: The GLOBE study of 62 societies*. Thousand Oaks, CA: Sage.

House, R. J., Spangler, W. D., & Woycke, J. (1991). Personality and charisma in the US Presidency: A psychological theory of leader effectiveness. *Administrative Science Quarterly*, *36*, 364–96.

Houtman, I., Kornitzer, M., De Smets, P., Koyungu, R., De Backer, G., Pelfrene, E., Romon, M., Boulenguez, C., Ferrario, M., Origgi, G., Sans, S., Perez, I., Wilhelmsen, L., Rosengren, A., Isacsson, S.-O., & Östergren, P.-O. (1999). Job stress, absenteeism, and coronary heart disease European study (the JACE study). *European Journal of Public Health*, *9*, 52–7.

Howard, A. (Ed.) (1995). *The changing nature of work*. San Francisco, CA: Jossey-Bass.

Howell, J. M., & Frost, P. J. (1989). A laboratory study of charismatic leadership. *Organizational Behavior and Human Decision Processes*, *43*, 243–69.

Howell, J. M., & Hall-Merenda, K. E. (1999). The ties that bind: The impact of leader–member exchange, transformational and transactional leadership, and distance on predicting follower performance. *Journal of Applied Psychology*, *84*, 680–94.

Hoyer, W. J. (1998). Commentary: The older individual in a rapidly changing work context: developmental and cognitive issues. In K. W. Schaie & C. Schooler (Eds.), *Impact of work on older adults*. New York: Springer.

Huff, A. S. (Ed.), (1990). *Mapping strategic thought*. Chichester, UK: Wiley.

Huffcutt, A. I., & Arthur, W., Jr. (1994). Hunter and Hunter (1984) revisited: Interview validity for entry-level jobs. *Journal of Applied Psychology, 79*, 184–90.

Hughes, E. C. (1971). *The sociological eye: Selected papers*. Chicago: Aldine-Atherton.

Hulin, C. L., & Judge, T. (2003). Job attitudes. In W. C. Borman, D. R. Ilgen, & R. J. Klimoski (Eds.), *Handbook of psychology Vol. 12, Industrial and organizational psychology* (pp. 225–54). New York: Wiley.

Hulzebosch, R., & Jameson, A. (1996). FACE: A rapid method for evaluation of user interfaces. In P. W. Jordan, B. Thomas, B. A. Weerdmeester, & I. L. McClelland (Eds.), *Usability evaluation in industry* (pp. 195–204). London: Taylor and Francis.

Hunsaker, Cooms in S. Cartwright, C. L. Cooper. (1999). *Managing mergers, acquisitions and strategic alliances: Integrating people and culture* (2nd edn.). Oxford: Butterworth-Heinemann.

Hunt, R., & Shelley, J. (1988). *Computer and common sense* (4th edn.). Hemel Hempstead, UK: Prentice-Hall.

Hunter, J. E., & Hunter, R. F. (1984). Validity and utility of alternative predictors of job performance. *Psychological Bulletin, 96*, 72–98.

Hunter, J., & Schmidt, F. L. (1990). *Methods of meta-analysis: Correcting error and bias in research findings*. Newbury Park, CA: Sage.

Hunter, J., & Schmidt, F. L. (2004). *Methods of meta-analysis: Correcting error and bias in research findings* (2nd edn.). Newbury Park, CA: Sage.

Hunton, J. E., & Harmon, W. K. (2004). A model for investigating telework in accounting. *International Journal of Accounting Information Systems, 5*, 417–27.

Huws U., Korte W. B., & Robinson S. (1990). *Telework: Towards the elusive office*. Chichester, UK: Wiley.

Huws, U. (1993). *Teleworking in Britain*. Sheffield: Department of Employment.

Hyötyläinen, R. (2000). *Development mechanisms of strategic enterprise networks. Learning and innovation in networks*. VTT publications 417. Espoo: Technical Research Centre of Finland.

Ibarra, H. (1995). Race, opportunity, and diversity of social circles in managerial networks. *Academy of Management Journal, 38*, 673–703.

Iles, P. A., & Robertson, I. T. (1997). The impact of personnel selection procedures on candidates. In N. Anderson & P. Herriot (Eds.), *International handbook of selection and assessment*. Chichester, UK: Wiley

Ilgen, D. R., & Pulakos, E. D. (Eds.) (1999). *The changing nature of performance*. San Francisco: Jossey-Bass.

Ilinitch, A. Y., Lewin, A. Y., & D'Aveni, R. A. (1998). Introduction. In A. Y. Ilinitch, A. Y. Lewin, & R. A. D'Aveni (Eds.), *Managing in times of disorder: Hypercompetitive organizational responses*. London: Sage.

Illegems, V., & Verbeke, A. (2004). Telework: What does it mean for management? *Long Range Planning, 37*, 319–34.

Industrial Society. (1997). *Appraisal*. Report no. 37. London: Industrial Society.

Industrial Society. (2001). Managing best practice. *Occupational Stress, 83*, 4–23.

International Herald Tribune. (1992). A giant that helps IBM think small. March 3, p. 10.

ISO 9241 (1997). *Guidance on usability*. Final draft 9241, Part II, 24 pp. Geneva: International Standards Organisation.

Ivancic, K., & Hesketh, B. (2000). Learning from errors in a driving simulation: Effects of driving skill and self-confidence. *Ergonomics*, *43*, 1966–84.

Jacinto, C., & Aspinwall, E. (2004). A survey on occupational accidents' reporting and registration systems in the European Union. *Safety Science*, *42*, 933–60.

Jackson, P. B., Thoits, P. A., & Taylor, H. F. (1995). Composition of the workplace and psychological well-being: The effects of tokenism on America's Black elite. *Social Forces*, *74*, 543–57.

Jackson, S. E. (1983). Participation in decision making as a strategy for reducing job–related strain. *Journal of Applied Psychology*, *68*, 3–19.

Jacobs, R., Kafry, D., & Zedeck, S. (1980). Expectations of behaviourally anchored rating scales. *Personnel Psychology*, *33*, 595–640.

Jacoby, L. L., Lindsay, D. S., & Toth, J. P. (1992). Unconscious preferences revealed: Attention awareness and control. *American Psychologist*, *47(6)*, 766–79.

Jacqes, E. (1970). *Work creativity, and social justice*. London: Heinemann.

James, J. R., & Tetrick, L. E. (1986). Confirmatory analytic tests of three causal models relating job perceptions to job satisfaction. *Journal of Applied Psychology*, *33*, 77–82.

Jarvenpaa, S. L., & Leidner, D. E. (1998). Communication and trust in global virtual teams. *Journal of Computer-Mediated Communication*, *3*, 1–38.

Jehn, K. (1997). A qualitative analysis of conflict types and dimensions in organizational groups. *Administrative Science Quarterly*, *42*, 530–57.

Jemison D., & Sitkin, S. (1996). Corporate acquisitions. *Academy of Management Review*, *11(1)*, p. 145.

Jeurissen, T., & Nyklícek, I. (2001). Testing the Vitamin Model of job stress in Dutch health care workers, *Work & Stress*, *15(3)*, 254–64.

Johnson, G., & Scholes, K. (1999). *Exploring corporate strategy: Text and cases* (5th edn.). London: Prentice-Hall.

Johnson, G., Scholes, K., & Whittington, R. (2005). *Exploring corporate strategy: Text and cases* (7th edn.). London: FT Prentice-Hall.

Johnson, J. V., & Hall, E. M. (1988). Job strain, work place social support, and cardio-vascular disease: A cross-sectional study of a random sample of the Swedish working population. *American Journal of Public Health*, *78*, 1336–42.

Jones, E. E., Farina, A., Hastorf, A. H., Markus, H., Miller, D. T., & Scott, R. A. (1984). *Social stigma: The psychology of marked relationships*. New York: Freeman.

Jones, F., & Fletcher, B. C. (1996). Job control and health. In M. J. Schabracq, J. A. M. Winnubst, & C. L. Cooper (Eds.), *Handbook of work and health psychology* (pp. 33–50). Chichester, UK: John Wiley.

Jones, J., & Wuebker, L. (1985). Development and validation of the safety locus of control scale. *Perceptual and Motor Skills*, *61*, 151–61.

Jonge, J. de & Dormann, C. (2003). The DISC Model: Demand-induced strain compensation mechanisms in job stress. In M. F. Dollard, H. R. Winefield, & A. H. Winefield (Eds.), *Occupational stress in the services professions* (pp. 43–74). London: Taylor & Francis.

Jonge, J. de, & Dormann, C. (2004). Matching demands, resources, and strains: A test of the Demand-induced strain compensation model in three different countries. *International Journal of Behavioral Medicine*, *11*, Supplement, 187.

Jonge, J. de, & Dormann, C. (2005, in press). The demand-induced strain compensation model: Renewed theoretical considerations and empirical evidence. In M. Sverke,

J. Hellgren, & K. Näswall (Eds.), *Balancing work and well-being: The individual in the changing working life.*

Jonge, J. de, & Dormann, C. (2006). Stressors, resources, and strain at work: A longitudinal test of the Triple Match Principle. *Journal of Applied Psychology, 91,* 1359–1374.

Jonge, J. de & Kompier, M. A. J. (1997). A critical examination of the Demand–Control–Support Model from a work psychological perspective. *International Journal of Stress Management, 4,* 235–58.

Jonge, J. de & Schaufeli, W. B. (1998). Job characteristics and employee well-being: A test of Warr's Vitamin Model in health care workers using structural equation modelling. *Journal of Organizational Behavior, 19,* 387–407.

Jonge, J. de, Schaufeli, W. B., & Furda, J. (1995). Job characteristics: Psychological work vitamins? *Paper presented at the IV ENOP Conference, Munich,* Germany.

Jordan, P. W. (1998). *An introduction to usability.* London: Taylor & Francis.

Joshi van, A., & Jackson, S. E. (2003). Managing workforce diversity to enhance cooperation in organizations. In M. A. West, D. Tjosvold, & K. G. Smith (Eds.), *International handbook of organizational teamwork and cooperative working* (pp. 277–96). Chichester, UK: Wiley.

Judge, T. A., & Piccolo, R. F. (2004). Transformational and transactional leadership: A meta-analytic test of their relative validity. *Journal of Applied Psychology, 89,* 755–68.

Judge, T. A., Bono, J. I., Ilies, R., & Gerhard, M. W. (2002). Personality and leadership: A qualitative and quantitative review. *Journal of Applied Psychology, 87,* 765–80.

Judge, T. A., Piccolo, R. F., & Ilies, R. (2004). The forgotten ones? The validity of consideration and initiating structure in leadership research. *Journal of Applied Psychology, 89,* 36–51.

Judge, T. A., Thoresen, C. J., Bono, J. E., & Patton, G. K. (2001). The job satisfaction–job performance relationship. A qualitative and quantitative review. *Psychological Bulletin, 127,* 376–407

Kaber, D. B., & Endsley, M. R. (2004). The effects of level of automation and adaptive automation on human performance, situation awareness and workload in a dynamic control task. *Theoretical Issues in Ergonomics Science, 5,* 113–53.

Kahneman, D. (1971). Remarks on attentional control. In A. F. Sanders (Ed.), *Attention and performance III.* Amsterdam: North Holland.

Kahneman, D. (1973). *Attention and effort.* Englewood Cliffs, NJ: Prentice-Hall.

Kahneman, D., & Tversky, A. (1979). Prospect Theory: An analysis of decision under risk. *Econometrica, 47,* 263–92.

Kahneman D., & Tversky A. (1984). Choices, values and frames. *American Psychologist, 39,* 341–50.

Kahneman, D., Slovic, P., & Tversky, A. (Eds.) (1982). *Judgment under uncertainty: Heuristics and biases.* Cambridge: Cambridge University Press.

Kahnweiler, W. M., & Kahnweiler, J. B. (2005). *Shaping your hr role, succeeding in today's organizations.* Burlington: Elsevier Butterworth-Heinemann.

Kaminski, M. (2001). Unintended consequences: Organizational practices and their impact on workplace safety and productivity. *Journal of Occupational Health Psychology, 6,* 127–38.

Kandola, R., & Fullerton, J. (1998). *Diversity in action: Managing the mosaic.* London: Institute of Personnel and Development.

Kandola, R., & Galpin, M. (2000). 360-degree feedback goes under the microscope. *Insights*, Volume 1, pp. 6–7. Oxford: Pearn Kandola.

Kanfer, R., & Ackerman, P. L. (2004). Aging, adult development and work motivation. *Academy of Management Review*, 29, 440–58.

Kanter, R. M. (1977). *Men and women of the corporation*. New York: Basic Books

Kantowitz, B., & Sorkin, R. (1987). Allocation of functions. In G. Salvendy (Ed.), *Handbook of human factors*. New York: Wiley.

Karasek, R., Brison, C., Kawakami, N., Houtman, I., Bongers, P., & Amick, B. (1998). The Job Content Questionnaire (JCQ): An instrument for internationally comparative assessments of psychosocial job characteristics. *Journal of Occupational Health Psychology*, 3, 322–55.

Karasek, R. A., & Theorell, T. (1990). *Healthy work: Stress, productivity and the reconstruction of working life*. New York: Basic Books.

Karau, S. J., Markus, M. J., & Williams, K. D. (2000). On the elusive search for motivation gains in groups: Insights from the Collective Effort Model. *Zeitschrift für Sozialpsychologie*, 31, 179–90.

Karau, S. J., & Williams, K. D. (1993). Social loafing: A meta-analytic review and theoretical integration. *Journal of Personality and Social Psychology*, 65, 681–706.

Karoly, P. (1993). Mechanisms of self-regulation: A systems view. *Annual Review of Psychology*, 44, 23–52.

Karwowski, W. (1991). Complexity, fuzziness, and ergonomic incompatibility issues in the control of dynamic work environments. *Ergonomics*, 34, 671–86.

Kasl, S. V. (1987). Methodologies in stress and health: Past difficulties, present dilemma's future directions. In S. V. Kasl & C. L. Cooper (Eds.), *Job control and worker health* (pp. 161–89). Chichester, UK: Wiley.

Kasl, S. V. (1996). The influence of the work environment on cardiovascular health: A historical, conceptual, and methodological perspective. *Journal of Occupational Health Psychology*, 1, 42–56.

Katz, D., & Kahn, R. L. (1978). *Social psychology of organizations* (2nd edn.). New York: Wiley.

Katz, P. J., Simanek, A., & Townsend, B. J. (1997), Corporate mergers and acquisitions: One more wave to consider, *Business Horizons, January–February*, 32–40.

Katzell, R. A., & Austin, J. T. (1992). From then to now: The development of industrial–organizational psychology in the United States. *Journal of Applied Psychology*, 77, 803–35.

Kay, E., Meyer, H. H., & French, J. R. P. (1965). Effects of threat in a performance appraisal interview. *Journal of Applied Psychology*, 49, 311–17.

Keenan, T. (1995). Graduate recruitment in Britain: A survey of selection methods used by organizations. *Journal of Organizational Behavior*, 16, 303–17.

Keenan, T. (1997). Selecting for potential: The case of graduate recruitment. In N. Anderson & P. Herriot (Eds.), *International handbook of selection and assessment*. Chichester, UK: Wiley.

Keith, N., & Frese, M. (in press). Performance effects of error management training: A meta-analysis.

Keith, N., & Frese, M. (2005). Self-regulation in error management training: Emotion control and metacognition as mediators of performance effects. *Journal of Applied Psychology*, 90, 677–691.

Kelloway, E. K., Mullen, J., & Francis, L. (2006). Divergent effects of transformational and passive leadership on employee safety. *Journal of Occupational Health Psychology*, *11*, 76–86.

Kelly, G. A. (1955). *The psychology of personal constructs* (2 vols.). New York: Norton.

Kern, H., & Schumann, M. (1984). *Das Ende der Arbeitsteilung*. Munich: Beck.

Kerr, N. L. (1983). Motivation losses in small groups: A social dilemma analysis. *Personality and Social Psychology*, *45*, 819–28.

Kerr, S., & Jermier, J. M. (1978). Substitutes for leadership: Their meaning and measurement. *Organizational Behavior and Human Performance*, *22*, 375–403.

Kieser, A. (2002). On communication barriers between management science, consultancies and business organisations. In T. Clark & R. Fincham (Eds.), *Critical consulting, new perspectives on the management advice industry* (pp. 206–7). Oxford: Blackwell.

Kiesler, S., Siegel, J., & McGuire, T. W. (1984). Social psychological aspects of computer–mediated communication. *American Psychologist*, *39*, 1123–34.

Kim, S., & Feldman, D. C. (2000). Working in retirement: The antecedents of bridge employment and its consequences for quality of life in retirement. *Academy of Management Journal*, *43*, 1195–1210.

King, N. (1970). Clarification and evaluation of the two-factor theory of job satisfaction. *Psychological Bulletin*, *74*, 18–31.

Kinsman, F. (1987). *The telecommuters*. Chichester, UK: Wiley.

Kirakowski, J., & Corbett, M. (1988). Measuring user satisfaction. In D. M. Jones & R. Winder (Eds.), *People and computers IV* (pp. 329–340). Cambridge, UK: University Press.

Kirakowski, J., & Corbett, M. (1993). SUMI: The software usability measurement inventory. *British Journal of Educational Technology*, *24*, 210–14.

Kirchmeyer, C., & Cohen, A. (1992). Multicultural groups: Their performance and reactions with constructive conflict. *Group and Organisation Management*, *17*, 153–70.

Kirkpatrick, D. L. (1976). Evaluation of training. In R. L. Craig (Ed.), *Training and development handbook: A guide to human resource development* (pp. 18.11–27). New York: McGraw-Hill.

Kitou, E., & Horvath, A. (2003). Energy-related emissions from telework. *Environment, Science and Technology*, *37*, 3467–75.

Kling, R. (1980). Social analyses of computing: Theoretical perspectives in recent empirical research. *Computing Surveys*, *12*, 61–110.

Kluger, A. N., & DeNisi, A. (1996). The effects of feedback interventions on performance: A historical review, a meta-analysis, and a preliminary feedback intervention theory. *Psychological Bulletin*, *119*, 254–84.

Kluger, A. N., & Rothstein, H. R. (1993). The influence of selection test type on applicant reactions to employment testing. *Journal of Business and Psychology*, *8*, 3–25.

Knights, D., & Raffo, C. (1990). Milk round professionalism in personnel recruitment: Myth or reality? *Personnel Review*, *19*, 28–37.

Kohn, M. L., & Schooler, C. (1983). *Work and Personality: An inquiry into the impact of social stratification*. Norwood, NJ: Ablex Publishing.

Kolb, D. A. (1984). *Experiential learning: Experience as the source of learning and development*. Englewood Cliffs, NJ: Prentice-Hall.

Kompier, M. A. J., & Kristensen, T. S. (2000). Organizational work stress interventions in a theoretical, methodological and practical context. In J. Dunham (Ed.), *Stress in the workplace: Past, present and future* (pp. 164–90). London: Whurr.

Kompier, M., & Cooper, C. (1999). *Preventing stress, improving productivity*. London: Routledge.

Konovsky, M. A., & Cropanzano, R. (1991). Perceived fairness of employee drug testing as a predictor of employee attitudes and job performance. *Journal of Applied Psychology, 76*, 698–707.

Konrad, A. M., & Linnehan, F. (1995). Formalised HRM structures: Coordinating equal employment opportunity or concealing organisational practices? *Academy of Management Journal, 38*, 787–820.

Korman, A. K. (1968). The prediction of managerial performance: A review. *Personel Psychology, 21*, 259–322.

Korsgaard, M. A., Brodt, S. E., & Sapienza, H. J. (2003). Trust, identity, and attachment: Promoting individuals' cooperation in groups. In M. A. West (Ed.), *Handbook of work group psychology*. Chichester, UK: Wiley.

Kostera, M., & Wicha, M. (1996). The "divided self" of Polish state–owned enterprises: The culture of organizing. *Organisation Studies, 17*, 83–105.

Kotter, J. P. (1973). The psychological contract: Managing the joining-up process. *Californian Management Review, XV(3)*, 91–9.

Kozlowski, S. W., Chao, G. T., Smith, E. M., & Hedlund, J. (1993). Organizational downsizing: Strategies, interventions, and research implications. In C. L. Cooper & I. T. Robertson (Eds.), *International review of industrial and organizational psychology 1993* (pp. 263–332) Chichester, UK: Wiley.

Kraiger, K. (2003). Perspectives on training and development. In W. C. Borman, D. R. Ilgen, & R. J. Klimoski (Eds.), *Handbook of psychology. Volume 12: Industrial and organizational psychology* (pp. 171–92). Hoboken, NJ: Wiley.

Kramer, A. F. (1991). Physiological metrics of mental workload: A review of recent progress. In D. L. Damos (Ed.), *Multiple-task performance*. London: Taylor & Francis.

Krause, N., Dasinger, L., & Neuhauser, F. (1998). Modified work and return to work: A review of the literature. *Journal of Occupational Rehabilitation, 8*, 109–39.

Krieger, L. H. (1998). Civil rights perestroika: Intergroup relations after affirmative action. *California Law Review, 86*, 1251–1333.

Kristensen, T. S. (1996). Job stress and cardiovascular disease: A theoretic critical review. *Journal of Occupational Health Psychology, 1*, 246–60.

Kubeck, J. E., Delp, N. D., Haslett, T. K., & McDaniel, M. A. (1996). Does job-related training performance decline with age. *Psychology and Aging, 9*, 539–53.

Kuhn, T. M. (1962). *The structure of scientific revolutions*. Chicago: University of Chicago Press.

Kurland, N. B., & Bailey, D. E. (1999). When workers are here, there, and everywhere: A discussion of the advantages and challenges of telework. *Organizational Dynamics, 28*, 53–68.

Kurz, R., & Bartram, D. (2002). Competency and individual performance: Modeling the world of work. In I. T. Robertson, M. Callinan, & D. Bartram (Eds.), *Organizational effectiveness: The role of Psychology*. New York: Wiley.

Labiancia, G., Gray, B., & Brass, B. J. (2000). A grounded model of organizational schema change during empowerment. *Organization Science, 11*, 235–57.

LaMarsh, J. (1995). *Changing the way we change. Gaining control of major operational change*. Reading, MA: Addison-Wesley.

Landis, R. S., Fogli, L., & Goldberg, E. (1998). Future-oriented job analysis: A description of the process and organizational implications. *International Journal of Selection and Assessment, 6*, 192–7.

Landsbergis, P. A. (2003). The changing organisation of work and the safety and health of working people: a commentary. *Journal of Occupational Environmental Medicine, 45*, 61–72.

Landy, F. J. (1997). Early influences on the development of industrial and organizational psychology. *Journal of Applied Psychology, 82*, 467–77.

Landy, F. J., & Farr, J. L. (1980). Performance rating. *Psychological Bulletin, 87*, 72–107.

Langer, E. J. (1975). The illusion of control. *Journal of Personality and Social Psychology, 32*, 311–38.

Lankau, M. J., & Scandura, T. A. (2002). An investigation of personal learning in mentoring relationships: Content, antecedents and consequences. *Academy of Management Journal, 45*, 779–90.

Lant, T. K., & Baum, J. C. (1995). Cognitive sources of socially constructed competitive groups: Examples from the Manhattan hotel industry. In W. R. Scott and S. Christensen (Eds.), *The Institutional Construction of Organizations: International and Longitudinal Studies*. Thousand Oaks, CA: Sage.

Lasn, K. (2005). Merger mania, filtering out dessenting voices. http://www.adbusters. org/magazine/30/merger

Latack, J. C., & Havlovic, S. J. (1992). Coping with job stress: A conceptual evaluation framework for coping measures. *Journal of Organizational Behavior, 13*, 479–508.

Latham, G. P., Erez, M., & Locke, E. A. (1988). Resolving scientific dispute by the joint design of crucial experiments by the antagonists: Application to the Erez–Latham dispute regarding participation in goal setting. *Journal of Applied Psychology, 73*, 753–72.

Latham, G. P., & Frayne, C. A. (1990). Increasing job attendance through training in self management: A review of two field experiments. In H. H. Quast, H. Thierry, & H. Häcker (Eds.), *Work motivation* (pp. 822–32). Hillsdale, NJ: Erlbaum.

Latham, G. P., & Saari, L. M. (1979). Application of social learning theory to training supervisors through behavioral modelling. *Journal of Applied Psychology, 64*, 239–46.

Lau, D. C., & Murnighan, J. K. (1998). Demographic diversity and faultlines: The compositional dynamics of organizational groups. *Academy of Management Review, 23*, 325–40.

Lave, J., & Wenger, E. (1991). *Situated learning: Legitimate peripheral participation*. New York: Cambridge University Press.

Lawrence, B. S. (1988). New wrinkles on the theory of age: Demography, norms, and performance ratings. *Academy of Management Journal 31*, 309–37.

Lawrence, P., & Lorsch, J. (1967). *Organization and environment*. Homewood, IL: Irwin.

Lawton, R. (1998). Not working to rule: Understanding procedural violations at work. *Safety Science, 28*, 77–95.

Lawton, R., & Ward, N. J. (2005). A systems analysis of the Ladbroke Grove rail crash. *Accident Analysis and Prevention, 37*, 235–44.

Lazarsfeld, P. F., & Merton, R. K. (1954). Friendship as a social process: A substantive and methodological analysis. In M. Berger, T. Abel, & C. H. Page (Eds.), *Freedom and control in modern society*. New York: Van Nostrand.

Lazarus, R. S., & Folkman, S. (1984). *Stress, appraisal and coping*. New York: Springer.

Lee, C., & Gray, J. A. (1994). The role of employee assistance programmes. In C. L. Cooper & S. Williams (Eds.), *Creating healthy work organizations* (pp. 215–42). Chichester, UK: John Wiley.

Lennerlöf, L. (1988). Learned helplessness at work. *International Journal of Health Services, 18, 2,* 207–22.

LePine, J. A., & Van Dyne, L. (2001). Voice and cooperative behavior as contrasting forms of contextual performance: Evidence of differential relationships with Big Five personality characteristics and cognitive ability. *Journal of Applied Psychology, 86,* 326–36.

Leventhal, G. S. (1980). What should be done with equity theory? New approaches to the study of fairness in social relationships. In C. Gergen, M. M. Greenberg, & R. Willis (Eds.), *Social exchange: Advances in theory and research* (pp. 27–55). New York: Plenum.

Levine, E. L., Spector, P. E., Menon, P. E., Narayanon, L., & Cannon-Bowers, J. (1996). Validity generalization for cognitive, psychomotor, and perceptual test for craft jobs in the utility industry. *Human Performance, 9,* 1–22.

Levinson, H. (1962). *Men, management and mental health*. Cambridge, MA: Harvard University Press.

Lewin, K. (1938). *The conceptual representation and the measurement of psychological forces*. Durham, NC: Duke University Press.

Lewin, K, Lippitt, R., & White, R. K. (1939). Patterns of aggressive behavior in experimentally created social climates. *Journal of Social Psychology, 10,* 271–99.

Lewis, D., & Sargeant, M. (2007). *Essentials of employment law* (9th edn.). London: Chartered Institute of Personnel and Development.

Licht, W. (1983). *Working for the railroad*. Princeton, NJ: Princeton University Press.

Lievens, F. (2001). Assessor training strategies and their effects on accuracy, interrater reliability, and discriminant validity. *Journal of Applied Psychology, 86,* 255–64.

Lievens, F., Harris, M. M., Van Keer, E., & Bisqueret, C. (2003). Predicting cross-cultural training performance: The validity of personality, cognitive ability, and dimensions measured by an assessment center and a behavior description interview. *Journal of Applied Psychology, 88,* 476–89.

Light, D. A. (2001). Who goes, who stays? *Harvard Business Review*, Jan., 35–44.

Lilischkis, S. (2003). *More yo-yos, pendulums and nomads: Trends of mobile and multi-location work in the information society*. STAR (Socio-economic trends assessment for the digital revolution). Issue report no 36, www. databank.it/star

Lipnack, J., & Stamps, J. (2000). *Virtual teams. People working across boundaries with technology*. New York: Wiley.

Lippitt, G. (1986). Guidelines for international consulting. In G. Lippitt & R. Lippitt (Eds.), *The consulting process in action* (2nd edn.). San Francisco: Jossey-Bass/Pfeiffer.

Lippitt, G., & Lippitt, R. (1986). *The consulting process in action* (2nd edn.). San Francisco: Jossey-Bass/Pfeiffer.

Lobard, M., & Ditton, T. (1997). At the heart of it all: The concept of presence. *Journal of Computer-Mediated Communication, 3,* 2.

Locke, E. A., & Latham, G. P. (1990). *A theory of goal setting and task performance.* Englewood Cliffs, NJ: Prentice Hall.

Locke, E. A., & Latham, G. P. (2002). Building a practically useful theory of goal setting and task motivation. *American Psychologist, 57,* 705–17.

Locke, E. A., & Latham, G. P. (2004). What should we do about motivation theory? Six recommendations for the twenty-first century. *Academy of Management Review, 29,* 388–403.

Lockhart, J. M., Strub, M. H., Hawley, J. K., & Tapia, L. A. (1993). Automation and supervisory control: A perspective on human performance, training, and performance aiding. *Proceedings of the Human Factors and Ergonomics Society 37th Annual Meeting.*

London, M., & Larsen, H. H. (1999). Relationships between empowerment, feedback, and self-management for career development. *Group and Organization Management, 24,* 5–27.

London, M., & Mone, E. M. (1999). Continuous learning. In D. R. Ilgen & E. D. Pulakos (Eds.), *The changing nature of performance. Implications for staffing, motivation, and development* (pp. 119–53). San Francisco: Jossey-Bass.

London, M., & Smither, J. W. (1999). Career–related continuous learning: Defining the construct and mapping the process. In G. R. Ferris (Ed.), *Research in personnel and human resources management* (pp. 81–121). Stamford, CT: JAI Press.

Longenecker, C. O. (1989). Truth or consequences: Politics and performance appraisals. *Business Horizons,* Nov./Dec, 1–7.

Longenecker, C. O., Liverpool, P. R., & Wilson, K. A. (1988). An assessment of managerial/subordinate perceptions of performance appraisal effectiveness. *Journal of Business and Psychology, 2,* 311–20.

Lopez, F. M. (1988). Threshold trait analysis system. In S. Gael (Ed.), *The job analysis handbook for business, industry and government* (Vol. 2, pp. 880–901). New York: Wiley.

Lord, R. G., DeVader, C. L., & Alliger, G. M. (1986). A meta-analysis of the relation between personality traits and leadership: An application of validity generalization procedures. *Journal of Applied Psychology, 71,* 402–10.

Lord, R. G., & Maher, K. J. (1991). *Leadership and information processing: Linking perceptions and performance.* Boston: Unwin-Hyman.

Lowe, K. B., Kroeck, K. G., & Sivasubramaniam, N. (1996). Effectiveness correlates of transformational and transactional leadership: A meta-analytic review of the MLQ literature. *Leadership Quarterly, 7,* 385–425.

Luke, R. A. (2000). Managing the older worker. In R. T. Golembiewski (Ed.), *Handbook of organizational consultation* (pp. 691–2). New York: Marcel Dekker.

Lundberg, U., & Frankenhaueser, M. (1978). Psychophysiological reactions to noise as modified by personal control over noise intensity. *Biological Psychology, 6,* 51–9.

Mabey, C., Salaman, G., & Storey, J. (1998). *Human resource management, A strategic introduction.* Oxford: Blackwell.

Mackie, D. M., Hamilton, D. L., Susskind, J., & Rosselli, F. (1996). Social psychological foundations of stereotype formation. In C. N. Macrae, C. Strangor, & M. Hewstone (Eds.), *Stereoypes and stereotyping* (pp. 41–78). New York: Guildford.

Macleod, M., Bowden, R., Bevan, N., & Curson, I. (1997). The MUSiC performance measurement method. *Behaviour and Information Technology, 16*, 279–93.

Macrae, C. N., Bodenhausen, G. V., Milne, A. B., & Jetten, J. (1994). Out of mind but back in sight: Stereotypes on the rebound. *Journal of Personality and Social Psychology, 67*, 808–17.

Macrae, C. N., Bodenhausen, G. V., Milne, A. B., Thorn, M. J. T., & Castelli, L. (1997). On the activation of social stereotypes: The moderating role of processing objectives. *Journal of Experimental Social Psychology, 33*, 471–89.

Macy, B. A., & Izumi, H. (1993). Organizational change, design and work innovation: A meta-analysis of 131 North American field studies, 1961–1991. *Research in Organizational Change and Development, 7*, 235–313.

Mankeltow, J., Brodbeck, F. C., & Anand, N. (2005). *How to lead: Discover the leader within you*. Swindon, UK: Mind Tools.

Mann, R. D. (1959). A review of the relationships between personality and performance in small groups. *Psychological Bulletin, 56*, 241–70.

Marks, M. A., Mathieu, J. E., & Zaccaro, S. J. (2001). A temporally based framework and taxonomy of team processes. *Academy of Management Review, 26*, 356–76.

Marks, M. L., & Mirvis, P. H. (1998), *Joining forces*. San Francisco: Jossey-Bass.

Martell, R. F., Lane, D. M., & Emrich, C. (1996). Male–female differences: A computer simulation. *American Psychologist, 51*, 157–8.

Martin, R. L., & Moldoveanu, M. C. (2003). Capital versus talent: The battle that's reshaping business. *Harvard Business Review*, July, 36–41.

Martins, L. L., Gilson, L. L., & Maynard, M. T. (2004). Virtual teams: What do we know and where do we go from here? *Journal of Management, 30*, 805–35.

Marx, K. (1932). *Capital and other writings* (Ed. Max Eastman). New York: The Modern Library.

Maslach, C., & Jackson, S. E. (1986). *Maslach Burnout Inventory*. Palo Alto, CA: Consulting Psychologists Press.

Maslow, A. H. (1943). A theory of human motivation. *Psychological Review, 50*, 370–96.

Mason, E. (1957). *Economic concentration and the monopoly problem*. Cambridge, MA: Harvard University Press.

Mathieu, J. E., & Martineau, J. W. (1997). Individual and situational influences on training motivation. In J. K. Ford, S. W. J. Kozlowski, K. Kraiger, E. Salas, & M. S. Teachout (Eds.), *Improving training effectiveness in work organizations* (pp. 193–221). Mahwah, NJ: Erlbaum.

Mathieu, J. E., & Zajac, D. M. (1990). A review and meta-analysis of the antecedents, correlates and consequences of organizational commitment. *Psychological Bulletin, 108*, 171–94.

Matthews, G. (2002). Towards a transactional model of driver stress and fatigue. *Theoretical Issues in Ergonomic Science, 3*, 195–211.

Maule, A. J. (1995). Framing elaborations and their effects on choice behavior: A comparison across problem isomorphs and subjects with different levels of expertise. In J.-P. Caverni, M. Bar-Hillel, F. H. Barron, & H. Jungermann (Eds.), *Contributions to decision research 1*. Amsterdam: Elsevier.

Maule, A. J., & Hodgkinson, G. P. (2002). Heuristics, biases and strategic decision making. *The Psychologist, 15*, 68–71.

Maule, A. J., & Hodgkinson, G. P. (2003). Re-appraising managers' perceptual errors: A behavioural decision making perspective. *British Journal of Management, 14,* 33–7.

Maume, D. J. (1999). Glass ceilings and gals escalators: Occupational segregation and race and sex differences in managerial promotions. *Work and Occupations, 26,* 483–509.

Maurer, T. J., Mitchell, D. R. D., & Barbeite, F. G. (2002). Predictors of attitudes toward 360-degree feedback system and involvement in post-feedback management development activity. *Journal of Occupational & Organizational Psychology, 75,* 87–107.

Maurer, T. J., & Rafuse, N. (2001). Learning not litigating: Managing employee development and avoiding clains of age discrimination. *Academy of Management Executives, 15,* 110–21.

Maurer, T. J., Weiss, E. M., & Barbeite, F. G. (2003). A model of involvement in work–related learning and development activity: The effects of individual, situational, motivational, and age variables. *Journal of Applied Psychology, 88,* 707–24.

Mayer, R. C., & Davis, J. H. (1999). The effect of the performance appraisal system on trust for management: A quasi-experiment. *Journal of Applied Psychology, 84,* 123–36.

Maznevski, M. M., & Chuboda, K. M. (2000). Bridging space over time: global virtual team dynamics and effectiveness. *Organization Science, 11,* 473–92.

McBrien, J. L., & Brandt, R. S. (1997). *The language of learning: A guide to education terms.* Alexandria, VA: Association for Supervision and Curriculum Development.

McCauley, C. D., Lombardo, M. M., & Usher, C. J. (1989). Diagnosing management development needs: An instrument based on how managers develop. *Journal of Management, 15,* 389–403.

McCauley, C. D., Ruderman, M. N., Ohlott, P. J., & Morrow, J. E. (1994). Assessing the developmental components of managerial jobs. *Journal of Applied Psychology, 79,* 544–60.

McClelland, D. C. (1961). *The achieving society.* Princeton, NJ: van Nostrand.

McClelland, D. C. (1965). N achievement and entrepreneurship: A longitudinal study. *Journal of Personality and Social Psychology, 1,* 389–92.

McClelland, D. C. (1975). *Power: The inner experience.* New York: Irvington.

McClelland, D. C. (1980). Motive dispositions: The merits of operant and respondent measures. In C. Wheeler (Ed.), *Review of personality and social psychology* (Bd. 1). Beverly Hills, CA: Sage.

McClelland, D. C. (1985). *Human motivation.* Glenview, IL: Scott Foresman.

McClelland, D. C., & Boyatzis, R. E. (1982). Leadership motive pattern and long-term success in management. *Journal of Applied Psychology, 67,* 737–43.

McCloskey, D. W., & Igbaria, M. (1998). A review of the empirical research on telecommuting and directions for future research. In M. Igbaria & M. Tan (Eds.), *The virtual workplace.* Hershey, PA: Idea Group Publishing.

McConahay, J. B. (1986). Modern racism, ambivalence and the Modern Racism Scale. In J. F. Dovidio & S. L. Gaertner (Eds.), *Prejudice, discrimination and racism* (pp. 91–125). New York: Academic Press.

McCormick, E. J. (1976). Job and task analysis. In M. D. Dunnette (Ed.), *Handbook of industrial and organizational psychology* (pp. 651–97). Chicago: Rand McNally.

McCormick, E. J., DeNisi, A. S., & Shaw, J. B. (1979). Use of the Positional Analysis Questionnaire for establishing the job component validity of tests. *Journal of Applied Psychology*, *64*, 51–6.

McCormick, E. J., Jeanneret, P. R., & Mecham, R. C. (1972). A study of job characteristics and job dimensions as based on the Positional Analysis Questionnaire (PAQ). *Journal of Applied Psychology*, *56*, 347–68.

McDaniel, M. A., Morgeson, F. P., Finnegan, E. B., Campion, M. A., & Braverman, E. P. (2001). Use of situational judgment tests to predict job performance: A clarification of the literature. *Journal of Applied Psychology 86*, 730–40.

McDaniel, M. A., Whetzel, D. L., Schmidt, F. L., & Maurer, S. (1994). The validity of employment interviews: A comprehensive review and meta-analysis. *Journal of Applied Psychology*, *79*, 599–616.

McDonald, D. G., & Hodgdon, J. A. (1991). *Psychological effect of aerobic fitness training: Research and theory.* New York: Springer.

McDowell, A., & Fletcher, C. (2004). Employee development – An organizational justice perspective. *Personnel Review*, *33*, 8–29.

McEvoy, G. M., & Cascio, W. F. (1989). Cumulative evidence of the relationship between employee age and job performance. *Journal of Applied Psychology*, *74*, 11–17.

McGee, J., & Thomas, H. (1986). Strategic groups: Theory, research and taxonomy. *Strategic Management Journal*, *7*, 141–60.

McGrath, J. E. (1991). Time, interaction, and performance (TIP). A theory of groups. *Small Group Research, 22*, 147–74.

McIntosh, P. (1993). White privilege and male privilege: A personal account of coming to see correspondences through work in women's studies. In A. Minas (Ed.), *Gender basics* (pp. 30–8). Belmont, CA: Wadsworth.

McLoughlin, I., & Clark, J. (1994). *Technological change at work* (2nd edn.). Buckingham: Open University Press.

McNamara, G., Vaaler, P. M., & Devers, C. (2003). Same as it ever was: The search for evidence of increasing hypercompetition. *Strategic Management Journal*, *24*, 261–78.

McNulty, T., & Ferlie, E. (2004). Process transformation: Limitations to radical organisational change within public service organisations. *Organisation Studies*, *25*, 1389–1412.

Medawar, P. B. (1969). *Induction and intuition in scientific thought.* London: Methuen.

Mehra, A., Kilduff, M., & Brass, D. J. (1998). At the margins: A distinctiveness approach to the social identity and social networks of underrepresented groups. *Academy of Management Journal*, *41*, 441–52.

Meijman, T. F., Mulder, G., van Dormelen, M., & Cremer, R. (1992). Workload of driving examiners: A psychophysiological field study. In H. Kragt (Ed.), *Enhancing industrial performance.* London: Taylor & Francis.

Merton, R. K. (1957). *Social theory and social structure.* Glencoe, IL: Free Press.

Messinger, G. S. (1985). *Manchester in the Victorian age.* Manchester: Manchester University Press.

Metzger, U., & Parasuraman, R. (2005). Automation in future air traffic management: Effects of decision aid reliability on controller performance and mental workload. *Human Factors, 47*, 35–49.

Meyer, C., Herrmann, D., & Hüneke, K. (2001). Medien- un Kommunikationskompetenz – Schlüsselqualifikation für die Zusammenarbeit auf Distanz. *Wirtschaftspsychologie, 10(4)*, 12–20.

Meyer, J. P., Becker, T. E., & van Dick, R. (2006). Social identities and commitments at work: Toward an integrative model. *Journal of Organizational Behavior, 27*, 1–19.

Miller, D., & Toulouse, J. M. (1986). Chief executive personality and corporate strategy and structure in small firms. *Management Science, 32*, 1389–1409.

Milliken, F. J., & Martins, L. L. (1996). Searching for common threads: Understanding the multiple effects of diversity in organizational groups. *Academy of Management Review, 21*, 402–33.

Mintzberg, H. (1994). *The Rise and fall of strategic planning.* London: Prentice-Hall.

Mintzberg, H., Ahlstrand, B., & Lampel, J. (1998). *Strategy safari: A guided tour through the wilds of strategic management.* London: Prentice-Hall.

Misumi, J., & Peterson, M. (1985). The performance-maintenance (PM). theory of leadership: Review of a Japanese research program. *Administrative Science Quarterly, 30*, 198–223.

Mitchell, J. L., & McCormick, E. J. (1979). *Development of the PMPQ: A structural job analysis questionnaire for the study of professional and managerial positions.* (Report No. 1). Lafayette, IN: Occupational Research Center, Department of Psychological Studies, Purdue University.

Mitchell, T. R. (1987). Motivation: New directions for theory, research and practice. In R. M. Steers & L. W. Porter (Eds.), *Motivation and work behavior* (pp. 292–302). New York: McGraw-Hill.

Mitchell, T. R., & Wood, R. E. (1980). Supervisors' responses to subordinate poor performance: A test of the attributional model. *Organizational Behavior and Human Performance, 25,* 123–38.

Mohrman, S. A., Cohen, S. G., & Mohrman, A. M., (1995). *Designing team-based organizations: New forms for knowledge work.* San Francisco: Jossey-Bass.

Mokhtarian, P. L., & Bagley, M. N. (2000). Modeling employees' perceptions and proportional preferences of work locations: The regular workplace and telecommuting alternatives. *Transportation Research, Part A, 34*, 223–42.

Mokhtarian, P. L., & Salomon, I. (1996). Modelling the choice of telecommuting 2: A case of the preferred impossible alternative. *Environment and Planning, Part A, 28*, 1859–76.

Mokhtarian, P. L., & Sato, K. (1994). A comparison of the policy, social, and cultural contexts for telecommuting in Japan and the United States. *Social Science Computer Review, 12*, 641–58.

Montreuil, S., & Lippel, K. (2003). Telework and occupational health: A Quebec empirical study and regulatory implications. *Safety Science, 41*, 339–58.

Moray, N. (1999). Human operators and automation. In *Proceedings of People In Control (PIC). Conference.* Publication No. 463. London: IEE.

Mor-Barak, M. E., & Cherin, D. A. (1998). A tool to expand organizational understanding of workforce diversity: Exploring a measure of inclusion–exclusion. *Administration in Social Work, 22(1)*, 47–64.

Moreland, J. P. (1987). *Scaling the secular city.* Grand Rapids, MI: Baker Book House.

Morgerson, E. P., & Campion, M. A. (1997). Social and cognitive sources of potential inaccuracy in job analysis. *Journal of Applied Psychology, 82*, 62–5.

Morgeson, F. P., & Campion, M. A. (2003). Work design. In W. C. Borman, D. R. Ilgen, & R. J. Klimoski (Eds.), *Handbook of psychology Vol. 12, Industrial and organizational psychology* (pp. 423–524). New York: Wiley.

Moroney, W. F., Biers, D. W., & Eggemeier, F. T. (1995). Some methodological considerations in the application of subjective workload measurement techniques. *The International Journal of Aviation Psychology, 5,* 87–106.

Morris, J. A., & Feldman, D. C. (1996). The dimensions, antecedents, and consequences of emotional labour. *Academy of Management Review, 21(4),* 986–1010.

Morris, N. M., Rouse, W. B., & Ward, S. L. (1988). Studies of dynamic task allocation in an aerial search environment. *IEEE Transactions on Systems, Man and Cybernetics, 18,* 376–89.

Morrison, A. M., White, R. P., & Van Velsor, E. (1987). Executive women: Substance plus style. *Psychology Today, 21,* 18–26.

Morrison, E. W. (1993). Longitudinal study of the effects of information seeking on newcomer socialization. *Journal of Applied Psychology, 78,* 173–83.

Motowidlo, S. J., & Van Scotter, J. R. (1994). Evidence that task performance should be distinguished from contextual performance. *Journal of Applied Psychology, 79,* 475–80.

Mount, M. K., Barrick, M. R., & Stewart, G. L. (1998). Five-factor model of personality and performance in jobs involving interpersonal interactions. *Human Performance, 11,* 145–65.

Muchinsky, P. M. (2003). *Psychology applied to work* (7th edn.). Belmont, CA: Tomson Wadsworth.

Mueller, L., DaSilva, N., Townsend, J., & Tetrick, L. (1999). An empirical evaluation of competing safety climate measurement models. Paper presented at the annual meeting of the Society for Industrial and Organizational Psychology, Atlanta, GA.

Murphy, K. R. (1986). When your top choice turns you down: Effects of rejected offers on the utility of selection tests. *Psychological Bulletin, 99,* 133–8.

Murphy, L. R. (2003). Stress Management at work: Secondary prevention of stress. In M. J. Schabracq, J. A. M. Winnubst & C. L. Cooper (Eds.), *Handbook of work and health psychology* (2nd edn., pp. 533–48). Chichester, UK: John Wiley.

Nahapiet, J., & Ghoshal, S. (1998). Social capital, intellectual capital, and the organizational advantage. *Academy of Management Review, 23,* 242–66.

Navon, D., & Gopher, D. (1979). On the economy of the human information processing system. *Psychological Review, 86,* 214–55.

Neal, A., & Griffin, M. A. (2006). A Study of the lagged relationships among safety climate, safety motivation, safety behavior, and accidents at the individual and group levels. *Journal of Applied Psychology, 91,* 946–53.

Neal, A., Griffin, M. A., & Hart (2000). The impact of organizational climate on safety climate and individual behaviour. *Safety Science, 34,* 99–109.

Nebeker, D. M., & Mitchell, T. R. (1974). Leader behaviour: An expectancy theory approach. *Organisational Behaviour and Human Performance, 11,* 355–67.

Nelson, D. L., & Simmons, B. L. (2004). Eustress: An elusive construct, an engaging pursuit. In P. L. Perrewé & D. C. Ganster (Eds.), *Emotional and physiological processes and positive intervention strategies. Research in occupational stress and well-being* (Vol. 3, pp. 265–322). Oxford, UK: Elsevier.

Nicholson, N. (1998). How hardwired is human behavior? *Harvard Business Review*, 76, 135–47.

Nicholson, N., & West, M. (1989). Transition, work histories, and careers. In M. B. Arthur, D. T. Hall, & B. S. Lawrence (Eds.), *Handbook of career theory*. Cambridge: Cambridge University Press.

Nielsen, J. (1993). *Usability engineering*. London: Academic Press.

Niles, J. S. (1994). *Beyond telecommuting: A new paradigm for the effect of telecommunications on travel*. Washington, DC: Office of Energy Research.

Nilles, J. M. (1998). *Managing telework. Strategies for managing the virtual workforce*. New York: Wiley.

Noe, R. A., Wilk, S. L., Mullen, E. J., & Wanek, J. E. (1997). Employee development: Issues in construct definition and investigation antecedents. In J. K. Ford, S. W. J. Kozlowski, K. Kraiger, E. Salas, & M. S. Teachout (Eds.), *Improving training effectiveness in work organizations* (pp. 153–89). Mahwah, NJ: Lawrence Erlbaum.

Nohria, N., & Ghoshal, S. (1997). *The Differentiated Network: Organizing Multinational Corporations for Value Creation*. San Francisco: Jossey-Bass.

Nonaka, I., Toyama, R., & Konno, N. (2000). SECI, *ba* and leadership: A unified model of dynamic knowledge creation. *Long Range Planning*, 22, 5–34.

Norman, D. A. (1998). *The invisible computer*. Cambridge, MA: MIT Press.

Norman, D. A., & Bobrow, D. G. (1975). On data-limited and resource-limited processes. *Cognitive Psychology*, 7, 44–64.

Noyes, J. M. (2001). *Designing for humans*. Chichester, UK: Psychology Press.

Noyes, J. M., & Baber, C. (1999). *User-centred design of systems*. London: Springer.

Nunes, F. (2005). Most relevant enablers and constraints influencing the spread of telework in Portugal. *New Technology, Work and Employment*, 20, 133–49.

O'Driscoll, M. P., & Cooper, C. L. (1996). Sources and management of excessive stress and burnout. In P. Warr (Ed.), *Psychology at work*. London: Penguin.

O'Donnell, R. D., & Eggemeier, F. T. (1986). Workload assessment methodology. In K. R. Boff, L. Kaufman & J. P. Thomas (Eds.), *Handbook of perception and human performance, Vol. 2: Cognitive processes and performance*. New York: Wiley.

Oldham, G. R. (1996). Job design. In C. L. Cooper & I. T. Robertson (Eds.), *International Review of Industrial and Organizational Psychology* (Vol. 11, pp. 35–60). New York: Wiley.

Oldham, G. R., & Cummings, A. (1996). Employee creativity: Personal and contextual factors at work. *Journal of Applied Psychology*, 39, 607–34.

Oliver, A., Cheyne, A., Tomas, J. M., & Cox, S. (2002). The effects of organizational and individual factors on occupational accidents. *Journal of Occupational and Organizational Psychology*, 75, 473–88.

Olszewski, P., & Mokhtarian, P. (1994). Telecommuting frequency and impacts for state of California employees. *Technology Forecasting and Social Change*, 45, 275–86.

Omoto, A. M., & Borgida, E. (1988). Guess who might be coming to dinner? Personal involvement and racial stereotyping. *Journal of Experimental Social Psychology*, 24, 571–93.

Ones, D. S., & Anderson, N. (2002). Gender and ethnic group differences on personality scales in selection: Some British data. *Journal of Occupational and Organizational Psychology*, 75(3), 255–76.

Organ, D. W., & Ryan, K. (1995). A meta-analytic review of attitudinal and dispositional predictors of organisational citizenship behavior. *Personnel Psychology, 48*, 775–802.

Paas, F. G. W. C., Camp, G., & R., R. (2001). Instructional compensation for age-related cognitive declines: Effects of goal specificity in maze learning. *Journal of Educational Psychology, 93*, 181–6.

Parasuraman, R., & Mouloua. M. (Eds.). (1996). *Automation and human performance.* Hillsdale, NJ: Erlbaum.

Parasuraman, R., & Riley, V. A. (1997). Humans and automation: Use, misuse, disuse, abuse. *Human Factors, 39*, 230–53.

Park, D. C. (1994). Aging, cognition, and work. *Human Performance, 7*, 181–205.

Parker, S., Axtell, C., & Turner, N. (2001). Designing a safer workplace: Importance of job autonomy, communication quality, and supportive supervisors. *Journal of Occupational Health Psychology, 6*, 211–28.

Parker, S. K., & Sprigg, C. A. (1999). Minimizing strain and maximizing learning: The role of job demands, job control, and proactive personality. *Journal of Applied Psychology, 84*, 925–39.

Parker, S. K., & Wall, T. D. (2001). Work design: Learning from the past and mapping a new terrain. In N. Anderson, D. S. Ones, H. K. Sinangil, & C. Viswesvaran (Eds.), *Handbook of industrial, work and organizational psychology* (Vol. 1, pp. 91–109). Thousand Oaks, CA: Sage.

Parker, S. K., Wall, T. D., & Jackson, P. R. (1997). "That's not my job: Developing flexible employee work orientations. *Academy of Management Journal, 40*, 899–929.

Parkes, K. R. (1994). Personality and coping as moderators of work stress processes: Models, methods and measures. *Work & Stress, 8*, 110–29.

Patterson, F. (Ed.). (2001). Emerging issues and future trends in work psychology. *Journal of Occupational and Organizational Psychology, 74(4)*, 379–562.

Patterson, M., West, M., Lawthom, R., & Nickell, S. (1998). *Issues in people management.* IPD Report No 22. London: Chartered Institute for Personnel and Development.

Payne, J. W., Bettman. J. R., & Johnson, E. J. (1993). *The adaptive decision maker.* Cambridge: Cambridge University Press.

Payne, R. (1988). Individual differences in the study of occupational stress. In C. L. Cooper & R. Payne (Eds.), *Causes, coping and consequences of stress at work* (pp. 209–32). Chichester, UK: John Wiley.

Pazy, A. (1994). Cognitive schemata of professional obsolescence. *Human Relations, 47*, 1167–99.

Pazy, A. (1996). Concept and career-stage differentiation in obsolescence research. *Journal of Organizational Behavior, 17*, 59–78.

Pazy, A. (2004). Updating in response to the experience of lacking knowledge. *Applied Psychology: An International Review, 53*, 436–52.

Pearce, J. L., & Porter, L. W. (1986). Employee responses to formal appraisal feedback. *Journal of Applied Psychology, 71*, 211–18.

Peiró, J. M. (1999). El modelo AMIGO: Marco contextualizador del desarrollo y la gestión de recursos humanos en las organizaciones. *Papeles del Psicólogo, 72*, 3–15.

Peiró, J. M. (2000). Assessment of psychosocial risks and prevention strategies: The AMIGO model as the basis of the prevenlab/Psychosocial methodology. *Psychology in Spain, 4*, 139–66, www. psychologyinspain.com/content/full/2000/12frame.htm

Peiró, J. M., González-Romá, V., & Cañero, J. (1999). Survey feedback as a tool for changing managerial culture. Focusing on users' interpretations. A case study. *European Journal of Work and Organizational Psychology, 8*, 537–50.

Pérez, M. P., Sanchez, A. M., & de Luis Carnicer, M. P. (2002). Benefits and barriers of telework: perception differences of human resources managers according to company's operations strategy. *Technovation, 22*, 775–83.

Perry, E. L., Davis-Blake, A., & Kulik, C. T. (1994). Explaining gender-based selection decisions: A synthesis of contextual and cognitive approaches. *Academy of Management Review, 19*, 786–820.

Perry Wooten, L., & Hayes James, E. (2005). Challenges of organisational learning: Perpetuation of discrimination against employees with disabilities. *Behavioural Sciences and the Law, 23*, 123–41.

Peter, R., Geissler, H., & Siegrist, J. (1998). Associations of effort–reward imbalance at work and reported symptoms in different groups of male and female public transport workers. *Stress Medicine, 14*, 175–82.

Peter, R., & Siegrist, J. (1997). Chronic work stress, sickness absence, and hypertension in middle managers: general or specific sociological explanations? *Social Science & Medicine, 45*, 1111–20.

Peteraf, M., & Shanley, M. (1997). Getting to know you: A theory of strategic group identity. *Strategic Management Journal, 18* (Summer Special Issue), 165–86.

Peters, L. H., Hartke, D. D., & Pohlmann, J. T. (1985). Fiedler's contingency theory of leadership: An application of the meta-analysis procedures of Schmidt and Hunter. *Psychological Bulletin, 97*, 274–85.

Peters, P., Tijdens, K. G., & Wetzels, C. (2004). Employees' opportunities, preferences, and practices in telecommuting adoption. *Information and Management, 41*, 469–82.

Peterson, S. J., & Spiker, B. K. (2005). Positive contributory value of older workers: A positive psychology perspective. *Organizational Dynamics 34*, 153–67.

Pettigrew, T. F. (1997). Generalized intergroup contact effects on prejudice. *Personality and Social Psychology Bulletin, 23*, 173–85.

Pettigrew, T. F. (1998). Intergroup contact theory. *Annual Review of Psychology, 49*, 65–85.

Pettitrew, T. F., & Martin, J. (1987). Shaping the organisational context for Black American inclusion. *Journal of Social Issues, 43*, 41–78.

Pettigrew, T. F., & Tropp, L. R. (2004). A meta-analytic test of intergroup contact theory. Manuscript submitted for publication.

Picard, R. W. (1997). *Affective computing.* Cambridge, MA: The MIT Press.

Picard, R. W., & Healey, J. (1997). Affective wearables. *Personal Technologies, 1*, 231–40.

Picot, A., Reichwald, R., & Wigand, R. T. (2001). *Die grenzenlose Unternehmung.* Gabler, Wiesbaden.

Pieper, M., & Hermsdorf, D. (1997). BSCW for disabled teleworkers: Usability evaluation and interface adaptation of and internet-based cooperation environment. *Computer Networks and ISDN Systems, 29*, 1479–87.

Pierce, C. L., & Sims, H. P. (2000). Shared leadership: Toward a multi-level theory of leadership. *Team Development, 7*, 115–39.

Pierce, J. L., & Newstrom, J. W. (2003). *Leaders & the leadership process: Readings, self-assessments & applications*. New York: McGraw-Hill/Irwin.

Pinder, C. C. (1998). *Work motivation in organizational behavior*. Upper Saddle River, NJ: Prentice-Hall.

Ployhart, R. E., & Harold, C. M. (2004). The Applicant Attribution–Reaction Theory (AART): An integrative theory of applicant attributional processing. *International Journal of Selection and Assessment, 12(1)*, 84–98.

Ployhart, R. E., & Ryan, A. M. (1997). Toward an explanation of applicant reactions: An examination of organizational justice and attribution frameworks. *Organizational Behavior and Human Decision Processes, 72*, 308–35.

Ployhart, R. E., & Ryan, A. M. (1998). Applicants' reactions to the fairness of selection procedures: The effects of positive rule violation and time of measurement. *Journal of Applied Psychology, 83*, 3–16.

Ployhart, R. E., Ryan, A. M., & Bennett, M. (1999). Explanations for selection decisions: Applicants' reactions to informational and sensitivity features of explanations. *Journal of Applied Psychology, 84*, 87–106.

Pomfrett, S. M., Olphert, C. W., & Eason, K. D. (1985). Work organisation implications of word processing. In B. Shackel (Ed.), *Human–computer interaction* (pp. 847–54). Amsterdam: Elsevier.

Popper, K. (1991). *The poverty of historicism*. London: Routledge. (First published 1957.)

Popuri, Y., & Bhat, C. R. (2003). On modeling choice and frequency of home-based telecommuting. *Transportation Research Record, 1858*, 55–60.

Porac, J. F., & Thomas, H. (1990). Taxonomic mental models in competitor definition. *Academy of Management Review, 15*, 224–40.

Porac, J. F., & Thomas, H. (1994). Cognitive categorization and subjective rivalry among retailers in a small city. *Journal of Applied Psychology, 79*, 54–66.

Porac, J. F., & Thomas, H. (2002). Managing cognition and strategy: Issues, trends and future directions. In A. Pettigrew, H. Thomas, & R. Whittington (Eds.), *Handbook of strategy and management*. London: Sage.

Porac, J. F., Thomas, H., & Baden-Fuller, C. (1989). Competitive groups as cognitive communities: The case of Scottish knitwear manufacturers. *Journal of Management Studies, 26*, 397–416.

Porac, J. F., Thomas, H., Wilson, F., Paton, D., & Kanfer, A. (1995). Rivalry and the industry model of Scottish knitwear producers. *Administrative Science Quarterly, 40*, 203–27.

Porac, J. F., Ventresca, M. J., & Mishina, Y. (2002). Interorganizational cognition and interpretation. In J. A. C. Baum (Ed.), *The Blackwell companion to organizations*. Oxford: Blackwell.

Porras, J. I., & Robertson, P. J. (1992). Organizational development: Theory, practice, and research. In M. D. Dunnette & L. M. Hough (Eds.), *Handbook of industrial & organizational psychology* (pp. 719–822). Palo Alto, CA: Consulting Psychologists Press.

Porras, J. I., & Silvers, R. C. (1991). Organisation development and transformation. *Annual Review of Psychology, 42*, 51–78.

Porter, M. E. (1980). *Competitive strategy: Techniques for analyzing industries and competitors*. New York: Free Press.

Porter, M. E. (1981). The contributions of industrial organization to strategic management. *Academy of Management Review*, *6*, 609–20.

Porter, M. E. (1985). *Competitive analysis*. New York: Free Press.

Poulton, E. C. (1970). *Environment and human efficiency*. Springfield, IL: Thomas.

Powell, A., Piccoli, G., & Ives, B. (2004). Virtual teams: A review of current literature and directions for future research. *The DATA BASE for Advances in Information Systems*, *35*, 6–36.

Preece, J., Rogers, Y., Sharp, H., Bunyon, D., Holland, S., & Carey, T. (1994). *Human–computer interaction*. Wokingham: Addison-Wesley.

Premack, S. Z., & Wanous, J. P. (1985). A meta-analysis of realistic job preview experiments. *Journal of Applied Psychology*, *70*, 706–19.

Price, H. E. (1985). The allocation of functions in systems. *Human Factors*, *27*, 33–45.

Primoff, E. S., & Eyde, L. D. (1988). Job element analysis. In S. Gael (Ed.), *The job analysis handbook for business, industry and government* (Vol. 2, pp. 807–24). New York: Wiley.

Prinzel, L. J., Scerbo, M. W., Freeman, F. G., & Mikulka, P. J. (1995). A bio-cybernetic system for adaptive automation. *Proceedings of the Human Factors and Ergonomics Society 39th Annual Meeting*, 1365–9.

Pritchard, R. D., Jones, S. D., Roth, P. L., Stuebing, K. K., & Ekeberg, S. E. (1988). Effects of group feedback, goal setting, and incentives on organzational productivity. *Journal of Applied Psychology*, *73*, 337–58.

Probst, T. M., Brubaker, T. L., & Barsotti, A. (2006). Organizational injury rate underreporting: The moderating effect of organizational safety climate. Paper presented to the Society of Industrial and Organizational Psychology, Dallas, Texas.

Prooijen, J. -W. van, Van den Bos, K., & Wilke, H. A. M. (2004). Group belongingness and procedural justice: Social inclusion and exclusion by peers affects the psychology of voice. *Journal of Personality and Social Psychology*, *87*, 66–79.

Pulakos, E. D., Arad, S., Donavan, M. A., & Plamondon, K. E. (2000). Adaptability in the workplace: Development of a taxonomy of adaptive performance. *Journal of Applied Psychology*, *85*, 612–24.

Quick, J. C., Quick, J., Nelson, D. L., & Hurrell, J. J. (1997). *Preventive stress management in organizations*. Washington, DC: American Psychological Association.

Raabe, B., Frese, M., & Beehr, T. A. (2007). Action regulation theory and careers: Antecedents and consequences of career self-management behaviors. *Journal of Vocational Behavior*, *70*, 297–311.

Raghuram, S., London, M., & Larsen, H. H. (2001). Flexible employment practices in Europe: country versus culture. *International Journal of Human Resource Management*, *12*, 738–53.

Raghuram, S., Wiesenfeld, B., & Garud, R. (2003). Technology enabled work: The role of self-efficacy in determining telecommuter adjustment and structuring behaviour. *Journal of Vocational Behavior*, *63*, 180–9.

Ragins, B. R. (1999). Gender and mentoring relationships: A review and research agenda for the next decade. In G. N. Powell (Ed.), *Handbook of gender and work* (pp. 347–70). Thousand Oaks, CA: Sage.

Ragins, B. R., & Sundstrom, E. (1989). Gender and power in organisations: A longitudinal perspective. *Psycholgical Bulletin*, *105*, 51–88.

Rasmussen, J. (1986). *Human information processing and human machine interaction.* Amsterdam: North Holland.

Rasmussen, J. (1990). Human error and the problem of causality in analysis of accidents. *Philosophical Transactions of the Royal Society London B, 327,* 449–62.

Rasmussen, J., & Jensen, A. (1974). Mental procedures in real-life tasks: A case study of electronic trouble-shooting. *Ergonomics, 17,* 293–307.

Raymark, P. H., Schmit, M. J., & Guion, R. M. (1997). Identifying potential useful personality constructs for employee selection. *Personnel Psychology, 50,* 723–36.

Reason, J. T. (1990). *Human error.* Cambridge: Cambridge University Press.

Reason, J. T. (1997). *Managing the risks of organizational accidents.* Aldershot: Ashgate.

Reason, J. T., Parker, D., & Lawton, R. (1998). Organizational controls and safety: The varieties of rule-related behaviour. *Journal of Occupational and Organizational Psychology, 71,* 289–304.

Ree, M. J., & Carretta, T. R. (1991). Predicting training success: Not much more than g. *Personnel Psychology, 44,* 321–32.

Ree, M. J., & Carretta, T. R. (1998). General cognitive ability and occupational performance. In C. L. Cooper & I. T. Robertson (Eds.), *International review of industrial and organizational psychology* (Vol. 13, pp. 159–84). London: John Wiley.

Reger, R. K., & Huff, A. S. (1993). Strategic groups: A cognitive perspective. *Strategic Management Journal, 14,* 103–24.

Reger, R. K., & Palmer, T. B. (1996). Managerial categorization of competitors: Using old maps to navigate new environments. *Organization Science, 7,* 22–39.

Reger, R. K., Gustafson, L. T., DeMarie, S. M., & Mullane, J. V. (1994). Reframing the organization: Why implementing total quality is easier said than done. *Academy of Management Review, 19,* 565–84.

Rehmann, J. T., Stein, E. S., & Rosenberg, B. L. (1983). Subjective pilot workload assessment. *Human Factors, 25,* 297–307.

Reid, G. B., & Nygren, T. E. (1988). The subjective workload assessment technique: A scaling procedure for measuring mental workload. In P. A. Hancock & N. Meshkati (Eds.), *Human mental workload.* Amsterdam: North-Holland.

Reilly, R. R., & Chao, C. T. (1982). Validity and fairness of some alternative employee selection procedures. *Personnel Psychology, 35,* 1–62.

Reiss, S. (2000). *Who am I? – The 16 basic desires that motivate our actions and determine our personality.* New York: Tarcher/Putnam.

Reynolds, P. D., Bygrave, W. D., Autio, E., Cox, L. W., & Hay, M. (2002). *Global entrepreneurship monitor – 2002 executive report.* London: London Business School.

Rheinberg, F. (2004). *Motivation (5. Aufl.).* Stuttgart: Kohlhammer.

Rheinberg, F., Vollmeyer, R., & Engeser, S. (2003). Die Erfassung des Flow-Erlebens (The measurement of flow). In J. Stiensmeier-Pelster & F. Rheinberg (Eds.), *Diagnostik von Motivation und Selbstkonzept* (p. 261–79). Göttingen: Hogrefe.

Rice, R. E. (1992). Task analyzability, use of new medium and effectiveness: A multi-site exploration of media richness. *Organization Science, 3,* 475–500.

Rice, R. W. (1978). Construct validity of the least preferred co-worker score. *Psychological Bulletin, 85,* 1199–1237.

Richter, A., Van Dick, R., & West, M. (in press). The relationship between group and organizational identification and effective intergroup relations, *Academy of Management Journal*.

Rieger, C. A., & Greenstein, J. S. (1982). The allocation of tasks between the human and computer in automated systems. In *Proceedings of the IEEE 1982 International Conference on Cybernetics and Society*, Seattle, WA, pp. 204–8.

Rifkin, J. (1995). *The end of work*. New York: Jeremy Tarcher/Putnam.

Rijk, A. E. de, Blanc, P. M. Le, Schaufeli, W. B., & Jonge, J. de (1998). Active coping and need for control as moderators of the Job Demand–Control Model: Effects on burnout. *Journal of Occupational and Organizational Psychology*, *71*, 1–18.

Riordan, C. M., Schaffer, B. S., & Stewart, M. M. (2005). Relational demography within groups: Through the lens of discrimination. In R. L. Dipboye & A. Colella (Eds.), *Discrimination at work* (pp. 37–61). Mahwah, NJ: Lawrence Erlbaum.

Riordan, C. M., & Shore, L. M. (1997). Demographic diversity and employee attitudes. An empirical examination of relational demography within work units. *Journal of Applied Psychology*, *82*, 342–58.

Riordan, C. M., & Shore, L. M. (2000). Relational demography within groups: Past developments, contradictions, and new directions. *Research in Personnel and Human Resources Management*, *19*, 131–73.

Rissler, A., & Jacobson, L. (1987). Cognitive efficiency during high workload in final system testing of a large computer system. In H. J. Bullinger & B. Shackel (Eds.), *Human computer interaction (Interact '87)*. Amsterdam: Elsevier-North Holland.

Robertson, I. T. (1993). Personality assessment and personnel selection. *European Review of Applied Psychology*, *43*, 187–94.

Robertson, I. T., & Smith, J. M. (1989). Personnel selection. In J. M. Smith & I. T. Robertson (Eds.), *Advances in Selection and Assessment*. Chichester, UK: John Wiley.

Robinson, S. L., & Morrison, E. W. (2000). The development of psychological contract breach and violation: a longitudinal study. *Journal of Organizational Behavior, 21(5)*, 525–46.

Rodger, A., & Cavanagh, P. (1962). Training occupational psychologists. *Occupational Psychology*, *36*, 82–8.

Rodgers, R., & Hunter, J. E. (1991). Impact of management by objectives on organizational productivity. *Journal of Applied Psychology, 76(2)*, 322–36.

Roe, R. A. (2002). What makes a competent psychologist? *European Psychologist, 7(3)*, 192–202.

Rogelberg, S. G., Barnes-Farrell, J. L., & Lowe, C. A. (1992). The stepladder technique: An alternative group structure facilitating effective group decision making. *Journal of Applied Psychology*, *77*, 730–7.

Rogers, C. (1957). The necessary and sufficient conditions of therapeutic personality change. *Journal of Counseling Psychology*, *21*.

Rogers, W. A., Lamson, N., & Rousseau, G. K. (2000). Warning research: An integrative perspective, *Human Factors, 42(1)*, 102–39.

Rothlauf, J. (1999). *Interkulturelles Management*. München/Wien: R. Oldenbourg Verlag.

Rotter, J. (1966). Generalised expectancies for internal versus external locus of control. *Psychological Monographs*, *80*, whole no. 609.

Rouse, W. B. (1981). Human–computer interaction in the control of dynamic systems. *ACM Computing Surveys, 13*, 71–99.

Rouse, W. B. (1988). Adaptive aiding for human–computer control. *Human Factors, 30*, 431–43.

Rousseau, D. M. (1995). *Psychological contracts in organizations: Understanding written and unwritten agreements*. Thousand Oaks, CA: Sage.

Rousseau, D. M. (2001). Schema, promise and mutuality: The building blocks of the psychological contract. *Journal of Occupational and Organizational Psychology, 74*, 511–41.

Ruderman, M. N., Ohlott, P. J., Panzer, K., & King, S. N. (2002). Benefit of multiple roles for managerial women. *Academy of Management Journal, 45*, 369–86.

Rudman, L. A. (1998). Self-promotion as a risk factor for women: The costs and benefits of counter stereotypical impression management. *Journal of Personality and Social Psychology, 74*, 629–45.

Rush, M. C., Thomas, J. C., & Lord, R. G. (1977). Implicit leadership theory: A potential threat to the internal validity of leader behavior questionnaires. *Organizational Behavior and Human Performance, 20*, 93–110.

Rutte, C. G. (2003). Social loafing in teams. In M. A. West, D. Tjosvold, & K. G. Smith (Eds.), *International handbook of organizational teamwork and cooperative working* (pp. 361–78). Chichester, UK: Wiley.

Rutter, M., & Rutter, M. (1992). *Developing minds. Challenge and continuity across the life span*. London: Penguin Books.

Ryan, A. M., & Ployhart, R. E. (2000). Applicants' perceptions of selection procedures and decisions: A critical review and agenda for the future. *Journal of Management, 26*, 565–606.

Ryan, A. M., & Sackett, P. R. (1987). Pre–employment honesty testing: Fakability, reactions of test takers, and company image. *Journal of Business and Psychology, 1*, 248–56.

Rybowiak, V., Garst, H., Frese, M., & Batinic, B. (1999). Error orientation questionnaire (EOQ): Reliability, validity, and different language equivalence. *Journal of Organizational Behaviour, 20*, 527–47.

Rynes, S. (1993). Who's selecting whom? Effects of selection practices on applicant attitudes and behavior. In N. Schmitt & W. Borman (Eds.), *Personnel selection in organizations*. San Francisco: Jossey-Bass.

Rynes, S. L., & Connerley, M. L. (1993). Applicant reactions to alternative selection procedures. *Journal of Business and Psychology, 7(3)*, 261–77.

Rynes, S. L., Gerhart, B., & Parks, L. (2005). Personnel psychology: Performance evaluation and pay for performance. *Annual Review of Psychology, 56*, 571–600.

Sackett, P. R., DuBois, C. L. Z., & Noe, A. W. (1999). Tokenism in performance evaluations: The effects of work group representation on male–female and white–black differences in performance ratings. *Journal of Applied Psychology, 76*, 263–7.

Sackett, P. R., & Mullen, E. J. (1993). Beyond formal experimental design: Towards an expanded view of the training evaluation process. *Personnel Psychology, 46*, 613–27.

Sadler-Smith, E., Down, S., & Lean, J. (2000). "Modern" learning methods: Rhethoric and reality. *Personal Review, 29*, 474–90.

Salas, E., & Cannon-Bowers, J. A. (2001). The science of training: A decade of progress. *Annual Review of Psychology, 52*, 471–99.

Salgado, J. F. (1998). The Big Five personality dimensions and job performance in army and civil occupations: A European perspective. *Human Performance, 11*, 271–88.

Salgado, J. F. (1999). Personnel selection methods. In C. L. Cooper & I. T. Robertson (Eds.), *International review of industrial and organizational psychology* (Vol. 14, pp. 1–53). Chichester, UK: Wiley.

Salgado, J. F. (2002). The Big Five personality dimensions and counterproductive behaviors. *International Journal of Selection and Assessment, 10*, 117–25.

Salgado, J. F. (2003). Predicting job performance using FFM and non-FFM personality measures. *Journal of Occupational and Organizational Psychology, 76*, 323–46.

Salgado, J. F., & Anderson, N. (2002). Cognitive and GMA testing in the European Community: Issues and evidence. *Human Performance, 15(1–2)*, 75–96.

Salgado, J. F., & Anderson, N. (2003). Validity generalization of GMA tests across countries in the European Community. *European Journal of Work and Organizational Psychology, 12*, 1–18.

Salgado, J. F., Anderson, N., Moscoso, S., Bertua, C., & De Fruyt, F. (2003). International validity generalization of GMA and cognitive abilities: A European Community meta-analysis. *Personnel Psychology, 56*, 573–605.

Salgado, J. F., Anderson, N., Moscoso, S., Bertua, C., De Fruyt, F., & Rolland, J. P. (2003). A meta-analytic study of general mental ability validity for different occupations in the European Community. *Journal of Applied Psychology, 88(6)*, 1068–81.

Salgado, J. F., & De Fruyt, F. (2005). Personality in industrial, work and organizational psychology. In A. Evers, N. Anderson, & O. Smit–Voskuyl (eds.), *Handbook of Selection*. Oxford: Blackwell.

Salgado, J. F., & Moscoso, S. (2002). Comprehensive meta-analysis of the construct validity of the employment interview. *European Journal of Work and Organizational Psychology, 11*, 299–324.

Salgado, J. F., Viswesvaran, C., & Ones, D. S., (2001). Predictors used for personnel selection: An overview of constructs, methods, and techniques. In N. Anderson, D. Ones, H. K. Sinangil, & C. Viswesvaran (eds.), *Handbook of industrial, work, and organizational psychology*, Vol. 1. London: Sage.

Salminen, S., Saari, J., Saarela, K. L., & Rasanen, T. (1993). Organizational factors influencing occupational accidents. *Scandanavian Journal Work Environ Health, 19*, 352–57.

Salminen, S., & Tallberg, T. (1996). Human errors in fatal and serious occupational accidents in Finland. *Ergonomics, 39*, 980–8.

Salmon, P. (2001). Effects of physical exercise on anxiety, depression and sensitivity to stress: a unifying theory. *Clinical Psychology Review, 21*, 33–61.

Salomon, I. (1998). Technological change and social forecasting: the case of telecommuting as a travel substitute. *Transportation Research Part C, 6*, 17–45.

Salomon, I., & Salomon, M. (1984). Telecommuting: the employees' perspective. *Technological Forecasting and Social Change, 25*, 15–28.

Salthouse, T. A., Hambrick, D. Z., Kristen, E. L., & Dell, T. C. (1996). Determinants of adult differences in synthetic work performance. *Journal of Experimental Psychology: Applied, 2*, 305–29.

Sampson, E. E. (1999). *Dealing with difference*. Fort Worth, TX: Harcourt Brace.

Sanchez, J. I. (2000). Adapting work analysis to a fast-paced electronic business world. *International Journal of Selection and Assessment, 8*, 207–15.

Sanchez, J. I., & Levine, E. L. (1999). Is job analysis dead, misunderstood, or both? New forms of work analysis and design. In A. Kraut & A. Korman (Eds.), *Evolving practices in human resource management*. San Francisco: Jossey-Bass.

Sanchez, J. I., & Levine, E. L. (2001). The analysis of work in the 20th and 21st centuries. In N. Anderson, D. S. Ones, H. K. Sinangil, & C. Viswesvaran (Eds.), *Handbook of industrial and organizational psychology: Vol. 1, Organizational psychology* (pp. 71–89). London: Sage.

Sarter, N. B., Woods, D. D., & Billings, C. E. (1997). Automation surprises. In G. Salvendy (Ed.), *Handbook of human factors and ergonomics* (2nd edn.). New York: Wiley.

Sauer J., & Rüttinger B. (2004). Environmental conservation in the domestic domain: The influence of technical design features and person-based factors. *Ergonomics, 47(10)*, 1053–72.

Sauer, J., Wiese, B. S., & Rüttinger, B. (2004). Ecological performance of electrical consumer products: The influence of automation and information-based measures. *Applied Ergonomics, 35(1)*, 37–47.

Saunders, C., Van Slyke, C., & Vogel, D. R. (2004). My time or yours? Managing time visions in global virtual teams. *Academy of Management Executive, 18*, 19–31.

Schabracq, M. J., & Cooper, C. L. (2001). *Stress als keuze. Werkboek persoonlijk stress-management* (Stress as a choice: workbook for personal stress management). Schiedam: Scriptum.

Schabracq, M. J., Maassen van den Brink, H., Groot, W., Janssen, P., & Houkes, I. (2000). *De prijs van stress* (The price of stress). Amsterdam: Welboom-Elsevier Reed.

Schaffers, H. (2005). Innovation and systems change: The example of mobile, collaborative workplaces. *AI & Society, 19*, 334–47.

Schaufeli, W. B. (2005). The future of occupational health psychology. *Applied Psychology: An International Review, 53*, 502–17.

Schaufeli, W. B., & Bakker, A. B. (2004). Job demands, job resources and their relationship with burnout and engagement: A multi-sample study. *Journal of Organizational Behavior, 25*, 293–315.

Schaufeli, W. B., & Enzmann, D. U. (1998). *The burnout companion to study and practice: A critical analysis*. London: Taylor & Francis.

Schaufeli, W. B., Salanova, M., Gonzalez–Roma. V., & Bakker, A. B. (2002). The measurement of engagement and burnout: A confirmative analytic approach. *Journal of Happiness Studies, 3*, 71–92.

Schaufeli, W. B., Taris, T. W., Le Blanc, P. Peeters, M. Bakker, A., & De Jonge, J. (2001). Maakt arbeid gezond? Op zoek naar de bevlogen werknemer (Does work make one happy? In search of the engaged worker). *De Psycholoog, 36*, 422–8.

Schein, E. H (1996), Three cultures of management: The key to organizational learning, *Sloan Management Review, 38*, 19–20.

Schein, E. H. (1990). Organisational culture. *American Psychologist, 45*, 109–19.

Schein, E. H. (1999). *Process Consultation Revised, Building the Helping Relationship*. Reading: Addison-Wesley.

Schellekens, J. M. H., Sijtsma, G. J., Vegter, E., & Meijman, T. F. (2000). Immediate and delayed after-effects of long lasting mentally demanding work. *Biological Psychology, 53*, 37–56.

Schiffman, S. S., Reynolds, M. L., & Young, F. W. (1981). *Introduction to Multidimensional Scaling*. New York: Academic Press.

Schinkel, S., Van Dierendonck, D., & Anderson, N. (2004). The impact of selection encounters on applicants: An experimental study into feedback effects after a negative selection decision. *International Journal of Selection and Assessment, 12(1–2)*, 197–205.

Schippmann, J. S. (1999). *Strategic job modeling: Working at the core of integrated human resources*. Mahwah, NJ: Lawrence Erlbaum Associates.

Schippmann, J. S., Ash, R. A., Battista, M., Carr, L., Eyde, L. D., Hesketh, B., et al. (2000). The practice of competency modelling. *Personnel Psychology, 53*, 703–39.

Schmalt, H.-D. (1999). Assessing the achievement motive using the Grid technique. *Journal of Research in Personality, 33*, 109–30.

Schmidt, F. L., & Hunter, J. (1977). Development of a general solution to the problem of validity generalization. *Journal Applied Psychology, 62*, 529–40.

Schmidt, F. L., & Hunter, J. E. (1998). The validity and utility of selection methods in personnel psychology: Practical and theoretical implications of 85 years of research findings. *Psychological Bulletin, 124*, 262–74.

Schmidt, R., & Wolf, G. (Eds.). (1997). *Polikom Konferenz*. Berlin: Projekttraeger Informationstechnik des BMBF bei der DLR.

Schmidt-Brasse, U. (2006). Going International – Auswirkungen auf die Arbeit von Organisationsberatern. In E. Bamberg, K. Hänel, & J. Schmidt (Eds.), *Beratung – counseling – consulting. Anforderungen und Kompetenzentwicklung bei der Organisationsberatung*. Göttingen: Hogrefe.

Schmitt, N. (1976). Social and situational determinants of interview decisions: Implications for the employment interview. *Personnel Psychology, 29*, 79–101.

Schmitt, N., & Chan, D. (1998). *Personnel selection: A theoretical approach*. Thousand Oaks, CA: Sage.

Schmitt, N., Ford, J. K., & Stults, D. M. (1986). Changes in self-perceived ability as a function of performance in an assessment centre. *Journal of Occupational Psychology, 59*, 327–35.

Schmitt, N., Gooding, R. Z., Noe, R. A., & Kirsch, M. (1984). Meta-analysis of validity studies published between 1964 and 1982 and the investigation of study characteristics. *Personnel Psychology, 37*, 407–22.

Schneider, B. (1987). The people make the place. *Personnel Psychology, 40*, 437–53.

Schneider, B. S., & Konz, A. M. (1989). Strategic job analysis. *Human Resource Management, 28*, 51–63.

Schneider, B., Kristof-Brown, A. L., Goldstein, H. W., & Smith, D. B. (1997). What is this thing called fit? In N. Anderson & P. Herriot (Eds.), *International handbook of selection and assessment*. Chichester, UK: Wiley.

Schönpflug, W. (1983). Coping efficiency and situational demands. In G. R. J. Hockey (Ed.), *Stress and fatigue in human performance*. Chichester, UK: Wiley.

Schönpflug, W. (1985). Goal-directed behavior as a source of stress: Psychological origins and consequences of inefficiency. In M. Frese & J. Sabini (Eds.), *The concept of action in psychology* (pp. 172–88). Mahwah, NJ: Lawrence Erlbaum.

Schooler, C., Mulatu, M. S., & Oates, G. (2004). Occupational self-direction, intellectual functioning, and self-directed orientation in older workers: findings and implications for individuals and societies. *American Journal of Sociology 110*, 161–97.

Schraeder, M., & Self, D. R. (2003), Enhancing the success of mergers and acquisitions: An organizational culture perspective. *Management Decision, 41(5)*, 511–22.

Schroth, H. A., & Shah, P. P. (2000). Procedures: Do we really want to know about them? An Examination of the effects of procedural justice on self-esteem. *Journal of Applied Psychology, 85(3)*, 462–71.

Schuler, H. (1993). Social validity of selection situations: A concept and some empirical results. In H. Schuler, C. J. L. Farr, & M. Smith (Eds.). *Personnel selection and assessment: individual and organizational perspectives.* Mahwah, NJ: Lawrence Earlbaum.

Schuler, R., & Jackson, S. (2001). HR issues and activities in mergers and acquisitions, *European Management Journal, 19(3)*, 239–53.

Schulte, C. (2005). Arbeitszufriedenheit über die Lebensspanne (Job satisfaction over the life-span). Lengerich: Pabst.

Schultz, P., & Schönpflug, W. (1982). Regulatory activity during states of stress. In W. Krohne & L. Laux (Eds.), *Achievement, stress and anxiety.* Washington, DC: Hemisphere.

Schwenk, C. R. (1984). Cognitive simplification processes in strategic decision making. *Strategic Management Journal, 5*, 111–28.

Seligman, M. E. P., & Csikszentmihalyi, M. (2000). Positive psychology: An introduction. *American Psychologist, 55*, 5–14.

Selye, H. (1956). *The stress of life.* New York: McGraw-Hill.

Semini, G., & Glendon, A. I. (1973). Polarization and the established group. *British Journal of Social and Clinical Psychology, 12*, 113–21.

Semmer, N. (2003). Individual differences, work stress and health. In M. J. Schabracq, J. A. M. Winnubst, & C. L Cooper (Eds.), *Handbook of work and health psychology* (2nd edn., pp. 51–86). Chichester, UK: Wiley.

Semmer, N. (2003). Job stress interventions and organization of work. In J. C. Quick & L. E. Tetrick (Eds.), *Handbook of occupational health psychology* (pp. 325–53), Washington, DC: American Psychological Association.

Senior, B. (2002). *Organisational change* (2nd edn.). Harlow: Pearson Education.

Shackel, B. (1981). The concept of usability. In *Proceedings of IBM Software and Information Usability Symposium* (pp. 1–30). Ploughkeepsie, NY.

Shackel, B. (1986). Ergonomics in design for usability. In M. D. Harrison and A. F. Monk (Eds.), *Proceedings of the 2nd Conference of the BCS HCI Specialist Group.* Cambridge, UK: Cambridge University Press.

Shackleton, V. J., & Newell, S. (1997). International selection and assessment. In N. Anderson & P. Herriot (Eds.), *International handbook of selection and assessment.* Chichester, UK: Wiley.

Shamir, B., House, R. J., & Arthur, M. B. (1993). The motivational effects of charismatic leadership: A self-concept based theory. *Organization Science, 4*, 577–94.

Shane, S. (1993). Cultural influences on national rates of innovation. *Journal of Business Venturing, 8*, 59–73.

Shannon, H. S., Mayr, J., & Haines, T. (1997). Overview of the relationship between organizational and workplace factors and injury rataes. *Safety Science, 26*, 201–17.

Sharfman, M. P., & Dean, J. W. (1991). Conceptualizing and measuring the organizational environment: A multidimensional approach. *Journal of Management, 17*, 681–700.

Sharit, J. (1997). Allocation of functions. In G. Salvendy (Ed.), *Handbook of human factors.* New York: Wiley.

Shaw, J. B. (1990). A cognitive categorization model for the study of intercultural management. *Academy of Management Review, 15,* 626–45.

Shebilske, W. L., Jordan, J. A., Goettl, B. P., & Day, E. A. (1999). Cognitive and social influences in training teams for complex skills. *Journal of Experimental Psychology: Applied, 5,* 227–49.

Sheehy, N., & Chapman, A. (1987). Industrial accidents. In C. L. Cooper & I. T. Robertson (Eds.), *International Review of Industrial and Organizational Psychology.* New York: Wiley.

Sheehy, N., & Gallagher, T. (1996). Can virtual organizations be made real? *Psychologist, 9,* 159–62.

Shepherd, A. (2001). *Hierarchical task analysis.* New York: Taylor & Francis.

Sheridan, T. (1980). Computer control and human alienation. *Technology Review, 10,* 61–73.

Sheridan, T. B. (2000). Function allocation: Algorithm, alchemy or apostasy? *International Journal of Human–Computer Studies, 52,* 203–16.

Shimazu, A., Shimazu, M., & Odahara, T. (2005). Divergent effects of active coping on psychological distress in the context of the Job Demands Control Support Model: The roles of job control and social support. *International Journal of Behavioral Medicine, 12,* 192–8.

Shimmin, S., & Wallace, D. (1994). *Fifty years of occupational psychology in Britain.* Leicester: Division and Section of Occupational Psychology, the British Psychological Society.

Shingledecker, C. A. (1987). In-flight workload assessment using embedded secondary radio communications tasks. In A. H. Roscoe (Ed.), *The Practical assessment of pilot workload* (pp. 11–14). AGARD monograph No. 282. Neuilly Sur Seine: AGARD.

SHL. (1998). *Work profiling system: User (analyst's) guide & technical manual.* Thames Ditton, UK: Author.

Shore, L. M., Tetrick, L. E., Coyle-Shapiro, J. A.-M., & Taylor, M. S. (2004). Directions for future research. In J. A.-M. Coyle-Shapiro, L. M. Shore, M. S. Taylor, & L. E. Tetrick (Eds.), *The employment relationship: Examining psychological and contextual perspectives.* Oxford: Oxford University Press.

Shore, M. L., Cleveland, J. N., & Goldberg, C. B. (2003). Work attitudes and decisions as a function of manager age and employee age. *Journal of Applied Psychology, 88,* 529–37.

Short, J., Williams, E., & Christie, B. (1976). *The social psychology of telecommunications.* London: Wiley.

SIBIS. (2003). New eEurope Indicator Handbook. www. sibis–eu.org.

Sidanius, J., Devereus, E., & Pratto, F. (2001). A comparison of symbolic racism theory and social dominance theory as explanations for racial policy attitudes. *The Journal of Social Psychology, 132,* 377–95.

Sieck, W., & Yates, J. F. (1997). Exposition effects on decision making: choice and confidence in choice. *Organizational Behavior and Human Decision Processes, 70,* 207–19.

Siegel, H. P. (2000). Using peer mentors during periods of uncertainty, *Leadership & Organization Development Journal, 21(5),* 243–53.

Siegrist, J. (1996). Adverse health effects of high-effort/low-reward conditions. *Journal of Occupational Health Psychology, 1,* 27–41.

Simon, H. (1996). *Die heimlichen Gewinner* (The secret winners). Frankfurt: Campus.

Simon, H. A. (1955). A behavioral model of rational choice. *Quarterly Journal of Economics, 69,* 99–118.

Simon, H. A. (1956). Rational choice and the structure of the environment. *Psychological Review, 63,* 129–38.

Simon, H. A. (1997). *Administrative behavior* (4th edn.). New York: Macmillan.

Simpson, L., Daws, L., Pini, B., & Wood, L. (2003). Rural telework: Case studies from the Australian outback. *New Technology, Work and Employment, 18,* 115–26.

Sinangil, H. K., & Ones, D. S. (2001). Expatriate management. In N. Anderson, D. S. Ones, H. K. Sinangil, & C. Visvesvaran (Eds.), *Handbook of industrial, work and organizational psychology,* Vol. 1. London: Sage.

Singh, S., & Gupta, B. S. (1977). Motives and agricultural growth. *British Journal of Social and Clinical Psychology, 16,* 189–90.

Sivasubramaniam, N., Murry, W. D., Avolio, B. J., & Jung, D. I. (2002). A longitudinal model of the effects of team leadership and group potency on group performance. *Group & Organization Management, 27,* 66–96.

Smith, M., & Robertson, I. T. (Eds.) (1989). *Advances in selection and assessment.* London: Wiley.

Smith, M., & Robertson, I. T. (Eds.) (1993). *The theory and practice of systematic personnel selection,* 2nd edition. London: Macmillan.

Smith, M., & Smith, P. (2005), *Testing people at work.* Oxford: BPS/Blackwell.

Smith, P. M. (1995). Leadership. In A. S. R. Manstead & M. Hewstone (Eds.), *The Blackwell encyclopedia of social psychology* (S. 358–62). Oxford: Blackwell.

Smith, S. P. C., & Kendall, L. M. (1963). Retranslation of expectations. *Journal of Applied Psychology, 47,* 149–55.

Smither, J. W., London, M., & Reilly, R. R. (2005). Does performance improve following multi-source feedback? A theoretical model, meta-analysis and review of empirical findings. *Personnel Psychology, 58,* 33–66.

Smither, J. W., Reilly, R. R., Millsap, R. E., Pearlman, K., & Stoffey, R. W. (1993). Applicant reactions to selection procedures. *Personnel Psychology, 46,* 49–76.

Soane, E., & Chmiel, N. (1999). *Emotional risk communication and the adoption of safety precautions in a safety-critical workplace.* Proceedings of the British Psychological Socirty Annual Psychology Conference, Belfast.

Soane, E., & Chmiel, N. (2005). Are risk preferences consistent? The influence of decision domain and personality. *Personality & Individual Differences, 38,* 1781–91.

Sonnentag, S., & Kleine, B. M. (2000). Deliberate practice at work: A study with insurance agents. *Journal of Occupational and Organizational Psychology, 73,* 87–102.

Sonnentag, S., Niessen, C., & Ohly, S. (2004). Learning at work: Training and development. In C. L. Cooper & I. T. Robertson (Eds.), *International review of industrial and organizational psychology* (Vol. 19, pp. 249–89). Chichester, UK: Wiley.

Sparrow, P. R. (1996). Too good to be true? *People Management,* 5 Dec., 22–9.

Sparrow, P. R., & Bognano, M. (1993). Competency requirement forecasting: Issues for international selection and assessment. *International Journal of Selection and Assessment, 1,* 50–8.

Sparrow, P. R., & Cooper, C. L. (2003). *The employment relationship: Key challenges for HR.* Oxford: Butterworth Heinemann.

Spataro, Sandra, E., (2005). Diversity in context: How organisational culture shapes reactions to workers with disabilities and others who are demographically different. *Behavioural Sciences and the Law*, *23*, 21–38.

Spector, P. E. (2002). Individual differences in health and well being in organizations. In D. A. Hoffman & L. E. Tetrick (Eds.), *Individual and organizational health*. San Francisco: Jossey Bass.

Spector, P. E., & O'Connell, B. J. (1994). The contribution of personality traits, negative affectivity, locus of control and Type A to the subsequent reports of job stressors and job strain. *Journal of Occupational and Organizational Psychology*, *67*, 1–11.

Spender, J. C. (1989). *Industry recipes: The nature and sources of managerial judgement*. Oxford: Blackwell.

Sperandio, J. (1978). The regulation of working methods as a function of workload among air traffic controllers. *Ergonomics*, *21*, 195–202.

Spinks, W. A., & Wood, J. M. (1996). Implementation of office-based Telecommuting: A Japanese and Canadian Case Study. In The First Asia Pacific DSI conference, Hong Kong, pp. 1057–66.

Stahl, M. J. (1983). Achievement, power, and managerial motivation: Selecting managerial talent with the job choice exercise. *Personnel Psychology*, *36*, 775–89.

Stanney, K. M., Maxey, J., & Salvendy, G. (1997). Socially centred design. In G. Salvendy (Ed.), *Handbook of human factors and ergonomics* (2nd edn.). New York: Wiley.

Staples, S. D., Hulland, J. S., & Higgins, C. A. (1999). Self-efficacy theory explanation for the management of remote workers in virtual organizations. *Organization Science*, *10*, 758–76.

Starbuck, W. H. (1976). Organizations and their environments. In M. D. Dunnette (Ed.), *Handbook of industrial and organizational psychology*. Chicago, IL: Rand McNally.

Stasser, G., & Stewart, D. (1992). Discovery of hidden profiles by decision–making groups: Solving a problem versus making a judgment. *Journal of Personality and Social Psychology*, *63*, 426–34.

Steele, C. M., & Aronson, J. (1995). Stereotype threat and the intellectual test performance of African Americans. *Journal of Personality and Social Psychology*, *69*, 797–811.

Steers, R. M., Mowday, R. T., & Shapiro, D. L. (2004). The future of work motivation theory. *Academy of Management Review*, *29(3)*, 379–87.

Steiner, D. D., & Gilliland, S. W. (1996). Fairness reactions to personnel selection techniques in France and the United States. *Journal of Applied Psychology*, *81*, 134–41.

Steptoe, A. (1983). Stress, helplessness and control: The implications of laboratory studies. *Journal of Psychosomatic Research*, *27*, 361–7.

Sternberg, R. J. (1997). *Thinking styles*. New York: Cambridge University Press.

Sterns, H. L., & Miklos, S. M. (1995). The aging worker in a changing environment: organizational and individual issues. *Journal of Vocational Behavior 47*, 248–68.

Stevens, M. J., & Campion, M. A. (1994). The knowledge, skill, and ability requirements for teamwork: Implications for human resource management. *Journal of Management*, *20*, 503–30.

Stevens, M. J., & Campion, M. A. (1999). Staffing work teams: Development and validation of a selection test for teamwork settings. *Journal of Management*, *25*, 207–28.

Steward, B. (2000). Changing times: The meaning, measurement and use of time in teleworking. *Time and Society*, *9*, 57–74.

Stogdill, R. M. (1948). Personal factors associated with leadership: A survey of the literature. *Journal of Psychology, 25,* 35–71.

Stokes, G. S., Hogan, J. B., & Snell, A. F. (1993). Comparability of incumbent and
applicant samples for the development of biodata keys: The influence of social desir-
ability. *Personnel Psychology, 46,* 739–62.

Stone, D. L., & Jones, G. E. (1997). Perceived Fairness of biodata as a function of the
purpose of the request for information and gender of the applicant. *Journal of Business
and Psychology, 11(3),* 313–23.

Storey, J. (Ed.) (1994). *New wave manufacturing strategies.* London: Paul Chapman.

Straus, S. G., & McGrath, J. E. (1994). Does the medium matter? The interaction of
task type and technology on group performance and member reactions. *Journal of
Applied Psychology, 79,* 87–97.

Strube, M. J., & Garcia, J. E. (1981). A meta-analytic investigation of Fiedler's contingency model of leadership effectiveness. *Psychological Bulletin, 90,* 307–21.

Sturgeon, A. (1996). Telework: threats, risks and solutions. *Information Management
and Computer Security, 4,* 27–38.

Sullivan, C. (2003). What's in a name? Definitions and conceptualisations of teleworking
and homeworking. *New Technology, Work and Employment, 18,* 158–65.

Sullivan, C., & Lewis, S. (2001). Home-based telework, gender and the syncronization
of work and family. *Gender, Work and Organization, 2,* 123–45.

Sullivan, M., Mahmassani, H., & Yen, J. (1993). Choice model of employee participation
in telecommuting under a cost-neutral scenario. *Transportation Research Record, 1413,*
42–8.

Summers, B., Williamson, T., & Read, D. (2004). Does method of acquisition affect the
quality of expert judgment? A comparison of education with on-the-job learning.
Journal of Occupational and Organizational Psychology, 77, 237–58.

Sutcliffe, K. M., & Huber, G. P. (1998). Firm and industry as determinants of
executive perceptions of the environment. *Strategic Management Journal, 19,* 793–
807.

Svenson, O. (1979). Process description of decision making. *Organizational Behaviour
and Human Performance, 23,* 86–122.

Tajfel, H. (1978). Social categorization, social identity, and social comparison. In H.
Tajfel (Ed.), *Differentiation between social groups: Studies in social psychology of intergroup relations* (pp. 61–76). London: Academic Press.

Tajfel, H., & Turner, J. (1979). An integrative theory of intergroup conflict. In W. G.
Austin & S. Worchel (Eds.), *The social psychology of intergroup relations* (pp. 34–47).
Monterey, CA: Brooks/Cole.

Talaga, J., & Beehr, T. A. (1989). Retirement: a psychological perspective. In C. Cooper,
& I. T. Robertson (Eds.), *International Review of Industrial and Organizational Psychology.* Chichester, UK: Wiley.

Tannenbaum, S. I., & Yukl, G. (1992). Training and development in work organizations.
Annual Review of Psychology, 43, 399–441.

Taris, T. W., Kompier, M. A. J., de Lange, A. H., Schaufeli, W. B., & Schreurs, P. J. G.
(2003). Learning new behavior patterns: A longitudinal test of Karasek's active learning
hypothesis among Dutch teachers. *Work and Stress, 17,* 1–20.

Tattersall, A. J., & Fairclough, S. H. (2003). Adaptive automation and modes of control.
In G. R. J. Hockey, A. W. K. Gaillard & O. Burov (Eds.), *Operator functional state:*

The assessment and prediction of human performance degradation in complex tasks. Amsterdam: IOS Press.

Tattersall, A. J., & Foord, P. S. (1996). An experimental evaluation of instantaneous self-assessment as a measure of workload. *Ergonomics, 39,* 740–8.

Tattersall, A. J., & Hockey, G. R. J. (1995). Level of operator control and changes in heart rate variability during simulated flight maintenance. *Human Factors, 37,* 682–98.

Tattersall, A. J., & Morgan, C. A. (1997). The function and effectiveness of dynamic task allocation. In D. Harris (Ed.), *Engineering psychology and cognitive ergonomics: Integration of theory and application.* Aldershot: Avebury.

Taylor, F. (1911). *The principles of scientific management.* New York: Harper.

Taylor, P. J., Russ-Eft, D. F., & Chan, D. W. L. (2005). A meta-analytic review of behavior modeling training. *Journal of Applied Psychology, 90,* 692–709.

Teo, T. S. H., Lim, V. K. G., & Wai, S. H. (1998). An empirical study of attitudes towards teleworking among information technology personnel. *International Journal of Information Management, 19,* 329–43.

Terry, D. J., & Callan V. J. (1998). In-group bias in response to an organizational merger. *Group Dynamics: Theory, Research and Practice, 2,* 67–81.

Tharenou, P. (2001). The relationship of training motivation to participation in training and development. *Journal of Occupational and Organizational Psychology, 74,* 599–621.

Tharenou, P., & Burke, E. (2002). Training and organizational effectiveness. In I. T. Robertson, M. Callinan, & D. Bartram (Eds.), *Organizational effectiveness: The role of psychology.* Chichester, UK: Wiley.

Theorell, T., & Karasek, R. A. (1996). Current issues relating to psychosocial job strain and cardiovascular disease research. *Journal of Occupational Health Psychology, 1,* 9–26.

Thomas, D. A. (2001). The truth about mentoring minorities: Race matters. *Harvard Business Review, 79,* 98–107.

Thomas, K. M., & Chrobot-Mason, D. (2005). Group level explanations of workplace discrimination. In R. L. Dipboye & A. Colella (Eds.), *Discrimination at work* (pp. 63–88). Mahwah, NJ: Lawrence Erlbaum.

Tjosvold, D. (1991). *Team organisation: An enduring competitive advantage.* Chichester, UK: John Wiley.

Tjosvold, D. (1998). Cooperative and competitive goal approaches to conflict: Accomplishments and challenges. *Applied Psychology: An International Review, 47,* 285–342.

Tougas, F., Lagagé, M., De la Sablonnière, R., & Kocum, L. (2004). A new approach to the link between identity and relative deprivation in the perspective of ageism and retirement. *International Journal of Aging, & Human Development 59,* 1–23.

Tracey, J. B., Tannenbaum, S. I., & Kavanaugh, M. J. (1995). Applying trained skills on the job: The importance of work environment. *Journal of Applied Psychology, 80,* 239–52.

Tremblay, D. G. (2003). Telework: A new mode of gendered segmentation? Results from a study in Canada. *Canadian Journal of Communication, 28,* 461–78.

Triplett, H. (1897). The dynamogenic factors in pace making and competition. *American Journal of Psychology, 9,* 507–33.

Trist, E. L., & Bamforth, K. W. (1951). Some social and psychological consequences of the long-wall method of coal-getting. *Human Relations, 4,* 3–38.

Trompenaars, F., & Hampden-Turner, C. (1998). *Riding the waves of culture – Understanding diversity in global business* (2nd edn.). New York: MacGraw-Hill.

Tsui, A. S., Egan, T. D., & O'Reilly, C. A. (1992). Being different: Relational demography and organizational attachment. *Administrative Science Quarterly, 37,* 547–79.

Tsui, A. S., & O'Reilly, C. A. (1989). Beyond simple demographic effects: The importance of relational demography in superior–subordinate dyads. *Academy of Management Journal, 32,* 402–23.

Tsutsumi, A., & Kawakami, N. (2004). A review of empirical studies on the model of effort–reward imbalance at work: reducing occupational stress by implementing a new theory. *Social Science and Medicine, 59,* 2335–59.

TUC. (2000). Stress at work tops safety poll. www. tuc.org.uk/h_and_s/tuc–2390–fo.cf

Tuckman, B. W. (1965). Developmental sequences in small groups. *Psychological Bulletin, 63,* 348–99.

Tuckman, B. W., & Jensen, M. A. (1977). Stages of small-group development revisited. *Group & Organization Studies, 2,* 419–27.

Tung, R. L., Walls, J., & Frese, M. (2007). Cross-cultural entrepreneurship: The case of China. In J. R. Baum, M. Frese, & R. A. Baron (Eds.), *The Psychology of Entrepreneurship.* Mahwah, NJ: Lawrence Erlbaum.

Tupes, E. C., & Christal, R. E. (1992). Recurrent personality factors based on trait ratings. *Journal of Personality, 60,* 225–51.

Turner, N., Chmiel, N., & Walls, M. (2005). Railing for safety: Job demands, job control, and safety citizenship role definitions. *Journal of Occupational Health Psychology, 10,* 504–12.

Tversky, A., & Kahneman, D. (1974). Judgment under uncertainty: Heuristics and biases. *Science, 185,* 1124–31.

Tversky, A., & Kahneman, D. (1981). The framing of decisions and the psychology of choice. *Science, 211,* 453–8.

Tziner, A., & Eden, D. (1985). Effects of crew composition on crew performance: Does the whole equal the sum of its parts? *Journal of Applied Psychology, 70,* 85–93.

Uhlenbruck, K., Meyer, K. E., & Hitt, M. A. (2003). Organisational transformation in transition economies: Resource-based and organisational learning perspectives. *Journal of Management Studies, 40,* 257–82.

UK Department for Transport. (2002). Electronic communications and travel. www.dft.gov.uk/stellent/groups/dft_transstrat/documents/page/dft_transstrat_504911–04.hcsp

Ulrich, D. (1997). *Human resources champions, the next agenda for adding value and delivering results.* Boston: Harvard Business School Press.

Umbers, I. G. (1979). Models of the process operator. *International Journal of Man–Machine Studies, 11,* 263–84.

Ursin, H. (1986). Energetics and the self regulation of activation. In G. R. J. Hockey, A. W. K. Gaillard, & M. G. H. Coles (Eds.), *Energetics and human information processing.* Dordrecht: Marinus Nijhoff Publishers.

Ursin, H., Baade, E., & Levine, S. (1978). *Psychobiology of stress.* New York: Academic Press.

Uslu, A. T. (1997). Strategic mergers as an important tool in internationalizm (In Turkish: Uluslararasilasmada önemli bir araç olarak stratejik birlesmeler). *Öneri Journal* (Marmara University Institute of Social Sciences), *2(7)*, 21.

Van Dam, K. (2004). Antecedents and consequences of employability orientation. *European Journal of Work and Organizational Psychology, 13*, 29–51.

Van de Ven, A. H., & Poole, M. S. (1995). Explaining development and change in organisations. *Academy of Management Review, 20*, 510–40.

Van den Bos, K., Vermunt, R., & Wilke, H. A. M. (1997). Procedural and distributive justice: What is fair depends more on what comes first than on what comes next. *Journal of Personality and Social Psychology, 72*, 95–104.

Van der Doef, M., & Maes, S. (1998). The Job–Demand–Control(–Support) model and physical outcomes: a review of the strain and buffer hypotheses. *Psychology and Health, 13*, 909–36.

Van der Doef, M., & Maes, S. (1999). The Job–Demand–Control(–Support) model and psychological well being: A review of 20 years of empirical research. *Work and Stress, 13*, 87–114.

Van der Heijden, K. (1996). *Scenarios: The art of strategic conversation.* Chichester, UK: Wiley.

Van der Hiejden, K., Bradfield, R., Burt, G., Cairns, G., & Wright, G. (2002). *The sixth sense: Accelerating organizational learning with scenarios.* Chichester, UK: Wiley.

Van der Schaaf, T., & Kanse, L. (2004). Biases in incident reporting databases: an empirical study in the chemical process industry. *Safety Science, 42*, 57–67.

Van der Vlist, R. (1998). Planned change in organisations and organisational development in the 1990s. In P. J. D. Drenth, H. Thierry, & C. J. de Wolf (Eds.), *Handbook of work and organisational psychology* (Vol. 4, pp. 161–92). New York: Psychology Press.

Van Dyck, C., Frese, M., Baer, M., & Sonnentag, S. (2005). Organizational error management culture and its impact on performance: A two-study replication. *Journal of Applied Psychology, 90(6)*, 1228–40.

Van Eerde, W., & Thierry, H. (1996). Vroom's expectancy models and work-related criteria: A meta-analysis. *Journal of Applied Psychology, 81*, 575–86.

Van Gerven, P. W. M., Paas, F. G. W. C., Van Merrienboer, J. J. G., & Schmidt, H. G. (2002). Cognitive load theory and aging: Effects of worked examples on training efficiency. *Learning and Instruction, 12*, 87–105.

Van Knippenberg, D., De Dreu, C. K. W., et al. (2004). Work group diversity and group performance: An integrative model and research agenda. *Journal of Applied Psychology, 89*, 1008–22.

Van Sell, M., & Jacobs, M. (1994). Telecommuting and quality of life: a review of the literature and a model for research. *Telematics and Informatics, 11*, 81–95.

Van Vegchel, N., de Jonge, J., & Landsbergis, P. A. (2005). Occupational stess in (inter)action: The interplay between job demands and job resources. *Journal of Organizational Behavior, 26*, 535–60.

Van Vegchel, N., De Jonge, J., Bosma, H., & Schaufeli, W. (2005). Reviewing the Effort–Reward Imbalance model: Drawing up the balance of 45 empirical studies. *Social Science & Medicine, 60*, 1117–31.

Vancouver, J. B., Thompson, C. M., Tischner, E. C., & Putka, D. J. (2002). Two studies examining the negative effect of self-efficacy on performance. *Journal of Applied Psychology, 87*, 506–16.

Vartiainen, M. (2006). Mobile virtual work – Concepts, outcomes and challenges. In E. Andriessen & M. Vartiainen (Eds.), *Mobile virtual work: A new paradigm?* Heidelberg: Springer.

Vartiainen, M., Hakonen, M., Koivisto, S., Mannonen, P., Nieminen, M. P., Ruohomäki, V., & Vartola, A. (2007). *Distributed and mobile work – Places, people and technology.* Helsinki: Gaudeamus.

Veldman, H. (1992). *Hidden effects of noise as revealed by cardiovascular analysis.* Doctoral dissertation, University of Groningen, The Netherlands.

Venkatesh, V., & Johnson, P. (2002). Telecommuting technology implementations: A within- and between-subjects longitudinal field study. *Personnel Psychology*, 55, 661–87.

Verhaeghen, P., & Salthouse, T. A. (1997). Meta-analysis of age–cognition relations in adulthood: Estimates of linear and nonlinear age effects and structural models. *Psychological Bulletin, 122,* 231–49.

Vincente, K. (1999). *Cognitive work analysis.* Mahwah, NJ: Lawrence Erlbaum.

von Hippel, W., Sekaquaptewa, D., & Vargas, P. (1995). On the role of encoding processes in stereotype maintenance. In M. P. Zanna (Ed.), *Advances in experimental social psychology* (Vol. 27, pp. 177–254). San Diego: Academic Press.

Vredenburgh, A. G. (2002). Organizational Safety: Which management practices are most effective in reducing employee injury rates? *Journal of Safety Research, 33,* 259–76.

Vroom, V. H. (1964). *Work and motivation.* New York: Wiley.

Vroom, V. H. (1966). Organizational choice: A study of pre- and post-decision processes. *Organizational Behavior and Human Performance, 1,* 212–25.

Vroom, V. H. (1995). *Work and motivation.* San Francisco: Jossey-Bass.

Vroom, V. H. (2000). Leadership and the decision making process. *Organizational Dynamics, 28,* 82–94.

Vroom, V. H., & Yetton, P. W. (1973). *Leadership and decision making.* Pittsburgh: University of Pittsburgh Press.

Waalevijin, P., & Segaar, P. (1993). Strategic management. *Long Range Planning, 26(2),* 24.

Wagenaar, W. A. (1992). Risk taking and accident causation. Jn J. F. Yates (Ed.), *Risk-taking behaviour.* Chichester: John Wiley & Sons.

Wagenaar, W. A., & Groeneweg, J. (1987). Accidents at sea: Multiple causes and impossible consequences. *International Journal of Man–Machine Studies, 27,* 587–98.

Wagenaar, W. A., Groeneweg, J., Hudson, P. T. W., & Reason, J. T. (1994). Promoting safety in the oil industry. *Ergonomics, 37,* 1999–2013.

Wagenaar, W. A., Hudson, P. T. W., & Reason, J. T. (1990). Cognitive failures and accidents. *Applied Cognitive Psychology, 4,* 273–94.

Wahba, M. A., & Bridwell, L. G. (1987). Maslow reconsidered: A review of research on the need hierarchy theory. In R. M. Steers & L. W. Porter (Eds.), *Motivation and work behavior* (pp. 51–9). New York: McGraw-Hill.

Waldman, D., & Avolio, B. J. (1986). A meta-analysis of age differences in job performance. *Journal of Applied Psychology 71,* 33–8.

Walker, T. G., & Main, E. C. (1973). Choice shifts in political decision making: Federal judges and civil liberties cases. *Journal of Applied Social Psychology, 3,* 39–48.

Wallace, J. C., Popp, E., & Mondore, S. (2006). Safety climate as a mediator between foundation climates and occupational accidents: A group-level investigation. *Journal of Applied Psychology, 91,* 681–8.

Walters, D., Halliday, M., & Glaser, S. (2002). Creating value in the new economy. *Management Decision, 40(8)*, 775–81.

Wang, Z. M. (1994). Culture, economic reform and the role of industrial/organizational psychology in China. In H. C. Triandis, M. D. Dunnette, & L. M. Hough (Eds.), *Handbook of industrial organizational psychology*, Vol. 4. Palo Alto, CA: Consulting Psychologists Press.

Wanous, J. P., Poland, T. D., Premack, S. L., & Davies, K. S. (1992). The effects of met expectations on newcomer attitudes and behaviours: A review and meta-analysis. *Journal of Applied Psychology, 77*, 288–97.

Warr, P. (1987). *Work, unemployment, and mental health*. Oxford: Clarendon Press.

Warr, P. (1990). Decision latitude, job demands, and employee well-being. *Work and Stress, 4(4)*, 285–94.

Warr, P. (1990). The measurement of well-being and other aspects of mental health. *Journal of Occupational Psychology, 63*, 193–210.

Warr, P. (1994). A conceptual framework for the study of work and mental health. *Work and Stress, 8*, 84–97.

Warr, P. (1994). Age and employment. In H. C. Triandis, M. D. Dunnette, & L. M. Hough (Eds.), *Handbook of industrial and organizational psychology*. Palo Alto, CA: Consulting Psychologists Press.

Warr, P. (1998). Age, work, and mental health. In K. W. Schaie & C. Schooler (Eds.), *The impact of work on older adults* (pp. 252–303). New York: Springer.

Warr, P. (1999). Job performance and the aging workforce. In N. Chmiel (Ed.), *Introduction to work and organizational psychology*. Oxford: Blackwell Publishers.

Warr, P. (2001). Age and work behaviour: Physical attributes, cognitive abilities, knowledge, personality traits and motives. In C. L. Cooper, & I. T. Robertson (Eds.), *International Review of Industrial and Organizational Psychology* (Vol. 16, pp. 1–36). London: Wiley.

Warr, P., & Allan, C. (1998). Learning strategies and occupational training. In C. L. Cooper & I. T. Robertson (Eds.), *International review of industrial and organizational psychology* (Vol. 13, pp. 83–121). Chichester, UK: Wiley.

Warr, P., Allan, C., & Birdi, K. (1999). Predicting three levels of training outcome. *Journal of Occupational and Organizational Psychology, 72*, 351–75.

Warr, P., & Birdi, K. (1998). Employee age and voluntary development activity. *International Journal of Training and Development, 2*, 190–204.

Warr, P., & Bunce, D. (1995). Trainee characteristics and the outcomes of open learning. *Personnel Psychology, 48*, 347–75.

Warr, P., & Downing, J. (2000). Learning strategies, learning anxiety and knowledge acquisition. *British Journal of Psychology, 91*, 311–33.

Warr, P., & Fay, D. (2001). Age and personal initiative at work. *European Journal of Work and Organizational Psychology, 10(3)*, 343–53.

Warr, P., & Pennington, J. (1994). Occupational age-grading: Jobs for older and younger nonmanagerial employees. *Journal of Vocational Behavior 45*, 328–46.

Watson Fritz, M. B., Narasimhan, S., & Rhee, H. S. (1998). Communication and coordination in the virtual office. *Journal of Management Information Systems, 14*, 7–28.

Watson, W. E., Kumar, K., & Michaelsen, L. K. (1993). Cultural diversity's impact on interaction process and performance: Comparing homogeneous and diverse task groups. *Academy of Management Journal, 36*, 590–602.

Weber, B. & Hertel, G. (2007). Motivation gains of inferior group members: A meta-analytic review. *Journal of Personality and Social Psychology, 93*, 973–93.

Weber; Y. (1996). Corporate cultural fit and performance in mergers and acquisitions. *Human Relations, 49(9)*, 119–27.

Weckerle, J. R., & Schultz, K. S. (1999). Influences on the bridge employment decision among older USA workers. *Journal of Occupational and Organizational Psychology, 72*, 317–29.

Weddle, M. G. (1996). Reporting occupational injuries: The first step. *Journal of Safety Research, 27*, 217–33.

Wegman, D. H., & McGee, J. P. (Eds.) (2004). *Health and safety needs for older workers.* Washington, DC: National Academies Press.

Wegner, D. M., Schneider, D. J., Carter, S., & White, L. (1987). Paradoxical effects of thought suppression. *Journal of Personality and Social Psychology, 53*, 5–13.

Weick, K. E. (1979). *The social psychology of organizing* (2nd edn.). Reading, MA: Addison-Wesley.

Weick, K. E., & Quinn, R. E. (1999). Organisational change and development. *Annual Review of Psychology, 50*, 361–86.

Weiner, B. (1985). An attributional theory of achievement motivation and emotion. *Psychological Review, 92*, 548–73.

Weiner, B. (1986). *An attributional theory of motivation and emotion.* New York: Springer.

Weinstein, N. D. (1988). The precaution adoption process. *Health Psychology, 7*, 355–86.

Welford, A. T. (1976). Ergonomics: Where have we been and where are we going: 1. *Ergonomics, 19*, 275–86.

Wellman, B., Salaff, J., Dimitrova, D., Garton, L., Gulia, M., & Haythornthwaite, C. (1996). Computer networks as social networks: Collaborative work, telework, and virtual community. *Annual Review of Sociology, 22*, 213–38.

Welsh, E. T., Wanberg, C. R., Brown, K. G., & Simmering, M. J. (2003). E–learning: Emerging uses, empirical results and future directions. *International Journal of Training and Development, 7*, 245–58.

Wenger, E., McDermott, R., & Snyder, W. M. (2002). *Cultivating communities of practice: A guide to managing knowledge.* Boston, MA: Harvard Business School Press.

Wenzel, H., Hausschild, M., & Alting, L. (1997). *Environmental assessment of products*, Vol. 1. London: Chapman & Hall.

West, M. A. (2002). Sparkling fountains or stagnant ponds: An integrative model of creativity and innovation implementation in work groups. *Applied Psychology: An International Review, 51*, 355–86.

West, M. A., & Allen, N. A. (1997). Selecting for teamwork. In N. Anderson & P. Herriot (Eds.), *International handbook of selection and assessment* (pp. 493–506). Chichester, UK: John Wiley.

West, M. A., & Borrill, C. A. (2005). Understanding doctors' performance. In J. Cox, J. King, A. Hutchinson, & P. McAvoy (Eds.), *The influence of team working* (pp. 106–18). London: Radcliff.

West, M. A., Borrill, C. S., Dawson, J. F., Brodbeck, F. C., Shapiro, D. A., & Haward, B. (2003). Leadership clarity and team innovation in health care. *Leadership Quarterly, 14*, 393–410.

West, M. A., Borrill, C., Dawson, J., et al. (2002). The link between the management of employees and patient mortality in acute hospitals. *The International Journal of Human Resource Management, 13(8)*, 1299–1310.

West, M. A., Garrod, S., & Carletta, J. (1997). Group decision-making and effectiveness: Unexplored boundaries. In C. L. Cooper & S. E. Jackson (Eds.), *Creating tomorrow's organizations* (pp. 293–317). Chichester, UK: Wiley.

West, M. A., & Markiewicz, L. (2003). *Building team-based working. A practical guide to organizational transformation.* Oxford: Blackwell.

West, M. A., Tjosvold, D., & Smith, K. G. (Eds.) (2003). *The international handbook of organizational teamwork and cooperative working.* Chichester, UK: Wiley.

West, M., & Johnson, R. (2002). A matter of life and death. *People Management, 21*, Feb.

Westfall, W. D. (2004). Does telecommuting really increase productivity? *Communications of the ACM, 47*, 93–96.

Wheeler, M. E., & Fiske, S. T. (2005). Controlling psychological prejudice. *Psychological Science, 16*, 56–63.

Wickens, C. D. (1984). *Engineering psychology and human performance.* Columbus, OH: Merrill.

Wickens, C. D., & Hollands, J. G. (2000). *Engineering psychology and human performance* (3rd edn.). New York: Harper Collins.

Wiegmann, D. A., Zhang, H., & von Thaden, T. (2001). *Defining and assessing safety culture in high reliability systems: An annotated bibliography.* Technical report ARL–01–12/FAA–01–4, Aviation Research Lab, Institute of Aviation, University of Illinois.

Wiener, E. L. (1985). Beyond the sterile cockpit. *Human Factors, 27*, 75–90.

Wiener, E. L. (1988). Cockpit automation. In E. L. Wiener & D. C. Nagel (Eds.), *Human factors in aviation.* San Diego, CA: Academic Press.

Wierwille, W. W., & Casali, J. G. (1983). A validated scale for global mental workload measurement applications. *Proceedings of the 27th meeting of the Human Factors Society.* Santa Monica, CA: Human Factors Society.

Wiesenfeld, B. M., Raghuram, S., & Garud, R. (2001). Organizational identification among virtual workers: the role of need for affiliation and perceived work-based social support. *Journal of Management, 27*, 213–29.

Wigand, R., Picot, A., & Reichwald, R. (1997). *Information, organization and management.* Chichester, UK: Wiley.

Wildman, S. M. (1996). Privilege in the workplace: The missing element in anti-discrimination law. In S. M. Wildman (Ed.), *Privilege revealed: How invisible preference undermines America* (pp. 25–42). New York: New York University Press.

Wilkes, R. B., Frolick, M. N., & Urlwiler, R. (1994). Critical issues in developing successful telework programs. *Journal of Systems Management, 45*, 30–4.

Williams, J. R., Miller, C. E., Steelman, L. A., & Levy, P. E. (1999). Increasing feedback seeking in public context: It takes two (or more) to tango. *Journal of Applied Psychology, 84*, 969–76.

Williams, K. D., & Karau, S. J. (1991). Social loafing and social compensation: The effects of expectations of co-worker performance. *Journal of Personality and Social Psychology, 61*, 570–81.

Williams, K. Y., & O'Reilly, C. A. (1998). Demography and diversity in organizations: A review of 40 years of research. *Research in Organizational Behavior, 20*, 77–140.

Wilson, G. F., & Eggemeier, F. T. (1991). Psychophysiological assessment of workload in multi-task environments. In D. L. Damos (Ed.), *Multiple-task performance*. London: Taylor & Francis.

Wilson, M., & Greenhill, A. (2004). Gender and teleworking identities in the risk society: A research agenda. *New Technology, Work and Employment, 19,* 207–21.

Winkler, B. (2002). Enhancing performance through training. In S. Sonnentag (Ed.), *Psychological management of individual performance* (pp. 267–91). Chichester, UK: Wiley.

Winter, D. G. (1991). A motivational model of leadership: Predicting long–term management success from TAT measures of power motivation and responsibility. *Leadership Quarterly, 2(2),* 67–80.

Woehr, D. J., & Huffcutt, A. I. (1994). Rater training for performance appraisal: A quantitative review. *Journal of Occupational and Organizational Psychology, 67,* 189–206.

Wofford, J. C., & Liska, L. Z. (1993). Path–goal theories of leadership: A meta-analysis. *Journal of Management, 19,* 857–76.

Wohlgemuth, A. C. (1991). Der Makrotrend in der ganzheitlichen Organisationsberatung In M. Hofmann (Ed.), *Theorie und Praxis der Unternehmensberatung.* Heidelberg: Physica Verlag.

Womack, J. P., Jones, D. T., & Roos, D. (1990). *The machine that changed the world.* New York: Rawson.

Wood, R. E., Mento, A. J., & Locke, E. A. (1987). Task complexity as a moderator of goal effects: A meta-analysis. *Journal of Applied Psychology, 72,* 416–25.

Woodruffe, C. (1997). *Assessment centres: Identifying and developing competence.* London: Institute of Personnel Management.

Woodruffe, C. (2000). *Development and assessment centres: Identifying and developing competence.* London: CIPD.

Wooten, L. P., & James, E. H. (2005). Challenges of organisational learning: Perpetuation of discrimination against employees with disabilities. *Behavioural Sciences and the Law, 23,* 123–41.

Workman, M., & Bommer, W. (2004). Redesigning computer call center work: A longitudinal field experiment. *Journal of Organizational Behavior, 25,* 317–37.

Workman, M., Kahnweiler, W., & Bommer, W. (2003). The effects of cognitive style and media richness on commitment to telework and virtual teams. *Journal of Vocational Behavior,* 199–219.

Wuebker, L. (1986). Safety locus of control as a predictor of industrial accident and injuries. *Journal of Business and Psychology, 1,* 19–30.

Xie, J. L., & Johns, G. (1995). Job scope and stress: Can job scope be too high? *Academy of Management Journal, 38,* 1288–1309.

Yap, C. S., & Tang, H. (1990). Factors associated with attitudes towards teleworking. *Information and Management, 19,* 227–35.

Young, R. A., & Collin, A. (2004). Introduction: Constructivism and social constructivism in the career field. *Journal of Vocational Behavior 64,* 373–88.

Yukl, G. (2005). *Leadership in organizations* (6th edn.). Upper Saddle River, NJ: Prentice-Hall.

Yukl, G., & Falbe, C. M. (1991). Importance of different power sources in downward and lateral relations. *Journal of Applied Psychology, 76,* 416–23.

Yukl, G., & Tracey, B. (1992). Consequences of influence tactics used with subordinates, peers, and the boss. *Journal of Applied Psychology, 77*, 525–35.

Yukl, G., & Van Fleet, D. D. (1992). Theory and research on leadership in organizations. In M. D. Dunnette & L. M. Hough (Eds.), *Handbook of industrial and organizational psychology* (Vol. 3, S. 147–97) Palo Alto, CA: Consulting Psychologists Press.

Zacharatos, A., Barling, J., & Iverson, R. D. (2005). High-performance work systems and occupational safety. *Journal of Applied Psychology, 90*, 77–93.

Zajac, E. J., & Bazerman, M. H. (1991). Blindspots in industry and competitor analysis: Implications of interfirm (mis)perceptions for strategic decisions. *Academy of Management Review, 16*, 37–56.

Zapf, D., Bechtoldt, M., & Dormann, C. (in press). Instrument zur Stress-bezogenen Arbeitsanalyse (ISTA), Fragebogen Version 6.0 (Instrument for stress-related job analysis (ISTA) questionnaire version 6.0). *Zeitschrift für Arbeits- und Organisationspsychologie.*

Zohar, D. (1980). Safety climate in industrial organisations: Theoretical and applied implications. *Journal of Applied Psychology, 65*, 96–102.

Zohar, D. (2000). A group-level model of safety climate: Testing the effect of group climate on microaccidents in manufacturing jobs. *Journal of Applied Psychology, 85*, 587–96.

Zohar, D. (2002). Modifying supervisory practices to improve subunit safety: A leadership-based intervention model. *Journal of Applied Psychology, 87*, 156–63.

Zohar, D., & Luria, G. (2003). The use of supervisory practices as leverage to improve safety behavior: A cross-level intervention model. *Journal of Safety Research, 34*, 567–77.

Zohar, D., & Luria, G. (2005). A multilevel model of safety climate: Cross-level relationships between organizational and group-level climates. *Journal of Applied Psychology, 90*, 616–28.

Index